Published by K · G · Saur

INTERNATIONAL COUNCIL ON MONUMENTS AND SITES
CONSEIL INTERNATIONAL DES MONUMENTS ET DES SITES
CONSEJO INTERNATIONAL DE MONUMENTOS Y SITIOS
МЕЖДУНАРОДНЫЙ СОВЕТ ПО ВОПРОСАМ ПАМЯТНИКОВ И ДОСТОПРИМЕЧАТЕЛНЫХ МЕСТ

HERITAGE AT RISK

Patrimoine en Péril / Patrimonio en Peligro

ICOMOS WORLD REPORT 2004/2005 ON MONUMENTS AND SITES IN DANGER

ICOMOS rapport mondial 2004/2005 sur des monuments et des sites en péril

ICOMOS informe mundial 2004/2005 sobre monumentos y sitios en peligro

edited by Marilyn Truscott, Michael Petzet and John Ziesemer

Published by K · G · Saur

Heritage at Risk edited by ICOMOS

ICOMOS is very grateful to the German Federal Government Commissioner for Cultural Affairs and the Media, the UNESCO Division of Cultural Heritage, and to the Messerschmitt Foundation for their generous support of this publication

Die Beauftragte der Bundesregierung
für Kultur und Medien

EDITORS: Marilyn Truscott, Michael Petzet, John Ziesemer

TRANSLATIONS: José Garcia, Gaia Jungeblodt, Claudia de Sevilla, Marilyn Truscott, Olivia de Willermin, John Ziesemer

LAYOUT: Michael Petzet, Detta Petzet
TYPESETTING & SCANS: FotoSatz Pfeifer GmbH, Gräfelfing bei München
PRINTING & BINDING: Strauss GmbH, Mörlenbach

Front and Back Cover: The historic city of Bam (Iran) before and after its destruction (photos: Yasuyoshi Okada)
Inside Front Cover: Salvaging fragments of the Great Buddha of Bamiyan
Inside Back Cover: Provisional fixing of plaster fragments on the back wall of the Small Buddha of Bamiyan

Photo Credits

Many photo credits can be found in the captions. Most other pictures were provided by the various committees or individual members of ICOMOS. In addition we received pictures from the following people and institutions: J. Michel (pp. 82/83), B. Imam (pp. 95-103), G. Jonas/E. Sassen (p. 104), World Monuments Fund (p. 109), U. Ghaidan/N. Al-Dabbagh (pp. 112-121), G. Palumbo/A. Baldioli/M. Acri (p. 127), M. Eiden (p. 144), W. Wedekind (pp. 151-156), J.-M. Deom (pp. 157-160), Cultural Heritage without Borders (pp. 161-164), K. Merten (p. 200).

ISBN 3-598-24243-3

CONTENTS

FOREWORD

Heritage at Risk 2004/2005 groups national and regional reports on monuments and sites in danger, highlighting threats and risks affecting cultural heritage worldwide and diffusing this information. Subjects include wars, interethnic conflict, barbaric acts, plundering and pillage, natural catastrophes, atmospheric pollution, urban development and inappropriate planning regulations, not to mention neglect, uncontrolled tourism and inaccurate restorations. The publication of the 2004/2005 Report shows how many countries have reacted positively to this initiative since its first appearance in 2000. It also highlights how assessment, regular monitoring and planning of long-term programmes are not only necessary but indispensable for the protection of cultural heritage worldwide. So too are strengthening national legislation on cultural property and continued cooperation from international bodies. UNESCO through its World Heritage Committee and ICOMOS through its National Committees are strongly committed to reducing the impact of threats and destruction and I wish to thank ICOMOS and its President, Michael Petzet, for their efforts to maintain this regular reporting of conditions of cultural heritage worldwide. A number of other NGO's are also currently active on this matter, like the WMF and Heritage without Borders.

On the subject of natural disasters, who can forget the tsunami tragedy which hit the coasts of several countries of Asia and Africa on 26 December 2004, killing so many, destroying infrastructures and devastating the natural and cultural landscapes of several countries. The total loss cannot yet be assessed. Speaking at a press conference at the *Mauritius International Meeting on Small Island Developing States* on 5 January 2005, Mr Matsuura, Director-General of UNESCO, stressed the need of a strategic and systematic approach at national level to help countries in terms of risk preparedness. UNESCO, along with experts from the World Heritage community and local authorities, is mobilizing all efforts to evaluate damage to the sites inscribed on UNESCO's World Heritage List located in the regions hit by the earthquake and tsunami. Information is currently being collected and missions will be dispatched in coordination with the national authorities as soon as possible to decide on appropriate action. UNESCO is proposing expert assessment missions to Sri Lanka and Indonesia to assess the situation of the affected cultural and natural World Heritage properties, notably the Old Town of Galle and its Fortifications and the Tropical Rainforest Heritage of Sumatra. Emergency assistance will also be available through the World Heritage Fund to help the affected countries establish detailed damage assessments and rehabilitation plans. These UNESCO expert assessment missions will fall under the joint declaration of cooperation between UNESCO and the Government of Italy on emergency actions in countries affected by conflicts or natural disasters for the safeguarding, rehabilitation and protection of cultural and natural heritage. On the policy level, an important advance has been made on the occasion of the Meeting on Cultural Heritage Risk Management, organized by the UNESCO World Heritage Centre in collaboration with the Agency for Cultural Affairs of Japan, ICCROM and ICOMOS in the framework of the UN World Conference on Disaster Reduction (Kobe, Japan, 18–22 January 2005). The Recommendations resulting from this event (Cf. http://www.unisdr.org/wcdr/thematic-sessions/thematic-reports/report-session-3-3.pdf) have stressed the proactive role of heritage as a contributor to sustainable development and disaster reduction, as well as the importance of traditional knowledge systems and intangible heritage in mitigating and/or preventing disasters.

Iraq after years of embargo and war

This fourth world report gives an assessment of Iraqi's cultural heritage, in the wake of the conflict and more than ten years of embargo. The chapter entitled "State of Ecology and Built Heritage After Four Decades of Adversity" includes five case-studies (the Marshlands of South Iraq; the Kurdish Countryside; the Old Town of 'Ana on the Euphrates; the Citadel of Arbil; and the Ottoman *Saray* Administrative Complex in Baghdad) and an overview of restoration and reconstruction works carried out in the country. 2005 will mark soon two years after the looting of the Iraq Museum in Baghdad and of many other Iraqi cultural institutions in Baghdad and around the country (April 2003). The entire structure of the cultural heritage of Iraq – archaeological sites and historic buildings, museums and cultural institutions, libraries and archives, and the intangible heritage – has been badly affected, thereby causing an irreversible loss to Iraqi people and, in particular, children who are stewards of cultural heritage for future generations.

Looting of archaeological sites and plundering of historic buildings continue unabated. While it is now possible to determine the number of artefacts that disappeared from the Iraq Museum of Baghdad, it is quite impossible to assess the number of objects that have been illicitly removed from archaeological sites and sold off. More than 10,000 archaeological sites have been identified and included in the inventory prepared by the Iraqi State Board of Antiquities and Heritage, with many others not yet listed. These include the well-known remains of Ashur, Ctesiphon, Eridu, Hatra, Isin, Khorsabad, Kish, Lagash, Larsa, Nimrud, Nineveh, Samarra, Ur and Uruk. Two sites have been inscribed on the UNESCO World Heritage List: Hatra in 1985, and Ashur in 2003. Illicit excavation at archaeological sites continues to destroy the Iraqi heritage, in particular in the southern region, at such important sites as Isin, Umma and Umm Al-Aqarib. The installation of military bases close to or at archaeological sites, as in the cases of Hatra, capital of the Parthian Empire, and Babylon, capital of the Neo-Babylonian king, Nabuccodonosor II (604–562 BC), calls for urgent attention, as these may cause irreversible damage.

UNESCO's action to protect the Iraqi cultural heritage

Protection, like rehabilitation, is a long-term process calling for international efforts and long-term strategies. Since April 2003 UNESCO is committed to devising an overall strategy to protect the Iraqi cultural heritage. Two expert missions visited the country in May and June 2003 to begin defining priority domains of intervention in close cooperation with the Iraqi authorities. Three international expert meetings took place between April a few days after the looting of the Iraq Museum and August 2003. The resulting programme for culture was included in the global strategy for the rehabilitation of Iraq, drawn up by the United Nations System in February 2004.

Following the third UNESCO expert meeting in Tokyo in August 2003, the participants recommended that the Director-General of UNESCO set up an International Coordination Committee for the Safeguarding of the Cultural Heritage of Iraq. Under the auspices of the Ministry of Culture of Iraq and UNESCO, the Committee was created in September 2003 in order to allocate international assistance according to needs and plan a programme following the highest international standards. Its first Plenary Session took place in May 2004 at UNESCO Headquarters and led to a number of recommendations, that are now receiving the attention of the UNESCO Secretariat in order to ensure an appropriate follow-up.

Financial contributions to implement field projects have been made to UNESCO by the Governments of Italy, Japan, Switzerland, Flanders, Norway, Turkey, Czech Republic and Latvia. Other UNESCO Member States, including Germany, Belgium, Denmark, France, Greece, Hungary, Latvia, the Islamic Republic of Iran, Netherlands, Poland, the Czech Republic, United Kingdom, United States of America, Jordan, Egypt, Spain, and Switzerland have expressed their willingness to contribute to protecting the Iraqi cultural heritage by means of technical assistance. Moreover, UNESCO has received contributions to its Special Account for Iraqi cultural heritage, in particular from Greece and the Holy Sea, while Saudi Arabia has pledged financial assistance.

Thanks to these contributions, and in spite of the state of insecurity in the country, during the last two years UNESCO has been active in Iraq and is today implementing fourteen projects for a total amount of more than eight million dollars. These involve several fields: archaeological sites, historic buildings, cultural institutions and museums, libraries and archives, and the safeguarding of intangible cultural heritage. The "Iraqi Maqam" was proclaimed as Masterpiece of the Oral and Intangible Heritage of Humanity in 2003 and Iraq benefited from financial assistance of the UNESCO/Japanese Funds-in-Trust for the Intangible Cultural Heritage for the preparation of this candidature.

The main aims of these UNESCO projects are the fight against illicit traffic of the Iraqi cultural heritage, the rehabilitation of premises and provision of equipment to enable cultural institutions to become fully operational as soon as possible, and capacity-building and training for professional staff, in order to update their skills in various fields.

Among its activities to combat illicit traffic of Iraqi cultural property, UNESCO is working closely with INTERPOL on the basis of an agreement signed in July 2003, to track archaeological objects, illicitly exported from Iraq, on the art market. In this regard, documentation on cultural property is an essential tool: a training course in basic standards for documentation of movable properties (Object-ID Standard) for the State Board of Antiquities and Heritage staff was held in Amman in December 2004. Two other training courses were organised simultaneously in Amman with the assistance of WMF/GCI on the use of GIS and preparation of an archaeological sites database. Vehicles and equipment to strengthen security are being provided at endangered sites under the United Nations Development Group (UNDG) programme for protection of the Iraqi cultural heritage. A training course for border patrols and site guards to stop illicit traffic in cultural artefacts and provide security at archaeological sites was held in Amman in October-November 2004 thanks to a contribution by the Government of Italy and the assistance of the Italian Carabinieri. As part of the activities for the rehabilitation of the Iraq National Museum in Baghdad, and with the aid of a contribution by the Swiss Government, UNESCO is providing a museum collection and information management database, as well as hardware with which to operate the system. The first session of a training course in documentation using photogrammetry took place in Riga in June 2004 and concentrated on archaeological sites and historic buildings.

Among the projects aiming at rehabilitation of premises and provision of equipment, UNESCO is providing equipment for the maintenance and patrolling of the site of Nineveh in northern Iraq which was the imperial capital of the Biblical Assyrian King Sennacherib in the 8th century BC. Specialized publications on museum studies have also been delivered to the Iraq Museum in Baghdad, while, thanks to a contribution pledged by the Government of Japan, UNESCO is assisting the Iraqi authorities in the rehabilitation of the conservation laboratories of the museum. Under the UNDG programme to protect the Iraqi cultural heritage, the first phase of the projects for the rehabilitation of the Regional Centre for the Conservation of Cultural Property in the Arab Countries, and of the Child Museum, both of which are in Baghdad, began in 2004. The rehabilitation of the Melodic Institute and provision of equipment for the National Library and National Archives in Baghdad are also planned in the UNDG programme.

Mounir Bouchenaki
Assistant Director-General for Culture
UNESCO, Paris

AVANT-PROPOS

Patrimoine en péril 2004/2005 est une publication qui réunit des rapports nationaux et régionaux sur les monuments et les sites en péril, attire l'attention sur les menaces et les risques qui pèsent sur le patrimoine culturel dans le monde et diffuse ces informations. Sont traités des sujets comme les guerres, les conflits interethniques, les actes de barbarie et de pillage, les catastrophes naturelles, la pollution atmosphérique, le développement urbain et les réglementations inappropriées en matière d'aménagement, sans oublier le manque d'entretien, le développement touristique incontrôlé et les restaurations inopportunes. Le rapport 2004/2005 fait état du nombre de pays qui ont répondu favorablement à cette initiative depuis son lancement en 2000. Il montre aussi comment l'évaluation, le suivi régulier et la planification des programmes à long terme sont non seulement nécessaires mais indispensables à la protection du patrimoine culturel mondial. Tout aussi importants sont le renforcement des législations nationales sur les biens culturels et la poursuite de la coopération avec les organismes internationaux. L'UNESCO avec son Comité du patrimoine mondial et l'ICOMOS au travers de ses comités nationaux se sont fermement engagés à réduire l'incidence des risques et des destructions, et je tiens à remercier l'ICOMOS et son Président, M. Michael Petzet, des efforts qu'ils fournissent pour actualiser en permanence les informations sur la situation du patrimoine culturel dans le monde. Un certain nombre d'autres ONG mènent aussi actuellement des activités dans ce domaine, par exemple WMF et Patrimoine culturel sans frontières.

En ce qui concerne les catastrophes naturelles, qui pourra oublier la tragédie du tsunami qui a frappé les côtes de plusieurs pays d'Afrique et d'Asie le 26 décembre 2004, causant la mort d'innombrables personnes, détruisant des infrastructures et ravageant les paysages naturels et culturels de plusieurs pays ? On ne peut pas encore évaluer l'ampleur de ces pertes. S'exprimant lors d'une conférence de presse à l'occasion de la *Réunion internationale sur les petits États insulaires en développement*, tenue à Maurice le 5 janvier 2005, M. Matsuura, directeur général de l'UNESCO, a souligné la nécessité d'adopter une approche stratégique et systématique à l'échelon national pour aider les pays dans le domaine de la prévention des risques. L'UNESCO, en coopération avec des experts de la communauté du patrimoine mondial et les autorités locales, met tout en œuvre pour évaluer les dégâts subis par les sites inscrits sur la Liste du patrimoine mondial dans les régions frappées par le tremblement de terre et le tsunami. Des informations sont en train d'être recueillies et des missions seront envoyées sur place dès que possible, en coordination avec les autorités nationales, pour arrêter des mesures appropriées. L'UNESCO se propose d'envoyer au Sri Lanka et en Indonésie des missions d'experts chargés d'évaluer la situation des sites du patrimoine mondial culturel et naturel qui ont été atteints, notamment la vieille ville de Galle et ses fortifications et le Patrimoine des forêts tropicales ombrophiles de Sumatra. Une aide d'urgence sera également débloquée par le Fonds du patrimoine mondial pour aider les pays touchés à procéder à des évaluations détaillées des dégâts et à élaborer des plans de réhabilitation. Ces missions d'évaluation de l'UNESCO s'inscriront dans le cadre de la déclaration commune de coopération entre l'UNESCO et le Gouvernement italien prévoyant des actions d'urgence dans des pays frappés par des conflits ou des catastrophes naturelles en vue d'assurer la sauvegarde, la réhabilitation et la protection de leur patrimoine culturel et naturel. Au niveau des pouvoirs publics, un pas important a été franchi à l'occasion de la Réunion sur la gestion des risques pour le patrimoine culturel organisée par le Centre de l'UNESCO pour le patrimoine mondial en collaboration avec l'Agence pour les affaires culturelles du Japon, l'ICCROM et l'ICOMOS, dans le cadre de la Conférence mondiale des Nations Unies sur la prévention des catastrophes (Kobe, Japon, 18–22 janvier 2005). Les recommandations issues de cette manifestation (voir http://www.unisdr.org/wedr/thematic-sessions/thematic-reports/report-session-3-3.pdf) ont mis en évidence le rôle proactif du patrimoine en tant qu'acteur du développement durable et de la réduction des catastrophes ainsi que l'importance des savoirs traditionnels et du patrimoine immatériel dans l'atténuation ou la prévention des catastrophes.

L'Iraq après des années d'embargo et de guerre

Ce quatrième rapport mondial évalue le patrimoine culturel iraquien à la suite du conflit et après plus de dix années d'embargo. Le chapitre consacré à l'état de l'environnement et du patrimoine bâti après quatre décennies d'adversité comprend cinq études de cas (les zones marécageuses du sud de l'Iraq ; la campagne kurde ; la vieille ville d'Ana sur l'Euphrate ; la citadelle d'Arbil et le centre administratif ottoman de Saray à Bagdad) et une présentation des travaux de restauration et de reconstruction entrepris dans le pays. En 2005, il y aura deux ans que le Musée national de Bagdad et bon nombre d'autres institutions culturelles iraquiennes à Bagdad et dans le reste du pays ont été pillés (avril 2003). Toute la structure du patrimoine culturel iraquien – sites archéologiques et bâtiments historiques, musées et institutions culturelles, bibliothèques, archives et patrimoine immatériel – a été gravement touchée, avec les pertes irréversibles que cela signifie pour le peuple iraquien et en particulier les enfants qui sont les gardiens de ce patrimoine pour les générations futures.

Les actes de pillage de sites archéologiques et de bâtiments historiques se poursuivent avec la même intensité. S'il est désormais possible de déterminer le nombre d'artefacts qui ont disparu du Musée national de Bagdad, il est tout à fait impossible d'évaluer le nombre d'objets qui ont été illicitement enlevés des sites archéologiques et vendus. Plus de 10.000 sites archéologiques ont été identifiés et inscrits sur la liste établie par le Conseil national iraquien des antiquités et du patrimoine, et de nombreux autres n'ont pas encore été recensés. Parmi eux, les célèbres vestiges d'Assour, Ctésiphon, Eridu, Hatra, Isin, Khorsabad, Kish, Lagash, Larsa, Nimrud, Ninive, Samarra, Ur et Uruk. Deux sites ont été inscrits sur la Liste du patrimoine mondial de l'UNESCO : Hatra en 1985 et Assour en 2003. Les fouilles illicites sur les sites archéologiques continuent de détruire le patrimoine iraquien, en particulier dans le sud du pays, sur des sites aussi importants que Isin, Umma et Umm Al-Aqarib. L'installation de bases militaires sur des sites archéologiques ou à proximité, comme à Hatra, capitale de l'Empire parthe, et à Babylone, capitale du roi néo-babylonien Nabuchodonosor II (604–562 av. J.-C.) doit appeler l'attention sans délai car elle risque de causer des dégâts irréversibles.

Action de l'UNESCO visant à protéger le patrimoine culturel iraquien

La protection, tout comme la restauration est un processus qui s'inscrit dans la durée et appelle des initiatives à l'échelon international et des stratégies à long terme. Depuis le mois d'avril 2003, l'UNESCO s'emploie à élaborer une stratégie globale de protection du patrimoine culturel iraquien. Deux missions d'experts se sont rendues dans le pays en mai et juin 2003, afin de commencer à définir les domaines d'intervention prioritaires en étroite coopération avec les autorités iraquiennes. Trois réunions internationales d'experts ont eu lieu entre le mois d'avril, la première quelques jours après le pillage auquel a été soumis le Musée national, et le mois d'août 2003. Le programme culturel auquel ont abouti ces initiatives a été intégré dans la stratégie globale de reconstruction de l'Iraq formulée par le système des Nations Unies en février 2004.

À l'issue de la troisième réunion d'experts de l'UNESCO tenue à Tokyo en août 2003, les participants ont recommandé au Directeur général de l'UNESCO de créer un Comité international de coordination pour la sauvegarde du patrimoine culturel de l'Iraq. Sous les auspices du Ministère de la culture de l'Iraq et de l'UNESCO, le Comité a été établi en septembre 2003 dans le but de répartir l'aide internationale en fonction des besoins et de planifier un programme d'aide à mettre en œuvre conformément aux normes internationales les plus élevées. Sa première session plénière, qui s'est déroulée en mai 2004 au Siège de l'UNESCO, a débouché sur un certain nombre de recommandations qui font actuellement l'objet de l'attention du Secrétariat de l'Organisation afin de mettre en œuvre les activités de suivi voulues.

Des contributions financières destinées à l'exécution de projets sur le terrain ont été versées à l'UNESCO par les gouvernements des pays suivants : Italie, Japon, Suisse, Flandres, Norvège, Turquie, République tchèque et Lettonie. D'autres États membres de l'UNESCO, parmi lesquels l'Allemagne, la Belgique, le Danemark, la France, la Grèce, la Hongrie, la Lettonie, la République islamique d'Iran, les Pays-Bas, la Pologne, la République tchèque, le Royaume-Uni, les États-Unis d'Amérique, la Jordanie, l'Égypte, l'Espagne et la Suisse ont exprimé la volonté de contribuer à la protection du patrimoine culturel iraquien par le biais d'une assistance technique. En outre, des contributions ont été versées au Compte spécial pour le patrimoine culturel iraquien de l'UNESCO, notamment par la Grèce et le Saint-Siège, et l'Arabie saoudite a annoncé le versement d'une aide financière.

Grâce à ces contributions, et malgré la situation d'insécurité que connaît le pays, l'UNESCO a joué un rôle actif au cours des deux dernières années en Iraq où elle exécute actuellement quatorze projets représentant un montant total de plus de huit millions de dollars. Ceux-ci portent sur des éléments différents du patrimoine, à savoir des sites archéologiques, des monuments historiques, des institutions culturelles et des musées, des bibliothèques et des archives, ainsi que le patrimoine culturel immatériel. Le Maqâm iraquien a été proclamé chef-d'œuvre du patrimoine oral et immatériel de l'humanité en 2003 et l'Iraq a bénéficié, pour la préparation de son dossier de candidature, du soutien financier du fonds-en-dépôt UNESCO/Japon pour le patrimoine culturel immatériel.

Ces projets de l'UNESCO ont pour principaux objectifs la lutte contre le trafic illicite de biens culturels iraquiens, la restauration de bâtiments et la fourniture de matériel devant permettre aux institutions culturelles de devenir dès que possible pleinement opérationnelles ainsi que le renforcement des capacités et la formation de personnels spécialisés afin de mettre à jour leurs compétences dans divers domaines.

Dans le cadre de ses activités visant à lutter contre le trafic illicite de biens culturels iraquiens, l'UNESCO collabore étroitement avec INTERPOL sur la base d'un accord conclu en juillet 2003, pour retrouver, sur le marché de l'art, des objets archéologiques exportés illicitement d'Iraq. La documentation relative au patrimoine culturel constitue à cet égard un instrument essentiel : un stage de formation consacré à l'utilisation des normes fondamentales de description des biens mobiliers (norme Object-ID) a été organisé à Amman en décembre 2004, à l'intention du personnel du Conseil national iraquien des antiquités et du patrimoine. Deux autres stages de formation ont été simultanément organisés à Amman avec le concours du WMF (World Museum Fund)/du GCI (Getty Conservation Institute) sur l'utilisation du GIS (Geographic Information System – système d'information géographique) et l'établissement d'une banque de données sur les sites archéologiques. Des véhicules et du matériel visant à renforcer la sécurité des sites menacés sont fournis par le biais du programme pour la protection du patrimoine culturel iraquien du Groupe des Nations Unies pour le développement (GNUD). Un stage de formation de patrouilles frontalières et de gardiens de sites, ayant pour objet d'empêcher le trafic d'objets culturels et de garantir la sécurité des sites archéologiques, a eu lieu à Amman en octobre-novembre 2004, grâce à une contribution du Gouvernement de l'Italie et avec le concours des carabiniers italiens. Dans le cadre des activités de restauration du Musée national iraquien de Bagdad, et avec l'aide d'une contribution du Gouvernement suisse, l'UNESCO met actuellement en place une base de données sur la gestion des collections du musée et de l'information, et fournit les logiciels nécessaires à son fonctionnement. La première session d'un stage de formation à la documentation utilisant les techniques photogrammétriques, tenue à Riga en juin 2004, a été centrée sur les sites archéologiques et les monuments historiques.

S'agissant des projets visant à la restauration de sites et à la fourniture de matériel, l'UNESCO fournit des équipements au titre de la sauvegarde et de la surveillance par des patrouilles du site de Ninive, capitale impériale du roi assyrien biblique Sennacherib au VIIIe siècle av. J.-C., au nord de l'Iraq. Des publications spécialisées en muséologie ont par ailleurs été remises au Musée national de Bagdad et une contribution du Gouvernement du Japon permet à l'UNESCO d'aider les autorités iraquiennes à restaurer les laboratoires de conservation du Musée. Comme prévu dans le programme pour la protection du patrimoine culturel iraquien du GNUD, la première phase des projets de remise en état du Centre régional pour la conservation des biens culturels dans les pays arabes ainsi que du Musée des enfants, tous deux situés à Bagdad, a débuté en 2004. La remise en état de l'Institut d'études musicales et la fourniture de matériel pour la Bibliothèque nationale et les Archives nationales de Bagdad sont également prévues dans le programme du GNUD.

Mounir Bouchenaki
Sous-Directeur général pour la culture
UNESCO, Paris

PRÓLOGO

Heritage at Risk/Patrimonio en peligro 2004/2005 contiene informes nacionales y regionales sobre monumentos y sitios en peligro, en los que se destacan las amenazas y riesgos que afectan al patrimonio cultural en todo el mundo con objeto de difundir esta información. Los temas abarcan las guerras, los conflictos interétnicos, los actos de barbarie, el saqueo y el pillaje, las catástrofes naturales, la contaminación atmosférica, el desarrollo urbano y las normas de planificación inadecuadas, por no mencionar la negligencia, el turismo incontrolado y las restauraciones equivocadas. La publicación del Informe 2004/2005 pone de manifiesto la cantidad de países que reaccionaron positivamente a esta iniciativa desde su primera edición, en 2000. Evidencia asimismo cómo la evaluación, la vigilancia permanente y la planificación de programas a largo plazo son no sólo necesarias sino imprescindibles para la protección del patrimonio cultural en el mundo. También lo son el fortalecimiento de la legislación nacional sobre los bienes culturales y la constante cooperación de los organismos internacionales. La UNESCO por conducto de su Comité del Patrimonio Mundial y el ICOMOS a través de sus Comités Nacionales están firmemente empeñados en atenuar las consecuencias de las amenazas y la destrucción, y quisiera dar las gracias al ICOMOS y su Presidente, Michael Petzet, por sus esfuerzos encaminados a perpetrar estos informes periódicos sobre la situación del patrimonio cultural en el mundo. Varias otras organizaciones no gubernamentales también trabajan activamente en este ámbito, como el World Monuments Fund (WMF) y Patrimonio sin Fronteras.

Tratándose de las catástrofes naturales ¿quién puede olvidar la tragedia del tsunami que azotó las costas de varios países de Asia y África el 26 de diciembre de 2004, causando tantas muertes, destruyendo infraestructuras y devastando los paisajes naturales y culturales de diversos países? Aún no se pueden evaluar las pérdidas totales. Expresándose en una conferencia de prensa en la *Reunión Internacional de Mauricio sobre los Pequeños Estados Insulares en Desarrollo* el 5 de enero de 2005, el Sr. Matsuura, Director General de la UNESCO, recalcó la necesidad de un planteamiento estratégico y sistemático en el plano nacional para ayudar a los países en materia de prevención de riesgos. La UNESCO, junto con especialistas de la comunidad del patrimonio mundial y las autoridades locales, está promoviendo múltiples iniciativas para evaluar los daños en los sitios inscritos en la Lista del Patrimonio Mundial de la UNESCO situados en las regiones afectadas por el sismo y el tsunami. Se está acopiando información y se enviarán cuanto antes misiones, en coordinación con las autoridades nacionales, para definir las intervenciones apropiadas. La UNESCO propone misiones de evaluación de expertos a Sri Lanka e Indonesia para examinar la situación de los bienes culturales y naturales del patrimonio mundial afectados, en especial la Ciudad Vieja de Galle y sus fortificaciones y los bosques tropicales lluviosos de Sumatra. Asimismo, se prestará asistencia de emergencia mediante el Fondo del Patrimonio Mundial para ayudar a los países afectados a establecer evaluaciones pormenorizadas de los daños y planes de rehabilitación. Estas misiones de evaluación de especialistas de la UNESCO se efectuarán en el marco de la declaración conjunta de cooperación entre la UNESCO y el Gobierno de Italia sobre operaciones de emergencia en pro de la salvaguardia, rehabilitación y protección del patrimonio cultural y natural en países víctimas de conflictos o catástrofes naturales. En materia de políticas, se ha hecho un importante paso adelante con motivo de la Reunión sobre gestión de riesgos del patrimonio cultural, organizada por el Centro del Patrimonio Mundial de la UNESCO en colaboración con el Organismo de Asuntos Culturales de Japón, el ICCROM y el ICOMOS en el marco de la Conferencia Mundial de las Naciones Unidas sobre la Reducción de los Desastres (Kobe, Japón, 18–22 de enero de 2005). En las recomendaciones formuladas en esa ocasión (véase http://unisdr.org/wcdr/thematic-sessions/thematic-reports/report-session-3-3.pdf) se subrayó la función dinámica del patrimonio como elemento que contribuye al desarrollo sostenible y la reducción de los desastres, así como la importancia de los sistemas tradicionales de conocimiento y el patrimonio inmaterial para mitigar y/o prevenir catástrofes.

Iraq tras años de embargo y guerra

En este cuarto informe mundial se presenta una evaluación del patrimonio cultural iraquí tras el conflicto y más de diez años de embargo. En el capítulo relativo a la situación ecológica y el patrimonio construido al término de cuatro decenios de adversidad figuran cinco estudios monográficos (las marismas del Sur de Iraq, la campiña kurda, la ciudad vieja de Ana a orillas del Éufrates, la ciudadela de Arbil y el Complejo Administrativo Otomano Saray en Bagdad) y un panorama de las obras de restauración y reconstrucción realizadas en el país. En 2005 se cumplirán próximamente dos años del saqueo del Museo de Iraq en Bagdad y de muchas otras instituciones culturales iraquíes en Bagdad y en todo el país (abril de 2003). El conjunto del patrimonio cultural de Iraq – sitios arqueológicos y edificios históricos, museos y entidades culturales, bibliotecas y archivos y el patrimonio inmaterial – ha sido gravemente afectado, causando una pérdida irreversible al pueblo iraquí y, en especial, a los niños que deberán hacerse cargo del patrimonio cultural para las generaciones futuras.

El saqueo de los sitios arqueológicos y el pillaje de edificios históricos no han disminuido en lo más mínimo. Aunque ahora se puede determinar el número de objetos que desaparecieron del Museo de Iraq en Bagdad, es absolutamente imposible evaluar el número de objetos extraídos ilícitamente de sitios arqueológicos y vendidos. Se han localizado e incluido en el inventario preparado por el Consejo Estatal Iraquí de Antigüedades y Patrimonio más de 10.000 sitios arqueológicos, pero quedan muchos otros por inscribir. Cabe mencionar entre ellos los conocidos vestigios de Ashur, Ctesifon, Eridu, Hatra, Isín, Jorsabad, Kish, Lagash, Larsa, Nimrud, Nínive, Samarra, Ur y Uruk. Se inscribieron dos sitios en la Lista del Patrimonio Mundial de la UNESCO: Hatra en 1985 y Ashur en 2003. Las excavaciones ilícitas en sitios arqueológicos siguen destruyendo el patrimonio iraquí, sobre todo en el Sur, en sitios tan importantes como Isín, Umma y Umm Al-Aqarib. La instalación de bases militares cerca de sitios arqueológicos o en ellos, como en los casos de Hatra, capital del imperio parto y Babilonia, capital del rey neobabilonio Nabucodonosor II (604–562 A.C.), requiere urgentemente atención, ya que pueden producirse daños irreversibles.

Acción de la UNESCO para proteger el patrimonio cultural iraquí

La protección, como la rehabilitación, es un proceso a largo plazo para el cual se necesitan iniciativas internacionales y estrategias a largo plazo. Desde abril de 2003 la UNESCO se ocupa de elaborar una estrategia global para proteger el patrimonio cultural iraquí.

Dos misiones de expertos visitaron el país en mayo y junio de 2003 para empezar a definir campos de intervención prioritarios en estrecha cooperación con las autoridades iraquíes. Tres reuniones internacionales de expertos tuvieron lugar entre abril, pocos días después del saqueo del Museo de Iraq, y agosto de 2003. El programa resultante relativo a la cultura se integró en la estrategia global para la rehabilitación de Iraq, elaborada por el sistema de las Naciones Unidas en febrero de 2004.

Tras la tercera reunión de expertos de la UNESCO en Tokio en agosto de 2003, los participantes recomendaron que el Director General de la UNESCO estableciera un Comité Internacional de Coordinación para la Salvaguardia del Patrimonio Cultural Iraquí. El Comité se creó en septiembre de 2003 bajo los auspicios del Ministerio de Cultura de Iraq y la UNESCO, a fin de canalizar la asistencia internacional en función de las necesidades y planificar un programa basado en las normas internacionales más rigurosas. Su primera reunión plenaria se celebró en mayo de 2004 en la Sede de la UNESCO y dio lugar a una serie de recomendaciones, de las que la Secretaría de la UNESCO se está ocupando para darles un seguimiento apropiado.

La UNESCO recibió contribuciones financieras destinadas a ejecutar proyectos sobre el terreno de los Gobiernos de Italia, Japón, Suiza, Flandes, Noruega, Turquía, República Checa y Letonia. Otros Estados Miembros de la UNESCO, entre ellos Alemania, Bélgica, Dinamarca, Francia, Grecia, Hungría, Letonia, la República Islámica del Irán, los Países Bajos, Polonia, la República Checa, el Reino Unido, los Estados Unidos de América, Jordania, Egipto, España y Suiza expresaron su deseo de contribuir a la protección del patrimonio cultural iraquí mediante una asistencia técnica. Además, la UNESCO recibió contribuciones en su Cuenta Especial para el patrimonio cultural iraquí, en especial de Grecia y la Santa Sede, mientras que Arabia Saudita ha prometido prestar ayuda financiera.

Gracias a esas contribuciones y pese a la situación de inseguridad del país, en los dos últimos años la UNESCO ha trabajado en Iraq y sigue realizando 14 proyectos, por una cuantía total de más de ocho millones de dólares, que abarcan distintos ámbitos: sitios arqueológicos, edificios históricos, instituciones culturales y museos, bibliotecas y archivos, y la salvaguardia del patrimonio cultural inmaterial. El "Maqam Iraquí" fue proclamado obra maestra del patrimonio oral e inmaterial de la humanidad en 2003; en la preparación de esta candidatura Iraq recibió asistencia financiera a través del Fondo Fiduciario japonés para el patrimonio cultural inmaterial.

Estos proyectos de la UNESCO tienen como principales objetivos luchar contra el tráfico ilícito de bienes culturales iraquíes, rehabilitar locales y suministrar equipo para que las instituciones culturales puedan reanudar cuanto antes todas sus actividades, y proporcionar capacitación y formación al personal profesional a fin de actualizar sus competencias en distintos campos.

Entre las actividades que realiza para combatir el tráfico ilícito de bienes culturales iraquíes, la UNESCO colabora estrechamente con INTERPOL en virtud de un acuerdo firmado en julio de 2003, a fin de rastrear en el mercado del arte objetos arqueológicos exportados ilícitamente de Iraq. A este respecto, la documentación sobre los bienes culturales es un instrumento esencial: en diciembre de 2004 se celebró en Ammán un curso de formación sobre normas fundamentales para la documentación de bienes muebles (norma Object-ID) en beneficio del personal del Consejo Estatal de Antigüedades y Patrimonio. Otros dos cursos de formación se organizaron simultáneamente en Ammán con la asistencia del WMF y el Getty Conservation Institute (GCI) sobre la utilización del Sistema de Información Geográfica (SIG) y la preparación de una base de datos relativa a sitios arqueológicos. En el marco del programa del Grupo de las Naciones Unidas para el Desarrollo (GNUD) se están proporcionando vehículos y equipo para reforzar la seguridad en los sitios en peligro a fin de proteger el patrimonio cultural iraquí. En octubre-noviembre de 2004, gracias a una contribución del Gobierno de Italia y a la asistencia de los "carabinieri" italianos, tuvo lugar un curso de formación para patrullas de fronteras y guardianes de sitios a fin de detener el tráfico ilícito de objetos culturales y brindar seguridad a los sitios arqueológicos. Entre las actividades encaminadas a rehabilitar el Museo Nacional de Iraq en Bagdad, y con la ayuda de una contribución del Gobierno de Suiza, la UNESCO está proporcionando una base de datos para la gestión de las colecciones y la información del museo, así como equipos informáticos con los cuales hacer funcionar el sistema. En junio de 2004 se celebró en Riga la primera sesión de un curso de formación sobre documentación mediante fotogrametría, centrado en los sitios arqueológicos y los edificios históricos.

Entre los proyectos destinados a rehabilitar locales y suministrar equipo, la UNESCO facilita material para el mantenimiento y la vigilancia del sitio de Nínive en el Norte de Iraq, antigua capital imperial del rey asirio bíblico Senaquerib en el siglo VIII a.C. También se han entregado al museo de Iraq en Bagdad publicaciones especializadas sobre estudios museológicos mientras que, gracias a una contribución prometida por el Gobierno de Japón, la UNESCO presta asistencia a las autoridades iraquíes para la rehabilitación de los laboratorios de conservación del museo. En el marco del programa de protección del patrimonio cultural iraquí del GNUD, se inició en 2004 la primera fase de los proyectos de rehabilitación del Centro Regional para la Conservación de los Bienes Culturales en los Países Árabes y del Museo del Niño, ambos situados en Bagdad. En ese mismo programa del GNUD se prevé asimismo la rehabilitación de la Academia de Música y el suministro de equipo a la Biblioteca Nacional y los Archivos Nacionales en Bagdad.

Mounir Bouchenaki
Subdirector General de Cultura
UNESCO, París

INTRODUCTION

This new ICOMOS *World Report on Monuments and Sites in Danger*, with some 60 separate reports from 45 countries or fields of expertise, shows once again that many monuments and heritage sites are threatened worldwide even if they are on the World Heritage List and that the losses caused not only by natural disasters but also by man are immense. Faced with the gigantic tsunami catastrophe, which hit humankind exactly one year after the terrible Bam earthquake (26 December 2003, see pp. 105–110) and while this report was already being printed, we hope that the professional network of ICOMOS will prove successful in view of this tremendous challenge (see message by the President, pp. 23–25).

The annual report by ICOMOS on Heritage at Risk is intended to highlight problems and issues threatening monuments and sites around the world, and where possible to present case studies from various countries to share possible solutions with other areas of the world. This meets ICOMOS' objectives to serve as a forum for professional dialogue and exchange, and to disseminate information on conservation principles, techniques and policies.

In presenting these reports from many parts of the world, ICOMOS recognises that they are a mere drop in the bucket of the risks, threats and damage to individual sites and monuments and general patterns in the treatment of cultural heritage places that risks their fabric, their cultural integrity and the special values they have for associated communities. The reports are a snapshot, depicting issues considered to be important, pressing and serious to those reporting; they do not pretend to be comprehensive or present statistical trends and pressures.

Even so, this 2004/2005 *Heritage at Risk* report shows clearly that heritage protection and conservation / preservation still has a long way to go, before ICOMOS can be assured of a consistent worldwide recognition and concern for our monuments and sites, cultural landscapes and all kinds of heritage places. It appears that cultural heritage still does not gain the level of commitment that the international conventions for its protection might suggest. In many countries archaeological sites continue to be plundered by illegal excavations, and the illicit traffic of works of art represents a continuous loss of cultural goods that from a preservation perspective should be preserved on their original site. Not only paintings, sculptures and the artefacts of cult sites are being decimated in many countries through theft, but art monuments are actually being destroyed in order to gain fragments for the market: temple complexes are being looted, sculptures decapitated, frescoes cut up. Whilst damage from war and natural disasters gain international headlines, the enclosed reports show that just as great risks are more insidious and incremental. These dangers result from a lack of knowledge about what heritage there is, a lack of awareness of its value to our society, a lack of understanding of how it may be protected whilst allowing certain developments, including a lack of appreciation of technical solutions and conservation standards.

Analysis of the reports in this volume shows that apart from the general risks to heritage from natural disasters and physical decay of structures, there are certain patterns in human activity that risk our heritage. These are among others: war and inter-ethnic conflicts, development, tourism and redundancy.

Risks from war

The risks to heritage places due to conflicts such as war and inter-ethnic conflict have been demonstrated in the previous three *Heritage at Risk* reports. Again in this 2004 report, there are several instances of damage from warfare, including Afghanistan, Iraq, Kosovo or Palestine. Such war damage and destruction to cultural heritage hits the headlines of the media around the world; it is shocking, dramatic and often directed at precious and unique icons of past and present cultures. It may be deliberately aimed at such monuments, for example to the Bamiyan Buddhas, or in Kosovo, for reasons of iconoclasm or centuries old internecine conflicts. In such cases, ICOMOS has been active, meeting its aim in putting the expertise of its highly qualified conservation experts at the service of the international community and the countries concerned to restore the damage. This volume's report on ICOMOS' activities at Bamiyan in Afghanistan is such an example. The ongoing conflict in Iraq has meant that little has been achieved on the ground to mitigate the ongoing damage to its heritage, despite strong international horror and good intentions about saving Iraq's millennia of monuments and sites.

Preventative measures against future destruction in times of conflict are harder to achieve, despite ICOMOS' support of the International Committee of the Blue Shield. Longer-term strategies, such as measures to celebrate and share the importance of such places with others, for example by World Heritage listing, may be one way to build bridges between previously polarised communities, breaking down longstanding enmities that can result in attacks on the cultural heritage of another group.

Risks from development

Whilst war, including the damage and looting of hundreds of important archaeological sites in Iraq, and natural destruction such as the earthquake destruction of the significant earthen city of Bam, are dramatic and lead to urgent actions at an international level, more insidious damage is taking place daily in many countries as part of the normal planning and building processes.

So again this 2004/2005 *Heritage at Risk* report raises concerns from several national committees about such risks from inappropriate development of heritage areas, impacting on their significance. This is especially the case in historic city centres. Austria and the Czech Republic both raise the threat to inner city streetscapes from the development of roof areas, changing the nature of the roofline and damaging the architectural heritage qualities. In Cyprus, the risk of development in areas where the full cultural history is not understood is risking earlier cultural phases of Nicosia, emphasising the need to identify all historic phases in urban areas and having protected zones of cultural and archaeological sensitivity.

In such urban areas, as mentioned in several country reports, a key issue may not be inadequate legislation, but the ineffectual application of such statutory regulations, either for a lack of understanding of the risks to the heritage values or the greater pressure exerted by the profit motive of property development. Italy shows that it is not necessarily developing countries where authorities lack the force or resources to stop inappropriate or frankly illegal developments, that both impact the general urban amenity as well as heritage values. Needed are case studies demonstrating how a successful balance was achieved between the retention of heritage values and development that ICOMOS could disseminate to its members and to countries and regions struggling to protect heritage against such development pressures. A serious and severe example is in the Casa Antiguo World Heritage site in Panama, where historic façades were demolished, and in the World Heritage centre of Avila, Spain, where the insertion of new housing and carparks is seen as destroying the city's historic integrity.

Urban sprawl is another development that is mentioned by many national committees as impacting on the surroundings of urban centres, damaging the relationship between city and its rural surroundings, its landscape setting. Andorra, Australia, and Norway all mention aspects of this issue, whilst New Zealand mentions the destruction of the individual character of small towns in the trend to inserting notional 'heritage' features such as lighting, paving and shopfronts, causing them all to look the same and quite out of keeping with their historic style and fabric.

All the examples demonstrate how important it is to fully understand the reason buildings, structures, entire quarters of a city may be heritage listed, not just for their historical importance, but for values associated with the relationship to each other, integrity of scale and design, and for the memories and meanings such areas have for the local population. If such values are well understood by all, they stand a better chance of being maintained, and proposed new developments amended to limit their impact, even enhance the heritage sites. Again, the examples given, such as high-rise buildings threatening the visual integrity of Cologne in Germany, or Prague in the Czech Republic, highlight the risks of incremental change. However, development is not restricted to such urban areas, and can result in large swathes of country landscapes being irretrievably changed. These include large-scale mining, windfarms, increasingly wide and straight highways and bridges, dams, open mining, and increasingly invasive agricultural practices. Countries such as Australia, Germany, Serbia and Montenegro, and the Archaeological Heritage committee have noted the impact in rural areas to cultural landscape values as well as the ongoing risk to sub-surface archaeological sites, for example in New Zealand, Poland, and Japan, so destroying important evidence of cultures and times past. The description of how much of the historic Jain route in India has been destroyed or is at risk from dam building is sobering.

Tourism

Tourism development is actually a sub-set of the above problem, but deserves separate mention as it is so widespread and so often cited by national committees in their *Heritage at Risk* reports. In many developing countries, international tourism is seen as a major source of income and major developments, such as along coastal areas, are dedicated to the pleasure of foreigners. Such developments are hardly compatible with the protection of the way of life, cultural traditions and cultural heritage of local communities. Even remote heritage sites are no longer protected by their isolation, on the contrary, their very distance from settlement places them at risk, often resulting in either accidental damage, rubbish pollution and even vandalism. This is reported from Kazakhstan, regarding the rock engravings at Tamgaly-Tas, or the stone arrangements (geoglyphs) at the Trujillo ceremonial sites in the northern Peruvian desert, damaged by vehicles running over the sites, in this latter case also damaged by mining development. Visitation numbers and uncontrolled tourism are also risks to heritage as shown in the reports from Costa Rica, where inappropriate tourism development is destroying the integrity of the town of Liberia.

As was stated in the 2002-03 *Heritage at Risk* report, ICOMOS is disappointed at the lack of commitment to heritage by the tourism industry, which is still exploiting it through over-use, not contributing to the protection and conservation of cultural heritage from its profits. It should however also be noted, that the sooner it is understood that tourism is not the automatic solution to heritage conservation and heritage funding, or the economic well-being of a local community, the more considered might be any tourism development of our precious and non-renewable heritage sites and landscapes.

Redundancy

Social, economic and technical changes often result in certain structures no longer being used or useful. This is a normal result of change, but in recent decades such changes are often rapid or imposed from outside an area with little opportunity to slowly incorporate them into the existing systems and structures, resulting in their lying empty and abandoned. Examples from big industry, Hungary, Germany and elsewhere, all point to the difficulty of finding adaptive reuses for such large complexes, for presenting them as industrial museums or even residential areas, cannot be applied to all. The report from Belgium highlights another issue related to redundant industrial complexes, that of the pollution and ongoing toxic impact on the surrounding environment, with potential conflicts between environment conservationists and heritage conservators.

Military installations are also increasingly going out of use with changed technology. This is described for Poland, which outlines the problems of keeping places that are no longer useful, including the lack of physical maintenance, lack of funds, and the difficulty of finding a future use and purpose. Previous *Heritage at Risk* reports have shown how manor houses in Eastern European countries are faced with such problems, their going out of government hands, often resulting in inappropriate development or their decay. A report from Russia shows that these risks are also threatening the integrity of former palaces, until now protected and managed by the state. Italy also reports on concern about the sale of heritage places by the government and the public response to this.

The Ottoman churches of Turkey form another such redundant type of heritage at risk, for due to demographic and social changes, these buildings are no more being used and may not be valued as part of the historic heritage of Turkey. Highlighting their plight is a first step in raising awareness, which should be followed by an appreciation of their importance in the diversity of the cultural landscape.

Changes in agricultural practice has meant that farmsteads, the complexes of residence, barns, sheds and other outhouses, are also falling out of use, as most clearly described in The Netherlands and in Finland. Norway also describes this process, and raises the issue of abandoned farms being overgrown by forest, that is disappearing traces of human activity of the formerly rural landscapes, as well as resulting in a loss of biodiversity.

Changes in lifestyle and technology are also resulting in certain building forms and styles going out of fashion and use. Previous *Heritage at Risk* reports have described how this is resulting in a shift away from traditional, vernacular building forms, perhaps because they are not thought 'modern', or because they require more effort to construct and maintain. Either way, the change results in a more homogenous built landscape around the world, often resulting in forms that are less suited to the local environment and climate. It is often only after the change is irreparable that local communities realise what they have lost by way of unique signatures of their cultural landscape. Examples in the 2004/2005 report include the mudbrick vernacular courtyard houses of Sardinia, Italy, adobe structures in Mexico, and wooden suburban housing in Vilnius, Lithuania.

Both the Dutch and Mexican reports describe measures to maintain and appreciate traditional styles, in Mexico, using vernacular adobe building techniques for modern and inexpensive adobe housing, and in Holland, an active program of the 'Year of the Historic Farmhouse' in 2003, and holding an ICOMOS Vernacular Architecture conference, were able to raise awareness and a wider support for this traditional built form in the landscape.

Other risks

Not knowing about heritage is of course a key risk, and remote areas or particular types of heritage can be neglected. Central Asian countries such as Kyrgyzstan and Tajikistan both have reports on remote Buddhist or Islamic sites that without detailed recording or conservation currently taking place with foreign funding would not be documented; nonetheless, the risk is that once such special projects are completed, the site may still not be sufficiently well managed for any long-term protection or survival. Ukraine highlights the frustration of apathy or lack of funding for its wide range of heritage sites, representing its diverse ethnic history as a crossroads between East and West. Guinea's important Slave Sites, evidence of a particularly brutal phase in African history, are at risk from lack of expertise and funding. An international effort is needed in the long-term, for these sites are part of humanity's reminder of past brutal times, they are not only Guinea's responsibility.

Another threat mentioned by both Sweden and Australia is the issue of delegating heritage management and conservation to local authorities. This trend in many countries, which whilst benefiting from the local community's knowledge of its history, their local attachment and connection, may risk a loss or fragmentation of centralised conservation expertise and knowledge of and access to solutions in other regions.

Whilst the above analysis of risks has focused on those caused by human activity, natural disasters continue to damage heritage, as outlined in the Czech report on the 2002 flood damage to numerous heritage buildings throughout the countryside. It is difficult to know how to prevent such damage, although the report from Japan provides an excellent study for the prevention and mitigation of earthquake damage, particularly affecting historic wooden buildings around the historic city of Kyoto. This case study is one that could be applied for heritage places in other earthquake zones. However, how to protect against for example global warming is a longer term issue that has barely been addressed internationally in regard to cultural heritage protection; the risks of rising sea levels are however already visible in the Polar regions as shown in this report, and also mentioned by New Zealand.

ICOMOS, the International Council on Monuments and Sites with some 8000 members organised in 125 National Committees and 25 International Scientific Committees is the advisory body for UNESCO on issues concerning the World Cultural Heritage, in particular the evaluation of monuments and sites that have been placed on the World Heritage List or are under consideration for listing. On the whole, the UNESCO Convention for the Protection of the World Cultural and Natural Heritage remains one of the few successful efforts at world cultural politics directed at saving humankind's historic heritage, and ICOMOS is proud to be able to work with UNESCO as an advisory body. The monuments and sites, historic districts and cultural landscapes that are entered on UNESCO's World Heritage List should in fact be numbered among the non-endangered monuments, but our reports show that here, too, there are cases of substantial danger.

So the *Heritage at Risk Report* 2004/2005 is proof that the situation of the cultural heritage is still highly critical in many regions of the world. While time and again billions are being invested into the preparation of war and destruction, the responsible often lack the necessary commitment when it comes to preserving the threatened heritage of past centuries and millennia. Therefore, we can only hope that the H@R report will inspire further commitments on national and international levels, generate new initiatives in preservation, and provide an additional positive impulse for existing institutions such as the ICOMOS-supported International Committee of the Blue Shield. The effect should also extend to international foundations that are involved in preservation such as the Getty Foundation or the World Monuments Fund. Their good example could also influence other internationally operating sponsors, now that there is also increased awareness of the economic importance of heritage conservation and its special role in terms of "sustainable development". In this sense, with its *Heritage at Risk* Report ICOMOS hopes not only to gain the moral support of the world public in the battle against all kinds of threats, but also to achieve practical results in co-operation with all forces that are interested in preservation/conservation of the cultural heritage.

Acknowledgments

Unlike the previous *Heritage at Risk* reports, this 2004/2005 volume was not produced by the earlier taskforce of members from Australia, Canada and Germany, but steered by members of the Editorial Board, particularly under the guidance of the President of ICOMOS International. The report includes not only contributions from national committees and a few of the International Scientific Committees, but some reports by individual experts. I would also like to thank the 45 experts from 29 countries and eight scientific committees, as well as the Holy See and ICCROM, who attended a workshop held in Bergen, Norway, on 6 September 2004 during the ICOMOS Advisory Committee meeting. Their contributions as well as those of the "Heritage at Risk" workshop at Victoria Falls in October 2003 are important to this publication. Whilst commending the input from all ICOMOS colleagues and committees it is also noted, in line with ICOMOS policy, that the information provided for this publication reflects the independent view of each committee and the different authors.

Our experienced editorial team had very committed support from our Australian colleague Marilyn Truscott who edited the English texts, translated some of the French texts and co-ordinated and edited other translations. John Ziesemer once again dedicated considerable time to the overall production of this publication. I also would like to thank Hannelore Puttinger from the ICOMOS Secretariat in Munich, as well as Gaia Jungeblodt and the staff of the International Secretariat in Paris, especially Olivia de Willermin, Melanie Grywnow, and Claudia de Sevilla and José Garcia, who added the material to the ICOMOS website. The publication of the 2004/2005 World Report would not have been possible without the financial and organisational framework provided by ICOMOS Germany and made possible through the generous support of the German Federal Government Commissioner for Cultural Affairs and the Media as well as of the Messerschmitt Foundation. Furthermore, we also need to thank UNESCO Cultural Heritage Division and the Ministry of Culture and Communication of France for their financial support. Finally, I once again extend my thanks to the K.G. Saur publishing company, particularly Manfred Link, for facilitating the printing of this publication.

As previous reports, this 2004/2005 report is also available on the Internet at www.international.icomos.org/risk.

Michael Petzet
December 2004

INTRODUCTION

Cette nouvelle édition du *rapport mondial ICOMOS sur les monuments et les sites en péril*, constitué de 60 rapports individuels provenant de 45 pays ou domaines d'expertise différents, montre une nouvelle fois qu'un grand nombre de monuments et de sites sont en péril à travers le monde même s'ils sont inscrits sur la liste du Patrimoine mondial, et que les pertes dues non seulement aux catastrophes naturelles mais aussi à l'homme sont immenses. Devant la catastrophe gigantesque causée par le tsunami qui a frappé le monde exactement un an après le terrible tremblement de terre de Bam (26 décembre 2003, voir p. 105–110), et alors que ce rapport était déjà en cours d'impression, nous espérons que grâce à l'ensemble du réseau professionnel de l'ICOMOS nous réussirons à faire face à ce défi majeur. (voir message du Président p. 23–25)

Le rapport annuel sur le Patrimoine en péril publié par l'ICOMOS a pour objectif de mettre l'accent sur les problèmes et les enjeux qui menacent les monuments et les sites de par le monde, et quand c'est possible de présenter des études de cas de divers pays pour partager les éventuelles solutions avec d'autres régions du monde. Ceci rejoint l'objectif de l'ICOMOS d'agir en tant que forum pour le dialogue et l'échange entre professionnels et de diffuser l'information sur les techniques, principes et politiques de conservation.

En présentant ces rapports provenant des quatre coins du monde, l'ICOMOS reconnaît qu'ils ne représentent qu'une goutte dans l'océan de risques, menaces et dommages subis par les sites et monuments individuels et ne montrent que des tendances générales dans le traitement des lieux du patrimoine culturel dont sont mis en péril à la fois le tissu même, mais aussi leur intégrité culturelle et les valeurs spécifiques qu'ils représentent pour les communautés concernées. Ces rapports sont des prises de vue qui illustrent des enjeux considérés comme importants, urgents et sérieux par ceux qui préparent les rapports. Ils n'ont pas la prétention d'être exhaustifs ou de présenter des données statistiques.

Néanmoins, ce rapport *Patrimoine en péril* 2004-2005 montre clairement que la protection et la conservation du patrimoine culturel a encore du chemin à faire avant que l'ICOMOS soit assuré de la reconnaissance systématique mondiale de nos monuments et sites, paysages culturels et toutes sortes de lieux du patrimoine. Il semble que le patrimoine culturel ne suscite pas encore le niveau d'attention que les conventions internationales créées pour sa protection peuvent laisser penser. Dans beaucoup de pays, les sites archéologiques sont encore pillés par des fouilles illégales et le trafic illicite des œuvres d'art provoque une disparition permanente de biens culturels qui, du point de vue de la conservation, devraient demeurer sur leur site d'origine. Non seulement les peintures, les sculptures et les objets des lieux de culte sont décimés par le vol, mais les monuments artistiques sont détruits afin que des fragments soient mis sur le marché : des temples sont dynamités, des sculptures décapitées, des fresques découpées. Alors que les dommages causés par des guerres et des désastres naturels font les unes de la presse internationale, ce rapport montre qu'il existe des risques aussi grands qui sont plus insidieux et progressifs. Ces dangers viennent d'un manque de connaissance des différents type de patrimoine, d'un manque de sensibilité envers la valeur qu'il a pour notre société, d'un manque de compréhension de comment on peut le protéger tout en permettant certains développements, ainsi qu'un manque de compréhension des solutions techniques possibles et des normes de conservation en vigueur.

L'analyse des rapports de cette édition montre qu'en dehors du risque général pour le patrimoine culturel dû aux désastres naturels et à la détérioration physique des structures, il existe des modes d'activité humains qui mettent en danger notre patrimoine. Ceci sont entre autres : la guerre et le conflit interethnique, le développement, le tourisme et l'abandon des structures dû au changement d'usage.

Les risques dus à la guerre

Les menaces qui pèsent sur le patrimoine à cause de conflits comme la guerre et les conflits interethniques ont été démontrées dans les trois précédents volumes du rapport *Patrimoine en péril*. En 2004-2005 de nouveau, il y a plusieurs cas concernant des dommages dus à la guerre, comprenant l'Afghanistan, l'Iraq, le Kosovo et la Palestine. Ces dommages et destructions dues à la guerre, choquants et dramatiques, font la une de l'actualité dans les médias à travers le monde et souvent les cibles sont des symboles précieux et uniques des cultures présentes et passées. Des monuments peuvent être pris délibérément pour cible, par exemple les Bouddhas de Bamiyan ou, comme au Kosovo, être victime d'un iconoclasme ou de conflits intestins datant de plusieurs siècles. Dans ces cas, l'ICOMOS a agi en offrant l'expertise de ses éminents experts en conservation au service de la communauté internationale et des pays concernés pour réparer les dommages. Le rapport sur les activités de l'ICOMOS à Bamiyan en Afghanistan inclus dans ce volume en est un exemple. Le conflit continu en Iraq a eu pour conséquence le peu de progrès réalisés sur place pour atténuer les dommages continuels subis par son patrimoine, malgré l'indignation internationale et les bonnes intentions de sauver les monuments et sites millénaires de l'Iraq.

Des mesures préventives contre des destructions futures durant des conflits sont plus difficiles à mettre en œuvre, malgré le soutien de l'ICOMOS pour le Comité International du Bouclier Bleu. Des stratégies à long terme, telles que des initiatives pour célébrer et partager l'importance de ces lieux avec d'autres, par exemple à travers l'inscription au Patrimoine mondial peuvent être un des moyens de rapprocher des communautés auparavant divisées, pour vaincre des inimitiés de longue date qui peuvent avoir pour conséquence des attaques sur le patrimoine culturel d'un autre groupe.

Les risques dus au développement

Alors que la guerre en Iraq, qui inclut des dommages et pillages de centaines de sites archéologiques importants, et que la destruction naturelle de la citadelle bâtie en terre de Bam dévastée par un tremblement de terre sont dramatiques et suscitent des actions d'urgence au niveau international, des dommages plus insidieux ont lieu tous les jours dans beaucoup de pays dans le cadre des processus normaux de construction et d'aménagement.

Le rapport *Patrimoine en péril* 2004-2005 traite des préoccupations énoncées par plusieurs comités nationaux sur les risques dus au développement inadapté de zones historiques, qui à un impact sur leur valeur. Ceci est notamment le cas dans les centres villes historiques. L'Autriche et la République Tchèque signalent la menace qui pèse sur les paysages urbains des centres villes due aux transformations au niveau des toitures qui modifient la ligne de faîte de la ville et endommagent la qualité de son patrimoine architectural. À Chypre, la pression du développement dans des zones où l'histoire culturelle n'est pas entièrement documentée met en danger des phases culturelles plus anciennes de Nicosie. Ceci met en évidence le besoin d'identifier toutes les strates historiques dans les zones urbaines et de protéger les zones d'importance culturelle et archéologique.

Comme plusieurs rapports le soulignent, dans ces zones urbaines la question centrale n'est pas une législation insuffisante mais une mise en œuvre inefficace des normes légales, soit à cause d'un manque de compréhension pour les risques qui pèsent sur les valeurs patrimoniales soit à cause de la pression croissante exercée par la recherche de profit des promoteurs immobiliers. L'Italie montre que ce n'est pas nécessairement uniquement dans des pays en voie de développement que les autorités manquent de puissance ou de moyens pour faire arrêter des projets inappropriés ou franchement illégaux, qui affectent à la fois les équipements urbains en général mais aussi les valeurs patrimoniales. Il est nécessaire d'établir des études de cas qui montrent comment un équilibre réussi pourrait être atteint entre le maintien des valeurs patrimoniales et le développement. Celles-ci pourraient être diffusées par l'ICOMOS à ces membres et aux pays et régions qui luttent pour protéger le patrimoine contre cette pression de développement. Un exemple sérieux et grave est le site du Patrimoine mondial du centre historique de Panama où des façades historiques ont été démolies, et le centre ville d'Avila en Espagne, également inscrit au Patrimoine mondial, où la construction de parkings et de nouveaux immeubles de logement détruisent l'intégrité historique de la ville. L'étalement des villes est un autre développement qui est mentionné par beaucoup de Comités comme ayant un impact sur les alentours des centres urbains, portant atteinte à la relation entre la ville et son environnement rural, son cadre paysager. L'Andorre, l'Australie, la Norvège tous mentionnent des aspects de cette problématique, alors que la Nouvelle Zélande parle de la destruction du caractère individuel des petites villes due à une tendance à insérer des éléments soit disant de patrimoine comme l'éclairage, le pavement, les devantures de magasins, ayant pour résultat une uniformisation de ces villes sans lien avec leur tissu et leur style historiques. Tous ces exemples illustrent l'importance de comprendre pleinement la raison pour laquelle des édifices, des structures ou des quartiers entiers sont inscrits en tant que patrimoine, pas seulement pour leur importance historique, mais aussi pour des valeurs liées à la relation qu'ils ont entre eux, pour l'intégrité de leur dimension et de leur conception et pour les souvenirs et significations que ces zones ont pour la population locale. Si ces valeurs sont bien comprises par tous, elles ont une meilleure chance d'être maintenues, et les nouveaux projets de développement proposés ont plus de chance d'être modifiés pour limiter leur impact, même parfois pour mettre en valeur des sites historiques. Encore une fois, les exemples présentés tels que les tours qui menacent l'intégrité visuelle de la ville de Cologne en Allemagne ou à Prague en République Tchèque, soulignent les risques dus aux changements progressifs. Cependant, le développement ne concerne pas uniquement ces zones urbaines, et peut conduire à une transformation irrémédiable de pans entiers de paysages ruraux. Ceci peut inclure l'exploitation minière à grande échelle et à ciel ouvert, les sites à éoliennes, des autoroutes de plus en plus larges et droites, ainsi que des ponts, des barrages, et aussi des techniques agricoles de plus en plus invasives. Des pays comme l'Australie, l'Allemagne, la Serbie et le Monténégro, ainsi que notre Comité sur le patrimoine archéologique ont mentionné l'impact que ces développements ont dans les zones rurales sur les valeurs des paysages culturels et le risque qu'ils représentent pour les sites archéologiques enfouis, par exemple en Nouvelle Zélande, en Pologne et au Japon, en détruisant des témoignages importants des cultures et temps passés. La description de la destruction de la route historique du Jaïnisme en Inde ou de sa mise en péril à cause de la construction de barrages donne à réfléchir.

Le Tourisme

Le développement touristique est en effet une sous catégorie du problème mentionné ci-dessus, mais mérite quand même d'être évoqué séparément étant donné sa diffusion et le fait qu'il est très souvent cité par les comités nationaux dans leurs rapports *Patrimoine en péril*. Dans beaucoup de pays en voie de développement, le tourisme international est considéré comme une source majeure de revenus. Des projets de développement d'infrastructure importants, par exemple le long des zones côtières, sont dédiés entièrement aux plaisirs des étrangers. De tels développements sont difficilement compatibles avec la protection des modes de vie, des traditions et du patrimoine culturel des communautés locales. Même des sites historiques éloignés ne sont plus protégés par leur isolement. Au contraire, leur éloignement de toute habitation les met en danger, avec pour résultat fréquent des dommages accidentels, une pollution par des déchets et même du vandalisme. De tels cas se sont produits au Kazakhstan, notamment sur les gravures rupestres de Tamgaly-Tas, ou les dispositions de pierres (géoglyphes) des sites cérémoniels de Trujillo dans la zone désertique du nord du Pérou, endommagées par les véhicules qui traversent les sites, et dans le second cas également par l'exploitation minière. Un grand nombre de visiteurs et un tourisme incontrôlé représentent un risque pour le patrimoine comme on peut le voir dans les rapports du Costa Rica qui expliquent qu'un développement inadapté du tourisme est en train de détruire l'intégrité de la ville de Liberia.

Comme cela a déjà été évoqué dans le rapport *Patrimoine en péril* de 2002-2003, l'ICOMOS est déçu par le manque d'engagement de l'industrie touristique envers le patrimoine, par le fait qu'elle continue à l'exploiter excessivement, sans contribuer avec ses profits à sa protection et sa conservation. Cependant, on devrait également noter que plus tôt on aura compris que le tourisme n'est pas la solution automatique pour la conservation du patrimoine et son financement, ni pour le bien-être économique des communautés locales, plus les aménagements touristiques de nos précieux et irremplaçables sites et paysages patrimoniaux seront mieux pensés.

Les structures ayant perdu leur usage

Les changements sociaux, économiques et techniques ont souvent pour conséquence l'abandon de certaines structures. Ceci est un résultat normal du changement, mais dans les décennies récentes ces transformations se sont faites rapidement ou ont parfois été imposées de l'extérieur avec peu d'occasion de les incorporer progressivement dans des systèmes et structures existants, qui par la suite restent inoccupés ou sont abandonnés. Des exemples issus des industries lourdes en Hongrie, en Allemagne et également ailleurs, présentent la difficulté de trouver de nouveaux usages pour ces grands ensembles, car ils ne peuvent pas tous être transformés en musées industriels ou en quartiers d'habitation. Le rapport de la Belgique met en exergue une autre problématique liée aux complexes industriels abandonnés, celle de la pollution et de l'effet toxique à long terme sur les environs, avec des conflits possibles entre les conservateurs de l'environnement et les conservateurs du patrimoine.

Les installations militaires commencent également a être désaffectées à cause des évolutions technologiques. Ceci est le cas en Pologne, dont le rapport décrit les problèmes du maintien des lieux devenus inutiles, incluant le manque d'entretien, le manque d'argent et la difficulté à trouver des usages futurs. Les rapports *Patrimoine en péril* précédents ont montré comment des manoirs dans les pays d'Europe de l'Est font face aux mêmes problèmes. Aussitôt cédés par le gouvernement, ils subissent des développements inadaptés ou sont laissés à l'abandon. Un rapport de la Russie montre comment ces risques peuvent aussi menacer l'intégrité d'anciens palais, auparavant protégés et gérés par l'État. L'Italie fait également état de ventes de lieux historiques par le gouvernement et la réaction publique que cela suscite.

Les églises ottomanes de la Turquie sont un autre exemple de ce patrimoine mis en péril à cause des changements d'usage. Les changements démographiques et sociaux ont pour conséquence l'abandon et la dépréciation de ces édifices qui ne sont plus considérés comme faisant partie du patrimoine historique de la Turquie. Souligner leur situation désespérée est un premier pas vers la sensibilisation, qui doit être suivie par une prise en compte de leur importance dans la diversité du paysage culturel.

Les changements dans les pratiques agricoles ont entraîné l'abandon des fermes, ainsi que des habitations associées, des granges, remises et autres dépendances, comme le décrivent clairement les rapports soumis par les Pays-Bas et la Finlande. La Norvège parle également de ce processus en évoquant des fermes laissées à l'abandon et envahies par la forêt, ce qui signifie la disparition des traces d'activité humaine dans cet ancien paysage rural, ainsi qu'une perte de la biodiversité.

Les changements dans les modes de vie et la technologie font aussi que certaines formes et certains styles de construction ne sont plus à la mode ou ne plus utilisés. Les rapports *Patrimoine en Péril* précédents ont décrit comment ceci s'est traduit par un délaissement des formes traditionnelles vernaculaires de construction, peut être parce qu'elles ne sont plus considérées comme étant « modernes » ou parce qu'elles nécessitent un plus grand effort dans la construction et l'entretien. De toute manière, ce changement a pour conséquence une uniformisation du paysage bâti à travers le monde, souvent aboutissant à des formes de construction moins adaptées à l'environnement et au climat local. C'est souvent uniquement suite à des changements irréversibles que les communautés locales s'aperçoivent de ce qu'elles ont perdu, c'est-à-dire leur signature unique dans le paysage culturel. Les exemples recensés dans le rapport 2004-2005 incluent les maisons vernaculaires en brique crue avec cour en Sardaigne, Italie, des structures en adobe du Mexique, et les habitations en bois qui se trouvent dans les faubourgs de Vilnius en Lituanie.

Le rapport hollandais ainsi que celui du Mexique décrivent les mesures prises pour maintenir les styles architecturaux traditionnels et sensibiliser les populations ; au Mexique avec l'utilisation de techniques vernaculaires de construction en adobe pour créer des habitations modernes et bon marché, et aux Pays-Bas, à travers la tenue d'une « Année de la ferme historique » en 2003 ainsi qu'une conférence sur l'architecture vernaculaire organisée par l'ICOMOS, qui a pu sensibiliser davantage et susciter un soutien plus large pour cette forme de bâtiment traditionnel dans le paysage.

D'autres risques

La méconnaissance du patrimoine est bien évidement un risque majeur, et des régions éloignées ou des types particuliers de patrimoine peuvent ainsi être négligés. Les pays de l'Asie centrale, comme le Kirghizistan et le Tadjikistan font rapport sur des sites Bouddhistes ou Islamiques isolés qui n'auraient jamais été documentés sans les actuels programmes de relevés et de conservation mis en œuvre avec des financements étrangers. Le danger est qu'une fois que ces projets ponctuels sont terminés, ces sites ne soient toujours pas suffisamment bien gérés pour garantir leur protection à long terme et leur sauvegarde. L'Ukraine constate sa frustration face à l'apathie et au manque de moyens dont sont victime la grande variété de ses sites historiques issus d'une histoire ethnique diverse au croisement de l'Orient et de l'Occident. Les sites importants liés à l'esclavage en Guinée, témoignages d'une phase particulièrement brutale de l'histoire Africaine, sont en péril à cause d'un manque d'expertise et de financement. Un effort international à long terme est nécessaire car ces sites rappellent un passé violent à l'ensemble de l'humanité et ne sont pas uniquement de la responsabilité de la Guinée.

Une autre menace mentionnée à la fois par la Suède et l'Australie est le fait que la gestion et la conservation du patrimoine sont déléguées aux autorités locales. Cette tendance présente dans beaucoup de pays peut amener à une perte ou une fragmentation de l'expertise centralisée de la conservation et de la connaissance et de l'accès à des solutions rencontrées dans d'autres régions, mais elle bénéficie de la connaissance de la communauté locale, de son histoire, de son attachement et de son lien à son patrimoine. L'analyse des risques faite jusqu'ici se concentre sur ceux causés par l'activité humaine. Cependant, les désastres naturels continuent à endommager le patrimoine, comme l'expose le rapport de la République Tchèque sur les dommages causés par les inondations en 2002 sur de nombreux édifices historiques à travers le pays. Il est difficile de savoir comment prévenir de tels dégâts, mais le rapport fourni par le Japon contient une excellente étude sur la prévention et la réduction des dommages dus aux tremblements de terre, particulièrement en ce qui concerne les bâtiments historiques en bois dans le centre historique de Kyoto. Cette étude de cas pourrait être appliquée à d'autres sites historiques dans des zones sismiques. Par contre, comment se protéger contre les effets du réchauffement planétaire est une problématique à long terme qui n'a quasiment pas été abordée au niveau international en ce qui concerne la protection du patrimoine culturel. Les risques dus à la montée du niveau de la mer sont néanmoins déjà visibles dans les régions polaires comme le démontre le rapport de cette région, et sont aussi évoqués par la Nouvelle Zélande.

Comptant quelques 8000 membres regroupés en 125 Comités Nationaux et 25 Comités Scientifiques Internationaux, l'ICOMOS, Conseil International des Monuments et des Sites, est l'organe consultatif de l'UNESCO en matière de patrimoine culturel mondial, particulièrement en ce qui concerne l'évaluation des monuments et des sites inscrits sur la Liste du Patrimoine mondial ou dont l'inscription sur celle-ci est envisagée. Dans l'ensemble, la Convention de l'UNESCO pour la Protection du Patrimoine Culturel et Naturel Mondial, adoptée en 1972, demeure l'un des rares efforts réussis de politique culturelle mondiale visant à sauvegarder le patrimoine historique de l'humanité, et l'ICOMOS est fier de travailler, en tant qu'organe consultatif, aux côtés de l'UNESCO. Les monuments et sites, centres historiques et paysages culturels inscrits sur la Liste du Patrimoine mondial de l'UNESCO devraient de fait figurer parmi les monuments non menacés, mais notre rapport indique qu'on y observe pourtant certains cas de grand danger.

Le rapport *Patrimoine en péril 2004-2005* est la preuve que la situation du patrimoine culturel est toujours critique dans de nombreuses régions du monde. Alors que maintes et maintes fois des milliards sont investis dans la préparation de la guerre et la destruction, l'engagement nécessaire lorsqu'il s'agit de protéger le patrimoine menacé des siècles et millénaires passés fait souvent défaut aux responsables. Par conséquent, nous ne pouvons qu'espérer que le rapport *Patrimoine en péril* inspirera d'autres engagements, à l'échelle nationale et internationale, donnera naissance à de nouvelles initiatives de conservation et insufflera un nouvel élan aux institutions existantes, telles le Comité International du Bouclier Bleu soutenu par l'ICOMOS. Son impact devrait également s'étendre aux fondations internationales concernées par la conservation, comme la Fondation Getty ou le World Monuments Fund. Leur excellent exemple pourrait également influencer d'autres sponsors internationaux, alors même que chacun prend de plus en plus conscience de l'importance économique de la conservation du patrimoine, et du rôle majeur qu'elle a à tenir dans le cadre de ce « développement durable ». Avec son *rapport mondial sur les monuments et sites en péril*, l'ICOMOS espère non seulement obtenir le soutien moral du public dans la bataille contre les menaces de toutes sortes, mais aussi obtenir des résultats pratiques en coopération avec toutes les forces intéressées à la préservation du patrimoine culturel.

Remerciements

À la différence des rapports Patrimoine en péril précédents, cette édition 2004-2005 n'a pas été préparée par le groupe de travail constitué des membres de l'Australie, du Canada et de l'Allemagne, mais piloté par un comité de rédaction sous la direction du Président de l'ICOMOS International. Le rapport n'inclut pas seulement les contributions des Comités Nationaux et de certains Comités Scientifiques, mais aussi des rapports d'experts individuels. Je souhaite remercier les 45 experts des 29 pays et huit Comités scientifiques, ainsi que le Saint-Siège et l'ICCROM qui ont participé à l'atelier de travail qui s'est tenu à Bergen en Norvège le 6 septembre 2004 durant la réunion du Comité consultatif de l'ICOMOS. Leurs contributions aussi que les contributions de l'atelier „Heritage at Risk" pendant l'Assemblée Générale à Victoria Falls en octobre 2003 ont été importantes pour cette publication. Tout en rendant hommage à la participation de tous les collègues et comités de l'ICOMOS, il faut aussi souligner qu'en accord avec la politique de l'ICOMOS, les informations fournies dans cette publication reflètent l'opinion indépendante de chaque comité et des différents auteurs.

Notre équipe de rédaction expérimentée a bénéficié du soutien très engagé de notre collègue australienne, Marilyn Truscott qui a édité les textes en anglais, traduit certains des textes Français et a co-ordonné et édité d'autres traductions. John Ziesemer a une fois encore consacré un temps considérable à l'édition de cette publication. Je souhaite également remercier Hannelore Puttinger du secrétariat ICOMOS de Munich, ainsi que Gaia Jungeblodt et l'équipe du Secrétariat International de Paris, spécialement Olivia de Willermin, Melanie Grywnow et Claudia de Sevilla ainsi que José Garcia, qui a mis les documents sur le site internet de l'ICOMOS. La publication du *rapport mondial 2004-2005* n'aurait pas été possible sans le soutien financier et logistique fourni par ICOMOS Allemagne et sans le soutien généreux du Commissaire aux Affaires Culturelles et aux Médias du Gouvernement Fédéral d'Allemagne ainsi que la Fondation Messerschmitt. Nous devons également remercier la division du Patrimoine culturel de l'UNESCO et le ministère de la Culture et de la Communication français pour son soutien financier. Enfin, j'exprime une fois encore mes remerciements à la maison d'édition K.G. Saur, notamment à Manfred Link, pour avoir facilité le tirage de cette publication.

Comme tous les rapports précédents, cette édition 2004-2005 est aussi disponible sur Internet à l'adresse suivante : www.international.icomos.org/risk.

Michael Petzet
Décembre 2004

INTRODUCCION

Esta nueva edición del *Informe Mundial de ICOMOS sobre Monumentos y Sitios en Peligro,* que incluye unos 60 reportajes de 45 países o campos especializados, demuestra una vez más que muchos bienes patrimoniales están amenazados en todo el mundo, incluso hallándose inscritos en la Lista del Patrimonio Mundial; y, además, que las pérdidas causadas, no sólo por desastres naturales sino también por la acción del hombre, son inmensas. Frente a la gigantesca catástrofe del *tsunami*, que golpeó a la humanidad exactamente un año después del terrible terremoto de Bam (26 de diciembre de 2003, ver pp. 105–110), y mientras este Informe se prepara para ser impreso, esperamos que la red profesional del ICOMOS demuestre su capacidad de reaccionar positivamente ante este enorme desafío (ver el mensaje del Presidente en pp. 23–25).

El Informe anual del ICOMOS sobre *Patrimonio en Riesgo* tiene por objeto destacar los problemas y los factores que amenazan a los monumentos y sitios en todo el mundo y, en lo posible, presentar casos de estudio en diversos países, con el fin de compartir posibles soluciones con otras áreas del planeta. Se cumplen así los objetivos del ICOMOS de servir como un foro para el diálogo profesional y el intercambio, y para difundir información sobre principios, técnicas y políticas de la conservación.

Al presentar estos informes de diferentes partes del mundo, ICOMOS reconoce que éstos vienen a representar sólo algo así como una gota de agua dentro del mar de riesgos, amenazas y daños que se ciernen sobre sitios y monumentos concretos, así como unos rasgos generales del tratamiento aplicado a lugares de valor patrimonial que ponen en peligro su tejido, su integridad cultural y los valores especiales que entrañan para las comunidades que los habitan. Los informes son como instantáneas, que reflejan unos conflictos considerados importantes, apremiantes y serios en el contexto en el que se producen; no pretenden ser exhaustivos, ni presentar las tendencias y las presiones desde un punto de vista estadístico.

Aun así, este Informe de *Patrimonio en Riesgo* 2004/ 2005 demuestra claramente que la protección y la conservación patrimonial todavía tienen que recorrer un largo camino antes de que el ICOMOS pueda estar seguro de que efectivamente existe un reconocimiento y una preocupación a escala mundial en torno a nuestros monumentos y sitios, paisajes culturales y toda clase de lugares con valor patrimonial. Es evidente que el patrimonio cultural todavía no goza del nivel de compromiso que podría esperarse de las Convenciones Internacionales para su protección. En muchos países, los sitios arqueológicos siguen siendo expoliados por excavaciones ilegales, y el tráfico ilícito de obras de arte representa una pérdida continua de bienes culturales que, atendiendo a su preservación, deberían ser conservados en su emplazamiento original. No sólo se han visto diezmados por los robos las pinturas, las esculturas y los objetos pertenecientes a lugares destinados al culto en muchos países, sino que actualmente se están destruyendo monumentos artísticos con el objeto de conseguir fragmentos destinados al mercado. Este es el caso de los templos saqueados, las esculturas decapitadas y los frescos arrancados. Mientras que los daños provocados por las guerras y los desastres naturales ganan los titulares de los medios, los informes aquí incluidos muestran otros grandes riesgos más insidiosos y en incremento. Estos peligros resultan del desconocimiento sobre qué es patrimonio, de la inexistencia de una conciencia acerca de su valor para nuestra sociedad, de la ausencia de comprensión sobre cómo puede ser protegido permitiendo al mismo tiempo su adecuación a las necesidades actuales, y también del desprecio a las soluciones técnicas y a las pautas establecidas para su conservación.

El análisis de los informes incluidos en este volumen demuestra que, además de los riesgos generales que entrañan los desastres naturales y de la decadencia física de las estructuras, hay ciertas facetas características de la actividad humana que ponen en peligro nuestro patrimonio. Entre otras, podemos citar las guerras y los conflictos interétnicos, el desarrollo, el turismo y la obsolescencia.

Los Riesgos de la Guerra

Los riesgos a los que se hallan expuestos los lugares de valor patrimonial debido a problemas tales como la guerra y los conflictos interétnicos han quedado demostrados en los tres Informes anteriores de *Patrimonio en Riesgo*. Otra vez, en este Informe de 2004 se incluyen varios casos de daños de guerra relativos a Afganistán, Irak, Kosovo o Palestina. Las noticias sobre tales daños y destrucción del patrimonio cultural golpean en los titulares de los medios alrededor del mundo; son daños impactantes, dramáticos, que a menudo afectan a iconos preciosos y únicos de culturas pasadas y presentes. A veces, estos ataques se dirigen deliberadamente a determinados monumentos como, por ejemplo, en el caso de los Budas de Bamiyan, o en el de Kosovo, por razones iconoclastas, o por viejos conflictos seculares y fratricidas. En tales casos, ICOMOS ha actuado eficazmente en cumplimiento de su objetivo, poniendo la experiencia de sus expertos, altamente cualificados en el campo de la conservación, al servicio de la comunidad internacional y de los países afectados, para restaurar el daño causado. Las actividades realizadas en Bamiyan, Afganistán, que se presentan en este volumen son un claro ejemplo. El conflicto en curso en Irak demuestra lo poco que se ha avanzado en el fondo para mitigar el persistente daño sobre el patrimonio, a pesar del gran horror internacional y de las buenas intenciones dirigidas a salvar los milenarios monumentos y sitios de valor patrimonial de Irak.

Las medidas preventivas contra la destrucción futura en casos de conflicto armado son difíciles de alcanzar, a pesar de la ayuda de ICOMOS al Escudo Azul. Las estrategias a más largo plazo, tales como las medidas dirigidas a encomiar y compartir la importancia de tales lugares con otros, por ejemplo a través de la Lista del Patrimonio Mundial, pueden ser un camino para construir puentes entre comunidades previamente polarizadas y poner fin a largas enemistades potencialmente generadoras de ataques contra el patrimonio cultural de otro grupo.

Los Riesgos del Desarrollo

Mientras que la guerra, incluyendo el daño y el saqueo de centenares de sitios arqueológicos importantes en Irak y la destrucción natural como en el caso del terremoto en la valiosa ciudad de tierra de Bam, son dramáticas y conducen a acciones urgentes a escala internacional, en muchos países se producen diariamente daños más insidiosos como parte de los procesos normales de planeamiento y construcción.

Nuevamente, este Informe de *Patrimonio en Riesgo* 2004/ 2005 pone de manifiesto la preocupación de varios Comités nacionales del ICOMOS ante tales riesgos, derivados del desarrollo inapropiado de las áreas patrimoniales, que afectan a su significación. Este caso afecta específicamente al centro de las ciudades históricas. En Austria y la República Checa se ha incrementado la amenaza a los paisajes urbanos de los centros históricos a causa del desarrollo de la edificación en altura, cambiando así la naturaleza del perfil urbano y dañando las calidades arquitectónicas del patrimonio. En Chipre, el riesgo de desarrollo de áreas donde la historia cultural completa no ha sido suficientemente comprendida, está amenazando fases culturales tempranas de Nicosia, por lo que debe remarcarse la necesidad de identificar todas las etapas históricas de las áreas urbanas y de proteger zonas culturales y arqueológicas especialmente sensibles.

En tales áreas urbanas, tal y como se refleja en los informes de varios países, puede ser que la cuestión clave no consista en la existencia de una legislación inadecuada, sino en la falta de aplicación eficaz del marco normativo, bien sea por una falta de comprensión de los riesgos que afectan a los valores patrimoniales o, más aún, por la gran presión ejercida por las expectativas de beneficio que genera el desarrollo inmobiliario. Italia demuestra que no son necesariamente los países en vías de desarrollo donde las autoridades carecen de fuerza o de recursos para detener procesos inadecuados, o francamente ilegales, de desarrollo que impactan tanto en el encanto general de la atmósfera urbana como en los valores patrimoniales. Es necesario que el ICOMOS difunda, no sólo entre sus miembros, sino también entre los países y las regiones que luchan por proteger el patrimonio contra las presiones del desarrollo, aquellos casos de estudio que demuestran cómo conseguir un equilibrio acertado entre la salvaguarda de los valores del patrimonio y el desarrollo. Un ejemplo serio y contundente nos lo ofrece el Casco Antiguo de la ciudad de Panamá, inscrito en la Lista del Patrimonio Mundial, cuyas fachadas históricas han sido demolidas, y otro caso es el del Centro de Ávila, España, que también forma parte de dicha Lista, donde la inserción de nuevos edificios y aparcamientos de vehículos destruyen la integridad histórica de la ciudad.

Muchos comités nacionales hacen referencia a la urbanización irregular como otra forma de desarrollo que afecta negativamente a los alrededores de los centros urbanos al dañar la relación entre la ciudad y su entorno rural, a su asentamiento armonioso dentro del paisaje. Andorra, Australia y Noruega mencionan aspectos de este conflicto, mientras que Nueva Zelanda se refiere a la destrucción de la personalidad propia de pequeñas ciudades, provocada por la tendencia a introducir "características teóricas de patrimonio", tales como iluminación, pavimentación y frentes comerciales, con el resultado de que todas ellas terminan ofreciendo un aspecto similar y muy distinto de su verdadero estilo y tipo de construcción históricos.

Todos los ejemplos demuestran cuán importante es entender de forma integral la razón por la que los edificios, las estructuras, así como sectores o barrios completos de una ciudad pueden ser valorados desde el punto de vista patrimonial, no sólo por su importancia histórica, sino por los valores asociados a las relaciones existentes entre unos y otros, por la integridad de la escala y el diseño, y por los recuerdos y significados que tales áreas tienen para la población local. Si tales valores son bien entendidos por todos, habrá mayores oportunidades de que se mantengan, así como de que se introduzcan enmiendas a los nuevos planes de desarrollo que limiten su impacto, e incluso realcen el valor patrimonial de los lugares. Una vez más, los ejemplos aportados, como es el caso de los edificios en altura que amenazan la integridad visual de Colonia en Alemania, o Praga en la República Checa, enfatizan los riesgos por incremento de alturas. Sin embargo, el desarrollo no se restringe a tales áreas urbanas, y puede dar lugar a grandes devastaciones de los paisajes rurales que están sufriendo cambios irreversibles. Éstos incluyen la explotación minera a gran escala, las fincas de producción de energía eólica, el trazado, cada vez más amplio y recto, de las autopistas y los puentes, las represas, la explotación minera a cielo abierto, y las prácticas agrícolas con un efecto invasor cada vez mayor. Países tales como Australia, Alemania, Serbia y Montenegro, y el Comité del Patrimonio Arqueológico, han observado el impacto causado a los valores culturales del paisaje en áreas rurales, así como también el riesgo existente para los sitios arqueológicos situados en superficie, por ejemplo en Nueva Zelanda, Polonia, y Japón, de modo que se destruyen evidencias importantes de culturas y de épocas pasadas. Un ejemplo alarmante de ello es el Itinerario Cultural de Jain, en la India, cuya descripción permite ver lo que se ha destruido, o está en vías de serlo, por la construcción de una represa.

El Turismo

El desarrollo del turismo es realmente un subconjunto del problema anterior pero merece una mención separada, por estar tan extendido y ser tan a menudo citado por los Comités nacionales en sus Informes de *Patrimonio en Riesgo*. En muchos países en vías de desarrollo, el turismo internacional se considera como una fuente importante de ingresos y de progreso, tal como ocurre a lo largo de áreas costeras dedicadas a su disfrute por los extranjeros. Tales progresos son difícilmente compatibles con la protección del modo de vida, de las tradiciones culturales y del patrimonio cultural de las comunidades locales. Incluso los sitios patrimoniales con una ubicación remota no resultan más protegidos en virtud de su aislamiento; por el contrario, su misma distancia de lugares habitados los sitúa en una posición de riesgo que a menudo da por resultado daños de carácter accidental, así como contaminación por desperdicios, e incluso acciones de vandalismo. De esto se informa en el caso de Kazajstán, con respecto a los grabados rupestres de Tamgaly-Tas, o a los dibujos en la piedra (petroglifos) de los lugares ceremoniales de Trujillo, en el desierto peruano norteño, dañados por los vehículos que circulan sobre los propios sitios; en este último caso también se encuentran afectados por el desarrollo minero. La cantidad de visitas y el turismo incontrolado representan igualmente riesgos para el patrimonio, según se demuestra en los informes de Costa Rica, donde el desarrollo turístico inadecuado está destruyendo la integridad de la ciudad de Liberia.

Como se indicaba en el Informe de *Patrimonio en Riesgo* 2002–03, ICOMOS está decepcionado ante la falta de responsabilidad de la industria del turismo respecto al patrimonio, al que sigue explotando con una carga de uso excesivo, y sin contribuir a su protección y conservación con los beneficios que obtiene del mismo. Sin embargo, es preciso observar que cuanto antes se entienda que el turismo no constituye la solución automática para lograr la conservación del patrimonio y los fondos necesarios para ello, o para conseguir el bienestar económico de una comunidad local, antes podrá prestarse una consideración adecuada al desarrollo turístico de nuestros preciados y no renovables lugares y paisajes patrimoniales.

La Obsolescencia

Frecuentemente, los cambios sociales, económicos y técnicos dan lugar a que ciertas estructuras resulten inútiles o dejen de ser utilizadas. Esto es una consecuencia normal de tales cambios pero, en las últimas décadas, estos suelen producirse de forma rápida, o vienen impuestos por factores externos a un área que tiene pocas posibilidades de incorporarlos paulatinamente a los sistemas y las estructuras existentes, lo que torna a éstas en elementos vacíos y abandonados. Hay ejemplos de las grandes industrias de Hungría, Alemania y otros lugares, cuyo problema radica en la dificultad de hallar nuevos usos adaptables a esos grandes complejos, o en convertirlos en museos industriales, o incluso en áreas residenciales, ya que éstas no son soluciones aplicables a todos los casos. El informe de Bélgica ilustra otro caso relacionado con el de los complejos industriales de carácter obsoleto, como es la contaminación y el impacto tóxico que producen en el ambiente circundante, con conflictos potenciales entre los conservacionistas del ambiente y los conservadores del patrimonio.

Con los cambios de la tecnología, las instalaciones militares también van quedando cada vez más fuera de uso. Esto se describe en el caso de Polonia, que destaca los problemas que representa conservar los lugares que ya no son de utilidad, entre los que se señala la falta de mantenimiento físico, la carencia de fondos, y la dificultad de encontrarles un destino y un uso futuros. Los informes anteriores de *Patrimonio en Riesgo* han demostrado que las fincas solariegas de los países del este europeo se enfrentan a este tipo de problemas a partir de su salida de manos del gobierno, lo que a menudo conduce a su inadecuado desarrollo, o a su decaimiento. Un informe de Rusia demuestra que estos riesgos también están amenazando la integridad de antiguos palacios que hasta ahora estaban protegidos y gestionados por el Estado. Italia también expresa su preocupación sobre la venta de lugares patrimoniales por parte del gobierno y la respuesta pública que ello genera.

Las iglesias otomanas de Turquía responden a otro tipo de obsolescencia del patrimonio en riesgo ya que, a causa de los cambios demográficos y sociales, estos edificios no se usan ya y quizás no se valoren como parte de la herencia histórica del país. Desvelar su situación es un primer paso para incrementar su conocimiento, lo que debería dar lugar a una consiguiente estimación de la importancia que revisten dentro de la diversidad del paisaje cultural.

Los cambios en las prácticas agrícolas han significado que las casas de labranza, los caseríos, graneros, pajares, abrevaderos y apriscos, así como otras dependencias, también están cayendo en desuso, según se describe con toda claridad en el caso de los Países Bajos y Finlandia. Noruega también describe este proceso, y plantea el tema de las granjas abandonadas que son invadidas por el bosque, haciendo desaparecer rastros de la actividad humana de los paisajes antes rurales y provocando una pérdida de la biodiversidad.

Los cambios en la forma de vida y en la tecnología están generando también ciertas formas de edificación y de estilos basados en la moda y en el uso. En anteriores informes de *Patrimonio en Riesgo* se ha descrito cómo se están dejando de lado las formas tradicionales de la construcción vernácula, quizá porque se estima que ya no son "modernas" o porque exigen un mayor esfuerzo en su construcción y mantenimiento. En cualquier caso, el cambio da lugar a un paisaje construido más homogéneo en todo el mundo, y que con frecuencia se traduce en unas formas menos adaptadas al ambiente local y al clima. Es habitual que las comunidades locales se den cuenta de lo que han perdido, en términos de rasgos exclusivos de su paisaje cultural, sólo después de que el cambio resulte irreversible. Los ejemplos incluidos en el informe de 2004/2005 incluyen casas vernáculas de patio de ladrillo de arcilla de Cerdeña, Italia; estructuras de adobe en México, y casas suburbanas de madera en Vilnius, Lituania.

Tanto los informes holandeses como los mexicanos describen medios para mantener y apreciar los estilos tradicionales. En México, mediante el uso de técnicas vernáculas de construcción en adobe para edificar casas modernas y baratas, y en Holanda con un activo programa llamado "Año de la Casa Rural Histórica", desarrollado en 2003, así como con la celebración de un congreso de ICOMOS sobre Arquitectura Vernácula que contribuyó a despertar la conciencia y a conseguir un apoyo más amplio para esta forma de construcción tradicional en el paisaje.

Otros Riesgos

No tener conocimientos sobre el patrimonio representa, sin lugar a dudas, un riesgo capital, y así algunas áreas remotas o tipos especiales de patrimonio pueden sufrir de falta de cuidados. Los países de Asia central, tales como Kirguistán y Tayikistán, han hecho informes sobre lugares lejanos con patrimonio budista o islámico que, de no contar con una catalogación adecuada o con la conservación que actualmente se lleva a cabo con fondos exteriores, no estarían documentados; no obstante, el riesgo consiste en que una vez que dichos proyectos especiales se culminan, el sitio puede no estar suficientemente bien gestionado tanto por lo que se refiere a la necesidad de contar con algún tipo de protección como a su supervivencia a largo plazo. Ucrania destaca la frustración que surge de la apatía o de la carencia de medios económicos en lo que se refiere al amplio repertorio de lugares con valor patrimonial que representan la pluralidad étnica de su historia como una encrucijada entre el este y el oeste. Los importantes lugares patrimoniales de Guinea que están ligados a la Esclavitud y atestiguan una fase particularmente brutal en la historia africana se encuentran en situación de riesgo, debido a la carencia de expertos y de cobertura económica. Se requiere un esfuerzo internacional a largo plazo, ya que estos sitios son parte de la memoria de la humanidad sobre un pasado brutal y no son responsabilidad exclusiva de Guinea.

Otra amenaza a la que hacen referencia tanto Suecia como Australia es el problema que plantea la delegación de la gerencia y la conservación del patrimonio en las autoridades locales. Esta tendencia que está vigente en muchos países, supone por una parte la posibilidad de beneficiarse del conocimiento que la comunidad local posee sobre su propia historia, así como de sus vinculaciones y su raigambre local, pero entraña el riesgo de pérdida o fragmentación de la experiencia que proporciona la conservación centralizada y de saber cómo acceder a las soluciones adoptadas en otras regiones.

Mientras que el anterior análisis de riesgos se centra en los que se derivan de la actividad humana, los desastres naturales continúan dañando al patrimonio, como se señala en el informe de la República Checa acerca de las inundaciones padecidas en 2002 por muchos edificios patrimoniales a lo largo y ancho de sus áreas rurales. Resulta difícil prever cómo evitar tales daños, aunque el informe de Japón nos proporciona un estudio excelente sobre el modo de prevenir y mitigar los derivados de los terremotos, especialmente en lo que se refiere a los edificios históricos de madera de los alrededores de la ciudad de Kyoto. Se trata de un caso de estudio que podría aplicarse a los lugares patrimoniales situados en otras zonas vulnerables a los terremotos. Sin embargo, hay aspectos como, por ejemplo, la protección contra el calentamiento global que constituye un tema de estudio a plazo más largo y que apenas se ha tratado a escala internacional por lo que se refiere a la protección del patrimonio. No obstante, como se indica en este informe, los riesgos de elevación del nivel del mar ya son visibles en las regiones polares, y así lo señala también Nueva Zelanda.

El ICOMOS, Consejo Internacional de Monumentos y Sitios, con unos 8000 miembros organizados en 125 Comités Nacionales y 25 Comités Científicos Internacionales, es el órgano consultivo de la UNESCO en materia de conservación y de protección del patrimonio cultural mundial y, en particular, en lo referente a la evaluación de monumentos y sitios que han sido incluidos en la Lista del Patrimonio Mundial, o cuya inclusión está en estudio. En general, la Convención de la UNESCO para la Protección del Patrimonio Cultural y Natural Mundial, establecida en 1972, sigue siendo uno de los pocos esfuerzos realizados con éxito en el ámbito de la política cultural mundial para salvaguardar el patrimonio histórico de la humanidad, e ICOMOS está orgulloso de trabajar con la UNESCO, en tanto que órgano consultivo. Los monumentos y sitios, barrios históricos y paisajes culturales incluidos actualmente en la Lista de Patrimonio Mundial de la UNESCO deberían en realidad figurar entre los monumentos fuera de peligro, pero nuestro informe indica que también aquí se observan casos de riesgo sustancial.

El informe de *Patrimonio en Peligro* 2004/2005 es una prueba de que la situación del patrimonio cultural es aún muy grave en muchas regiones del mundo. Mientras una y otra vez se invierten billones en la preparación de la guerra y la destrucción, a menudo no existe un compromiso necesario por parte de los responsables cuando se trata de preservar el patrimonio de siglos y milenios pasados amenazado de peligro. Por tanto, sólo nos cabe esperar que el Informe sobre Patrimonio en Peligro inspire mayores compromisos a nivel nacional e internacional, genere nuevas iniciativas en el campo de la preservación y dé un impulso positivo adicional a las instituciones existentes, tales como el Escudo Azul apoyado por ICOMOS. El efecto debería extenderse también a fundaciones internacionales comprometidas en la preservación, tales como la Fundación Getty o el World Monuments Fund. Sus buenos ejemplos podrían también influir en el ánimo de otros patrocinadores que operan a nivel internacional, ahora que crece la conciencia sobre la importancia económica de la conservación del patrimonio y su papel fundamental en el tan mencionado 'desarrollo sostenible'. Por eso, con su Informe Mundial sobre Monumentos y Sitios en Peligro, ICOMOS espera no sólo lograr el apoyo moral del público de todo el mundo en la batalla contra todo tipo de amenazas, sino también alcanzar resultados prácticos en colaboración con todas las fuerzas interesadas en la conservación/ preservación del patrimonio cultural.

Agradecimientos

Este Informe de *Patrimonio en Riesgo* 2004/2005, a diferencia de los que lo precedieron, no ha sido realizado por el anterior grupo de trabajo compuesto por miembros de Australia, Canadá y Alemania, sino que ha sido dirigido por los miembros del Comité Editorial, especialmente bajo la dirección del presidente internacional del ICOMOS. El informe incluye no solamente contribuciones de los Comités nacionales y de algunos de los Comités Científicos Internacionales, sino también algunos informes de expertos individuales. Además, quisiera dar las gracias a los 45 expertos de 29 países y a los 8 Comités científicos, así como a la Santa Sede y al ICCROM, que participaron en un taller realizado en Bergen, Noruega, el 6 de septiembre, durante la reunión del Comité Consultivo del ICOMOS. Sus contribuciones, asi como las contribuciones del taller "Patrimonio en riesgo" durante la Asamblea General en Victoria Falls en octubre de 2003 son importantes para esta publicación. Al mismo tiempo que elogiamos la participación de todos los compañeros y Comités del ICOMOS, también señalamos que, de acuerdo con la política del ICOMOS, la información proporcionada para esta publicación refleja la opinión independiente de cada Comité y de sus diversos autores.

Nuestro experimentado equipo editorial contó con la abnegada ayuda de nuestra compañera australiana Marilyn Truscott que, además de compilar los textos en inglés y traducir alguno de los textos franceses, coordinó y dirigió otras traducciones. Juan Ziesemer dedicó nuevamente un tiempo considerable a todo el proceso de publicación de esta obra. También quisiera dar las gracias a Hannelore Puttinger, de la Secretaría del ICOMOS de Munich, así como a Gaia Jungeblodt y al personal de la Secretaría Internacional de París, especialmente a Olivia de Willermin, Melanie Grywnow, Claudia de Sevilla y José García, que introdujeron el material en el Sitio de Internet de ICOMOS. La publicación del Informe Mundial 2004/2005 no habría sido posible sin contar con el apoyo económico y de organización que nos fue proporcionado por ICOMOS Alemania, gracias a la generosa ayuda recibida del Comisionado del Gobierno Federal Alemán para los Asuntos Culturales y los Medios, así como de la Fundación Messerschmitt. Igualmente debemos expresar nuestra gratitud a la División del Patrimonio Cultural de la UNESCO y al Ministerio de Cultura y Comunicación de Francia por su ayuda económica. Finalmente, extiendo una vez más mi agradecimiento a la empresa de publicaciones K.G. Saur, particularmente a Manfred Link, por facilitar la impresión de esta publicación.

Como los precedentes informes, este volumen 2004/2005 está también disponible en Internet en www.international.icomos.org/risk.

Michael Petzet
Diciembre de 2004

Message concerning the earthquake and ensuing tsunami in the Indian Ocean

ICOMOS joins the international community in deploring the tragic loss of life due to the tsunami which hit the coasts of several countries across Asia and Africa on Sunday 26 December 2004 and expresses its heartfelt sympathy to the populations and governments struck by this tragedy.

In these days all of our members are asking how we with our professional network can help those countries affected by the Tsunami disaster, and I am very grateful for the many constructive suggestions and ideas we have received. After the disaster of 26 December we tried at once to take up contact with the National Committees of the countries concerned and were extremely relieved to hear that, as far as we could find out, our colleagues had survived this gigantic human catastrophe and had already started making active contributions to saving their endangered cultural heritage. We received the most comprehensive news from ICOMOS Sri Lanka, the country where my predecessor as President of ICOMOS International, Roland Silva, organised the General Assembly of ICOMOS in 1993 - for many of us an unforgettable experience. ICOMOS Sri Lanka intends to present a first damage report by the end of this month.

In the present situation the alleviation of human suffering must of course be first priority. We are touched by a human tragedy of inconceivable dimensions, but we also feel our professional responsibility to assist the countries hit by the floods to save the damaged and endangered cultural heritage. After all, we believe that this cultural heritage in the form of monuments and sites has a vital role to play in reconstructing lost places and communities and that also after a disaster the preservation of local building traditions is of great importance for the identity of cultural regions. Some of our committees in the affected countries have therefore already started surveying and identifying heritage at risk, – this is urgent work which will continue.

The consequences of the tsunami disaster will also have to be on the agenda of the ICOMOS Executive Committee meeting in early February. At the same time there will also be a meeting of the International Committee of the Blue Shield, a committee bringing together ICOMOS with ICOM (the International Council of Museums), ICA (International Council on Archives) and IFLA (the International Federation of Library Associations and Institutions). For future actions in the regions harmed by the flood catastrophe a close co-operation with our partner organisations, in particular ICOM, makes sense, but of course as always in such cases we wish to work under the guidance of UNESCO, and we are also in contact with ICCROM (the International Centre for the Study of the Preservation and Restoration of Cultural Property in Rome), as well as with IUCN, the World Conservation Union, the latter two

Dickwella on the southern coast of Sri Lanka, the building has collapsed, but the statues are intact

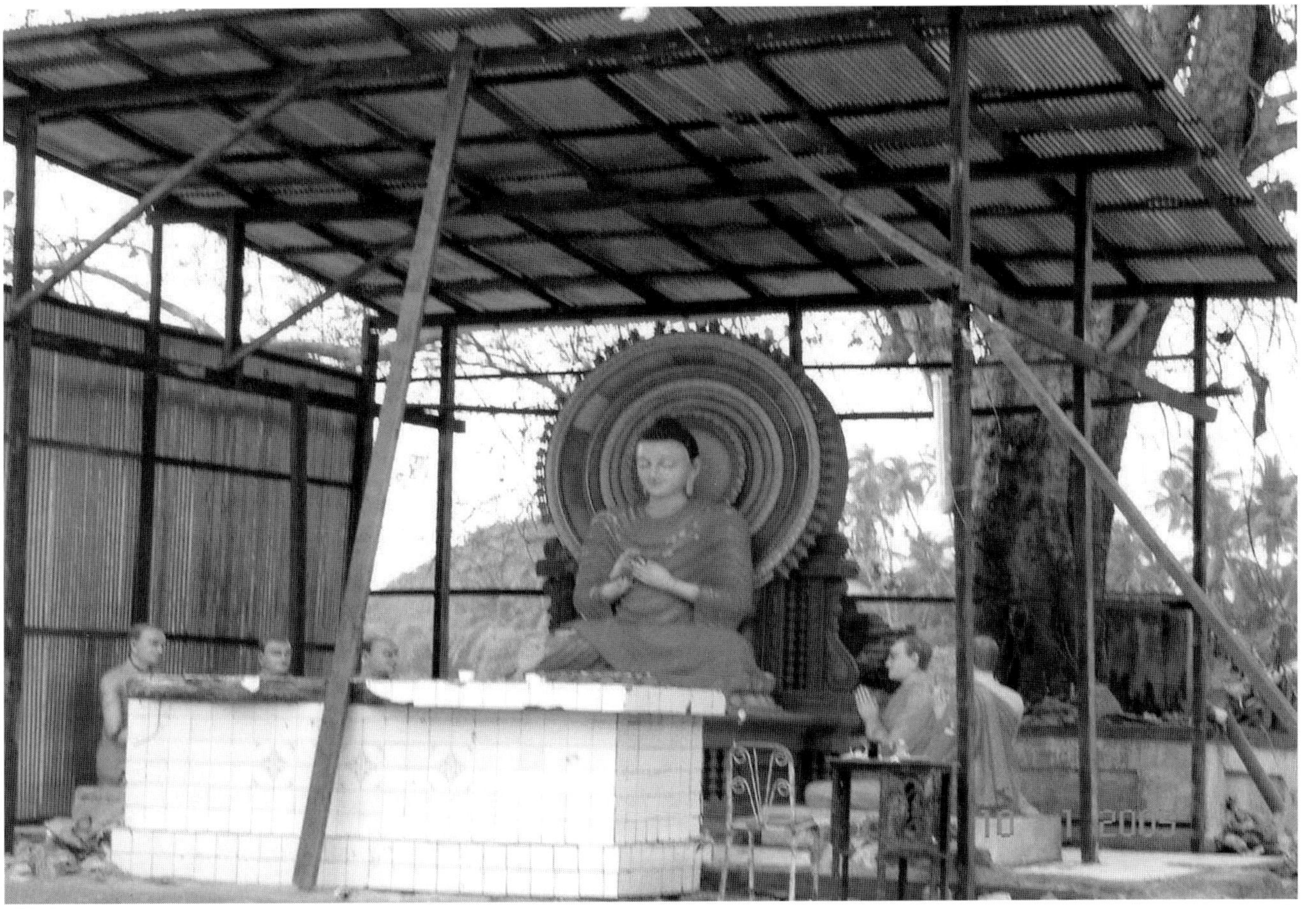

being our partners as advisory bodies of UNESCO within the framework of the World Heritage Convention.

Our new *Heritage at Risk Report* 2004/2005, which will come out in the coming weeks, will show once again that many monuments and historic sites are threatened world-wide even if they are on the World Heritage List and that the losses caused not only by natural disasters but also by man are immense. Faced with the gigantic Tsunami catastrophe, which hit mankind exactly one year after the terrible Bam earthquake (26 December 2003), we have to concentrate for the time being on compiling information in order to then be able to start actions under the guidance of the relevant National Committees. No doubt, some of our International Scientific Committees, eg the Committee for Earthen Architecture, will also be able to make contributions. So I sincerely hope that with the help of all of you the professional network of ICOMOS will prove to be successful even in view of this tremendous challenge.

The International Monuments Day on 18 April 2005, initiated by ICOMOS, will offer many of our committees an extra opportunity to point out the consequences of the tsunami disaster for the cultural heritage.

Paris, 7 January 2005

Michael Petzet
President of ICOMOS

Message concernant le tremblement de terre et le tsunami dans l'Océan Indien

L'ICOMOS se joint à la communauté internationale et déplore les tragiques pertes en vies humaines à la suite du tsunami qui a dévasté les côtes de plusieurs pays d'Asie et d'Afrique le dimanche 26 décembre 2004 et exprime sa profonde sympathie aux populations et gouvernements éprouvés par cette tragédie.

A présent, tous nos membres nous demandent comment notre réseau de professionnels peut aider les pays sinistrés par le récent tsunami, et je remercie tous ceux qui nous ont envoyé des idées et suggestions très constructives. A la suite de cette catastrophe survenue le 26 décembre, nous avons immédiatement essayé de prendre contact avec les Comités Nationaux dans les pays affectés. Nous sommes extrêmement soulagés d'apprendre qu'à notre connaissance tous nos collègues ont survécu à cette gigantesque catastrophe humaine et ont déjà commencé à œuvrer activement à la sauvegarde de leur patrimoine en danger. Nous avons reçu des informations très complètes du Sri Lanka, pays où mon prédécesseur en tant que Président d'ICOMOS international, Roland Silva, avait organisé notre Assemblée Générale en 1993, qui pour beaucoup d'entre nous reste une expérience inoubliable. L'ICOMOS Sri Lanka prévoit de présenter son premier rapport sur les dommages causés au patrimoine à la fin du mois.

Dans la situation actuelle, le soulagement de la souffrance des populations victimes doit de toute évidence être la priorité absolue. Nous sommes tous profondément touchés par cette tragédie humaine d'une dimension inconcevable, mais nous sentons aussi que notre responsabilité professionnelle est d'aider les pays touchés par ces inondations à sauver leur patrimoine endommagé ou mis en péril. Nous croyons que ce patrimoine culturel et les monuments et sites qui en sont une expression, joue un rôle vital dans la reconstruction des lieux et communautés sinistrés et aussi qu'à la suite d'un désastre, la sauvegarde des traditions de construction locales est très importante pour l'identité culturelle des régions affectées. Certains de nos Comités dans les pays touchés ont donc déjà commencé à documenter et identifier le monuments et sites endommagés ou en péril – une tâche urgente qui est en cours.

Les conséquences de cette catastrophe seront portées à l'ordre du jour de la réunion du Comité Exécutif de l'ICOMOS qui aura lieu début février. En même temps, il y aura une réunion du Comité International du Bouclier Bleu, qui rassemble l'ICOMOS, l'ICOM (Conseil international des musées), l'ICA (Conseil International des Archives) et l'IFLA (Fédération internationale des associations de bibliothécaires et des bibliothèques). Pour nos actions à venir dans les régions affectées par cette catastrophe, une coopération étroite avec nos organisations partenaires, en particulier l'ICOM s'impose et, comme toujours dans ces cas, nous souhaitons travailler en accord avec l'UNESCO et aussi en contact étroit avec l'ICCROM (le Centre international d'etudes pour la conservation et la restauration de biens culturels à Rome), ainsi qu'avec l'UICN (Union mondiale pour la conservation de la nature) - qui sont nos partenaires en tant qu'organes consultatifs dans le cadre de la Convention du patrimoine mondial.

Notre nouveau rapport Patrimoine en péril - Heritage at Risk 2004/2005, qui paraîtra dans quelques semaines, montrera encore une fois que beaucoup de monuments et sites historiques de par le monde sont en danger, même quand ils sont inscrits sur la Liste du Patrimoine mondial, et que les pertes dues aux catastrophes naturelles mais aussi à l'action de l'homme sont immenses. Face à cette catastrophe gigantesque, due au tsunami, qui à frappé le monde exactement un an après le terrible tremblement de terre à Bam (26 décembre 2003), nous devons à présent concentrer nos efforts sur la collecte d'informations qui nous permettra de mettre en place des actions concrètes sous la direction des Comités Nationaux dans les pays concernés. Sans aucun doute, certains de nos Comités Internationaux Scientifiques, par exemple notre Comité sur l'Architecture en terre, seront aussi en mesure de contribuer à cette tâche. J'espère donc qu'avec l'aide de tout notre réseau de professionnels de l'ICOMOS nous réussirons à faire face à ce défi majeur.

La Journée international des Monuments et Sites célébrée le 18 avril 2005, à l'initiative de l'ICOMOS, donnera aussi l'opportunité à nos Comités de faire connaître les conséquences de la catastrophe due au tsunami sur le patrimoine culturel.

Paris, 7 Janvier 2005

Michael Petzet
Président de l'ICOMOS

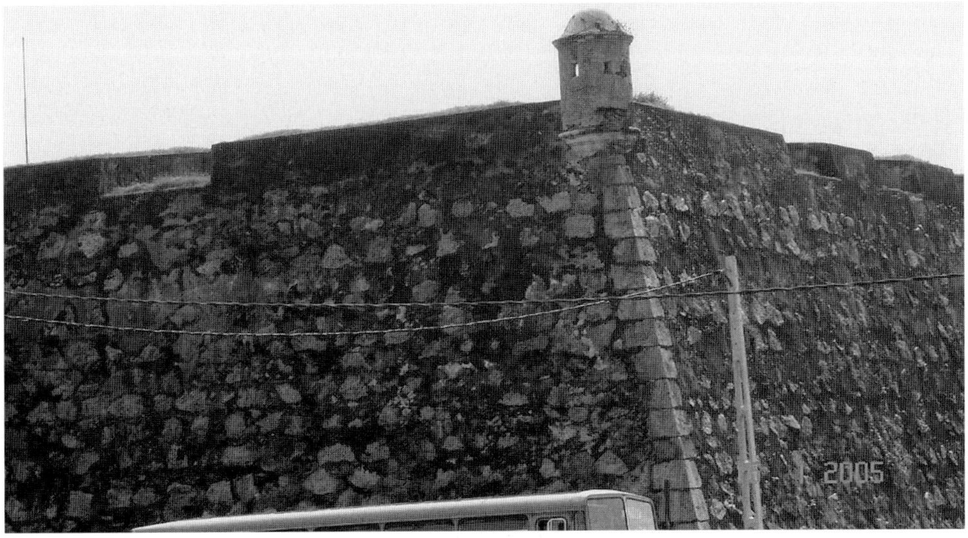

The historic fort in Galle (Sri Lanka) survived the tsunami of 26 December 2004

Mensaje sobre el terremoto y tsunami en el Océano Indio

ICOMOS se une a la comunidad internacional en el lamento de la trágica pérdida de vidas causada por el tsunami que golpeó la costa de varios países a lo largo de Asia y Africa el pasado 26 de Diciembre, y expresa sus condolencias a las poblaciones y gobiernos afectados por esta tragedia.

En estos tiempos nuestros miembros están preguntando cómo es posible que nuestra red internacional pueda ayudar a los afectados en el desastre del tsunami, y estoy agradecido por las sugerencias constructivas e ideas que hemos recibido. Después del desastre del 26 de Diciembre los Comités Nacionales de los paises afectados fueron contactados inmediatamente y nos sentimos extremadamente aliviados al saber que, hasta donde nos fue possible averiguar, nuestros colegas habían sobrevivido esta gigantezca catástrofe humana y habían ya comenzado a contribuir al salvataje de su patrimonio cultural en peligro de manera activa.

Recibimos noticias de ICOMOS en Sri Lanka, el país en donde mi predecesor como Presidente de ICOMOS Internacional, Roland Silva, organizó la Asamblea General de ICOMOS en 1993, para muchos de nosotros una experiencia inolvidable. ICOMOS Sri Lanka tiene le intención de presentar el primer reporte de daños para el fin de Enero.

No esta de mas destacar que en la situación actual el alivio del sufrimiento humano debe ser prioritario. Estamos siendo tocados por una tragedia humana de dimensiones inconcebibles, pero también sentimos por nuestra responsabilidad professional la necesidad de asistir a los países afectados en el salvataje de su patrimonio cultural dañado y en peligro. Después de todo, creemos que este patrimonio cultural, que toma la forma de monumentos y sitios, juega un papel vital en la reconstrucción de lugares y comunidades perdidas. Además, luego de tal desastre, la preservación de tradiciones de construcción es de gran importancia para la identidad cultural de cada region. Por lo tanto, algunos de nuestros comités en los países afectados han comenzado el relevamiento e identificación del patrimonio en riesgo – este trabajo urgente continuará.

Las consecuencias del desastre del tsunami también tendrán su lugar en la agenda del Comité Ejecutivo de ICOMOS en su reunión a principios de Febrero. Al mismo tiempo, habrá una reunión del Comité internacional del Escudo Azul (International Committee of the Blue Shield) que relaciona a ICOMOS con ICOM (el Consejo Internacional de Museos), IFLA (International Federation of Library Associations and Institutions) e ICA (Consejo Internacional de Archivos). Para nuestras acciones futuras en las regiones afectadas por la catástrofe, la cooperación con nuestras organizaciones colaboradoras, en particular ICOM, es necesaria, pero por supuesto como es habitual en estos casos deseamos trabajar bajo la tutela de UNESCO, y estamos también en contacto con ICCROM, el Centro Internacional de Restauración en Roma, y tambien IUCN la World Conservation Union, éstas dos ultimas organizaciones siendo nuestras colaboradoras como consejeras de UNESCO dentro del marco de la Convención del Patrimonio Mundial.

Nuestro nuevo *Heritage at Risk Report* del año 2004/2005 que será publicado en las próximas semanas, mostrará nuevamente que muchos de los monumentos y sitios historicos en el mundo están en peligro aún cuando son parte de la Lista de Patrimonio Mundial y que las perdidas no son solamente causadas por desastres naturales pero también en gran parte por el hombre. Enfrentándonos a la gran tragedia del tsunami, que golpeó a la humanidad exactamente un año después del gigantezco terremoto de Bam (26 de Diciembre 2003), tenemos que concentrarnos por el momento en la recopilación de información para poder comenzar acciones bajo la tutela del los Comités Nacionales relevantes. Sin duda, algunos de nuestros Comités Científicos Internacionales, como el Comité de Arquitectura en Adobe, tambien podrán contribuir. Asi espero sinceramente que con la ayuda de todos ustedes, la red profesional de ICOMOS se muestre exitosa incluso frente a este enorme desafío.

El Día Internacional de Monumentos el 18 de Abril del 2005, iniciado por ICOMOS, dará a muchos de nuestros Comités Internacionales una oportunidad extra de señalar las consecuencias del desastre del tsunami para el patrimonio cultural.

Paris, 7 de Enero del 2005

Michael Petzet
Presidente de ICOMOS

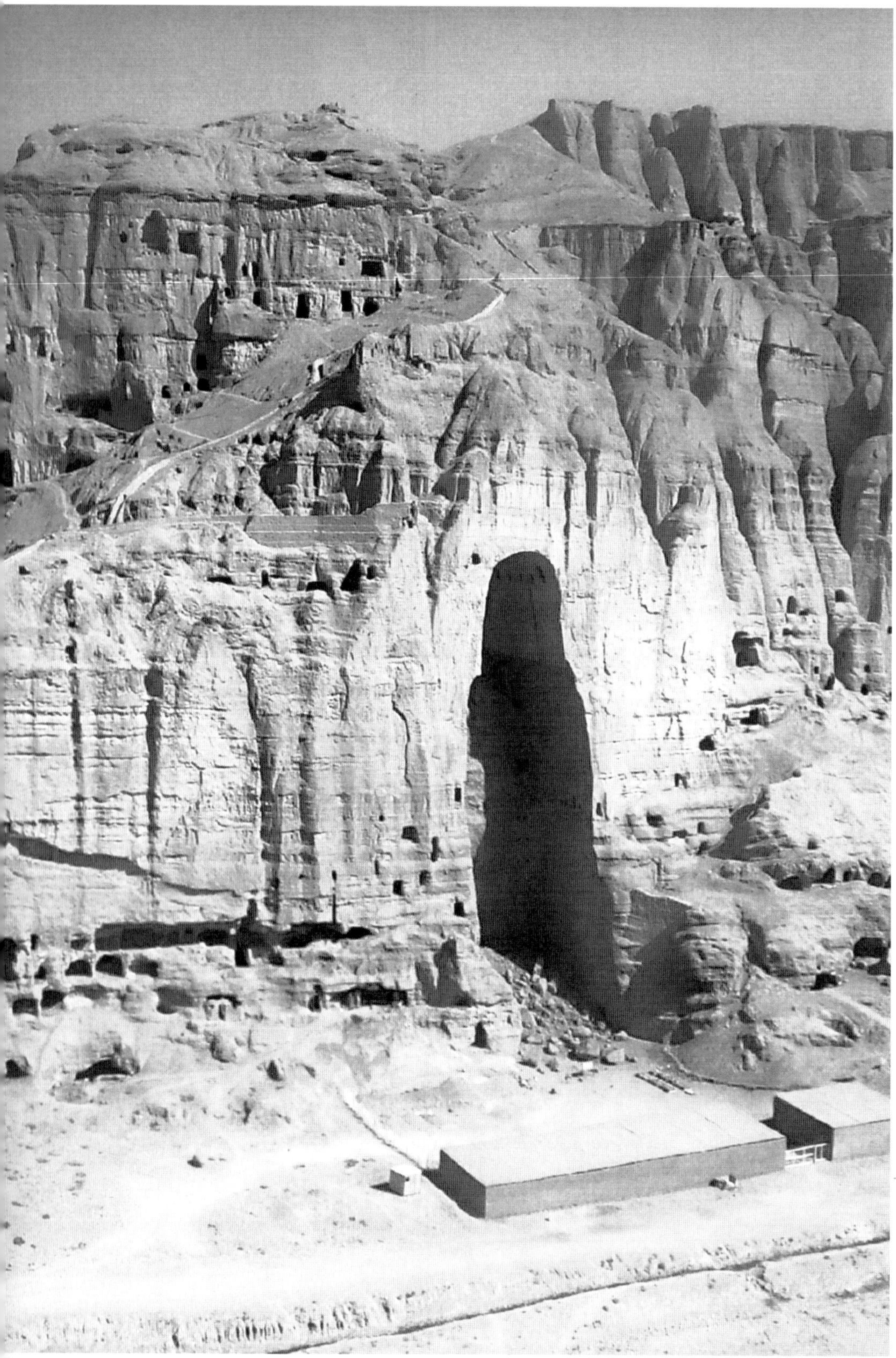

Niche of the Great Buddha, in the foreground the new shelters for storing the fragments

AFGHANISTAN
ICOMOS Actions in Afghanistan

As a result of funds provided by the German Foreign Office, ICOMOS was able to continue its work in Afghanistan in 2003-2004. In close co-operation with Professor Michael Jansen of the Technical University of Aachen, the national inventory of heritage places, monuments and sites, begun in 2002, could be further developed, initially on the basis of all available written sources. As practically all files of the Afghan State Conservation Office were lost during the war, the database currently being prepared is crucial for all future conservation work. Afghan colleagues, together with SPACH, are adding to this database on the spot by checking and documenting the present condition of sites. A special focus has been the documentation of earthen architecture in the Bamiyan valley, which was declared a World Heritage site in 2003.

The Babur Park project and the rehabilitation of the old quarter of Ashekan wa Arefan (*Heritage at Risk* 2002-2003, p. 16) was continued by the Aga Khan Trust for Culture, which in 2003 also took over the support of the expert originally employed by ICOMOS. Apart from the occasional expert advice on questions about stone conservation in the Babur Park, ICOMOS, under the guidance of UNESCO, has focussed of late on the Bamiyan valley.

The Second UNESCO/ICOMOS Expert Workshop on the Preservation of the Bamiyan Site (Munich, 18-20 December 2003), organised by ICOMOS Germany, reported on the progress made to date in Bamiyan (see attached Recommendations). In 2003, a complete survey recording of the topographical features close to and inside the niches of both the Great and the Small Buddha was done by engineering expert, Dr Mario Santana-Quintero, followed by a detailed survey of the rear walls of both niches undertaken by engineering and geology experts, Drs Pierre Smars (Belgium) and Michael Urbat from Cologne University. They were able to prepare a comprehensive stratigraphic mapping of the niche of the Great Buddha. In autumn 2003, preliminary consolidation began of the endangered cliff in the niche of the Small Buddha. This was based on the concept by Prof. Claudio Margottini and carried out by the Italian firm RODIO with funds from the Japan Fund in Trust of UNESCO.

Fragment Protection Mission in 2004

Only after the rear walls of the niches had been secured by steel nets in June 2004 to avoid the risk of falling stones, salvage of the decaying fragments of both statues could begin without risk to life. Thanks to funds provided by the German Foreign Office, a small ICOMOS team in co-operation with the Afghan authorities and the UNESCO office in Kabul made considerable progress between end-June and end-October 2004. At first it was most appropriate to safeguard those fragments of the Buddha Statues which show signs of original surface and to store them in a place protected from rain and snow. The restorers, Edmund Melzl and Engelbert Praxenthaler, as well as engineer Georgios Toubekis (Technical University Aachen) made the site ready and carried out the various tasks. Shelters were built in a suitable location in front of the Buddha niche to store the stone material, whilst finds of original plaster had to be secured and stored in boxes inside the mudbrick buildings near the Great Buddha, which had already been restored by ICOMOS in 2002. These buildings are now used for the local office of the Department of Historical Monuments in Bamiyan.

The new shelter structures consist of two rooms of 11 m x 9 m and 35 m x 9 m, both 3.80 m high and open to the front of the Great Buddha niche. The area has been secured by a surrounding fence with an entrance gate between the two buildings, so as not to obstruct the view towards the Buddha niche. To harmonise with the reddish appearance of the overall cliff-face and the general traditional architecture of the valley the construction was done in mudbrick with stone foundations and plastered with red mud. Care was taken not to disturb any archaeological sub-surface deposits. The lightweight roof construction was designed in such a way that it can be easily removed to give full access to the individual compartments.

The work was executed entirely by a local Bamiyan company under the supervision of the experts on site. Carpenters and locksmiths from the local bazaar [market] provided excellent pieces to solve construction details. Two employees of the national Monuments Department assisted in the entire process of the project. They supervised the local workers and were acquainted with international standards in documentation and conservation.

The niche of the Great Buddha measures approximately 300 cubic metres and the pile of rubble rises to 8 m above ground level so that about 1600 cubic metres are to be moved. Sand and crum-

Salvaging fragments of the Great Buddha

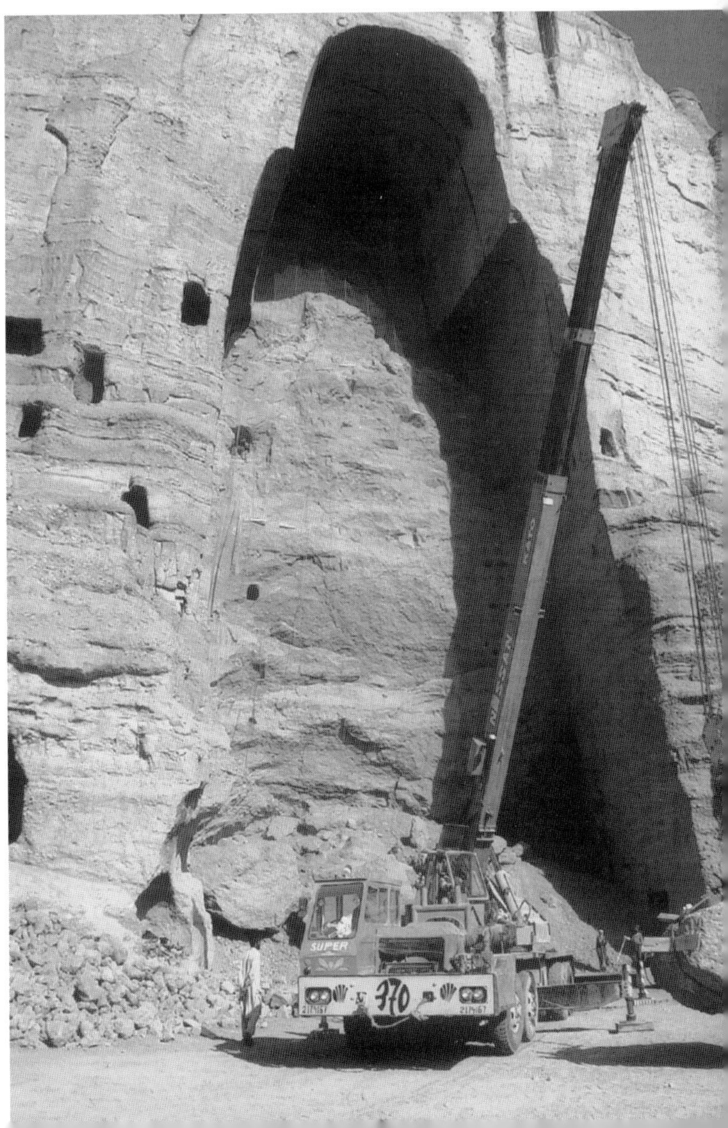

bling pieces of rock have been moved by hand and shovel and placed nearby the Buddha niche. A layer was laid down separating original ground surface and the niche material so as to be able to distinguish these materials from each other in the future. All pieces were checked for signs of original surface.

Security aspects determined any activity as it was known that the area of the niches served as ammunition stockpile in the years before the destruction. Throughout the progress of the works finds of battle as well as exploded and unexploded ordnance came to light. A de-mining expert assisted the works daily to remove dangerous artefacts and to check the metal finds.

All the debris was examined shovel by shovel by the workers in the search for remains of mud plaster and then carried by wheelbarrow to the western side of the fenced area. Pieces of stone showing signs of original surface were transferred to the shelters and stored on wooden palettes. Heavy fragments of rock were moved by a fork lifter or by a 30-ton crane to the shelters. The transport and movement of stone pieces had to be carried out very carefully because of the generally delicate condition of this material. Wooden boards placed between the steel rope and the boulders successfully prevented damage to the rock surface during movement. By using a fork lifter in combination with wooden boards, medium-sized fragments of up to about 8 tons could be lifted and carried without damage.

These fragments have been documented describing size, find location, surface condition, signs of carving and physical characteristics. Any original surface on smaller pieces could be identified by a change in colour whereas bigger fragments show holes of almost identical conical shape which used to hold wooden spikes anchoring the surface mud plaster.

The analysis of some mud plaster remains revealed the composition of the original plaster surface of the Buddhas. The examples found at the Small Buddha show a plaster in three layers. Organic parts such as straw, wooden sticks to reinforce the mud plaster, string and animal hair were found, which allowed Carbon14 dating. Now for the first time we have rather exact dates for both Buddhas: for the Small Buddha 507 AD +/– 15 years, for the Great Buddha 551 AD +/– 12 years. This means an age difference between the two statues of about half a century.

Besides, the larger plaster fragments from the clothing of the Small Buddha, which are still *in situ* on the rear wall of the niche, have been provisionally consolidated by Engelbert Praxenthaler, a safeguarding action at the last minute, because the precious plaster fragments were severely threatened. In 2004 only about a third of the fragments could be saved from the niche of the Great Buddha. Provided that similar funds will be available, ICOMOS hopes to complete the safeguarding of the fragments of both Buddhas in the year 2005. The consolidation of the rear walls, so far only provisionally secured by means of steel nets, is also extremely urgent. The recommendations of the Third Expert Working Group on the Preservation of the Bamiyan Site (Tokyo 18–20 December 2004) have encouraged ICOMOS to continue its concept:

1. *In 2005, the securing of fragments by the ICOMOS team should be continued at both niches. As soon as all the fragments are identified, documented and stored accordingly, the next steps should be decided by the Afghan authorities, assisted by international experts.*
2. *The ICOMOS conservation concept, in accordance with the relevant international guidelines (Charter of Venice etc), should be implemented. All fragments, sculptured and non-sculptured, should be preserved.*
3. *ICOMOS is encouraged to propose appropriate ways to conserve and to present the fragments. The technical possibilities of an anastylosis should be considered.*
4. *The Ministry of Information and Culture should reinforce cooperation with ICOMOS in the implementation of the conservation measures, also with regards to the facilitation of local administrative procedures.*
5. *ICOMOS should continue the important C14 analysis to date the plaster surface of the statues.*

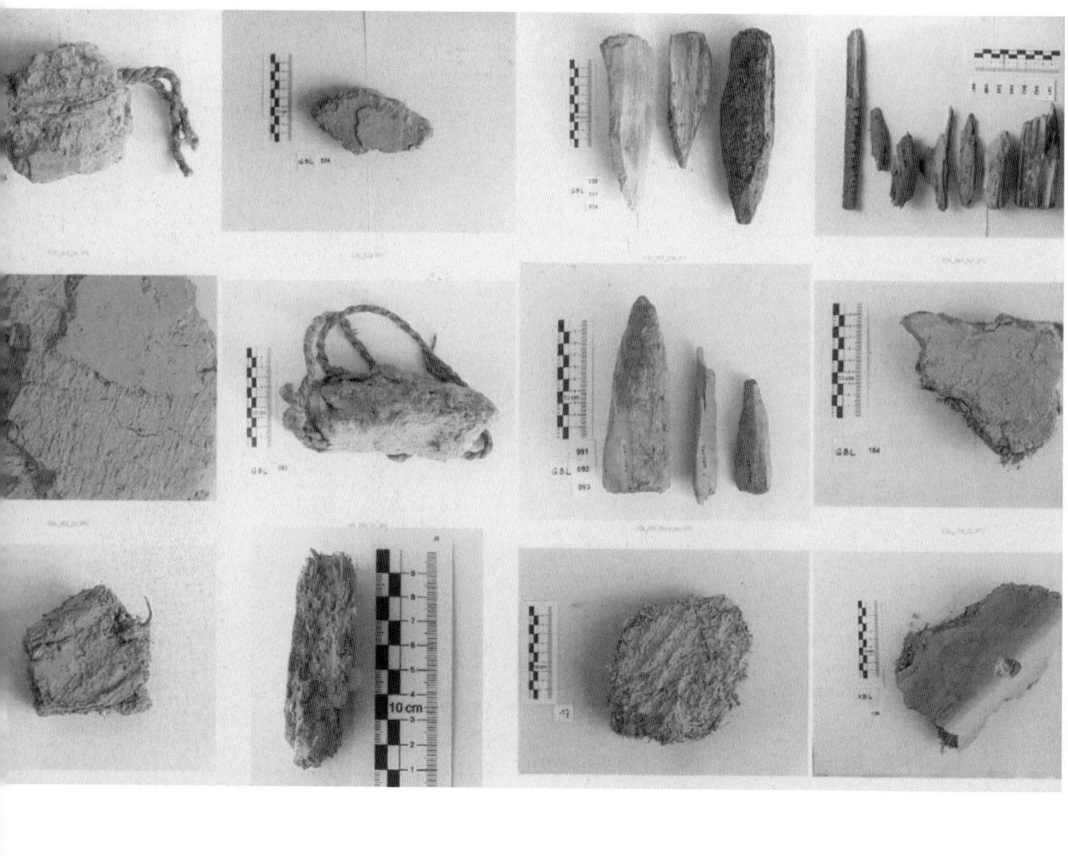

Rescued fragments of the Great and Small Buddhas, used for Carbon 14 dating (plaster fragments with string, pegs)

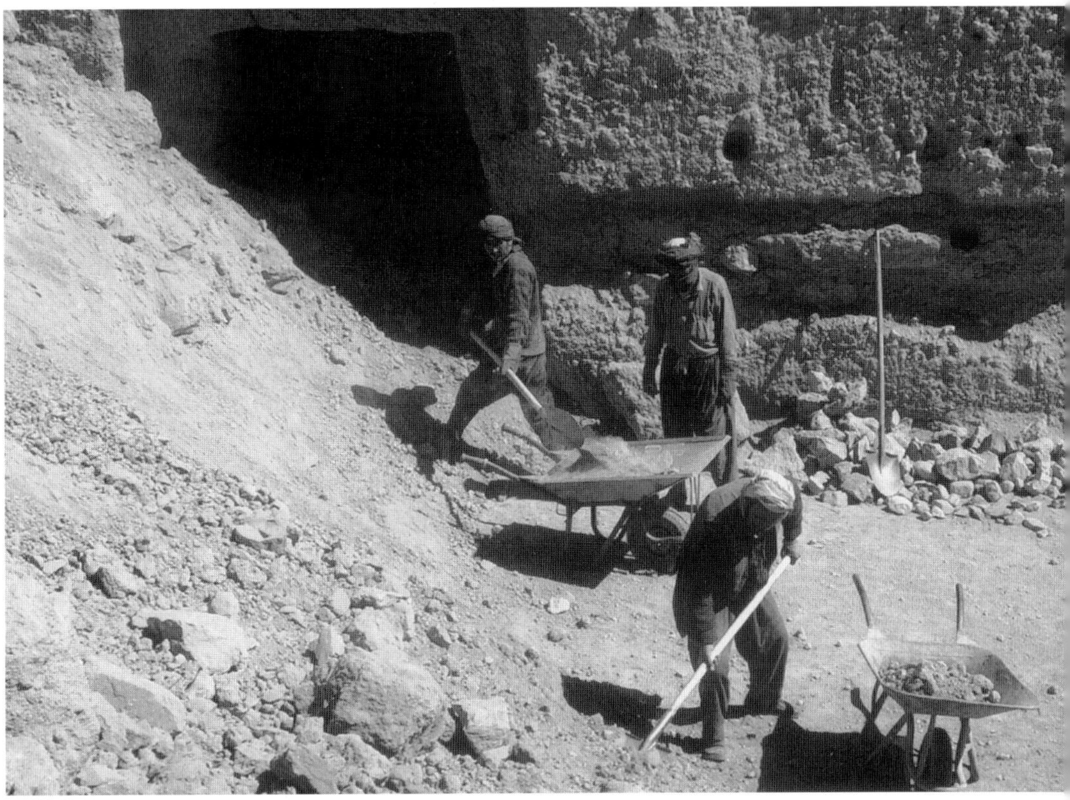

Salvaging fragments of the Great Buddha

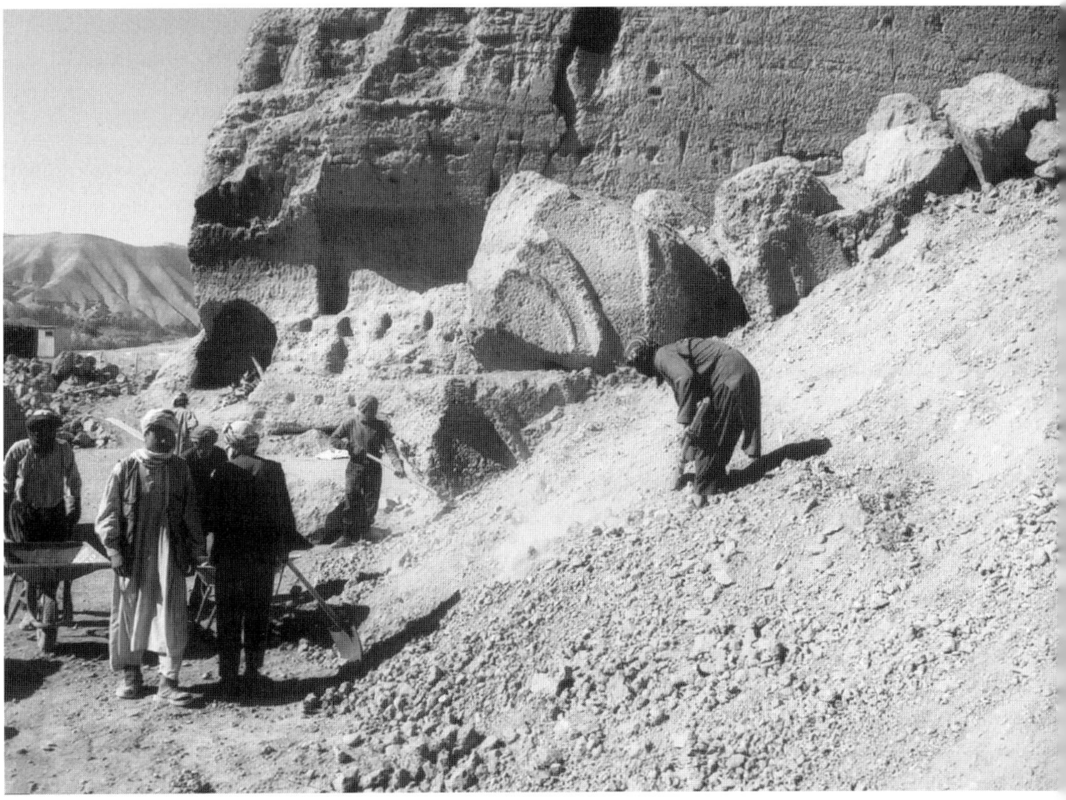

Salvaging fragments of the Great Buddha

Second UNESCO/ICOMOS Expert Working Group on the Preservation of the Bamiyan site

Munich/Germany, 18-20 December 2003

Recommendations

I. General

1. In view of the complexity of the safeguarding requirements of the Bamiyan site, an interdisciplinary approach should be pursued and a coordinated working schedule of the experts involved in the different aspects of the Bamiyan project should be drafted;
2. Reports on the safeguarding of the Bamiyan site and information on the history of restoration should be compiled and made available to the Afghan authorities and to experts involved in the Bamiyan project;
3. A tourist brochure on the site should be prepared;
4. The next Expert Working Group on the Preservation of the Bamiyan Site is expected to be held in November/December 2004 in Tokyo.

II. Consolidation of the cliffs and niches

1. General

a) In view of the presence of anti-personnel mines at the Bamiyan site, further demining should be an integral part of all consolidation efforts and be included in future budgets;
b) Information now available on the destructive effects of seismic hazards at the Bamiyan site should be included in future consolidation plans;
c) Investigations should be completed in areas that are not yet accessible, in particular in the lower eastern part of the Small Buddha, and in the lower western part of the Large Buddha. In addition, isostatic maps should be developed and tests on the effectiveness of grouting and anchoring, as well as on the compatibility of old and new materials and further rock mechanic laboratory tests, should be carried out;
d) A long-term monitoring system of the cliffs and weather conditions should be installed in 2004. It is essential to include capacity building programmes for the local community in the installation and maintenance of this monitoring system. It would also be desirable to install a basic earthquake monitoring unit and to carry out a study on the effect of the 1956 earthquake;
e) The Archaeological Survey of India will be consulted in order to obtain information on consolidation work carried out in Bamiyan in the 1970s.

2. Small Buddha niche

a) Plans for the preservation of the Buddha silhouette should be developed and emergency conservation measures started;
b) The final consolidation of the Small Buddha niche should be carried out, notably through stabilizing the remaining upper eastern part of the niche;
c) It is recommended that consolidation work start on the upper western part.

3. Large Buddha niche

a) Plans for the preservation of the Buddha silhouette should be developed and emergency conservation measures started;
b) Water infiltration should be limited.

III. Conservation of the fragments of the statues of the Buddha

1. The fragments of the statues should be covered during winter 2003/2004 in order to protect them from deterioration. ICOMOS will provide funds for this purpose to the Afghan Ministry of Information and Culture;
2. The safeguarding and conservation of the fragments will be a priority in 2004. Appropriate techniques for moving the fragments out of the niches should be studied, taking into account their fragility and their weight. The fragments should be protected by a temporary roof;
3. The fragments should be placed outside the niches under shelter. At the Small Buddha site, an appropriate location (possibly below the slope) will be determined in which to place them;
4. Detailed geological analysis of the back of the niches and the fragments should be carried out in order to determine the original position of the fragments. For this purpose, the 3-D documentation successfully carried out by the Japanese firm PASCO should be complemented by studies by ICOMOS in cooperation with the Universities of Aachen and Cologne. The Geological Department of the University of Kabul will be invited to cooperate. Training and capacity building for Afghan students should be included;
5. The appropriate conservation, notably the stabilization of this particular kind of rock, should be further studied by ICOMOS stone restorers;
6. Further studies of the presentation of the fragments *in situ* should be initiated.

IV. Preservation of the mural paintings

1. Conservation work on the mural paintings initiated in 2003 should be continued;
2. The remains of the structure of cave G should be preserved;
3. The remaining mural paintings still *in situ* should be consolidated in 2004, notably by fixing their edges;
4. The fragments of mural paintings collected should be further studied and an appropriate method for their conservation determined;
5. It is strongly recommended that international mural paintings experts be involved in the future National Centre for the Conservation of Mural Paintings in Bamiyan, whose establishment is planned by the National Federation of UNESCO Associations in Japan. This project should be discussed during the next Plenary Session of the *International Coordination Committee for the Safeguarding of Afghanistan's Cultural Heritage*;
6. Climatic conditions in the storage room used for fragments of mural paintings and archaeological objects at the local office of the Ministry of Information and Culture should be studied and enhanced if required.

V. General Master Plan

1. The development of a General Master Plan for the safeguarding of the site, presently being developed by the National Research Institute for Cultural Properties (NRICP), Tokyo, is of great importance and should be made available as soon as possible. Once UNESCO receives the preliminary General Master Plan drawn up by NRICP, it should be dispatched to international experts involved in the project in order to receive their comments and ensure coordination of efforts. A coordination meeting to discuss the preliminary General Master Plan should be held in Kabul;
2. The preliminary General Master Plan should be discussed in 2004 with the Afghan Ministry of Information and Culture. Local authorities to be involved in these discussions should be addressed through representatives of the Government of Afghanistan;
3. The development of the 3-D model and map successfully initiated by PASCO should be completed in 2004, and the data made available to the Afghan authorities and the experts involved in the Bamiyan project;

VI. Archaeological activities

1. The definition of the archaeological zones in the Bamiyan valley is a priority in view of ensuring its protection in the future. To this end, Professor Tarzi is ready to put his experience at the disposal of the experts of the National Research Institute for Cultural Properties (NRICP), Japan, and UNESCO, in order to jointly develop a historical map of the Bamiyan valley;
2. To ensure a coordinated effort in obtaining further knowledge of the archaeological remains of the Bamiyan valley, the Délégation Archéologique Française en Afghanistan (DAFA) and NRICP will cooperate. UNESCO will continue to play its role in coordinating archaeological activities in Bamiyan, in close cooperation with the Afghan National Institute of Archaeology, and it should therefore be informed by all institutions of ongoing and planned activities;
3. Historical photographs of the DAFA archives should be made available to all experts involved in the Bamiyan project;
4. General archaeological explorations should be continued by NRICP and DAFA in 2004. In areas where positive results have been achieved, detailed investigations should be carried out. In addition, test trenches could be excavated in order to complement results obtained by investigation;

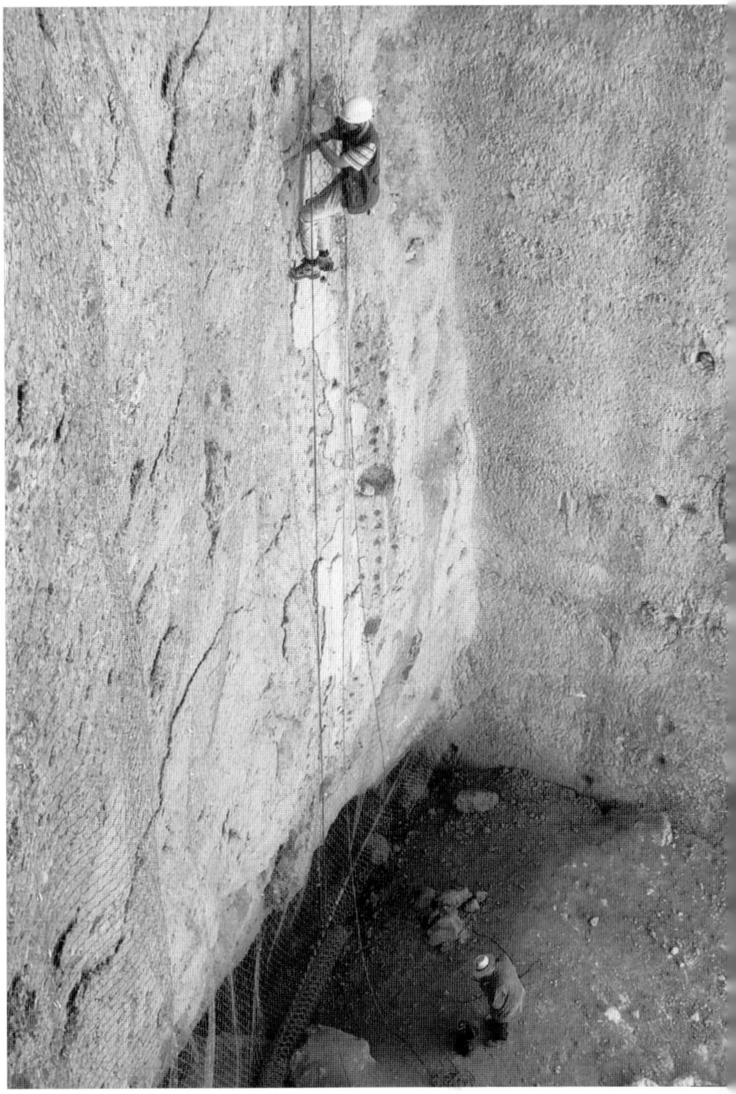

Provisional fixing of plaster fragments on the back wall of the niche of the Small Buddha, carried out by restorer E. Praxenthaler

5. Cooperation between experts from NRICP and ICOMOS should be initiated in order to obtain the maximum results for an archaeological survey of the Bamiyan valley;
6. It would be desirable to explore all the archaeological sites in the Bamiyan valley.

ALBANIA
The Mesi Bridge at Shkodra on the Kir river

In Albania arched bridges, built in various periods, occupy an important place among historic engineering items. In the mountainous country of Albania consisting of valleys and torrential streams, the bridges of stone or with arches were an imperial necessity. These bridges were built as a result of local funding and by the labour of the local inhabitants. The oldest remains take us back to Classical times, to the 1st century BC at the time of the Roman Empire.

Because of damaging factors, the stone bridges that survive today in Albania date to the 17th century, when the Balkans were under the protection of the Ottoman Empire. There are so many bridges of different periods, which are protected by the state and have the status of 'Cultural Monument'. In the north of Albania in the Shkoder region there are several medieval bridges because of the many rivers and streams. In the north-east, a few kilometres from the town of Shkoder on the Kir river, is the Mesi bridge near the village of Mesi, from which it takes its name. This bridge is 130 m long and is one of the biggest bridges in the Balkans. From the outset, the bridge was a colossal construction with its top reaching its full height at the keystone of the main arch.

Its origin cannot be older than the 18th century and it is not on the 1688 Carouell map, which includes all the bridges in this region. Various facts link this bridge with the works by the ruler of Pachalik of Shkoder, Mehmed Pacha Bushati (the Elder) in 1768, when he also built the Leaden Mosque in the Shkodra castle.

In its ground plan, the Mesi Bridge does not follow a completely straight line, but takes a change of direction of 14 degrees towards the lower side about 5 m to the right of the big arch, enforced by the massive rocks on the river-bed.

We can see from its building techniques that the Mesi Bridge has two construction phases. The first phase saw the building of the big central arch and three others alongside, two on the left and one on the right. In the second construction phase, the Kir river flow had outflanked the bridge and therefore the smaller arches were built at either end.

Today the bridge consists of 13 arches. The biggest is in the centre, with a span of 21.5 m, created by a double vault rib 108 cm wide. The bank is paved in river stones and is very uneven, later being reinforced with side bastions built of river stone.

Technically, the bridge has been damaged over time by devastating floods. Such conditions have resulted in floodwaters cutting away at the arches on the right side. This has caused cracks in the hang of the arch. Even the main arch has suffered from cracks that also jeopardise the bridge's stability.

The consolidation of the piers, the infill of the cracks from below and the creation of a hydrological system on the bridge in case of floods, are seen as necessary conservation actions. Doing these particular and technical works is pressing because of the eventual deterioration of this bridge.

Not implementing these works will cause damage to the very existence of this bridge, seen as cultural heritage at risk. We consider that the case of the Mesi Bridge merits being in the 2004 edition of *Heritage at Risk ICOMOS World Report of Monuments and Sites in Danger.*

The Mesi Bridge represents cultural heritage which extends beyond the national dimension. In this aim in mind, it is worth analysing it in the technical reports of international cultural organisations.

ICOMOS Albania

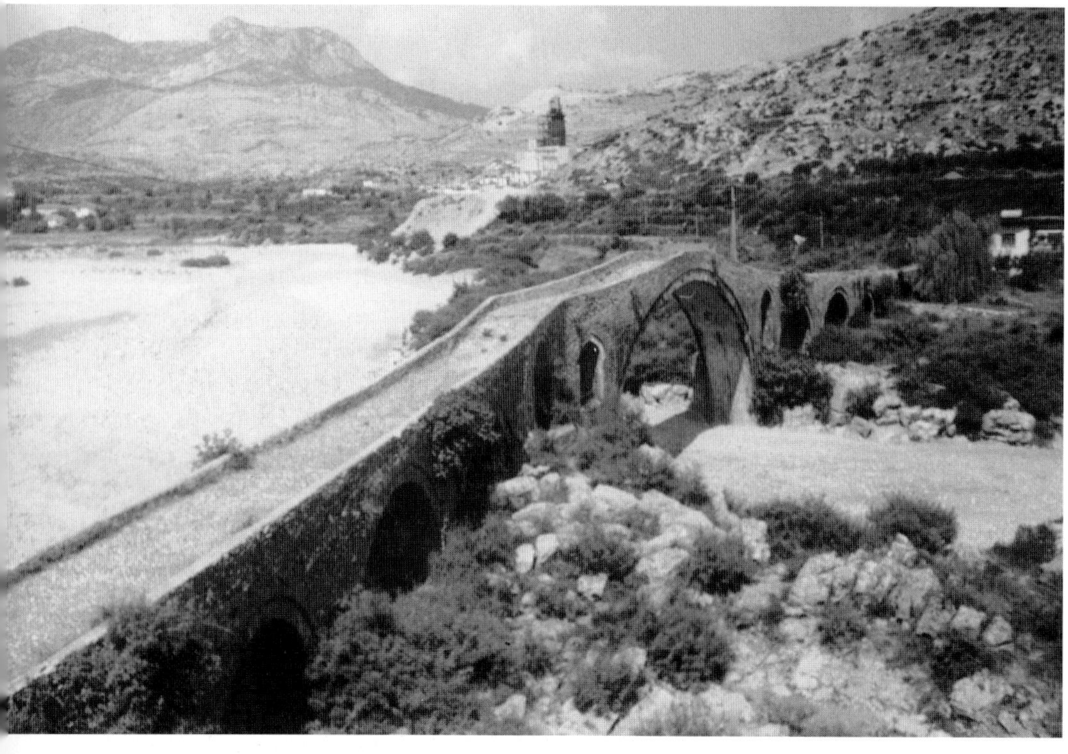

View of the Mesi Bridge at Shkodra

ANDORRA
A horizon of hope for heritage at risk

The *Heritage at Risk* program highlights the difficult cohabitation between cultural heritage and our model of industrial society. This power sharing is, moreover, more and more complicated because of the progressive, generalised spread of urban or developed areas. Andorra is a significant example of this model of progress and comfort as well as of the problems that it generates in cultural heritage management.

In 2000 the ICOMOS Andorra committee gave details in an alarming report: the largest metropolitan area in the Pyrenees with 70,000 inhabitants, subjected pressure on its heritage, whether it was central or on the outskirts. Whether it were the cultural landscape of the Madriu Valley, or the complex of the historic centre of Santa Coloma or even the 20th century urban heritage, it was running the risk of being changed without anyone's consideration, and that is still the current situation for some of it. Indeed real estate speculation continues to be very important in Andorra, troubling for built or landscape heritage.

Four years after the publication of that report, those sections of Andorran society inclined to recognise the importance of cultural heritage and to share in the responsibility and effort towards its protection for the benefit of future generations are slowly increasing. Whilst it is still impossible to talk of a deep and complete change in thinking, such as in other countries more involved in this field, civil society is becoming more and more aware of the need to assume the totality of the costs which progress calls for. A quality of life does not merely amount to stocking up on groceries, on water and on energy, nor of guaranteeing health and housing. Natural and cultural heritage are increasingly seen as another resource at the intended base to positively change the every day.

In Andorra, the consciousness of cultural heritage is revealed in a growing concern about the conservation of cultural assets, which enabled the passing of the Cultural Heritage Act of Andorra in 2003. Without taking account of the concepts, systems, norms and standards, that can always be improved, this act reduces the possibility of arbitrary decisions and, above all, it endows the country with the necessary instruments to change the awareness of individuals about cultural heritage in a significant and effective way. This act is a tool that will contribute to guide the country to a desirable growth in harmony with heritage protection.

In accordance with the new law, the not negligible wish to include part of 20th century heritage in the documented list of tangible assets, represented another advance in this sphere. Civil society has discovered the architectural value and the historic importance of a group of properties, that until then was without any apparent identity. On the one hand, the community has started to realise that cultural heritage and its protection is not only a matter for the government administration, but that it concerns all of us, and on the other hand, that the cultural estate does not only affect public buildings but also landscapes and private buildings. It is the beginning, admittedly still diffident, of taking collective responsibility for heritage protection.

It is clear that the declaration on 1 July 2004 of the Madriu-Perafita-Claror Valley as World Heritage in the cultural landscape category[1] marked a turning point in this long process of changing the thinking of the Andorran community. This declaration is determining for the group of this society that is thus keeping a long-range power of influence from around the planet, that is, international acknowledgement. The situation of the Madriu Perafita Claror Valley allows the practical implementing of the widely repeated idea that we must think globally, plan regionally and act locally.

The limited spread of this valley, 4,247 hectares, lets good management be brought to a satisfactory conclusion. Its proximity to the largest urban area in the Pyrenees can be an opportunity to highlight that there is another way of doing things. UNESCO's recognition is evidence of the confidence in the people of Andorra, and their wish to act in another way on Earth. It is clearly evident that the road to travel is long, that heritage consciousness is still not widespread, and that the legal instruments are still imperfect, but the beginning of the trail has been blazed: the dialogue and the debate which have been created in society are bearers of hope.

ICOMOS Andorra

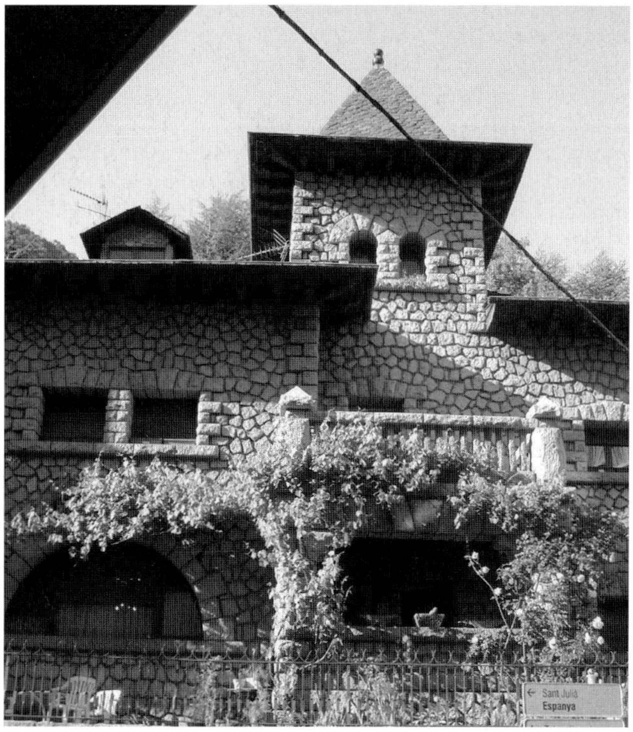

Xalet Casa Arajol

View of the Madriu Valley

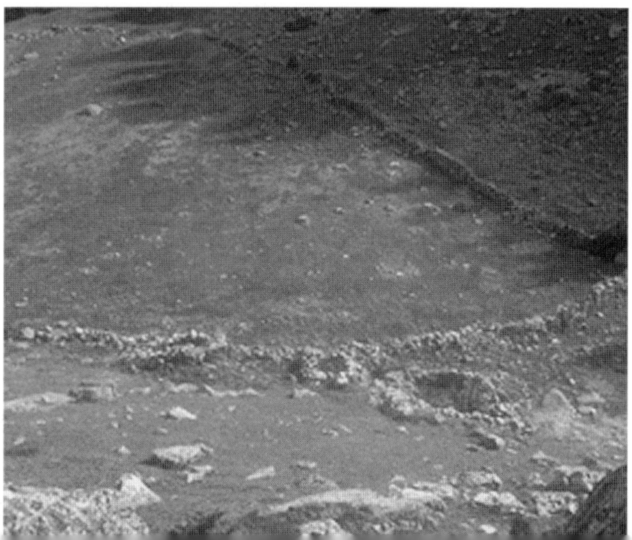

ANDORRE
Un horizon d'espoir pour le patrimoine en péril

Le programme 'Heritage at risk' met en évidence la cohabitation difficile entre le patrimoine culturel et notre modèle de civilisation industrielle. Cette cohabitation est, en outre, de plus en plus compliquée du fait de l'extension progressive généralisée des zones urbanisées ou exploitées. L'Andorre est un exemple significatif de ce modèle de progrès et de bien-être ainsi que des problèmes qu'il génère dans la gestion du patrimoine culturel.

L'an 2000 le comité andorran d'ICOMOS a élaboré un rapport alarmant : la plus grande conurbation des Pyrénées (70.000 habitants) subissait une pression sur son patrimoine, qu'il soit central ou périphérique. Que ce soit le paysage culturel de la Vallée du Madriu, ou l'ensemble du centre historique de Santa Coloma ou encore le patrimoine urbain du XX° siècle, courraient, et c'est toujours d'actualité pour certains d'entre eux, le danger d'être transformés sans considération aucune. La spéculation immobilière, en effet, continue d'être très importante en Andorre, provocant des troubles sur le patrimoine bâti ou paysager.

Quatre ans après la parution de ce rapport, les secteurs de la société andorrane disposés à reconnaître l'importance du patrimoine culturel et à partager la responsabilité et l'effort de sa protection au profit des générations futures augmentent lentement mais de jour en jour. Pourtant, s'il est encore impossible de parler d'un changement profond et global des mentalités, comme dans d'autres pays plus impliqués dans ce domaine, la société civile est de plus en plus sensible à la nécessité d'assumer la totalité des coûts que comporte le progrès. La qualité de vie ne se résume pas simplement à s'approvisionner en aliments, en eau et en énergie ni à garantir l'hygiène et le logement. Le patrimoine naturel et culturel est de plus en plus considéré comme un autre recours de base visant à changer positivement le quotidien.

En Andorre, la prise de conscience concernant le patrimoine culturel s'est manifestée par un intérêt croissant pour la conservation des biens. Ce qui a permis l'approbation l'an 2003 de la Loi du Patrimoine culturel d'Andorre. Sans tenir compte des concepts, des régimes, des normes ou des mesures, pouvant être toujours améliorés, cette loi réduit les possibilités de décisions arbitraires et elle dote surtout le pays des instruments nécessaires pour transformer la conscience des individus, sur le patrimoine culturel, de manière significative et efficace. Cette loi est un outil qui va contribuer à conduire le pays à une souhaitable croissance en harmonie avec la sauvegarde des lieux et des monuments.

Conformément à la nouvelle loi, la volonté d'inclure une part – non négligeable – du patrimoine urbain du XX° siècle dans la liste des biens immeubles inventoriés a représenté une autre avancée dans ce domaine. La société civile a découvert la valeur architectonique et l'importance historique d'un ensemble de biens, jusqu'alors sans identité apparente. D'une part, les citoyens ont commencé a prendre conscience que le patrimoine culturel et sa protection ne relève pas seulement de l'Administration mais qu'elle nous concerne à tous, et , d'autre part, que les biens culturels n'affectent pas uniquement les bâtiments publics mais aussi les paysages et édifices privés. C'est le début, bien que timide encore, de la prise en charge collective de la sauvegarde du patrimoine.

Il est évident que la déclaration, le 1er juillet 2004, de la Vallée de Madriu Perafita Claror patrimoine de l'humanité dans la catégorie de paysage culturel marquera un tournant dans ce long processus de changement de mentalité de la société andorrane. Cette déclaration est déterminante pour l'ensemble de cette société qui garde ainsi un pouvoir d'influence de la planète terre à long terme, c'est-à-dire la reconnaissance mondiale. La position de la Vallée du Madriu Perafita Claror permet de poser en pratique l'idée largement répétée qu'il faut penser globalement, planifier régionalement et agir localement.

L'extension limitée de cette vallée (4.247 hectares) permet de mener à bien une bonne gestion. Sa proximité de la plus grande conurbation des Pyrénées peut être une opportunité de mettre en évidence qu'il y a une autre manière de faire les choses. La reconnaissance de l'UNESCO est un témoignage de confiance aux citoyens andorrans et à leur volonté d'agir d'une autre manière sur la Terre. Il est tout à fait évident que le chemin à parcourir est long, que la prise de conscience n'est pas encore généralisée et que les instruments légaux sont encore imparfaits; les premiers jalons sont posés : le dialogue et le débat qui se sont instaurés dans la société sont porteurs d'espoir.

ICOMOS Andorre

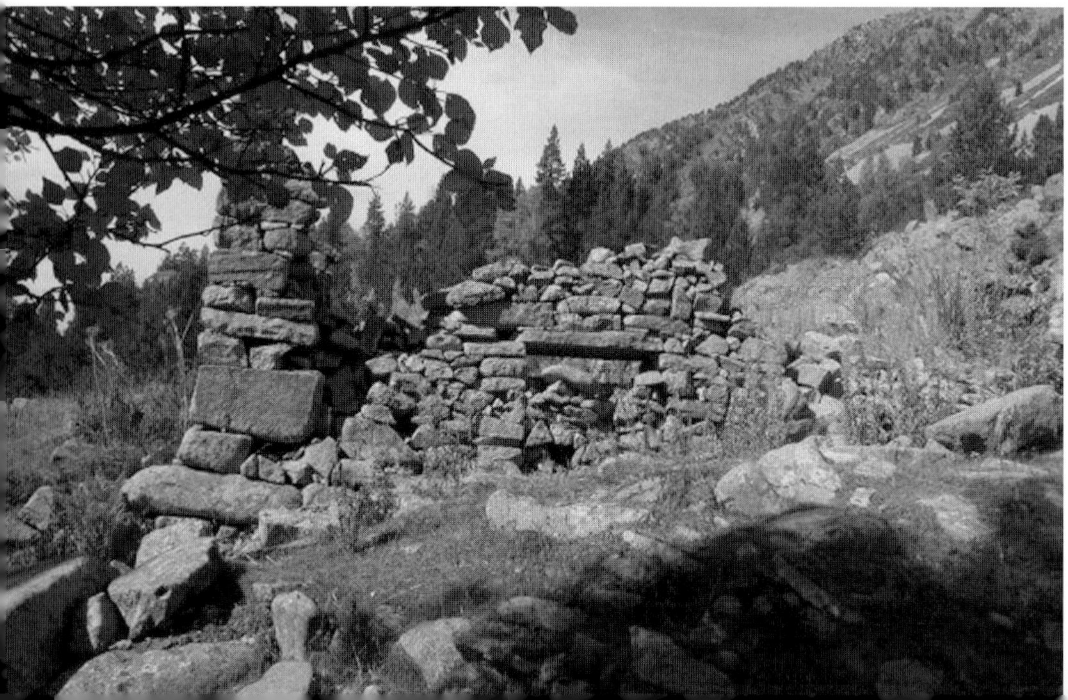

View of the Madriu Valley

AUSTRALIA
Heritage Landscapes and Gardens

Australia is the only nation that is a continent, with a vast array of different topographies, and an incredible biological and ecological diversity. All landscapes are layered with cultural memory and meaning, and there is a dawning realisation that the whole of the Australian continent can be seen as a 'cultural landscape' - arising from the very long and intertwined history of interaction between people and the environment.

Australian landscapes are unique, resulting from 80 million years of evolution of the land and its flora and fauna since Gondwana separated, at least 60,000 years of Indigenous occupation and more than 200 years of European contact, cultural diversity and multiple and shared histories.

Some of these special characteristics are at risk, becoming less sustainable in the face of change, or through a lack of appreciation or adequate protection of their heritage values. In other cases, planning and land use processes are not sufficiently integrated to fully recognise all aspects of our heritage, thus placing at risk elements of heritage values - natural and cultural, Indigenous and settler - within the broader landscape.

Australia ICOMOS sees these as key issues for conservation philosophy and practice, and therefore welcomes their exploration through the scientific symposium planned for the 15th ICOMOS General Assembly, to be held in Xi'an, China in 2005. Particular concerns, examples and solutions are presented in our report below, as well as further reading, to broadly contribute to that discussion.

Issues

Cultural landscapes can be significant for their designed, evolved or associative values. They can include large areas of land – sometimes difficult to perceive as 'bounded' places.

Cultural landscapes can be linear in form (such as in the case of cultural routes, roads, song lines, waterways), and can be associated with significant intangible cultural heritage.

Importantly, landscapes provide the physical, visual and experiential/sensory *setting* of individual heritage places. Travelling through landscapes can be an important aspect of their significance. In many cases, the significance of landscapes can be inseparably linked with continuing cultural traditions – including land use practices, rural technologies, vernacular architecture, cultural concepts of time and space, the performing arts, religious observances, and so on.

Risks to heritage landscapes arise from some of their characteristics as heritage places:

- Landscapes are dynamic and it can be difficult to manage their complexity and ongoing evolution.
- Landscapes are affected by a diversity of pressures, often outcomes are the result of cumulative and/or interactive influences.
- Landscapes often consist of land in a variety of present-day land tenure arrangements – integrated approaches to protection and management can be difficult to achieve where there is a mixture of private and public owners and managers.
- Landscapes and their multiple values are managed through many activities undertaken by different levels of government – and by different agencies within each level of government – typically without sufficient coordination and shared values and priorities.
- Landscapes can be affected through the incremental impact of a vast number of individual development approvals, occurring simultaneously at different levels of government, often without adequate coordination. In many of the most vulnerable areas – such as coastal landscapes within the urbanised east and south-east of the continent – the pace of change arising from multiple pressures is great.
- Landscapes currently suffer from a lack of broadly understood and applied methods for perceiving, valuing, and managing their heritage values. So, while there is a growing awareness of the importance of cultural landscapes within the community, and by heritage agencies, broad landscapes still tend to be in the 'too hard basket' in many instances.
- Landscapes – perhaps more than other heritage places – require the articulation of multiple narratives to be appropriately interpreted and celebrated.

In Australia, conservation practitioners have a wealth of experience of understanding and addressing these matters – at the global level (through for example the recognition of Uluru-KataTjuta as one of the first cultural landscapes recognised through the World Heritage Convention), and in local contexts. While there are many instances where excellent outcomes have occurred and best practice is being re-defined, it is also true that there are still many others where these factors present a considerable risk to the sustainability and viability of Australia's heritage.

This is a very broad theme for examining Heritage@Risk – a few examples have been selected to illustrate the issues, trends and potential solutions.

Drought, Fire and Climate Change

Throughout south-eastern Australia excessive drought believed to be related to global warming is having considerable impact on heritage gardens, avenues and landscapes. Impacts include loss of trees, increased vulnerability to bushfire, shortened life span of significant vegetation, and influences on planting choices in designed landscapes to incorporate new management regimes arising from water restrictions.

During the summer of 2002–2003, a vast area of south-eastern Australia was burned by wildfire, with the alpine region particularly affected. Loss of life and property was accompanied by significant losses of cultural and natural heritage. Again, in the summer of 2003–2004 bushfires affected areas of high conservation value – including Booderee National Park on the coast, with the loss of many trees and other vegetation.

Environmental change is insidious and is expected to ultimately have a considerable impact on significant landscapes and heritage settings. Because of this dilemma the 2004 national conference of the Australian Garden History Society was devoted to this topic - *Browned Off: Old Gardens in a New World,* held in Sydney in October, 2004 (see www.gardenhistorysociety.org.au/).

An example relates to Australia's unique and valued garden suburbs. The city of Canberra – Australia's federal capital – is a planned Garden City. Canberra was extensively planted with exotic trees and bushes, and is famous for its colourful spring and autumn, in a landscape otherwise typically eucalypt grey-green. Within this landscape, long-term water restrictions are having an impact on street trees. There are discussions about possibly replac-

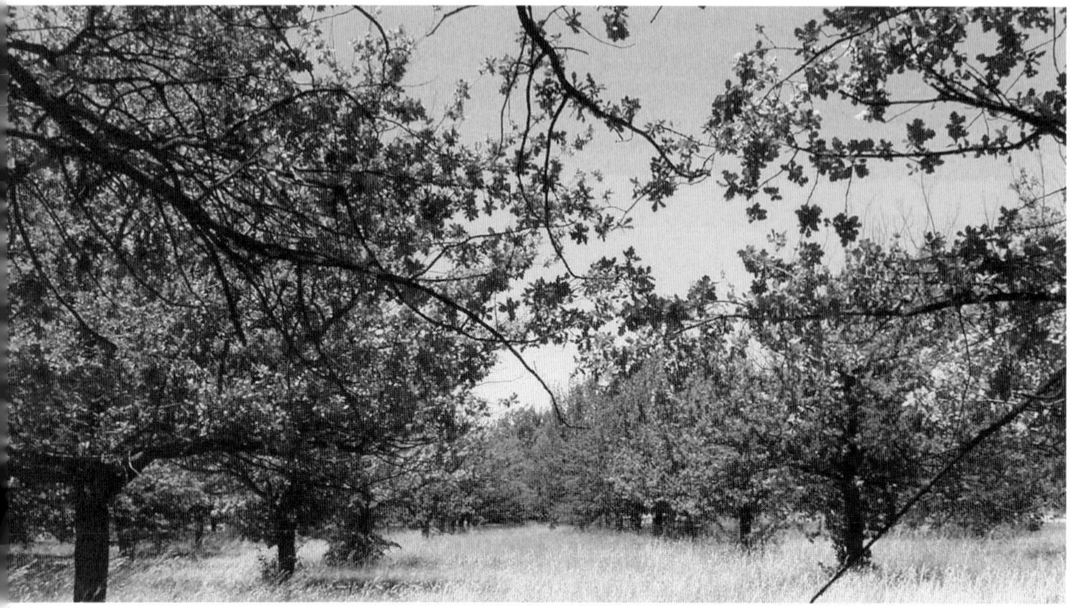

York Park historic oak trees, Canberra, Australia (photo: Duncan Marshall)

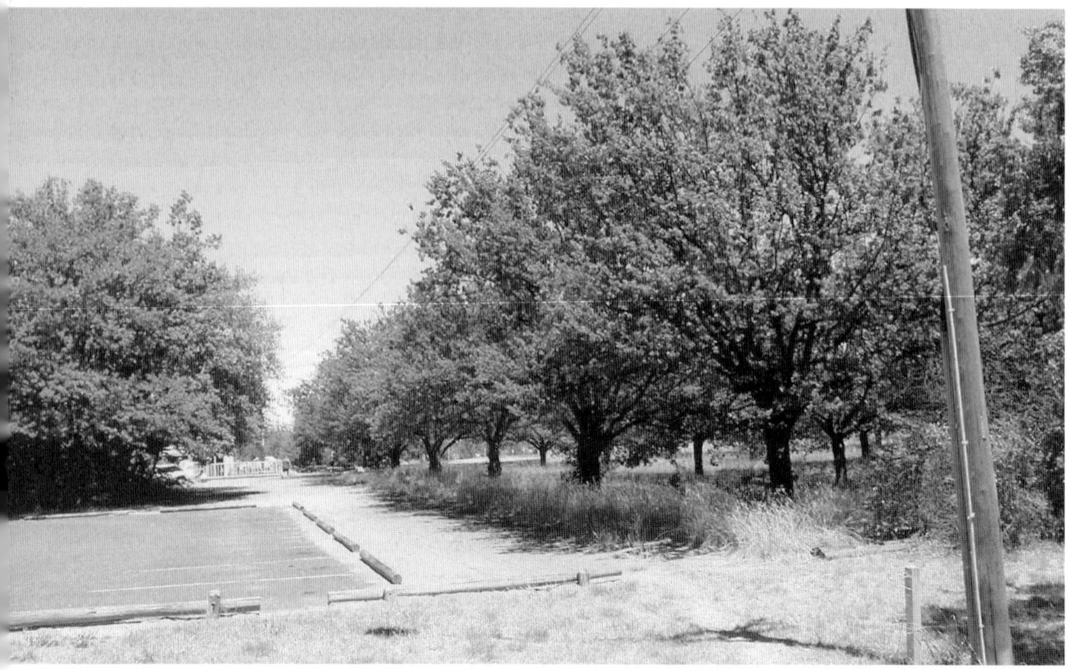

York Park historic oak trees, Canberra, Australia, damaged by parking (photo: Duncan Marshall)

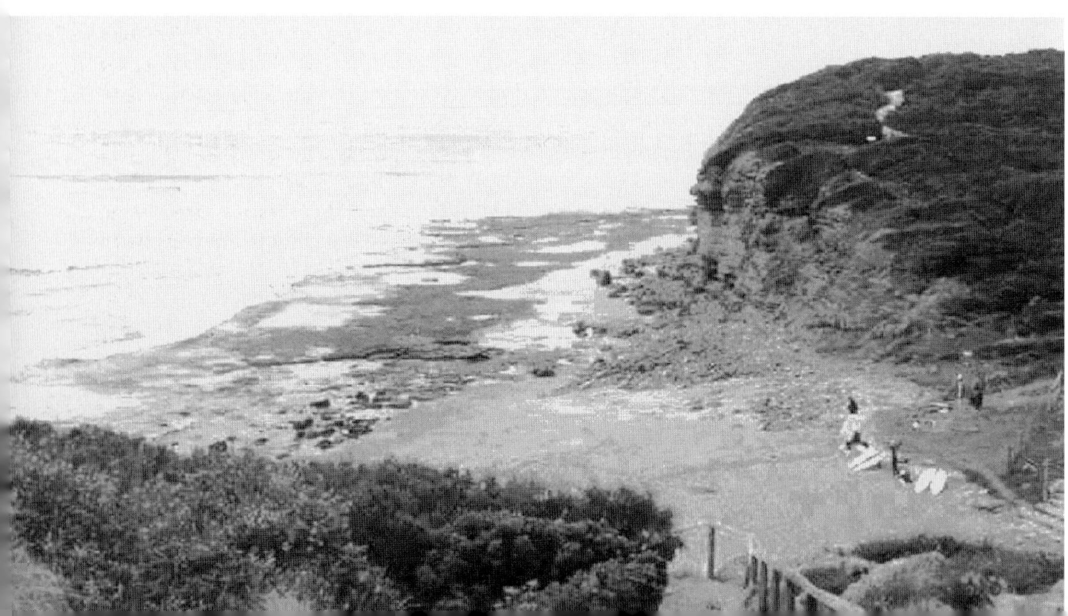

Bells Beach, near Torquay, Victoria – part of Australia's highly valued coastal landscapes. Included in the Victorian Heritage Register because of its iconic status within the history of the development of surfing in Australia (photo: Heritage Victoria)

ing the northern hemisphere deciduous trees with native species, so changing the entire look of the city.

Perhaps it was not this issue that was primarily a factor in a recent case threatening a copse of oak trees in Canberra, but certainly their bedraggled and drought-parched appearance did not help. The York Park Plantation is a small plantation of English Oak (*Quercus robur*) trees in Central Canberra. It has been included in the Commonwealth Heritage List, and has well-documented associations with the visit to Canberra by the Duke of York in 1927 for the opening of the new Parliament House. Although some trees have died, the plantation is intact.

In 2004, the National Trust included York Park in its *Endangered Places List* due to a proposed office and car park development. Intense lobbying by many people and community-based heritage groups such as the Australian Garden History Society and the National Trust of Australia has put the development proposal on hold. There is a current commitment to move the boundary of the car park to prevent further compaction under the trees, removal of invasive weed species, and appropriate tree pruning. Nonetheless, the case illustrates the vulnerability of our listed landscape heritage places.

Changes in garden 'fashion'

Whilst drought has hastened 'hard-landscaping' trends in gardens, with many areas of grass now being paved, such changes sit within a broader international shift to a more formal garden style, with regular paving and rigid furniture structures. This fashion can impact on heritage gardens.

The heritage-listed Old Parliament House Rose Gardens occupy a prominent and strategic location at the southern end of the main Land Axis of Walter Burley Griffin's design for Australia's federal capital city of Canberra. The Gardens have been recently redeveloped.

The new works included the removal of approximately 600 historic roses, in favour of hybrid varieties and inserted a new hard-edged style, currently in vogue and quite out of keeping with the original design of enclosed gardens reflecting an Edwardian garden style.

These works have seriously impacted upon the heritage integrity of the existing heritage precinct. This took place despite protests by heritage experts to the Canberra planning authority. The former value of the Gardens as an integral part of the design and use of Old Parliament House has been lost, and their potential to be acclaimed as major integral component of the early 20th century group of features in the Parliamentary Triangle has also been lost.

As well, the new and altered appearance of the Gardens has had an impact on their importance in providing the setting for Old Parliament House, and on the vistas that comprise the significant Parliamentary Triangle landscape.

Urban Expansion and Rural Landscapes

In Australia, a major risk to rural cultural landscapes in some regions is urban 'sprawl' arising from the accommodation of population growth on the low-density fringes of major metropolitan areas.

In Sydney, planning processes for growth have the potential to rapidly and dramatically change the character of areas known for their 'colonial landscape' values. Properties in these areas were manifest in a distinct style, derived from British 18th century pastoral landscapes.

The 2001 Australian State of the Environment report refers to the Southern Highlands region of NSW, where accelerated urban development is a potential risk to the modern-day 'hill station' character of the area. In recognition of these issues, and in response to related community concerns, the Wingecarribbee Shire conducted a study of historic rural landscapes during the 1990s. The study resulted in the establishment of landscape protection zones within the planning scheme, which has facilitated the retention of landscape integrity and created a synergy with policies to protect rural lands from fragmentation.

Coastal Landscapes

In many regions, community perceptions suggest that coastal landscapes are subject to risks through rapid changes in land use. Pressures on coastal environments are particularly evident in those regions close to major population centres. Risks to the heritage values of coastal environments are many, and include the individual and cumulative effects of:

- increased urbanisation in coastal areas (arising from the demand for seaside holiday houses/'weekenders', and through demographic change as more city dwellers and retirees seek lifestyle change through movement to coastal areas – the 'seachange' phenomenon);
- developments for recreation and tourism – including resort developments, golf courses;
- pressures for increased road capacity in scenic coastal areas;
- redevelopment of maritime infrastructure to enable Australian seaports to remain competitive within global transport markets;
- Increased erosion, storm damage and the other effects of climate change.

Another land use conflict in coastal areas has involved the energy sector, and the drive for improved energy efficiency and Government commitments to increase the provision of energy from sustainable and renewable sources.

The rapid uptake of wind energy in Australia is causing a major impact on valued landscapes in rural areas, particularly valued coastal areas of Australia. Wind farm installations have become a major community area of concern and protest. Not all wind farm developments occur in coastal areas – their placement and viability vary substantially – although those occurring in coastal areas seem to be particularly contentious.

Best practice standards have been set for the installation of wind farms with regard to general planning, visual impacts and some natural conservation considerations. However, a thorough investigation of landscape values that includes historic, social and aesthetic heritage values of landscapes was not part of the planning requirements.

Natural and cultural heritage therefore feature prominently in the language of this debate, and there is a lack of consistent and agreed approaches to landscape assessment – both at the strategic planning stage, and in relation to the siting and design of individual developments.

In recognition of this gap, a joint initiative of the Australian Wind Energy Association and the Australian Council of National Trusts has been supported by the Australian Greenhouse Office and the Heritage Division of the Department of the Environment and Heritage. While the project is still in its first stage, the aim is to develop a best practice national approach which has the agreement of the industry and heritage organisations. (see www.nationaltrust.org.au/media_whats_new.htm)

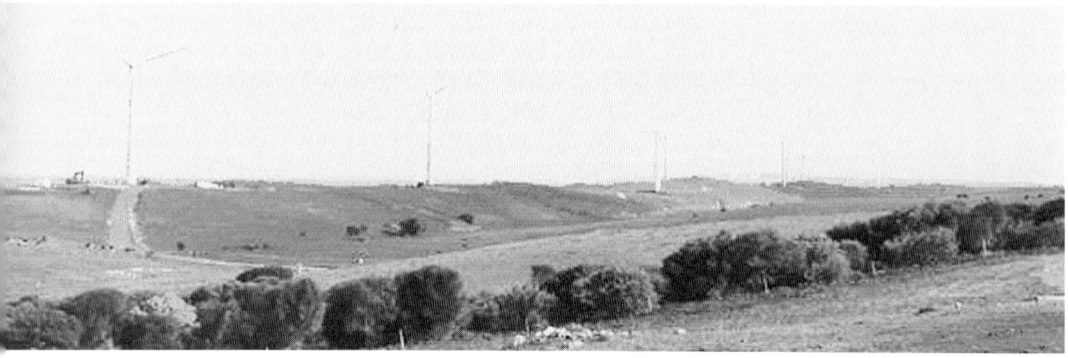

Wind Farm near Codrington in Western Victoria (photo: Codrington Wind Farm Tours http://www.myportfairy.com/windfarmtours)

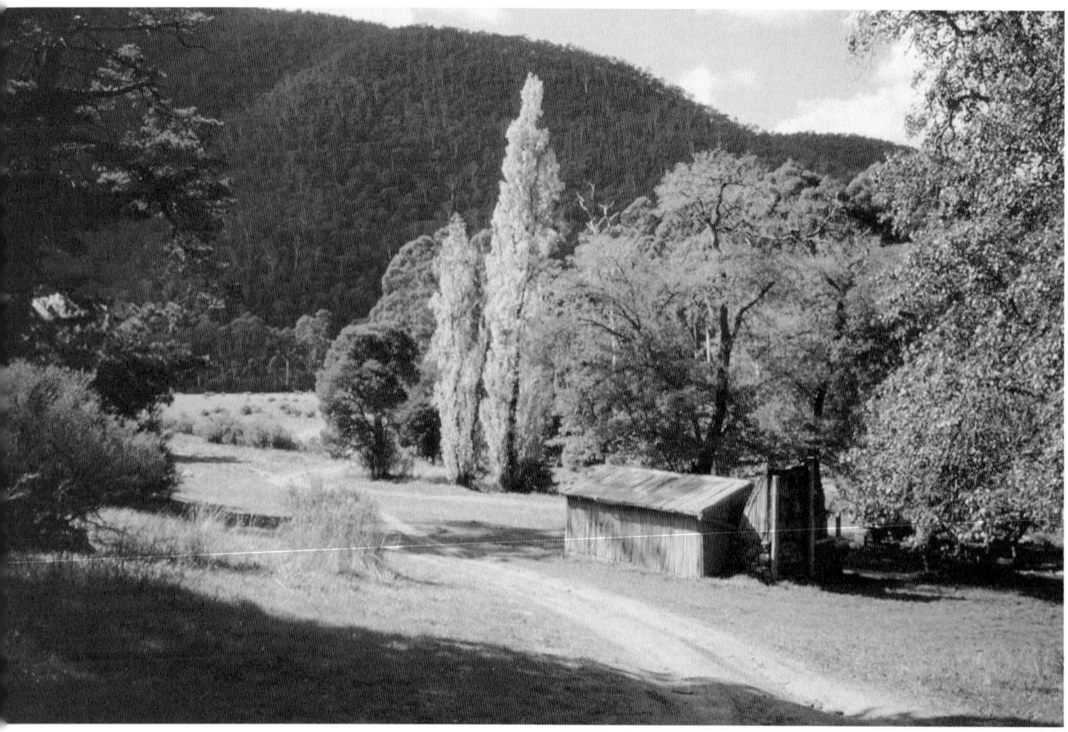

Wonnangatta Station

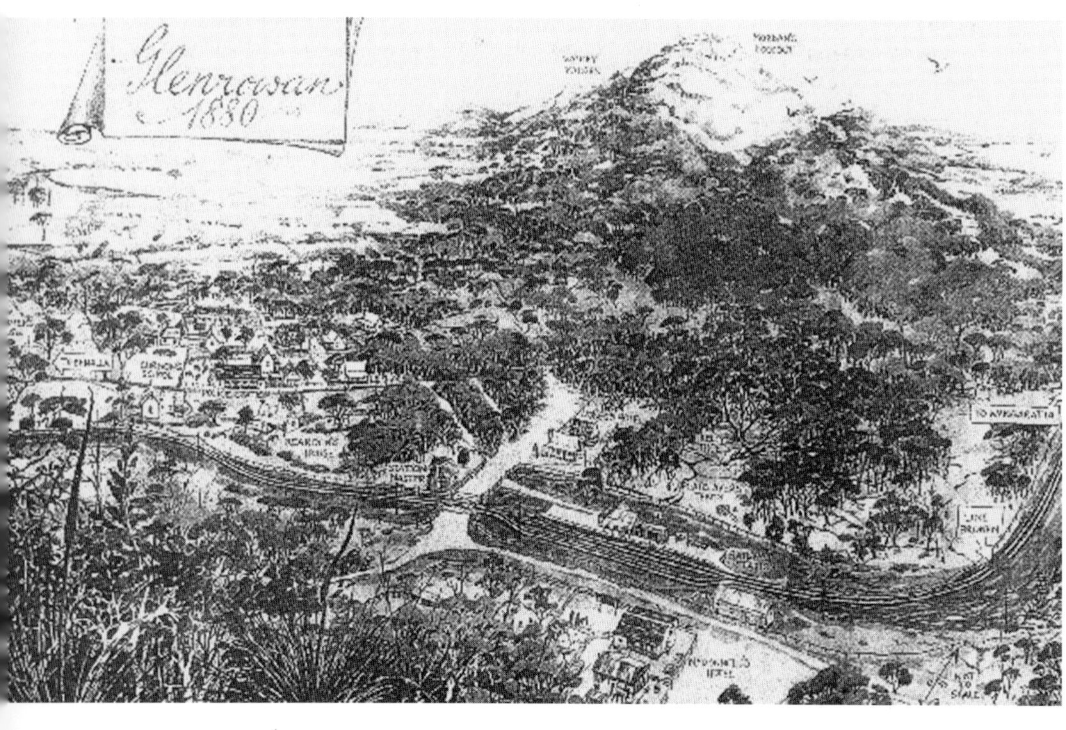

Historical Plan of Glenrowan (photo: Heritage Victoria)

Cultural or Natural?

Australia still suffers from a fragmentation of the protection of its natural and cultural heritage. Despite some excellent work in recent years on the integrated recognition of the values of landscapes, in the minds of many communities and government authorities, there is a persistent separation of Indigenous, post-contact ('historic') and natural places and values. This makes for cumbersome decision-making, and too often a 'dots on the map' approach to heritage listing and conservation.

An example of this divided approach is the tendency for national parks policies to require removal of exotic vegetation, and/or revegetation using native species, often without adequate assessment of the cultural values of the exotic plantings. This can result in the unintended and unrecognised loss of cultural heritage value within these layered landscapes.

This separation between natural and cultural heritage identification, protection and management has long been an issue within Australian land and heritage management. This occurs despite the fact that Indigenous people consider that cultural and natural landscapes are one and the same, and are indivisible. In many parts of Australia Indigenous people have an increasing role in owning and/or jointly managing national parks.

Recognising that 'natural areas' and 'wilderness' can and frequently do have important and under-recognised cultural heritage values has been promoted through various projects by Australia ICOMOS, including a major report with case studies. Another important initiative is the work by the Australian Heritage Council on the heritage values of 'inspirational landscapes', which is currently in its 2nd stage.

Transcending the artificial classifications of 'natural' and 'cultural' heritage within the landscape is therefore an important and long-standing challenge in Australia. At the start of 2004, a new and significantly different national heritage system commenced operation in Australia. One of the features of this new system is to include Australia's natural and cultural heritage within the definition of the 'environment' in the amendments to the *Environment Protection and Biodiversity Conservation Act* 1999. It is still too early to anticipate the impacts of this new national heritage system.

Setting

Landscapes function to provide the settings for important heritage places, and provide meaningful links between them. Settings are often not recognised as forming part of the values of heritage places, and protection measures are not well developed and inconsistently applied. Development approval processes often do not or cannot legally consider the broader landscape, linkages, setting or streetscape. Damage to heritage places and values can occur through attrition in such cases. This has long been recognised in Australia, but change to laws and systems can take time.

For many designed landscapes, capturing views, enframing vistas and incorporating borrowed scenery is an inherent component of the design. Many significant gardens not only capture significant viewscapes, but are themselves significant vista features – as silhouettes, for their visibility in different lights, and for different seasonal colours.

The landscape setting frequently provides an evocative journey to a heritage place – including places in urban, rural and 'natural' contexts. Climbing a mountain to a spectacular scenic viewpoint, to a Buddhist cave complex, or an historic pagoda are essential components of the experience of the place. Similarly, approaching a grand building along a major avenue, or approaching a historic house through historic laneways are significant aspects of the heritage values of these places. These include intangible and ephemeral elements – sounds and smells, light, shadow, bird life and plant details, 'empty' space, the textures of the surrounding environment.

Recognition of the heritage values of the setting also involves perceiving the patterns of settlement and the linkages between individual elements.

An example is Port Macquarie, NSW, where local planning instruments have no capacity to manage the archaeological remains of the historic convict-era penal settlement as a whole, no respect for the original street grid and town precincts, no willingness to use the original town layout as a starting point for new design. This important penal landscape is therefore masked and at considerable risk. This threat demonstrates the inadequate protection not only at the local level, but also through broad scale strategic planning and urban design processes. These often look only at individual sites in isolation, rather than perceiving the links and connections that often exist between them.

Intangible Heritage Values

Another major lack in most heritage planning processes and structures is considerable of intangible heritage values. This is despite changes to the national heritage standard, the Australia ICOMOS *Burra Charter*, which articulated these meanings and associations with place – 'social value' – more strongly. Many people working within the development industries, and in approvals agencies are still unaware of this facet of the heritage process, and do not have the tools or skills to undertake community consultation about intangible values and what impacts a development may have on them.

An example of a place with important intangible heritage values is the landscape associated with one of Australia's best-known folk heroes, Ned Kelly, a 19th century 'bush-ranger' (road bandit). This story has substantial cultural resonance for most Australians. One of the most evocative places in the stories about Ned Kelly is the 'siege' site in the town of Glenrowan where Ned was captured following a lengthy gun battle with the Police. Today there are almost no 'tangible' heritage elements associated with the siege, other than the broad lay-out of the landscape, including the sight lines between key points in the drama. Glenrowan, a small town, on the main north-south highway between Australia's two cities is working to build its image, distinctive character and economic prosperity on its associations with this story – the mythic subject of many films, books, ballads and fine art.

Understanding Indigenous Concepts of 'Country'

Indigenous concepts of 'country' and the rich cultural meanings embodied in the landscape are the basis for approaches to management of cultural heritage. This is illustrated through many examples – and in relation to the diversity of Indigenous cultural groups throughout the continent, living in many different social, cultural and environmental contexts.

One example of the breadth of the implications of embracing this landscape-based approach can be seen in the communiqué from the Indigenous participants to the *Celebrating Mountains* conference held in 2002 by the Australian Alps National Parks, in partnership with Australia ICOMOS.

The broad set of recommendations include commentary on the

inappropriate categorisation of 'natural' and 'cultural' heritage, access to country and to traditional plant and animal resources, place names, control of knowledge and intellectual property, interpretation, joint management, training and employment, and more.

Whilst such Indigenous cultural connections are better recognised by most Australians for 'traditional' Aboriginal people in the deserts and tropics of Australia's centre and north, it is still relatively rare in the south-east with longer and denser European settlement and a greater disruption between the past and present. Exceptions are occurring increasingly with a growing understanding of a strong cultural continuity demanding recognition. This is taking place, for example in the hand-back of national parks on the South Coast of NSW, where two sacred mountains, Biamanga (Mumbulla Mountain, and Gulaga (Mt Dromedary) are in the process of being returned to the Yuin people. Many Indigenous communities are taking greater control of decisions about their heritage place, being included in that process by changes to legislation, as well as receiving grants to conserve and develop them for cultural tourism. This is generally done in a way that integrates the site with its setting and the surrounding landscape, interpreting it and its meaning as well as for example, the traditional food and medicine plants.

Conclusion

It is likely that adoption of a holistic landscape approach will have benefits for understanding, conserving and interpreting all of Australia's heritage and appropriately perceiving heritage places within their settings.

It might be useful to draw more on the 'cultural landscape' way of thinking... The concept of cultural landscapes is a means of integrating, for any one place, aspects of natural, Indigenous and historic, aesthetic, scientific and social heritage values. It also makes us realise that the actual 'places' we have identified only represent selected concentrations of meaning or significance in a wider intellectual and cultural landscape context. Without a full appreciation of the heritage values of a cultural landscape the individual physical places within it could have no meaning. (Lennon et al 2001, p. 14)

It is hoped that heritage conservation in Australia will benefit through the insights gained from drawing on the multi-layered landscapes that surround us. As the above issues demonstrate we have some way to go.

References

Australia ICOMOS 1999, *The Burra Charter: the Australia ICOMOS Charter for Places of Cultural Significance.*(see www.icomos.org/australia)

Australia ICOMOS 2003, Guidelines for Cultural Heritage Places Damaged by the January 2003 Bushfires in South East Australia.

Australia ICOMOS 2003, *Historic Environment: Celebrating Mountains Issue* Vol 17(2). (see www.icomos.org/australia)

Australian Council of National Trusts 2004, *Endangered Places 2004.* Canberra. (available from www.nationaltrust.org)

Australian State of the Environment Committee 2001, *Australian State of the Environment Report, 2001.* CSIRO Publishing & Department of the Environment and Heritage, Canberra. (available from www.deh.gov.au/soe/)

Heritage Victoria 2002, *Landscape Assessment Guidelines.* (available from www.heritage.vic.gov.au) Jane Lennon & Associates and the University of Canberra 1999, *Conserving the Cultural Values of Natural Areas: A Discussion Paper.* Report to the Australian Heritage Commission and Australia ICOMOS. (available from www.icomos.org/australia)

Lennon, Jane, Michael Pearson, Duncan Marshall, Sharon Sullivan, P. McConvell, Warren Nicholls and David Johnson 2001, *Natural and Cultural Heritage: Australia State of the Environment Report 2001.* CSIRO Publishing & Department of the Environment and Heritage, Canberra. (available from www.deh.gov.au/soe/)

Lennon, Jane 2001, Identifying and assessing cultural landscapes: Australian practice in a global context. In *Heritage Landscapes: Understanding Place and Communities* (ed. Maria Cotter, Bill Boyd and Jane Gardiner), Southern Cross University, Lismore, NSW.

Ramsay, Juliet, *et al* 2004, Australian Cultural Landscapes: Heritage at Risk. Unpublished paper for Australia ICOMOS, prepared by the Historic Gardens and Cultural Landscapes Reference Group.

Walker, Meredith, and Peter Marquis-Kyle 2004, *The Illustrated Burra Charter: Good Practice for Heritage Places.* Australia ICOMOS.

NSW Heritage Office 2003, Cultural Landscapes Charette – background papers. (available from www.heritage.nsw.gov.au)

Planisphere 2004, Wind Farms and Landscape Values: Draft Issues Paper. Australian Wind Energy Association and Australian Council for National Trusts. (available from www.nationaltrust.org.au)

Australia ICOMOS

Authorship: This entry was prepared for Australia ICOMOS by Marilyn Truscott, Juliet Ramsay and Kristal Buckley, with input from Jane Lennon, members of Australia ICOMOS, and its Historic Gardens and Cultural Landscapes Reference Group.

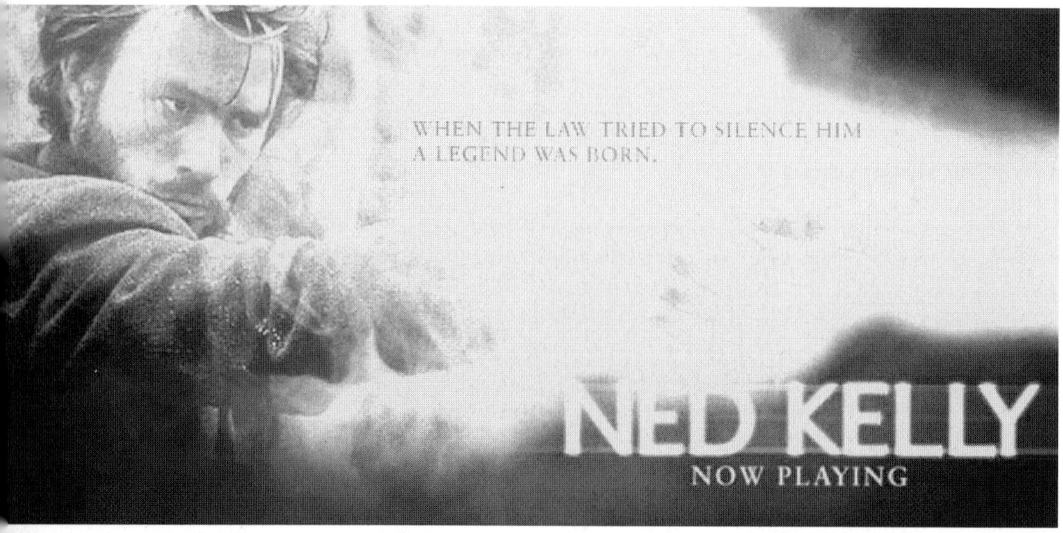

Advertising for the Universal Studios movie 'Ned Kelly' (2003), starring Heath Ledger, Orlando Bloom, Geoffrey Rush and Naomi Watts

AUSTRIA
Vienna's Roofscape and Roofspace

Cultural heritage in developed countries is in danger. Economic pressure, urban development and changes in use are the forces of social development. The dwindling significance and decreasing value of architectural heritage and the dominance of modernity and a modern lifestyle as aspects of social prestige represent major factors that are endangering such heritage. The seduction of technology, materials and design is obvious. In this context it seems ironic that it is not a lack of money that is a risk to architectural heritage, but rather the abundance of money. This means many investments in architectural works are against the interests of heritage preservation and conservation. One of the most noteworthy which has evolved as a field of its own is roofspace development.

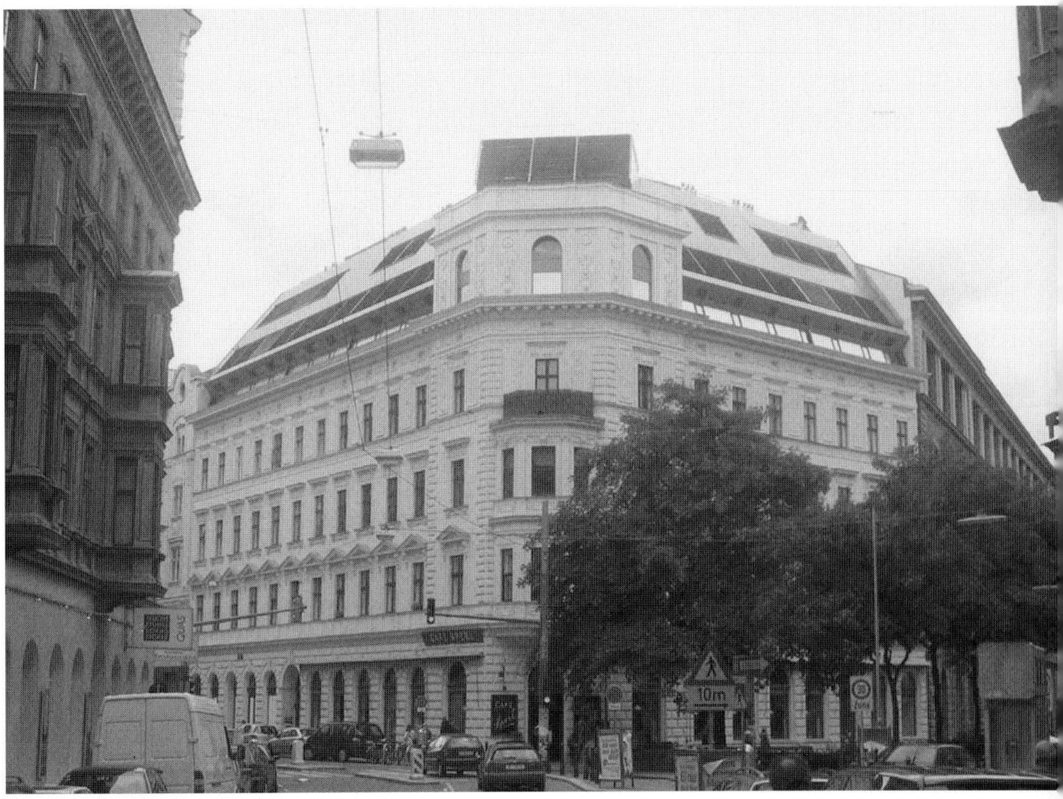

Vienna, Gumpendorfer Strasse (2002)

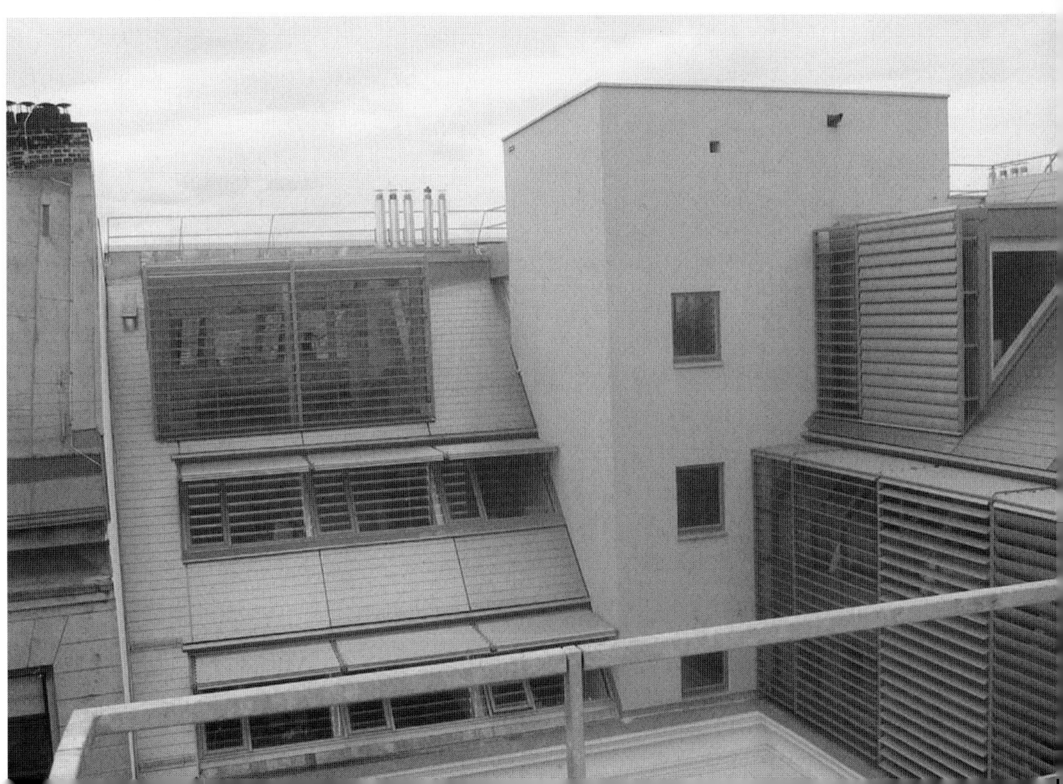

Vienna, Gumpendorfer Strasse (2002)

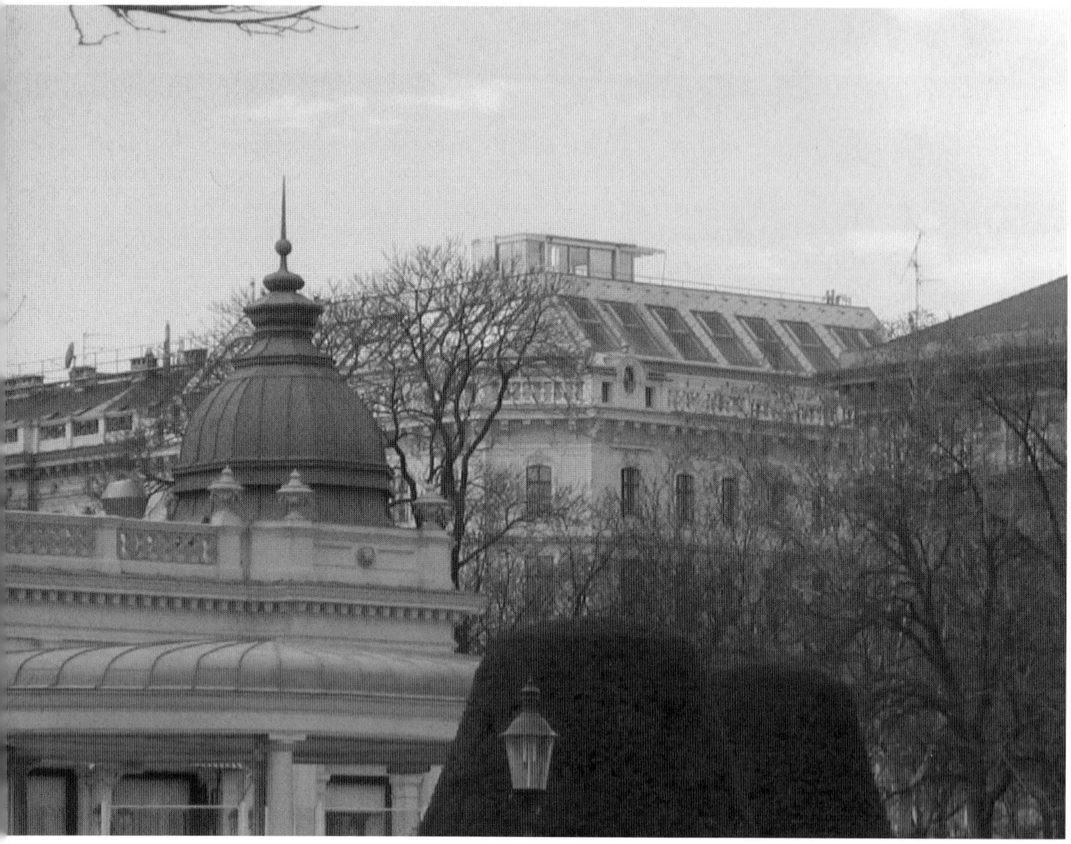

Vienna, Inner City

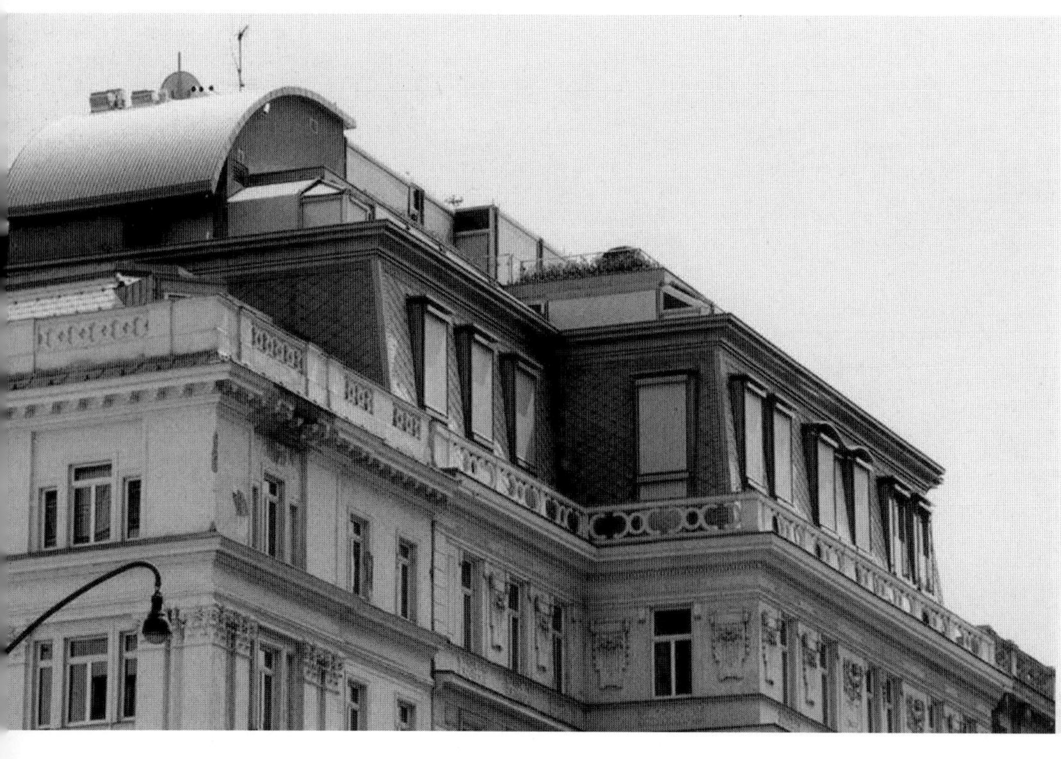

Vienna, Neuer Markt, Hotel Ambassador (2001-2002)

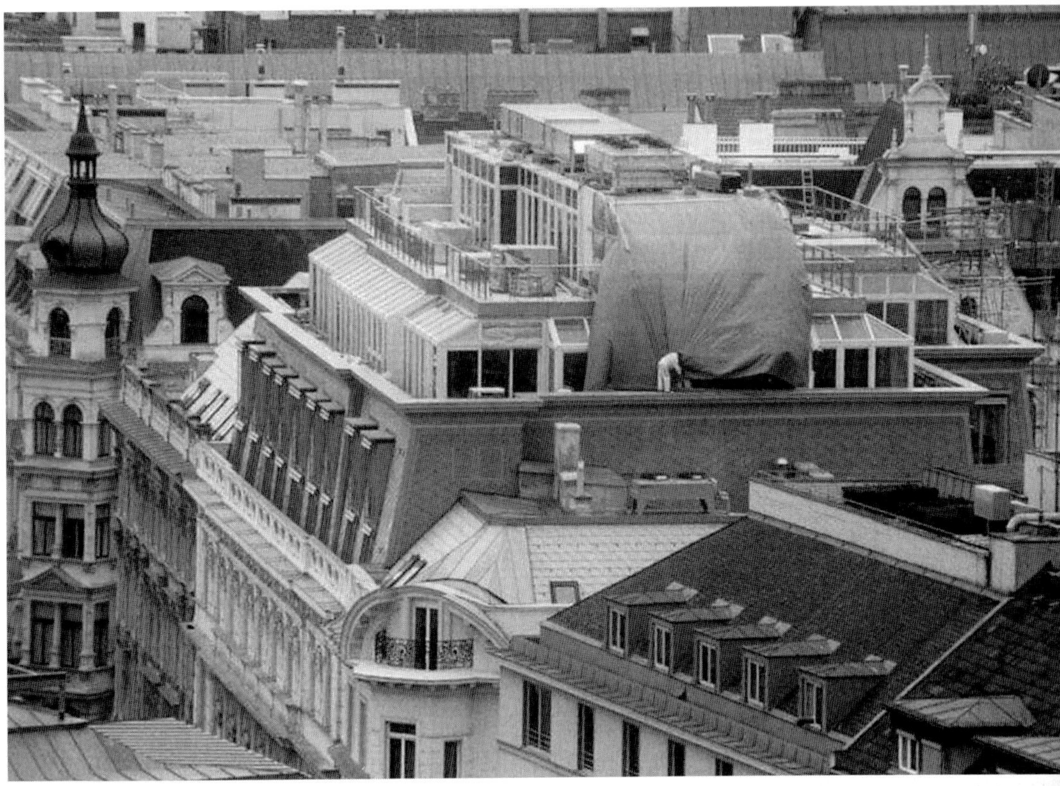

Vienna, Neuer Markt, Hotel Ambassador (2001-2002)

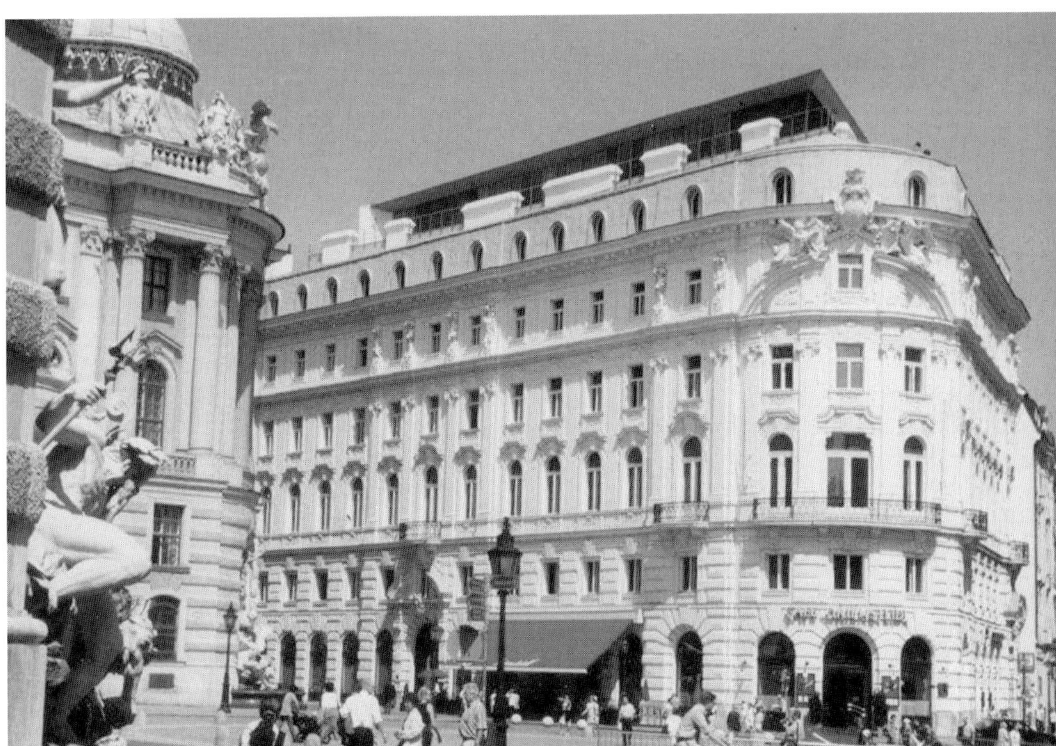

Vienna, Michaelerplatz, Palais Herberstein (2002)

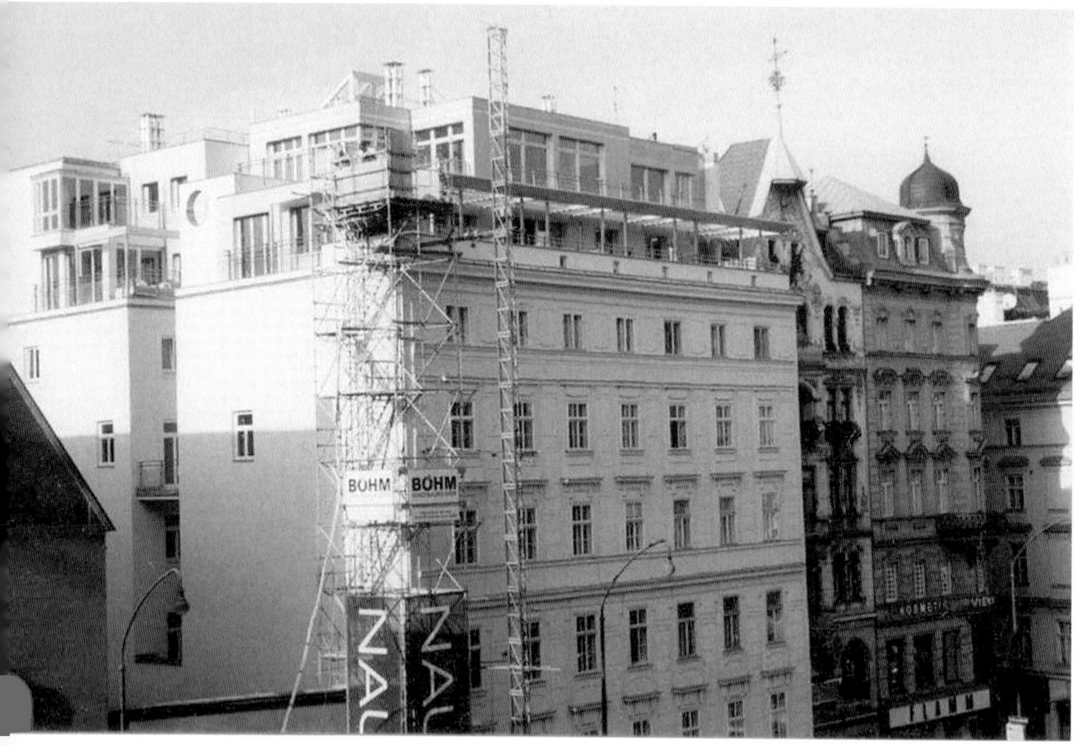

Vienna, Neuer Markt

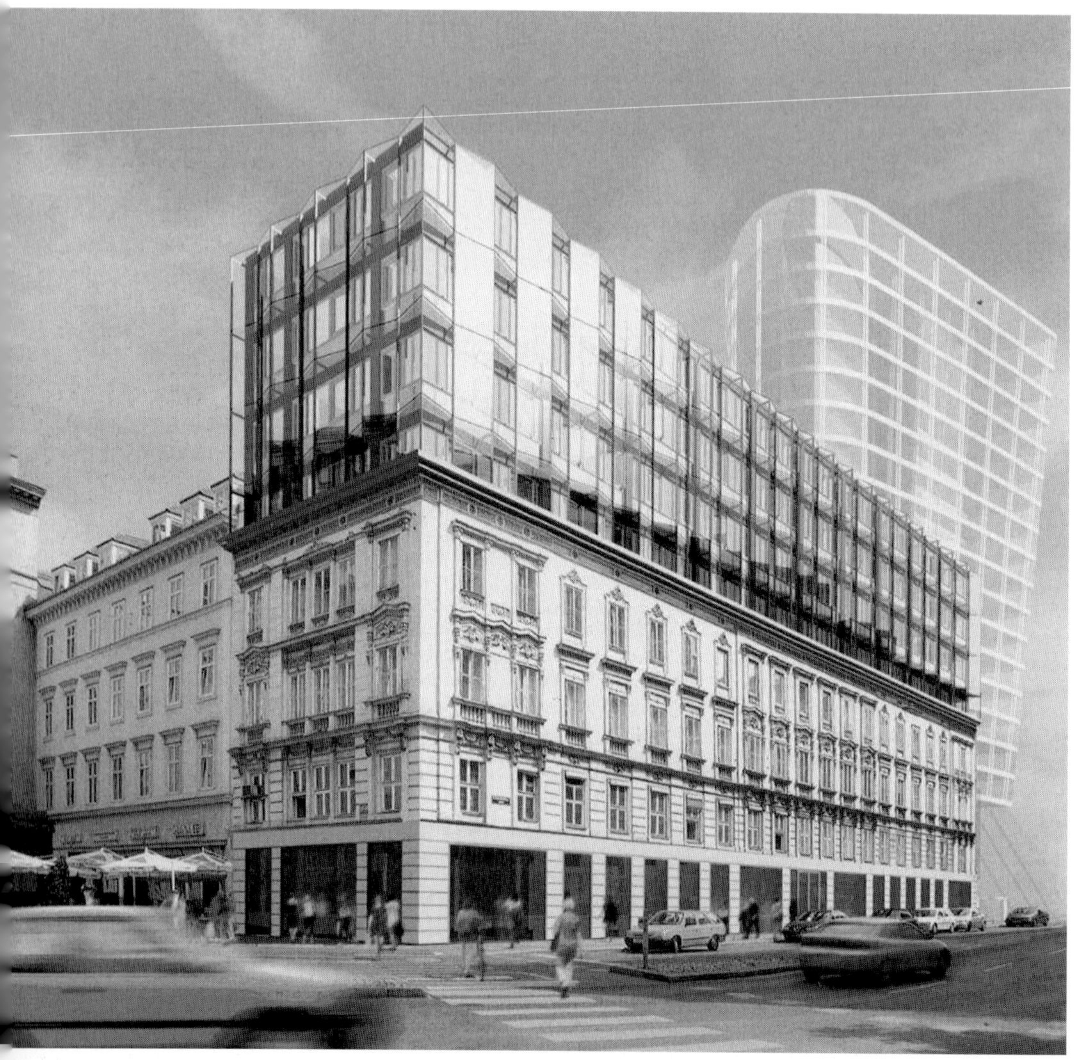

Vienna, Praterstrasse, Project

In particular, this has started to give Vienna a new face. Until the beginning of World War II, Vienna grew in area. Apart from the war damage, most of the rooftops, the roofscape, remained intact. It is only in the last few decades that the use of this space has taken place, showing dramatic effects in the past few years. This has resulted in new types of construction in the rooftops of Vienna. The 'city above the city' indicates how this newly discovered building zone is being dominated by the affluent society and their representatives and is in this sense an expression of social and economic strength. This means that socially and economically privileged groups shape the city. The 'city above the city' is in a sense a sort of 'gated community' which is located more than in a metaphorical sense 'above' the social and economic lower classes. Draufsetzen (to set up on), the name of an exhibition in Vienna in 2004, more or less presented this new building activity in a positive and animated way.

Viennese law supports this expansion if this type of construction is not subject to heritage laws. In certain circumstances, three levels are permitted above the cornice and it seems that official policy has supported this development up to now.

The only effective measure against this building activity would be the legal protection by heritage authorities (according to the Austrian Denkmalschutzgesetz – heritage legislation). But Austrian heritage law is primarily geared to single structures, and the protection of complexes, which would be the logical purpose, is therefore long needed. The legal protection of the urban environment and urban space is not effective enough.

Discussions about the Historic Centre of Vienna World Heritage property (Wien-Mitte) have resulted in a shift in this liberal policy. In the centre of the core zone of the World Heritage site, a reduction in the three floors which may be added has been achieved for future projects. But many applicants who applied before the introduction of this new policy are still permitted to carry out the additions according to the earlier three-floor rule. Negative results in roof expansion must therefore be expected.

Buildings that have been affected by these extreme additions are mainly those built during the second half of the 19th century. Although not usually subject to heritage laws, these historic buildings have without doubt fulfilled an important role in the city. With such roof additions, Vienna's general appearance with these buildings' original façades would lose the city's sense of continuity. A mixture of architecture would strongly disturb its built harmony and ruin the general historic authenticity that the city conveys.

Salzburg

During the final editing of the *Heritage at Risk* Report the demolition of the Kleines Festsspielhaus in the centre of the World Cultural Heritage zone in Salzburg began. This building is (or better was) a symbol of the world-famous Salzburger Festspiele and was planned by Clemens Holzmeister who was the congenial partner of Max Reinhardt, the founder and soul of this wonderful annual festival. This icon of Salzburg has now been destroyed. The reason for this unbelievable action was in the end to obtain a few dozen more seats. The irony of this is, that according to Austrian preservation law this demolition is regarded only as a mere alteration, because another part of the building complex of the Salzburger Festspielhaus still exists.

ICOMOS Austria

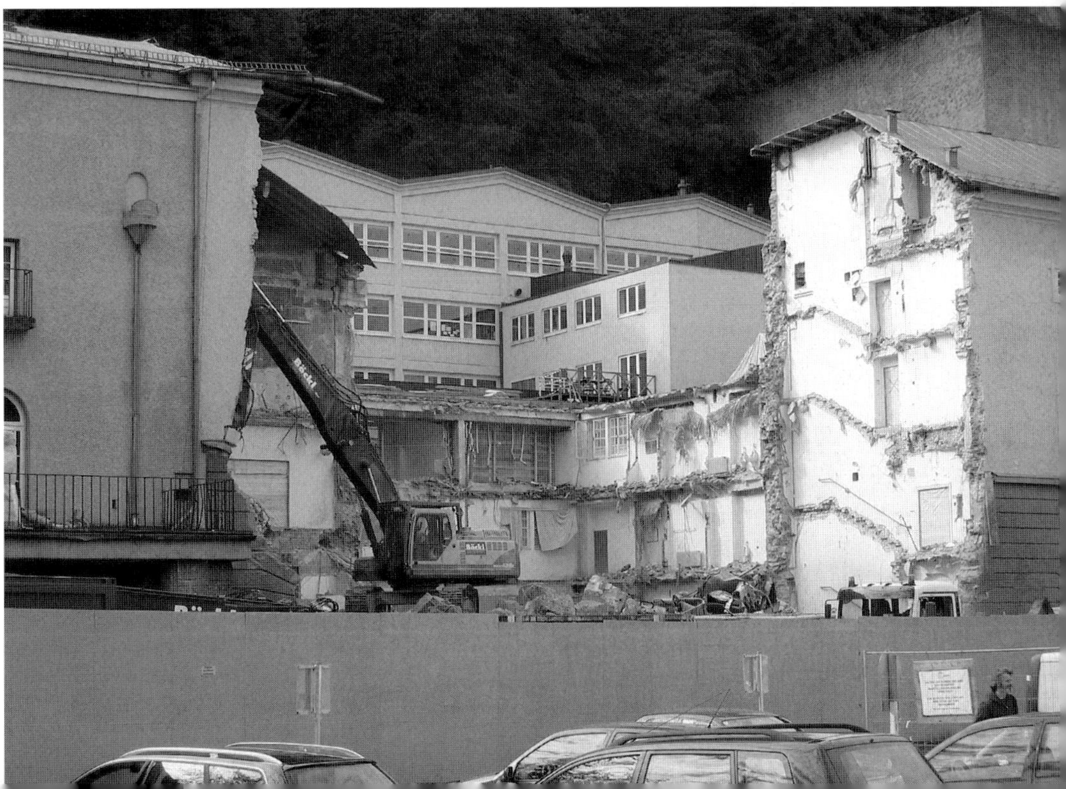

Salzburg, Neues Festspielhaus, demolition in October 2004

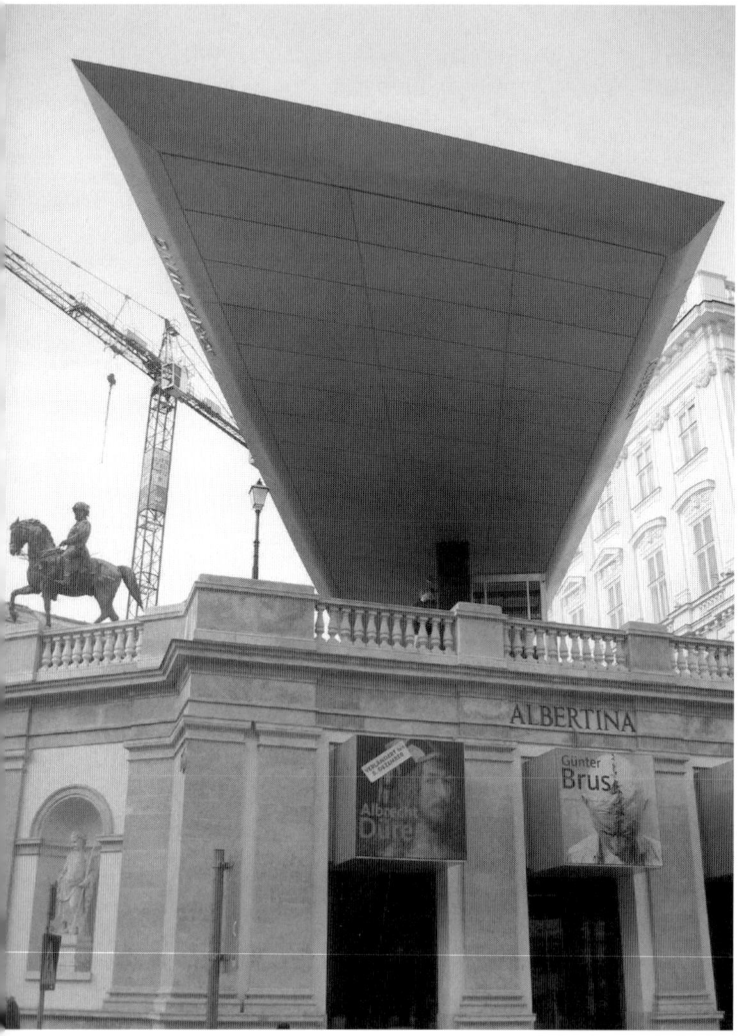

Vienna, Albertina, Museum of Graphic Arts. Fifty metre long overhanging roof, designed by the Austrian architect Hans Hollein, a symbol for the "roof-mania" in Vienna.

Vienna, Falkestrasse. The artificial initial of the "roof on roof" development in Vienna, erected 1984–1988 by the architects Coop-Himmelblau.

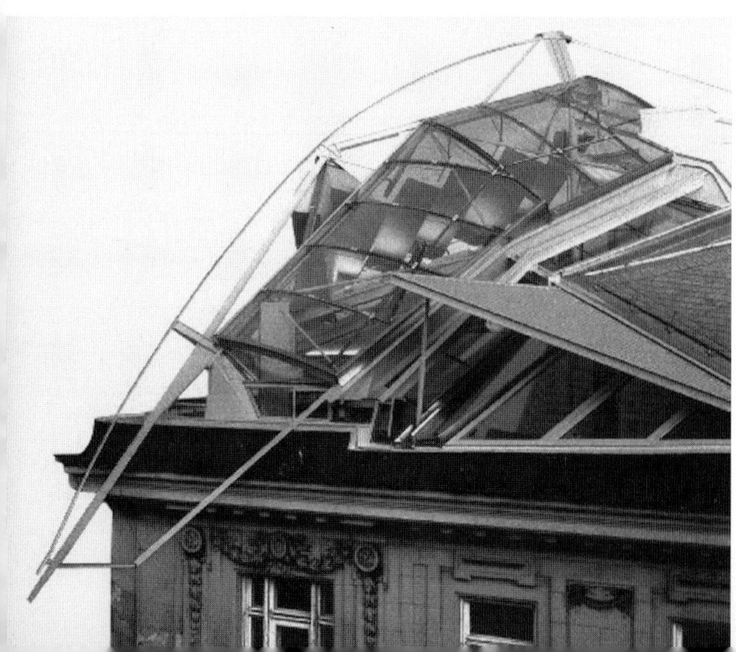

BELGIUM
Environment and Heritage

Humans have always interfered with the environment, with nature, since the beginning. In a sense, the extent to which we bend the biosphere to our will is the essence of culture or civilisation. By trial and error, humans have learned to control fire, to transform stone and other materials into tools and implements, and have started manufacturing new materials, bronze at first, iron and other metals later, and still later synthetic materials based on carbon compounds from crude oil. In doing so, humans have continuously bent nature to their will. Initially, such interference was not of such a proportion so as to disturb the balance in nature. Even after a catastrophic forest fire, nature recovers rapidly. However, as human technical capabilities improved, meddling with nature became more extreme. Raw materials that are less harmless to the environment were discovered and used. As early as the Middle Ages, white lead was used in making paint. Aggressive acids were used for tanning. From the 18th century on, huge quantities of highly toxic substances, such as cyanogen and cadmium, were used to mix textiles dyes. However, the situation became very serious in the 19th century, when industrial processes were introduced on an unprecedented scale and of an unparalleled intensity. New chemical processes were applied to the production of steel, cokes, gas and synthetic materials. Then we learned how to handle radioactive processes. All those new developments involved an unprecedented impact on the environment.

Environmental awareness

In the last fifty years, the West has seen a complete change in the perceptions of the relationship towards the environment. Until then, human beings had always thought to have unrestrained power over nature. But in the 1960s, the general public gradually became aware of the limitations to economic growth and the burden on the environment. Earlier, it was quite normal to discharge poisonous products into groundwaters, to bury them or to pile them up in the open. Environmental movements have made us aware that we cannot continue dumping waste in an uncontrolled way without adverse effects. In most western countries, legislation has been changed by now and more rigid environmental standards imposed. Almost everywhere, owners are obliged today to clean up polluted soils before land ownership can be transferred. In spite of the good intentions of this legislation, conflicts with cultural heritage conservation may arise.

Industrial archaeology

In the last thirty years, interest in our industrial heritage and in industrial culture has grown exponentially. An understanding that the industrial revolution has effected an unprecedented impact on the life of every human being, has aroused the interest of scientists and voluntary workers in the remains of this human activity. The interest in industrial archaeology, which originated in Europe in Great Britain in the early 1970s, has spread quickly. A considerable number of industrial sites, such as the lift locks on the *Canal du Centre* in Belgium's Walloon region, the mines and coke factory of *Zollverein* in the Ruhr area of Germany or the industrial landscape of Blaenvanon in Wales, Great-Britain, feature on the UNESCO World Heritage list. They are listed alongside the pyramids of Egypt and Mexico and the Angkor temples of Cambodia, illustrating the importance allocated to industrial heritage.

When studying industrial remains, we are automatically confronted with the environmental pollution produced by these industries. Whilst industrial heritage is considered to be an object of study by archaeologists and historians, pollution is an inherent part of the site. Just as an archaeological survey of medieval cesspools reveals a wealth of information about the everyday life of people living centuries ago, analysis of the soil pollution can provide us with large amounts of data on the former industrial activities on a specific area of land. It is precisely at this point that the historian collides with the current environmental legislation, which naturally aims to end all possible air, soil and groundwater pollution. However, in so doing, the historical significance the pollution may have is often ignored. Moreover, the legislation often stands in the way of an industrial site being legally protected as a heritage site. In giving priority to rigorous environmental decontamination, valuable elements of historical heritage are often destroyed and thus denied future generations.

We would like to illustrate this with a few examples from Flanders.

Case 1: Creosote Yard in Ostend

In 1995, the Flemish Minister of Culture signed the definitive protection order with regard to the Belgacom Creosote Yard. It concerned a plant in the back harbour of Ostend, where since the early twentieth century, telegraph poles and railway sleepers were treated against wood rot by impregnating them with creosote oil under pressure. The buildings housing the steamer, the steam pumps and the 21 meters long autoclave,[1] and the part of the site where treated and untreated wood was stored, were legally protected as a heritage site. As the site remained in use until only a few years earlier, it was fairly intact and certainly unique of its kind. The installation was the property of the Belgian telephone company (Belgacom), who no doubt did not give priority to actively managing its industrial heritage and opening it to the public. The company made an in principle agreement with the Flemish Association for Industrial Archaeology,[2] stipulating that the latter would take the site on a long lease for a peppercorn amount, with the aim of opening it to the public with the creation of a separate foundation. A few years ago, however, a law became effective in Flanders prescribing that everyone who transfers land ownership has to prove that the ground is free of contamination. This proved to be a problem in this case as for three-quarters of a century, poly-aromatic hydrocarbons had been used lavishly in this area on this plot of land. Creosote oil is of course a derivative of coal, obtained during coke production. Since the time of the site's legal protection, a number of expensive studies have been undertaken on the site and the remaining oil has been removed, which has already cost the owner a small fortune. And yet, no definitive solution has been reached. The ground should be dug up, the soil decontaminated and the original land relaid. Moreover, the heaviest pollution is said to be inside the building, around the autoclave where an underground oil reservoir was once located. This poses a huge technical problem in itself. How should one proceed to excavate the soil to a depth of two to three metres in a building of 30 m x 5 m, containing a steel tube of 2 m x 21 m, without endangering the building's stability? Technically, almost nothing is impossible but everything has its price. The present owner cannot take the financial risk to invest such an enormous amount of money in the block of land's clearing. Since the legal protection does not provide for a grant for such works, things are in abeyance pending some alternative ruling.

Case 2: Coke factory in Zeebrugge

In 2002, three Belgian regions, Flanders, Wallonia and Brussels-Capital, each inherited a disused coke factory from the obsolete industrial company Cockerill-Sambre. Flanders thus becomes the owner of a unique plant in the harbour of Zeebrugge, where since 1906 British coal is converted into coke for the Ruhr basin steel industry. The Public Flemish Waste Products Company (OVAM), a semi-public enterprise, is charged with the management of the site, with the aim of decontaminating it and bringing it back on the market as a harbour site. The Flemish Association for Industrial Archaeology once again sounded the alarm, and together with a few other associations, brought the historical value of the site to public attention. In December 2003, a proposal was submitted to protect the site as heritage because of its historical, technical and social interest. At the same time, some alternative adaptations were suggested.

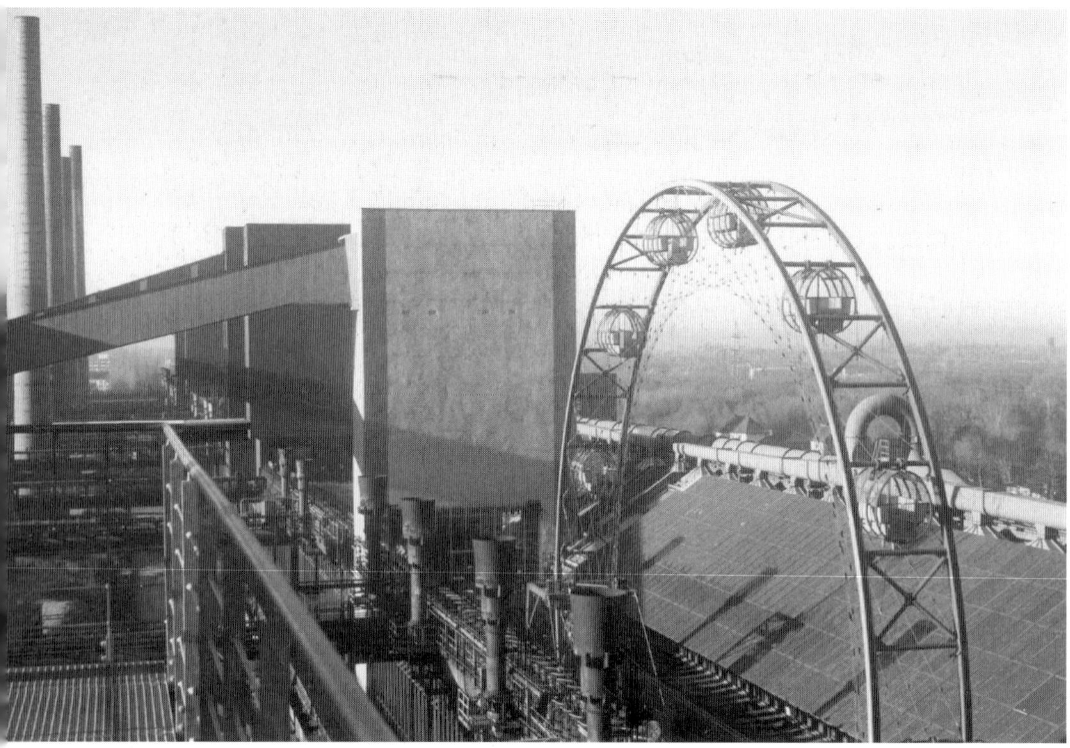

Former coke factory Zollverein, Germany. Since its listing as UNESCO World Heritage in 2001, it had already more than 500,000 visitors. Environmental burdens do not necessarily stand in the way of opening up a site to tourists.

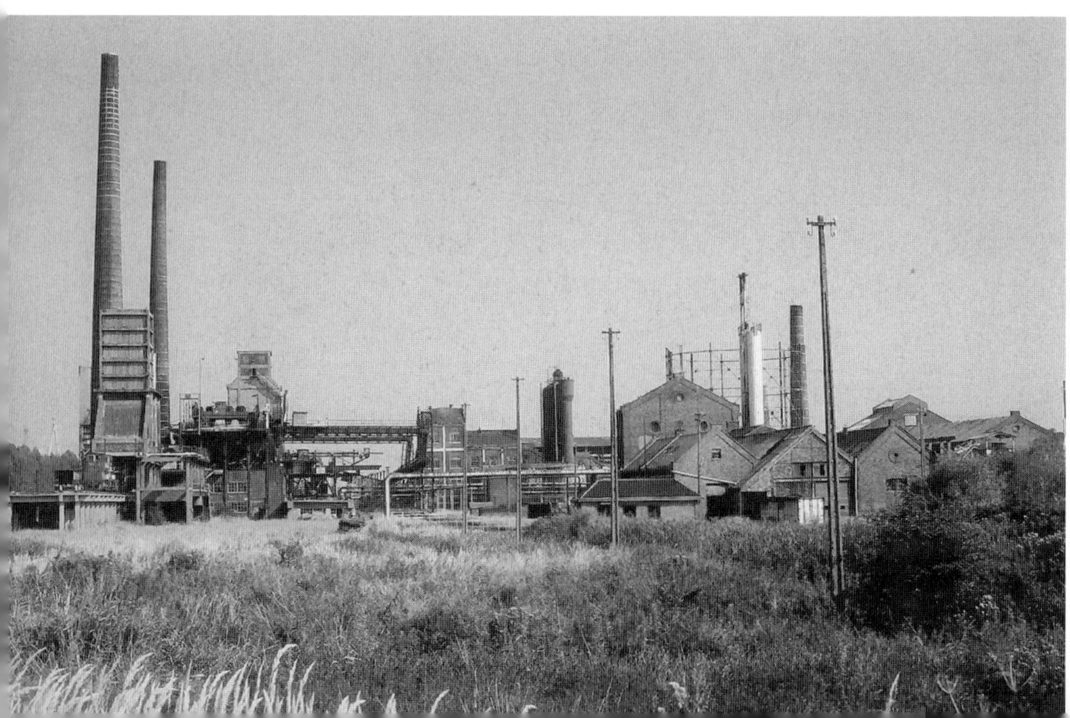

Coke factory Zeebrugge, Belgium. Because of environmental problems it does not qualify for protection as industrial heritage.

The Ground Decree has again played a damaging role in this case, since it prescribes that the soil be free of contamination when it changes ownership or use. Among others, the Bruges administration, in whose jurisdiction the land is located but which cannot be held responsible for funding the clean-up, is insisting on the implementation of the strictest possible environmental standards. Even though this business is situated within a harbour area, standards are required that are usually applied to residential areas. Because of the specific soil conditions, the ground should be dug up, at some places to a depth of even 10 metres, which would make the conservation of the buildings and the equipment impossible. This argument is now being put forward to refuse legal protection. The argument that protecting and converting the buildings might lead to a cheaper solution,[3] on the condition that reasonable environmental standards in keeping with a new function be applied, commands little or no esteem.

Towards an adapted regulation

Let us be clear: this is not a plea to abolish or mitigate environmental legislation. It is not our intention to engage in a controversy between environmental conservationists and heritage conservators. On the contrary, we plead for a dialogue between both, since their interests should not necessarily be incompatible.

Adapted standards

First and foremost, we wish to argue that other standards be applied to cleaning up the soil and the buildings in specific cases, such as when sites of an outstanding historic interest are concerned which qualify for legal protection as industrial heritage. These standards should be in accordance with the new purpose of the site. First, we are thinking of confining the particular area, combined with an adequate control and possible purification of the groundwater. In doing so, polluted groundwater contaminating adjacent ground can be prevented, to an extent that has not yet occurred before. If necessary, digging up of the surface soil, and storing and encasing the polluted soil on the spot, might prove a much cheaper alternative to requiring deep excavation and transport of the polluted soil, which also involves serious environmental risks. Would it not be advisable to apply other standards and to find out what the real health consequences are for those who will use and visit the site in the future, rather than continue to apply strict theoretical standards?

Adapted legislation

What prevents the legislator from making an exception to the Ground Decree for specific cases of land transfer which concerns the site's opening to the public? As long as a polluted site does not change ownership or function, soil sanitation is not required. Would it not be possible to state that there is no question of conversion when the workings of such an operation including its environmental pollution are shown to the public in a museological and educational context?

Environmental-educational surplus values

The opening to the public of such historically polluted sites under specific controlled conditions can even be invaluable in the environmental-educational field. Is there is better way to illustrate that the soil grows leaner under the influence of unrestrained industrialisation? Is there a better way to visualise the evolution in our environmental awareness, or to demonstrate the regenerating capacity of nature, than by means of authentic evidence? After all, the sterilised ground that is left behind after decontamination hardly lends itself to an enjoyable nature experience.

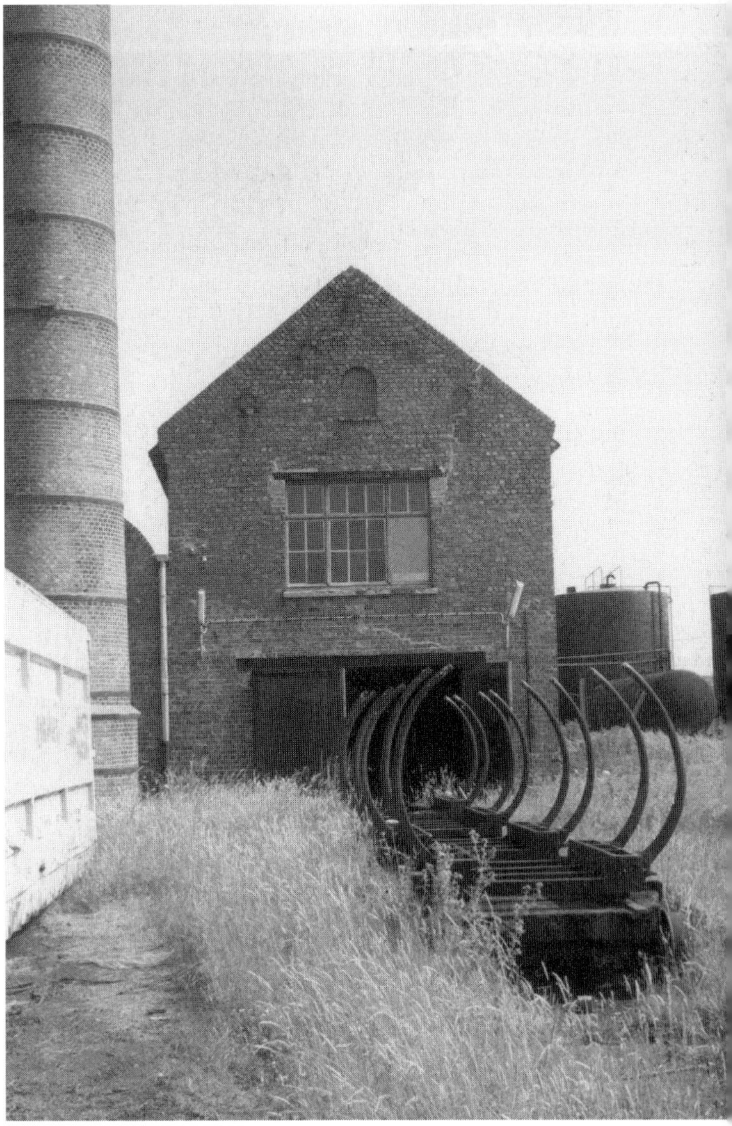

Former creosote yards at Ostend, Belgium. Legally protected as a heritage site, although not yet open to the public because of the environmental legislation.

ICOMOS Belgium
(with thanks to Stefaan Heyse,
Coordinator Flemish Association for Industrial Archaeology)

1 autoclave: a tubular steam kettle into which wood or other material is steamed under pressure for opening the cells.

2 VVIA: association of volunteer workers, founded in 1978. Forms a platform for local and thematic associations devoting themselves to the study and maintenance of industrial heritage in Flanders and Brussels.

3 Based on the current plans, the cost for decontamination and demolition is estimated as 50 million euros at the start of the works.

COSTA RICA
The case of Liberia, Costa Rica: preservation or progress?

Liberia, the 'White City' lies in Costa Rica's north-western Guanacaste savannah, surrounded by four volcanoes, Orosi, Tenorio, Rincón de la Vieja and Miravalles, that give the local soil its characteristic white colour. Its whitewashed adobe houses, which use the traditional *bahareque* technique of building in mud and bamboo, reveal colonial Spain's urban architectural influence.

Like most colonial towns in Latin America, the grid of narrow streets that defines the town has as its core a central square. This has its music pavilion where the municipal band performs at *recreos* (rests or breaks) on Sunday afternoons and *retretas* (from the French *retraite*, or retreat) on Thursday and Sunday nights. The square is also home to a vast, shady *guanacaste* tree (*Enterolobium ciclocarpum*), which gives its name to this north-western province and is Costa Rica's national tree.

On the southern side of the square, King's Road, the colonial highway to the city, runs toward the country's highlands. At its outset, the road flanks the adobe building of the former Governor's mansion, which has been proclaimed a historical and architectural heritage site as has the Zúñiga-Clachar house, also along this road. Both have been honoured with the Ministry of Culture's Save Our Heritage Award, the former in 2002, and the latter in 1995.

The Copa de Oro restaurant is further south along King's Road. On some moonlit evening in the 1930s, the composer and band leader Jesús Bonilla, a regular customer, was there when inspiration struck. Luna liberiana ('Liberian Moon'), one of Costa Rica's best-loved romantic ballads, describes the full moon over Liberia as 'a moon for loving', and calls the town itself 'a paradise granted us by God above, whose beautiful women know how to love'[1]. Continuing past the restaurant, several magnificent structures display Liberia's distinctive 'sun doors', or corner double doors.

This beautiful parade of heritage sites does not stop until King's Bridge, a historic landmark once marking the city's southernmost limits that now delineates its historic sector. Near King's Bridge, the local *cimarrona* brass bands provide slightly out-of-tune yet joyful accompaniment to the annual town fiesta each year as the run of the bulls takes place along King's Road. They are herded by *sabaneros*, Guanacaste's cowboys, who ride haughty *paso-fino* horses to a rodeo where crowds of cheering spectators applaud feats of riding, lassoing and bullfighting.

Liberia has preserved a significant share of its original urban structures in what is known as the 'Old Quarter', an architecturally homogeneous and largely unaltered area that has garnered the appreciation of Liberians and the desire to protect it. Liberia is a town with a consolidated spatial-cultural form.

In 1989, the Liberian municipal government and the town's residents asked the Ministry of Culture and the University of Costa Rica to sponsor a cultural inventory of Liberia's built environment, one of the first in the country. The report, presented to the local authorities, proposed a series of guidelines on how to interpret the city, to understand and respect its uniqueness.

On 18 April 1997, ICOMOS Costa Rica organised a symposium on adobe architecture in Liberia. Co-sponsored by the City Council and the local Cultural Committee, the event drew not only local participants but also national and international experts. These all unanimously signed the 'Liberian Charter on Heritage Preservation', committing all parties to the preservation and enhancement of Liberia's architectural legacy for the benefit of future generations.

In spite of all these efforts, educational and promotion activities have yet to produce sufficient numbers of people set on conservation. At the request of the local Cultural Committee and the Municipality, ICOMOS Costa Rica produced a scathing report in 1994 on the uncontrolled demolition taking place in Liberia. It also issued recommendations to the Municipality, the Costa Rican Housing and Urban Development Institute, and the Ministry of Health on the need to put an end to such destruction.

No local building codes, or urban development and land-use plans, exist to encourage a holistic approach to sustainable development, one that reconciles the demands of modernity with the conservation of the town's built heritage. Like any other historical heritage site, Liberia is subject daily to the degradation caused by a misunderstood notion of modernity and progress.

The town has also suffered very high rates of immigration in recent years, leading to extreme urbanisation and the rise of shanty-towns at its outskirts. As the provincial capital of Guanacaste and its political and administrative hub, it has grown in response to the need to house an ever-increasing number of government officials and the tradespeople and others who have followed.

Breathtaking tropical beaches, national parks, conservation areas, volcanoes (some of them very active) and other attractions have drawn ever-increasing plane-loads of tourists from around the world to Liberia and nearby locations. This is putting increasing pressure on accommodation, basic services, and the availability of affordable land, inflating real estate prices.

Multinationals have jumped into the fray, building identical modern hotels, apartment blocks, and other facilities that undermine the cultural foundations of the region. Sometimes they do not even take into account the local climate when designing their facilities, causing a waste of energy and other resources, even as they callously break with the existing architectural integrity of the surrounding community.

The siren calls of so-called modernity continue to whisper comfort and beauty, blinding the local citizenry to the value of their own heritage, as they rid themselves of buildings that were constructed in harmony with local environmental conditions and customs over generations.

Government officials, unenthusiastic, even lethargic about conserving the town's heritage, have shown remarkable zeal in promoting and facilitating the construction of these new structures. It is unlikely that they are motivated by destruction for destruction's sake or selfish desires. The reason may well be a lack of foresight and the absence of a systematic approach to urban development. Whatever the reason, it has led to a confrontation between these officials and a significant proportion of the local population that is deeply attached to its roots.

King's Bridge, a narrow, one-way metal structure dating back to the early 20th century, impedes high-volume vehicle movement along King's Road. Some local groups would like to see it demolished and replaced by a modern, multi-lane structure that can accommodate a much greater density of traffic. Should this happen, King's Road would lose its soul. The rather intimate charm of this historical and architecturally significant street would be lost to engine noise, exhaust fumes and honking horns. Cars and trucks would travel at high speed, pedestrians would hesitate before crossing the road, and the leisure embodied in the road's benches and trees would be disrupted for ever.

It would be entirely feasible to build a new bridge on any number of parallel sites that would not put Liberia's heritage at risk.

Conflict is unnecessary. Progress need not turn a blind eye to the virtues of conservation. Development need not entail the destruction of Liberia's architectural heritage. The town's extraordinary adobe houses, its characteristic 'sun doors', its whitewashed façades and red tiled roofs, need not fall victim to the juggernaut of modernity.

Erick Chaves Chaves and Miguel Chaves Fernández
ICOMOS Costa Rica

[1] The song was even recorded by the Caracas Academic Octet as part of a collection of 15 'Latin American popular classics' from such countries as Argentina, Brazil, Cuba, and Mexico. More information is at www.sincopa.com/ethnic/cdinfo1/octet_clasiclatin.htm.

COSTA RICA
El caso de Liberia, Costa Rica: ¿patrimonio o progreso?

Situada al norte de Costa Rica y en medio de la planicie guanacasteca, con terrenos blancos de origen volcánico, rodeada de los volcanes Orosi, Tenorio, Rincón de la Vieja y Miravalles, se encuentra la "Ciudad Blanca": Liberia, la que con sus blancas casas de bahareque encalado nos muestra su particular fisonomía urbano-arquitectónica de influencia colonial española. En medio de ella está el Parque Central, y en él, encontramos el quiosco donde la *banda* municipal ejecuta los *recreos* los domingos por la tarde y las *retretas* los jueves y domingos por la noche. También ahí se ubica el gran árbol de Guanacaste (*Enterolobium ciclocarpum*), símbolo nacional y monumento a la génesis de la ciudad.

Hacia el sur de ese parque y de ese Guanacaste, se encuentra la *Calle Real*, antigua vía de acceso al pueblo primigenio, que inicia con el edificio de adobes de la otrora Gobernación. A partir de él, continúa una serie de excelentes exponentes arquitectónicos como la casa de la familia Zúñiga Clachar, ambos declarados *patrimonio histórico-arquitectónico* y ganadores del premio "*Salvemos nuestro patrimonio*", otorgado por el Ministerio de Cultura de Costa Rica, en los años 2002 y 1995, respectivamente. Un poco más al sur encontramos el restaurante "*La Copa de Oro*" donde se inspiró don Jesús Bonilla para componer "*Luna Liberiana*", himno a la sensibilidad de los pobladores. Le siguen una serie de magníficos ejemplos caracterizados por la particular 'puerta del sol' o doble puerta esquinera. La hermosa secuencia remata en su extremo sur con el *Puente Real* hito histórico que definió el límite de la ciudad y, ahora, de su centro histórico. Este angosto puente funge hoy día como válvula que impide el paso de alto tránsito automotor y que, de no ser por él, trastocaría su más íntimo ser y se traería abajo este importante resabio de interés histórico – arquitectónico que se conoce como la 'Calle Real del barrio Condega'.

Es también en el extremo sur de Liberia, exactamente junto al Puente Real, de donde cada año parte el tope de toros los días de fiesta local, y es propiamente a lo largo de la Calle Real donde el arreo marcha al ritmo de las *cimarronas* o bandas improvisadas que van entonando las alegrísimas "parranderas" para los altivos sabaneros, que las flanquean en sus engalanadas monturas y briosos caballos, que van partiendo camino entre la mar de gente que se aglutina para disfrutar de los festejos y de los lances de monta, lazeo y toreo, a pie y a caballo.

Liberia conserva gran parte de su estructura urbana original en lo que se llama "El Casco Viejo". En él se encuentra un conjunto arquitectónico homogéneo y poco alterado que ha logrado resguardar los elementos fundamentales de la composición urbana y ha provocado el reconocimiento y la estima del liberiano que la vive y protege. Liberia es una ciudad con una estructura espaciocultural consolidada, pero que, al igual que cualquier otro sitio de interés histórico-patrimonial, está expuesta al deterioro causado por la inserción de una mal entendida modernidad, de un mal entendido progreso. También, al interior de la ciudad se suceden otros fenómenos nocivos para la salud citadina: la alta e indiscriminada inmigración que ha sufrido Liberia en los últimos años ha traido consigo un masivo proceso de urbanización, con manifestaciones extremas como la tugurización de algunas zonas. Además, dada su condición de capital de la provincia de Guanacaste y centro político-administrativo, en Liberia se instala necesariamente el equipamiento y la infraestructura necesarios para tratar de cubrir esas necesidades, trayendo consigo la impronta del sector comercial y del burócrata, pues lógicamente requieren se les supla de vivienda a la brevedad.

A las situaciones apuntadas ha de sumárseles el turismo masivo que, en constante crecimiento, produce una alta demanda de espacio y de servicios, acarreando también una mayor presión sobre los precios de la tierra. No en balde, Guanacaste es la provincia de mayor crecimiento turístico en los últimos años. Este flujo creciente de turismo ha producido la aparición de servicios y comercio de tipo 'transnacional', y ésto, a su vez, ha provocado un socavamiento de aquella sólida estructura cultural que mencionamos líneas arriba: aparecen nuevas edificaciones, modernas e indiferentes a la cultura ancestral, al entorno cultural y al clima, estructuras que no aportan absolutamente nada positivo al esquema urbano existente, que más bien lo rompen en su unidad. Pero, paradójicamente, estas nuevas estructuras sí son prioridad para algunos funcionarios públicos ya que proporcionan soluciones espaciales prototípicas de aquella modernidad mal entendida de la que hablábamos. Así las cosas, esta vorágine impensada está llevando a un enfrentamiento entre algunas autoridades y la población profundamente proclive a aquella realidad construida antaño y viva hoy día, enfrentamiento realmente producido por la falta de previsión y visión de conjunto y no por un deseo egoísta o destructivo.

Otro pequeño pero importante nubarrón se cierne sobre la *Calle Real*. Dijimos que ésta se inicia frente a la iglesia y termina pocas cuadras al sur, precisamente donde se encuentra el Puente Real: una angosta estructura metálica de comienzos del siglo XX y de un solo carril. Algunas fuerzas locales pretenden su demolición para dar paso franco a la modernidad, es decir, pretenden ampliarlo a varias vías para que se produzca un alto tránsito vehicular. Si esto se diera, la *Calle Real* perdería su espíritu: los automóviles transitarían a alta velocidad, los peatones no tendrían su espacio, sus bancas, sus arboledas y el ritmo vital de la calle se vería trastocado completamente. A todas luces, es innecesario perder la Calle Real por un puente que es perfectamente factible ubicar en alguno de muchos otros sitios paralelos.

En el año 1989 – y a solicitud del pueblo y del Municipio liberiano – se lleva a cabo el inventario de bienes inmuebles de la ciudad de Liberia, quizás uno de los primeros que se hicieron en el país. Fue patrocinado por el Ministerio de Cultura y la Universidad de Costa Rica y se entregó a las autoridades ofreciendo también una serie de valoraciones como medio para *leer* la ciudad, para comprenderla y respetarla. Posteriormente, en 1994, a solicitud del Comité de Cultura local y de la Municipalidad, el ICOMOS de Costa Rica brinda un revelador informe acerca de las demoliciones que acontecen en la ciudad y se brinda además una serie de consejos al Municipio, al Instituto de Vivienda y Urbanismo y al Ministerio de Salud para detenerlas. El 18 de abril de 1997, el ICOMOS de Costa Rica realiza el *Simposium sobre Arquitectura de Tierra en Liberia*, a solicitud del Consejo Municipal y del Comité de Cultura, con la asistencia mayoritaria de los ciudadanos locales pero también con la de expertos nacionales y extranjeros. Al final del evento se redactaría la "Carta de Liberia". Todas estas acciones han coadyuvado a fortalecer aquella sólida estructura espacio-social que mencionamos párrafos arriba, pero, aún así, la labor educativa y divulgativa nunca es suficiente.

La mal entendida '*modernidad*' pregona confort y estética, subvalorando lo propio, lo tradicional, dada la adopción de patrones constructivos exógenos que se abren paso a punta de la demolición de la arquitectura bien adaptada y del modo de vida ancestral. Sumado a esta complejidad de alto impacto, tenemos la inexistencia de normativas urbano-arquitectónicas que ayuden a poder implementar un modelo de desarrollo integral que lleve de la mano a esa modernidad con el patrimonio construído. He ahí el punto central: armonía y no antagonismo. Es necesario evitar que al paso de un malentendido progreso sigan haciendo desaparecer al panorama edilicio liberiano con sus extraordinarias casas de adobe y bahareque, con sus características *puertas del sol*, sus blancas fachadas y sus cubiertas de teja. El progreso debe ser cabal.

Arq. Erick Chaves Chaves
Arq. Miguel Chaves Fernández
ICOMOS de Costa Rica

CYPRUS

The archaeological heritage of Cyprus begins in the pre-Neolithic, in the 10th millennium BC and continues uninterrupted with numerous monuments and sites to modern times. In the Neolithic, the island acted as a staging post for the transmission of Neolithic culture from the Near East to Europe. It flourished as a cosmopolitan trading centre during the Bronze Age when exploitation of its copper resources reached its peak, attracting the attention of the Mycenaean Greeks who settled the island at the end of the Bronze Age, thus determining its future. The amalgamation of Aegean and Near Eastern cultural traits resulted in a uniquely local culture. Due to its strategically important position in the crossroads of Europe, Asia and Africa, Cyprus came under the domination of almost all the great powers that ruled over the Mediterranean – the Assyrians, Egyptians, Persians, the Ptolemaic kingdom of Egypt, and the Romans and in its later history it was dominated by the Lusignans, Venetians, and Ottomans, and formed part of the British Empire until its independence in 1960. The variety of sites and monuments, consisting of settlements, cemeteries, palaces, castles, churches and monasteries, some of which have been included in the World Heritage List, is the legacy of its turbulent history.

Development is one of the factors affecting the cultural heritage of the island. Due to the frequent occurrence of ancient remains during construction projects, there is a growing tendency to incor-

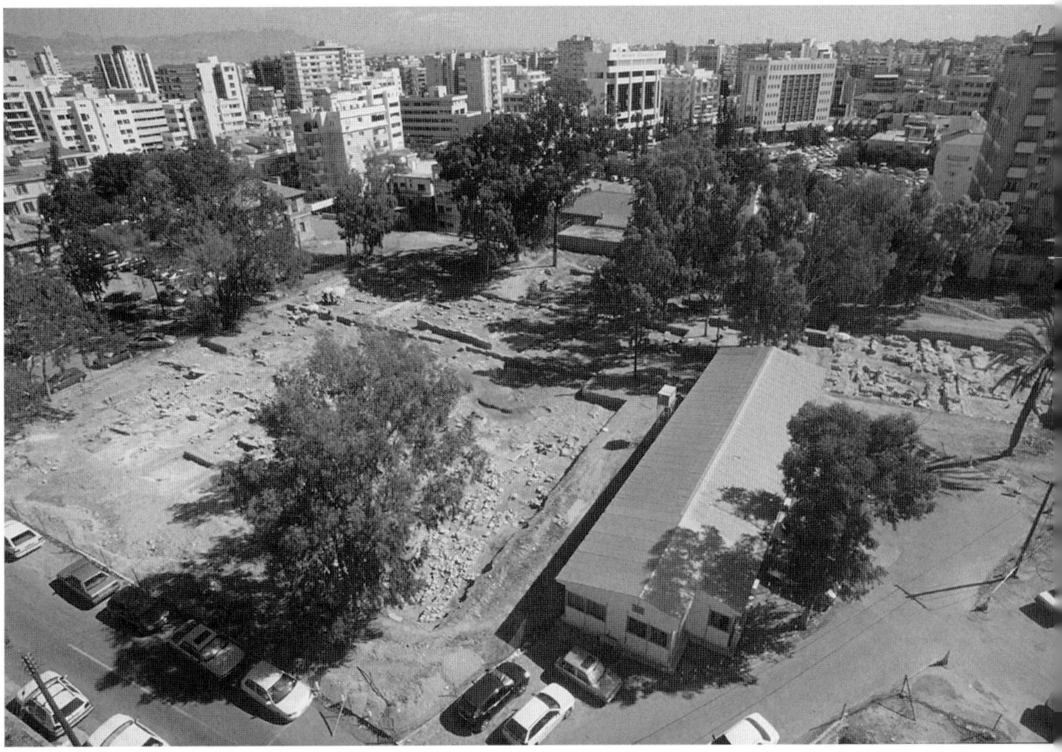

Hill of Agios Georgios, Nicosia – Byzantine and Medieval remains

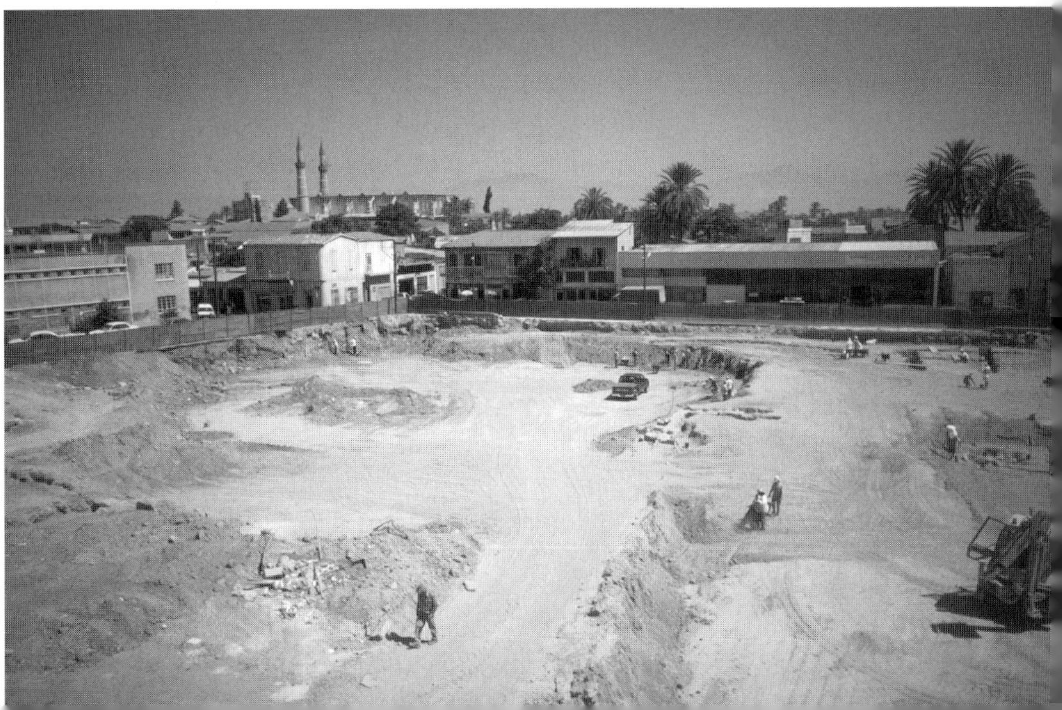

Early historical phases of Nicosia found at new Parliament building site, from the Late Chalcolithic period (mid-3rd millennium BC) to the present day

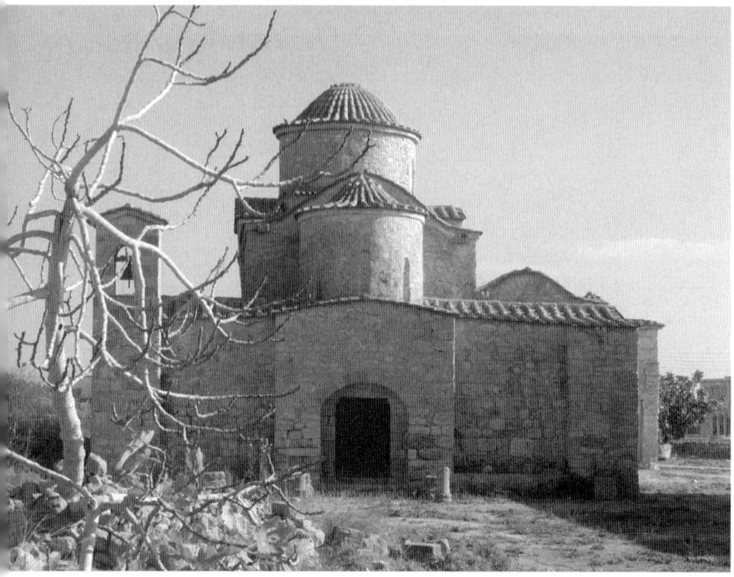

Church of Panagia Kanakaria, Lythrangomi, impacts of abandonment

porate ancient sites within modern projects, sometimes with detrimental results for both the ancient site and the new building. Two recent proposals to build the new House of Representatives on the Hill of Agios Georgios, Nicosia, and the new Town Hall in the old city of Nicosia, are problematic because antiquities have been found on both sites, in both cases after the plans for the buildings were approved. At the site of the new Parliament superimposed strata have been found belonging to the various historical phases of the city, beginning with the Late Chalcolithic period (mid-3rd millennium BC) to the present day.

The city's history, although one of the longest in the Mediterranean, was little known to its population as the modern city completely overlies its ancient forerunners and until recently no large-scale excavations had been held to document its history. The site of the proposed new town hall adds to the evidence found on the Hill of Agios Georgios and has brought to light important remains of the Byzantine and Medieval periods, times in which Nicosia was an important cosmopolitan commercial and artistic centre. However, as the largest part of the site has not yet been excavated and the archaeological deposits are quite deep, new information from earlier periods is likely to be brought to light in approaching months.

The pressures of pre-fixed excavation deadlines are detrimental factors that may lead to incomplete or inaccurate documentation and a consequent loss of information. In addition, the predetermined plans of the buildings – both winners of architectural competitions – restrict the number of modifications that may be made. In order to minimise the risks of potential damage, the ICOMOS National Committee is proposing a workshop between experts and the authorities with the aim to achieve the best possible solutions under the circumstances.

The ICOMOS Cyprus National Committee is also concerned with the state of conservation of monuments and sites in the north of the island, which has been under Turkish occupation since 1974. The opening in April 2003 of the barrier separating the Greek and Turkish communities enabled the people of Cyprus to visit heritage places all over the island but it also prompted the trafficking of illegally excavated antiquities. The Department of Antiquities, in an effort to mitigate the problem, issued information leaflets to make people aware that such objects were illegally obtained and should not be purchased. The risk of destruction to cultural heritage still continues as occasionally reported in the Turkish Cypriot press. It has come to our attention that the cemetery of Vounous, one of the major cemeteries of the mountain range of Pentadactylos, which yielded masterpieces of ceramic art now occupying an entire gallery in the Cyprus Museum, is to be developed. Although it is known that remaining tombs were looted, there may still be intact tombs and some investigation should at least be carried out before any development begins.

Another serious risk concerns the religious heritage sites of Early Christian, Byzantine and Medieval date in northern Cyprus, which have been abandoned since 1974. One of the most notable examples is the well-known church of Panagia Kanakaria in the village of Lythrangomi, where the wall mosaics dating to the 6th century and considered to be amongst the few surviving masterpieces of the period, were removed in 1979 and sold to an art dealer. The Republic and Church of Cyprus filed a lawsuit in the United States District Court of Indianapolis for the recognition of the mosaics' legal owners and for the mosaics' return to Cyprus. The case was won and a small number of the mosaics were returned in 1991. The church, however, continues to lie abandoned and the impacts are very visible.

ICOMOS Cyprus

Church of Panagia Kanakaria, Lythrangomi, remains of a mosaic

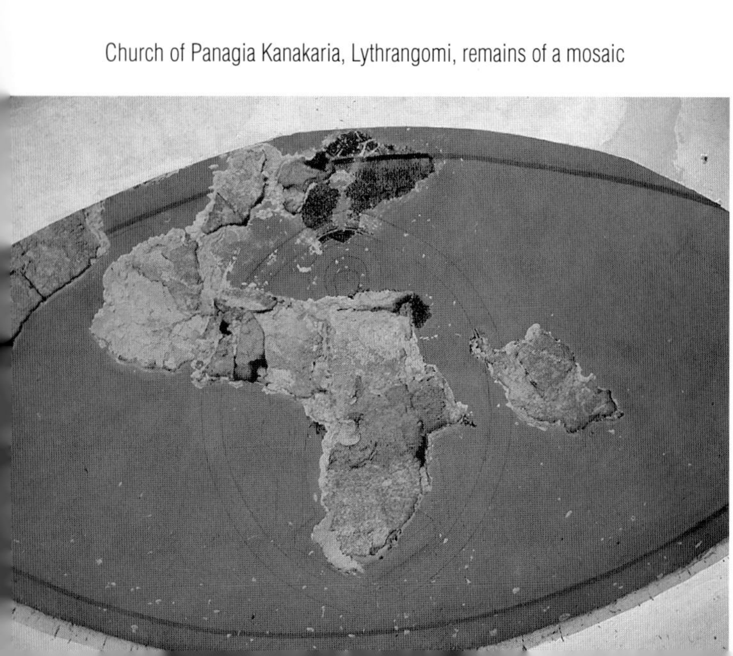

CZECH REPUBLIC
World Heritage and Development

Prague – a World Heritage Site in the Shadow of Commercial Projects

In the [northern] autumn of 2003, the President and three members of the Czech National Committee of ICOMOS visited the Lord Mayor of the City of Prague. They came to discuss with him the Czech Committee's serious concerns about some aspects of the present development of the city, including some particular projects endangering the values for which it was inscribed on the World Heritage List. Czech ICOMOS expressed disapproval that the municipal administration had gradually cancelled the function and authority of the Chief Architect of the City of Prague to coordinate the capital´s urban development and supervise the standard of new constructions. Further, the City Council had annulled a special Decree on the Building Development Regulation within the Prague Conservation Area and later decentralised decision-making on the granting of building permits. From the municipal authority, a centralised city body, power was transferred to 13 separate city quarters that form today's city.

The Czech ICOMOS committee sees in all these measures a loss of interest by the city's management to maintain the possibility and mechanisms to direct appropriately the flood of investments, to regulate the city´s urban development, to ensure the quality of new construction in its jurisdiction and to effectively protect its heritage buildings. In contrast, development is directed by the *laissez faire* principle, increasing the influence of investors with strong capital and allowing 'non-standard' methods to be used to force through their projects.

The Mayor and his deputy mayor were very polite and the discussion opened reciprocally. However, the participants did not arrive at an overall agreement or even partially constructive conclusions about the above issues. In contrast to the emphasis of Czech ICOMOS on the preservation of the heritage values, the Mayor set its development as the city's main priority. The deputy mayor replied to the Czech ICOMOS remark that in the case of Prague one of the main reasons for its listing as World Heritage site is Prague's extraordinary beauty in its urban integrity, meaning that its value is very vulnerable without efficient regulation, by stating that the listed area of the city is too large. In his opinion it was a mistake by previous city managers that its present representation would definitely not ever repeat, but had to cope with at present.

The results of this meeting are characteristic of Prague's present situation. In many respects it fulfils the prognoses and warnings by our Western European colleagues immediately after the 'Velvet Revolution'. At that time, we were full of euphoric, optimistic hopes and did not want to believe them. I am reminded of the outstanding international colloquy characteristically titled, *Prague, the Future of a Historical City*, organised in Prague in 1990. At that time, outstanding philosophers, historians, town-planners, architects and artists from France and several other Western European countries met Czech professionals (they included Jacques Derrida, Jean Viard, Michel Parent, Francois Choay, Leon Pressouyre and others).

Our Western European friends envisaged the threats to Prague in the following areas:

- in the capitalisation of Prague's unique beauty and atmosphere that may change into a sort of banal,
  consumer-oriented tourist attraction (Choay, Viard),
- in the 'triumphant scheming' that will radically change the multipliers of land values and result in the start of numerous tower blocks (Pressouyre). There is the threat that 'the new development will eclipse the city, will want to include into the saturated urban and architectural form, its new non-changing structures, escaping the ability to newly integrate with the primary whole' (Derrida).

The situation was summarised in a concise way by Leon Pressouyre: 'Today Prague is exposed to capitalist speculation and to the test of economic and social choice. That will exclude, undoubtedly, the aesthetic choice required by the city's unique significance'.

It is not possible to say unambiguously yet, whether Pressouyre was or was not right. It is certain that 'the world of money' fell upon the unprepared city with unusual power. The financially powerful foreign investors managed, in the first phase, to fill almost all vacant sites and open spaces in the historical centre with new buildings that are bulky, and unfortunately largely unsuccessful from an architectural design perspective. 'Façadism' was brought into Prague from Western Europe, having not been previously applied here, and leaving only the outer shell of the historical building, covering what is in fact a completely new building. Other investors persist in striving for the demolition of existing buildings so that they might erect more massive new buildings in their place or excise parcels from areas of municipal parkland.

The following selected cases, highlighting the greatest risks to the urban integrity of Prague, are especially characteristic and described in greater detail in the attachments to this report. They do not cover the extent of the problem. Apart from ostentatious investment projects about which they convey basic information, less striking changes are performed in Prague's historical centre, which are no less destructive to the authenticity of the historical urban fabric with irreversible cultural losses occurring. It is, most of all, the extensive construction of attic flats inserted into authentic historical roofspaces, with their often unthinkingly designed dormers, that is destroying the until recently extremely poetic 'roof landscape' of the Lesser Town and the Old Town. A number of new shops, restaurants or casinos have destroyed not only the atmosphere, but the authentic layout and built details of the parterres of historic houses, heavily damaging them with their insensitiveness. Lobby groups for building contractors seeking major state or municipal permits present a not insignificant risk. Perhaps the most eloquent example was the project for the technical and, at the same time, functionally completely unnecessary reconstruction of our most valuable industrial heritage site, the Charles Bridge – after a long struggle it was fortunately cancelled.

Despite this I do not think that the extreme pessimism of Leon Pressouyre's prognoses is warranted. Despite all the enterprise, materialism and hostile greed of our present conditions the 'aesthetic choice', that is respect for the beauty and uniqueness of historic Prague, has not yet been excluded from the process in today's changes. For the city's wonderful urban integrity has resisted so far. It has preserved its unique natural surrounds in the green hills and Vltava islands, its majestic historical outstanding places, and the balanced heights of its built areas. Most of all, the harmonic composition of the city centre has not yet been shattered by deficient new tower buildings, as has occurred in a number of historic towns of Western Europe.

Therefore, the wonder of Prague still exists. But this is not a result of the 'high culture' of our own and foreign investors, nor

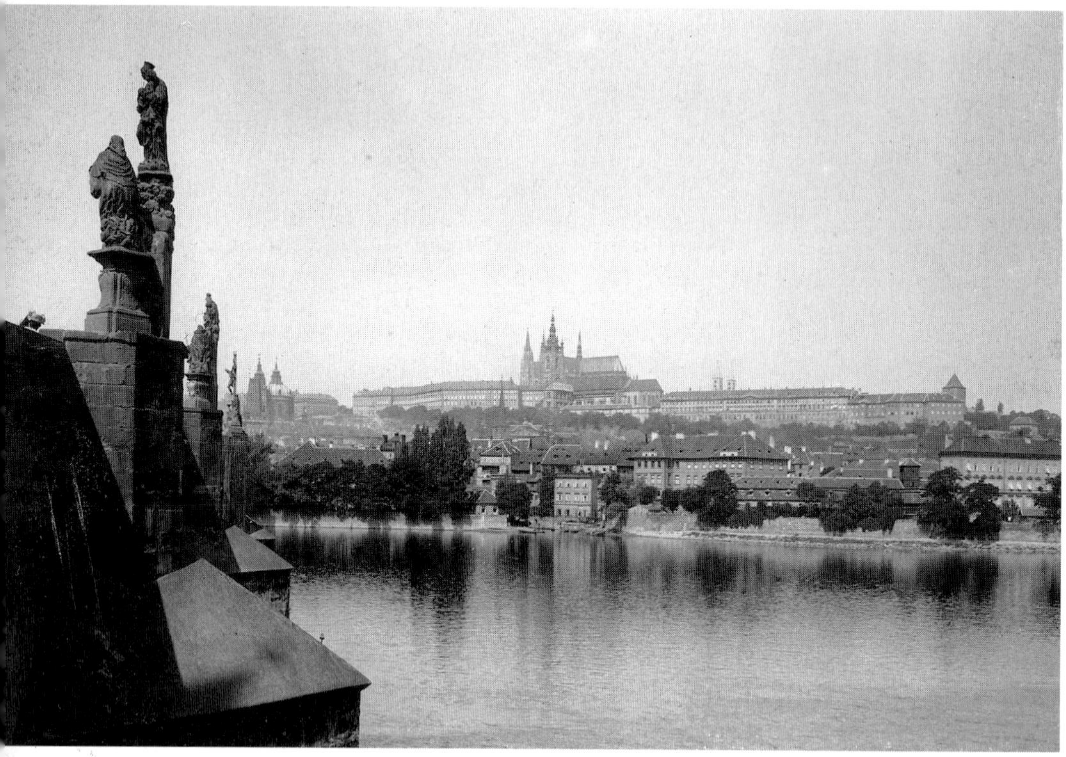

The photo dated to about 1905 records that the panorama of the City of Prague has not been changed in the course of the last one hundred years

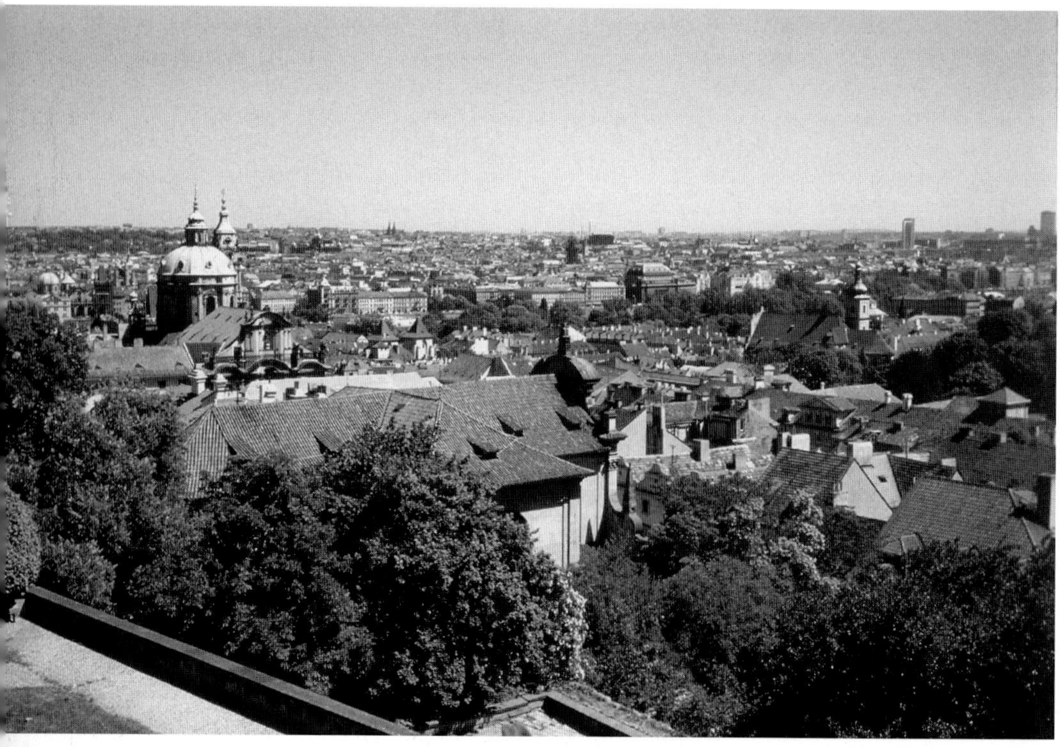

The view of Prague from the terrace of Prague Castle. The photograph shows the so far almost unspoilt heights of the built-up area on the horizon of which are the 'hollow teeth' of the unsuccessful tower buildings at Pankrác Plain.

due to some special wisdom, foresight and altruism of municipal representation and its administration. Nor can we overestimate the merits of the state heritage preservation institutions.

In my opinion, the greatest accolade for the current retention of historic Prague's integrity is owed to public opinion and elements of the original civic society – voluntary community associations, such as Klub Zastarou Prahu (The Club for Old Prague) with a hundred years of tradition, Deti zeme (Children of the Earth), Ceska umeleckohistoricka spolecnost (The Czech Art-Historians Society), Spolecnost pro trvale udrzitelny rozvoj (The Society for Sustainable Development) or community associations in local government areas. Also the media has become a large defender of historic Prague that largely stands for public opinion and particularly likes to publish the 'suspicious', 'atypical' or clear corruption cases. In many respects these elements actually replace the often ineffective state and municipal administration systems and, typically, the absence of clearly defined planning procedures to process developers starting projects in the city.

The struggle between the defenders of historic Prague and greedy investors continues and is often very intense. The first tower building or the first historic park sacrificed to speculation may become a precedent with unpredictable consequences. Nevertheless, I am properly entitled to optimism from existing campaigns. Today, not only associations and pressure groups of selfless defenders of historic Prague but also the wider public have begun to be aware of the unique, yet extremely vulnerable beauty and value of their city. People are waking out of their lethargy and community passivity forced on them over decades by a communist police regime.

I am convinced that we will not lose the struggle for historic Prague. This ancient, magically beautiful city will never be changed into a banal, standardised world metropolis, full of busyness, luxury and consumerism. I believe it will further preserve the testimony of its history, its beauty and its spiritual content.

Josef Stulc
Czech Republic ICOMOS

Endangering the Panorama of Prague

One of the most esteemed values of Prague as a historic city inscribed on UNESCO's World Heritage List is its famous and unmistakable panorama. The Prague Castle, with its almost theatrical effect, rises on its headland above the slopes covered by a dense historical built-up area. The panorama's foreground is formed by the wide and calm Vltava river in which the city is mirrored like a fairytale. For the entire past hundred years, since the neo-Gothic towers were built on St Vitus Cathedral at Prague Castle at the beginning of the 20th century, this panorama has miraculously remained unaffected by larger construction intrusions. It forms the worldwide known 'signature' of Prague, the mark that is recognisable to the entire cultural world. Sadder is the fact that efforts to yield the maximum commercial effect from these places in the city, highly attractive to tourists, above all present clear threats to Prague's panorama and built-up area on the riverbank. The original industrial items that traditionally belong to a historic town's riverbank – old mills, brickworks – gradually surrender not only to the pressure of new commercial and cultural and tourist use, which does not endanger them of itself, but are accompanied by attempts to forcefully adapt their volume, space and visual image to the new function.

The building of the Sova Mills, originally of the Renaissance and rebuilt and completed in the 1860s, was converted recently

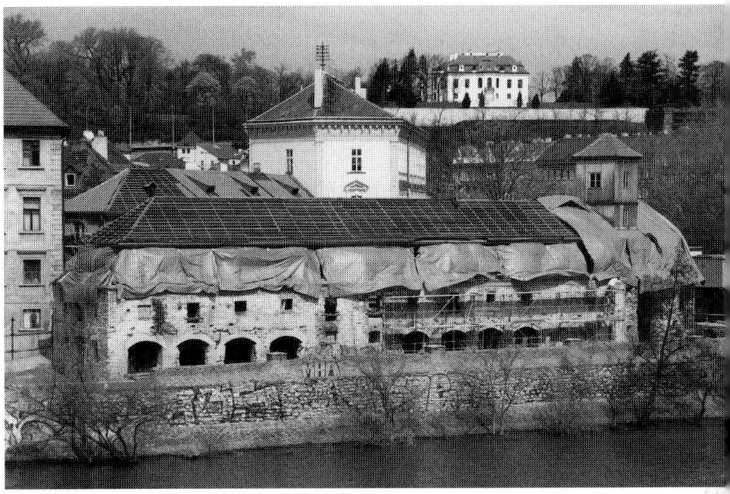

Prague, the large river bank area of the former Herget Brickworks in 2000. A typical picture of the forced re-adjustment of historic structure to new use

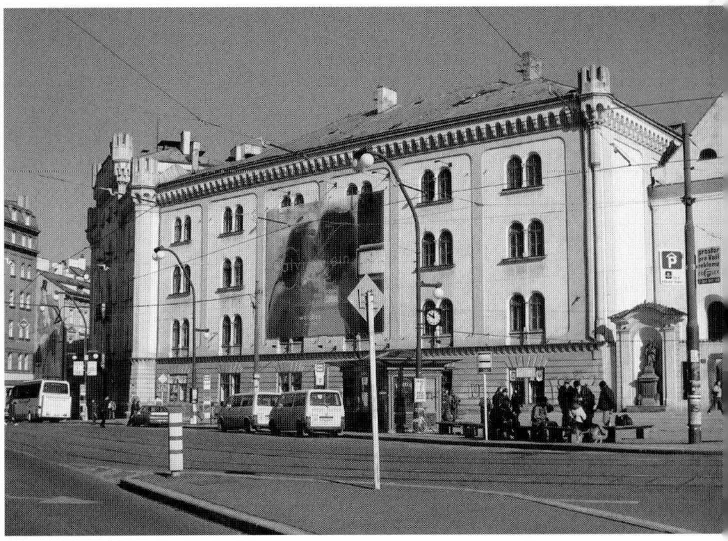

Prague, the historic Josefská Barracks from Republiky Square. The vacated building is ready for demolition. Only the façade is to be preserved.

Prague, the view over the former courtyard of the rear façade of the main building of the Josefská Barracks. The stables have been demolished already. At present rescue archaeological research is being done in the area. According to the house in the picture in the upper right sense can be made of the sizes of the parcels of land and the character of the surrounding built-up area. This can be compared with the planned new building that is to take up the whole free area in the photograph.

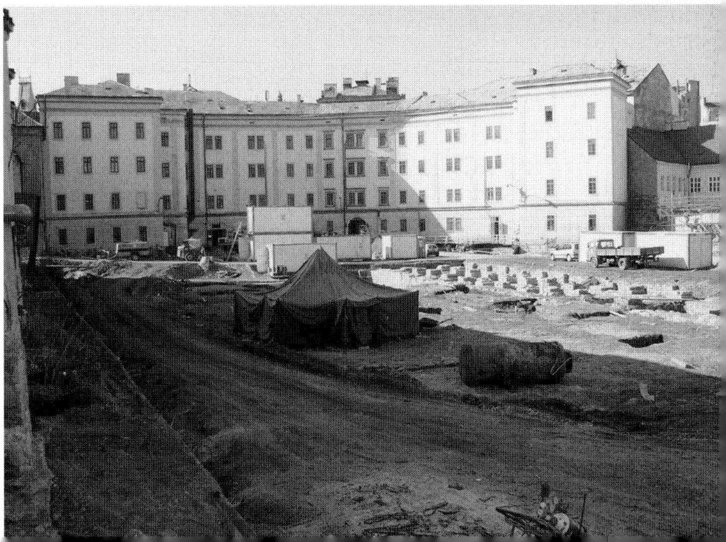

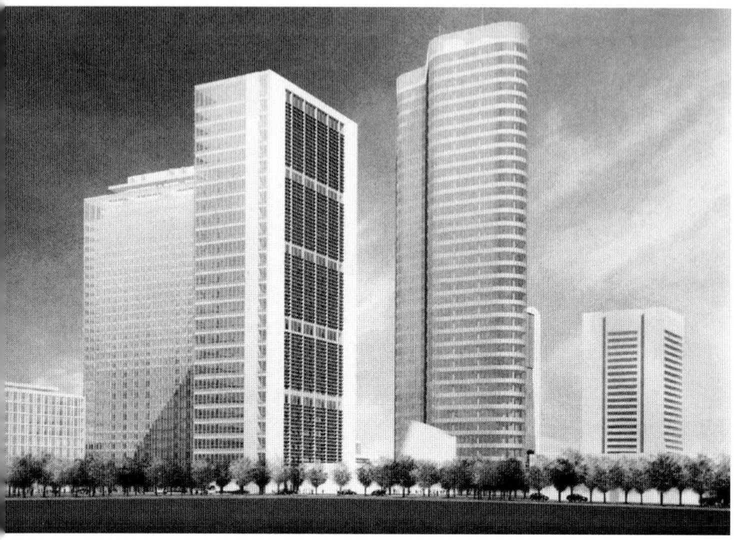

The model of the new group of still substantially taller high-rise buildings proposed for Pankrác Plain by Richard Meyer. A precedent that would find a number of eager successors.

into the museum of modern art (2002–2003). It was fitted with a bulky structure in the shape of a cube created in steel and glass, illuminated at night. Astonishing built adaptations to other parts of the building have already been designed.

The large area of riverbank of the former Herget Brickworks dating from the end of the 18th century was adapted during 2000–2003 for a completely new tourist use – restaurants and a commercial exhibition hall. As part of the reconstruction, historical vaults on the ground floor were vandalised by being torn down, and large openings were broken through the façade facing the river, in an originally solid wall, for the benefit of a view for the restaurant guests. Also, an apartment building with underground parking is planned to be built in the exclusive Herget Brickworks area.

The above-mentioned examples have the value of a tempting precedent for other subjects taking interest in the use and unsuitable structural adaptation of historic buildings in areas in Prague attractive to tourists. With the accomplishment of the two above-mentioned reconstructions the process has begun of a gradual interference with Prague's unique panorama – so sacrosanct that it should remain intact at any costs.

Katerina Beckova

The Planned Construction of the Giant Shopping Centre at the Republiky Square in Prague - a Crime Committed on the World Heritage Site

The intended rebuilding of the former Josefska Barracks at Republiky Square is so far the largest and most upsetting damage to the cultural values of the historic core of Prague since the fall of the communist regime in 1989. The area of the barracks was built up in 1857–61. It includes the main three-wing accommodation building near the square, the riding school along Na Porici street and the vast courtyard with free-standing stables. The area is protected as cultural heritage. In its place an enormously big shopping, entertainment and administrative centre is to be built. The total area of the site is expected to be built over. According to the project approval only the façade and some parts of the main building facing Republiky Square and the riding school are to be preserved. Behind the scenes a giant new building is planned with a total capacity of over 100,000 m^2 of commercial area, including underground parking for about 800 cars. The project also includes the construction of an underground space beneath Republiky Square and car ramps leading to Revolucni Street.

Prague's centre does not suffer from a lack of commercial-administrative areas. This proposed use is not needed in this area, on the contrary. While commercial-administrative areas may also be successfully built in other places, at Republiky Square they will take up an important site that could be used in a markedly more useful manner for the city.

The proposed size is far too large and will lead to increased traffic overload. The privately-owned, commercial fee-paying underground car-park will probably be only rarely used by local inhabitants. Instead, it will serve visitors, customers and staff of the future centre. The proposed large-capacity car-parks are not the solution to the current parking problems. In comparison to the current situation, they represent pollution from hundreds more cars. Those cars will not only park there, but will also arrive and leave. By closing Revolucni Street, cars that now pass through the square will not disappear but will arrive through the adjacent streets of the Old and New Towns. And what will be the result? It will be many more cars in the narrow residential alleys of the adjacent historic built area.

Access to the underground parking is planned by ramps from Revolucni Street. That street is a part of the bypass in the location of the fortifications between the Old and New Towns. The construction of the exit ramps means that this important road will no longer be a thoroughfare. Let us imagine that the ramps to private parking were to cut the Ringstrasse in Vienna – that is a comparable situation. The point is not the closing of this street to car traffic, it is that by building the drive-in ramps that closure will be permanent and there will be no chance to reassess it in the future if necessary.

The area of the former barracks is an exceptionally well-preserved and, therefore, an extraordinarily significant archaeological site. Apart from others, medieval structures are preserved underground. Excavations for the new basements will destroy everything.

In the context of a historic town every original building is irreplaceable. With the demolition of most of the barracks, an important historic building will cease to exist. At the same time, other potential investors will be given the signal that the responsible authorities tolerate such treatment of architectural and archaeological heritage in Prague.

According to the 1987 Washington Charter, the basic values of a historic site include the original land subdivision, the relationship between the open spaces and built areas, the form and characteristic appearance of the buildings. In all the above cases, the proposed construction is completely out of keeping with the design of the surrounding urban area. Instead of the usual arrangement of the individual houses, roofs, and courtyards, a huge structure is proposed that builds over 100% of the area corresponding in size to tens of historical parcels of land. This poorly designed, large, unstructured mass will have a negative appearance in the overall viewshed of the historical centre.

In Prague, many historic heritage places can be seen, some quite well repaired. Many things have improved or, at least, there is the hope that they will improve. Nevertheless, the above example may be the first of a series of larger stones in a rolling avalanche. If nothing is done, in the future only the ruins will remain of the heritage values of Prague's historic core for which it was declared a World Heritage site.

Milos Solar

Sky Scrapers at Pankrac Plain

Pankrac Plain is an upland separated by the valley of the Botic stream on the southern border of the historic New Town of Prague. It is a very exposed position in the entire city's panorama. Therefore, the area is included in the buffer zone of the Prague Conservation Area. After the construction of the bridge across the valley and the metro line being inserted into the area, in the mid-1970s it became a very attractive construction area because of its rapid connection to the city centre. During the 'normalisation' phase of the Communist regime following the Soviet invasion in 1968, Pankrac Plain was chosen by the Communist Party leaders as the most suitable part of Prague for efforts to 'make visible' the socialist presence with pretentious constructions. The Paris quarter, La Défense, was presented as the source of inspiration to achieve the planned new 'world repute' for Prague. However, that comparison which is still used, is far from an analogy, as it is as if La Défense were built just above Étoile Square and not more than 5 km from the historic city. At Pankrac, the Communists managed to build three tower buildings, some 100 m high with the shapeless mass of the Palace of Culture in their foreground. The people of Prague aptly called that unsuccessful urban design 'hollow teeth'.

In 2001, the firm ECM Radio Plazza announced the project for a further wave of filling Pankrac with high-rise buildings, this time as high as 150 m. The developer advanced skilfully using the world-renowned architect, Richard Meyer, as the Trojan horse, in setting out the project. His design has of course indisputably high qualities, if it were intended for another place. Also, the developer won very active support for the project from the mayor of the local city quarter Prague 4. The mayor self-confidently stated to the media that his quarter had the right to have its own 'Hradcany' (that is, its own 'Prague Castle' as the city's most visible structure). The comparison really gets to the core of the problem. Indeed, the project is trying, quite consciously and with breathtaking arrogance, to 'outdo' the Prague Castle in the current extremely impressive panorama of historic Prague. Apart from the mayor's support, the investor also achieved an unusual welcome from all sections of the Prague Municipal Authority responsible to approve the project.

In the project's extensive publicity and the reaction to it, it was mainly the opinions of members of the Czech Architects Community that clashed. The main supporter, spokesperson and, at the same time, direct participant in the project team was architect Vaclav Aulicky. He is the designer of the infamous, already obsolete, TV tower of the first half of the 1980s, that was panoramically completely unsuitable for historic Prague, and politically imposed despite the resistance of the state heritage conservation agencies and public opinion, although at that time nobody needed to ask for this latter. The tower's main mission was to interfere with television and radio signals and thus prevent the inhabitants of Prague and Central Bohemia from receiving free information. The main spokesperson of those against the Meyer project, apart from conservators with a unified view, was the well-known architect Vlado Milunic, co-designer with Frank Ghery on the original and also highly contextual project, the so-called Dance House on the Vltava river embankment in the city's historic centre.

Apart from the adversaries in the theoretical discussion, the developer faced unexpectedly tough resistance from not only the state heritage preservation institutions (it is worth mentioning that their voice is only advisory, the municipal administration takes the decisions), but also of Prague's inhabitants, most of all in Pankrac itself. In the restored democracy, decisions can no longer be made behind closed doors as under the Communists. At their request, participants in the approval procedure became the community body, Sdruzeni obyvatel Pankrace (Association of the Inhabitants of Pankrac) supported by other NGOs, Deti zeme (Children of the Earth) and Sdruzeni pro trvale udrzitelny rozvoj (Association for Sustainable Development). Despite the stubborn welcome to the project by the Municipal Authority officials, so far these NGOs have blocked the approval of the project successfully.

The problem is not yet resolved as to whether the new tower buildings will link back to the arrogance and arbitrary decisions of past Communist planners, and whether they will be built against the will of the local inhabitants and all lovers of historical Prague. Thanks to widespread publicity which we believe will not allow apparent corruption, the situation is mildly optimistic. Also the comparison helps with the recent, almost identical project of high-rise buildings near Vienna's central station, because of which that city almost lost its World Heritage status. Let us believe that the Prague administration will take a lesson from the Viennese precedent and will not expose its wonderful city to a similar risk.

Josef Stulc

Two Years After the Floods in Bohemia

The huge floods that hit much of Bohemia in August 2002 also deeply affected our cultural heritage, apart from human tragedies and considerable damage to the environment, factories, infrastructure and agricultural areas (see *Heritage at Risk, ICOMOS World Report 2002/2003*, pp. 71–81). Already during and immediately after the flood, various rescue operations started. The following brief case-studies inform you of some selected remarkable cases of these activities.

Prague, the Capital

The Restoration of the Old New Synagogue in Prague

The ancient Altnai (Old New) Synagogue, a remnant of the once important and large Jewish Ghetto of Prague, is a simple, oblong building with a high saddle roof finished with Late Gothic brick shields. The synagogue's two-aisled nave synagogue with six fields of Gothic five-part ribbed vaults on two buttresses with rich carved decoration on architectural details was built in the course of the second half of the 13th century. Low late medieval additions, serving as a hallway and a space for women, were gradually added to the southern, western and northern sides.

The latest major renewal of the structure was carried out 1997–1999, when the façades were repaired, the interior dried out, and the paving, plaster and furnishing, movable elements repaired, and the overall restoration carried out of all valuable stone elements, forged and girdlers' elements and of the entire tabernacle (*aron ha-kodesh*). All these works were performed with maximum technical precision under the supervision of the National Institute and with the participation of the best specialists.

In August 2002 water penetrated the Synagogue's newly restored interior during the large flood and inundated the interior to an approximate height of 1 m. Thanks to well-organised rescue works by Prague's Jewish Community, significant state financial

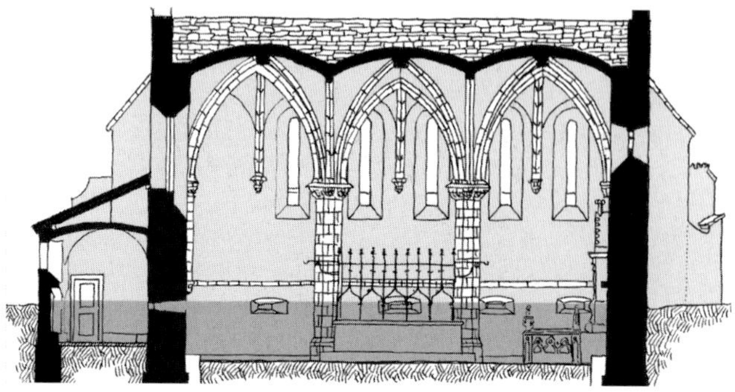

Prague, longitudinal section of the Altnai Synagogue shows the location of the two vast buttresses, almemor and the box for the torah (aron hakodesh). Marked in blue is the level of water during the 2002 flood.

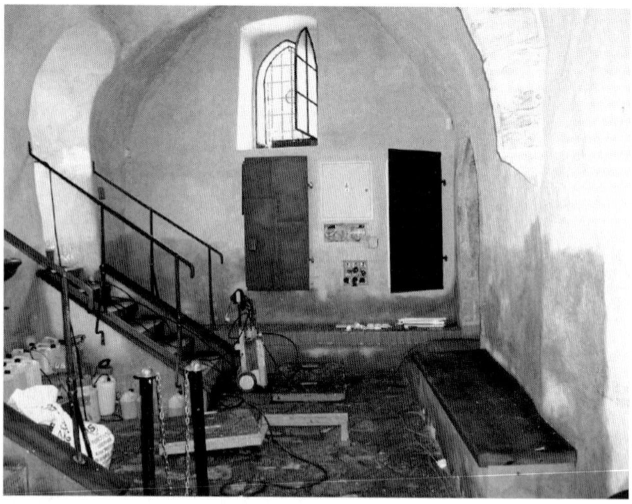

The southern hallway is the oldest addition to the Synagogue, it originated, evidently, already during the construction in the last quarter of the 13th century. The condition shortly after the falling off of water during the 2002 flood.

The most valuable part of the interior of the Altnai Synagogue from the liturgical and ancient monument point of view is the box for the torah (aron hakodesh). The condition after the performance of the conservators works in 2002 within the framework of the removal of the consequences of the flood.

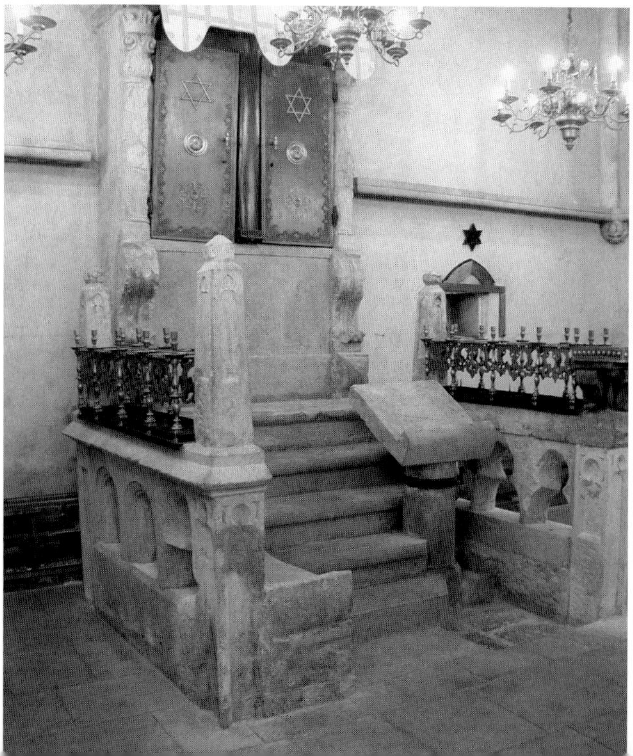

support and the professional approach by experts, the results of the damage were removed during 2002 and today once again visitors from the whole world can admire this extraordinary historic sanctuary.

Ondrej Sefcu

The Region of Central Bohemia

Roztoky, the mansion house

This late medieval stronghold and mansion of the 15th and 16th centuries was not damaged greatly by the flood and, fortunately, no significant structural problems appeared on the building of the neighbouring mill. Nevertheless, the buildings suffered considerable partial damage and had to undergo a general overhaul. That included, above all, the removal and cleaning of dirt and damaged plaster up to the level affected by water. A restoration survey was also conducted and valuable plaster layers from the oldest building stages were documented and made stable.

The former mansion is part of the Regional Museum of Central Bohemia, that also includes laboratories equipped with extremely valuable instruments. The laboratories served the entire region undertaking investigations, analytical tests and other operations as a part of the restoration of manuscripts, paintings, sculptures and other historical works of arts.

Damage caused to the laboratory equipment was considerable and the laboratory operations were practically destroyed. The irradiation room was silted with mud, and had to be cleaned and dried out. Only then could repairs begin, including a general reconstruction of the technology. Above all, the ionising radiation source including its protective container, the lifting device and the shield gate, complete electric installation, the air-conditioning and ventilation system and the security system were repaired. The equipment is now ready for further operation, necessary tests having been performed.

Dolni Berkovice, the Historic Country House Area

This manor is a late Renaissance building remodelled extensively in neo-Renaissance style in the mid-19th century.

The country house proper and its adjoining park were hit by the flood and had to be cleaned out and let dry before repairs could be started. Works for to stabilise the north-west corner of the house and the chapel have already been completed. Carpentry and new roofing repaired part of the roof. Plaster and floors were also repaired in the damaged part of the manor. The chapel furnishing was restored, that is the movable objects and decoration including hanging paintings and murals.

Libis, St James Church

The church is a simple Late Gothic structure from 1391, remarkable for its extremely well preserved series of Gothic mural paintings.

The medieval building's stability was not compromised. Thanks to its solid foundation and the building materials that had been used, the damage was limited to only its plaster. However, the interior furnishing and decoration and, above all, the medieval murals, were hit severely. Quite complicated and expensive

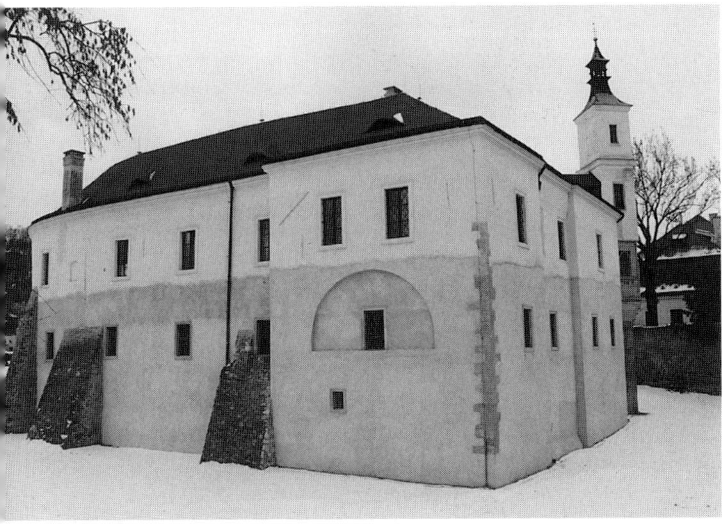

Roztoky, the manor house, an overall view of the main building at the premises

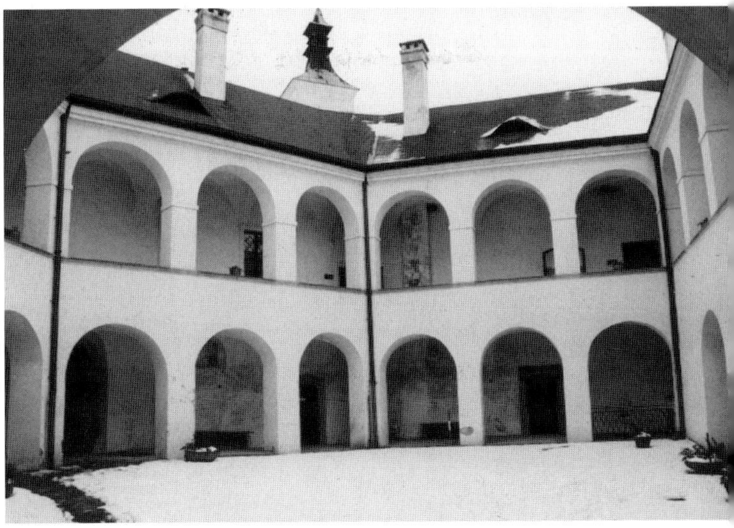

Roztoky, the manor house, the main building courtyard

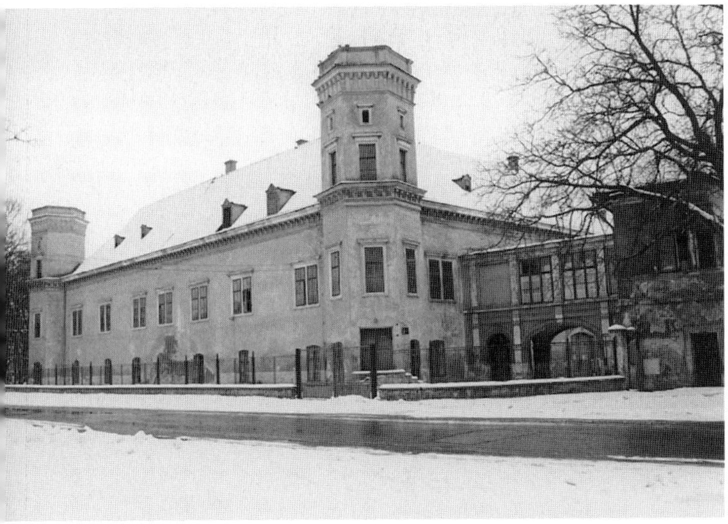

Dolní Beřkovice, the Historic Country House, an overall view

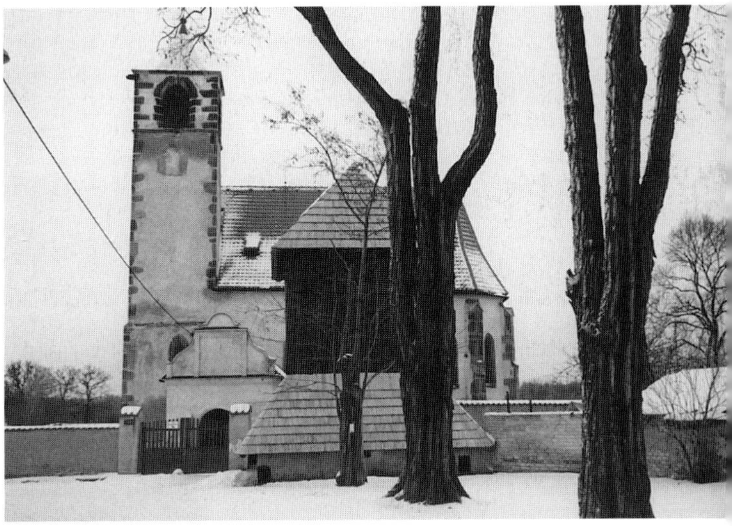

Libiš, an overall view of the church with the cemetery and the bell tower

Hořín, a view of the country house courtyard

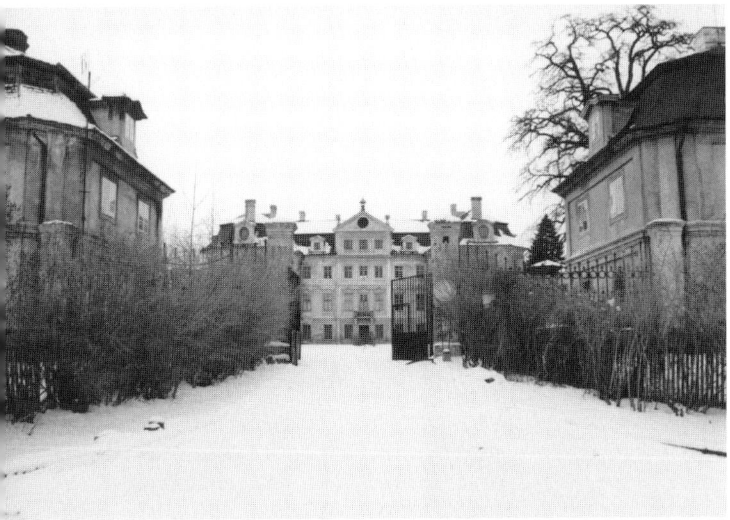

Hořín, the country house farmyard

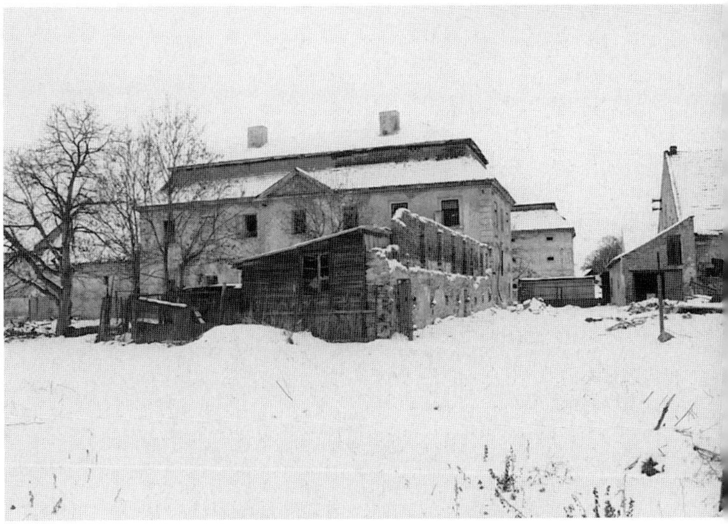

restoration works had to be carried out because of subsequent high humidity, which persisted for a long time. After the building was finally dried out, the church decoration was made stable.

The neighbouring wooden bell tower was overhauled, the repairs including the reinforcement of the wooden structure and renovation of the shingle roofing.

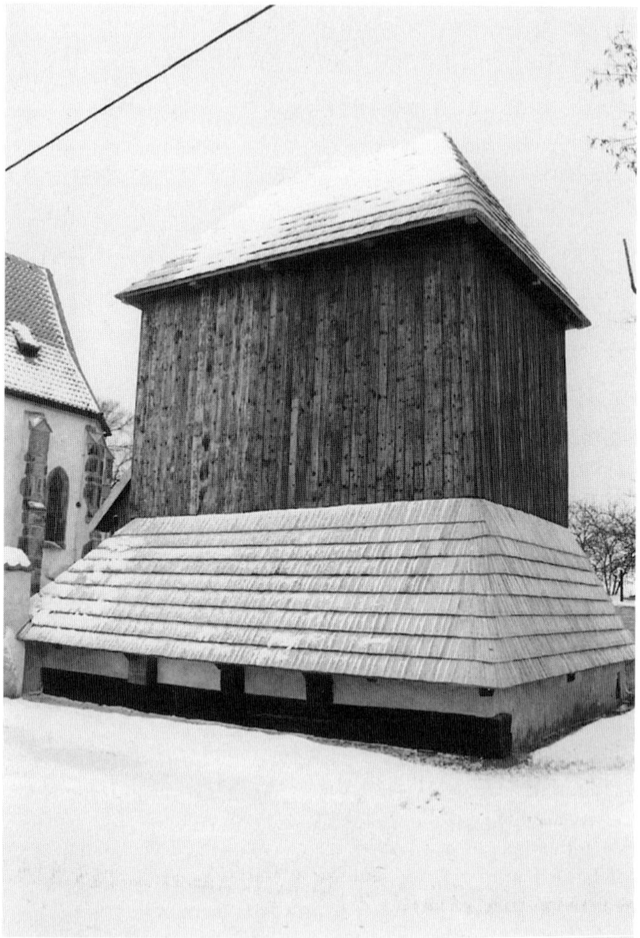

Libiš, the wooden bell tower

Horin, the Country House with St John of Nepomuk Chapel

Horin Manor is an important item of Bohemian Baroque of the 18th century with a very original architectural design and rich Rococo-style decoration in its interiors. The building located in the flood area was severely inundated.

Buildings on the premises were thoroughly cleared out of the flood deposits. Certain projects were planned for and preparatory works started. The most valuable interiors damaged by the flood were restored. The entire country house area has not however been used for a long time and is deteriorating slowly, a condition unrelated to the 2002 flood.

The original country house complex also includes a farmyard, most of which is neither used, nor secured. The condition of the farm will soon pose a risk to the existence of the entire heritage site. The condition is alarming for the splendid family vault from the first part of the 19th century, built in Italian Renaissance style. Regardless of its general deterioration, the family vault remains in its condition from the flood. The crypt with coffins was flooded and silted with mud, and has not been cleared out, nor secured from free access.

Libechov, the Historic Country House and Park

Originally a late medieval fortified mansion, the house was substantially rebuilt and completely remodelled in Baroque style in the 1730s. Interiors were redecorated in Romantic style in the 1840s.

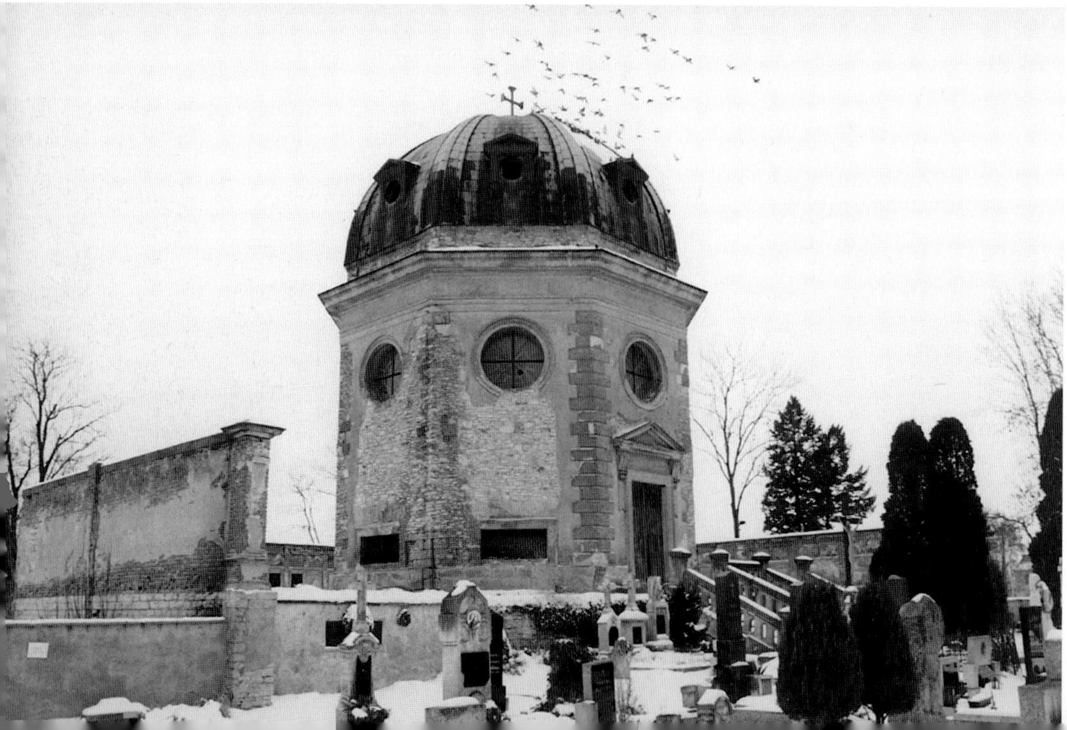

Hořín, the chapel with a vault at the cemetery

The flood caused considerable damage to the country house, its condition already requiring a general renovation before the flood. Now, it is being repaired in gradual stages. The premises were cleaned to remove the flood's direct effects. Numerous projects have been planned to save the house including its extensive premises and park with significant sculptures. Restoration inspections and basic physical security works have already been conducted to be followed, if possible, by further necessary stages. The manor's granary and probably the outbuildings in front also will undergo an overhaul this year. The Orangery remains one of the biggest problems, as the building was already badly affected before the flood and now it needs extensive repairs.

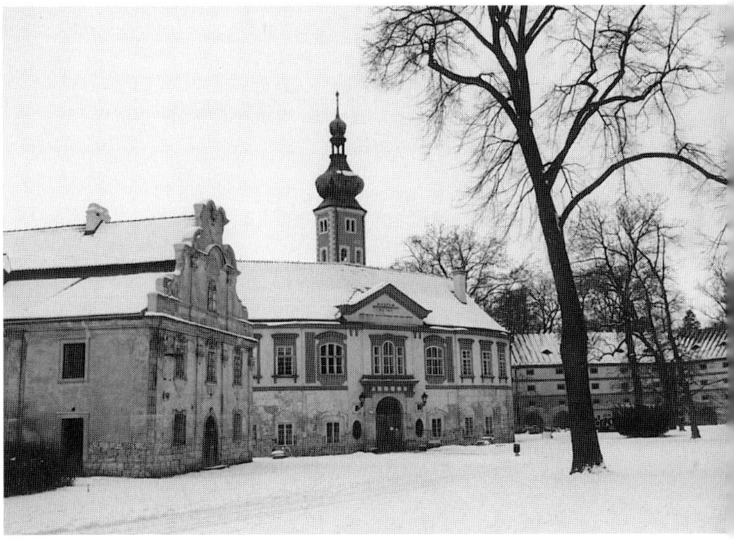

Liběchov, the country house premises with the main building and other buildings

Veltrusy, the Country House Area and Landscape Park

Veltrusy Country House, built in the 1730s, is a most remarkable piece of Bohemian Baroque architecture. The house with its very original layout and significant interior decoration is surrounded with an extensive landscape park and 'ferme ornée', the first of its kind in Bohemia.

In this case the flood damage was the heaviest in the region. The flood affected the ground badly, resulting in alterations in the worst hit area where the protective dike broke. The old, original trees, which withstood the torrent's surge and were not uprooted, are often dying from being waterlogged. Buildings were mainly structurally affected, in addition to direct damage to furnishings. Such damage is gradual and of long-term character.

In the first stage, repairs focused on the basic physical security of the place by replacing the destroyed dike at the river mouth. Silted sand and soil were removed and by contrast hollowed out areas were back-filled.

The country house and other buildings on the premises were immediately basically secured. The damage to the area inspired a greater interest in the place, which resulted in detailed surveys and preliminary works being conducted on a large scale. General repairs took place at the same time and necessary building started where essential. Given the extent of the needed repairs and adaptations, this is still merely the beginning of the general rehabilitation of the manor area. These efforts should result in putting the country house back to its original form from its historically most important period.

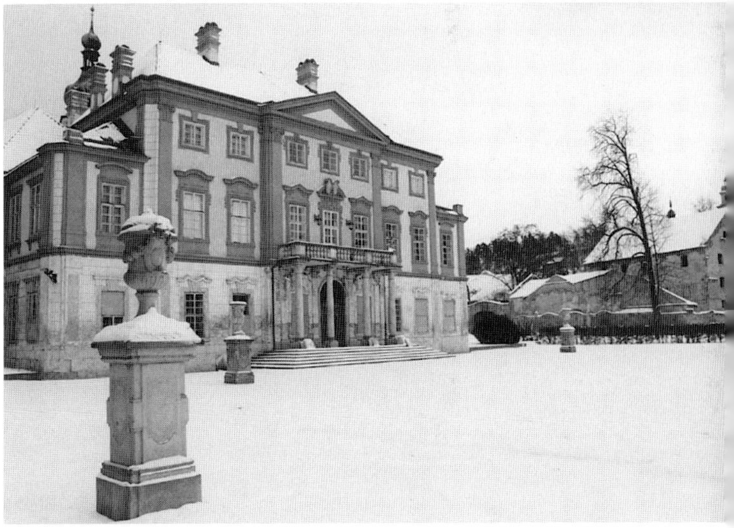

Liběchov, the garden front of the country house

Vsestudy, so-called Red Mill in the area of Veltrusy Historic Country House

The early Gothic-revival mill was located in a strong torrent of the swollen floodwaters and commensurate extensive damage resulted to the building. Therefore repairs had to focus on a general stabilisation of the building and on reconstructing its interior machinery. Difficult building works and interior adaptations have already been completed.

Jiri Mrazek

Veltrusy, a west view of the country house

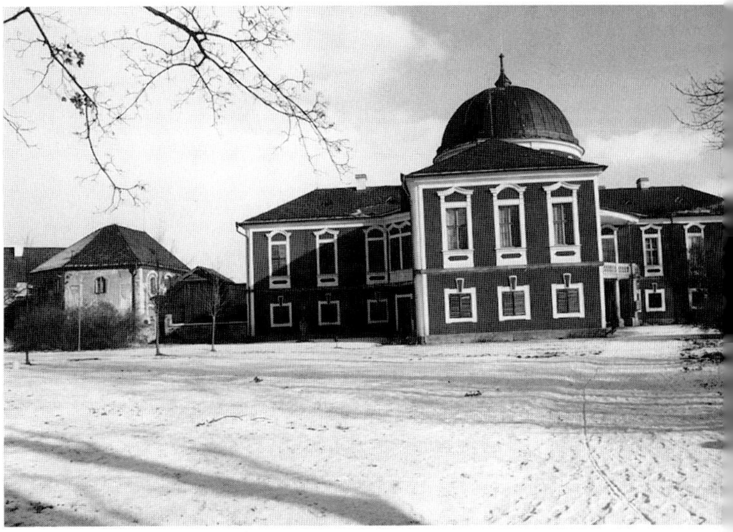

The Region of South Bohemia

Ceske Budejovice, the Historical Centre Conservation Area

In the administrative building of the Regional Unit of the National Institute for the Protection and Conservation of Monuments and

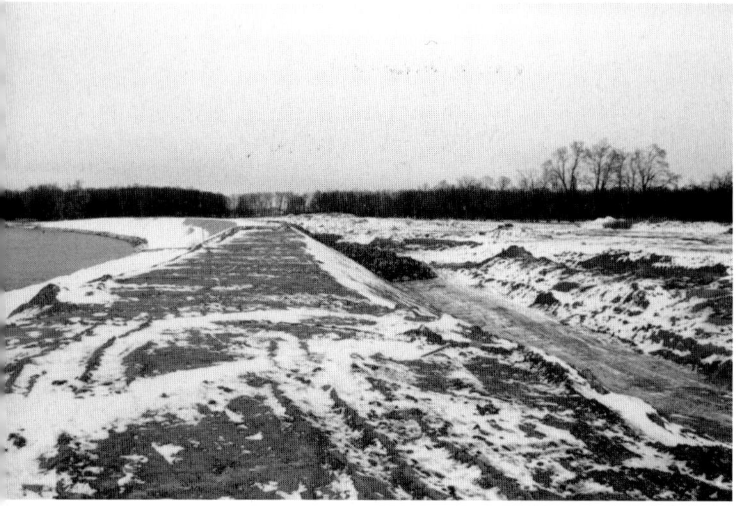

Veltrusy, a newly built dike on the western side of the park

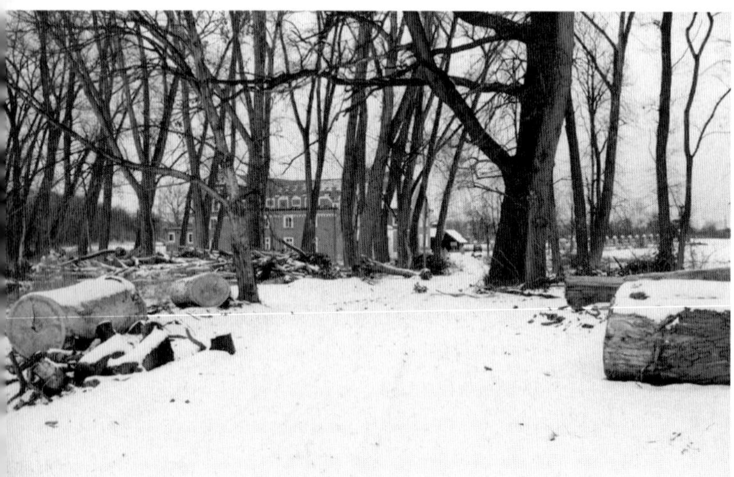

Všestudy, Red Mill at the premises of Veltrusy park

Všestudy, an overall view of Red Mill

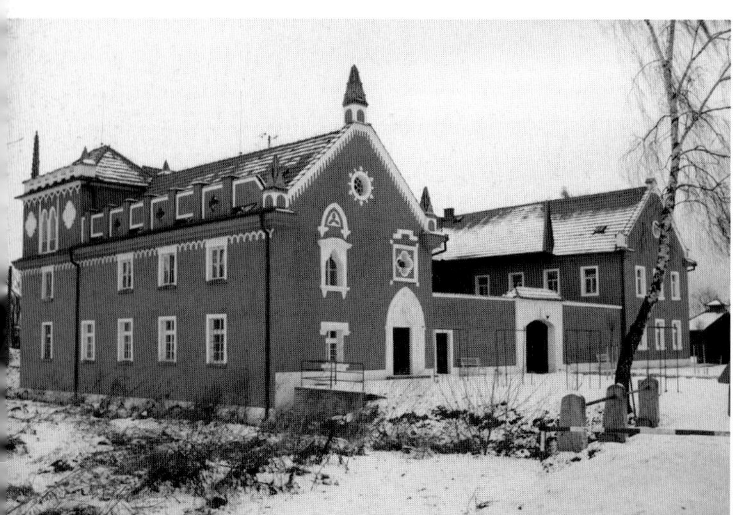

Sites at Senovazne Square, the files and plan archives were flooded and irreparable damage was caused by flood to the photographic archives. For almost a month the Institute's routine program was interrupted and the staff of the historic monuments conservation section, assisted by volunteers, both students and colleagues from unaffected localities, separated the saturated documentation files and dried out the archival materials on lines stretched in the lofts, corridors and empty offices. Although the premises of the Institute reminded one rather of a laundry drying room, more than 80% of the agenda files, including photographic documentation was successfully saved in this way.

In the building itself, the water pressure forced out the entry gate and carried it across the entire Senovazne Square, and sewage water damaged both outside and inside façades, including the windows and doors on the ground floor, the pavement, outside historic fence and greenery.

Research was undertaken, the damaged street façade restored and the clean-up took place of the interiors of all three branches of the National Institute, located in listed historic buildings in Ceske Budejovice.

Cesky Krumlov, the Historical Centre – a Conservation Area

The surroundings of the castle and the palace are inscribed on the World Heritage List.

The rocky headland above the Vltava river bearing the castle and palace of Cesky Krumlov protected that architectural jewel from the 13th to 18th centuries against direct damage to the buildings or the historically significant movable heritage in their interiors. The narrow rocky isthmus, however, is water-locked by the river from one side, and from the other side by the Polecnice brook. Across the artificially dug rampart, the inner palace is connected with the theatre building by the Plastov bridge pillars. Under them, on both sides of the rock, the approach road passes between Cesky Krumlov's centre and the car park in the neighbourhood called Jelenka formed by Rybarska and Hradni streets. The Polecnice floodwaters streamed through that vacant site towards the Vltava river. It hollowed a 2 m deep trough, uncovering the collector distributions and waved the road's asphalt covering like a ribbon. The strong flow of the Vltava river then eroded the bedrock and removed or deeply eroded part of the walls on the banks.

Only one month after the flood abatement, the Ministry of Culture of the Taiwanese Republic of China contributed financially to fix the destroyed electricity, water and sewerage networks and pledged the provisional pedestrian footbridge between the town centre and Jelenka. Works have continued on solidifying the banks, securing the eroded rock and building the bulk of the access road.

Trebon's Historical Pond System

The area of the Renaissance Trebon palace is near the Svet pond. In the 16th century the group of ponds of the South-Bohemian pond-diggers Stepanek Netolicky and Mikulas Ruthard of Malesov was completed by Jakub Krcin of Jelcany with the construction of the large water regulation system, draining the marshy landscape of the Trebon region. The ingenuity of the connection of the individual ponds by the Zlata stoka (Golden drain) and Nova Reka (the New River) was only shown during the crisis days of August, 2002. The water system took away, without causing any

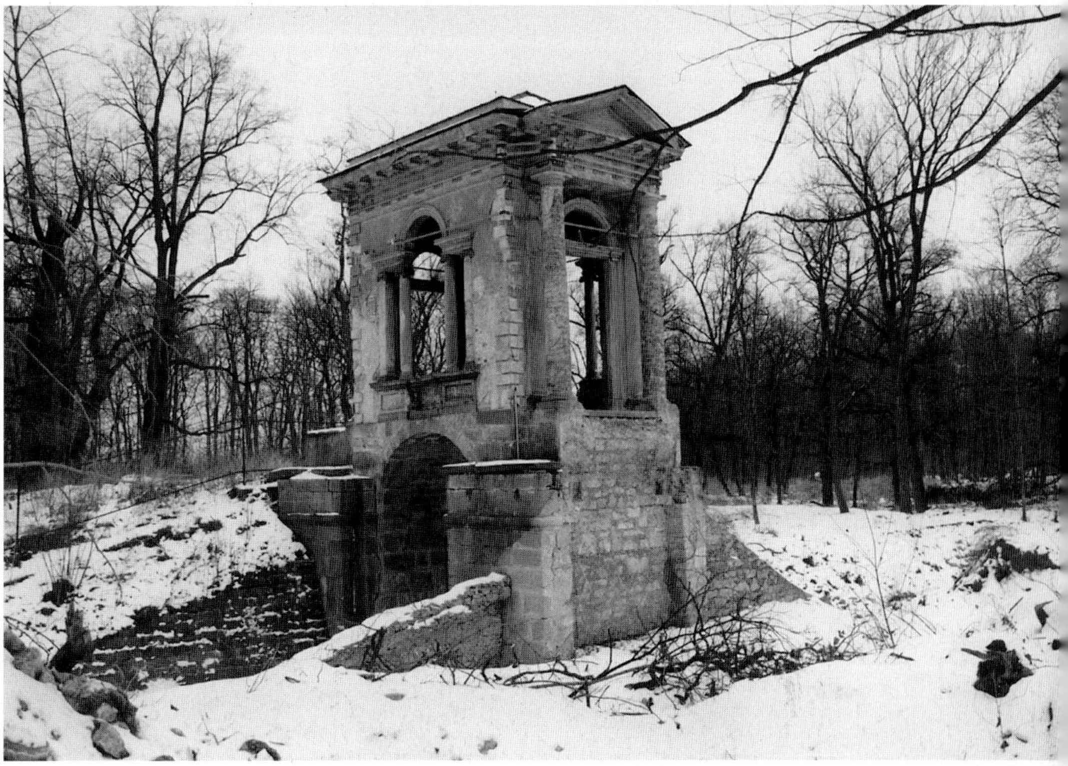

Veltrusy, Laudon's Pavilion in the park

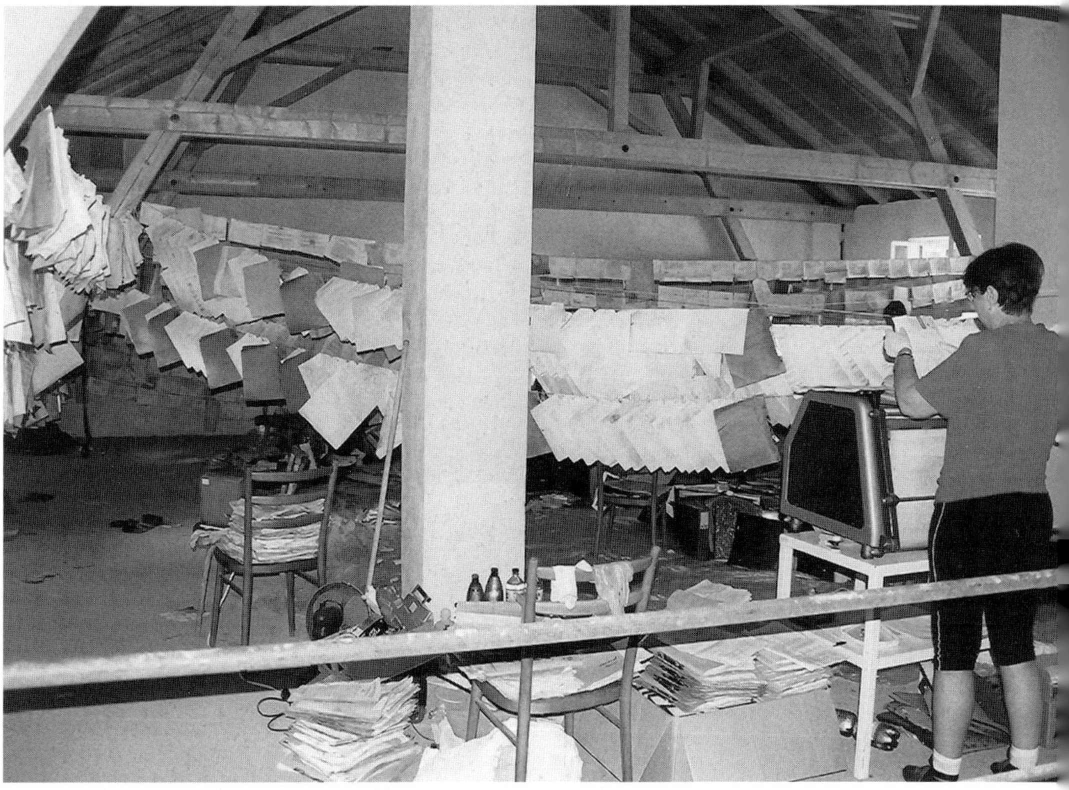

Ceské Budějovice, in the conference room of the institute the flooded files were dried

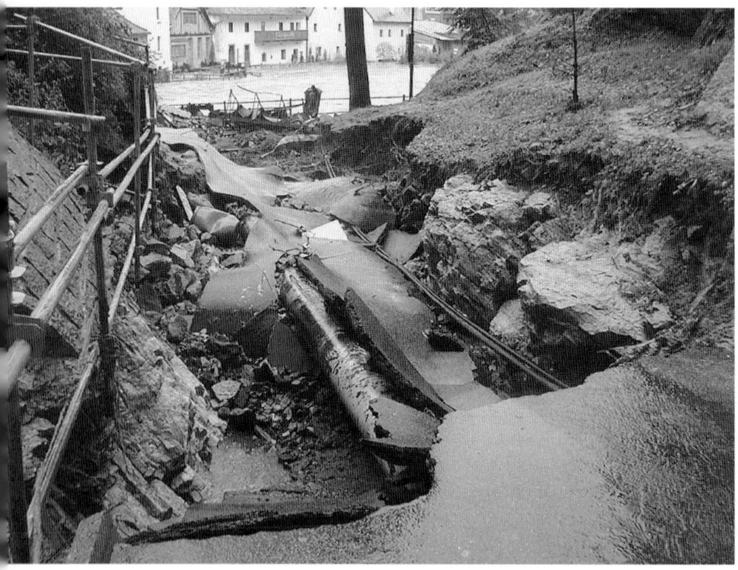

Ceský Krumlov, the condition of the access road under the Pláštový Bridge after the water falling off

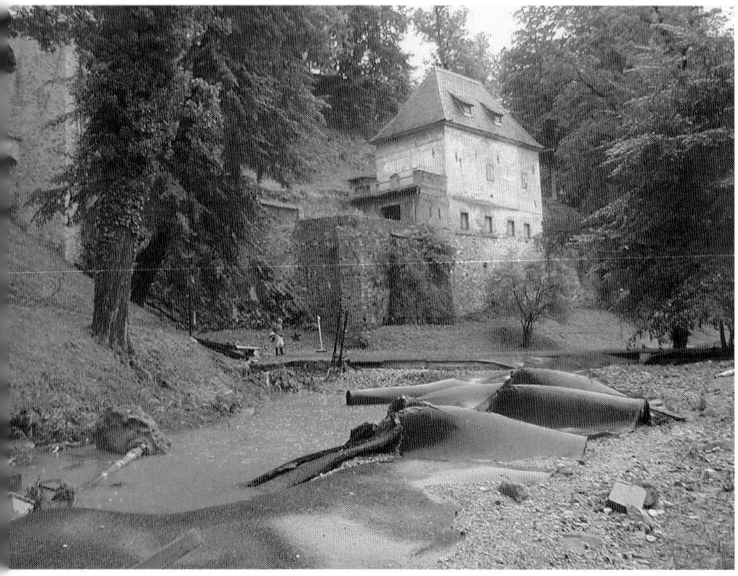

Ceský Krumlov, the brought down asphalt road in Jelenka

Kratochvíle, foundation of willow wattles on the bank of the brook near Kratochvíle

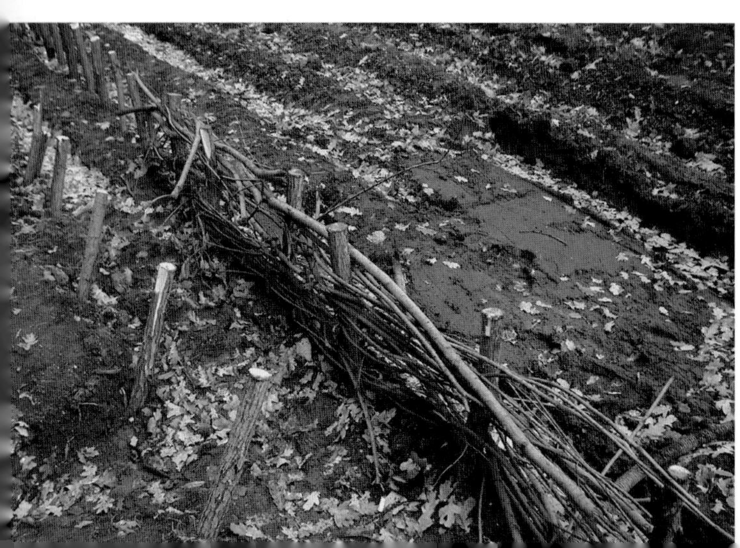

critical damage, more water than the Vltava cascade built in the 1950s and '60s. To prevent the break-up of the Svet dam, it was necessary to begin a controlled discharge of the stored waters through the palace park, spread out below the level of the pondage. The Svet pond waters then swamped the foundation and stone footings of the park fence and damaged most of the historical pool in the parterre part of the park. Extensive replacement of the fence footings took place and the pool was repaired, the works having to be performed very quickly given the closure of the road leading to the town's centre.

Kratochvile, the Historic Country House and Park

The flood had an impact also on the Kratochvile mansion, a jewel of late 16th century Renaissance art and architecture. Its neighbouring pond was built at the same time by the Lords of Rozmberk to supplying agricultural irrigation. However, the pond filled with the 2002 rain storm, overflowed the dam, flooded the area in front of the château and destroyed the stone banks of the stream in the south of the area. When considering the original damage, a procedure was selected that is not often used today, although proven in the past, of solidifying the banks with willow wattles. The historians were also greatly concerned about the strongly sodden surrounding mansion walls.

Maja Havlova

North Bohemia

Kresice – the Church of the Visitation of the Virgin Mary

The most heavily affected historic monument in the village of Kresice was the Baroque pilgrimage church of the Visitation of the Virgin Mary, built in 1729–1732 on the site of the older Baroque chapel by the renowned builder of Litomerice, Octavio Broggio. The building's structural stability was affected and the interior damaged by the flood, primarily the interior plaster and the movable items. The outer façade, repaired in 2001, survived the impact of water almost without any harm. The water that flooded the church was up to a height of 370 cm, and almost all inside features were seriously damaged. The main Baroque altar from 1763 with rich sculpted decoration was very seriously damaged as was the wooden pulpit of the third quarter of the 18th century. Both side altars of St Joseph and St Anna, in mid-19th century neo-Renaissance style, also suffered minor damage, as did the church pews and two confessional boxes.

In the face of the relatively extensive damage that the flood caused to the church of the Visitation of the Virgin Mary, demands for restoration for both the building itself and the movable items already began in 2003. Research on the building's stability was carried out, and on the basis of its results, securing of the vault ribs was started in 2004, along with minor mending of the lower rafters. Also subject to conservators' research was the interior painting and in the most damaged areas the paint was re-fixed. As part of the overall restoration, the damaged painting will be completely fixed and secured in 2004. The interior movable elements were already treated with biocides in [northern] autumn 2002 and in 2003 the restoration was started for the most significant historic features – the main altar and the pulpit. Both of these historic monuments were dismantled and moved to the conservation studio. Conservators' research on both historic features was undertaken that show older significant polychromy, and restoration was then begun. At present both historic features have been cleaned, and repainting and some retouch carving has been done. Conservation of the other movable heritage is also anticipated for completion in 2004, together with the overall restoration of the church.

Steti – the Church of St Simon and Judah

The late Baroque church of St Simon and Judah, built in 1785 after a large flood had destroyed an earlier church, was damaged, mostly its artistic fittings. The building itself was not seriously damaged, with the exception of the interior plaster, façades and entrances. However, in the interior the main altar of the second half of the 18th century was damaged, the marbling mainly suffering, as well as both of the side altars of St John Baptist and the Birth of the Lord. Fortunately, the altar pictures were not seriously damaged, but the painted illusory design of all the altars was more damaged. Unfortunately, this included the main painted illusory altar by one of the most significant Bohemian painters of late Baroque, Josef Kramolin. Major damage was suffered by the richly carved wooden pews of about 1730 brought here in the past from the church of St Franciscus in Prague and by the wooden Baroque pulpit of the second half of the 18th century, of which the lower part had almost completely disintegrated.

The restoration of the inside furnishings of the church was already started in [northern] autumn 2002 when the renewal and restoration of the marbling of damaged altars were undertaken and biocide conservation was begun of the illusory painted design. Over time, it became clear that the damage to that part of the church was the most serious, because despite repeated biocide treatment, mould on the paintings' surface kept reappearing. For this reason, the complex conservation has not been started yet, as its achievement is also dependent on amassing sufficient funds. However, in 2003 the overall restoration of the church pews and the pulpit was undertaken in the church interior, so that both of these items can now continue to serve their function as before. The completion of the restoration of the interior of the church, that is, the restoration of internal plasters, decoration, and so on, is planned for 2004.

Pocáply – the Church of St Adalbert

The architecturally unique church of St Adalbert in Pocáply built in the style of dynamic Baroque according to Kilian Ignaz Dienzenhofer's design from 1724 to 1726, was flooded to a height of about 130 cm. In the building itself the plaster, façades and entrances were damaged. In the interior the floor was damaged, sinking at the triumphal arch, and the movable items also damaged. The wooden refectories of the side altars from the period around 1735 with St Benedict and with the scene of Crucifixion was most badly affected. The pulpit of the first half of the 18th century and the Baroque carved pews of the same period were also markedly impacted. The main altar's painted illusory design by the painter of Litomerice, F Kutschera, was affected in a very similar manner as the altar of St Simon and Judah church in Steti.

The conservation and building restoration on the church structure were already started in [northern] autumn 2002. The early 21st century outer façade was not so seriously damaged and its treatment only needed cleaning and minor repairs. Already in [northern] autumn 2002, the most seriously damaged refectories of the side altars were brought to the conservation studio where they were restored at the turn of 2002–2003. Then during 2003 the overall treatment of the interior church furnishings was carried out. The church pews, the pulpit and the main altar were stabilised and cleaned. At the same time the floor was repaired. The restoration of the illusory-altar architecture by F Kutschera is planned for 2004.

Prosmyky – the Chapel of St Franciscus Seraphinus

The 1770s chapel of St Franciscus Seraphinus in Prosmyky was flooded up to a height of about 300 cm. The aggressive floodwaters caused considerable damage to the outer façade, which by contrast to the façades of the other churches, had not been recently repaired, and to the interior decoration. Due to damp's capillary action the wall and ceiling decorations of the second half of the 18th century were also damaged, although they were not directly flooded. Further, the building's stability was slightly weakened and the interior furnishings damaged, the greatest damage being suffered by the marble altar and pulpit of the second half of the 18th century.

The structural and conservation works in the chapel were mostly done in 2003. In both cases it was a total and complex restoration. The structural works included securing its stability, repairs to the truss, re-laying the roofing and repairing the outer façade, including its coating. The restorer´s work concentrated principally on the restoration of the fresco decoration of the vaults and walls, and at the same time the pulpit was restored and conservation started on the main altar. Also the interior door was restored, and the stone portals and stone grid separating the presbytery space. The overall treatment of the chapel of St Franciscus Seraphinus will be completed in 2004 with the complex restoration of the main altar.

Petr Hruby and Jakub Patek
Czech ICOMOS

The Imperial Mill in Prague 6 - Bubenec

Among the many examples from the Czech Republic, presented in the *Heritage at Risk 2002/2003* report in connection with the devastating floods of 2002, was the Imperial Mill, whose condition is still very alarming. This unique Renaissance building with its splendid entry gate based on designs by Sebastiano Serlio and a domed grotto was extensively described by Ivan Prokop Muchka (*Architecture of the Renaissance*, Prague 2001):

In 1584 the Czech Chamber bought an already existing mill which stood at the confluence of the Bubene stream with one of the branches of the Vltava, and work on Emperor Rudolf II's intention to build a kind of garden courtyard compound began almost immediately. Part of the cliff in the hill called Pecka, falling steeply into the water, was quarried out so that it would become accessible not only from the south, along the stream, but also from the middle of Stromovka park, from the summer palace. In this way, business operations could be separated from 'recreational' ones, which served only the ruler. Rudolf favoured this place because he could come here completely alone, on a path with beautiful scenery – the cliff overhang, tiny islands and the picturesque banks of the Vltava – and devote himself to observing the world of nature. (...) The layout of the 'recreational' part of the complex is very simple. It consisted of a two-storey building with a floor plan in the shape of the letter L; the longer side was in practice only an arcaded corridor. Both storeys ended on the west side with a shorter wing, on the ground floor with a passage to the business area and in the upper floor with a hall which could be heated by an 'Italian' fireplace. Unfortunately, in the second half of the 18th century the open arcades were walled in, and in the first half of the 19th century another storey was added. At the beginning of the 20th century the mill became redundant after the canalisation of the river and the complex was recently adapted for new intended uses.

FINLAND

Finland, with only 5.2 million inhabitants, is one of the largest countries in the European Community, located at the northern limits of settlement, being the northernmost agricultural country in the world. The climate is harsh for agriculture, and the Europe-wide directives have typically been planned for much warmer central European conditions. For these reasons up here the survival of the living countryside is critical.

Today we have an increasingly mechanised, semi-industrial countryside, marked by low-cost metal sheds, 'dryer' towers and rounded grain silos, as signs of a living countryside. A smaller and smaller workforce is required. The old wooden houses have a diminishing role in the new system; the built rural environment is in danger of losing its memory.

In the 19th century, just before the beginning of urbanisation and the mechanisation of agriculture, Finland's mostly rural population grew up in villages in ever larger houses. From the 1860s, this situation began to change. People moved to the rapidly growing industrial cities in Finland, but also went to the USA and Australia.

This process has increased since World War II. The modern motorised countryside did not need the number of horses or labourers. By leaving the traditional economy behind, we are losing many of our traditional rural log house types, such as boat houses (eg for wooden church boats), stables, cowsheds, sheds, various types of storehouses, barns, drying barns, smithies, even the number of 'pair-room houses', once so numerous, is diminishing in Finland. Wooden fences, piers and bridges are also in grave danger.

In the countryside, the old wooden main buildings are the last type to go, as buildings that are still in use survive the best. Often people have built their modern single-family houses next to them. Sometimes the old buildings are used as 'summer cottages'; sometimes not even for that purpose. In many cases people have left their farms altogether. Diminishing use also affects traditional open rural landscapes as in many cases they are closing in from vegetation regrowth.

As families may have lived on their farms for up to 20 consecutive generations, it is often emotionally difficult to rent them out, and quite impossible to sell the farms. As a result, even the main buildings are now threatened by a lack of maintenance.

Finland has several sub-cultures of extensive rural log houses, the best known in the Ostrobothnia and Carelia regions, but also elsewhere. The bigger the building, the more expensive is its upkeep – and the more likely its destruction. These large houses were originally built by large families, today there may be only one person with the upkeep of the place.

Problems with wooden buildings normally begin with leaking roofs - and taps. The basements tend to move due to frozen ground, and old, cracking chimneys are especially dangerous. However, renovation work can also be dangerous, as the wrong

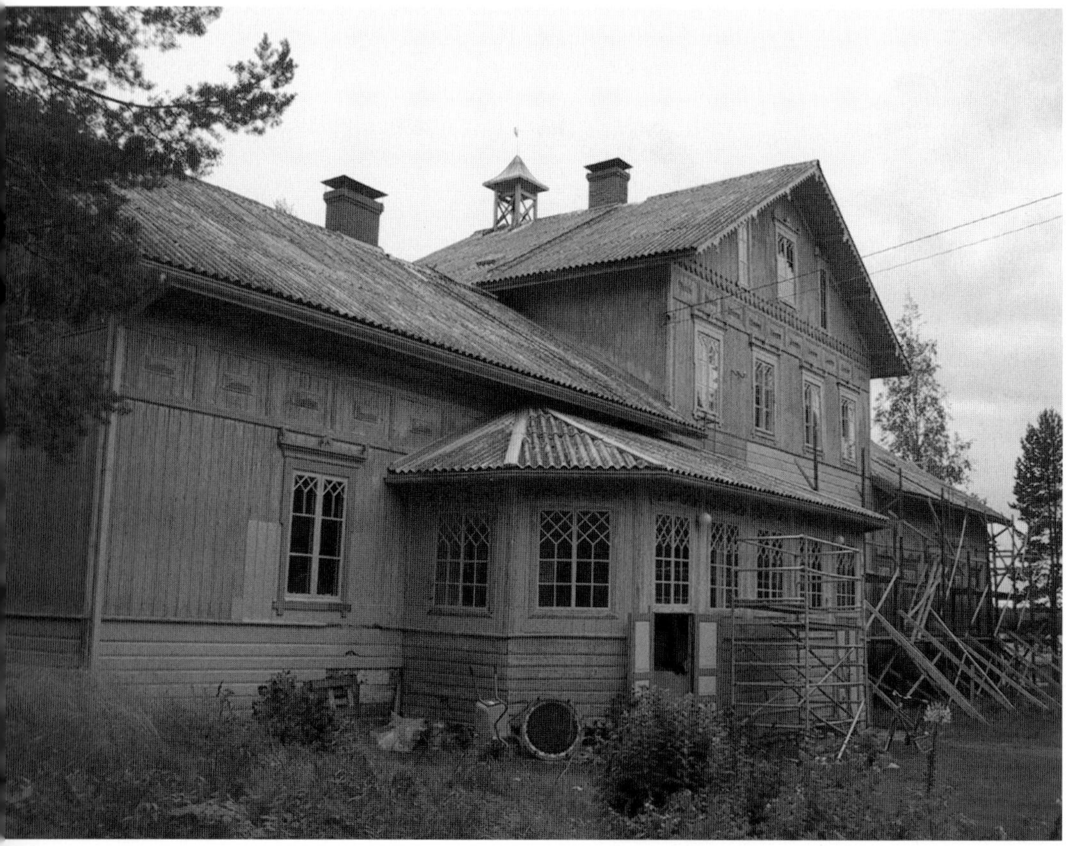

The West Façade of Isotalo ('Big House') at Tunkelo village. It is one of the biggest Finnish rural main buildings in central Finland (photo: Aaro Söderlund)

type of new windows and doors as well as crudely added external heat insulations too often distort and swell the fine old façades. Additions of modern sanitary services break up the floor plan, not to mention the effect of modern annexes. Even a new overly waterproof paint will effectively rot any wooden house.

Wooden buildings tend to be destroyed totally, whether by weathering or by burning, unlike stone houses, which can possibly be restored even after they have lost all their wooden parts.

Another clear speciality in the traditional Northern wooden building culture is that its building material has been in constant slow rotation. Houses were often moved as entire buildings to new sites and/or for new purposes, or as parts of buildings, or as logs for spare parts, from house to house, moving from a higher quality use down to lesser uses. Finally such reused building material became firewood. This explains why wooden buildings are often not 'authentic' as they tend to have elements from some other, older houses.

This suggests that there may even be room to adjust some international assumptions in restoration, such as expressed by the Venice Charter, that stresses an insistence on original building materials in a heritage site, based on the natural assumption that it would be built of solid, stable material like stone. The insistence of the authenticity of the building fabric would paradoxically end the authenticity of the wood building tradition based on recycling.

One may wonder what is the real Heritage at Risk. Should the risk be sudden, or can slow processes also cause acceptable risks? Perhaps we may agree that it does not really matter whether the risk is fast and noisy or silent and hard to notice, if we measure them by their results – built heritage that is irretrievably lost.

ICOMOS Finlan

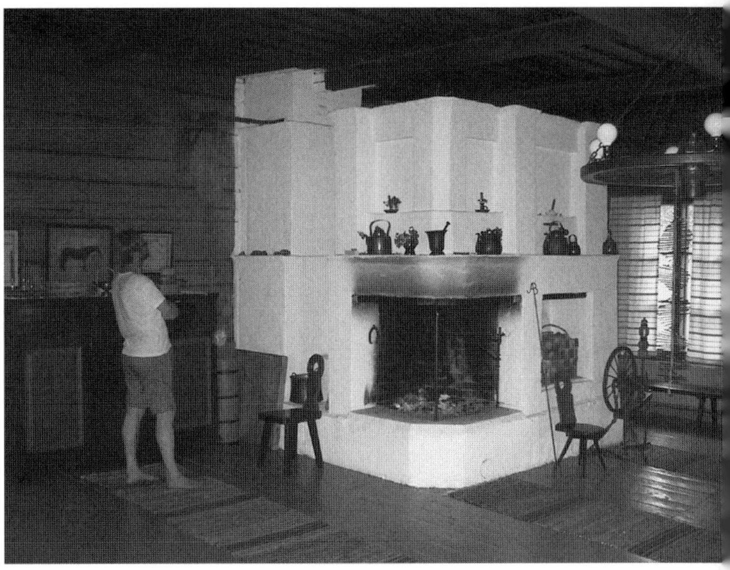

The Pirtti(Great Hall) and fireplace of Alanen farm's main building, near Isotalo (photo: Aaro Söderlund)

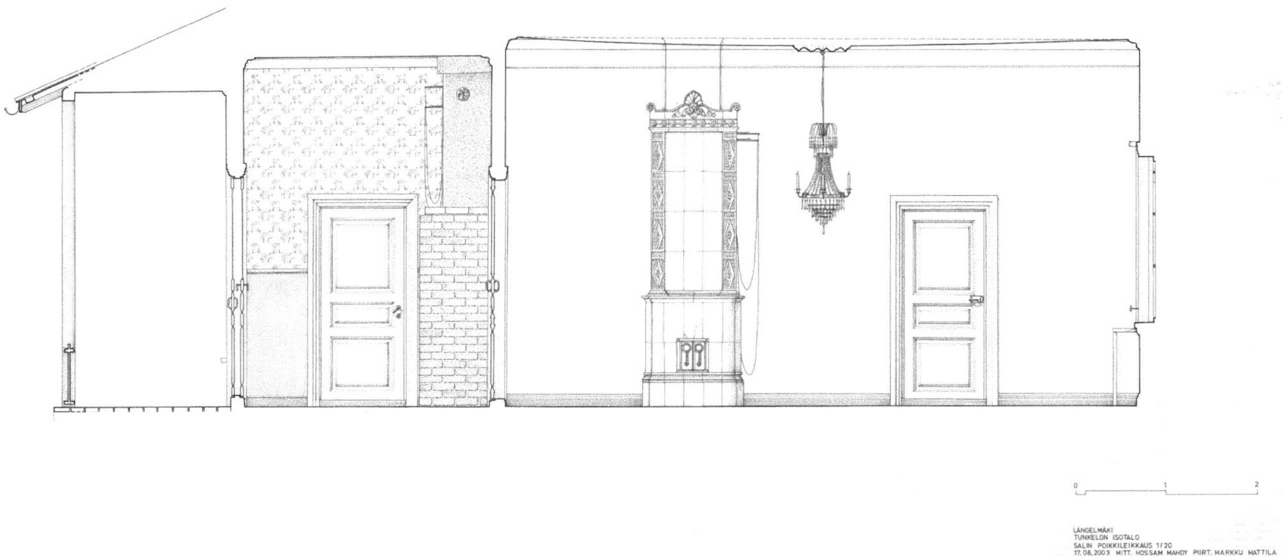

Section of the Salon of Tunkelo Isotalo (© Dr. Hossam Mahdy, Egypt and Markku Mattila, Finland 2003).

GERMANY

World Heritage site Weimar

Fire in the Anna-Amalia Library

In the previous edition of *Heritage at Risk* we gave an account of the devastating floods of August 2002 (see H@R 2002/2003, p. 25). In the meantime the damage to the historic building fabric in Saxony and Sachsen-Anhalt has largely been repaired. This year's report on conservation problems in Germany starts with the fire in the Anna-Amalia library in Weimar, which until the tragedy struck was a building and intact interior that had been an authentically preserved part of the World Heritage site (Classical Weimar, inscribed in 1998). The fire was a tragic accident which happened just when all the preparations had been made for the required

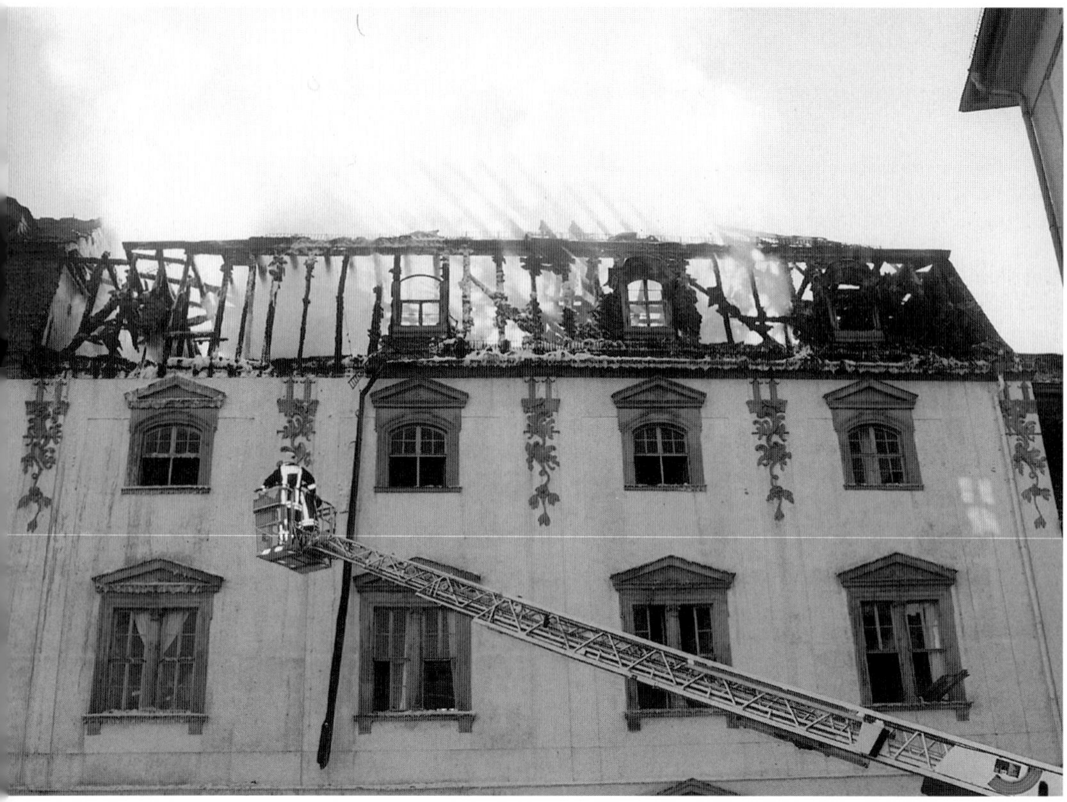

Weimar, Anna Amalia Library, west facade on the day after the fire (3 September 2004), smouldering fires not yet extinguished (photo: J. Seifert)

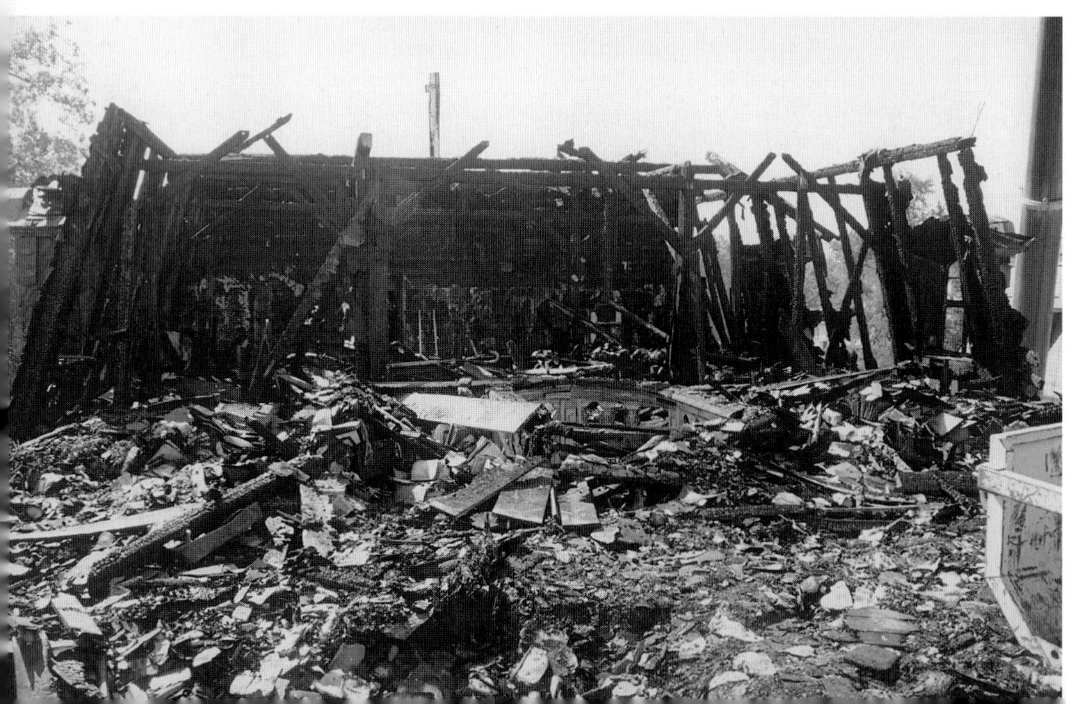

Top storey of the library building on the day after the fire. On the floor burnt shelves and books (photo: J. Seifert)

extensive restoration. Meanwhile the Federal Government and donors have provided considerable funds so that the building will probably be repaired soon. However, conserving the rescued books and manuscripts will take a very long time.

The fire in the Duchess Anna-Amalia Library in Weimar on the night of 2–3 September 2004 has affected a site symbolising in a unique way the intellectual world of German Enlightenment and the period of German classical literature. This library was founded by Grand Duchess Anna Amalia and directed by Goethe from 1797. The devastating fire in the attic which destroyed approximately 50,000 books, manuscripts and scores, for instance the larger part of the Duchess's collection of written music, also seriously damaged the exceptional library hall in the central area of the complex, built between 1761–66 based on designs by August Friedrich Strassburger. The hall's upper gallery in the mansard was lost with its ceiling painting by H. Meyer (after Caracci) as well as other paintings stored there.

However, the second gallery's stucco ceiling, which threatened to collapse, could be conserved. As a result, the Rococo hall's architecture that had its wooden elements saturated by water from fire-extinguishers remains largely intact and will be restored in the future.

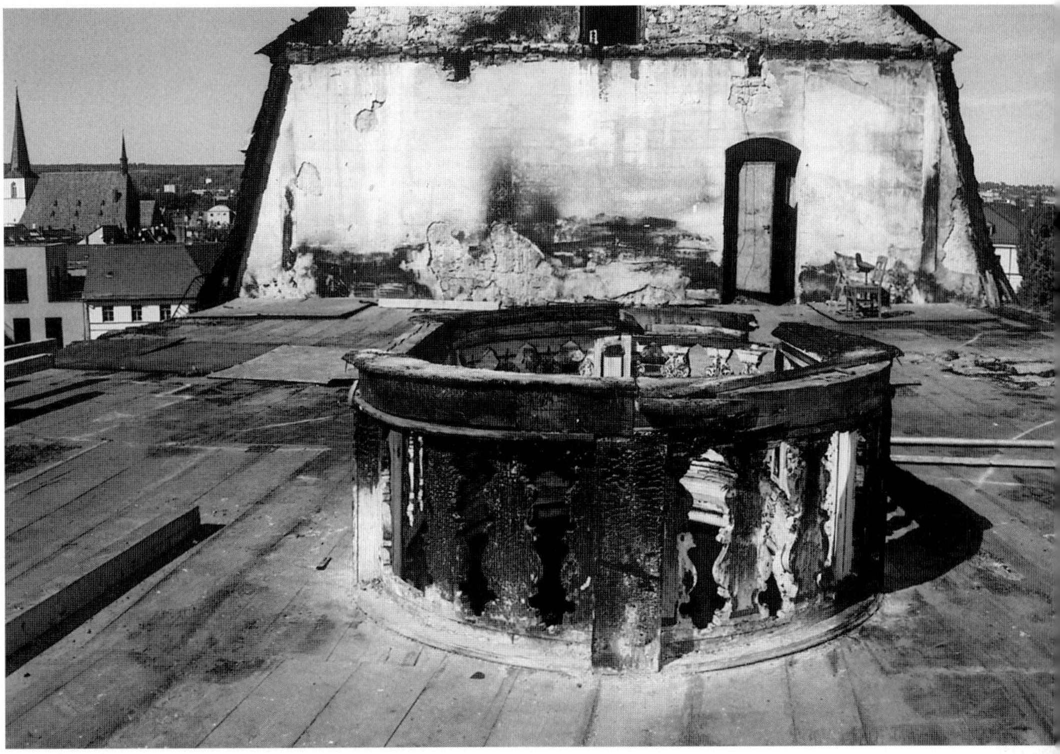

The cleared-out top storey of the library (photo: J. Seifert)

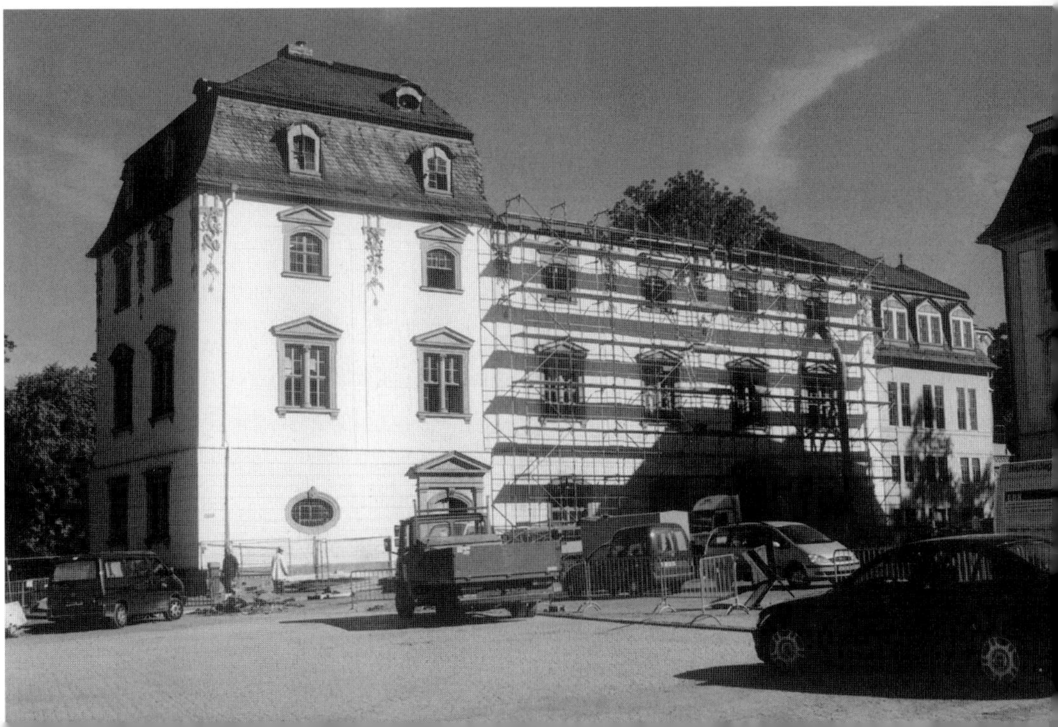

West facade with scaffolding for temporary roof (photo: J. Seifert)

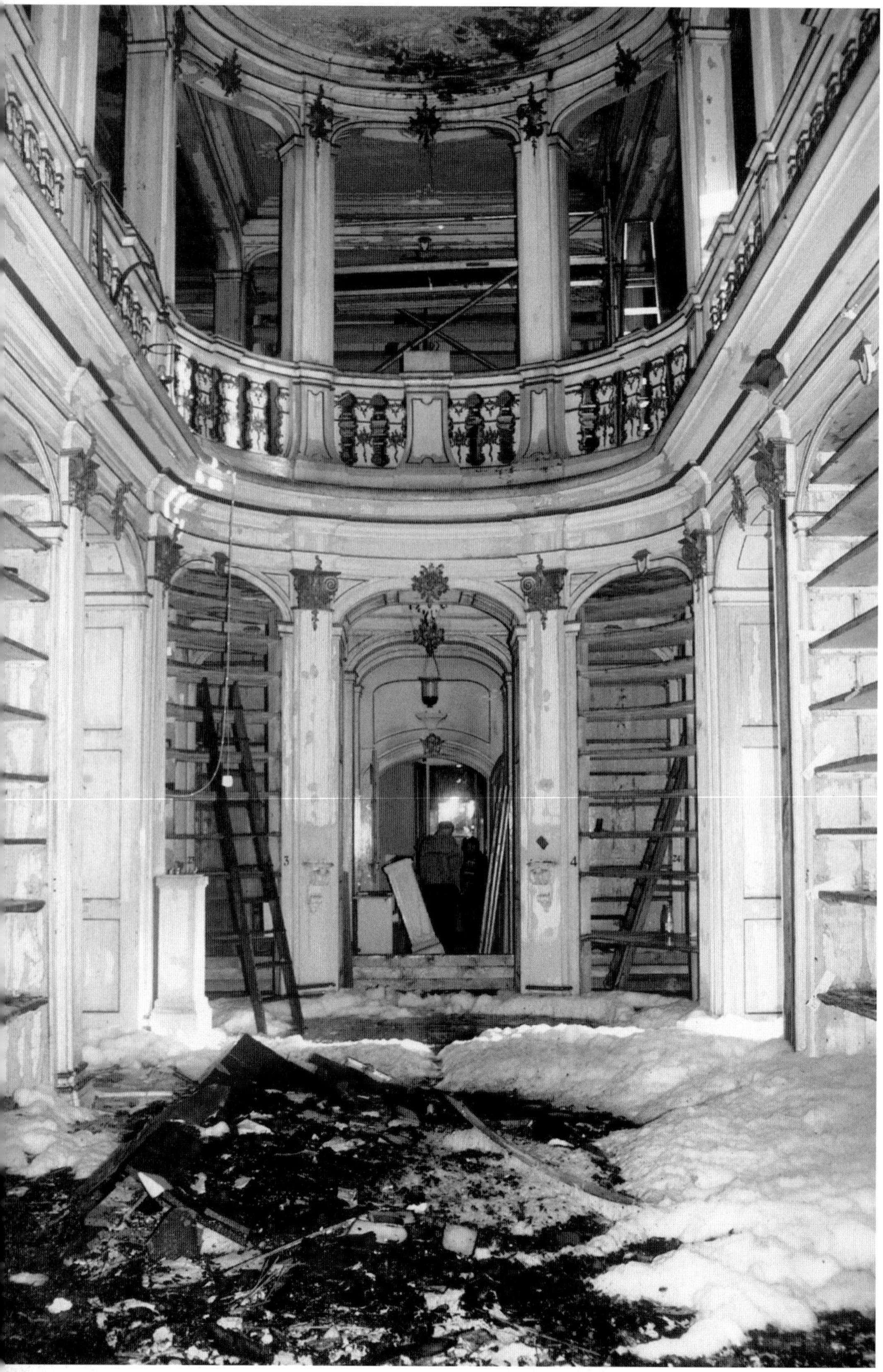

The cleared-out Rococo hall after the fire with remains of debris and foam as well as with provisional shoring (photo: J. Seifert)

Problems with high-rise buildings in Cologne and Munich

While the Wien-Mitte project, a cluster of high-rise buildings threatening the World Heritage site Historic Centre of Vienna and St. Stephen's cathedral in 2003, could be stopped (see *Heritage at Risk* 2002/2003, pp. 42–43), the City of Cologne has unfortunately not been willing to respect the visual integrity of Cologne Cathedral (see *Heritage at Risk* 2002/2003, p. 96). Despite all concerns, not only voiced by ICOMOS during a symposium on 14 November 2003 and despite public protest expressed at other conferences and in several newspaper articles, the City of Cologne approved its own high-rise building concept shortly afterwards without making any attempt to avoid or at least reduce the concept's negative impact on the World Heritage site Cologne Cathedral. Of course, this landmark of Cologne, which can be seen from afar, needs the buffer zone that was already required in 1996. Avoiding an appropriate buffer on the Deutz side of the river leaves the door open for the proposed cluster of five high-rise buildings up to 120 m high, which will probably dominate the cathedral on an east-west axis. The RZVK building is nearest the cathedral and beside the Hohenzollern bridge exit ramp, and at 104 m reaches the same height as the gallery at the base of the cathedral spire, whence countless visitors have enjoyed the panoramic view of the city.

Instead of taking UNESCO's and ICOMOS' frequently expressed concerns seriously and protecting the visual integrity of this unique architectural masterpiece, the City quickly made reality: the RZVK tower is almost completed. It remains an open question if, when and how the other clusters of 120 m high-rise buildings will be completed according to the plan accepted at the end of 2003. In view of these circumstances, the World Heritage Committee at its meeting on 5 July 2004 in Souzhou, China, inscribed Cologne Cathedral in its list of World Heritage in Danger.

The government of North Rhine-Westphalia has therefore set up a taskforce to prepare the report requested by the World Heritage Committee. This report will contain statements about establishing a buffer zone and the results of the 'townscape compatibility investigation', carried out by the University of Aachen.

The cathedral, situated by the Rhine river, a *masterpiece of human creativity* and *symbol of the endurance and steadfastness of*

Cologne, concept for high-rise buildings (2003)

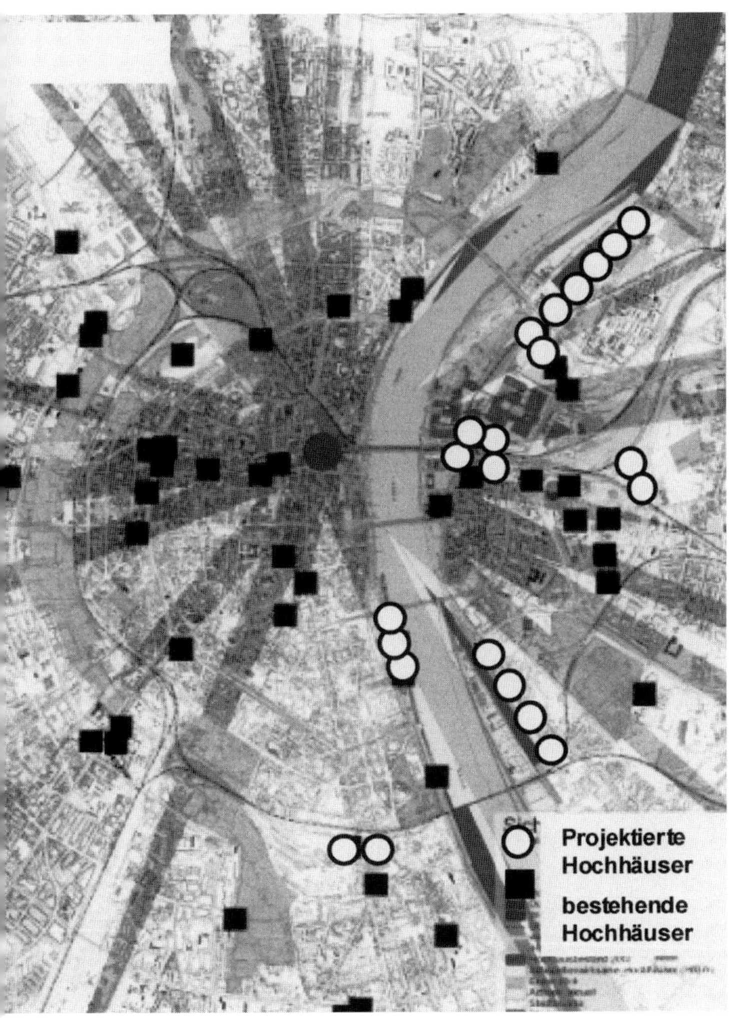

Cologne, project for the RZVK high-rise building with view towards the cathedral (computer simulation: Data Services GmbH)

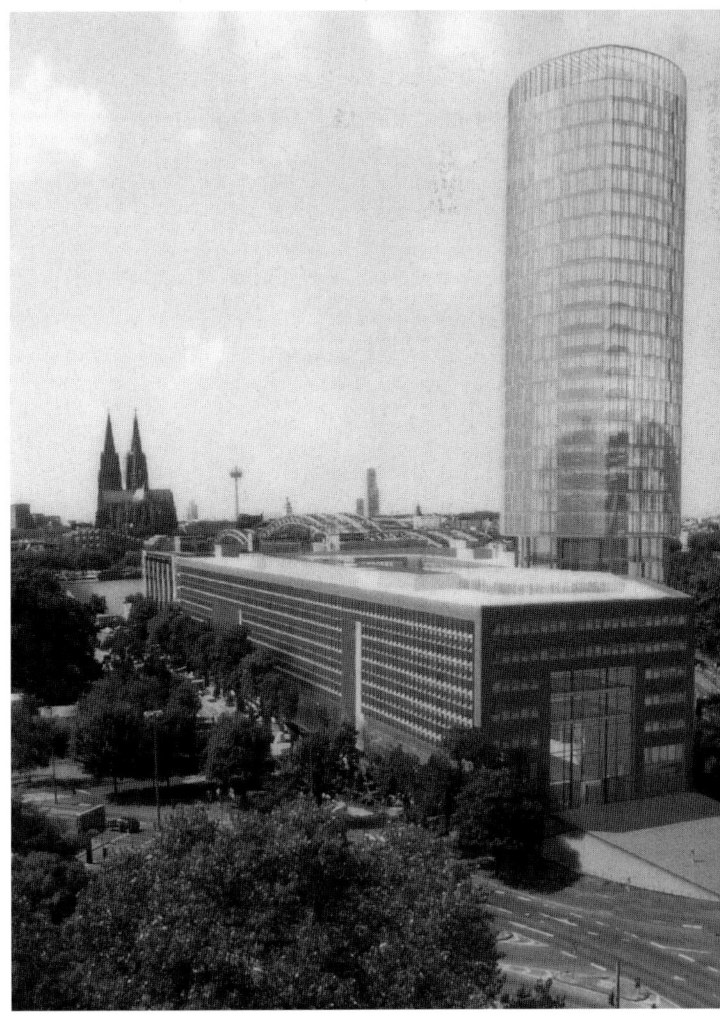

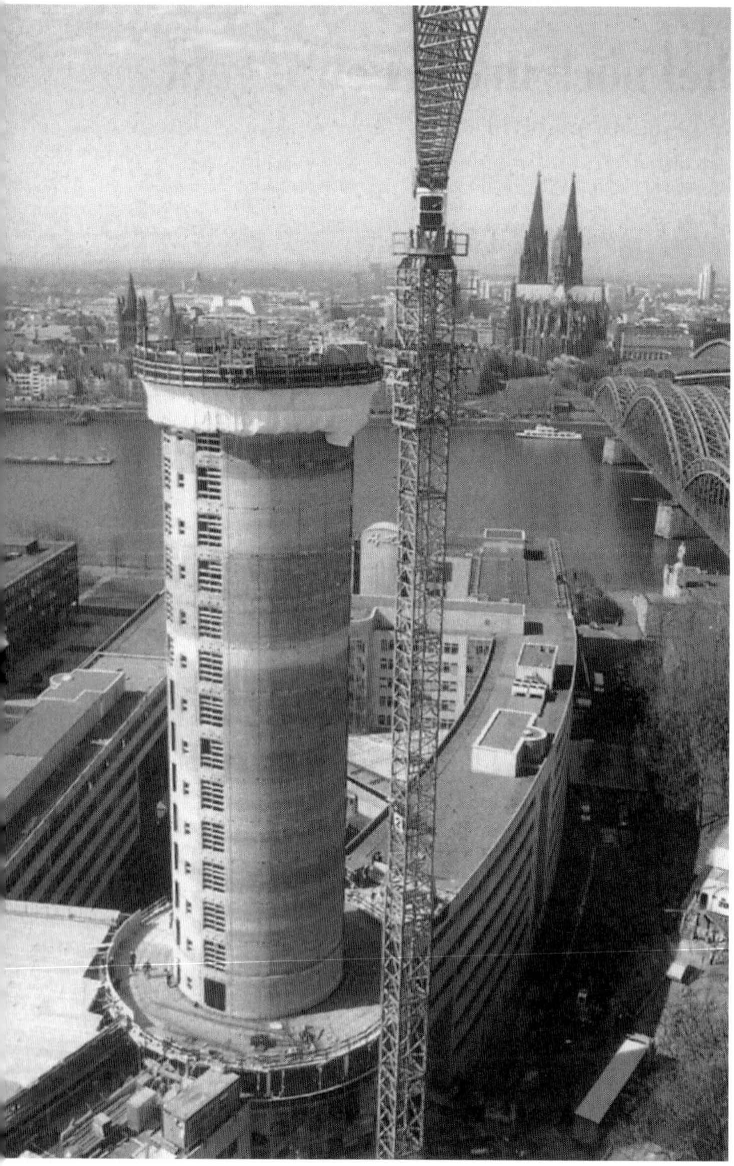

Cologne, the RZVK building during construction

Christian faith over seven centuries (text of inscription in the World Heritage List 1996), is one of the most outstanding examples of Gothic architecture in Europe, although the building, including the famous double steeple façade, was only completed in the 19th century, following the preserved medieval plan of the façade from about 1280. The cathedral's condition is relatively good and the building is very well looked after, in the tradition of cathedral stonemason lodges, by the Cathedral Conservation Organisation. As well, the condition of the area immediately surrounding the cathedral, also the subject of complaint for quite a while, is to be improved soon.

In Munich there was also fierce public discussion in 2004 about high-rise building projects, that threaten to disturb the visual integrity of important monuments and complexes. The Birketweg high-rise project, four buildings up to 120 m, would have towered above the pavilions around the crescent in front of Nymphenburg Palace and would have severely affected the outstanding complex of the palace and park. Public protest, also from ICOMOS, as well as a public petition announced in August 2004 led the city council to reduce the building heights to 60 m, so making way for a new development which will not disturb the Nymphenburg group.

However, the ruin of Ludwigstrasse, the magnificent famous avenue of King Ludwig I, cannot be restored any longer. This was caused by the so-called Highlight Towers designed by Helmut Jahn and constructed in the north of Munich near the exit to the Nuremberg motorway. When one looks from the Feldherrenhalle towards the triumphal arch *(Siegestor)* the two towers appear as if they accidentally stand next to the arch (see fig.). The Munich town-planning commission must have overlooked the consequences for this important axial view. Given such careless handling of high-rise projects, which could also threaten the famous city silhouette with the panorama of the Alps, an anti-highrise initiative has been successful: following a plebiscite on 21 November 2004, future multi-storey buildings in Munich are not allowed to be higher than the towers of the Church of Our Lady (99 m).

Cologne, the RZVK building during construction with the cathedral in the background

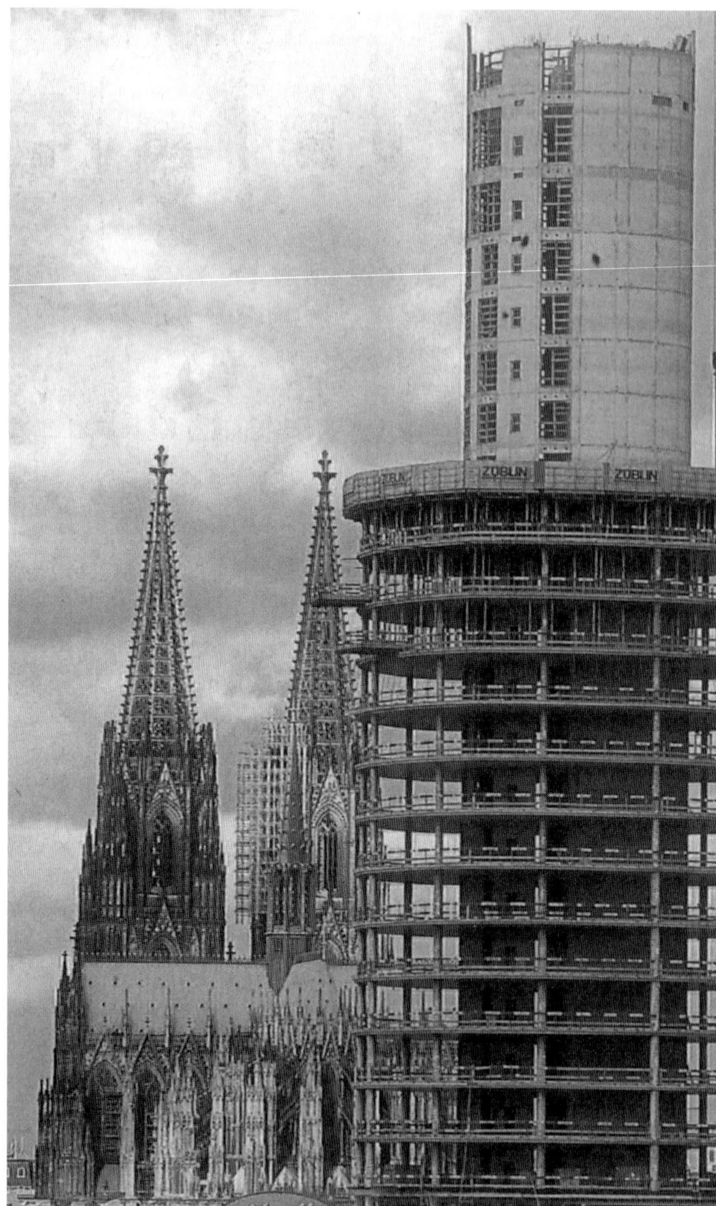

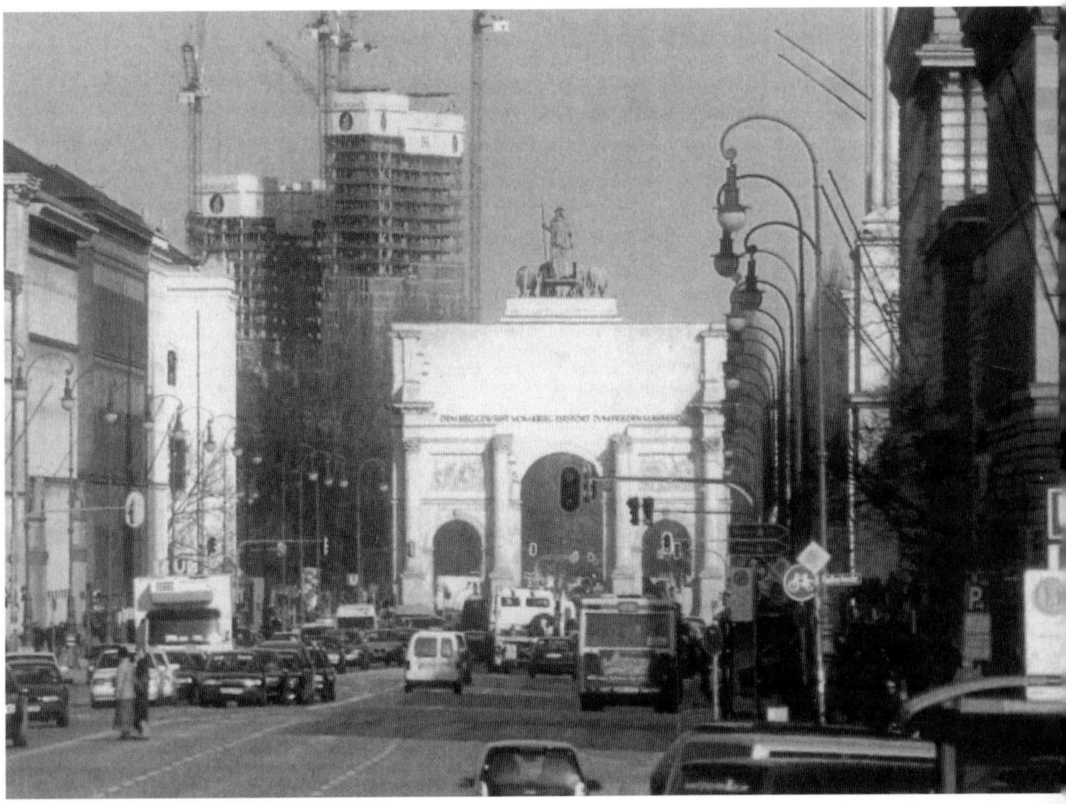

Munich, Ludwigstrasse with triumphal arch and the so-called Munich Highlight Towers under construction, February 2004 (photo: Heinz Gebhardt)

Munich, Nymphenburg palace ensemble threatened by four high-rise buildings in Birketweg (computer simulation: Planungsreferat Munich). Thanks to public protest this project was given up.

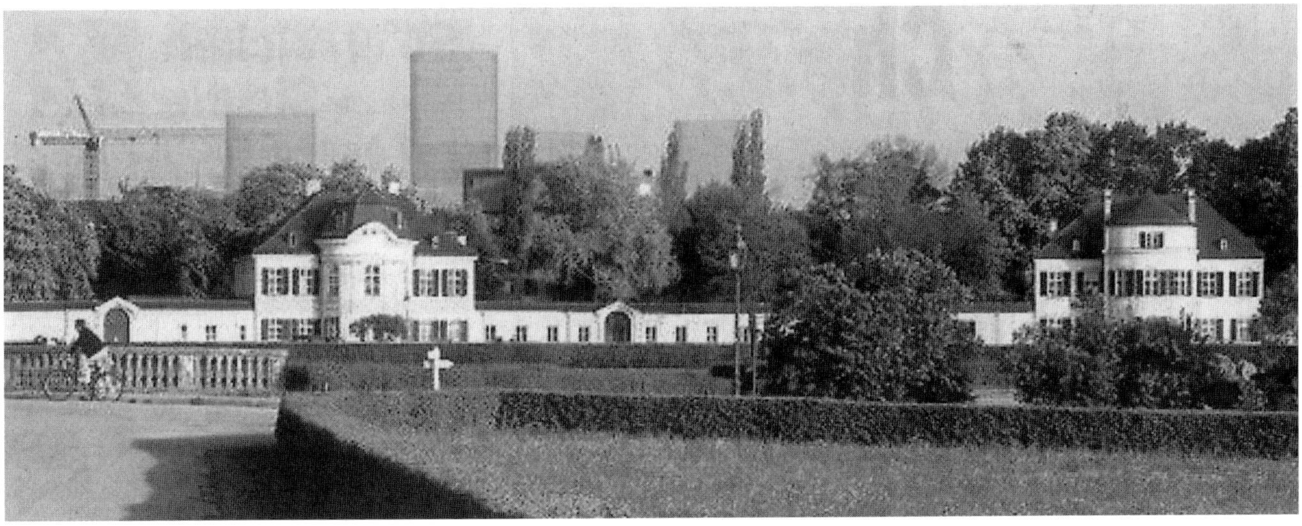

World Heritage site Quedlinburg

The unique Quedlinburg built assemblage, which with its numerous half-timber houses was inscribed in the World Heritage List in 1993, was literally saved from final decay at the very last minute. According to urban rehabilitation plans before the German reunification, entire old town quarters were meant to be replaced by prefabricated buildings, leaving only a few half-timber façades and thus destroying historic Quedlinburg. As a first step after reunification, the many dilapidated houses were provisionally covered and then repaired and restored one after the other – thanks to considerable funds from the Federal Government.

Initiatives by the Deutsche Stiftung Denkmalschutz, which chose Quedlinburg as one of its main funding projects, also need to be emphasised. However, here as in other historic town centres in the former German Democratic Republic, the declining population remains a problem that is difficult to solve as there is often an inadequate use for the historic fabric.

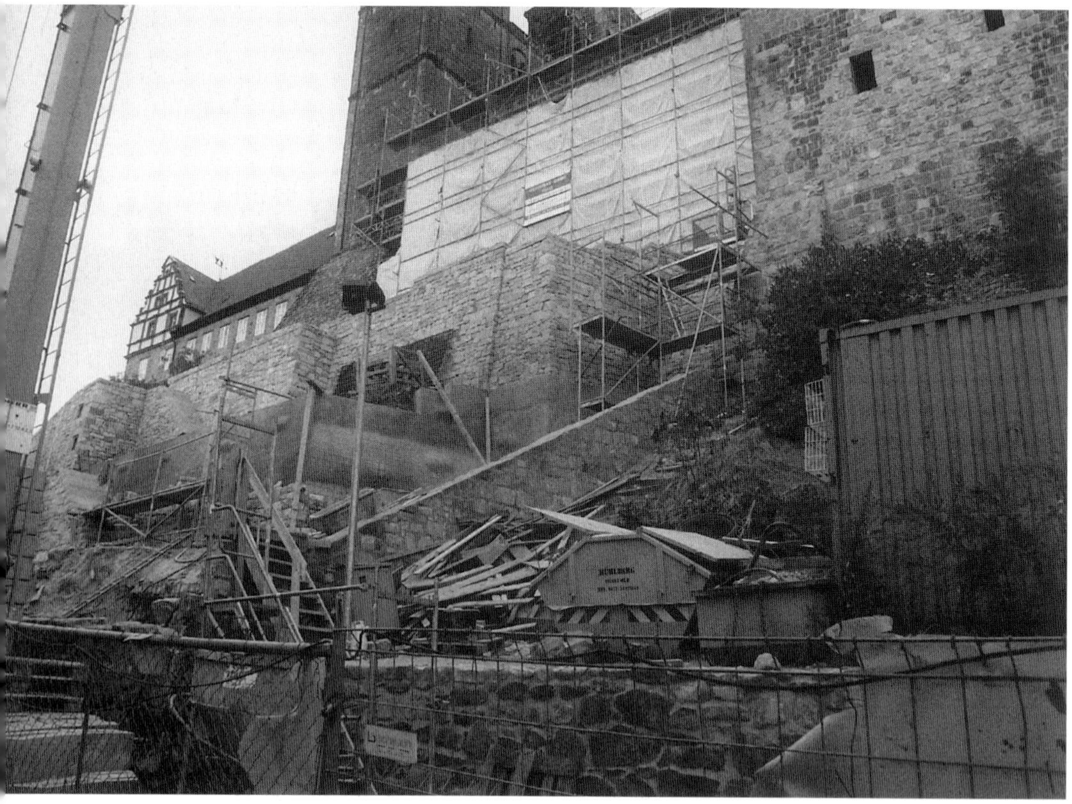

Quedlinburg, so-called Schlossberg, southern wall underneath the convent church during repairmeasures, October 2004 (photo: A. Hubel)

Currently, disquieting news is being spread that the so-called Schlossberg is at risk of collapsing, on which the former convent church of St Servatius and adjacent buildings are located. At the beginning of 2003, plans focussed on the urgent repair of parts of the retaining walls which surround almost the entire hill; at the moment extensive repairs of the stonework are being carried out on the particularly unstable southern side. Now it is even being said that the entire hill is at risk because underground watercourses are affecting its stability. Although no detailed evaluation is available yet, costs for the hill's stabilisation have already been identified: while the Deutsche Stiftung Denkmalschutz talks of 12 million euros, the local press states these measures will cost between 12 and 17 million euros. It seems advisable to consult more experts and to wait for their detailed investigations before decisions are made.

In all, the town suffers from a shift of retail trade from the old town to shopping centres and megastores erected outside the town on large empty blocks. These shopping areas absorb so much purchasing power that quite a number of town centre shops already stand empty. Furthermore, the usual discrepancy between ecological necessities and practical needs are found, as new estates and business parks have been erected in areas formerly used for farming, while no use is made of empty industrial sites. For instance, the buildings of the former seed growing company Mette (Harzweg 23) stood empty for years and were exposed to neglect and vandalism. Now permission has been given to demolish the majority of buildings, including the large extensions with Expressionist architectural details from the 1920s; only the main building from around 1900 is to remain. This large industrial complex near the old part of the town could have been used sensibly, even for a shopping centre. The buildings of the former infantry barracks, erected in 1909 in the triangular area between Gneisenaustrasse, Halberstädter Strasse and Schillerstrasse from designs by Knoch & Kallmayer are equally at risk. These two to four storeys build-

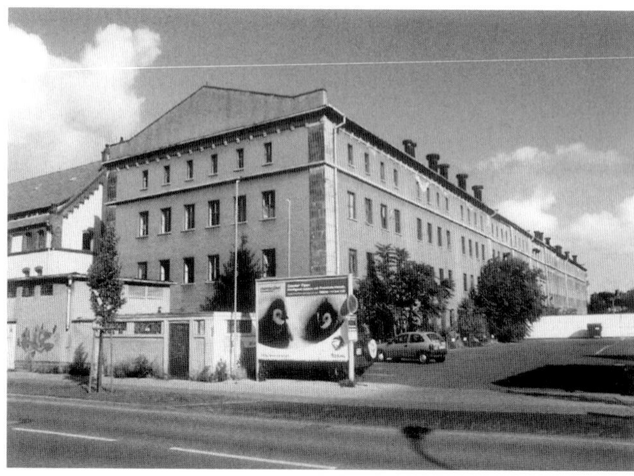

Quedlinburg, former seed growing company Mette (Harzweg 23), extensions from c. 1920 (photo: A. Hubel)

Quedlinburg, former infantry barracks, erected in 1909, buildings in Gneisenaustrasse, October 2004 (photo: A. Hubel)

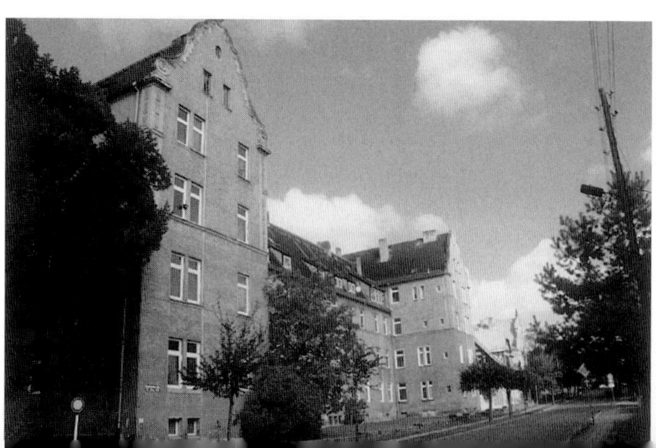

ings, now used for residential purposes, are a group with a unity of design, consisting of plastered façades and natural stone elements as well as gables with volutes and half-timbering. These details and the way the buildings were grouped make a very picturesque impression.

This group of buildings on the northern edge of the old town and its urban role must not be destroyed. The buildings where the *Bundesanstalt für Züchtungsforschung* (federal institute of breeding research) is still located, (Neuer Weg 22/23) are likely to face a similar fate. This complex comprises villas, banks and industrial buildings of the former Dippe Brothers company, which established a huge seed growing empire and erected the buildings between 1850 and 1910. The two villas built between 1893 and 1895 for the Dippe brothers in the Renaissance and Baroque styles are particularly splendid. As the federal institute has started to build a new building on the Moorberg near Quedlinburg, the result will be yet another abandoned industrial site, separated from the huge Mette industrial complex by only the river Bode and a road. The question arises whether it would not have been possible for the federal institute to remain in the town by using the grounds of both former companies.

World Heritage site Lübeck

Market Square

The problematic development of a department store on Lübeck's Market Square resulted in a UNESCO expert mission in 2002 to clarify whether the World Heritage status of the city would be affected by this construction project near the historic town hall and St Mary's church. This UNESCO mission concluded that the project would not threaten the World Heritage status. No representatives of UNESCO were consulted for the subsequent detailed designs of the department store. Instead, the City intends to invite a UNESCO delegation to Lübeck when the building opens in March 2005.

At present work is being carried out on the façades and in the interiors, while the aluminium roof has already been completed. The roof material which is atypical for Lübeck and the controversial shape of the roof emphasise the awkwardness of this building in the city's roofscape. Attempts are being made to meet UNESCO's demands for a 'diversity of use' on the ground floor by installing a bistro with tables on the market square and a small tea shop.

So far there are no plans for the adjacent plot of the former Stadthaus, demolished in 2002.

The Gründungsviertel (foundation quarter)

Another important urban project is situated in the *Gründungsviertel* close to the market square, the town hall and St Mary's church. This area was severely damaged during World War II and is not part of the designated World Heritage site. After the war, two vocational training schools were built in this area. These school buildings whose large size did not respect the historical town structure will be closed in the foreseeable future. In order to have some influence on future town planning in this area, the City of Lübeck commissioned an expert report, which recommends the demolition of the schools and the development of small plots for houses and shops. The frontages follow the historic courses of the streets, the plot structure however is based on a grid system using the measurements of the deep-level garages and not those of the widths of the historic blocks. This concept was developed in cooperation with the heritage conservation department and takes into account the historic mixture of residential and commercial occupancy as well as the possibility of erecting these buildings in stages.

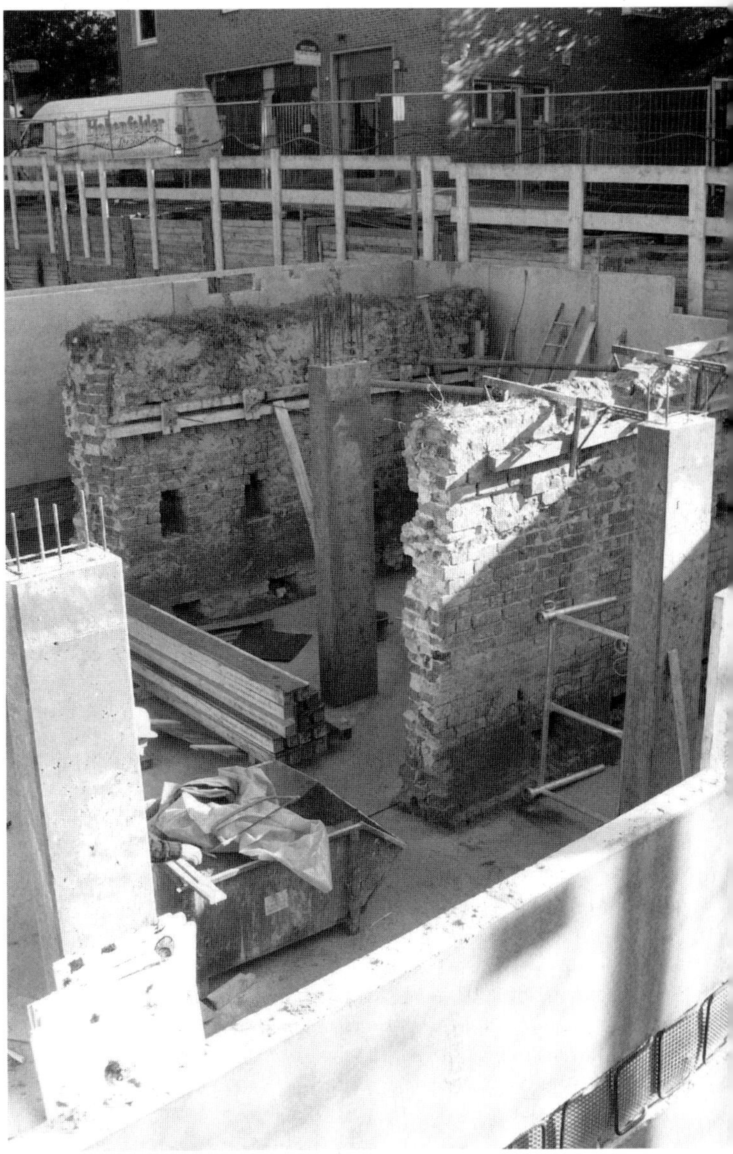

Preserved Gothic walls in the basement of the planned hall of residence (photo: Fröhlich/Reck)

Hall of Residence Alfstrasse / Fischstrasse

Despite the existing expert report, the City has in the meantime commissioned an investor to construct a large building in one part of this quarter. In this area where extensive excavations were carried out between 1984 and 1987, a hall of residence is currently being built. Before construction work began, archaeologists gave permission to remove the excavated medieval cellars, which contained relevant information on the City's history. Only thanks to the initiative of a concerned architect two Gothic cellar walls were left *in situ*. By removing all other finds, the cellar of Alfstrasse 9, which may be considered as one of the City's first vaulted cellars

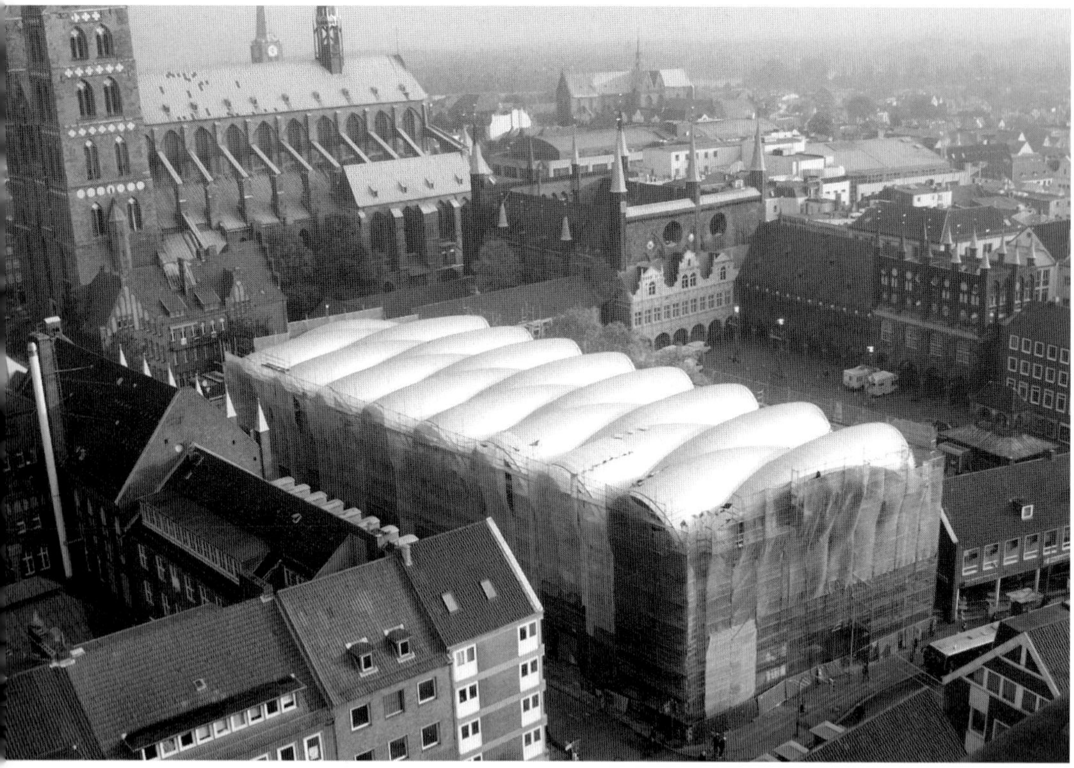

View towards the new department store at Lübeck's market square (photo: Fröhlich/Reck, October 2004)

dating from the 13th century, has also been lost. Given that the hall of residence is near public car parks and public transport the plan to build underground parking for 30 students could easily have been abandoned so that the remains could be preserved.

In spite of the careful integration of the hall of residence into the existing townscape a development similar to that on Market Square is to be feared. Again, under the pressure of potential investors, the City has given up its urban preplanning based on the historic plot structure, and instead has accepted large mono-structures.

For all building projects which may have an impact on the appearance of the historic city and its World Heritage status an advisory council was founded in 2003, consisting of independent architects, to give its expert opinion on such plans. So far all involved parties consider the work of the council as constructive and important. The UNESCO expert mission of 2002 recommended establishing a special World Heritage council, which is being set up.

Protection of the area and Management Plan

The heritage conservation legislation is supposed to be amended to include the protection of built complexes and particularly to improve the legal status of the old part of Lübeck. Nonetheless, this amendment has not yet been ratified as the legislator does not approve of the conservation department's proposal to distinguish between two zones, zone 1 being the old town on the island and zone 2 the surrounding water as well as the banks. In the latter zone alterations to buildings would only have to be announced, not require permits.

In 2002, the UNESCO Commission had recommended the preparation of a management plan. For other World Heritage sites such plans have already been developed, documenting the individual protected areas (for example, buffer zones), designating the World Heritage zone by all its various blocks and indicating the state of the inventory work as well as of the general development plans. Designating the banks which surround the old part of Lübeck as buffer zones would have meant that they would have the status of protected public space from where the skyline of the old town could be enjoyed. Such a buffer zone would have prevented the regrettable current development in the southern part of the embanked peninsula where the master plan has been altered to allow the construction of residential buildings right by the water.

World Heritage site Bamberg

There are still concerns about the World Cultural Heritage site of Bamberg regarding the present planning situation for the so-called 'City-Passage' in the area of Lange Strasse (street) and Franz-Ludwig-Strasse. The latest plans have given up the originally proposed carpark, but all the same still intend to completely infill the lots between Lange and Franz-Ludwig Streets. Yet there are buildings worth preserving and historically important architectural remains in this area, all of which are threatened by the planned development.

For instance, it is intended to demolish the rear buildings at 11 and 13 Heller Street, both of which have rich stucco ceilings and other interior decorations from the Baroque age. There are also remains of the old 13th–15th century city walls which should be preserved. Although up to now only four exploratory trenches have been undertaken to archaeologically investigate the area, the *mikwe* of the former synagogue has already been found. Other surface areas have not yet been excavated, although this is vital before any sub-surface disturbance can start. As all archival sources show that the former Jewish synagogue was located in the area of 11–15 Heller Street, it is highly likely that archaeological remains of this late medieval synagogue will also be found here.

Dieter Roth's Mould Museum in Hamburg demolished

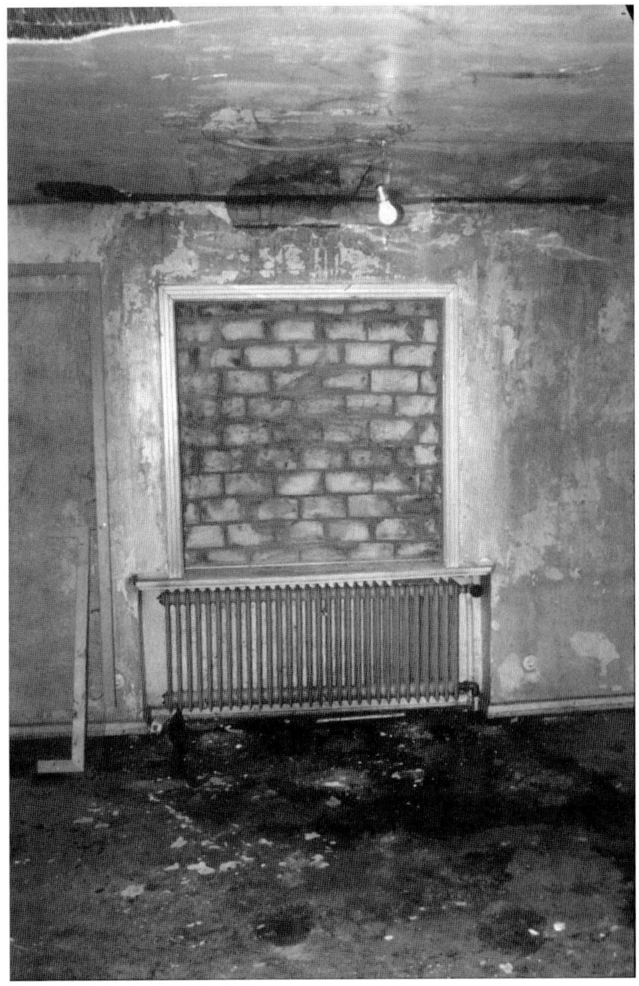

Situation before the demolition, room already cleared out, the frames removed (cf. Heritage at Risk 2002/2003, fig. on p. 97)

In the 1960s Dieter Roth (1930–98), whose work was recently fêted with a retrospective exhibition called *Roth-Zeit* in Basle, Cologne and New York, started to experiment with objects of chocolate and other perishable materials. His works of art were meant to be subject to a natural process of ageing and decay, even to total self-disintegration. This concept made him famous worldwide, but collectors and conservators have been faced with seemingly insoluble problems. From 1991, a Hamburg collector enabled the artist to install his mould museum in a former outbuilding in Hamburg's Alsterchaussee, setting up hundreds of objects mostly made of chocolate and cheese. The intention was to let the objects disintegrate, thus gradually including the entire building in the decay process. The mould museum was Dieter Roth's most important artistic legacy.

ICOMOS already reported on the mould museum and the threats to this *Gesamtkunstwerk* in the previous *Heritage at Risk* publication (see H@R 2002/2003, p. 97) – unfortunately in vain. In the meantime the museum has been demolished (beginning on 2 February 2004). While many objects had already been dismantled some time ago, the building itself was filleted wall by wall before the final demolition so as to gain further objects for exhibition. Apparently, there are plans to display the items in a nearby new building. But whoever believes that the exhibits gained from the

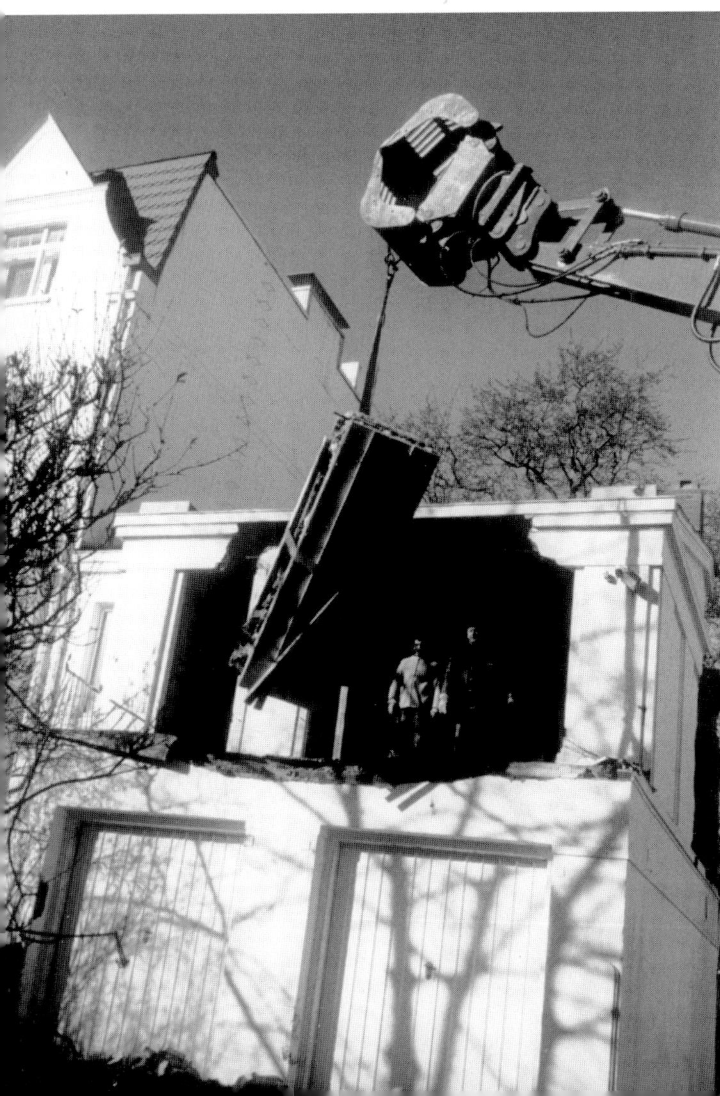

◀ Start of the filleting of the mould museum

Remains of the floor on the ground floor where the famous chocolate tower, which reached as far as the upper storey, was installed

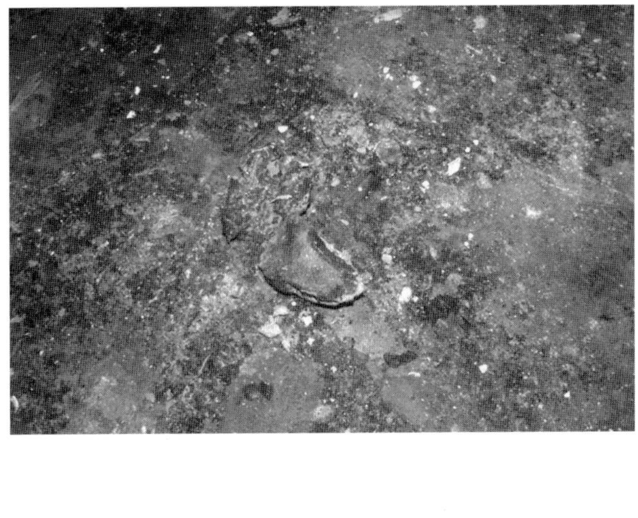

destruction of this synthesis have anything to do with the original idea of the mould museum has completely misunderstood the artist's intention. From an economic perspective isolated objects may have a much higher value than a decaying building, but the actual artistic idea was lost when the entire context was destroyed.

ICOMOS is documenting the end of the mould museum with a series of photographs, for this case illustrates the difficulties of preserving the cultural heritage of the 20th century.

ICOMOS Germany

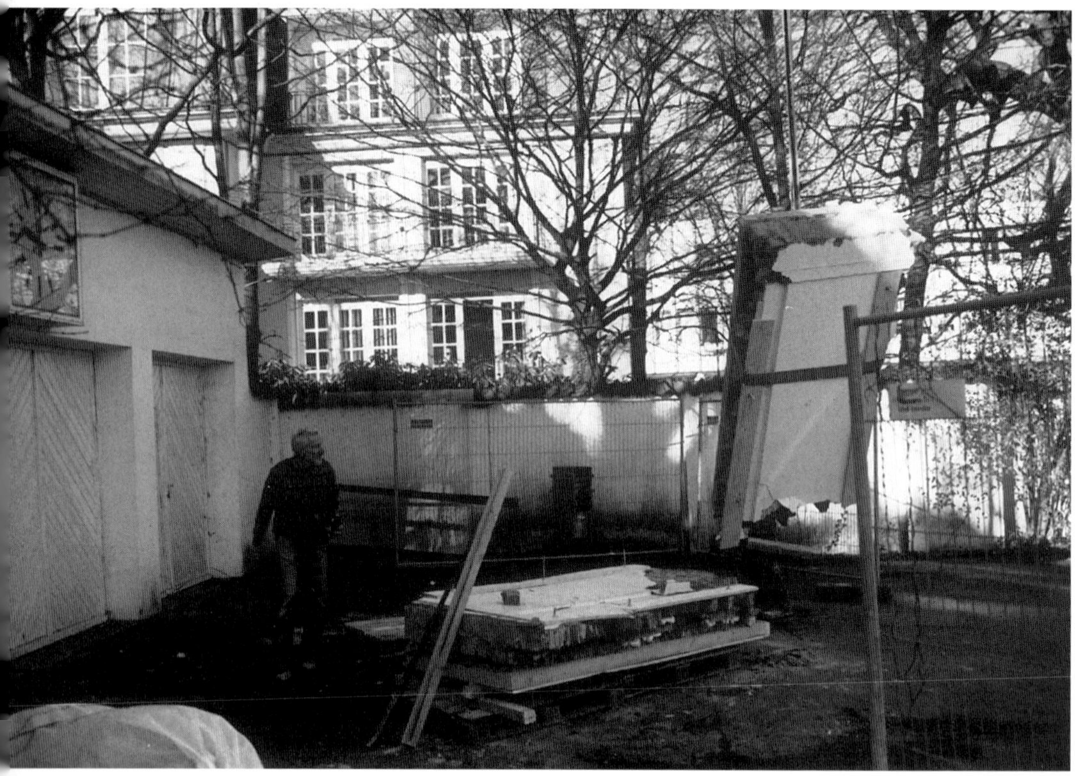

Cut-out wall pieces as future exhibition objects

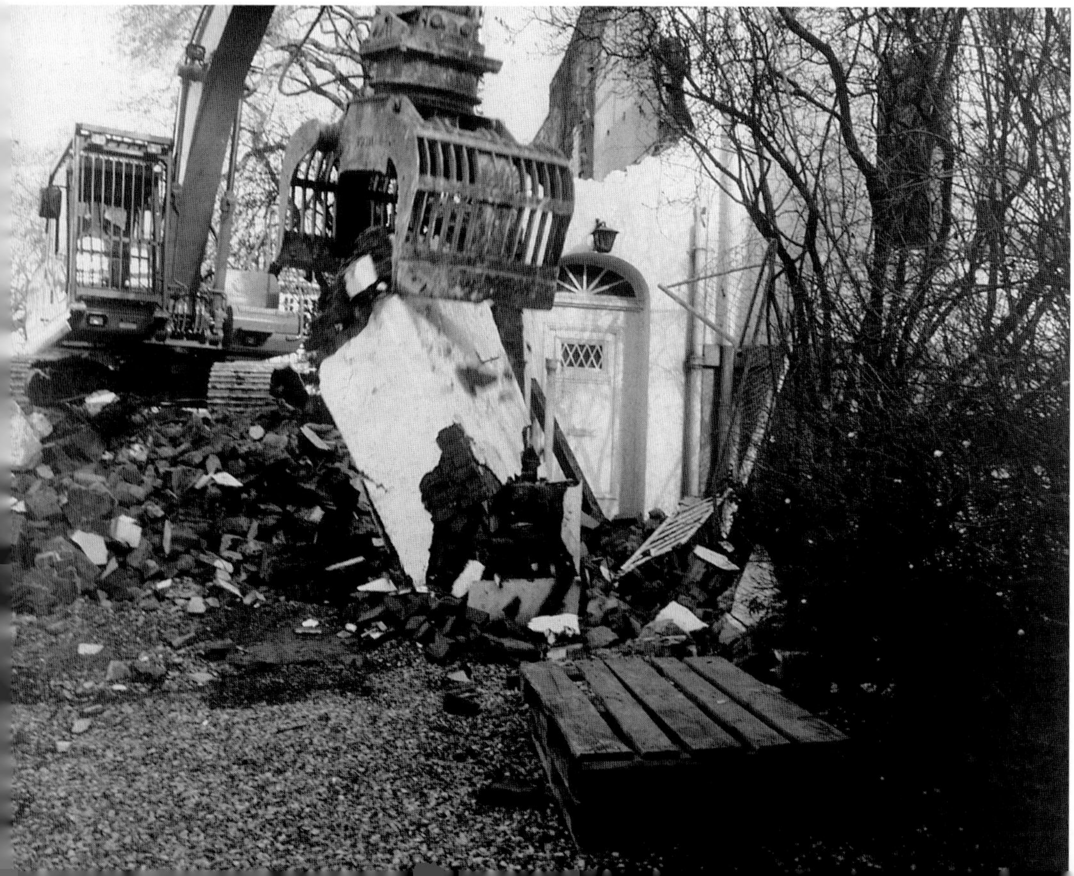

Demolition of the museum, on the left the former entrance

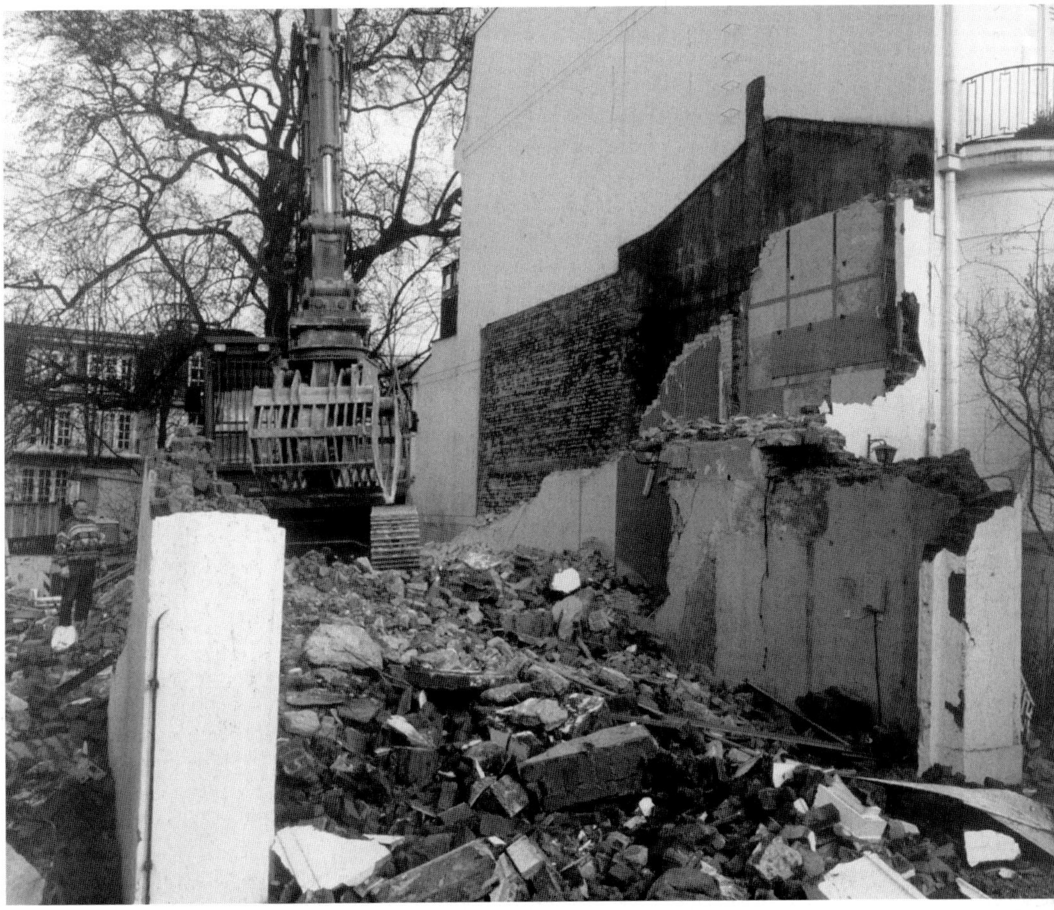

Demolition of the museum, on the remaining wall painted sections

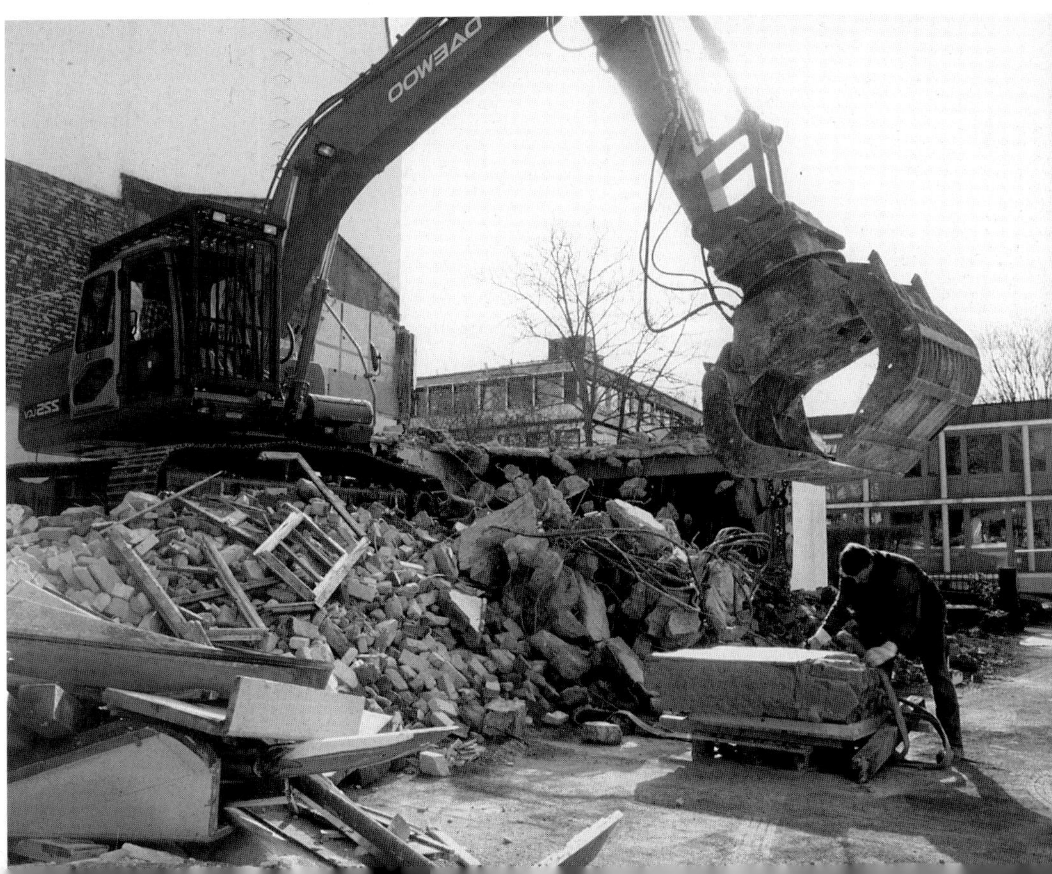

The demolition contractor rescues a remaining piece of wall with traces of the Gesamtkunstwerk

Historic Heuersdorf

Germany produces more than a quarter of its electricity from vast fields of low-grade lignite fuel. This 'brown coal' was formed during recent geological periods, permitting it to be extracted using surface mining techniques. The yearly earthmoving task of extracting 180 million tons of lignite from beneath 900 million tons of soil and rock is equivalent to excavating the original Suez Canal 15 times. This epic undertaking would deserve a gala performance of Giuseppe Verdi's *Aida* every four weeks, were it not for the relentless destruction of natural landscapes and historic monuments it entails.

Since 1924, over 300 villages have been devastated by gigantic bucket-wheel excavators burrowing through some of Germany's most fertile soil. The mining corporation RWE (operating in the Rhineland), the US-owned MIBRAG (in Middle Germany to the south of Berlin), and the Swedish state enterprise Vattenfall Europe (in Lusatia to the east) are planning new lignite power stations to compensate for the phase-out of nuclear energy. Only rarely are cultural landmarks spared or relocated in the process of mining. Most recently, despite nominal legal protection both as a historic architectural complex and as a Sorb minority community, the entire village of Horno near the Polish border was laid waste by Vattenfall.

Mining resettlement was instituted in the Third Reich as a wartime expedient. More than 100,000 people have since been relocated from their traditional homelands into new residential subdivisions. German federal and state authorities defend this policy as a necessary measure to enhance national energy security.

In the year 2000, however, the medieval community of Heuersdorf south of Leipzig won a milestone court case by demonstrating that European power trading had rendered its resettlement unnecessary. The 52 million tons of lignite beneath the village nevertheless equates to electricity sales exceeding two billion euros at the nearby Lippendorf power plant. The destruction of Heuersdorf thus remains a lucrative prospect for MIBRAG and the plant operator Vattenfall. A permission-to-destroy law (*Heuersdorfgesetz*), passed by Saxony's parliamentary assembly on 22 April 2004, is currently being contested by the village council before the state constitutional court.

Heuersdorf probably originated as a farming settlement that expanded into a rural community in the 12th or 13th century, when 4000 villages were chartered in the principality of Meissen. The oldest structure is the Emmaus Church, built largely of fieldstone, that was first chronicled in 1297. The absence of large windows identifies it as a fortified church, perhaps the oldest in Saxony. Carbon14 dating has yet to be performed on the rafter construction, which uses a remarkable arrangement of buttressing beams to support the cupola. Horizontal grooves chiselled into one cornerstone depict the devil's futile attempts to claw his way into the building. The church now defends the northern access to the town from the assault of MIBRAG excavating equipment. A number of sturdy three-sided brick farm-houses closer to the mine have however already been vacated.

The origins of the second, Tabor Church are difficult to unravel. The present structure is exemplary for regional period architecture of the 19th century, with opposing galleries suitable for performing the two-choir works of Johann Sebastian Bach. The previous building it replaced contained a bell inscribed with the year 1388. The church stands at the southern boundary in what was once Grosshermsdorf, which was administratively united with Heuersdorf to its north in 1935. A number of houses erected along the main connecting thoroughfare merged the villages, thus defining a distinct phase of development. A subsequent chapter is evi-

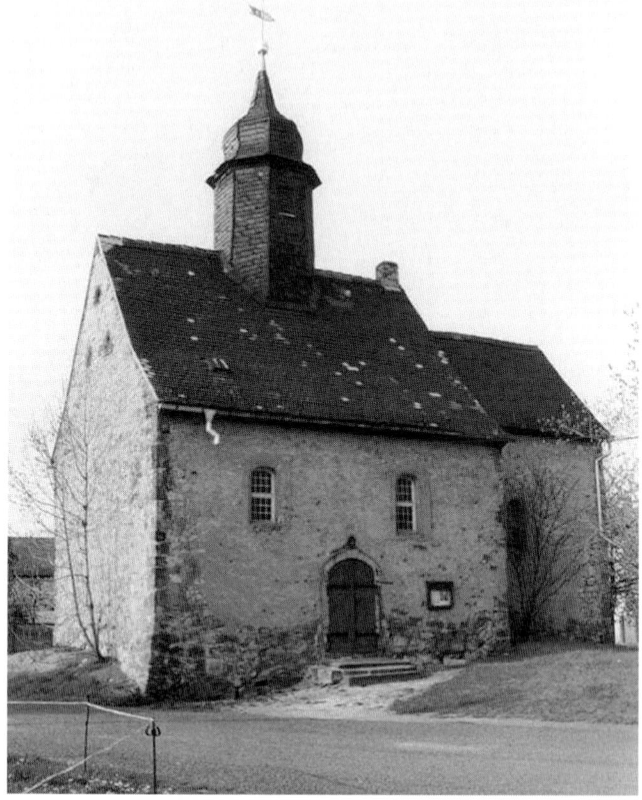

Heuersdorf, Emmaus church

Heuersdorf, Tabor church, interior

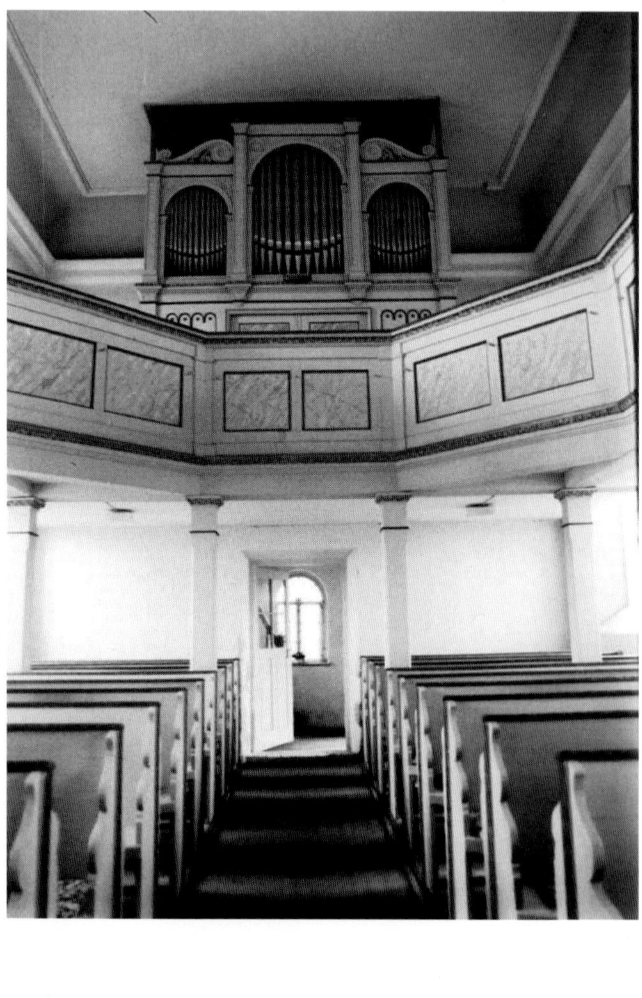

dent in scattered collectivised farm buildings added after World War II.

Heuersdorf remained an intact Christian community during the Marxist regime of 1945 to 1989, with congregation members maintaining and restoring both churches. Yet Lutheran officials are now condoning the demolition of these structures under the supposition of employment benefits. In fact, however, the devastation of the neighbouring village of Breunsdorf in 1995 has not diminished the emigration of young people from the region. The jobless rate persists at over 23 percent, or about 2.3 times the national average, because of mining rationalisation and limited employment alternatives.

A number of events surrounding Heuersdorf contribute to an understanding of German history. Grosshermsdorf was initially an outpost of a neighbouring town that was destroyed during the Hussite Wars in the early 15th century. Martin Luther's wife Katharina von Bora was born in Lippendorf and returned as a widow to the nearby farming manor at Zöllsdorf, which was devastated in 1981 by the same Schleenhain mine that currently encroaches on Heuersdorf. At least one Heuersdorf family traces its lineage to the Thirty Years' War. The villagers were forced to billet soldiers during the decisive battle of Lützen in 1632, at which the Swedish king Gustavus II Adolphus was killed shortly before his army swept to final victory.

Grosshermsdorf contains a feudal knight's brickwork residence (*Rittergut*) and the timbered homesteads of several farmers who succeeded in freeing themselves from his indenture. The burgeoning local economy attracted blacksmiths, saddlers, and other nonpropertied tradesmen to auxiliary buildings flanking the residence. A manor house on the opposite side of the courtyard was subsequently converted for use as a schoolhouse and town hall.

The most famous historic figure from the village is Alexander Clarus Heinze, a delegate to the Dresden Parliament of 1848–49 and the ill-fated commander of the Communal Guards in Germany's unsuccessful democratic revolution.

Heuersdorf has housed families displaced by mining and postwar refugees from Eastern Europe. In 2001, it was the venue of the Third Climate Conference of German Youth (after Bonn and Berlin) that analysed and criticised the excessive greenhouse gas emissions of lignite power generation.

Following German reunification in 1990, Heuersdorf had about 320 inhabitants. Its current population has been reduced to less than 150 by MIBRAG resettlement campaigns. The sizeable financial compensation offered by the mining company cannot be willed to heirs, explaining the predominance of elderly people who have left the village.

The remaining population is intent on preserving the 43 registered buildings in the embattled community. The legal outcome of this conflict could be of incalculable importance for maintaining the historic fabric of other regions. RWE plans the destruction of 18 further villages in the Rhineland for its Garzweiler II mine. MIBRAG and Vattenfall have not issued corresponding details for eastern Germany, but they have already announced the construction of three new lignite power plants.

Jeffrey H Michel
Energy Coordinator of Heuersdorf

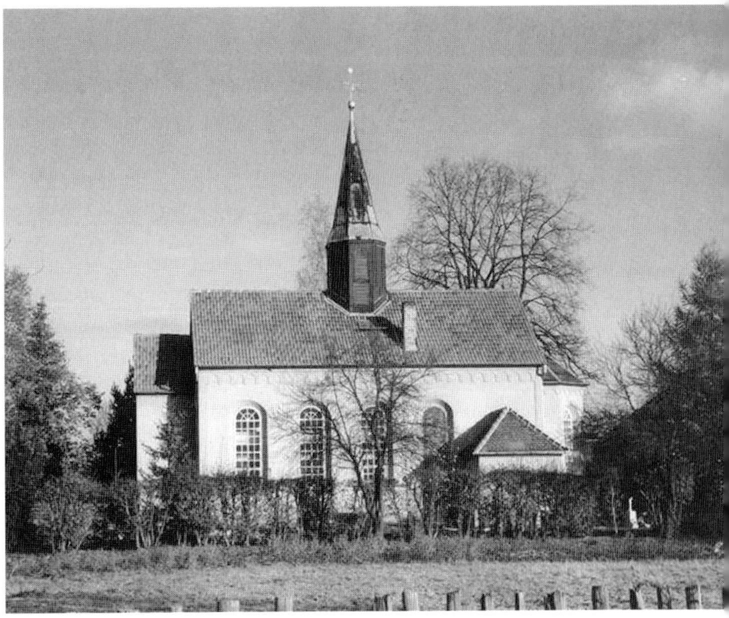

Heuersdorf, Tabor church

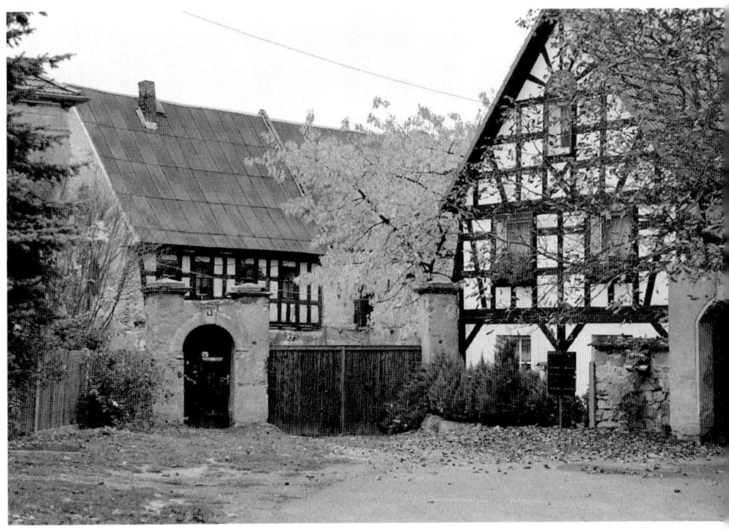

Heuersdorf, farmhouse

Feudal knight's farm

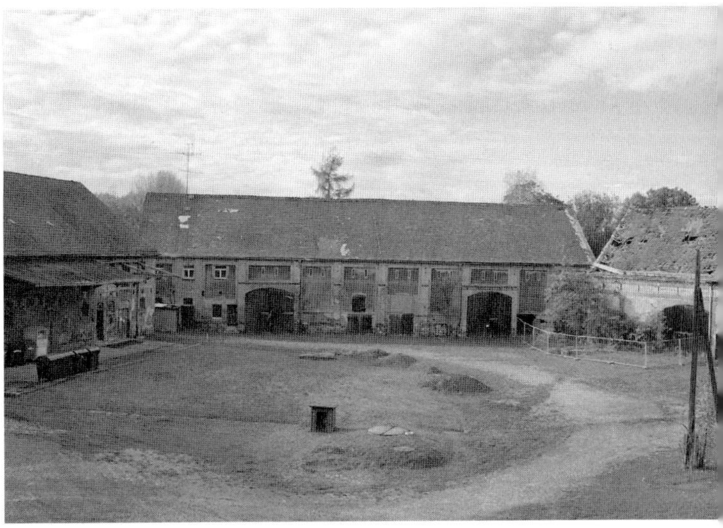

GUINEA
Sites and Monuments linked to Slavery

Dedicated to the International Year of the Campaign against Slavery and its Abolition

Framework and objectives

ICOMOS Guinea's current 2004–2005 report has at its aim to improve conditions for the conservation and improvement of heritage in Guinea, an African country, qualifying as the country that embodies West Africa, because of the richness of its natural and cultural heritage. The aims of this report are as follows:

- To participate in ICOMOS' regular assessment and awareness raising about the risks which cultural heritage suffers around the world
- To raise national awareness and for Guinea's development partners whilst at the same time to focus the international scientific community's attention on the particularly unfavourable conservation condition of cultural heritage places in this country.

The Committee chose to dedicate its report to the 2004 International Year of the Campaign against Slavery and its Abolition, proclaimed by the United Nations and organised by UNESCO. This choice is justified when one knows that in Guinea there are sites and monuments that are most important heritage places in this African region, whether well or little known, this refers to the phenomenon of slavery.

Choice of theme

The issue regarding the protection of cultural heritage places linked with the Negro Trade frequently returns to the agenda of ICOMOS Guinea meetings. However, unanimity was not free at the outset on the choice of this theme for the annual report.

This has prompted difficult discussions and three inclinations are outlined:

- the option of working on an 'ordinary' report about Guinean heritage places at risk, as previously in the 2001-2002 report,
- the choice of the theme recommended by ICOMOS for the celebration of the International Monuments Day 'Earth and Earthen Architecture',
- the option of joining the movement to celebrate the International Year of the Campaign against Slavery.

We confirm that in any case, the Guinea National Committee of ICOMOS does not have or practically has no means to carry out its plans and ideas, and thus can supply information that is more pertinent than contained in its preceding report. On the other hand, it is important to emphasise this aspect, in knowing the Committee has found itself confronted by real constraints and that its priority is to make sure of the best means to set this up and start. As a result, in the space of one year, it is inclined to deliver the information that reflects the approximate current condition of the country's cultural heritage sites. A consensus for the third option was finally reached, the report to be made on the state of cultural heritage slavery sites in Guinea.

Sources and sites of evidence of the Transatlantic Negro Trade

Finding any emerging remains is unlikely for the stream of Trans-Saharan deportation of Blacks which was made from the 2nd century BC, until about the 19th century. This is unlike the considerable evidence of the Transatlantic Trade in Blacks as well as a sort of 'interior trade' feeding 'domestic slavery'. The sources that are used, particularly the documentary records sources and oral history, bear witness to the past practice of these two last forms of slavery in the communities which peopled the four natural and cultural regions of the country, that is, Maritime Guinea (to the west, the region with first contact with European traders) Central Guinea, or Foutah Djalon (where there was domestic slavery until the 20th century), Forested Guinea (which was strongly touched by the Atlantic trade) and Upper Guinea (where since the Mansa period, there were the Mandingue sovereigns of the 13th to 15th centuries).

Several segments of the journeys linked the interior regions with the Atlantic coast, where slaves were embarked for the Americas. Of all the areas for the destination and embarkation of slaves, that of Rio Pongo (actually the Boffa Prefecture) presents the most characteristic site as this area was the most active during the Negro Trade.

In this region the trade was long-lasting and made the business of the Mulatto Families, of whom one was Lady Nyiara Lightburn, the famous 'Queen of Nyiara Belli', who died in 1880, at 120 years of age. This woman was renowned as one of the principal players in the slave trade in the 18th and 19th centuries. She lived in Faringhya, the 'slavers' city', located in the Rio Pongo swamp, between 10°17' latitude north and 13° 59' longitude west, and watered by two rivers, the Rio Pongo and the Fatala. She held the largest factory in the country with 6000 slaves under her command.

Both in the interior of Guinea as in the coastal zones of the destination, one notes the remarkable presence of Guinean cultural heritage slave sites and which have been the object of study of the first activities of the project 'The Slave Route' in Guinea. Mamadou Lefloch Camara and Mamadi Koba Camara, ICOMOS Guinea members, have undertaken historic research on the Negro trade in Maritime Guinea (Rio Nunez) and Upper Guinea (Baliya province) respectively. Other historians such as the Honorable feu Facinet Béavogui have also led similar research in other regions of the country.

Types of heritage places

The research has enabled the methods of capture and subjugation of the slaves, those involved and the routes to be dealt with. In each of the regions of the country one can gather the sequence of facts related to names and place names from local languages, which facilitated to some level the characteristic sites of the slave trade:

- The hunt and capture sites (alongside waterways, isolated spaces, platforms for the slave-traders …)
- Billeting quarters (outside permanent human settlement)
- Slave markets (of which some are located beyond inhabited sites ...)
- Conquest sites (stone scatter sites, some of flint-knapping)
- Slave holding centres and entrepôts

- Embarkation sites (wharves on the Rio Pongo, Boffa, the Rio Nunez, at Boké, and the Negro port of Benty …)
- Settlements and other elements of built cultural heritage
- Slave hunters' / kidnappers' camp-sites or assembly villages
- Trade routes

Risks affecting the physical integrity of heritage

In Guinea the evidence of cultural heritage places linked to slavery are generally in a deteriorated state and are constantly exposed to the following factors:

- The extreme elements, a condition of the natural environment (animal, vegetation or ecological) which are less and less propitious for site preservation – To note above all is the high humidity in Guinea's regions, especially Maritime Guinea, the region where the greatest number of cultural heritage places of the Negro trade are to be found, where there is heavy and frequent rain, as well as the impact in Upper Guinea where the large temperature swings during the 'inter-seasonal period 'of December-Januar, give rise to splits and cracking and other symptoms of decay on the structures
- The process of modernisation or of the spread of settlement areas/ and of primary production – Infrastructure works often risk reducing the area of certain sites, affecting their physical integrity and the structure of the cultural heritage place or in certain cases causing it to disappear completely
- Cases of illegal appropriation – Inappropriate treatment or other risks linked to use of the sites by the tenants or owners help in such cases also in limiting the area of certain sites.

The area Port Benty, which is an example of a 'Negro site' exposed to such types of threat, happens to be almost ruined. In such a condition, the human settlements, cultural landscapes, historic places, monuments, archaeological sites, linked to the Negro trace are on their way to disappearing, carrying with them irreplaceable evidence.

Factors indirectly worsening the condition of heritage

The complete abandonment of heritage sites and monuments, the underestimation or pure and simple lack of knowledge of their significance to cultural identity and for development, the inadequacy of skills in the area of conservation, the deficiencies at the professional level in heritage management organisations, the lack of follow-up of actions and the absence of coordination between the interested parties, these are the threats that aid a worsening of the condition of Guinea's heritage.

We must likewise remember that the results of the research undertaken by Guinean historians were presented at a seminar organised by UNESCO at Conakry, in Guinea on 24–26 March 1997, with the theme 'Oral Tradition and the Negro Trade'. The results are not well known to national users. Also, conservation activities and appropriate management have not followed up on this first work. As a result, the hope to see Guinean Slave heritage promoted has been blunted.

This research has been inadequate in practice, in comparison to the goal of making an actual inventory, of conserving and of sponsoring cultural heritage places – from the point of view of the participative and lasting development of the communities involved.

On this subject, the public authorities have done little to integrate this approach, yet the new national development policy, called 'Strategy for Poverty Reduction', prescribes advancing cultural heritage under the heading of development objectives:

*Tourism, the Arts, Cultural Heritage will become according to the facts of the sub-sectors, bearers of growth. It is necessary to work on promotion programs to support their development. These programs must place particular emphasis on … the translation of cultural heritage development activities into goals to reduce poverty …*Under this heading, we must *'support museum development and the enhancement of sites and monuments (protection, conservation and management)'*.

The Guinea ICOMOS Committee has often stressed the need to train specialists and technicians in conservation and site conservation management planning: '… *Indeed, if Guinea really possessed professionals in sufficient number, capable of making final statements on the values and significance of sites, however there is a severe lack of specialists in identification, research, conservation and cultural heritage place management.*' This is why the Committee has stressed in its plea broadcast on the occasion of International Monuments Day the necessity of *'work on a program of improving Guinean professionals and technical assistants in the conservation and management of cultural heritage places, with the purpose of forming successfully a team of experts and competent technicians that the country needs'.*

Elsewhere in this submission, it was also noted:

- The absence of coordination between the various development parties in their more or less direct actions at cultural heritage sites
- … the lack of budgetary allocation for the conservation and development of Guinea's cultural heritage places …
- … the urgency to implement a national conservation policy for the conservation and management of cultural heritage places, in allowing a participative and inter-sectoral approach as well as making known and adopting a framework legal protection.

Resources and Initiatives of ICOMOS Guinea

The ICOMOS Guinea Committee has decided to use its own skills. Two of its members have already enthusiastically initiated research on the 'Slave Route' (see above). Of its members and sympathisers there are architects, archaeologists, information officers and those responsible for tourism. Committee members have experience in doing inventories, conservation and working on site management plans.

The Guinea ICOMOS team intends to lead an awareness raising drive about cultural heritage in general and on the heritage sites linked to slavery in particular. It is making contact, physically and morally, with various persons, and for example, has been able to obtain the endorsement of the ministry of public works to collaborate with this department in taking on responsibility for its programs and projects in areas of heritage protection.

The priority projects, closely allied to ICOMOS Guinea's portfolio, centre on the protection of Guinea's heritage at risk, as follows:

- cross-sectoral heritage and lasting development (PIPDD) – The aim is to enhance Guinean natural and cultural heritage from the perspective of lasting development, taking into account the improvement of experts and the community's living conditions, the assertion of cultural identity, in the face of the hazard of globalisation, and the use of the significance of this heritage to promote peace and cultural diversity. The specific objectives are to work out and implement an IEC plan for heritage conservation and the fight against poverty. To put in place and strengthen an inter-sectoral, cross-institutional and participative collaborative framework for the protection, conservation and natural and cultural heritage management – Implement the Strategy Document for the Conservation and Management of Guinean Natural and Cultural Heritage, guided by the National Strategy for Poverty Reduction – Produce a rescue plan on the basis of judicious selection of sites and monuments at risk.

- Inventory project and the creation of a database on Guinean heritage at risk
- Seminar / workshop for those responsible and professionals on cultural heritage conservation
- A documentary film project of awareness raising on the conservation of sites and monuments of Negro trade in Guinea
- Revision of Guinea's indicative list for World Heritage (a project worked on for the Guinea Minister responsible for cultural heritage).

To conclude, the staff of ICOMOS Guinea considers they must emphasise that the programs on the Negro trade in Africa will only be partially achieved, if the considerable and outstanding evidence in Guinea is not sufficiently identified and enhanced, in the area of conservation and management plans, which must be worked on and implemented, according to the appropriate methodology on the subject.

It is with these aims that a cordial appeal from the ICOMOS Guinea Committee is directed with all good grace for an immediate surge of exchange and solidarity. The Committee is appealing to ICOMOS, and especially its brother national committees, to state-controlled and private parties, national and international, to assist in strengthening its capacity to intervene and make its actions eligible for the achievement of its mission.

Sékou Kobani Kourouma
President
ICOMOS Guinea

GUINEE
Les sites et monuments liés à l'esclavage

Dédié à l'Année internationale de la commémoration de la lutte contre l'esclavage et de son abolition

Cadre et Objectifs

Le présent rapport (2004-2005) du Comité Guinéen de l'ICOMOS (ICOMOS/GUINEE) a pour but de favoriser les conditions de conservation et de valorisation du patrimoine d'un pays africain, la Guinée, qualifié de «pays-synthèse de l'Afrique de l'Ouest », à cause de la richesse de son patrimoine culturel et naturel. Les objectifs de ce rapport sont les suivants :

- Participer à l'œuvre d'évaluation périodique et de sensibilisation de l'ICOMOS, sur les risques que subit le patrimoine culturel à travers le monde ;
- Sensibiliser l'opinion nationale et les partenaires au développement de la Guinée, en même temps polariser l'attention de la communauté scientifique internationale sur les conditions de conservation particulièrement défavorables du patrimoine culturel immobilier de ce pays.

Le Comité a choisi de dédier le rapport à l'«Année internationale (2004) de commémoration de la lutte contre l'esclavage et de son abolition », proclamée par l'ONU et organisée par l'UNESCO. Cette option se justifie quand on sait la présence en Guinée de sites et monuments des plus significatifs de la région africaine, cependant peu ou mal connus, se rapportant au phénomène de l'esclavage.

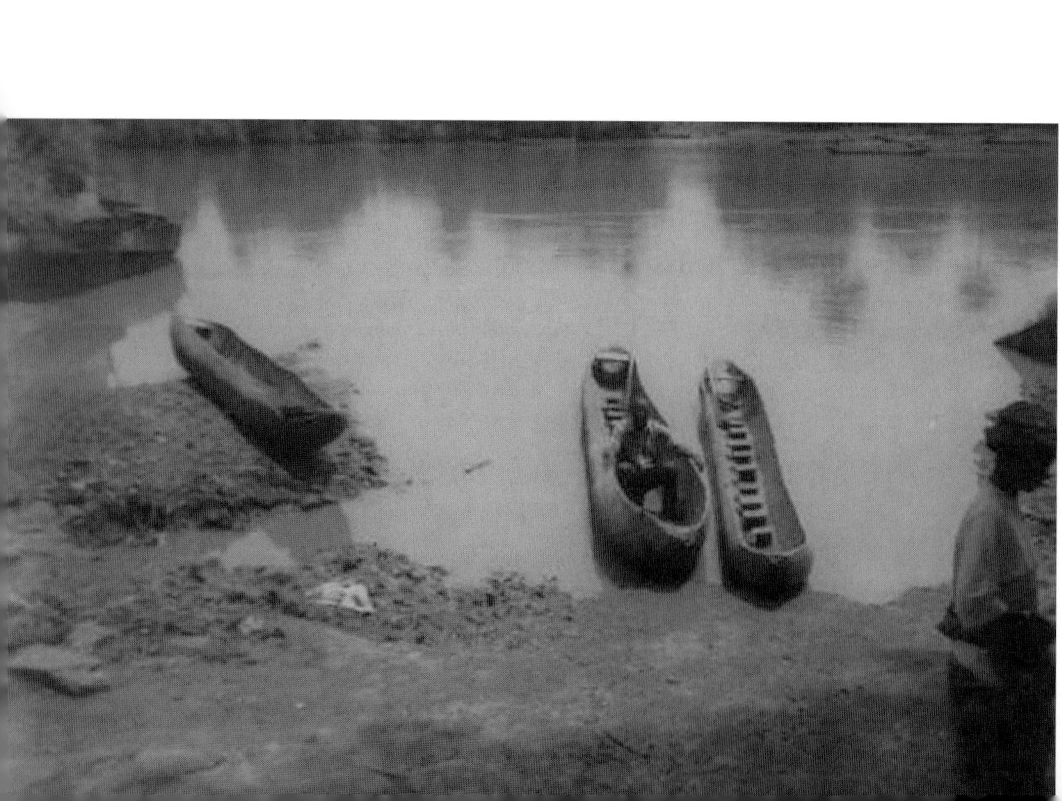

Landing place for the transport of slaves
Débarcadère pour le transfert des esclaves

Choix de thème

La problématique de la sauvegarde du patrimoine culturel immobilier lié à la « Traite négrière » revient souvent à l'ordre du jour des réunions d'ICOMOS GUINEE. Cependant, l'unanimité ne s'était pas dégagée au départ sur le choix de ce thème comme objet du rapport annuel.

Cela a suscité des discussions et trois tendances se sont dessinées :

- l'option pour l'élaboration d'un rapport « ordinaire » sur les sites et monuments guinéen en péril, tel que le rapport précédent de 2001-2002,
- le choix pour le thème recommandé par l'ICOMOS pour la célébration de la journée internationale des monuments et des sites : « ...Terre et architecture de terre... »,
- l'option de s'inscrire dans le mouvement de célébration de l 'année internationale sur la lutte contre l'esclavage.

Il s'est avéré que dans tous les cas, pour le moment, le Comité Guinéen de l'ICOMOS n'a pas tout ou presque pas les moyens de réaliser ses plans et projets, et pouvoir ainsi fournir des informations plus pertinentes que celles contenues dans son rapport précédent. Par ailleurs, il est important de souligner cet aspect, à savoir que le Comité se trouve confronté à des contraintes réelles et que sa priorité est de s'assurer les premiers moyens pour s'installer et démarrer ; par conséquent, en l'espace d'un an, il est enclin à livrer des informations ne reflétant de manière approximative l'état de conservation actuel des sites du patrimoine culturel du pays. Le consensus s'étant finalement dégagé sur la troisième option, le rapport fait état des héritages culturels liés à l'esclavage en Guinée.

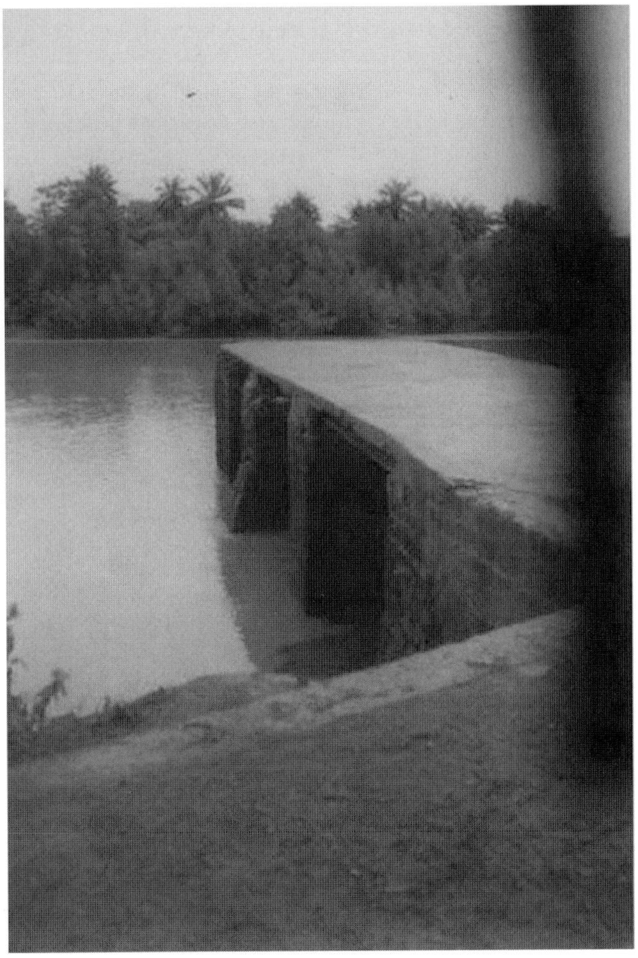

Bridge, trace of the slave trade, Rio Nunez
Pont, vestige de la traite négrière, Rio Nunez

Sources et lieux-témoins de la traite négrière transatlantique

Il est peu probable de trouver en Guinée des vestiges émergents du courant transaharien de déportation des Noirs, qui s'effectua depuis le 2ème siècle av.JC jusqu'aux environs du XIXè siècle. Contrairement, on y trouve de nombreux témoignages de la Traite des Noirs transatlantique et aussi d'une forme de « traite intérieure » nourrissant un « esclavage domestique ». Les sources dont on dispose (notamment les sources écrites et les sources orales) témoignent de la pratique par le passé de ces deux dernières formes de l'esclavage des communautés qui peuplent les quatre régions naturelles et culturelles du pays, à savoir, la Guinée Maritime (à l'ouest, région des premiers contacts avec les traitants européens), la Moyenne Guinée ou Foutah Djalon (où a subsisté jusqu'au 20è siècle l'esclavage domestique), la Guinée Forestière (qui avait été fortement atteinte par la traite atlantique) et la Haute-Guinée (où depuis l'époque des Mansa, souverains Mandingue du 13è- 15è siècle).

Plusieurs segments d'itinéraires reliaient les régions de l'intérieur à la côte atlantique, où les esclaves étaient embarqués pour les Amériques. De toutes les zones de destination et d'embarquement des esclaves celle du Rio Pongo (actuelle Préfecture de Boffa) présente les sites des plus caractéristiques car cette zone fut la plus active durant la «traite négrière».

Dans cette région la traite avait perduré et faisait l'affaire de «familles mulâtresses», dont Lady Nyiara Lightburn , la célèbre «Reine Nyiara Belli», morte en 1880, à 120 ans. Cette dame s'était illustrée comme l'un des principaux acteurs de la traite des esclaves entre le 18è et le 19è siècle. Elle résidait à Faringhya, «cité esclavagiste» située dans cette zone marécageuse du Rio Pongo; localité située entre 10°17' de latitude nord et 13° 59' de longitude ouest et arrosée par deux rivières: le Rio Pongo et la Fatala. «Elle tenait la plus grande factorerie du pays, avec 6 000 esclaves à ses ordres ».

Aussi bien à l'intérieur de la Guinée que dans les zones côtières de destination on remarque une présence remarquable des sites du patrimoine culturel guinéen, liés à la traite des esclaves et qui ont fait l'objet d'étude dans le cadre des premières activités du projet «La route de l'esclave» en Guinée, Mamadou Lefloch Camara et Mamadi Koba Camara, membres d'ICOMOS/GUINEE, ont effectué des recherches historiques sur la traite négrière respectivement en Guinée Maritime (Rio Nunez) et en Haute Guinée (province de Baliya). D'autres historiens comme l'Honorable feu Facinet Béavogui (1) ont mené des recherches semblables dans d'autres régions du pays.

Types de sites et de monuments

Les recherches ont permis d'aborder le point sur les méthodes de capture et de domptage des esclaves, les acteurs et les itinéraires. Dans chacune des régions du pays on peut recueillir des données d'ordre onomastique et toponymique, propres aux langues locales, qui permettraient d'élucider le point sur des lieux caractéristiques de la traite des esclaves :

- les aires de chasse et lieux de captures (abords de cours d'eau, espaces isolés des plateaux cuirassés,...)
- les lieux de cantonnement (en dehors des établissements humains permanents)
- les marchés d'esclaves, (dont certains sont placés au-delà des lieux habités..)
- les lieux de domptages (monuments lithiques, autels de phytolâtrie)
- les « esclaveries » et entrepôts
- les lieux d'embarcation (débarcadères sur le Rio Pongo, Boffa, le Rio Nunez, à Boké, port négriers de Benty...)
- les habitations et autres éléments du patrimoine historique bâti
- les lieux de campement ou hameaux de regroupement des kidnappeurs.
- Les itinéraires de traite.

Risques affectant l'intégrité physique des sites et monuments

En Guinée, les témoignages patrimoine culturel immobilier, liés à l'esclavage, se trouvent généralement dégradés et constamment exposés aux facteurs suivants :

- Les intempéries, un état de l'environnement naturel (animal, végétal et écologique) de moins en moins propice pour la conservation des sites – Il faut noter avant tout la forte humidité dans les régions de la Guinée, notamment en Guinée Maritime, où les pluies sont très fortes et très fréquentes, région où se retrouvent les sites le patrimoine immobilier le plus riche sur la traite négrière; il faut également l'impact des variations de température pendant l' «intersaison» (décembre-janvier) en Haute-Guinée occasionnant des fissures, craquelures ou autres formes de pathologie sur les structures;
- Les processus de modernisation ou à l'élargissement des zones d'habitat ou de production rurales – Des travaux d'infrastructure risquent souvent de réduire l'espace de certains sites, affectant l'intégrité physique et la structure du patrimoine culturel immobilier ou, dans certains cas, le fait carrément disparaître ;
- Des cas d'appropriation illégitime – On assiste, dans de tels cas aussi, à la restriction de l'espace de certains sites, des traitements inappropriés ou d'autres risques liés à l'utilisation des sites par des locataires ou propriétaires.

L'espace du port de Benty, qui est un exemple de « site négrier » exposé à ces formes de menace, se trouve aujourd'hui presque défiguré. Dans de telles conditions de conservation, des établissements humains, paysages culturels, places historiques, monuments, sites archéologiques liés à la traite négrière sont en passe de disparaître, emportant avec eux des témoignages irremplaçables.

Facteurs aggravant indirectement l'état du patrimoine

L'abandon pur des sites et monuments du patrimoine, la sous-estimation ou la méconnaissance pure et simple de leurs valeurs pour l'identité culturelle et pour le développement, l'insuffisance des compétences en matière de conservation, les insuffisances au niveau du cadre institutionnel de gestion, le manque de suivi des actions et l'absence d'une coordination entre les acteurs intéressés, telles sont les menaces favorisant l'aggravation de l'état de conservation du patrimoine en Guinée.

,.Par ailleurs, il faut rappeler que les résultats des recherches menées par les historiens guinéens ont été présentés à un Colloque organisé par l'UNESCO à Conakry Guinée, du 24 au 26 mars 1997, sur le thème «La tradition orale et la traite négrière». Ces résultats ne sont pas bien connus des utilisateurs nationaux; aussi, des activités de conservation et de gestion appropriées n'ont-elles pas suivi ces premiers travaux. Par conséquent, l'espoir de voir le patrimoine «esclavagiste» guinéen systématiquement promu s'est émoussé.

Ces recherches sont pratiquement insuffisantes, par rapport aux objectifs de l'inventaire proprement dit, de la conservation et de la mise en valeur du patrimoine culturel immobilier (dans l'optique d'un développement participatif et durable des communautés concernées).

A ce sujet, les pouvoirs publics ont peu intégré cette approche ; toutefois, la nouvelle politique de développement national libellée «Stratégie de Réduction de la Pauvreté», prescrit la mise en valeur du patrimoine culturel au titre des objectifs de croissance: *«Le tourisme, les arts, le patrimoine culturel deviennent à l'évidence des sous-secteurs porteurs de croissance. Il est nécessaire de mettre en oeuvre des programmes de promotion pour appuyer leur développement. Ces programmes doivent mettre un accent particulier sur (...) la traduction en objectifs de réduction de la pauvreté des activités de valorisation du patrimoine culturel ...»*A ce titre, il faut *«appuyer le développement des musées et la mise en valeur des sites et monuments (protection, conservation et gestion)»*

Le Comité Guinéen de l'ICOMOS a souvent souligné la nécessité de former des spécialistes et techniciens en conservation et mise en place de plans de gestion de sites. *«En effet, si la Guinée possède bien des disciplinaires en nombre suffisant, capables d'épiloguer sur des valeurs et significations des lieux, cependant elle manque cruellement de spécialistes en identification, étude, conservation et gestion du patrimoine culturel immobilier».* C'est pourquoi le Comité a souligné, dans son plaidoyer diffusé à l'occasion de la Journée Internationale du patrimoine culturel, sur la nécessité de *«mettre en œuvre d'un programme de perfectionnement des professionnels et techniciens guinéens en conservation et gestion du patrimoine culturel immobilier, aux fins de constituer à terme une équipe d'experts et techniciens compétents, dont le pays a besoin.»*

Par ailleurs, dans ce document de plaidoyer, il a été noté également

- « l'absence de coordination entre les différents acteurs de développement dans leurs actions plus ou moins immédiates sur les sites du patrimoine culturel... »,
- « ...le manque d'allocation budgétaire pour la conservation et la valorisation du patrimoine culturel immobilier guinéen... » et
- « ..l'urgence de mettre en place d'une politique nationale de conservation et de gestion du patrimoine culturel, privilégiant l'approche participative et intersectorielle ainsi que la mise à jour et l'adoption du cadre de protection juridique».

Ressources et initiatives du comité guinéen de l'ICOMOS

Le Comité Guinéen de l'ICOMOS a décidé de mettre à contribution les compétences en son sein. Deux de ses membres se sont déjà lancés dans la recherche sur « La Route de l'esclave » (cités plus haut). Au nombre de ses membres et sympathisants on compte des architectes, archéologues, Documentalistes, responsables du tourisme ; Des membres du Comité ont des expériences en inventaire, conservation et mise en œuvre de plans de gestion des sites.

L'équipe d'ICOMOS/GUINEE entend mener une offensive de sensibilisation sur le patrimoine culturel en général et en particulier les sites et les monuments liés à l'esclavage. Elle prends contact avec diverses personnes physiques ou morales et, par exemple, a pu obtenir l'aval du Ministère des travaux publics pour collaborer à la prise en compte dans les programmes et projets de ce département la dimension sauvegarde des sites et des monuments.

Les projets prioritaires, ficelés dans le portefeuille d'ICOMOS/GUINEE, portant sur la sauvegarde du patrimoine guinéen en péril, sont les suivants :

- Projet intersectoriel patrimoine et développement durable (PIPDD) – Le but à mettre en valeur le patrimoine naturel et culturel guinéen dans l'optique du développement durable, prenant en compte l'amélioration du cadre et des conditions de vie des populations, l'affirmation de l'identité culturelle face aux enjeux de la mondialisation et la mise à contribution des valeurs de ce patrimoine pour promouvoir la paix et la diversité culturelle. Les objectifs spécifiques sont : – Elaborer et mettre en œuvre un plan d'IEC pour la conservation du patrimoine et la lutte contre la pauvreté – Mettre en place et renforcer un cadre de collaboration intersectoriel, interinstitutionnel et participatif de protection, de conservation et de gestion du patrimoine naturel et culturel – Mettre en place un Document de Stratégie de Conservation et gestion du patrimoine naturel et culturel guinéen, orienté par la Stratégie nationale de réduction de la pauvreté – Réaliser un plan de sauvetage sur la base d'une sélection judicieuse de sites et monuments en péril
- Projet d'inventaire et création d'une base de données sur le patrimoine guinéen en péril
- Séminaire/atelier des responsables et professionnels sur la conservation du patrimoine culturel
- Projet de film documentaire de sensibilisation sur la conservation des sites et monuments de la traite négrière en Guinée
- Révision de la liste indicative de la Guinée pour le patrimoine mondial (projet élaboré à l'intention du Ministère guinéen en charge du patrimoine culturel).

Pour conclure, le staff d'ICOMOS/GUINEE estime devoir souligner que les programmes sur la traite négrière en Afrique n'auront été que partiellement réalisés tant que de nombreux et remarquables témoignages de la Guinée n'en sont pas suffisamment identifiés et valorisés, dans le cadre d'un plan de conservation et de gestion, dûment élaboré et mis en œuvre, selon la méthodologie appropriée en la matière.

C'est à ces fins qu'un appel cordial est lancé à toute les bonnes volontés pour un élan d'échanges et de solidarité à l'endroit du Comité Guinéen de l'ICOMOS ; le Comité lance un appel à l'ICOMOS, et notamment aux Comités nationaux frères, aux partenaires étatiques et privés, nationaux et internationaux, pour l'aider à renforcer ses capacités d'intervention et qualifier son action dans l'accomplissement de sa mission.

Sékou Kobani Kourouma
Le Président
ICOMOS Guinée

Références

ABOU SOUMAH, Etude littéraire de la Légende de Niara Beli, DES 1991, université de Conakry)

ABOU SOUMAH, SEKOU KOBANI KOUROUMA : «Farenghya, un haut-lieu de la traite négrière» Africa 2009 Newsletter N°4, 2004

ABOUBACAR TOURE : «La traite négrière dans la Mélacorée» (Colloque «Tradition orale et traite négrière» mars 1997)

ISMAËL BARRY : «Le Foutah de la traite négrière au 19è siècle. (Colloque« Tradition orale et traite négrière» mars 1997)

ICOMOS/GUINEE : «Plaidoyer : Conservons, protégeons et gérons notre patrimoine culturel et naturel, pour un développement humain, meilleur et durable …» Célébration de la Journée internationale du patrimoine. Conakry, 18 avril 2004

ICOMOS GUINEE, «Projet de formation en conservation et gestion des sites et monuments». Conakry, janvier 2002

J. S CANALE «Les origines ethniques des captifs du Foutah Djalon «in ''Notes africaines N° 123 juillet 1969

MAMADOU LEFLOCHE CAMARA : «L'aristocratie négrière du Rio Pongo (1807-1887) DEA, Sorbonne. Paris

MINISTERE DE L'ECONOMIE ET DES FINANCES. Rép. De Guinée : «'Document de Stratégie de réduction de la pauvreté». Conakry, janvier 2002

HUNGARY
Ózd – an Abandoned Industrial Site

Hungarian industry that developed in the second third of the 19th century produced innovations and products of an international standard. Our industrial heritage constitutes such an important part of our cultural heritage from a technological, industrial history and architectural point of view alike that saving and protecting it in the current situation requires a significant cultural policy decision.

State protection of industrial buildings is provided by local government regulations, or by the national heritage office. Now called the National Office of Cultural Heritage, in accordance with the Austrian model, this body has been functioning as a state office since 1872. Thus in Hungary, heritage protection always functions top down, on behalf of the state. It decides, prohibits or regulates matters, that also should be enforced by community decisions.

Difficulties met concerning the conservation and protection of industrial buildings are not merely theoretical or problems of differences of opinion. In Hungary, this type of heritage has always been more a part of economic than cultural life.

Ózd, view from the Big America Colony

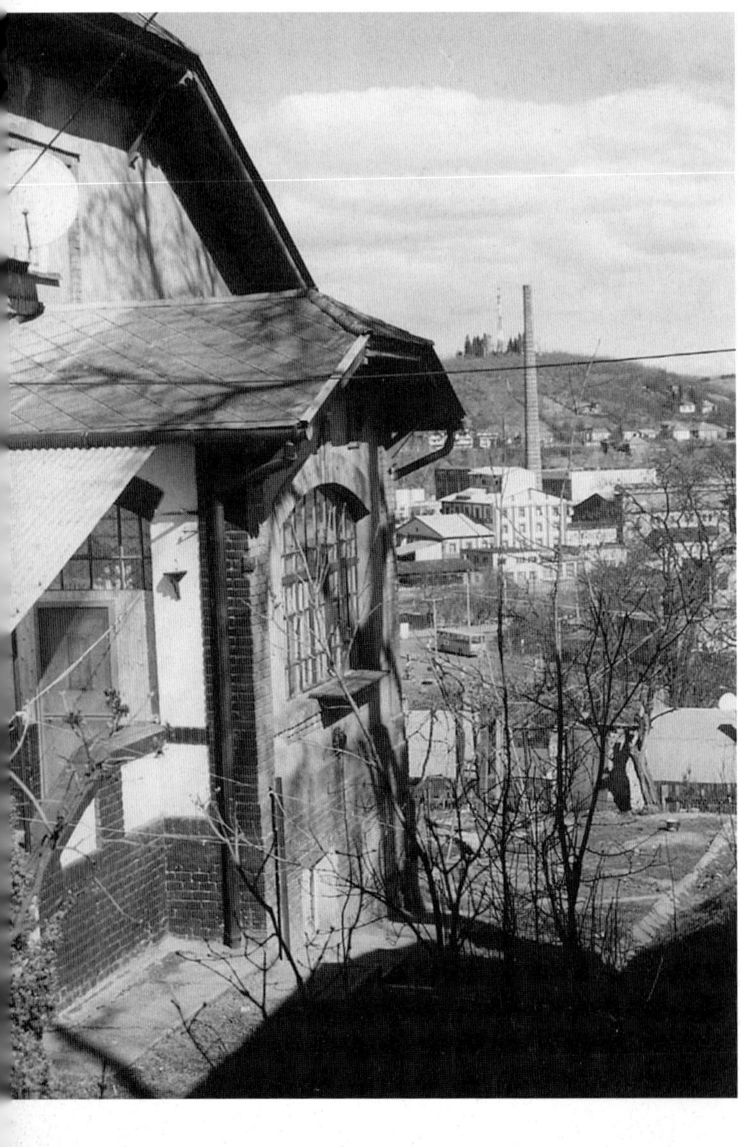

At the same time, the economic and political circumstances over almost the past twenty years started an extremely rapid and mass destruction in this legally unprotected area of our cultural heritage. This means the destruction of specific buildings, traditional industrial sites and regions characteristic of manufacturing industry. The 20th century buildings with their equipment and fittings, of the socialist large-scale industry, as well as traditionally renowned Hungarian technologies and products, are also ceasing to exist.

Whilst this phenomenon confronts Hungarian heritage protection with an extensive problem, which may be solved by getting ideas and models from our foreign colleagues, we must work out a special, central-eastern European manner of protection by ourselves. That is, while in western countries such buildings gradually become part of protected cultural values, which is the more usual, the situation is different in regards to this type of heritage in the ex-socialist countries. The collapse of large-scale industry, due to the economic consequences of the political changes, resulted in sudden and extensive numbers getting into such an economic state. Due to their mass privatisation, this risks their disappearance, transformation, or destruction in a way that cultural politics will not even be able to react.

On the basis of this, experts from the National Office of Cultural Heritage have prepared a pilot project this year in the industrial town of Ózd. The town and its surroundings contain all of the problems we are facing in this field. The challenge is not the importance or the significance of the task but the special atmosphere of the place. How does this show? The *genius loci* of a certain place is created by the complex entirety of its physical and spiritual manifestations, which were created in a specific medium, in a specific form, in specific place, creating something special, something unique, which is typical of that place alone. We can analyse and reveal the components of a special place, but we can only feel its complex entirety. Therefore, the conservation and revitalisation of a site are not only a great economic challenge but also a serious cultural and cultural-ethical task.

Ózd is 160 km from the Hungarian capital, Budapest, in the northern industrial centre of Hungary. Near the Bükk Mountains, 300-400 m high sections of hill formed, mostly of sandstone and clay. Brown coal is the most important asset and enabled industrial development; however, mining largely had ceased by the 1990s.

Iron industry is traditional in this area and can be dated back to the 14th century. As well as iron mining, small iron-smelting works, powered by water, were dominant at the beginning of the 19th century. These were replaced by large-scale industry in the mid-19th century, which was the era of the development of significant transport and railways infrastructure. Based on local coalmine production, the Ózd Ironworks became the country's first large-scale industrial factory, at a time when coal was considered one of the most up-to-date forms of energy.

The factory was built between 1846 and 1847 along the Hangony stream at the junction of the surrounding steep valleys. As we can see, the factory became the settlement's creator, the organising power of the centre's urban structure resulting from its extensive economic and social activity, which created and maintained the new settlement Ózd, the industrial town. Therefore the factory became the centre of the little villages situated in the adjoining valleys that provided the workers and became part of the urban structure of Ózd, whilst keeping their local architectural image. As a result, the centre of the town is not a historical town centre (in

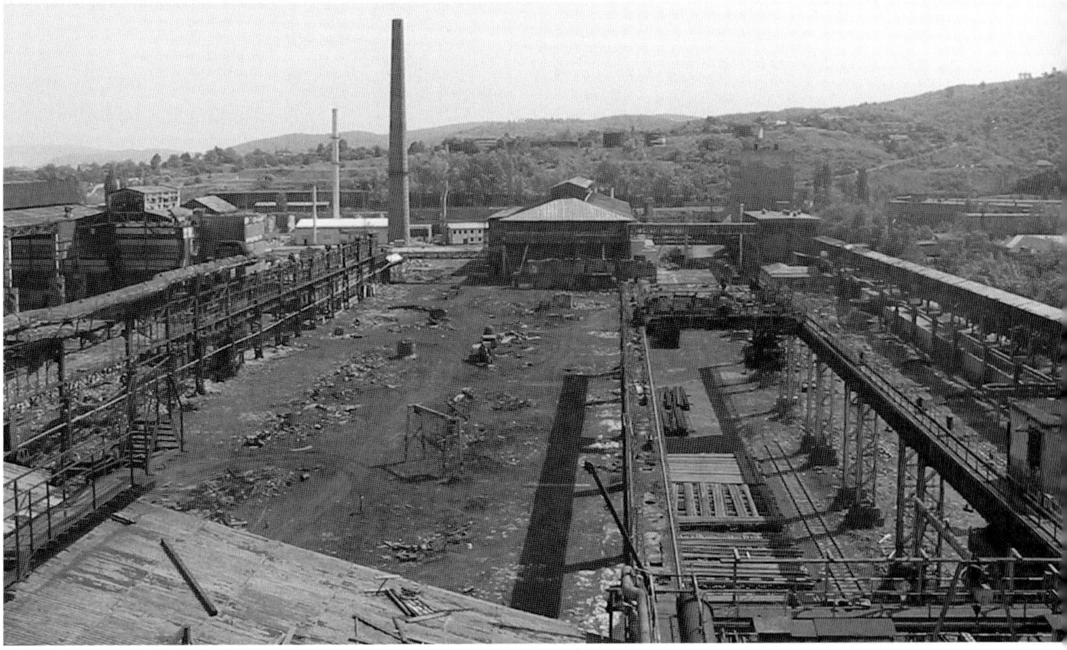

Òzd, the factory today

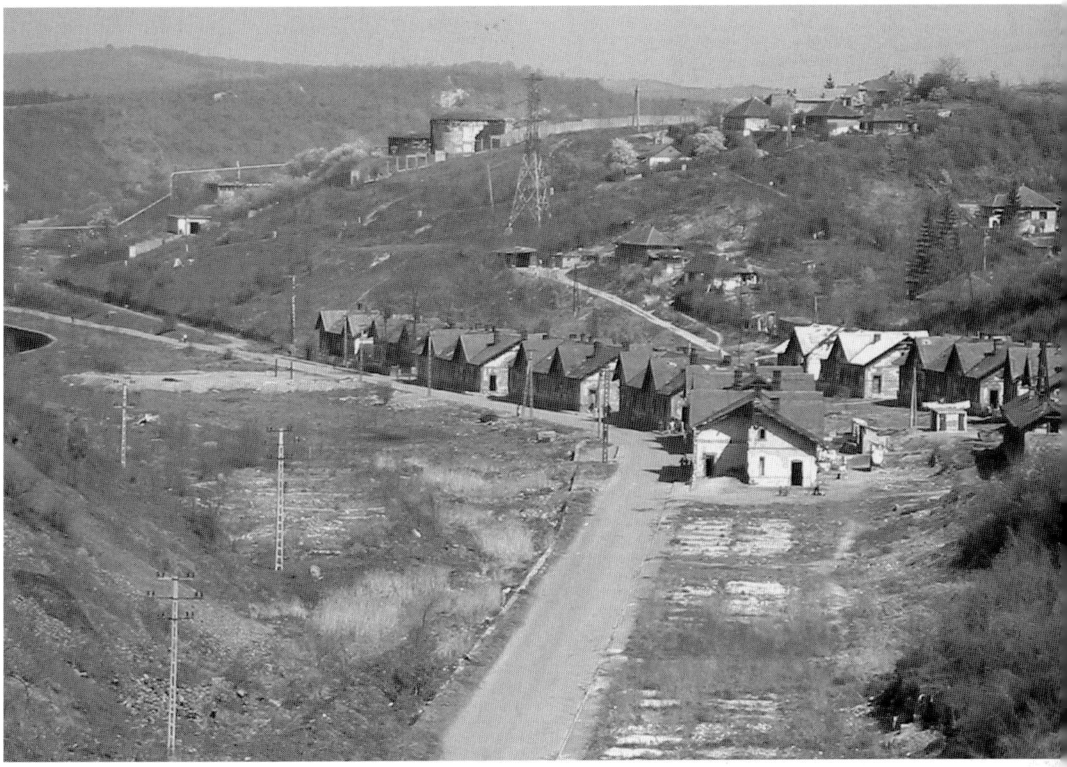

Ózd, one of the poorest colonies today

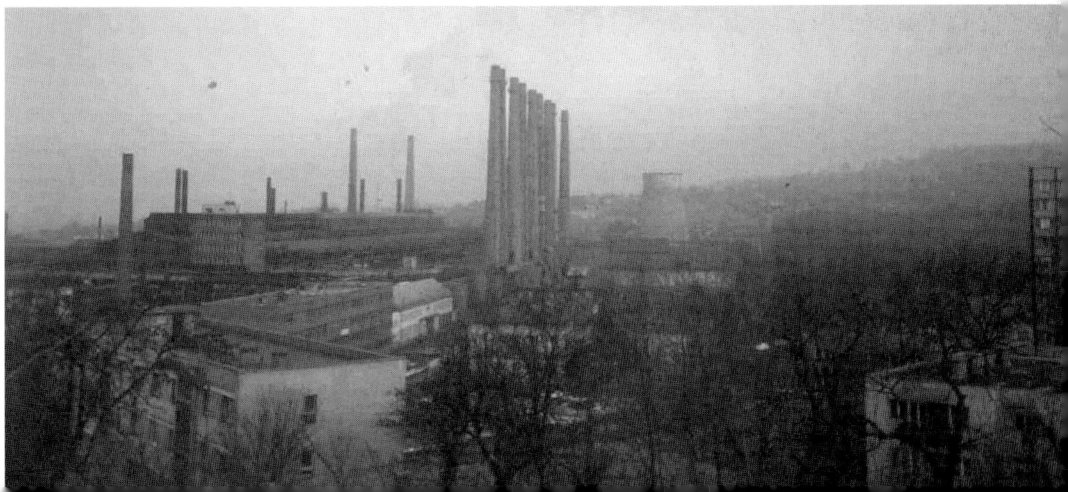

Ózd, the former 'Chimney Cathedral'

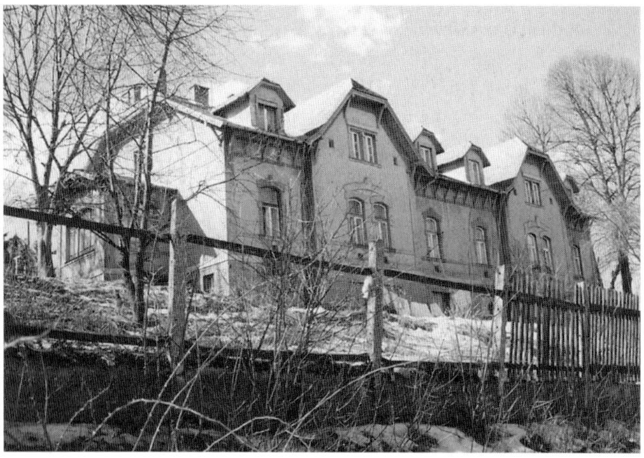

Ózd, the Big America Colony

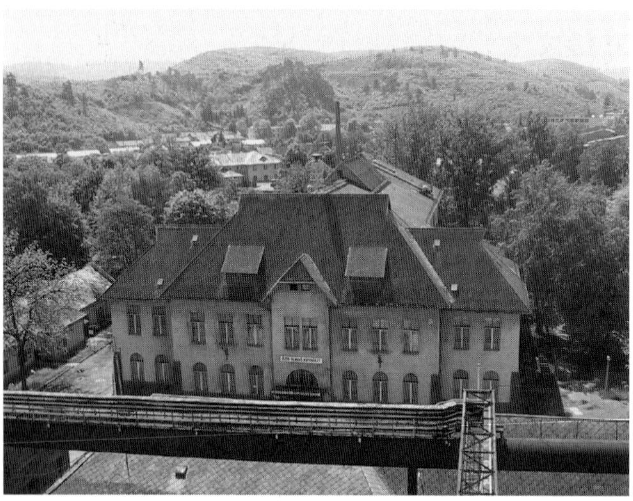

Ózd, the Reader's Club

Ózd, the swimming pool

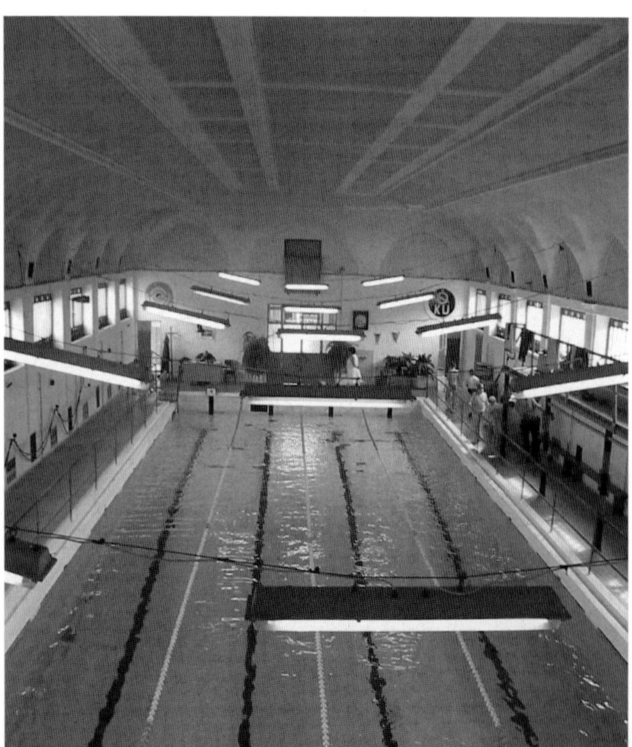

Hungary traditionally with a church and a main square) but a factory itself.

After the formation of another significant local factory, the Rimamurány-Salgótarján Ironworks SC, the Ózd factory had to be entirely restructured. Between 1861 and 1970, the factory established several residential areas for its workers around the factory. They were called „workers' colonies" or „workers' settlements". The colonies, which have shaped the special atmosphere of the town with their locations and names, were built at the end of the 19th century and at the turn of the century. The colonies' locations in the urban structure and the name of the different settlements reflected the social hierarchy, that was also manifested in their architecture. The location of the houses, the building size and quality was also formed according to this hierarchy.

So-called Big America (1913–1915) lies on the hill-top in front of the factory. It was built for the clerks and the directors of the factory. From these big houses, they had a view of so-called Little America (1898–1912), built for skilled workers. The differences are very clear, their names however express a particular and a typical local humour. There is a so-called Untidy colony (1882–1886) for unskilled workers and Venice colony (1922–1925), so-called because it was sited along a canal.

The factory also constructed public buildings in front of the row of the chimney-stacks. It was a sort of meeting place for young people, even 15 years ago rendezvous were decided in front of the chimneys. This street was the centre of the town's corporate life. One side had a row of imposing public buildings: the Reader's Club (1924), the Casino (1884), the building of the local museum (former school, 1896), the office block (1895), and opposite, the factory with the 'chimney cathedral', as the chimney-stacks were known by the local people. There was a beautiful swimming pool in the factory that at the turn of the century in Hungary was the first indoor swimming pool and bath in the provinces.

The factory showed itself in every aspect of life. As well, instead of a church bell, the sound of the factory hooter structured the town's time. There was a sound of hooter at 6 am, at 12 am, at 2 pm, at 6 pm and at 10 pm signalling the shifts and the time. A special sign language, which was used in the factory among workers, was used also in every day life; even children used it at school.

Ózd is a unique example of Hungarian large-scale industrial areas. It shows how industry and social conditions developed simultaneously. This development is seen in the area of civic facilities that has no doubt set an example for industrial companies in providing suitable residential facilities for their workers.

The 1850s began a time of development and prosperity that lasted for almost 150 years. In the 1990s however, with the change of political regime, large-scale industry ceased to exist in Hungary, leaving significant factories without work, including Ózd. Additionally, with the factory's decline, most of its workers became unemployed. Ózd lost its traditional dominance in the area.

These last ten years of decline have certainly had their impact on the town. The former 50 hectare central industrial area has seen many of its buildings demolished and several civic and residential buildings left abandoned and empty. The 'chimney cathedral', the symbol of Ózd was demolished. Even the most essential maintenance works have not been carried out and therefore most of the buildings have now reached a worrying physical state. As a result of the economic changes, the town's population decreased, many of the town's inhabitants left the area, especially young and educated people.

This process should be stopped as soon as possible. Otherwise it is feared that Ózd will not survive this phase of decline. But how can we preserve a town in its original form, with its special atmosphere, which also has lost its power to generate power in an economic, cultural and spiritual sense? Is it possible or even permissible to restore the social medium in which that special atmosphere was created? Today, the former workers' colonies are the poorest parts of the town. Inhabitants have changed. We have to face up to very difficult social and ethnic problems. So, how can we keep the built environment without maintaining the original social and economic power, given the original function has gone? These are very difficult economic questions, yet at the same time ethical ones. For preserving the *genius loci* means not only preserving material items: it means also preserving spiritual memory. But what can we do if this memory does not belong to the different inhabitants' memory? How can we restore, how can we re-create the special atmosphere of the place?

The initiation of the Ózd Project, begun in March 2004, reflects the intention of the National Office of Cultural Heritage to meet its commitment codified in the Act No. LXIV/2001, § 28 point c): „[the Office] combines the maintenance, development, conservation of values and management of areas protected for heritage features". In other words, the Office has to put effective tools into the hands of public players and private individuals responsible for the preservation of cultural values, widely serving the interests of this kind.

Aim of the project:

- Starting the cultural heritage-based revitalisation program of the recently redundant Ózd Industrial Region.

Content of the project:

- Exploration of potential domestic and international partners, and development of co-operational relationship with them;
- Exploration and recognition of the regional values;
- Analysis of opinions, intentions and potentialities on the basis of the explored values;
- Proposal for the regional revitalisation program and urban rehabilitation based on the integrated conservation.

As a first step we have identified heritage areas and started to survey individual buildings. This is in the central heritage area with the factory itself and the row of public buildings in front of it. We have proposed four individual buildings for listing in the area of the factory, and the building of the former Reading Club, the Casino, the former school, now the local museum, and the laboratories. They are all currently empty.

The other heritage units are the residential areas. They all still have their original architectural values: Venice Colony, New Colony, Big America, Vasvár, Várkony.

After large-scale industry ceased to exist in the area, large-scale demolition work was started in the factory. Almost half of the area was demolished and leveled in the hope that new small and medium-sized private businesses would locate there. The formerly busy town centre has become deserted and depopulated. Public buildings were scattered through the town, an insignificant shopping street becoming the main street of the town.

That is why we consider the factory and the row of public buildings in front of it to be the main heritage complex, which has to be dealt with organically. The basis and the main goal of the heritage-based strategy of the town's rehabilitation is that the factory and its surrounds regain and recover their original role in the urban structure as well as in the social and cultural life, which was so unique in Ózd.

Our aims are to open the factory to the town and that the empty space also provides opportunity to cultural and business re-use. Instead of the demolished chimney-stacks we plan chimneys of laser light as the symbol of Ózd's revitalisation. The site of the factory swimming pool must also be opened.

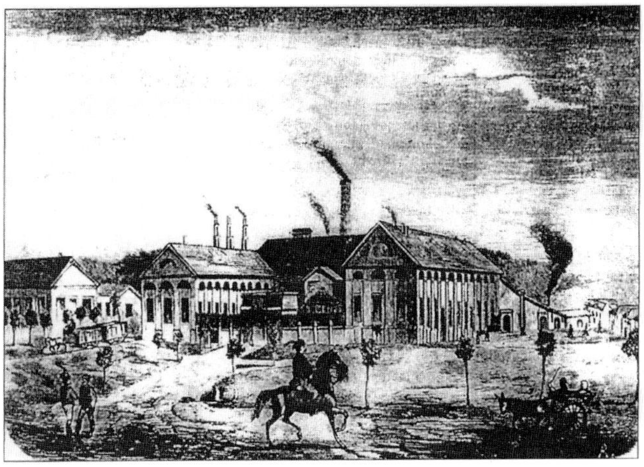

Ózd in1864

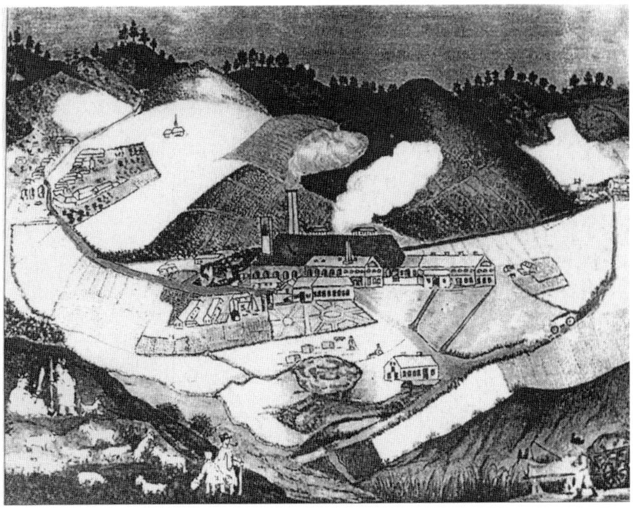

View of Ózd in 1847

As a first step of the rehabilitation of the residential areas we have three action displays along the three main roads leading from big towns into Ózd: Budapest Gate from the capital, Miskolc Gate and Eger Gate. These visual plans mark out the main principles of the maintenance of these sites, their connections to the urban structure and the environment.

As mentioned, we are at the very beginning of this work. We have just outlined the main principles of the work and started to build up partnerships. However, we hope that this demonstrates that our work can prove our basic aim, that culture is able to generate economic results.

Piroska Váczi
ICOMOS Hungary

INDIA
Threatened Jaina Heritage Route in Jharkhand and West Bengal

Buddhism and Jainism are very old traditions in the old district of Hazaribagh which included Shikarbhum, Manbhum, Dalbhum and adjoining East Singhbhum. The Jain heritage was more obvious in the three latter areas, while Buddhism was exclusively of Shikarbhum (Hazaribagh). The Lord Buddha was worshipped in Hazaribagh and the Upper Damodar Valley as Mahadeva. We still find names associated with Buddhism throughout the district as well as the physical presence of Buddhism in Buddhist sacred symbols found throughout the sacred village painting traditions of the great marriage mural art of *Khovar*, and the harvest mural art of *Sohrai*, for which Hazaribagh is justly famous.

In the Lower Damodar Valley there is the problem of destruction of ancient Jain temples in the score from flooding in dams such as the Panchet Dam on the river Damodar (1969), without recording over 20 temples and Chandil Dam on the river Suvarnarekha, (1985) without recording over 20 temples or more (Mitra 1969). The Chandil Dam alone drowned over a hundred villages in the birth-land of Vikramaditya the great Jain King, without archaeological salvage operations. Local villagers under the umbrella of the Aboriginal Society for Art and Recreation, Jamshedpur, managed to save scores of statues of *Tirthankaras*, and other granite and sand-stone statuary from Ichagarh, Dulmi, and a few adjoining villages, which are preserved in a small museum built by the Irrigation Department near the Chandil Dam. Chandil was also found to be a major Palaeolithic site (Ghosh 1970). This is an area of immense cultural and archaeological importance that has wilfully been flooded without any proper scientific examination. Hundreds of statues have reportedly disappeared from Ichagarh. The recurrent feature of destructive development is the lack of any investigation by the archaeological authorities.

The Maithon Dam on the Barakar river opposite Panchet must have similarly submerged several major temple sites. This dam is on the Barakar river that comes to Hazaribagh via the Tilaya Dam, along the old Pilgrim route from Pawapuri with Santal Parganas to the east and Shahabad to the West. It meets the Grand Trunk road at Asansol and continues south to Orissa and Singhbhum. We do not know how many Jain sites were submerged in the Tilaya Dam near Hazaribagh.

Similarly, no-one can guess how many such sites have been destroyed by submergence under the waters of the seven big dams made by the Damodar Valley Corporation *Tilaya Dam, Konar Dam, Patratu Dam, Maithon Dam, Lalpania Dam,* and *Panchet Dam, Tenughat Dam, Durgapur Barrage*. Some 8400 dams have additionally obviously had their impact on the watershed of the Damodar river. There are no figures of antiquities lost in the Icha Dam (West Bengal) which flooded eighty-seven villages in the Jaina heartland.

Along with dam flooding, archaeological and religious heritage has been devastated as a result of vast underground and opencast coal mining, that has set fire to the underground coal in the lower Damodar where huge underground flooded areas have been created by decades of old mine fires. Particularly impacted are the Jaina temples of the lower Damodar in Bokaro and Dhanban and along the Gowai, Kasai, Kangsabati, and Suvernarekha rivers in Manbhum, Saraikela Kharsawan, Purulia, and Singhbhum districts. This has been an enormous loss to the religious and cultural heritage of the community.

Presently the entire upper valley of the Damodar river in the North Karanpura Valley is under threat from the big dams for Super Thermal Power Projects (STPPs). Also, more than seventy opencast coal mines will destroy over two hundred villages and the Buddhist heritage of the valley. This includes a rich treasure of megalith sites, the Mauryan Period Buddhist sites, prehistoric rockart sites, and palaeo-archaeological sites. Both UNESCO and ICOMOS are aware of the matter and it has been published in the 2001–2002, 2002–2003 *Heritage at Risk* Reports.

The mining operations have been in their first stage since 1986 and already five mines have started and five more cleared, as well as two big dams and two STTPs. But there is still time if a strong international appeal is mounted.

The Jain and Buddhist heritage of Jharkhand and neighbouring West Bengal has been wilfully destroyed by so-called development projects such as big dams and mining in modern India. This heritage constitutes the most flawless traditions of sculpture found anywhere in the country. This is an interesting area of study for ethnographers for the Bhumij culture of Manbhum in Jharkhand in contact with Santal culture in Bengal during the revival of Jainism and Buddhism during the Pala Period 9th–12th centuries. The two great religions of India, Jainism and Buddhism were founded in the Damodar Valley which became the site of India's first great industrial model project (DVC) in 1947.

We may remember that in the light of the new district boundaries recently made between Jharkhand and West Bengal, the Purulia sites are now not in the Jharkhand district and so this state may care less for them, although they culturally belong to the ancient culture in Jharkhand. The same may be said of West Bengal in regard to Jaina sites just across the border in Jharkhand.

We may be reminded that in an age-old civilisation like India, there are only 10,000 protected heritage properties listed, compared with 500,000 such buildings protected by law in the United Kingdom, and over a million listed heritage sites in the USA which has over 2200 towns with heritage legislation. The only hope of bringing to light the wanton destruction of Jaina heritage sites in Jharkhand and West Bengal is an internationally-backed campaign.

The Jain sites of Jharkhand, West Bengal, and Orissa are crying out for a careful investigation by the international community as humanity's heritage. Most dates go back to the 8th–11th centuries, and those of the Pala Period, are very ancient sites millennia old. The following list gives the main sites already destroyed or neglected. Most of the destruction has been due to the large dams on the principal rivers of the region, and the dire neglect of the state authorities including the Archaeological Survey of India, although coal mines have destroyed equally vast areas in the same region, even before 1947. The total loss may only partially be reconstructed by referring to the oldest reports of British touring officials of the 19th century, generally the only reports available!

Threatened Sites

Arsa (Manbhum) Jain Temples

The Bengal List (p. 560) refers to a place called Arsa Karandi, about four miles southeast of Boram not far from the Kasai River which is famed as 'possessing ruins of temples' (ASI B.C.1903)

Anai

Three miles from Karcha, a few miles from Purulia, in the vicinity

MAP OF ARCHAEOLOGICAL SITES OF JAINA IMPORTANCE

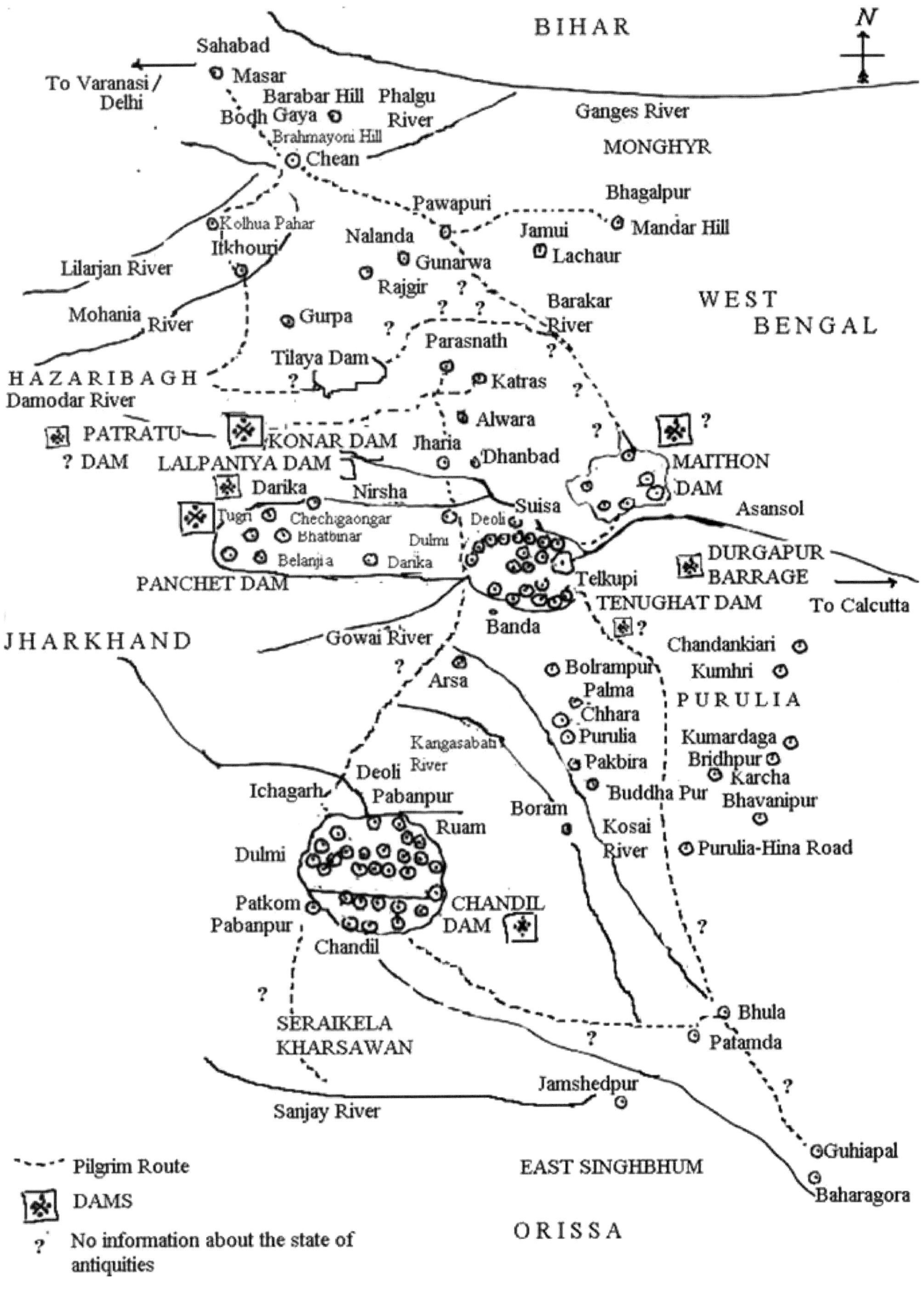

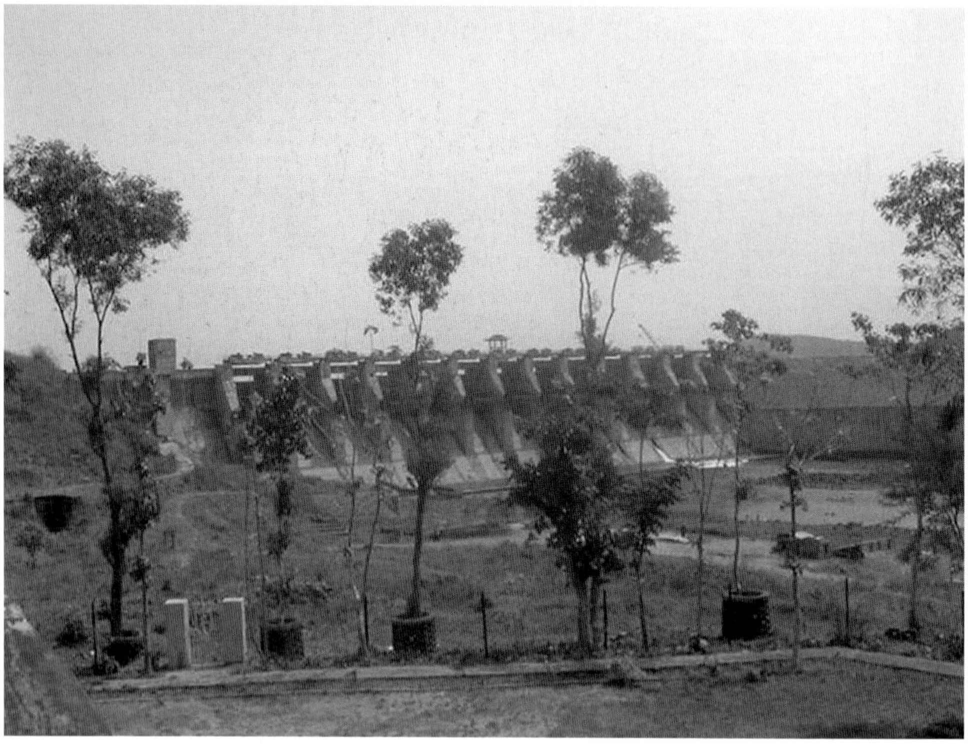

Chandil Dam

of this village there are a number of ruins of brick-built temples; two Jain temples were noted by Block.

Balrampur (Purulia) Jain Temple

The village is situated 4 miles to the southeast of Purulia. It was just noted by Colonel Dalton in 1866 as having two colossal statues of Tirthankaras.

Barida (Manbhum)

6 miles Southwest of Telkupi, this site may or may not have escaped flooding in the Panchet Dam on the Damodar River. The plan of the temple conforms to early Jain design.

Bridhpur

Near Pakbira, this site has a number of Jain images which are worshipped in an annual festival. Some of the images have reportedly been removed by people.

Bilonjia (Manbhum) Jain Temples/Tanks

It is situated 2 miles south of Chehgaongadh, ie fort Chechgaongadh is eight miles south-west of Katras on the banks of the river Damodar. Ruins here are of sixteen Jaina Temples representing a very large Jaina establishment which was described by Beglar in his report for 1872–1873. The fort of Chehgaongadh, the so called *garh*, is 1/2 mile by 1/4 mile in area and calls for extensive archaeological excavation and investigation. It needs investigation in view of flooding of 20 Jain temples in the Panchet Dam on the Damodar River in precisely this area which had a rich Bhumij tribal population. Carvings noted by Beglar was of very high workmanship comparable with Khajuraho and Udaypur. Rock-cut inscription reads *Srayaki Rachha bansidra* indicating Jain and Srawaki traditions.

Boram (new name Deulghat)(See Palma, Chhara, Pakbira)

This imposing site on the South bank of the Kangsabati River has numerous remains of Jaina temples, (nude male figures with Egyptian head-dresses according to F B Bradley Birt (*Chotanagpore* 1910, pp. 180–81), who places it on the Kosai river. Statues of *Trithankaras* wearing Gandharvan head-dresses. The sculptures are kept in a local Ashram and include *Risabhanatha, Chandraprabha,* and *Parsvanatha.* Closeby is another Jaina site named Ansa Karandi (Beglar 1878, p. 195). Several large stone statues have been found of *Risabhanatha, Chandraprabha, Parsvanatha, Uma-mahesvara.*

Bhavanipur

A few miles from Purulia and close to *Karcha*, this village has an image of Rishabanatha, *Padamvati-Dharanendra* (which is taken now as image of Shiv-Parvati). Beglar's list (1878) from Manbhum Jaina Sites includes the following:

- 1.Alwara (27 Jaina bronzes collected from Alwara were taken to the Patna Museum) (Saraswati 1975; Gupta1965, pp. 160-161);
- 2. Bhatbinor, 3. Tugri, 4. Chechgaongarh, 5. Darika
  Extra sites include: 1.Bilonjia (Two Large Jain temples); 2. Jarakhpur; and 3. Dulmi

Chandil (Singhbhum)

Two *Tirthankara* figures and a *Narasimha* figure remain in Chandil. One of the Tirthankara is *Adinatha.* Near the bridge over the Suvarnarekha there is a temple ruin which yielded at least one inscription and a number of sculptures (Chakrabarti 1993), the date assigned to the early Pala period (8th–9th cent. A.D.).

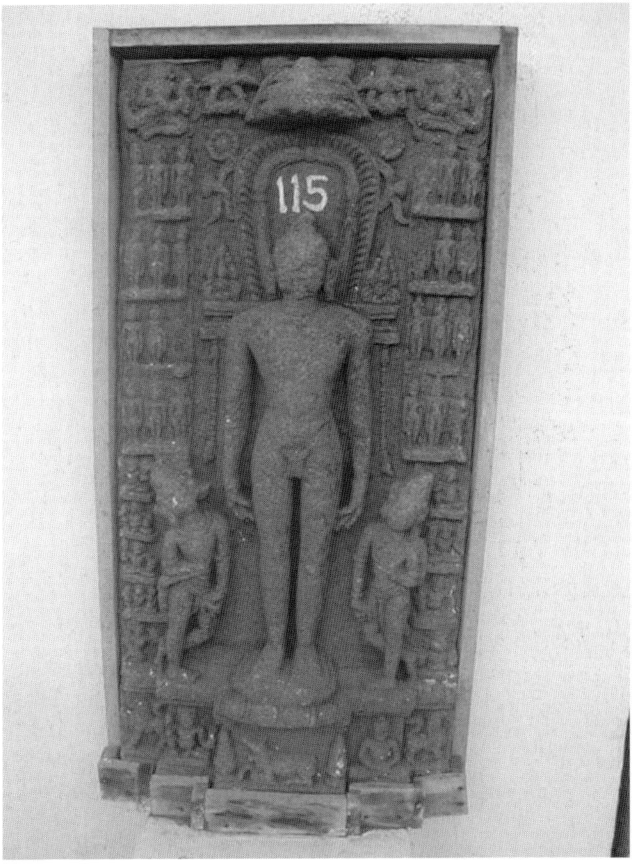

Chandil, salvaged Tirthankara figures

Chandankiari

A few miles from Purulia, head of the Manbhum district, a larger number of Jain antiquities were found. The collection of Jain Tirthankara images in Patna Museum are from this place. It is one of the finest collections of Jain antiquities in India. The sculpture in stone is exquisite and superb. They are dated to late Pala period (11th century). There are two other villages within five miles of Chandankiari *Kumhri* and *Kumardaga* where there are also some old Jain images.

Charra (Purulia) (See Palma, Pakbira, Boram)

Situated on the Kosai river, four miles northeast of Purulia on the road to Barakar. Beglar visited the site in 1872–73 and noted numerous Jain temples very elaborately carved, broken images, and votive *Chaitya.* According to the District Gazetteer originally as many as seven temples had stood over here. Five large *Tirthankara* statues have been found here. A ten-armed statue was found here by A Sastri in 1918. The site has also been noted by R D Bannerjee (1933, pp. 145–146) as having two temples of 50 feet high. Five large *Tirthankara* statues were found here. Two miles to the north another Jaina site, Gholamara, has been noted.

Deulbhira (Manbhum)

The site is on the bank of a small stream called the Hara; this is near Para. Remains of a temple and sculptures have been found, including a Tirthankara figure (height 79 cm), Uma-Masvara (height 95cm), a bull under the ten-armed Mahesvara and lion under the two-armed Uma, and an interesting figure of a goddess with four arms, the upper right and lower right respectively holding rosary and in blessing (*abhaya mudra)* and upper left and lower left respectively holding a lotus and lion below lotus (*Kamendalu*).

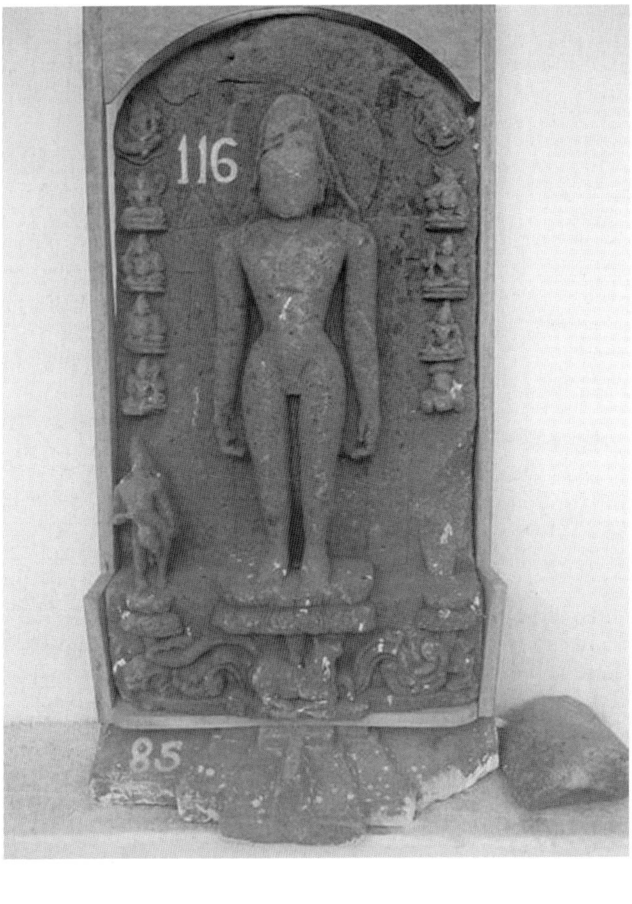

Darika

3 miles south-west of Chechgaongarh, there are old ruins, tanks, mounds, and cells. Beglar had noted a Jaina statue of black basalt.

Dulmi (Singhbhum)

On the north bank of the Suvernarakha river, it was first noted by Colonel Dalton in 1855, and visited by Beglar in 1872–73. It has *Chhatri* or umbrella with two stone columns supporting a triple umbrella. Beglar dates the ruins to the 10th century. Beglar also noted Bhumiya megalith graves near the place. This place requires investigation to see if it was submerged by the Panchet Dam on the Damodar River. Beglar assigns the date of the earlier Jain ruins to the 10th century, followed by Hindu in the 11th–12th centuries.

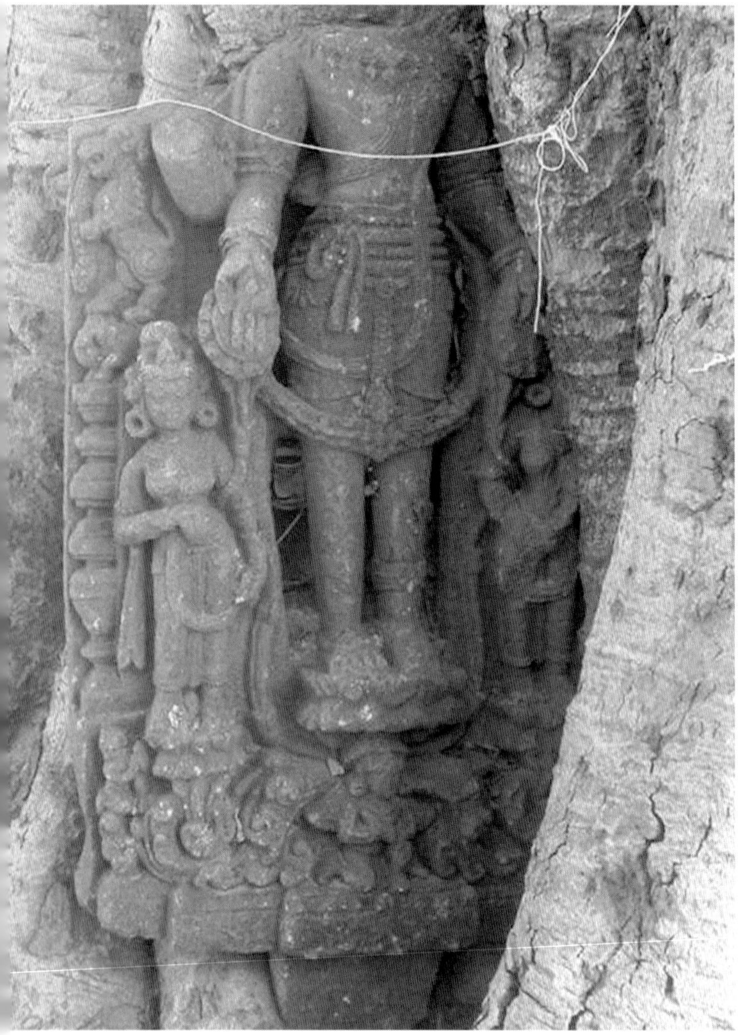

Dulmi, Jain ruins

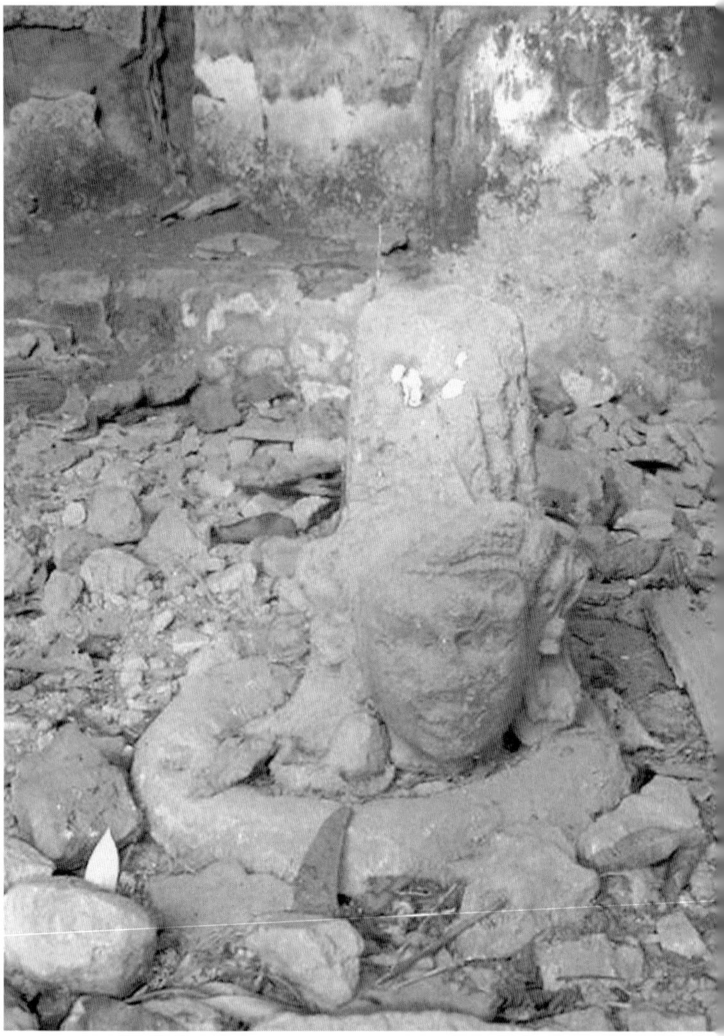

Dulmi, broken relics from Jain ruins

Two miles north-east of Sufaran. Beglar (1878) noted here a group of Jain temples under a Karam tree (*Adina Cordifolia*). The largest temple consisted of a sanctum, antarala, ardha-mandapa, mahamandapa, and so on. There may have been a portico. The site requires investigation if it is one of the 20 Jain temples flooded by the Panchet Dam referred to as Telkupi Jain temple complex on the South bank of Damodar River.

According to Beglar "The temple was once a very fine and large one, and had four subordinate temples near the four corners, of which two still exist." The tower had collapsed and in the shrine Beglar noted a Jain image three feet high with the figure of an antelope on the pedestal. It was being worshipped by the locals as Araniyanatha or 'forest god'. It is held sacred like the Tree God for females desiring offspring, who give it offerings. Beglar thought that many other Jain temples existed nearby. Little over a hundred yards away are two tanks known as Jora-pokhar on the banks of which was found a bas relief of elephant and rider.

Deoli (near Dutree)

When Beglar visited Deoli in 1876 he noted at Suisa a group of Jain temples.

Gholamara (Purulia)

A Jaina site two miles north-west of Chhara which itself is four miles north-east of Purulia.

Guhiapal (East Singhbhum)

80 km southeast of Jamshedpur and near Block Baharangora is Guhiapal, an archaeological site of Jaina importance, currently being excavated by the Archaeological Survey of India. At four specific sites in the region, Jaina images and structures of the 10th-11th centuries have been brought to light, and similar artefacts were also traced to the nearby villages of Barnipal, Jarapal, and Balijhuri. Baharagora is not far from the Suvarnarekha river as it flows into Bengal.

Ichagarh (Saraikela Kharsawan)

Hundreds of 9th–11th centuries (Pala Period) Jaina statuary are languishing in this area. The village and its heritage places are submerged in the Chandil dam which is nearby. Hundreds of large statues have already disappeared. It is from here the Aboriginal

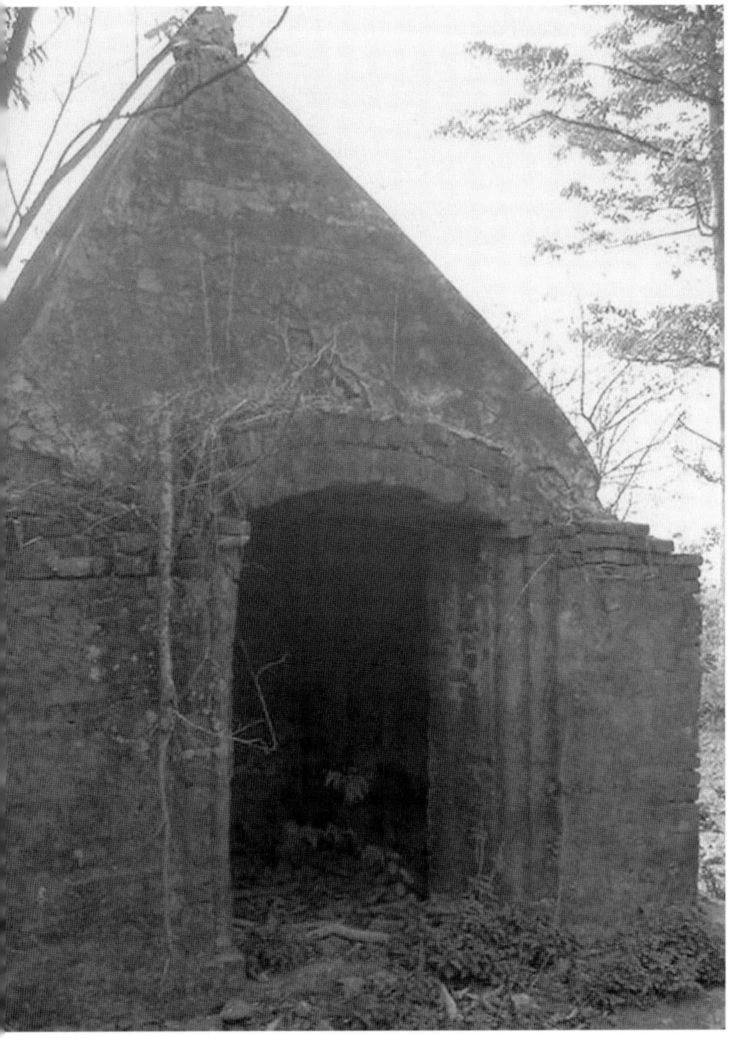

Dulmi, Jain temple

Society for Art in Jamshedpur collected the pieces which are preserved in the Patkum Museum. Some statues have been kept at the Tribal Welfare Research Institute Museum, Ranchi.

Jain site of importance. Part of relics submerged under the waters of Chandil Dam on the Suvernarekha River in East Singhbhum. This site is one of over 20 temple sites and 84 villages submerged by the waters of the Chandil Dam.

Itkhouri (Chatra district) (see also Sidpa below)

Itkhouri is a place strong in Buddhist Pali tradition as It-Khoi has been interpreted as *it-khoi*, meaning here the parting (khoi=loss) took place when Prince Siddhartha parted from his mother Mahamaya. It is directly on the pilgrim route from Varanasi to Hazaribagh, ten miles from Chauparan on the G.T.Road, and an equal distance from *Chatra,* an ancient Buddhist site where the Lord sat under the umbrella *(Chhatra)*

Itkhouri is situated on the Mohania river down which Prince Siddhartha wandered to the Gaya plain where he attained final enlightenment or *Nirvana.*

At the instance of INTACH, Hazaribagh Chapter's drawing attention to the site in 1994, a museum has been built to contain the thousands of pieces of red sandstone sculptures dated to the Pala period (9th -12th centuries). Excavation will undoubtedly reveal earlier relics to the Mauryan period. There seems a stylistic hunt of Jaina statuary, Uma-Mahesvari is also found; along with Surya.

Black basalt images of Surya, Shiv-Parvati, Nandi, and stupa with Buddha and Bodhisattvas have also been found at the site which have become the focal point of the Mahakali Hindu temple constructed at this place. Some of the sculpture in black stone from Rajmahal is obviously Jaina of Pala Period (8th–11th centuries)

Icha Dam

The Icha Dam which is contemporaneous with Chandil Dam in the so called Suvarnarekha Multipurpose Irrigation Project, flooded an unknown number of Jaina sacred sites in the West Bengal region. We only know that it drowned eighty-seven villages. All this is rather disconcerting, to say the least.

Jharia (Manbhum)

This region was probably the worst affected by the coal mining begun in 1903. It contains forts, buildings, and primitive burial mounds whose antiquity was noted by Beglar in 1872–73. Beglar noted that the name Jharkhand given by the Mughals to Kukrah (Chotanagpur) was an extension of Jharia-garh (Jharia Fort) to Jhar-Khand (Forest-neck, a sacred term used by the tribes, i.e. Bundel-Khand). The Khand is the ritual portion of the neck taken by the tribal priest from an animal killed in the animal hunt. Jharia has the remains of a Bhumij cemetery. This was originally a predominantly tribal area.

Karcha

This village is six miles from Purulia. There are many Jain statues and five mounds which require excavation. Other nearby Jain temple sites include Kumhri and Kumardaga, and two in Purulia town (Beglar 1878).

Kolhua Pahar (Chatra)

Some images cut into the rock on the stone of the western approaches of the hill have been described as of the Buddha by Dey. Kolhua Hill is situated six miles south-west of Hunterganj overlooking the valley of the Lilanjana River in the old Hazaribagh district bordering Magadh district and not over 60 km from Bodhgaya, the site of Lord Buddha's enlightenment..

A Buddhist Image found here by Aurel Stein is supposed to be the only Buddhist monument seen by him on the hill (D. R. Patil, Antiquarian Remains, p. 217).

Kolhua Hill is famed for its Jaina shrines rock-cut temples, Temple of Parasvanatha, (Jain) rock-cut sculptures of Jaina *Tirthankaras*, etc. It is a major Jain site of pilgrimage today but large quantities of Jaina stone antiquities have been the object of a thriving illegal trade for several decades with no effort to control the wanton loot going on. This has been typical of the open destruction of nearly all Jaina sites.

As per inscriptions found at the site it would be dated to the 7th or 8th Cent. A.D. Stein found reference to Kolhua in a Jain work called *Sri Tirtha-mala Amolakaranta* published in Hindi in 1983

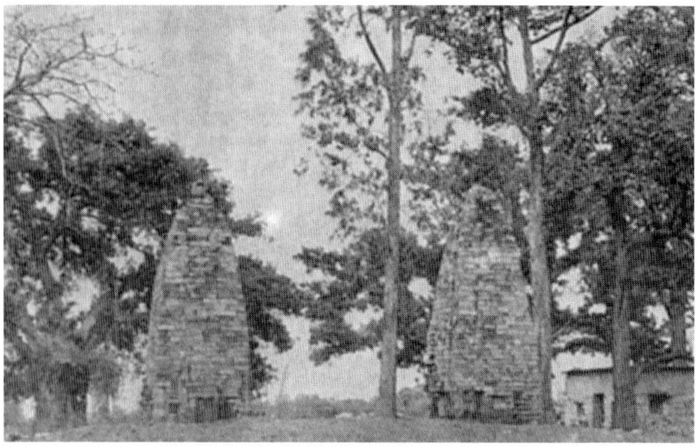

General view of Jain temple at Pakbira

by Rana Narayan Pal of Calcutta. According to the map given in this work the hill is mentioned as *Bhaddalapura-a-nagara* where it is stated the 10th *Tirthankara* Sitala-Swami was born. There are remains of a stone hill fort whose entrance faces to the west.

According to Bloch who visited the site in 1903 there were remains of two Temples in the village with ancient Jain statues, one having a figure wearing a crown, with a many-hooded cobra over the head. It probably represented Parasvanatha.

Khalbir-sthana (Purulia)

This is an interesting Jaina site where numerous votive Chaityas and the ruins of at least two temples in the nearby *Saal* jungles are to be found, one Saivite with the *Linga* in *situ* (Beglar 1878, p. 195).

Patkum (Important Site)

Patkum adjoins the Pabanpur Jaina site in pargana Manbhum attributed to the descendents of the legendary King Vikramaditya, which region was drowned in the Chandil dam (1985) on the river Suvarnarekha. As many as over twenty Jaina temples were submerged by the Chandil Dam. There had never been adequate archaeological survey in or any salvage operations, and all we know of them is from reports left by early British visitors such Beglar, Bloch, Hunter, and so on.

Patkum has become the site of a museum (established 1992) under the aegis of the Singhbhum Archaeology Preservation and Promotion Committee, of unique Jaina relics from the valley of the Suvarnarekha river, submerged by the Chandil Dam which destroyed over one hundred villages and attendant Jaina temples and statuary. The salvage by a concerned group of activists managed to bring about 150 large and small statues of Jain *Tirthanaras* and stone columns carved in granite and sandstone to the Patkum museum situated at a knoll just near the Dam. The Irrigation Department constructed a small museum here. Some pieces were taken to the Tribal Research Institute in Ranchi, it is reported. Jaina heritage at Ichagarh, Dulmi and adjoining villages are facing the rising waters of the Dam.

The remaining area requires extensive examination. Had investigation and highlighting of the Jain cultural heritage been done earlier it would have been a serious impediment to the Dam work begun in 1982 and avoided flooding of scores of villages and Jain sites and huge displacement of tribals of the area. No proper Archaeological survey was done before building the dam. Archaeological salvage is not used as a mandatory clearance for such destructive projects as big dams or mines. The negligence both of the Archaeological Survey of India and of individual scholars is brought to light along with India's policy of protecting non-Hindu sacred sites such as Jain and Buddhist sites of World Heritage.

Pandra (Manbhum)

Two miles behind Nirsha on the Grand Trunk road lies Pandra which has a large tank and Raja's palace, and temples of which one is a Jaina temple. The Telkupi group of temples submerged in the Panchet Dam is not far off. This entire area which is the heartland of the Bhumij tribes who once inhabited the area has faced complete destruction through the age old coal mining and the more recent dams on the Damodar river.

Pabanpur (Manbhum) Jaina Temple and Buddhist site (Important Site)

The village is located in Pargana Barabhum. The ruins contain highly artistic carvings. A miniature temple about two feet high containing representations of Jain Tirthankaras on the four sides was sent to the Indian Museum, Calcutta, for exhibition. Pabanpur requires inspection since Pabanpur adjoins the pargana of Patkum which has been submerged by the waters of the Suvarnerekha after the building of the Chandil Dam. The Pabanpur Temples are similar to the temples found at Dulmi and Telkupi attributed to Vikramaditya, the legendary ancestor of the Zamindars of Patkum. Nearby is the village of Bhula (meaning 'lost') up to which the ruins extend, and where there is a large burial ground attributed to the *Bhumiyas*. We may note that wherever extensive Jaina sites have been found the burial grounds of the Bhumij and Bhuiya have been found, indicating a tribal population which were under influence of the Jaina religion.

Pakbira (Purulia) Jaina Temples (see Chhara, Boram, Palma)

In Barabhum pargana the village is situated a mile east of Puncha and 25 miles southeast of Purulia on the Kosai river. The ruins were first noted by R C Beavan in 1865. They were later described by Beglar. The temple had collapsed but there was a tin shed which contained images, mostly of Jain tirthankaras, noteworthy being a colossal naked figure 7 1/2 feet high representing a Jain tirthankara Sreyamsanatha, with the lotus symbol on its pedestal. The foundations of the temple showed it was large, containing a *sanctum* and full complex of complementary chambers. The Temple faced to the West.

There are several temples at Pakbira, nearly two dozen according to Beglar, all built of stone, which indicates a large presence of stone cutters (Lohar or Asur) who would have presumably at that time adhered to the Jain religion. The masonry is carefully cut sandstone without any form of bonding. At a place near Pakbira is a hill between Pakbira and Baramasia which contains a cemetery of the Bhumiyas who were then probably Jains, and numerous votive Chaityas and oblong round stone blocks. These Bhumiyas were then most likely influenced by Jaina teaching.

The large stone images found here (height 2–28 m, width 38 cm) include those of Lord Mahavira, Lord Parsvanatha, Lord

Kunthunatha, Lord Neminatha, Lord Santinatha, and Lord Risabhanatha (10th century) and Lord Mahavira (9th century).

The Tirthankaras are in Karjotsaga yogi posture, on a double-petaled lotus, placed on a sapta-ratha (seven step) pedestal bordered by two bands in relief. The lanchana (Jain symbol) of the antelope, is shown in the centre of the pedestal. The miniature figures on the pedestal are the goat-headed deity Naigamesin who is the presiding deity of children. There are four female attendants performing anjali-mudra, similar to those found in the Mahabodi stupa sanctum floor at Bodhgaya. The Anjali-mudra is the offering of devotion to the Lord. At the base of the pedestal is a Kalasa (vase) on the left side and a linga (phallic emblem) on the right. The linga shows Hindu impact on Jaina statuary. The same was also faced by the Buddhist statuary.

The figure of Risabhanatha standing on a double-petaled lotus in Karjotsaga yogi posture is an exqunte specimen; attendant female figures with Chauris (small size) flank the figure. The Tirthankaras are backed by forty-eight smaller tirthankara images, in twelve rows of two on either side.

Palma (Purulia) Jain Temples and Memorial Stones (see Pakbira, Chhara, Boram)

Palma village is situated on the bank of river Kosai a few miles from Purulia. It has a large mound of a Jain Temple with images of Jain Tirthankaras scattered about. One of the images was larger than lifesize but broken in two. At the feet of each idol are two smaller figures carrying *Chowries* looking up at the figure. The entire area requires examination and excavation. Hunter refers to larger than life stone *tirthankaras* scattered about. It is clear that there are remains here of numerous Jain temples and their relics.

The temples are constructed of cut-stone and bricks, with quite a number of temples here, suggesting a Jain settlement nearby. Three colossal statues of Tirthankaras lay (two Agilnatha and one Satinatha) on the site when Block visited it in 1902. In 1937 Walsh reported the discovery of four memorial stones, which were moved to Patna Museum. The site requires fresh investigation. The Jina is pointed by a trefoil arch and surmounted by a curvilinear Sikahara of the Nagara older (Saraswati 1975, pp. 265–66)

Patamda (East Singhbhum)

At Bhula, six kilometres northeast of Patamda Block Office in East Singhbhum, many Jain sculptures were recovered in 1994 when canals were dug for the Suvarnarekha Multipurpose Project and Dam. 36 sculptures have been kept in front of Bhula Government Middle School at Bhula. The date of the sculptures is in the 9th–11th centuries (Pala Dynasty). The Patamda block is about 50 km north-east of Jamshedpur.

Parasnath Hill (Giridih district) Jain Temples

The Parasnath hill is now in Giridih district, formerly in Hazaribagh. Its height is 4481 feet. It is so named after Parasvanath, the 23rd Tirthankara of the Jains who attained Nirvana and died on the Hill. There is a group of Jain temples at Madhuban at the northern foot of the hill. Most temples on the hill have been constructed within the last few centuries. Beglar visited Parasnath but left no report of his impressions. No ancient religious monuments have been noted on the Hill beyond the 18th century. It is not presently threatened but is included as a major pilgrimage site of the Jains overlooking the Damodar river.

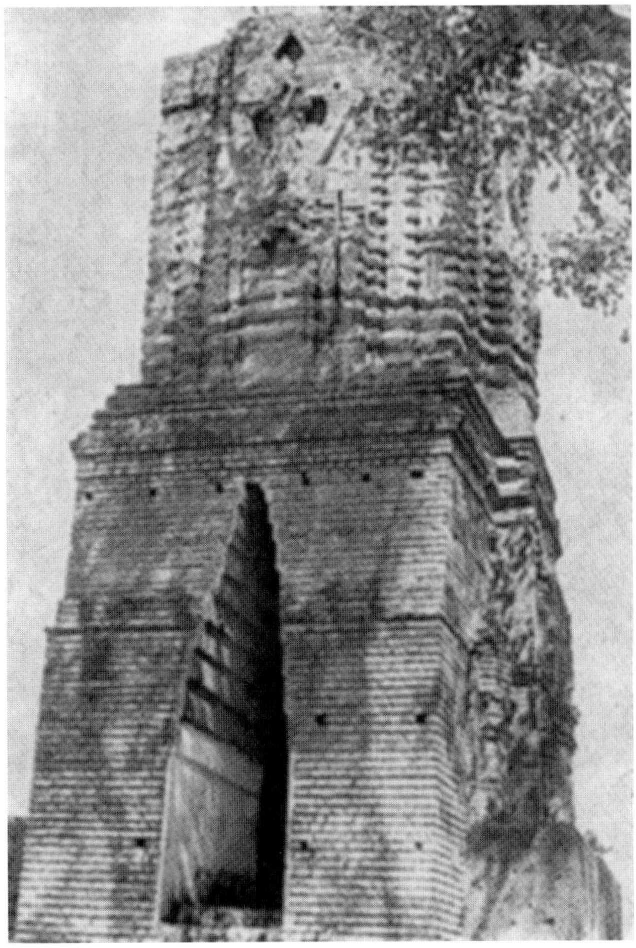

The early Jain temple at Para

The surviving Jain temple at Chharra

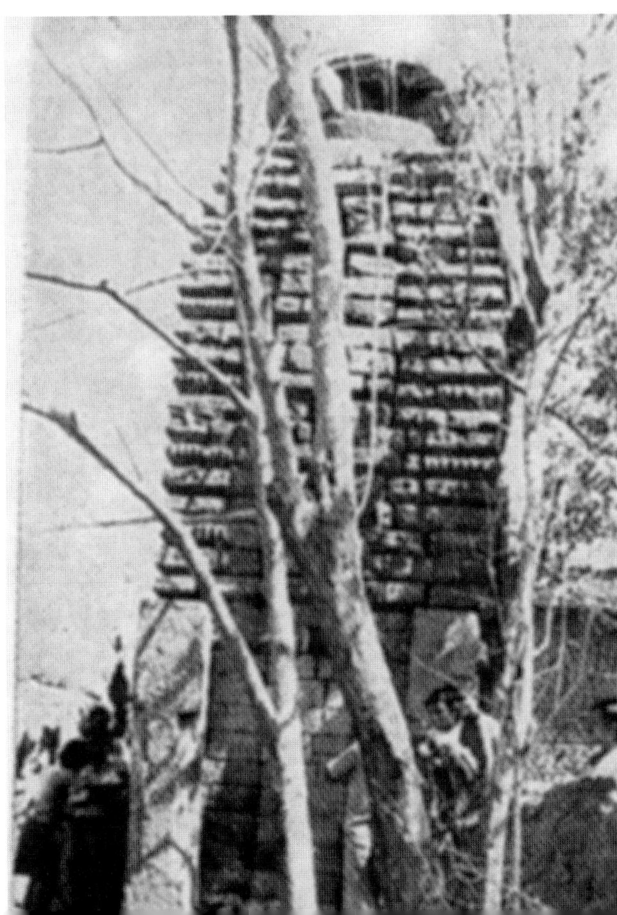

Ruam (Singhbhum)

This is an ancient Jaina site situated about two miles SW of Mahulia in Dalbhum area of the Singhbhum district. It was an important copper smelting centre and a former important settlement of Sravakas or Jains, with some old remains, tanks, and copper slag. O'Malley considers it to be an old Jaina *sravaka* settlement.

Ralibera (Manbhum)

Ralibera is near Anai-Jambal on Kangsabati River. Sculptures are in a mud hut in the school compound. They include Uma-Mahesvara on lotus with bull and lion *vimanas;* Risabhanatha height 1.32 m, width 63 cm with bull on pedestal below lotus.

Suisa (Manbhum)

No archaeological vestiges left except a group of sculptures and the remains of a Bhumiya cemetery as noted by Beglar (1878). Jain statues include *Risabhanatha* height 1.45 m, width 63 cm; *Parsvanatha* height 1.10 m, width 60 cm standing on a lotus with snake below; female deity height 1.10 m, width 59 cm standing on a lotus, with lion on pedestal indicating association with Lord *Mahavira.* Other include *Santinatha* on lotus, with deer below; *Mahavira* on lotus, with lion below; *Malinatha*, other female deities.

Suisa

This place is not far from Deoli and was visited by Beglar in 1876 when he found under a banyan tree a collection of Jain images.

Singhbhum

We can find the route of Jainism going from Magadha via Hazaribagh (Shikarbhum) and Katras to Purulia (Manbhum) which was the route to Orissa where Jaina carvings are found in Khandagiri caves. This district is also mentioned as Safa by Huen Tsiang (7th century), as well as its capital was noted by Cunningham to be at Barabazar in Barabhum Pargana, while Herbert identifies it with the Dalmi near Patkum. This area was purely an aboriginal population and was personally converted by Lord Mahavira himself.

Tuisama (Purulia)

Here Beglar noted a lot of Jain temples (1878:195)

Telkupi (Manbhum)

A village on the south bank of river Damodar, seven miles southeast of Chelrama. Beglar, Bloch, Hunter all visited the site between 1872–1902, and it is described as "the finest and largest number of temples within a small space to be found in Chutia Nagpur" (Beglar 1878). According to Bradley-Birt (1903) these were ancient Jain temples appropriated by the Hindus and that some Jaina images of *Tirthankaras* are being worshipped in the temples as Hindu deities. Beglar also noted an image of the Sungod (*Surya).*

Telkupi was important for being located on the trade/pilgrim route from Bihar to Orissa through Manbhum. Numerous mounds and tanks existed. Santals have a tradition of permitting a Santal girl promiscuous relations here once during her maidenhood at this place. It is said that King Vikramaditya used to come here for having oil put on his body before going to bathe at the Chhata Pokhar or Umbrella Tank at Dulmi 80 miles away. It is a link in the ancient tribal roots of Jainism in India. A most precious World Heritage site has been forever lost over here.

As in the report Chakrabarti et al (1993, p. 132) all 20 of the Telkupi group of Jaina temples on the South bank of the Damodar River were submerged under the waters of the DVC's Panchet Dam (1969) built 35 years ago on the Damodar River without any proper site recording or salvage operation. This conclusion was also the result of a study by Debala Mitra (1969), which noted in the Preface to her study that description of the temples was then largely posthumous because the entire area was already part of the Panchet Dam reservoir, which was the consequence of a big dam across the Damodar river near Panchet. She lists 26 temples of which her map of Telkupi Temples in the flooded area shows 20 out of 26 temples. In her report she lists a number of movable sculptures.

This bears a resemblance of over 20 Jaina temples under the waters of the Chandil Dam on the Suvernarekaha. And we do not know how much sacred heritage was lost in the nearby Maithon dam on the lower Barakar, the Konar dam on the Konar river, the Tilaya dam on the Upper Barakar, and the Lalpania dam on the Damodar river, and many, many other large dams and coal mines in the region. Now the attack of big dams, STTPs, and coal mines is on the Upper valley of river Damodar under the North Karanpura Coalfields Project (see ICOMOS *Heritage at Risk* Reports 2001/2002 – 2002/2003).

In the Upper Damodar Valley many rockart sites have iron slag in them. These sites have go back a long time to hunter-gatherer cultures (10-15,000 BC), but there may have been more recent markings by Jaina *sravakas,* which may be considered in view of the vast slag accumulations, and the great antiquity of the Jaina tribal culture in the remote past. The site of Isco is clearly a reference to copper mines (*ays*=copper, *Kho*=mine). Iron and copper remains have been found here also dating to earliest times (1500 BC).

More sites of Jaina heritage interest

The following sites are also of importance to Jain heritage:

- Manbhum & Purulia
- Jorakhpur
- Alwara
- Bhatnibor
- Dulmi
- Darika
- Kushjiri (Kashipur P.S.) (*Triratha* and *rekha* temple with richly carved stone figures)
- Ansar Karandi (near Boram) (Beglar 1878, p. 195)
- Pakhira (near Boram) (F.B.Bradley Birt)
- Para- (mounds)
- Garh-Jaipur
- Garh Panchet- (Fort of Panchet Hill)
- Ralibera- (across the river from Boram)

Updates

The stone/sand mining of rivers

One by one the hill rivers are being mined for stones and boulders at their sources. The forests on either side are stripped for several square kilometres around these areas. Additionally, the riverbeds are being dredged for sand. Special mention may be made for the following major rivers; Bokaro river at its source in Dhingura; Konar river near Gomia; Barakar river at its source below Lotia Dam (Tiger Pool).

Stone mining of Megaliths

Grave danger is posed to the stone mining rampantly on the increase throughout the Hazaribagh district. Major megalithic sites such as Banadag, Silvar, and other sites are in danger. Stone crushers are a big new business in Hazaribagh. The mining of Bawanbai Hill, a man-formed hill (2 km length, 1 km width, 325 ft height) has gouged out at least 20% of the hill on the east sides. If it is not contained, stone mining for commercial stone chips will completely wipe out the megaliths of the Hazaribagh District. All mining must be stopped subject to mandatory Ministry level archaeological clearance before mining which is not required in case of small mining projects currently.

Destruction of Adivasi villages religio-cultural landscapes, and archaeological sites in the North Karanpura Valley, for mines, dams, and Super Thermal Power Stations

At the western end of the Valley a big dam is being built on the Garhi river, a tributary of the Damodar, which will submerge four Mesolithic rockart sites and a major Mauryan site. The dam will also disrupt the migratory route of wild animals from Palamau to the west. Wildlife includes tiger and elephant. Over the years there has been a steady 'wearing down' of the environment's capacity to support big game or large wild animals. The Tandwa Super Thermal Power Project land has been arbitrarily acquired from the villagers and the STTP will be built alongside the dam. Over a dozen villages will be lost along with cultural and archaeological sites. In Balumath ten villages are presently under orders of being removed to make way for new mines.

At the eastern end of the valley, 40 km distant, a similar plan is being put into force by a project to place a big dam on the Badam river and place a Super Thermal Power Station adjacent to it at Gondalpura. Both the rivers (Garhi and Badam) are tributaries of the Damodar. Several decades back an STTP and big dam was built not far downstream at Patratu on the Saphe river, another tributary of the Damodar built by Russians.

Bulu Imam
Convener, INTACH (Hazaribagh Chapter)

References

Chakrabarti, Dilip K 1993, *Archaeology of Eastern India*, Munshiram Manoharlal Publishers Pvt.Ltd., New Delhi
Imam, Justin 2004, Patkum Museum Report, INTACH
Mitra, Debala 1969, PhD Thesis, Calcutta University
Patil, D R 1963, *Antiquarian Remains in Bihar*, K.P.Jayaswal Research Institute, Patna

Village of Biyanpura near Bhinbetka (Bhopal)

Bhinbetka has recently been inscribed in the World Heritage List of UNESCO. The site with wonderful rock paintings is situated in a remote area of the countryside. There are several villages nearby, barely influenced by 21st century life. One example is the village of Biyanpura (22° 56´16´´, 77° 36´50´´), which raises the serious question of what the cultural economic and social impact will be of an increase of tourism as a result of this World Heritage listing.

Michael Jansen
ICOMOS Germany

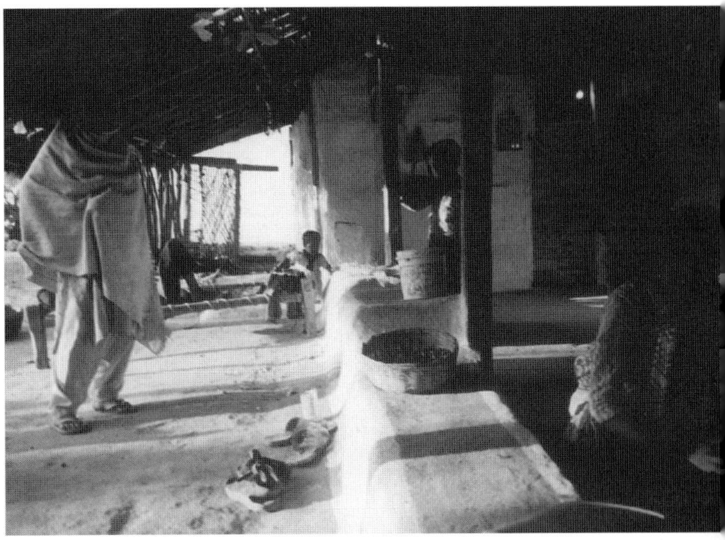

Views of Biyanpura

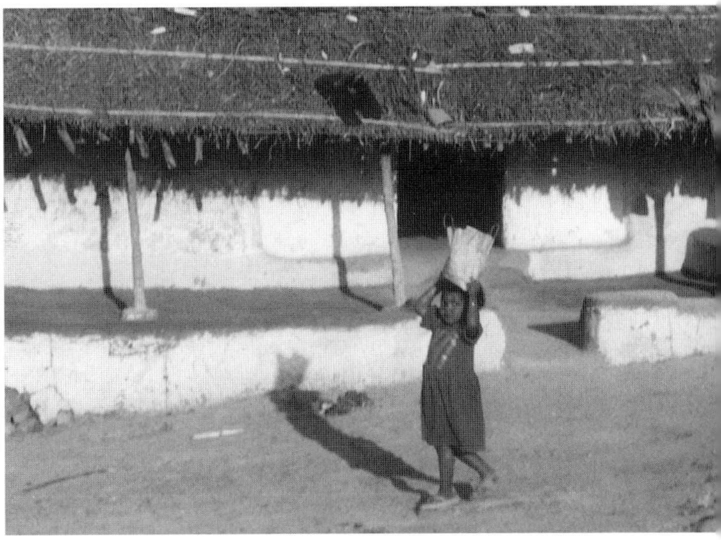

Merchants' houses (havelis) in the Shekhawati region, Northern India

The name of the Shekhawati region, situated in the desert zone between Delhi, Bikaner and Jaipur, is based upon the Rajput ruler Rai Shekaja, who founded a small princedom here in 1471. The Marwaris, the merchants of this province soon became very wealthy because of the favourable geographical position in the centre of important trade routes. This wealth was also reflected in the particularly opulent residential and shop buildings, the so-called *havelis*. After the decline of the caravan trade at the beginning of the 19th century the merchants moved their trade to the new metropoles Calcutta and Bombay, while their families remained in this region. With the money transferred to Shekhawati more fortification-like and richly decorated houses were erected.

In the period between 1750 and 1930 a great number of magnificent *havelis* were built, fitted with rich wooden and stone carvings and decorated with elaborate fresco paintings, both in the interiors as well as on the facades. The paintings, often covering every square centimetre of the walls, ceilings, columns and arches, deal with almost every topic which was important to people in that region: Apart from mythological scenes and traditional depictions of gods and saints, scenes from everyday life can be found. Especially the confrontation with the Western colonial power, its strange customs and technological achievements are often depicted, sometimes even explicitly as caricatures.

In the towns of this region (Jhunjhunun, Mandawa, Nawalgarh, Bissau, Churu, Dundlod, Fatehpur, Lakshamangarh, Nawalgarh, Ramgarh and Sikar) an abundance of *havelis* still exists. Although there are a few examples of beautifully restored *havelis* (in most cases serving as hotels or for other purposes), it is disturbing to see how many houses and their paintings are decaying. Entire streets can be found where every *haveli* is dilapidated.

The majority of these houses is still owned by the Marwari families, who, however, now live in the big cities or abroad. Many *havelis* are empty and are often plundered in search of antiques. Frescoes are cut from the walls, carved window frames and front doors are removed, and apparently entire sections of houses are demolished to be used again for new buildings. Frequently, frescoes on the facades have been painted over by advertisements or in the course of "repair work" have simply been plastered over. Countless posters for commercial and election purposes have also contributed to the poor state of the painted facades.

Gertraud Jonas
Edith Sassen

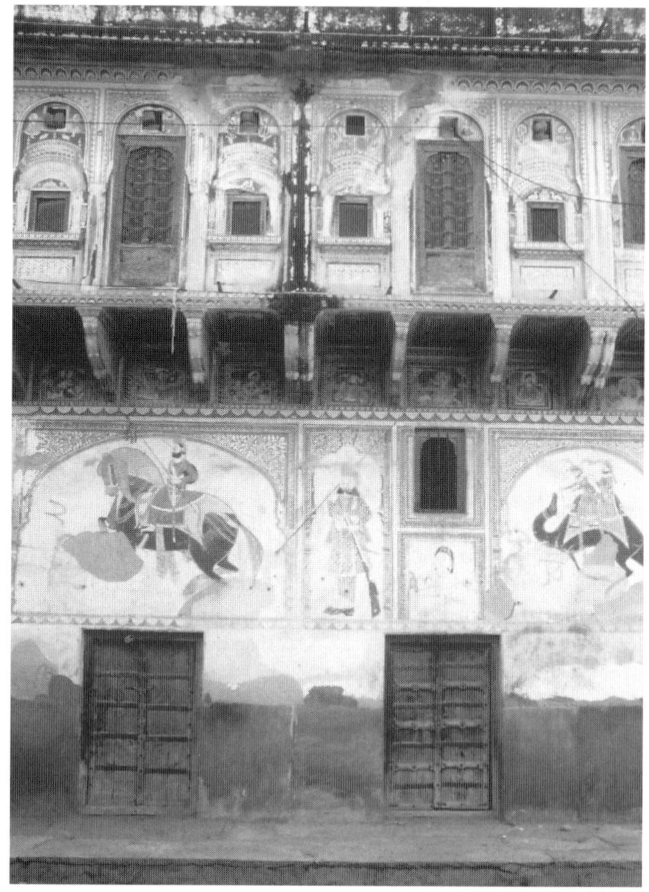

Havelis in the Shekhawati region

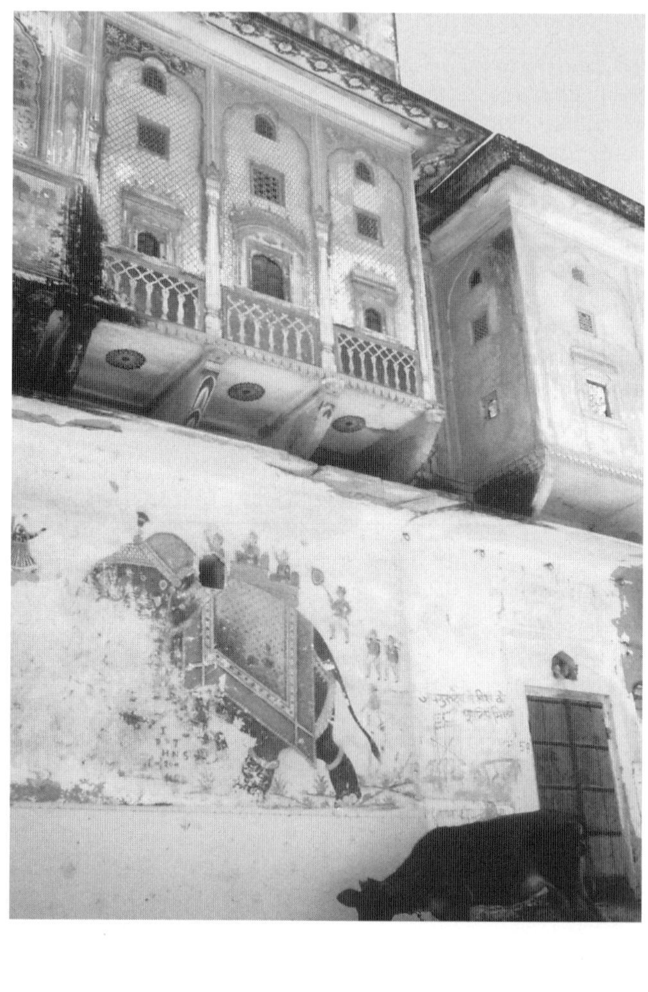

IRAN
The Bam Earthquake

The International Workshop on the Recovery of Bam's Cultural Heritage (17–20 April 2004, Bam, I.R. of Iran), co-organised by ICOMOS on the occasion of the International Day of Monuments and Sites (18 April 2004) adopted the following resolution in view of the devastating consequences of the earthquake on 26 December 2003:

The BAM Declaration and Recommendations

Preamble

The devastating earthquake of 26 December 2003 in the historic desert city of Bam, Islamic Republic of Iran, caused the tragic loss of many lives and the destruction of an overwhelming part of its cultural heritage. This natural disaster stirred a strong sense of solidarity in the international community for the people of Bam. This wish to aid was also particularly strong amongst institutions and professionals in the conservation of cultural heritage.

On the occasion of the International Day of Monuments and Sites (18 April), the Iranian Cultural Heritage Organization (ICHO), the United Nations Educational, Scientific, and Cultural Organization (UNESCO), and International Council of Monuments and Sites (ICOMOS) organized an International Workshop for the Recovery of Bam's Cultural Heritage between 17-20 April 2004 in Bam. 38 international and 23 Iranian expert participants and representatives of local and national authorities, and 31 ICHO members, gathered from Canada, France, Germany, Iran, Italy, Japan, Peru, Spain, the United Kingdom and the United States of America, as well as representatives of the Governments of France and Italy, International Centre for Earth Construction – Ecole d'Architecture de Grenoble – (CRATerre-EAG, France), the Getty Conservation Institute, World Monuments Fund, the International Centre for the Study of the Preservation and the Restoration of Cultural Property (ICCROM), ICOMOS, the World Bank, and UNESCO.

The workshop participants examined and reflected on the impact of the earthquake on Bam's heritage, notably Arg-e Bam and its related properties, the architecture and heritage assets which characterize this unique city, strategically located on the fringe of the desert;

Drawing from lessons learnt from previous natural disasters which affected built heritage in urban settings, such as the 1995 Kobe earthquake in Japan, and various earthquakes in India, Morocco, Turkey, and countries in North and South America,

Recognizing the universal nature of the ancient but still used earthen architecture as a living tradition adapted to desert environments, such as in Bam,

Noting with concern that human and natural threats continue to endanger Bam's heritage and realising the need for both urgent and long-term preventive considerations, which demand full coordination between all stakeholders,

Stressing the need to promote continued utilization of earth as a traditional building material for new constructions, thereby retaining and expanding the specialist skills and employment opportunities,

Emphasizing the fact that wisdom, knowledge and correct engineering principles must combine to create the required conditions for safe building, and it is not necessarily the implementation of material such as adobe which contributes to the failure of structures,

Recognizing the heroic and successful efforts by the authorities and professionals of Iran, in particular, the Iranian Cultural Heritage Organization, to effectively respond to the post-earthquake emergency needs of Bam's cultural heritage,

Noting that the crisis-response experience for Bam's cultural heritage could serve as a valuable and useful model at an international level after future disasters,

Calling upon all national and international partners and stakeholders to actively participate in the recovery process of Bam,

Recalling existing international conventions, recommendations, charters, and declarations favouring the integration of heritage conservation within the overall development process,

Adopted the following Declaration and Recommendations, for improved planning and conservation of Bam's heritage as an integral part of the recovery process and sustainable development process after the cataclysm, and called upon the Iranian authorities, ICOMOS and UNESCO to mobilize further co-operation at both national and international level to ensure that adequate steps are taken in the short, mid and long term, to provide further guidelines for preventive measures applicable to buildings, living settlements, archaeological sites of earthen architecture and cultural landscapes in Iran and around the world, and to encourage cooperation in the fields of research, education and training in relevant disciplines.

1. Conserving the full significance of Arg-e Bam and its setting

1.1 Arg-e Bam, whose strategic location was chosen for agricultural, economic and defensive reasons, is the cultural and spiritual landmark of the city of Bam and a dominant feature of its landscape. It is also a highly significant and exceptional record of many archaeological layers and historical periods, representing the long and rich civilization of this city, contributed to the evolution of earthen architecture and cultural development.

1.2 The earthquake caused major structural damage to Arg-e Bam and affected the visual and functional nature of its relation to the city and its traditions. It also exposed some of the archaeological features. A full understanding of the impact of the earthquake from a conservation and archaeological point of view is necessary to provide a comprehensive basis for specific interventions either to conserve the site, or to re-establish some of its pre-earthquake condition in concurrence with international conventions and charters.

1.3 The exceptional work achieved since the day of the earthquake by ICHO has taken into account the complex character of Bam's heritage, including the spiritual role of Arg-e Bam and its related properties in the life of the citizens of Bam. In particular, the Workshop participants took note of the rapid establishment of the access path within Arg-e Bam, which was planned with care and sensitivity, and of the other related facilities and safety measures.

1.4 The conservation and protection of Arg-e Bam requires a balanced approach with reference to scientific and cultural data to understand its place in the living culture and its contribution to the specific identity of Bam and the nature of its archaeological site. In this sense, archaeological research work and conservation should be considered as concurrent and complementary activities to be carried out on the property.

1.5 The significance of Arg-e Bam and its related properties, and the consequences of the earthquake both call for the establishment of a permanent centre dedicated to research and conservation. The elaboration of long term conservation strategies and time-restricted comprehensive management plans will contribute to the protection of Arg-e Bam, which the Government of Iran is presently proposing to be recognized as World Heritage property.

2. Conserving the character and the heritage of the city and landscape

2.1. The diverse tangible and intangible heritage resources of Bam express values associated with the long and complex history of the city. The heritage of Bam and its surrounding area are a cultural landscape composed of the desert environment, ingenious water use, management and distribution systems, (e.g. Qanats), agricultural land use, gardens, and built environment.

2.2. In the urgent recovery process of Bam city, the cultural, social, economic, and physical aspects must be addressed simultaneously with the conservation of Arg-e Bam. The absence of detailed and in-depth studies of the various cultural, social-economic and physical aspects of the city should not prevent recovery actions from taking place. Nevertheless they should be planned and implemented in a sensitive manner, in constant consultation with the heritage managers. Meanwhile, mid to long term planning and implementation to conserve the heritage of Bam, its character and cultural landscape should be undertaken. As part of this effort, an inventory of buildings, building elements and landscape features, should be prepared. All these efforts will provide information to implement awareness and social programmes for the people of Bam, and develop their understanding and appreciation of their earthen heritage.

2.3. Recovery planning and implementation should both refer to and be the subject to an integrated documentation programme. Considering the diversity of Bam's heritage and the challenges to the revitalization of Bam's cultural landscape, the techniques and media used for documentation should be appropriate to the objectives of the specified tasks at hand. All information should be incorporated into the information system of the larger management plan.

2.4. The foundation of Bam's strong identity is composed of gardens and plantations, monuments of religious and civil uses, traditional houses, public facilities and water systems, and such features as the walls of different types of earth constructions, for example "chiné", and all the manifestations of intangible heritage. The conservation, wherever possible, should be preferred and their reconstruction should be seen as a chance to perpetuate the living identity of Bam. Thus, through its urban landscape, there is an opportunity for real improvement in building technologies, and a reduction in vulnerability to natural forces, such as future earthquakes.

3. Integrating heritage in the recovery process and the future development of Bam

3.1. The conservation and revitalization of intangible and tangible heritage of Bam must be integrated within the General Master Plan which should be revised, as well as complementary support programmes and special projects contributing to the recovery process of post-earthquake Bam, in order to ensure that the unique identity and cultural character of Bam are retained and fully contribute to the restoration of the life of its citizens.

3.2. The cultural heritage, in particular the site of Arg-e Bam and the overall character of the city also constitute primary but non-renewable resources for the future social and economic development of the city, through tourism and other related activities. As such, their conservation and adequate management, including the perpetuation of skills and traditional know-how are to be considered as resources for the city's future development.

3.3. The recent development of tourism and its likely future expansion are not incompatible with the scientific and cultural objectives associated with the conservation and protection of Bam's cultural heritage and should be seen as complementary. While tourism infrastructures should be planned and developed so as to limit or eliminate their potentially negative visual or physical impacts on cultural heritage, the benefits of tourism should be shared with the local economy and contribute to the conservation of the cultural resources. Finally, the interpretation or presentation of the sites should include reference to the earthquake and its consequences for the local population.

4. Preserving and enriching the tradition of earthen architecture

4.1. The impact of the earthquake on the built heritage of Bam and its infrastructures demonstrated that it was the lack of quality of construction and engineering of the buildings that was the main cause of damage rather than the construction materials themselves. This also demonstrates the need to document and understand building and material performance properly. This is particularly important in the development of seismic earthen architecture technology for future use in Bam and elsewhere in Iran.

4.2. It is important to upgrade the social image of vernacular architecture among the local people, without which this kind of architecture will be inevitably lost due to the loss of the relevant traditional skills and know-how.

5. Protecting and preventing damage to earthen heritage in seismic areas

5.1. The collapse of structures and the debris resulting from earthquakes are serious risks to human life and to cultural heritage.

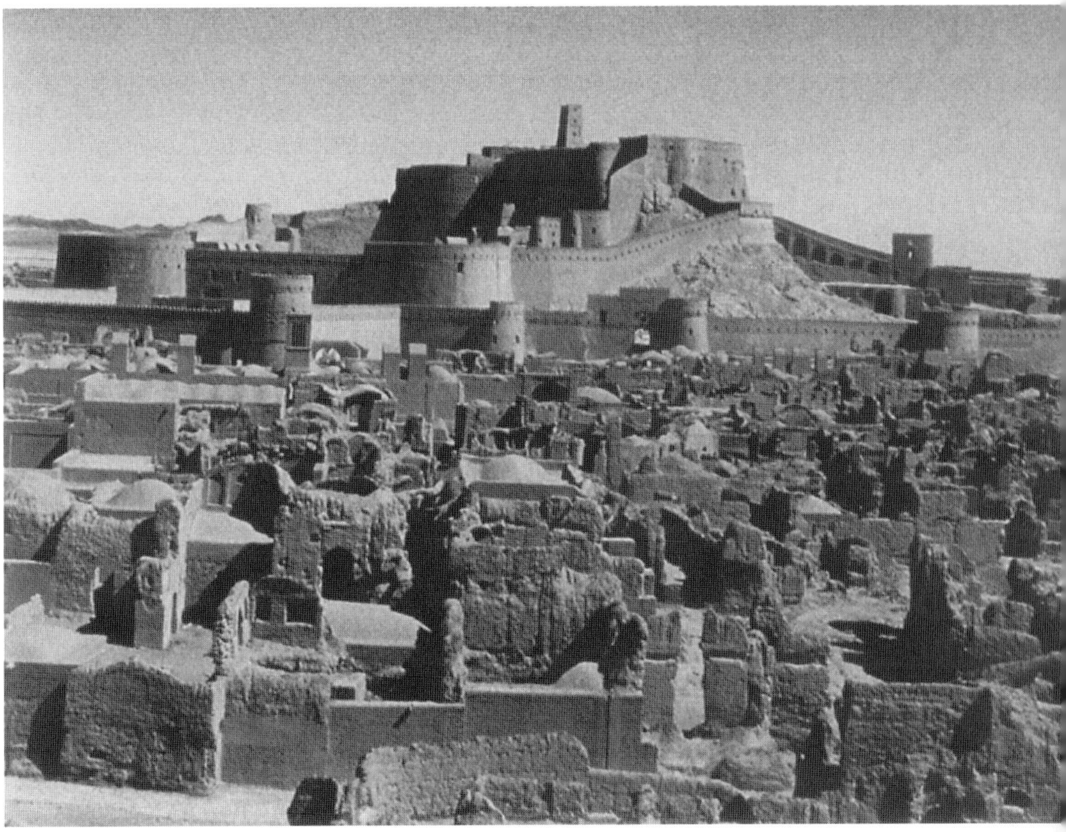

Bam before the earthquake

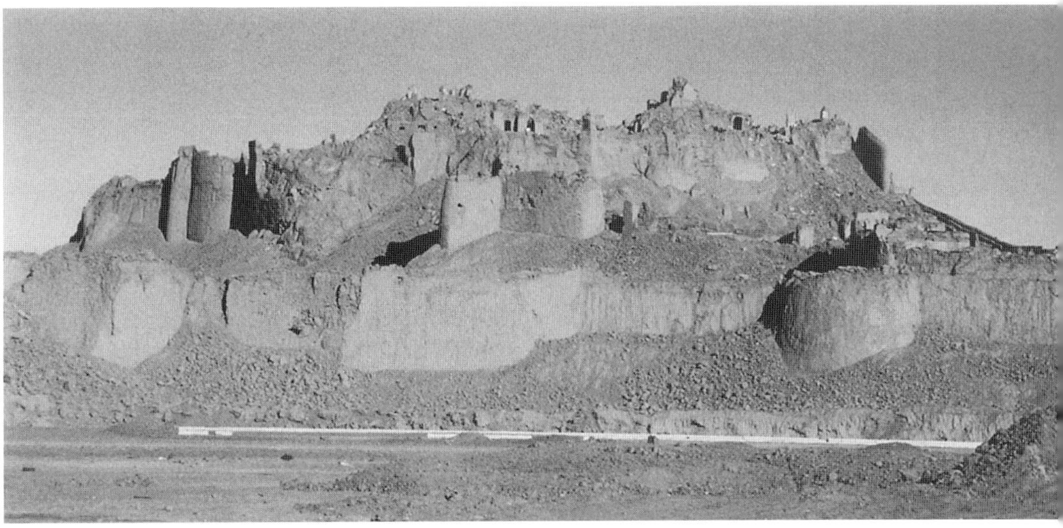

The Citadel at Bam after the earthquake

It is now recognized that protection against such cataclysms must be considered both for historic and contemporary structures. In light of this, it should be the practice in heritage environments to go beyond the confines of standard present-day engineering analysis and design techniques. This should include a full understanding and possible use of the earthquake performance characteristics of traditional anti-seismic construction practices of the regions and nations involved.

5.2. To facilitate the protection and prevention of damage to earthen heritage, it is essential to:
a. Increase understanding of the complete behaviour and performance of the earth material, structure, and construction in seismic areas;
b. Document the traditional cultures and architectures where earth is the principle building material, paying special attention to their specific responses and relationships to the needs of the inhabitants, and environments;
c. Document the different types of existing earthen materials and building systems, to understand and develop a glossary for the processes of decay;
d. Maintain and monitor all types of earthen structures;
e. Ensure that a full understanding and appreciation of earthen architecture, building materials and structures is integrated into the documentation used by all involved in conservation activities.

6. Sustaining co-operation to realize the conservation goals

6.1. The diversity of cultural, scientific, educational and management issues of Bam and the effects of the earthquake call for sustained co-operation at different levels, the sharing of concerns and knowledge in order to increase the capacity required for the realisation of specific projects.

6.2. At the local level, the recovery of Bam's cultural heritage requires the development of an integrated approach that is transparent and open towards the population. Basing itself on information and the processes of education, consultation, and participation, this approach should take into account the perspective of the local population, acknowledging the specific responsibilities of the institutions and professionals entrusted with the care, maintenance and accessibility of Arg-e Bam and other elements of Bam's cultural heritage.

6.3. Co-operation among governmental and non-governmental institutions and associations, at the national and international levels is essential to carry on specific tasks, such as the development of a comprehensive information system. Moreover, an interdisciplinary approach is necessary to address the various scientific, educational and conservation needs of Bam's cultural heritage. The setting up of appropriate tools and mechanisms to facilitate and sustain such national and international co-operation is required and must be implemented.

6.4. Co-operation must be developed with other organizations, especially those usually involved in restoration, archaeology and conservation of heritage, as well as those working in the fields of urban planning, housing, tourism and funding activities.

7. Recommendations

7.1. Recommendations for immediate action:
a. Document, identify and analyse initial risks and implement emergency stabilisation treatments.
b. Secure and stabilise the parts of Arg-e Bam which are vulnerable to aftershocks.
c. Provide adequate, sensitively designed and safe access to conservation professionals, the general public, and to the citizens of Bam who will continue to utilize the Arg-e Bam for traditional and religious activities.

7.2. Recommendations for short-term actions (2004–2005):
a. Define criteria and procedures for managing debris, taking into full consideration, on a case by case basis, the structural implications any interventions may cause on the heritage resources.
b. Continue with rigour the consultation process between ICHO and the relevant authorities in ensuring that the Master Plan for the Reconstruction of Bam City respects the heritage areas of Bam, as defined within the core and buffer zones, which are being proposed for World Heritage inscription. In addition, the panoramic views and cultural landscape surrounding Arg-e Bam and its related properties must be taken into account within the Master Plan.
c. Strengthen and continue the comprehensive management planning process in a short to medium time frame, for Arg-e Bam and its surrounding areas.
d. Develop plans for visitor access and orientation, including exhibition of pre and post-earthquake events and heritage assets.

7.3. Recommendations for mid-term actions (2004–2010):
a. Develop and implement a site management plan for Arg-e Bam and its surrounding areas. The plan must address and establish policies for conservation, archaeological researches, rehabilitation, cultural landscape protection, site interpretation, access, circulation and safety. Furthermore, the plan should guarantee compatibility with the General Master Plan being developed for Bam's reconstruction.
b. Develop a conservation programme, which includes a comprehensive analysis resulting in interventions based on the identification of the complete range of values in accordance with international charters.
c. Implement an open information management system to ensure access to information and to prevent wastes of effort. To this end, standard criteria for data collection, classification and entry must be established. These standards must take into consideration the needs of multiple disciplines.

7.4. Recommendations for long-term actions (2004–2015):
a. Assess the objectives of the site management plan of Arg-e Bam, the effectiveness of the policies within the management plan, and the compatibility with the expected outcomes from the General Master Plan.
b. Conduct scientific investigations to address issues related to the long term conservation of earthen architecture in Arg-e Bam. This could contribute, in a broader national and international context, to the development of adapted use of earthen architecture techniques for seismic areas and for contemporary needs.

8. Sustaining the momentum and focus to implement the present Declaration and Recommendations

8.1. Establish a permanent research centre for Arg-e Bam in particular, and on earthen architecture in general, which may also

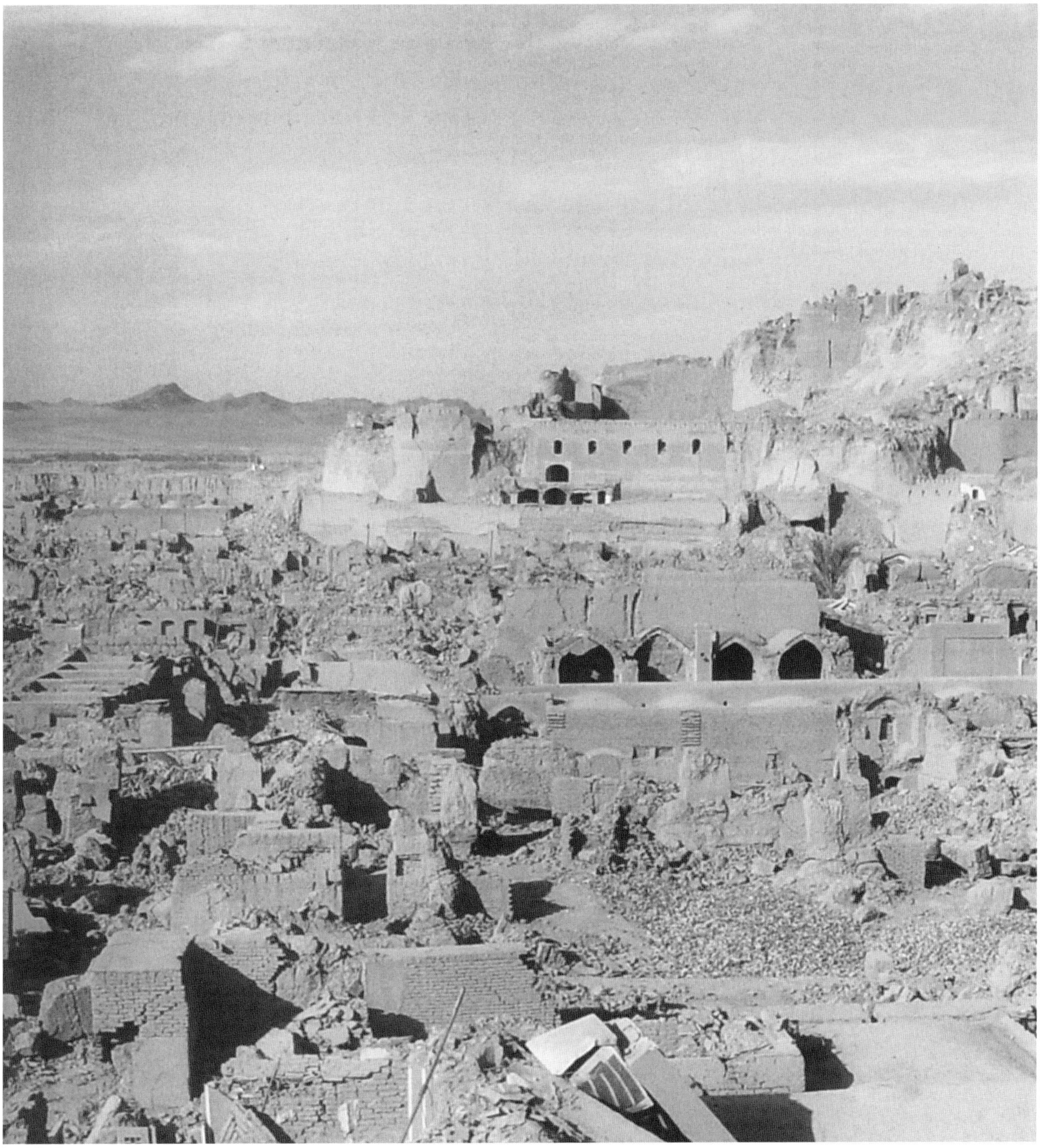

Bam, damages caused by the earthquake

promote the use of Arg-e Bam as a training and research centre of national significance.

8.2. To provide Bam and its heritage with the necessary support, the participants agreed that it would be essential for ICHO, ICOMOS and UNESCO to continue their co-operation to ensure the results of this workshop are effectively responded to. The documentation resources drawn from the information management system of Bam's heritage should comprise the foundation for sustainable conservation work. Special attention to the development of user interface design appropriate to professional communities, public outreach programmes, and pedagogical usage should be given priority. The appropriate cultural contexts and technological infrastructures can be instrumental in the dissemination strategies in this stage of implementation.

8.3. The urgent creation of a fund by UNESCO for streamlining assistance to Bam's heritage was recommended.

Finally, the participants of the Workshop expressed their deep appreciation to the Iranian Cultural Heritage Organization and the Iranian authorities, ICOMOS and UNESCO for jointly hosting and organizing this timely and important Workshop. Furthermore, gratitude was expressed to the Government of Japan, UNESCO and its World Heritage Committee, and the World Bank, for their generous technical and financial assistance to realize this Workshop, and to the Governments of Canada, France and Italy, the Getty Conservation Institute, and the World Monuments Fund for their technical co-operation.

Adopted in Bam, Iran, on 20 April 2004

A series of new dams is submerging archaeological sites throughout Iran

Ambitious hydro-electric programme is pushed ahead regardless of heritage fears

Iran's cultural heritage is facing almost unquantifiable damage from an ambitious programme of dam building. There are currently 85 dams under construction across the country, part of a programme that the Iranian government promotes with a considerable amount of national pride. It is an understandable concern in a dry country, parts of which are recovering from a seven-year drought. The dams are also connected to a programme of hydro-electric production that is seen as an essential part of a process of modernisation and industrialisation regularly highlighted by government issued targets and figures. By March of this year, hydro-electric power is expected to produce around 5,500 megawatts of electricity, rising to 14,000 megawatts by 2021, representing 20% of Iran's total usage.

In its desperate attempts to mount salvage operations, the Iran Cultural Heritage Organisation (ICHTO) has found itself not only obstructed by the Energy Ministry, but close to being in open opposition to the government. With little time remaining to survey the sites under threat, it is possible that the true extent of what will be submerged beneath the waters of these reservoirs will never be known, a potential cultural tragedy in a country often referred to as the cradle of civilisation.

At least five dams, all in advanced stages of construction, have been identified as threatening sites of particular importance. On 8 November, the waters began rising in the reservoir behind the biggest and most advanced of these projects, the Karun-3 Dam, on the Karun River, around 28 kilometres east of the ruins of the ancient city of Izeh. In a clear display of dissent, ICHTO officials refused to attend the opening ceremony attended by Energy Minister Habibollah Bitaraf. By 14 November, the historic Shalu Bridge, Iran's first suspension bridge, had already been submerged.

Of greater significance are the early archaeological sites in the area. In late September, a desperate plea for assistance was posted on the internet by A. Dashizadeh, an Iranian archaeologist directing an ICHTO salvage team, which was given a single month to survey the 50 kilometre-long river valley by Ab-Niroo, the company responsible for building the dam. Mr Dashizadeh said that the team had already located 18 sites from the Epipaleolithic period (20,000-10,000 BC), including 13 caves and four rockshelters. The river valley is also rich in rock-carved reliefs, graves, ancient caves and other remains from the Elamite era (2700BC- 645BC) many of which are now underwater.

At the time of writing archaeological salvage operations were continuing around the clock, with four to six months remaining before the water rises to its maximum level. However, Mahmud Mireskandari of the ICHTO's underwater archaeology team said that his team possesses neither the equipment nor the expertise necessary to save these sites, and without foreign assistance they will be lost. This assistance has yet to materialise and Faramarz Khoshab, president of Izeh's Cultural Heritage Association says that looting is already a problem.

US archaeologist Dr Henry Wright of the Museum of Anthropology at the University of Michigan, who surveyed the Karun river area in 1973, told The Art Newspaper that in addition to the early archaeological sites, other significant losses could include castles or qaleh from the Islamic period as well as extraordinary late Islamic cemeteries. „To see this happening breaks my heart," he said.

By far the most famous site under threat is Pasargadae, ancient capital of the Achaemenids in the sixth century BC and residence of Cyrus the Great, which was registered on Unesco's World Heritage List last July. Situated in Fars province, it is only four kilometres away from the Teng-e Bolaghi gorge, once part of the renowned Imperial route to Persepolis and Susa, which will be flooded by the Polvar River when the Sivand Dam is completed in March 2005. Part of the ancient city will be buried under mud, and even the mausoleum of Cyrus the Great is believed to be at risk. Beginning in January 2005, a salvage team consisting of French, German, Italian, Japanese and Polish archaeologists will collaborate with their Iranian counterparts in a joint operation to save an estimated 100 archaeological sites in the area.

Another major project, the Sarhand Dam near Hashtrud in East Azerbaijan Province, which will also become operational next year, threatens at least 10 important archaeological sites and substantial archaeological losses are also expected in Gilan Province.

This potential archaeological tragedy has received little media coverage in the west, and many of the areas have never been properly surveyed. What has emerged thus far may just be the tip of the iceberg, and in the process of attempting to transform itself into a modern industrial state, Iran seems set to obliterate a significant part of its cultural heritage.

Lucian Harris in *The Art Newspaper* (20 December 2004)

IRAQ
State of Ecology and Built Heritage after Four Decades of Adversity

In 1925, Baghdad City Council wanted to demolish the famous 14th century mosque of al-Marjan as part of a street widening project, but a public campaign, supported by the press, forced it to reverse the decision and the monument was saved. In a press conference the next day, the Mayor addressed the leaders of the campaign as follows: "Understand this: we were willing to build a bigger and better mosque in its place, of concrete. That you prefer an old ruin over a modern concrete building is truly astounding."

Disregard for the shared heritage and ignorance of its potential to forge and sustain a uniting identity for all sections of the population have prevailed, in varying degrees, among all the rulers of Iraq ever since its creation in 1921. However, empathy between the rulers and the past reached an all-time low during the decades of the dictatorship. This article highlights some of the consequences of that for Iraq's historic building stock and natural environment. A general historical overview is followed by more detailed presentations in five case studies where the damage was so serious that one can talk of cultural genocide.

Overview

Iraq came to occupy a position of prominence in Islamic history when Umayyad rule came to an end and the seat of the Caliphate moved to it from Syria in 750. Nearly all the surviving historic buildings were built after that date. The relatively fragile building materials used in their construction, namely sun dried bricks, fired bricks and wood, and prolonged exposure to the region's great temperature fluctuations and frequent floods make the task of maintaining them extremely difficult. This work is the responsibility of the State Board of Antiquities and Heritage (SBAH), which was initially established in 1923 to oversee excavations in Iraq's numerous archaeological sites and this continues to be its principal preoccupation. This is understandable in a country which possesses more than 10,000 unexplored sites. Despite this however, the Board's achievements in the field of rehabilitating historic monuments is impressive. Many heritage sites have been identified, surveyed and restored to their original state. In 1975, the Board with help from UNESCO established the Regional Centre for the Conservation of Cultural Property in the Arab Countries (RCCCP), which provided support in the form of consultancies, laboratory tests and training.

What is missing from the work of the Board in this field however, is a preventive maintenance strategy based on regular inspections of all sites by qualified staff who record their observations on specially prepared inventory forms. The inspections are repeated at intervals determined to suit each site in order to update the information. Based on these findings appropriate preventive repairs are carried out before decay sets in. Absence of such a strategy is responsible for the loss of many fine heritage sites, among them three 14th century minarets, and threatens others with the same fate.

The work of the Board is regulated by the Heritage Site Law No 55, promulgated in 2002, that defines the various categories of heritage sites and sets out procedures for dealing with them. It is an iniquitous law because it gives all the rights to the government and puts the entire responsibility on the shoulders of the citizen. It makes no provision, for example, for any form of help to owners of listed monuments or buildings of merit who cannot afford to preserve them. As a result many unique examples have been lost or deteriorated.

Impact of the Iran-Iraq War

Almost immediately after the war began in 1980, concern about heritage disappeared from the national political agenda. The RCCCP was closed down in 1993 and the SBAH lost a large chunk of its budget. Many of its employees were sent to the front and many others left the country to seek employment elsewhere. Restoration activities were limited to urgent maintenance of care for important heritage places. Even in such cases, constraints of budget and manpower sometimes forced SBAH staff to ignore the rules of sound practice. When cracks developed in the brick vault above the western *iwan* of the 13th century al-Madrasa al-Mustansiriyya in Baghdad the entire vault was removed and replaced by a reinforced concrete slab.

While battles were raging on the front the leaders in Baghdad were gripped by a hysterical spasm of mega construction projects. Public parks, playgrounds, schools, sport fields, even privately owned sites were seized to build palaces for the ruling family and the big-wigs of the Ba'ath Party and turned into no-go zones. Major planning decisions, frequently breaking fundamental taboos, were taken arbitrarily and in direct contravention of approved land use patterns. The riverside cafés along Abu Nouas Street, among the Middle East's most famous leisure centres, specialised in serving *masguf,* the renowned smoked carp, were closed down and a hedge of water hyacinth (*eichhornid crassipes*), a thick fast growing bush, was planted in their place, totally cutting off the street from the view of the river.

A rational, preplanned strategy to destroy monuments and other cultural vestiges was followed to severe Iraqis from the elements that connected them with their pre-Ba'athist past, as the examples below show:

- Guest workers from Egypt and elsewhere, with little knowledge of urban life, brought to replace Iraqis who had been drafted, were settled in the oldest and most traditional quarters of central Baghdad. The social pressures that followed forced the original inhabitants to leave their homes and a unique close-knit society, heir to a way of life over twelve centuries old was torn apart.
- In 1995 the traditional 19th and early 20th century courtyard houses of al-Shawwakah in west Baghdad were demolished and replaced by a line of concrete apartments, 15 storeys high copied from Europe of the 1950s, years after they had been condemned there as social disasters. They are out of keeping with the scale of the city and bear no relation to the life style of their occupants.
- In Rashid Street, the capital's main shopping centre, scores of old shops dating back to the 1940s were demolished to make room for a contemptible statue of a Ba'ath Party member who had been killed in that spot in 1959 while attempting a terrorist attack against the then prime minister.
- Iraq's Unknown Soldier Monument designed by one of the country's foremost architects and built in 1959, was demolished in 1982 and replaced by a presidential statue which became the focus of international media attention when American soldiers pulled it down in April 2003. A telling case of going from the sublime to the ridiculous.

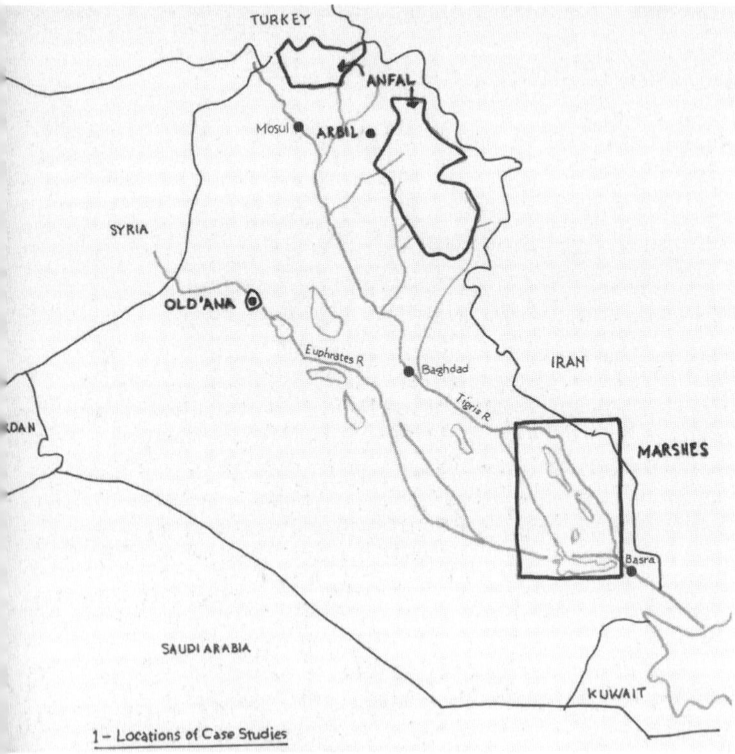

Map 1: Locations of case studies

Five Case Studies

The locations of the case studies are shown on map No 1. The first case study sets forth the draining of the interconnected marshes and lakes of south Iraq that has caused what the United Nations Environment Program (UNEP) has called 'one of the world's greatest environmental disasters'. Case study 2 describes the devastation that the Iraqi army visited on Kurdish towns, villages and farms, laying to waste about half of Iraq's productive farmland. Case study 3 is a eulogy to the old town of 'Ana, on the upper Euphrates which was submerged when the construction of al-Qadisiyya dam was completed in 1987. The ancient Qala'a (Citadel) of Arbil, the oldest continuously occupied site in the world, is the subject of case study 4. The last case study focuses on the Saray Administrative Complex, a group of mainly Ottoman buildings just inside the northwestern corner of Baghdad's 11th century wall, which eighteen weeks of post-war ransacking left in shambles.

1 Draining the Marshlands of South Iraq

Situation before the 1990s

The marshlands of south Iraq are located at the confluence of the Tigris and the Euphrates, between latitudes 32°30' and 30°0' and stretch from the Iraq-Iran border in the east to altitude line 40°30' in the west. They were made up of several permanent lakes and stretches of seasonal marshes interconnected with lagoons and watercourses. Covering an area of up to 20,000 km^2 during the flood season, they were the largest wetlands in the Middle East and among the most important in the world. A study of early Islamic documentary records and Sumerian cylinder seals that depict canoes similar to those used by the marsh dwellers, show that the marshes of Iraq were in existence for 5000 years or more before they were made to disappear.

They were home to about 400,000 Madan, who lived in arched reed houses on islets and moved by poling *mashhufs* (canoes), made locally of wood and reed mats waterproofed with bitumen. They lived by fishing and kept water buffalos for milk and yogurt. Produce of the marshes consisted of cereals (wheat, barley and rice), buffalo skins and bones, fish, dates, bamboo and woven mats. Ecologists have compared them to great mega deltas such as the Yangtze and Amazon in view of their interaction within regional and world ecosystems. They were the natural habitat of rare species of mammals, way station to migratory birds between Siberia and South Africa and they acted as a great water treatment system that released clean water into the Gulf.

Marshlands in 2001

The marshes began to decline in the 1970s as dam building in Syria and Turkey attenuated the flow of the two rivers. The situation worsened in 1990 when the gigantic Ataturk Dam in Turkey was completed, the first phase of the Southeast Anatolia project. Sub-

Map 2: Extent of marshes in 1985

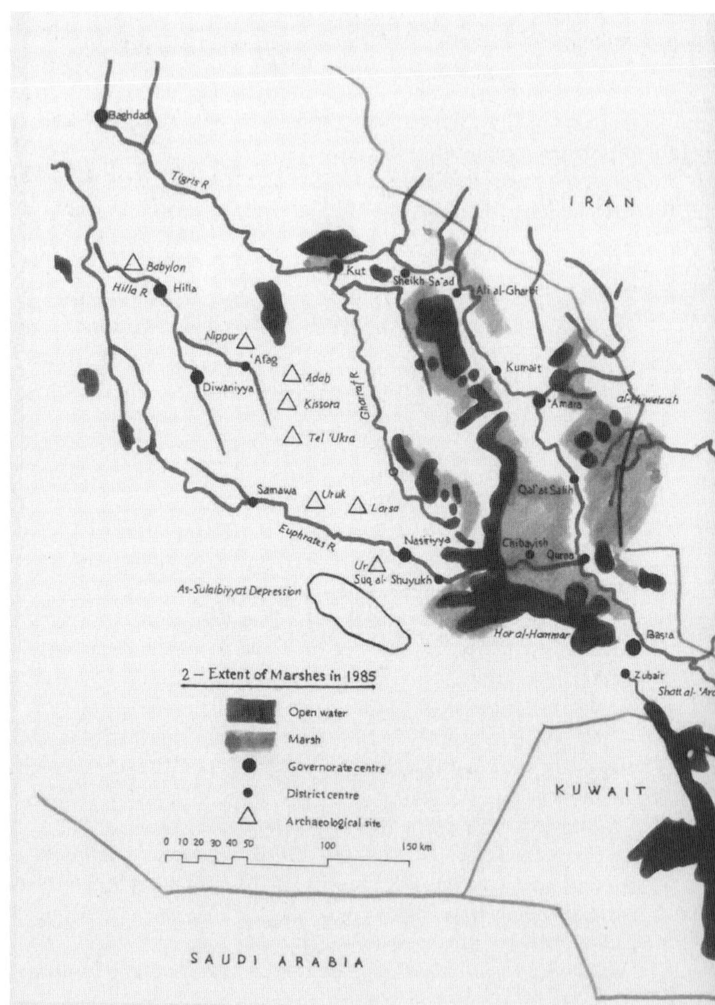

sequent phases of that project include the construction of 22 dams and 19 hydraulic stations.

In 1991, the previous government, as part of its systematic targeting of internal opposition groups, began constructing an intricate system of diversionary canals to drain the life-giving waters in order to force the inhabitants to evacuate the area. Some of the drained water has been harnessed to irrigate major farms with a total area of over 2000 km^2, which the government distributed among farmers from tribes loyal to it.

In 2000 UNEP reported that 90% of the marshes had disappeared and studies presented at the Worldwide Forum three years later indicated that a third of the remaining 10% had disappeared. The immediate result has been the displacement of about 300,000 Madan after their habitat was destroyed, and the loss of vital agricultural land and products. The draining has had other far-reaching environmental consequences. Among them:

- Disappearance of endemic flora and fauna. According to UNEP, forty birds types are in danger of extinction and rare species of fish-eating water animals have all but died out.
- Disappearance of way stations for migratory birds.
- Contamination of rivers with toxins from industry, sewerage and agriculture.
- Intrusion of saltwater into Shat-al-Arab causing disruption of fisheries in the Persian Gulf.

Map 3: Extent of marshes in 2000

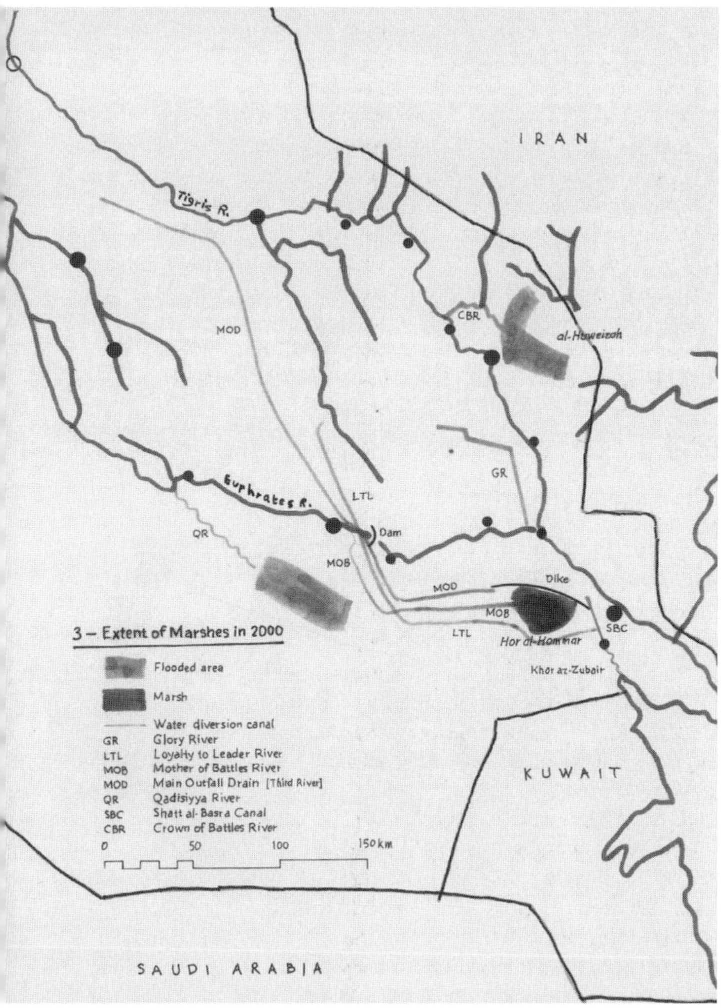

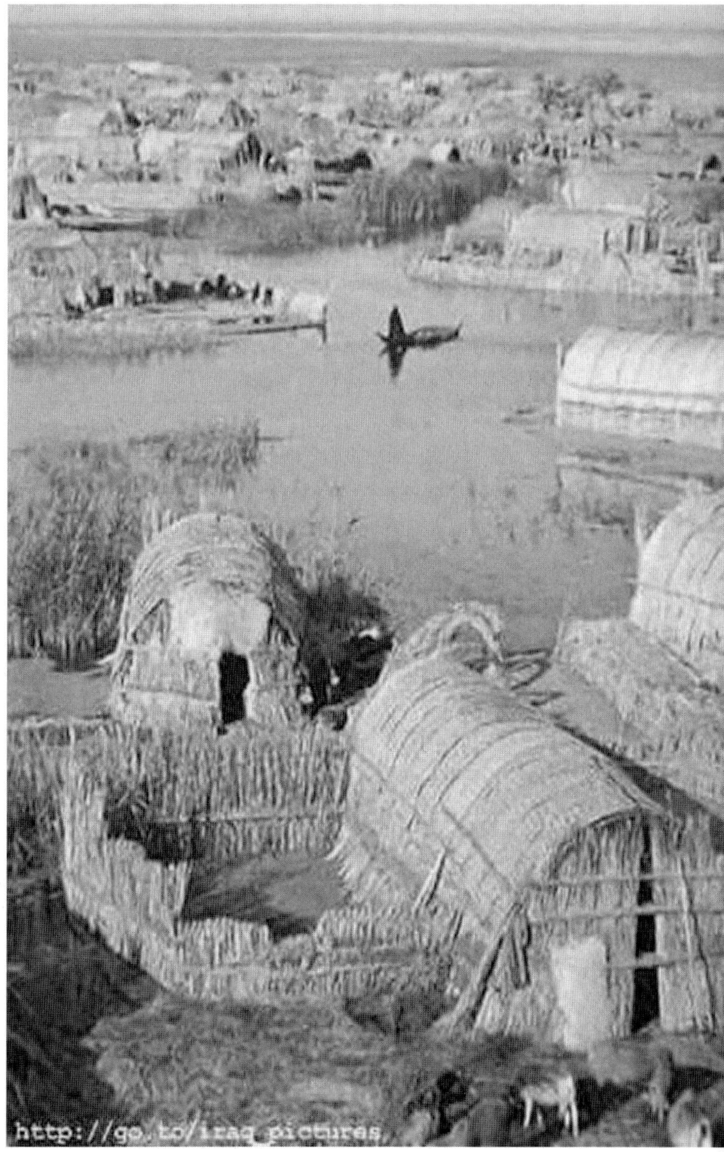

Marsh village, before 1985

Restoring the marshes

The central marsh between the two rivers has turned into a complete dust bowl. It is covered by a salt crust, 60 cm thick in places, due to the rapid evaporation of brackish water. Hor al-Hammar, west of Shat al-Arab still has some remaining lush areas where date palms are in cultivation and sizable segments of marsh remain in al-Huweizah, east of the Tigris where returnees have reintroduced their water buffalo. The current Iraqi interim government, with help from UNEP, USAID, international NGO's and universities, plans to make al-Huweizah a seed source for pilot projects that will lead to restoring as much as possible of the lost marshes. The implementation involves the following activities:

- Removal of about 800 km of diversionary canals.
- Rebuilding Iraq's damaged research infrastructure, particularly the Marine Science Centre of the University of Basra, which was looted after the war.
- Training Iraqi marine biologists and zoologists in wetlands ecology and management.

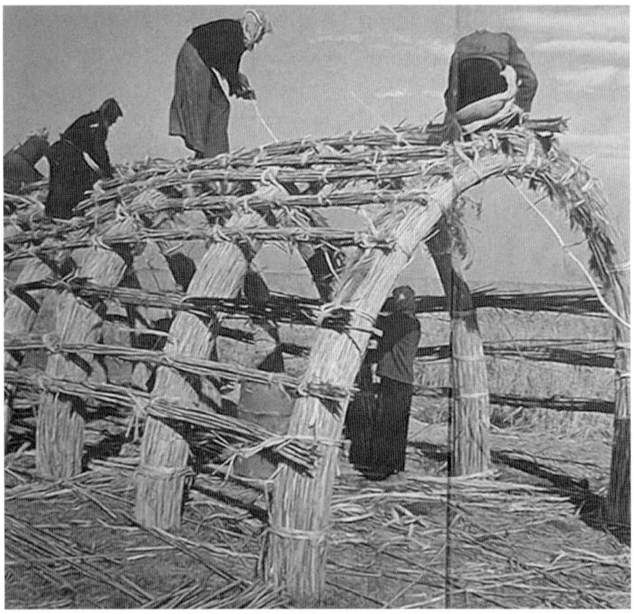

Reeds house under construction

The main restraining factor in this effort is the availability of water. The region is in the grip of a water crisis, therefore it is going to prove difficult to persuade Iraq's neighbours to heed the United Nations' call to reconsider their water policies to avoid further damage.

2 The Kurdish Countryside

The terrain

The fertile plains of Kurdistan begin to rise gently from the northern foothills of the arid Hamrin Hills towards the cold and snowy mountainous terrain in the northeast whose highest peak of Hasar Rost is over 3700 m. The climate of the plains is fairly rainy and Mediterranean, the produce is tobacco, cereals, wood, vines, fruit, hides, wool, mutton and goat meat, eggs and dairy produce.

In certain areas the sub-soil is very rich, especially in iron and chrome, but it is not properly exploited. The country's great source of wealth is obviously oil, a resource from which the Kurdish people draw very little benefit.

Iraqi Kurdistan covers an area of about 74,000 km^2, 15% of that of Iraq, the population is about four million, which is just over 18% of that of Iraq, more than half of it is rural. It occupies a central position in Greater Kurdistan whose population of about 25 million is divided among Turkey, Iran, Iraq and Syria.

Historical background

The Treaty of Sèvres, signed by the Turkish Empire and the United Kingdom in August 1920 gave the Kurds the opportunity to form an independent state in Kurdistan, in the parts formerly belonging to the Ottoman Empire but subsequent events in Turkey rendered the treaty inoperative. With help from Russia, the Kurds proclaimed in December 1945 the Mahabad Republic, which lasted for a year, until the Shah's troops overran it and executed its leaders. Since then Kurds in Iraq have been struggling for self-determination. The events that bear directly on our subject begin in 1970.

In that year the Iraqi Government granted the Kurds a considerable degree of autonomy. Soon after, it reneged on the covenant by evicting Kurdish farmers from the oil-producing areas of Kurdistan and replacing them with tribal Arab families. In March 1974 the Kurds rose up against the government, which turned into a full-scale war the following year. In 1975, the Algiers agreement between Iraq and Iran put an end to the struggle.

Tens of thousands of villagers in northeast Kurdistan were forcibly removed from their homes and relocated in barren sites in the desert in southwest Iraq. In 1976 the Iraqi Government secured the approval of Turkey and Iran to create a *cordon sanitaire,* 5-15 km wide along their borders. Between 1975 and 1978 an estimated 250,000 people were cleared out of this zone and relocated in crude concrete encampments built on the main highways in army-controlled areas. From 1982 onwards more villages, lying outside the *cordon sanitaire* were cleared. By the beginning of 1987 it was becoming evident that a carefully calculated ethnic cleansing strategy was being implemented. In the first phase, carried out between April and June of that year, 711 villages were burned and bulldozed. The subsequent phases took place seven months later under the code name of Anfal.

The Anfal campaigns

The first Anfal campaign began in February 1988 and the eighth and last campaign was completed on 6 September of the same year. There were six target zones covering an area of over 40,000 km^2 or more than half the total area of Iraqi Kurdistan. Every campaign began with multiple blitzes, which were accompanied in five of the six cases by bombardments using chemical weapons, followed by ground troops and pro-government militias moving in to destroy human habitation, loot possessions and animals and set fire to homes before the demolition crews were called to blast larger buildings such as schools, clinics and similar structures. An estimated 50,000 rural Kurds perished in the Anfal and more than 1270 villages were destroyed (only large villages are shown on Map No. 4), bringing the total number of destroyed villages since the 1970s to more than 3500. This represents 80% of the total number of villages in Iraqi Kurdistan.

Resettlement Programs

After the establishment of the safe haven in north Iraq by the US, UK, France and the Netherlands in April 1991, there were over 700,000 internally displaced people (IDPs) waiting to be resettled and the numbers continued to grow with the eviction of Kurds from Kirkuk and towns to the south. UN Habitat was tasked with managing the resettlement program. A number of specialised NGOs also helped by providing shelter and rebuilding villages. In 2003 one such NGO, Mission East, with help from other NGOs and funds from UNHCR, undertook a pilot project to rehabilitate a village in the Governorate of Dohuk. The water supply network of the village was rebuilt and 32 houses and a school erected. The group is planning to rehabilitate 20 more villages and similar activities are in progress in Sulaimaniyah and Arbil.

However, despite the availability of funds and expertise only a small proportion of families has been resettled. In the Governorate of Dohuk, for example, an average of 800 houses per year were

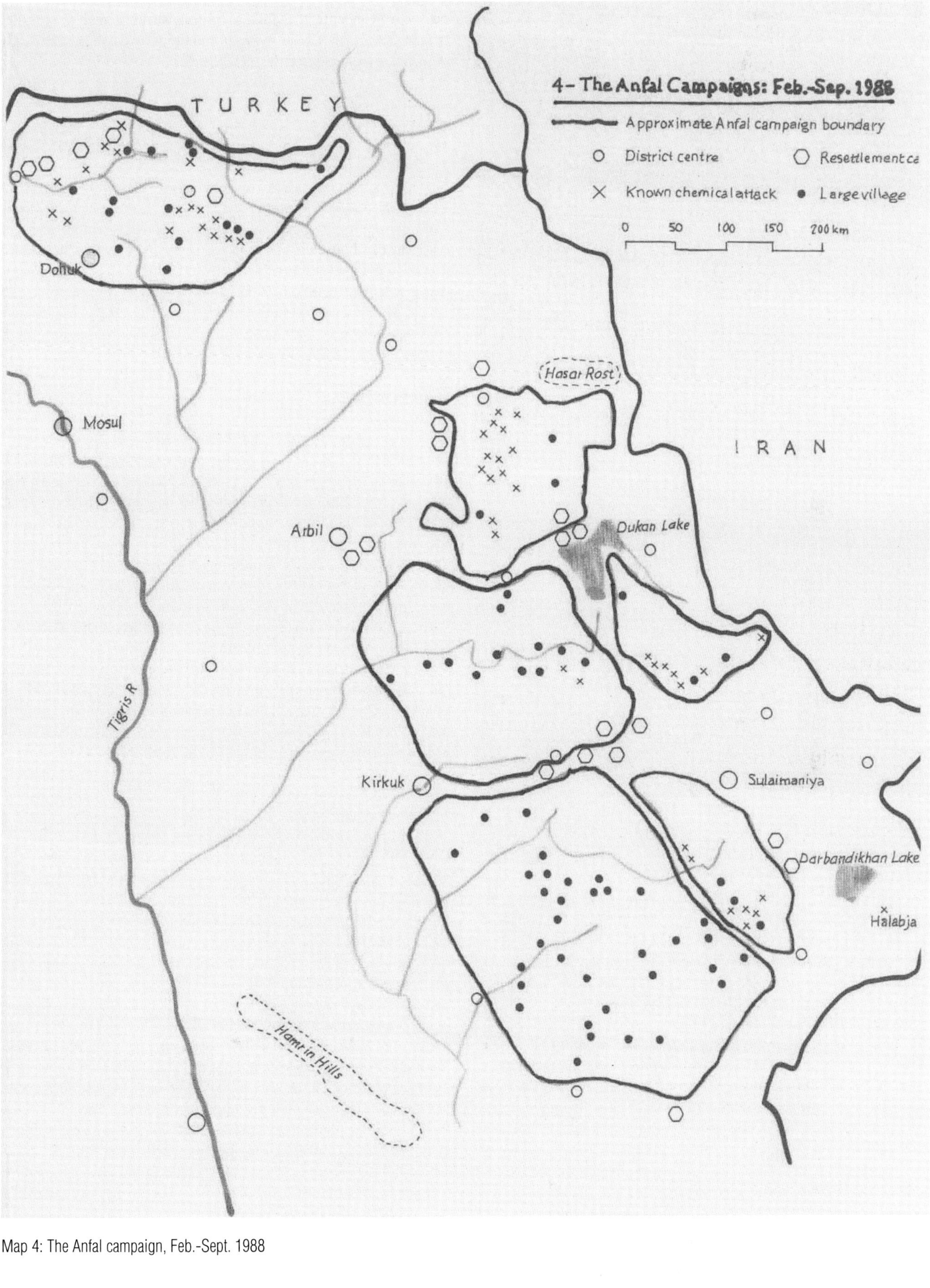

Map 4: The Anfal campaign, Feb.-Sept. 1988

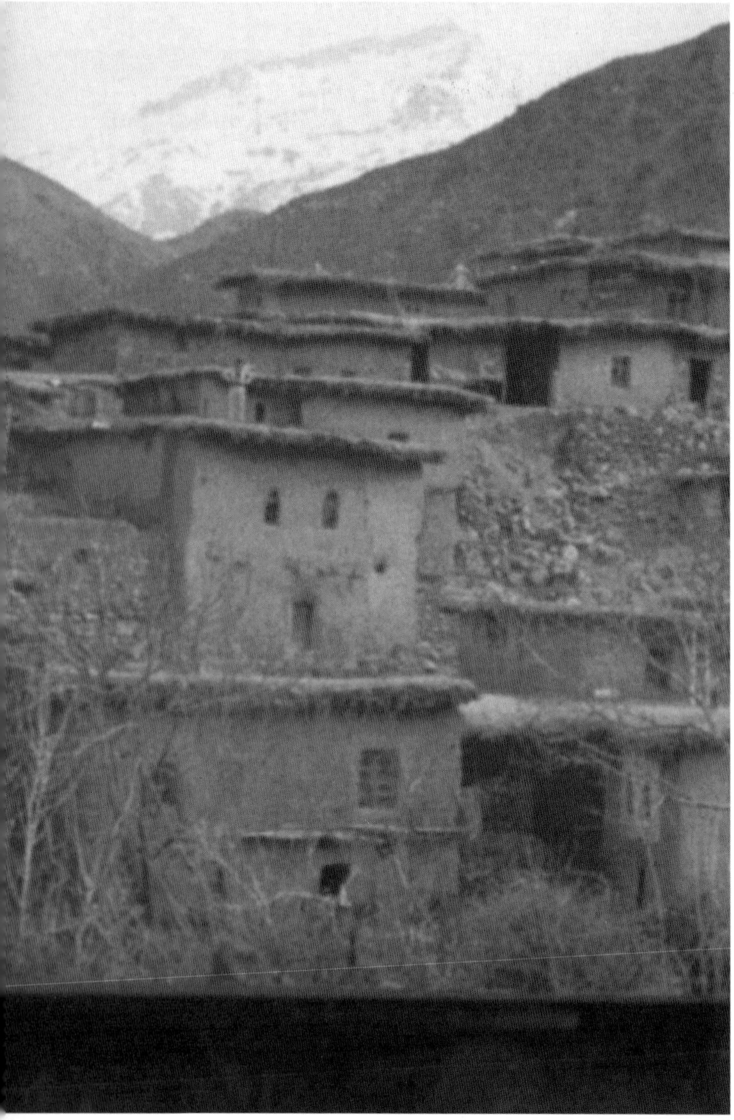

House in Haj Omran, North Iraq, built of stone and mud bricks (photo: Nik Wheeler)

built between 1996 and 2003. According to the Director of the Regional Government's Reconstruction Department, 6000 units per year are needed to resettle the IDPs living in public buildings, tents and collective villages.

Efforts to maintain the momentum of the program have been impeded by the use of conventional forms of contracts, applying urban type building standards and specifying factory manufactured building materials such as concrete blocks; all of which are inappropriate to the scale of the task. The huge volume of buildings demanded can only be implemented in the short time available by involving the beneficiaries themselves in the house production process. The obvious way to achieve this is through aided self-help schemes, whereby each family is given a site, complete with boundary walls, services and wet rooms plus cash grants to complete the construction. This will save time and cost, and create opportunities for employment. The walls can be constructed of stone, if locally available, or sun-dried bricks, to be manufactured in situ using stabilised soil. Kurds are familiar with these two materials and know how to maintain them. With some training, and expeditious management, teams of masons can be taught how to build small span arches, vaults and domes, which are needed to implement the proposed design.

3 The Old Town of 'Ana

The site of the old town of 'Ana lay on the west side of the Euphrates, about 80 km east of the Syrian border. It is the northernmost among a multitude of towns and villages that grew on both shores of the river attracted by the availability of water, fertile soil and mild climate. It stretches from west to east along a bend in the river extending about 12 km along a narrow strip of land, 200-250 m wide, squeezed between the Euphrates in the north and a high ridge of rocky hills in the south.

Historical note

'Ana was known to the Babylonians and the Assyrians. It is described as a fortress town in the records of Emperor Julian the Apostate's campaign against the Sassanians in 363. When the Italian traveler Pietro Della Valle visited it around 1620, it was a major entrepôt and virtually autonomous. Its leaders controlled the riparian and overland trade routes between Aleppo and Baghdad. The town was evidently also an important centre of learning, for Della Valle met a Scottish physician who had taken up residence there to study Arabic. Its size grew as trade brought more prosperity. Francis Rawdon Chesney, the British explorer and soldier, who was there at the beginning of the 19th century, tells us that it had 1800 houses, 3 mosques and 16 water wheels to irrigate its fruit gardens. A hundred years later the number of water wheels quadrupled indicating increased agricultural activity. Until its demise in 1987, 'Ana was a district centre belonging to the Governorate of al-Anbar with a population of about 7000.

Structure of the town

Until the 1930s, the Euphrates was a major trade artery. The town's linear shape and long quay provided maximum space for moorings, loading and unloading. With the advent of overland transport, riparian trade came to an end. The frontage was used to build more water wheels to irrigate the farms and orchards through open canals, which run along the alleyways. These are large vertical wooden wheels, attached around shafts, placed in the stream and turned by the river's motion. Flowing water strikes a series of buckets attached to the perimeters of the wheels. The shafts then rotate and the motion lifts the buckets full of water and empties them one by one in an open aqueduct.

Houses are of one or two storeys. The other two building types are public bathhouses and mosques, of which there are over twenty. These act as the public spaces where the men folk meet. There is no traditional covered *suq*, because most families have farms where they grow enough food and keep enough livestock to fulfill their needs. There are two longitudinal streets that run parallel to the riverbank and several transverse streets and canals which carry irrigation water from the aqueducts into the farms.

Houses are arranged in extended family clusters. Access to the units of the cluster is from a common courtyard that also serves as a meeting place for the womenfolk. The units within the cluster are grouped loosely, leaving enough room for expansion when required.

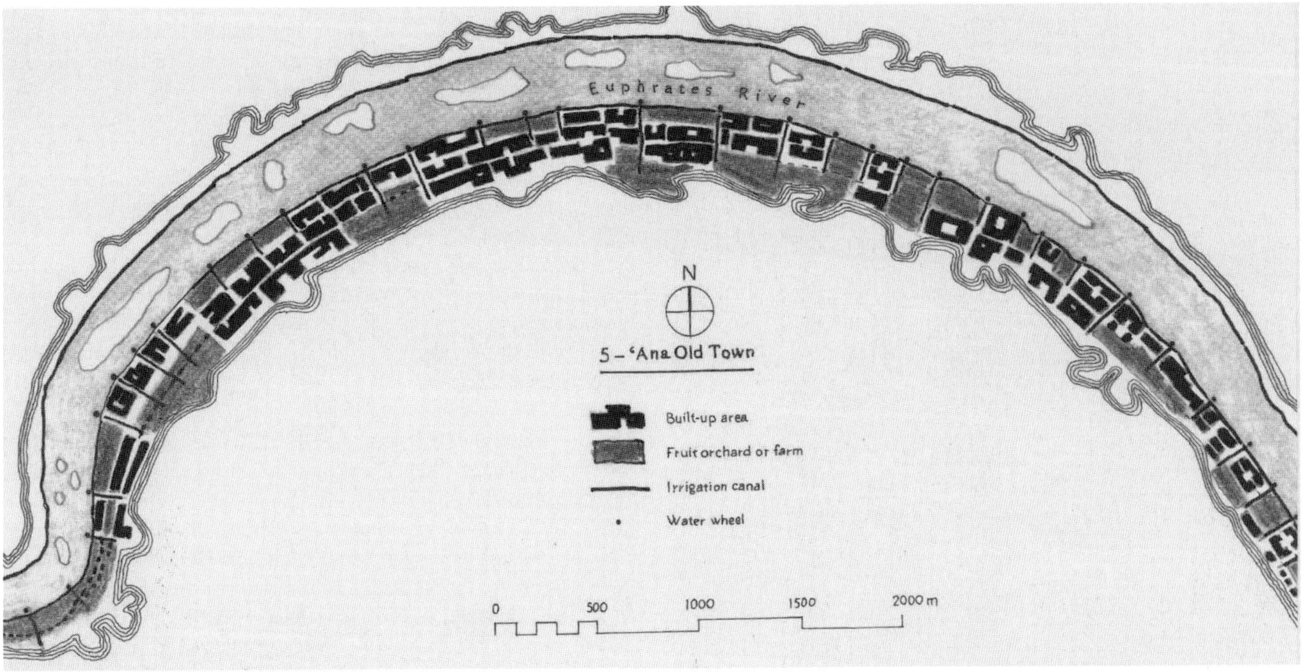

Map 5: Ana Old Town

Ana Old Town, Friday mosque

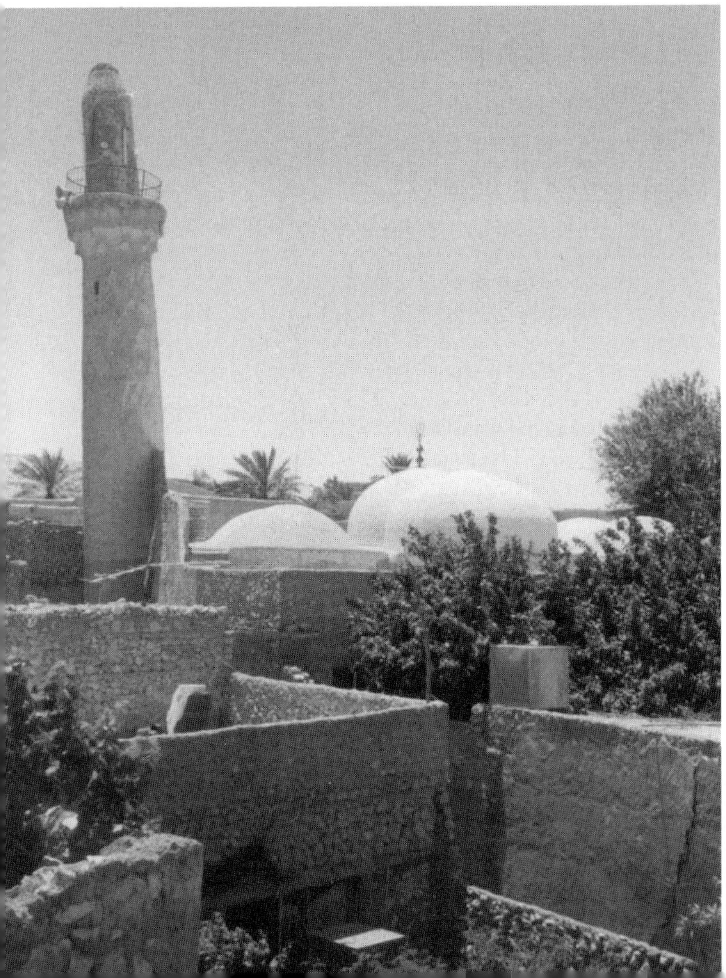

Street in Ana Old Town (photo: Saieb Khalil)

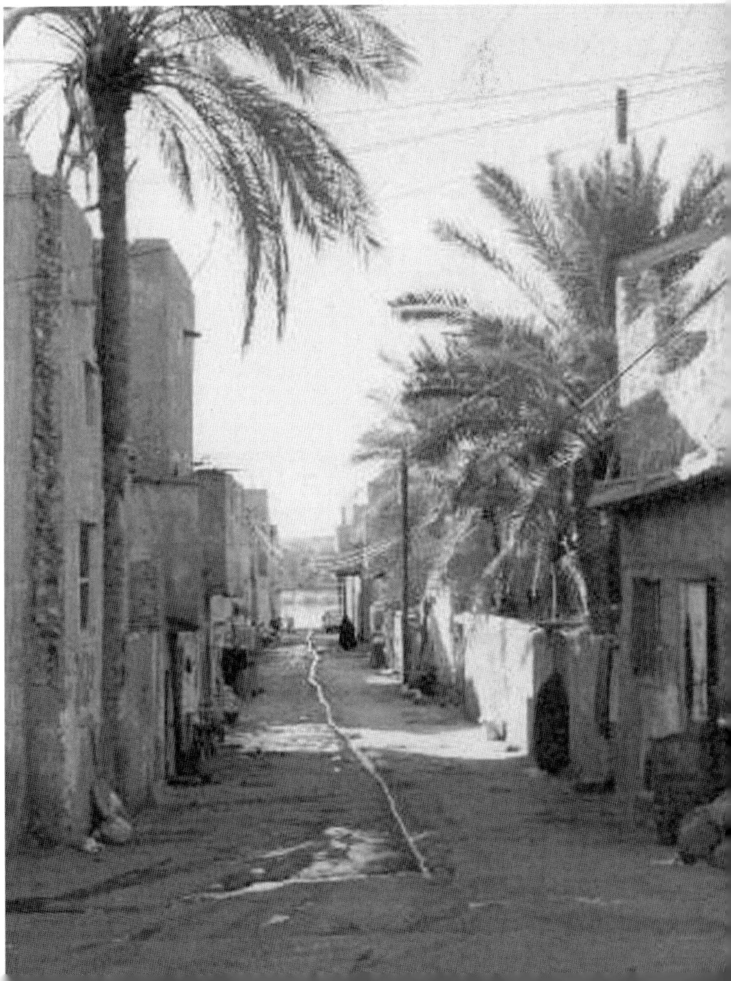

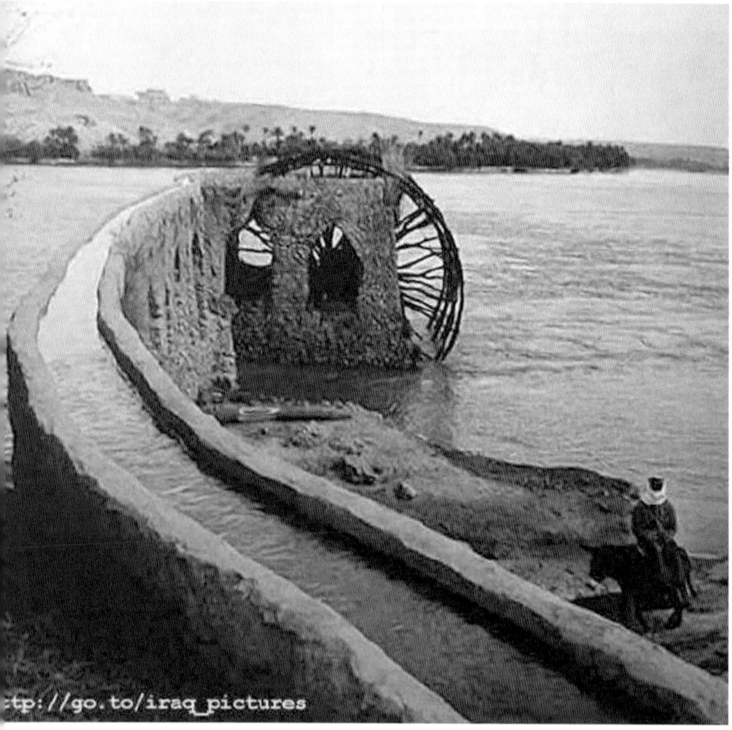

Water wheel in Ana Old Town (photo: Saieb Khalil)

Walls are thick, built of stone and plastered with lime mortar. Roofs are of mud carried on woven mats placed above wooded joints. Windows are small and directed towards the prevailing breeze. These features provide thermal comfort without recourse to electricity.

No hard boundaries separate the built-up zone from the agricultural zone. This marriage of town and country produced a balanced life capable of bringing the faculties of the inhabitants to perfection. It is no wonder that this little town produced many of Iraq's creative men and women, among them the country's foremost dramatist.

New town

The old town that had remained in existence for forty-one centuries disappeared when it was submerged in the waters of the al-Qadisiyyah reservoir in 1987. The inhabitants were resettled in a new town hurriedly constructed on a barren plateau, 14 km to the west of the old site. Many important considerations were sacrificed in order to meet the tight construction schedule. Prefabricated concrete panels, used to minimise assembly time, have produced monotonous lines of identical and garish white facades. There is no possibility of expansion. The courtyards have gone and with them the women's social life. Streets are wide and open spaces that cannot be planted for lack of topsoil, contrast sharply with the intimate spaces of old 'Ana where green spaces and water produced a unique life-centred environment. Large openings, no green areas and structures with low thermal capacity make users totally dependent on electric power for cooling, which is expensive and unreliable. Sadly, a valuable opportunity to apply lessons developed over centuries of trial and error in a creative manner has been missed.

4 Citadel of Arbil

Description

Arbil Citadel, house interior

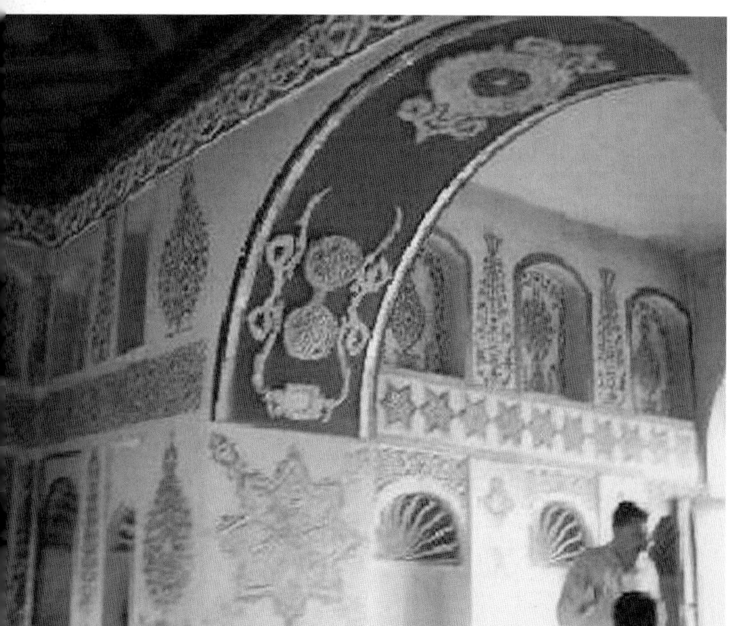

The Erbil Citadel is more than 8000 years old making it the longest continuously inhabited site in the world. This was made possible by the existence of abundant ground water, which has sustained the population throughout its long history. The Citadel rises 28-32 m above the surrounding city, and overlooks the wheat fields, which extend all the way to the Greater Zab River 30 km to the west. The mound has been formed by successive layers of settlements: Assyrian, Akkadian, Babylonian, Persian and Greek. In 331 BC, Alexander the Great defeated the Persian King Darius the Great in a battle which was fought thirty kilometres north of Arbil. The area of the Citadel is over ten hectares; the population is about 5400, only a fifth of whom are descendents of original families. There are just over 800 dwellings; most of them are courtyard houses with brick walls and mud roofs on timber joists, one-or-two storeys high, some of them have basements. About half of the houses are privately owned and the rest belong to the local and central governments. There are two mosques and one public baths. The citadel is accessible by a vehicular road and two pedestrian ramps. Water is supplied from elevated steel tanks and electricity through an overhead network. There is no sewage system; pit-latrines are used throughout.

Condition

During the 1920s a part of the western side of the citadel was removed to make room for shops which were later pulled down

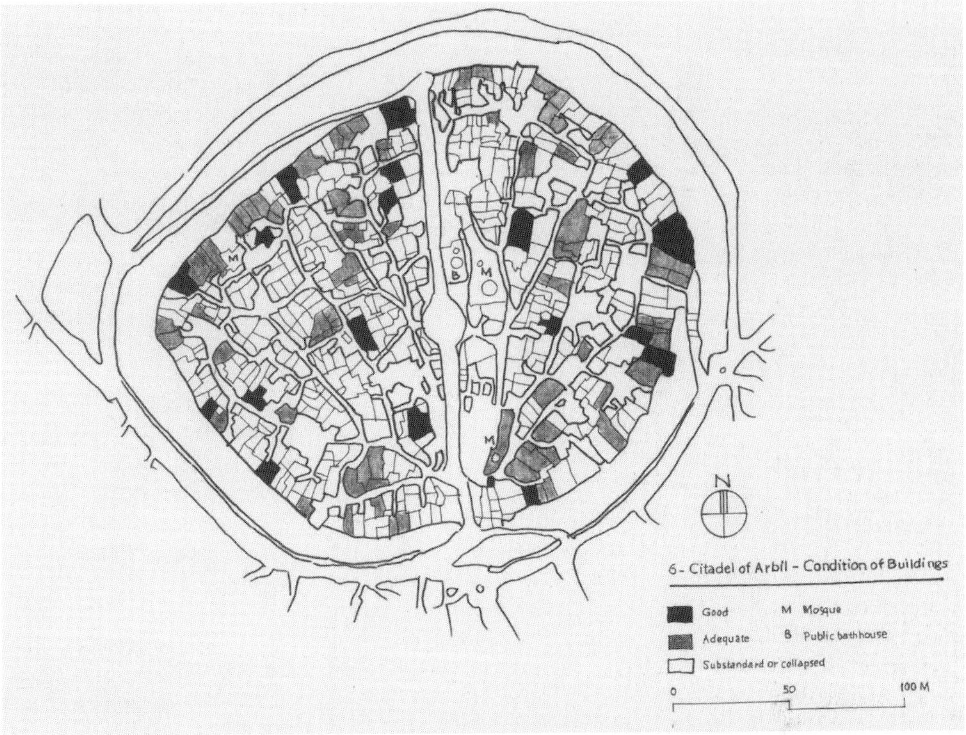

Map 6: Citadel of Arbil, condition of buildings

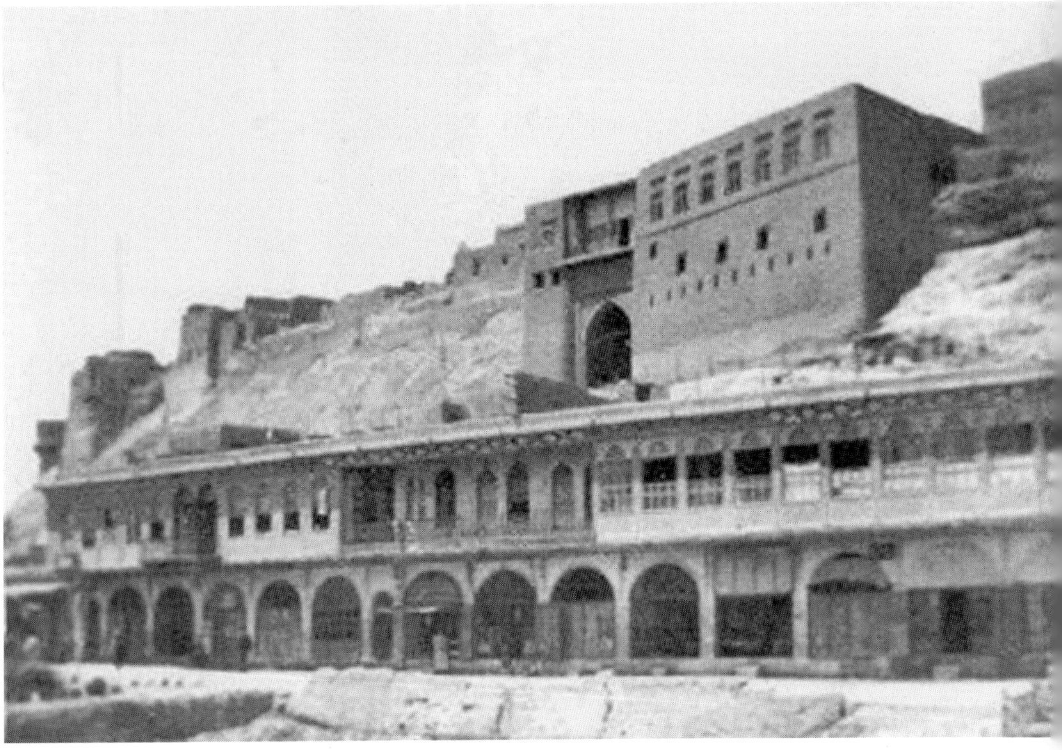

Arbil citadel

and their area added to the road which encircles the Citadel. The road was enlarged three more times causing erosion to the side of the mound.

Of the 800 houses no more than twenty are in an acceptable state. Their walls are adorned with brightly coloured niches, carved doors and upper verandas carried on columns made of timber or marble. The larger houses have fountains in the courtyards and their top floor veranda runs along 2 or 3 sides. In 1982, the SBAH rehabilitated seven houses. The only other conservation work carried out was the addition of a monumental arched entrance at the southern part of the wall.

5 Saray Administrative Complex

Description

The complex consists of five adjoining buildings along the eastern bank of the Tigris River. Four of them are Ottoman, built in the middle of the 19th century; the fifth dates from the 1930s and is British Colonial in style. Until March 2003 government departments occupied them.

They are located in the capital's old cultural and administrative centre, surrounded by structures representing almost every period of Iraq's past. Here is the 12th century Abbasid Palace, the 16th century Saray Mosque built for Sultan Süleiman 'the Magnificent',[1] al-Wazir Mosque, named after the Ottoman Governor who restored it in 1599, the Mandate era Ministry of defence and many early Hashemite buildings including the General Library and Parliament House. Here too is Suq al-Saray, arguably the oldest book market in the Islamic world, occupying a covered pedestrian street which connects the complex with the country's oldest existing Islamic University, the 14th century al-Madrasa al-Mustansiriyya.

Between them, the buildings in this historic zone chronicle all the planning patterns and architectural features which Iraq's historic building heritage has produced: closed courtyards, three-sided courtyards, *iwans*, grids, domes, vaults, stone walls, *chaf qim* (facing bricks) and so on, all of which are of superior quality.

The SBAH renovated the five buildings in 1989. In the early 1990s the extreme austerity measures as a response to the UN sanctions and the fall in oil revenues, meant that no further maintenance work could be carried out. In the chaos which followed the occupation of Baghdad in April 2003, every one of these buildings was plundered, at least one was bombed and several were set on fire. During 12 weeks, gangs of looters emptied all the five buildings of furniture, equipment, fixtures and fittings, doors, windows, wall panelling and floor tiles. In some buildings even the steel floor beams were removed. Appeals to the cultural committee of the Coalition Provisional Authority to provide protection were fruitless.

Rehabilitation

The conservation of the Saray Complex was the subject of a seminar organised by the Ministry of Culture last April. Many arguments were put forward in favour of their rehabilitation. Among them were:

- Upgrading will revive the district generally and restore to it its past function of Baghdad's cultural centre.

Baghdad, Qushla building in Saray complex

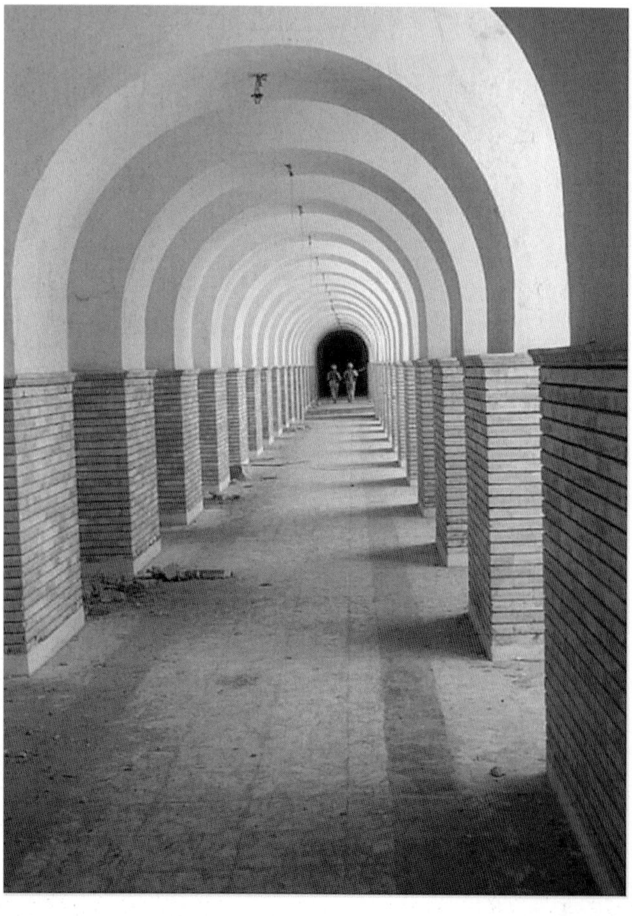

Baghdad, looted building in Saray complex

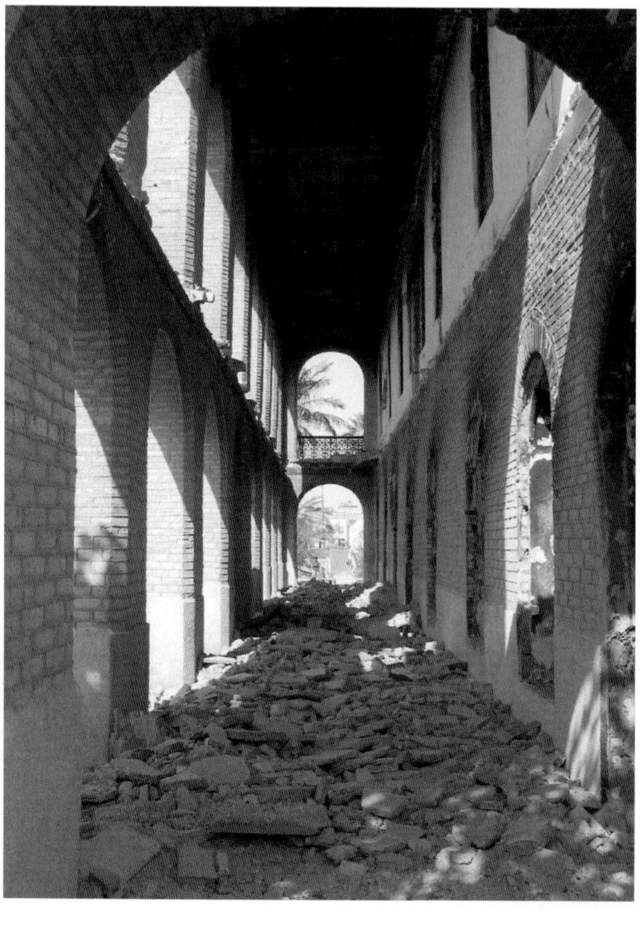

- Rehabilitating the gardens, which overlook the Tigris will provide public open space in one of Baghdad's most congested districts.
- Paving the access road and limiting it to pedestrians will provide quality space for the book vendors whose kiosks now crowd the pavements of the neighbouring main road.

The five buildings offer office space in a prime location in access of 30,000 m^2. Their rehabilitation is therefore not only desirable because they are visual reminders of the peoples' past, but also because it makes sense economically.

Conclusions

The culture of Iraq is in distress. Museums have been looted, libraries set on fire, historic buildings plundered and attrition continues to act on archaeological sites. But it is too early to write the obituary. Today the world has a far more effective system of protection for important monuments and sites than it used to have. UNESCO, together with many specialised international organizations now lists monuments, monitors threats and helps sustain sites more comprehensively than in the past. The opposition to the willed destruction of heritage is growing and it is organised.

The world has reacted positively and quickly to the cultural tragedy in Iraq and that has given Iraqis hope to rebuild their culture, which means rebuild their lives. Their country is a unique union of races, languages and religions. Much energy is currently being directed at the cleavage lines seeking to take the components apart. Let us hope that the riveting power of Iraq's culture, with the help of the international community will succeed in dissolving those energies into oblivion.

Usam Ghaidan and Nayab Al-Dabbagh

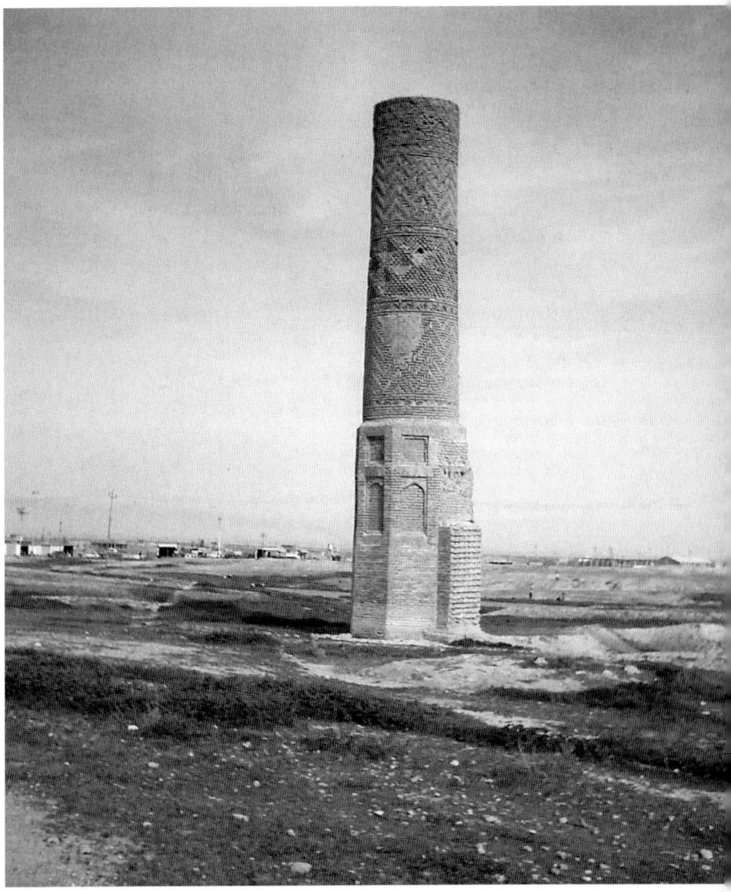

Stub of collapsed 14th century minaret in Arbil city

Leaning minaret of 12th-century Al-Nuri mosque in Mosul

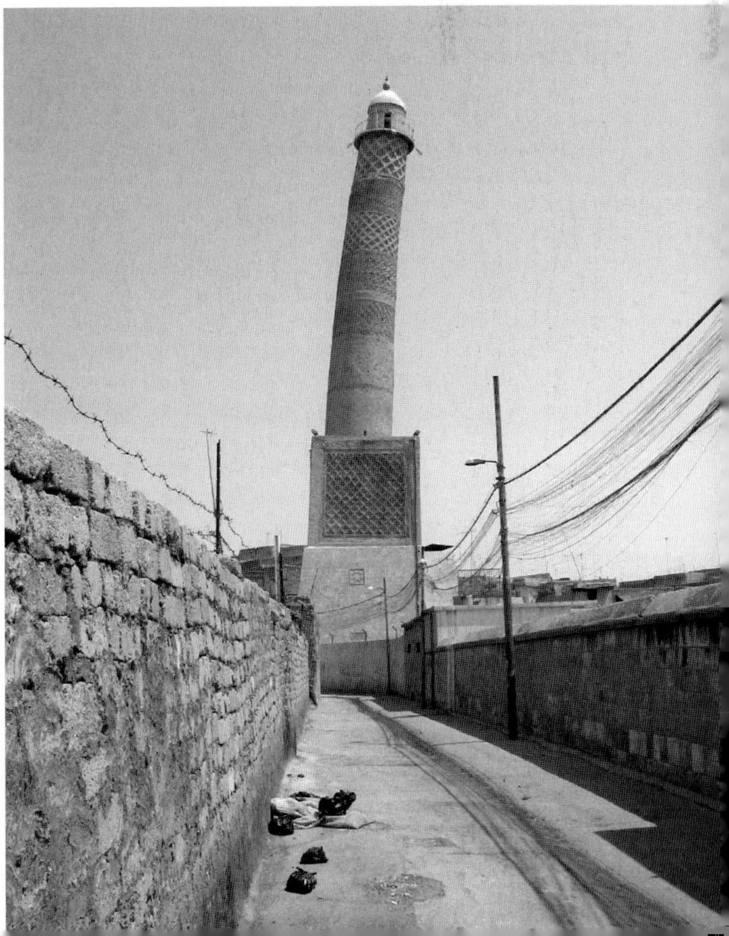

References

The Anfal Campaigns:
Middle East Watch: *The Anfal Campaign Against the Kurds.* 1998.
Khalid Salih, Anfal 1995 The Kurdish Genocide in Iraq. *Digest of Middle East Studies.* Spring 1995

The Old Town of 'Ana:
Ali Qahraman Hassan, Architect Structure of 'Ana Town as Reflection of its Ecology, M.Sc Thesis
presented to Department of Architecture at the Technological University in Baghdad (Arabic).
Professor Jala Muhammad al-Makhzumi 1988 Old 'Ana, Habitat and Region. Imara, *Architectural Quarterly*, May 1998, Baghdad, (Arabic).

Citadel of Arbil:
Professor Shireen Sherzad December 1979 *Architectural Design of the Historic Citadel of* Arbil- *Iraq.*
M.A. Thesis presented to the University of Colorado at Denver.

Sarai Administrative Complex:
Professor Haytham Khorsheed Said March 2004 *Rehabilitating the Qushla Building.* Seminar paper. Baghdad (Arabic).

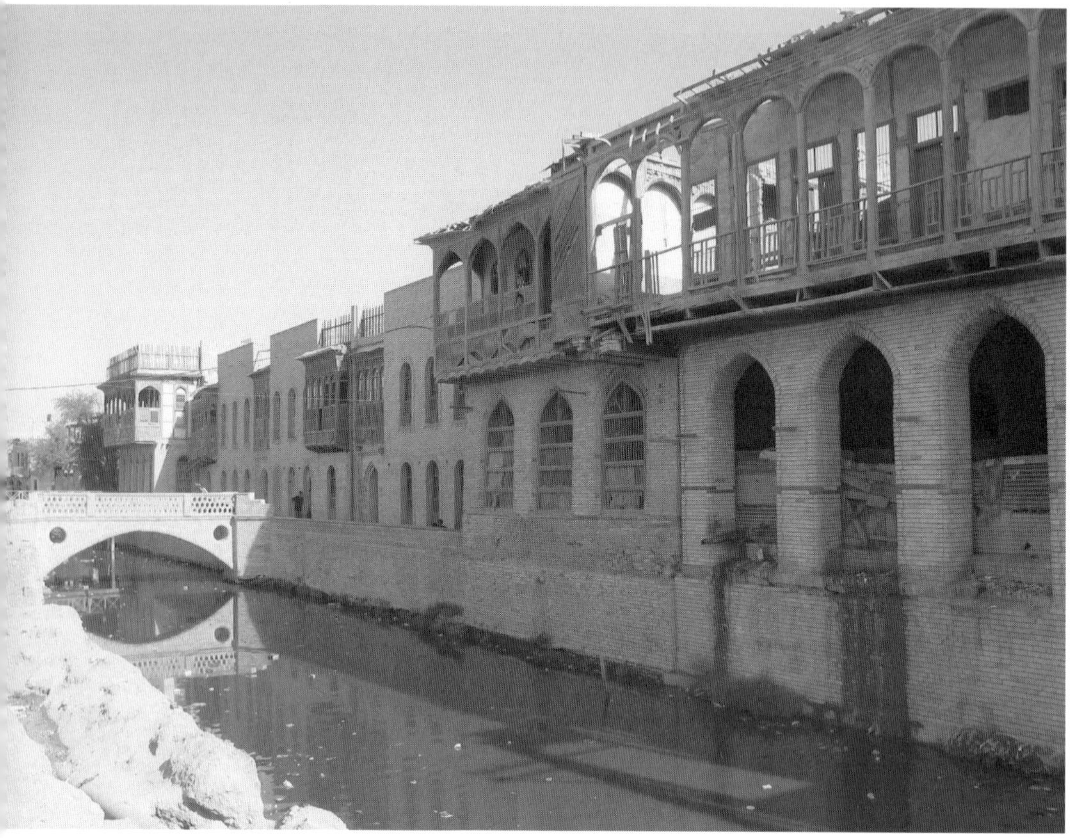

Houses in Basra (photo: Ingolf Thuesen)

Iraq's Cultural Heritage: Loss and Destruction - The Case for Restoration and Reconstruction

These days we hear a lot about oil and Iraq's other natural resources, and how Iraq has the second largest oil reserves in the world and so on. Well, while this may be true, let me tell you, at the outset, that Iraq is, more importantly, number one in cultural resources. It is, as all historians and archaeologists would agree, the cradle of civilisation and possesses some of the oldest and rarest cultural heritage of humanity.

Most developed nations today regard their cultural heritage, in all its various manifestations, especially their archaeological and architectural property, as a major irreplaceable national resource that has to be thoroughly documented, protected and enhanced. Some nations have gone as far as reconstructing whole historic areas that have been destroyed by wars or other disasters basing their work on measured drawings and old photographs. In contrast, Iraq has witnessed some of the worst cultural crimes in recent history.

Situated at a nexus of contending powers, rival religions, competing trade routes, and much sought after natural resources, it is not surprising that its history is riven with conflicts and destruction. Geography played a decisive role in the evolution of its culture in general and architecture in particular. Being largely an alluvial plain with two great rivers, the Euphrates and the Tigris, offered very suitable locations for human habitat and settlement but not for natural defences against foreign invaders. Some of the earliest and greatest civilisations developed here along the shores of these two rivers, Sumeria, Babylonia and Assyria. The interaction between the ingenuity of Mesopotamians and land gave rise to some of the most profound inventions in history – agriculture, the wheel, and writing to name but a few examples.

In the art and technology of building there were some tremendous innovations. These included the invention of the mud brick, baked brick, mosaics, ceramic tiles and bricks. In architecture, they included the logic of functional space planning, axiality, symmetry, formal composition, façade design, and the internal open courtyard. Structural elements such as load bearing walls, columns, pillars, multi-storey buildings, round arches, vaults and domes were all first introduced in Mesopotamia. For thermal comfort, several passive cooling techniques were developed. These included the use of thick mud walls and earth covered roofs for insulation, correct solar orientation, small outside openings, ventilated subterranean rooms, and the internal courtyard for better ventilation and cooling.

From the very first villages on earth, founded in northern Mesopotamia some 10,000 years ago to the more recent history of the last century, Iraq has been endowed with an extremely rich and varied cultural heritage. One may classify this heritage into four major groups:

Archaeological Monuments and Sites

More than 10,000 archaeological sites have been identified and officially registered. Most remain, however, unprotected and unexcavated. The real number of sites is much bigger, perhaps even closer to 50,000. Only a few sites attract public attention and therefore deserved official care and protection. These include Babylon, Nineveh, Nimrod, Khorsobad, Hatra, Assur, Samarra, Ctesiphon, Ukhaidir and Ur. Most other sites are subject to looting and erosion.

Historic Urban Centres

These include all the old and historic centres of most cities in Iraq. There are some 50 or so such centres. These include: Baghdad (Rusafa, Karkh, Kadhimiya, and Aadhamiya), Mosul, Basra, Kufa, Najaf, Karbala, Hilla, Kifil, Amara, Kut, Samarra, Hit, Tikrit, Telaafar, Sinjar, Sulaimaniya, Arbil, Kirkuk, Amadiya, Bashiqa, Qosh, Qara-qosh, Aqra, Kwaisanjaq, Dhok, and Zakho. Nearly all of these cores remain largely unprotected or documented. Most have lost as much as 60% of their historic fabric due to direct demolition, decay, and modern redevelopment.

Buildings and Monuments

The exact number of buildings and monuments of historic and architectural interest is unknown but run into thousands. These include mosques, churches, suqs, khans, caravanserais, hammams, madrasas, takyas, palaces and houses. The number could possibly approach 30,000 or even more. There is yet no national register of these important buildings. The database employed by the relevant official agencies is primitive and documentation is weak, unsystematic, and not computerised. Consequently, a very large number of these important buildings has fallen victim to the bulldozer including some very significant monuments such as Abbasid Bab Al-Muadham, Bab Al-Sharqi, and Maaruf Al-Karkhi in Baghdad. As for traditional houses and other smaller buildings they are being lost at an alarming rate.

Villages and Landscapes

The exact number of villages of cultural interest remains unknown but must run into the hundreds. There has been very little interest in them by officials, architects or historians. Similarly, there has been no attempt to protect landscapes and areas of outstanding natural beauty and declare them as national parks etc. These could include areas such as the southern marshes, the palm groves of the Basra region, some mountainous areas of the north, and some outstanding villages such as the domed village of Kimbetler near Kirkuk, Alus and Jubba on the Euphrates to name but a few.

The Ineffectiveness of the Present Protective System

The establishment of the first Iraqi National Museum and the Directorate of Antiquities back in 1923 by Gertrude Bell and Sati Al-Husari with the aim of protecting Iraq's rich cultural heritage marked a hopeful milestone. However, since then there have been some terrible losses to this heritage. The 'protective' official system also includes all municipalities, Amanat Al-Assima of Baghdad, the Ministry of Awqaf (Religious Endowments), and the Directorate of Tourism. The legal framework for the protection of Iraq's cultural heritage goes back to the first Antiquities Law of 1924, which was then refined in 1936. It defined 'antiquities' then as 'anything made by the hands of man before 1700 AD, such as buildings, coins, sculptures, manuscripts, and such objects that are illustrative of sciences, arts, crafts, literature, religion, customs, morals and politics in past age…' This arbitrary figure of 1700 meant that most historic centres and traditional buildings were excluded from protection legally! An amendment to this law was passed in 1974, which allowed the government to protect buildings and artefacts of a more recent date.

However, due to the weakness of the existing protective machinery, in terms of its technical, financial, and administrative skills and resources, the various official agencies have largely failed to live up to expectations. In addition, there has been little coordination between them to avoid conflict of interests and wasteful duplication of work. There has never been, for example, a national council for cultural heritage, which would have been responsible for the coordination of all protective efforts on a regional and national level. There has never been a ministry for heritage, Iraq deserves one. Political corruption and totalitarian measures played a major role in the destruction of heritage. Large areas of very important historic and cultural value were bulldozed, ostensibly for 'security' reasons. These included: The Citadel of Kirkuk, the area west of Imam Ali's Shrine in Najaf, the area between the two Shrines in Karbala, the surrounding area around Kadhimain Shrine, and also around the Gailani Shrine in Baghdad, to name only a few examples.

Similarly, much blame should be put upon the hundreds of NGOs in Iraq. Professional unions, associations and societies have been largely uninterested in Iraq's heritage, let alone to lobby for its protection. This also applies to Iraqi academics including historians and archaeologists who are supposed to be in the forefront of this important aspect of public lobbying and participation.

The Muslim clergy too has shown little, if any interest in preserving Iraq's outstanding Islamic monuments such as mosques, *madrasas*, *hussainiyas*, and *takyas*. Indeed, one can say that the Ministry of Awqaf itself has been instrumental in neglecting and even demolishing a great number of historic mosques and other *waqf* buildings. Great historic mosques such as the Mirjaniya Mosque (built 1356) and Maaruf Al-Karkhi (built 1215) were demolished and rebuilt completely new, in 1947 and 2000 respectively. In addition, the overwhelming majority of historic mosques have undergone major 'repair' work, which in reality meant ill-advised restoration or the inappropriate introduction of foreign and modern elements and materials. In fact, the Ministry does not even have a full documentary record of its properties. In conclusion, while it may be said that this 'protective' machinery has done some good work in safeguarding some of Iraq's architectural heritage, it has been largely ineffective and even destructive.

The Directorate of Antiquities has a similar negative and even destructive history. It has been too weak as the main official agency for the protection of heritage. It has succumbed so often to unlawful political pressures from corrupt leaders and political opportunists. A glaring example of its weakness and even apathy has been its inability to stop or divert destructive mega projects such as dams, highways, and other large-scale works which it knew would cause damage to historic sites and monuments. Examples are too numerous to mention here. But glaring ones would have to include: the construction of a pharmaceutical factory some 400 m away from the spiral minaret of Samara, the construction of a huge museum building close to the Arch of Ctesiphon, the rebuilding of Babylon, the reconstruction of several monuments in Abassid Samarra, the demolition of the historic citadel of Rawa to make way for a new Presidential Palace, and the drowning of the old towns of Ana and Rawa by the Qadisiya Dam in 1987. Incidentally, the rebuilding of Babylon included the insertion of thousands of bricks inscribed with the name of the last President!

Alarming Loss of Heritage

Due to the lack of an effective protective machinery, general ignorance and public apathy mentioned earlier, Iraq, it may be concluded, is also 'number one' in the world in the way it has allowed its heritage to be eroded. It is committing cultural suicide, gradually but surely. It is estimated that most historic towns have lost as much as 60% of their historic fabric, and even more in some cases. What remains now are only a few monuments and traditional buildings scattered here and there. The historic context has been lost or severely disrupted. This self-inflicted damage goes on today unabated. The remaining heritage is now under serious threat of being lost or distorted forever. Most people are alarmed when told that what remains from the once Capital of the Abbasid Empire and the world are only 7 monuments most of which have been altered or heavily restored. They are the Abbasid Palace, Mustansiryia Madrasa, the minaret of Khafafin Mosque, the minaret of Qumriya Mosque, Zumarrad Khatun's Shrine, Omar Al-Sahrawardi's Shrine and Mosque, and the Wastani Gateway.

Most of this loss took place during the past fifty years. The causes of this incredible destruction include:

- Ineffective and corrupt official protective agencies,
- Negligence and decay,
- Bad restorations and reconstructions,
- Looting and illicit excavations of sites,
- Mega projects,
- Wars (Iraq is a veteran!).

The Future of Iraq's Past

As was stressed earlier, Iraq is 'number one' in world heritage but also *number one* in the destruction of its own cultural heritage. The scale of its loss and destruction has been incomprehensible and unbelievable. And most of this irreplaceable loss had been easily avoidable, including the frequent wars! If one were to draw a list of all countries of the world according to their heritage losses during the last 50 years or so, Iraq would surely be somewhere at the top of that list.

What happens now that Iraq is under foreign occupation and there is so much talk about massive reconstruction? Is the future of Iraq's past ensured? Or the prevailing instability and power vacuum offers great opportunity for looters and other cultural offenders? The answer to these questions lies in Iraq's immediate political future developments. If things go well, and this is a big if, the new situation in Iraq could offer good possibilities for the country's cultural patrimony. Some areas of concern and top urgency would have to include the following measures:

- The formulation of new national and regional development policies and strategies with a new integrated protective system;
- New physical planning policies and development plans for all urban centres, towns, and villages, using GIS techniques, to ensure the conservation of the remaining historic fabric;
- The promulgation of new and more stringent laws to stop further losses or encroachments;
- The preparation of a national register or record of cultural heritage, including the designation of historic areas, areas of outstanding natural beauty, and the classification of all buildings and monuments according to their architectural or historic interest;
- The initiation of national programs for the protection, restoration, and even the reconstruction of lost monuments.

Ihsan Fethi

1 Possibly designed by the great ottoman architect Sinan. Its use of multi domes is reminiscent of Sinan's design for the Süleymaniye complex in Istanbul.

ITALY
Cultural Heritage at Risk

Introduction

Italy, commonly known as the *bel paese* because of its long-standing cultural heritage, can be proud of an outstanding tradition in the field of conservation and management of cultural heritage. Italy and its conservation professionals took a decisive part in the refinement of modern western trends for conservation, by designing specific legislation in the first decades of the 20th century which could be defined as pioneering in the field. Italy also took a lead in academic research, continuously improved and translated into practice, and by actively participating in international discussion on the topic, such as for the Charter of Athens in 1931 and the Venice Charter in 1964.

We may argue that the growing interest in conservation depended on the extensive cultural heritage in Italy, uniquely varied as well as historically very multi-layered, but also in the shared sense of belonging to common roots, to be protected and transmitted to future generations.

However, despite its leading role on the international academic scene, Italy is facing serious problems in protecting and managing its cultural heritage, whose natural deterioration is being irreversibly accelerated by managerial blindness. Despite innovative legislative achievements in 1939[1], Italian architectural, archaeological and environmental heritage has been facing a process of decline and deterioration which does not result from scarce economic and practical resources, but also from the Italian Governments' and people's incapacity to give value to their cultural potential.

Illegal development and speculation

The end of the World Wars represented an inevitable opportunity for uncontrolled development. The force of such development on the one hand allowed an immediate shared and high level of well-being, but on the other increased a tendency to lack respect for the law. In the field of preservation and care of cultural and natural heritage, this process has meant a very low standard in urban planning and a pressing demand-supply for industries and infrastructure[2]; illegal constructions dominating the urban and rural landscape of the peninsula.

However, once the economic 'boom' ended, Italy has had to face the environmental disaster resulting from this indiscriminate development without having the necessary tools for the long-term restoration and regeneration of wasted land. Although opposed by certain sectors of the Italian population, the first condono (the Italian term addressing the remission for building illegality) was adopted in 19853. This condono was proposed as a provisional measure in planning, it pardoned illegalities in various protected areas, through concessions by local authorities and territorial bodies of the Ministry of Culture (Soprintendenze). The community's adoption of this legislative measure was in light of its announced ambition to delegate direct responsibilities to the local level4. Most 'necessary' illegal residences became officially legal resulting in the landscape being irreversibly devastated.

However, such illegal treatment continued, as whatever was included in the 1939 laws – archaeological sites, coasts, national parks – was subjected to deregulated exploitation. This was even in the absence of primary needs, with the highest percentage taking place in the southern regions. After the wholehearted initiative of some local authorities and community representatives, who had the courage to reverse the acquiescence of this situation by ordering the demolition of illegal buildings, the situation returned to 'normal', culminating in a second *condono* in 1994[5], while in 2003 a third was announced and approved[6]. This is probably the worst of all because for the first time it allows for illegal buildings built on public land to be 'pardoned' and made legal.

In addition, new amendments to article 181 of the cultural heritage law were approved recently by the government (designed by the Minister and endorsed by the Senate on 1 May 2004). These amendments permit, at article 36 and especially 37, the pardon of illegal construction in protected environmental areas, if completed before 30 September 2004. This also gave transgressors the opportunity to complete and in some cases add to their treachery.

Why have another concession, the third one in less than twenty years? Referring to an appeal launched by various environmental associations[7] the risks of an additional general pardon do not simply include the cultural dimension of development, but also the social and economic ones, destabilising the sustainability of a process regulated with institutional consent.

Considering the social dimension and the Government's duty of care role, the continuous and repeated pardons of illegal development results in an increase in speculation and illegal construction, which is often part of a process of organised crime aimed at recycling dirty money. The highest percentage of illegal construction and speculation is registered in the south of Italy, where organised crime has its historical roots. The acceptance of illegality creates moreover inequalities among citizens, clearest to those who act legally. Last but not least, the act of condoning the illegality fundamentally threatens the authority and social balance of the law, given the presupposition of the Italian law that illegal acts against the cultural heritage should be pursued in court.

Also, the local situation may be critical because of an overload from an excessive amount of *condono* applications. This trend runs the risk of speeding up assessments and lowering requirements and permit criteria. In such a case, an excessive number of permits could be accompanied with a drop in controls.

Moving to the economic dimension, we should stress that the immediate proportional taxation revenue from a remission is considerably lower than the total investment necessary for the supply of infrastructure, such as pipelines, streets, electricity, and so on, necessary for legal and regular planning and to be undertaken by the local government, that is by the local community[8].

When discussing the impact that illegal construction and speculation has on cultural heritage, whether tangible or intangible heritage, the Italian paradox is even more frustrating, because it emphasises a perverse carelessness towards what is often considered the country's highest potential, both in economic and social terms. As an immediate visual reaction, it is easy to emphasise how uncontrolled planning negatively shapes and deprives cultural landscapes of their integrity as historically formed entities that have grown slowly and in keeping with natural inputs. They are non-reproducible, unique and their damage or loss is irreversible.

Such uncontrolled occupation of land which does not respect regulated interim plans or guidelines, nor takes safety measures into account, often drastically increases the risk of natural disasters, which could have consequences not only on human lives but also on existing cultural heritage. Furthermore, the costs of legalising illegal development, for example by providing them with regular sewage, electricity, and so on, creates a shortage of financial resources in local communities, with a direct impact on the already scarce resources which would normally be used to maintain cultural heritage. In addition, the acceptance of low-quality buildings, the hallmark of illegal development, will reduce investment in future high-quality buildings, as the architectural market becomes saturated. Unfortunately this also points to an impoverishment of research in architectural design or, even worse, a massive escape to foreign countries of honest and enthusiastic young architects. The paradox is that in a few years these buildings may also be covered by existing heritage protection laws, as they currently apply to buildings 50 years after their construction, after which it has to meet special permit procedures before being demolished or modified. It is easy to imagine the immense additional workload which the already stretched Soprintendenze will be submitted to.

Not to be excessively critical, we are also pleased to highlight government efforts to safeguard the quality of architecture, urban planning and environment by the release of the *legge quadro sulla qualità architettonica* (February 27th 2004), which aims at increasing project design standards for the built environment and infrastructure, to improve life quality and to preserve and prevent landscapes and skylines from 'aesthetic pollution'. It is particularly significant for architectural design competitions, because it encourages the involvement of young professionals who were often excluded in the past decade. We are reminded of the perverse and united unofficial Italian tradition by which new professionals, mostly in architecture, were considered amenable to work for free or for ridiculous salaries, and often without being acknowledged in the projects in which they participated, in a sort of ill-defined apprenticeship. It is also remarkable in its specific procedures for the recognition of contemporary architectural masterpieces through the 'declaration of important artistic nature' under agreed criteria and standards. This interesting approach consists in having financial contributions allocated to the buildings included in the list for their consolidation, restoration and maintenance.

Unfortunately, these efforts seem to be isolated, in the absence of a long-term comprehensive approach towards the creation of the necessary conditions for success. The impression is that one law alone cannot be effective while other laws permit the opposite.

Privatisation

The uproar caused by the Italian Government's recent moves to sell public properties to private individuals or corporations has found its way to the international press. It must be said that many countries have always bought and sold land and buildings, and recently France has moved to a very similar scheme of selling off a number of unprofitable buildings, including many that are definitely of cultural significance. The difference is the way the Italian government has announced it, consisting of a very complex scheme of the property's economic valuation, of the verification of values other than economic ones, and of its sale by either competitive bidding or direct agreements that in most cases violates the established rules of heritage protection.

Here we are not discussing the privatisation of services to a cultural attraction such as ticketing, restaurants, general maintenance and upkeep, museum shops, security, or recording and conservation. Privatisation here refers to the sale of a building or site of cultural heritage value, for which a change in use is allowed, or of a heritage place to a private company so that it can transform it into a tourist attraction.

The proponents of the sale of heritage sites maintain that the State is not able to adequately protect this vast heritage, and that the involvement of private money is necessary. They maintain that it is better to sell less important heritage so that the more important can be adequately protected.

The argument that a change of ownership does not necessarily modify a town's physical design, does not hold if the change in ownership also includes radical changes of use and the commercialisation of public spaces (Hassler, Algreen-Ussing, Kohler 2002). The privatisation of cultural heritage may have some short term economic advantages for the State and private concerns but in the long term it may weaken or even destroy the trust that citizens have in the State as the steward of public good (Throsby 2002). It may be more expensive in the long term for the State, if legislation forces the State to continue tax incentives in favour of the owner or to direct protective interventions if the site becomes endangered.

Cultural heritage economists have also pointed out that it is not correct to give only market value to cultural heritage, as there are other non-measurable or parameters that are more difficult to measure that have an influence on the way heritage is perceived and valued locally and globally (Throsby 2002, Klamer and Zuidhof 1999). The cultural and environmental potential of heritage to contribute to local communities' wellbeing is in fact broad and differentiated. While the economic value of goods is traditionally recognised as decisive when measuring its impact on transformations, we cannot neglect the existence of additional values whose evaluation methods are not established yet in economic terms. We should include use value, characterising a good for the range of possible uses it offers, social value, seen as its contribution to the community, to the creation of a common sense of belonging together, educational value, being the eternal educational role, direct and indirect, played by a cultural good, representative value, being how a good can be a symbol of a society and its past. Stressing that there are several indirect benefits of built heritage to society, its sale would have merely a single short-term effect.

The present trend to privatise cultural heritage sites risks the loss of its significance, as a balance and expression of different values, and the loss of its authenticity. In the longer term, this translates into decreasing community interest, as the resource no longer 'belongs' to them, and decreasing visitor satisfaction. This has dire consequences for a site that a private owner no longer sees as profitable, so encouraging a process of rapid sale of non-profitable properties, or of their contents, such as furniture or art objects, with the purpose of finding cash for repairs (English Heritage 2002). This has serious consequences for State authorities' capacity to direct that heritage legislation be respected (in the UK, for example, many manors and villas were destroyed by owners that were not able to maintain them, until specific legislation had to be introduced (Settis 2002)).

The danger is falling into a site-by-site approach, assessing each and every site in its existing context. There are hundreds of hill towns in Italy where perhaps there is not a single 'monument' of national heritage value, but where the context, the urban texture, the quality of life and the relationship with the landscape and the cultural traditions of that area create heritage and give value to the entire village. The balance between public and private, between community and individual was in many cases arrived at as a consequence of long-term historic processes, which the rapid and irreversible sale will disrupt. From this point of view there is no major and minor heritage, but a continuum that in Italy is particularly strong in its deep layerings. The risk of separating major and minor heritage is also in isolating 'major' heritage, transforming it into a mock-up of itself, and favouring the site's aesthetic value over any other value it may have.

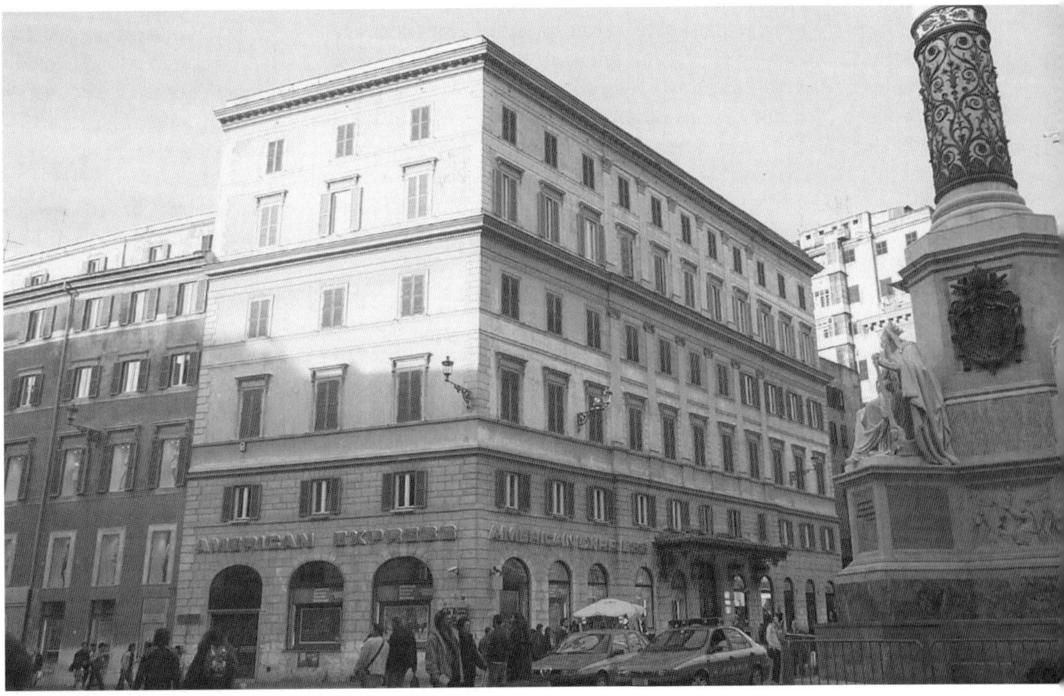

Rome, Piazza di Spagna – Piazza Mignanelli (example of building at risk of sale)

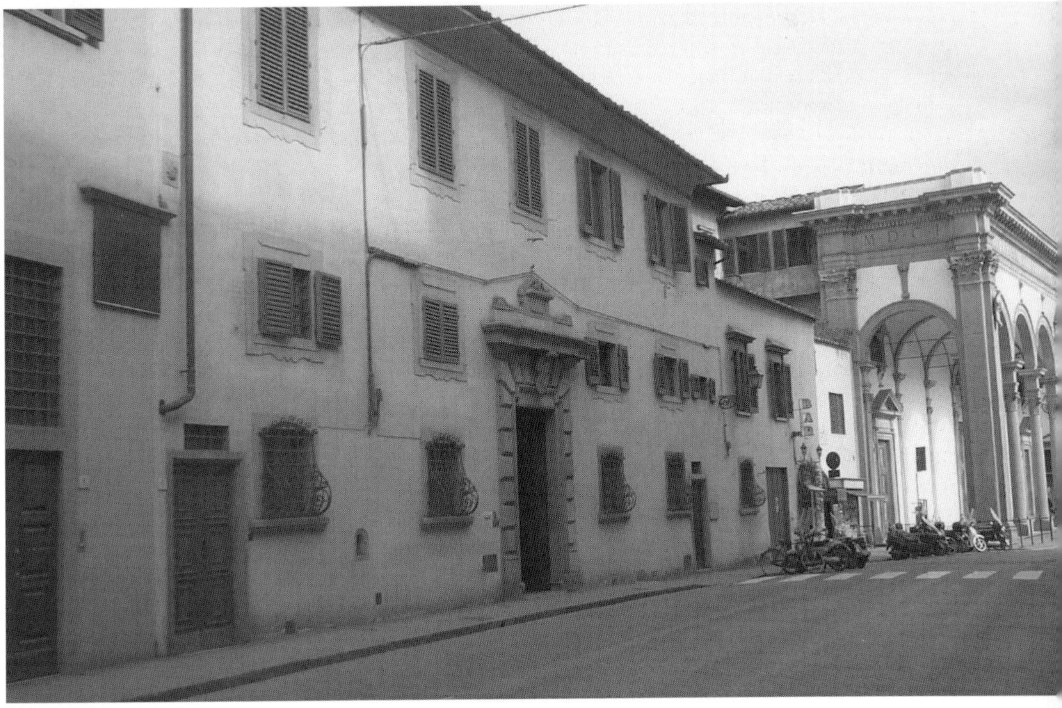

Florence, Via C. Battisti near Piazza della SS. Annunziata (example of building at risk of sale)

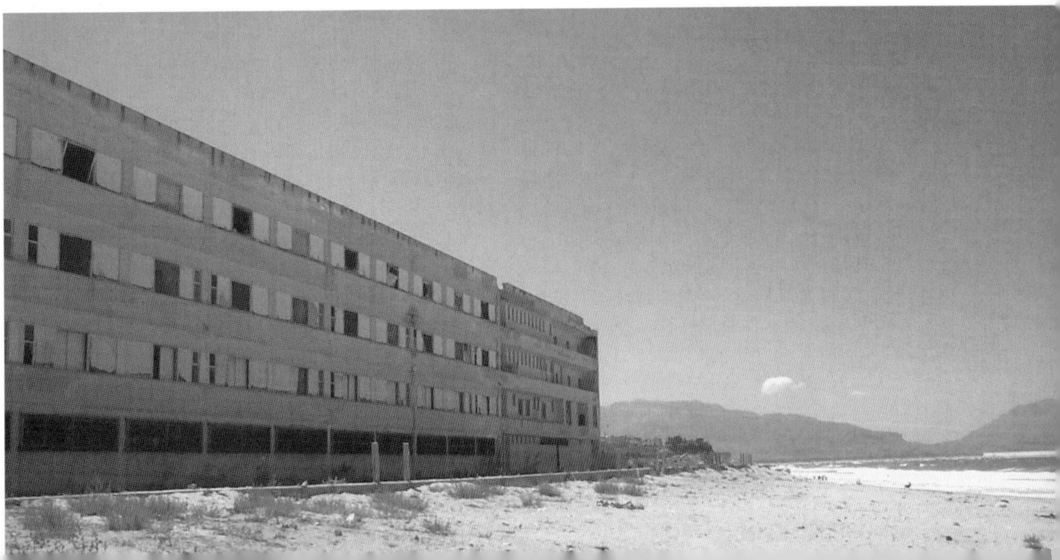

Sicily, North-West coast (near Palermo) spoilt by modern constructions

Going back to the Italian situation, the government's attempt to find financial support for its large program of new infrastructure development and tax reduction is based on this following scheme, the creation of a new company, *Patrimonio SpA*, which we can translate as Heritage Inc., to which state properties could be transferred by a decree signed by the Minister of Finance, and endorsed by the Ministers of Culture and of Environment, in the case of properties with a recognised cultural heritage value. The properties on this list could be sold or given by concession to private companies. By a simple signature, the Minister of Finance could also transfer any of these properties to another company, *Infrastrutture SpA* (Infrastructures Inc). The market value of this company's properties was intended for use to issue bonds and to receive bank loans. The bank would then become the new owner of the property, until the loan repayment.

This approach is accepting significant clauses which make its application dangerous. First, many culturally significant buildings were included in the 'shopping list', surprising given the availability of many State-owned buildings and areas of land of no cultural or environmental value. This reflects an incapacity to distinguish between cultural and non-cultural properties, as well as a lack of understanding of values other than purely economic ones. In addition, the laws accompanying the creation of these companies, as well as those authorising the direct sale of State properties to private companies, explicitly deny the Ministry of Cultural Heritage the right of first refusal. This Ministry is however responsible for confirming the cultural importance of heritage. In fact, the present evaluation of the market value of the State properties made by the *Demanio dello Stato*, the authority that administers State-owned buildings and land, is accompanied by a time-limit of 120 days for the *Soprintendenze* to declare whether a site is worth State protection or can be sold, and if there is no answer within that period, the assumption is that the site can be sold. Only 120 days to evaluate what it took centuries to build! Even admitting that each Soprintendenza in Italy, roughly one for each of 20 regions, has a work force able to carry out such a study for every site or building for which historic and architectural records have to be found or produced, the sheer number of pending actions shows that this is an impossible task. In Lombardy, each of the 12 architects working at the Soprintendenza has 1946 pending assessments! (Emiliani 2004). Although in theory 120 days would allow such an assessment to be carried out, in practical terms it is totally insufficient, given the overwork of every *Soprintendenza* in Italy. The invitation of the Minister of Culture to the *Soprintendenti* to take a site off the list of what can be sold if in doubt, does not relieve critics' misgivings about this law's consequences in the long term, given the parallel and explicit invitation to the *Soprintendenti* by higher State hierarchies to use this power with discretion.

So far we have discussed the theoretical possibilities that this new legislation introduces. But recent sales of buildings through private negotiations or competitive bids have included properties protected for their cultural heritage value within a scheme for the rapid sale of buildings belonging to State-owned insurance and social security companies.

To this legislative proposal, we should add the Italian Government's most recent initiative, which in article 30 of the Finanziaria 2005, foresees the possibility to grant the use of protected cultural resources by private parties, after the payment of a rent. These should then be responsible for the implementation of restoration and maintenance works, whose costs will be deducted from the rent, which is to be determined by the local Soprintendenza. It is stressed that private grantees will have to make the item *available* to the public in accordance with the rules agreed in the contract.

Although this legislative measure holds the positive potential to contribute to the conservation of the cultural heritage, it falls as an additional drop into an already full vase. As stated above, the operating conditions of local designated heritage management authorities were already stretched years ago, they cannot be efficient when overwhelmed by tons of records to check and complete. In Italy's dramatic cultural heritage management situation and in the absence of real strategic policies for conservation at a national level, this theoretically positive step sounds destructive and irreversible. Who will take responsibility for approving a conservation project? Who will monitor its application? The Soprintendenze, today, are not enabled to operate properly given their chronic lack of financial resources, although they can often count on highly professional, although demoralised personnel.

A characteristic example recalled by S Settis applies to the introduction in December 2002 of an urgent sale of cultural heritage, based on private negotiation, of monuments in several Italian heritage cities, in particular the sale of Manifattura Tabacchi, a huge industrial complex completed during the Fascist era in Florence, which had an order placed on it by the Ministry on the basis of its historic importance in Italian industrial development. The local authorities had already planned an important integrated project for the site aimed at establishing a cultural centre, hosting the national archive, the Opificio delle Pietre Dure Institute, and other cultural institutes of the city, a project which could not be realised as a result.

Another example of unbalanced privatisation is the Aeolian Islands, a UNESCO World Heritage site since 2000, which are considered natural heritage at risk. With a recent administrative measure, the Regional Assembly of Sicily (legge regionale n.6 2001) approved the normative law that authorises pumice quarrying despite UNESCO's request and the guidelines of the 'Piano paesistico' (a mandatory zoning plan) to stop the exploitation.

Sicily's finance law has provided for other regional measures during 2003, including authorising the trading of public land to the advantage of private bodies. The leading businesses in pumice extraction now have the right to purchase portions of volcanoes that together represent invaluable geomorphological heritage. Proposals to stop this happening are being put forward by the Legambiente di Filicudi, Stromboli e Ginostra.

The situation should be seen also in light of the national cultural and natural heritage management policy, that has indirectly introduced a differentiation between responsibilities for heritage, those for heritage conservation being the State, while its development has been assigned to the Regions, proposing a confused coordination and co-operation between State (with *Soprintendenze* which are acting regionally) and regions.

As far as positive initiatives are concerned, in March 2004, the Italian Ministry of Culture with the Agenzia del Demanio, passed a decree to improve inspection procedures for the buildings and properties to be transferred to the lists of buildings for sale prior to competitive bidding[9]. This allows *Soprintendenti* to express their concern and apply protection orders before the State properties are sold. The required documentation and formats meet acceptable standards, but the technical committee of the Ministry and State property office underestimated the Soprintendenze's technical and time resources to take care of the bureaucratic procedures (see above).

Italia Nostra denounced the procedure's complexity and its failure in an initial application attempt between February 6th and April 2nd 2004 and again reiterated that the Soprintendenze are overwhelmed by workloads. Not only is the number of superintendents insufficient to cover all duties related to heritage protection but an endless change in directives, staff re-organisation and nominations (someone has even called it a 'dismantling of the Soprintendenze') could finally bring chaos and an upset to all positive expectations.

Conclusions

It should be useful to remember the proposals put forward by Marco Dezzi Bardeschi (2003) and Salvatore Settis (2002). Both would be in favour of a closer cooperation between universities and Soprintendenze, at least to complement and update inventories and documentation as well as monitoring the condition of remote and neglected monuments. For example, the risk map, a great achievement of the *Instituto Centrale del Restauro* in the last quarter of last century, should be used more to coordinate professionals and government bodies with the support of public and private organisations. Possibly new resources should be made available to finance the creation of coordination-offices that would act as *facilitators* between governmental institutions, academies and the private sector (bank foundations, and so on). The latter is investing a considerable amount of funds in arts and conservation but to date there is neither a strategic will for a fair distribution of the grants nor an interaction between parties and institutions that are keen to allocate funds on the basis of clear priorities.

Examples of similar cases worldwide show that the State's hands-off policy towards cultural heritage does not pay in the long term. Partnerships between State and private bodies in protecting and managing cultural properties are definitively positive, with an understanding that the advantage to the private bodies comes especially from tax incentives, rather than theoretical, and often illusory, direct economic advantage. The result would be a general improvement in the social and economic condition of the community in which the site is located, because of a conservation approach that is more balanced than an aggressive strategy to obtain revenue. The recent adoption in Italy of new cultural heritage legislation[10] is a sign of the interest that the country has towards its heritage, alongside its commitment to assist UNESCO as one of that organisation's main donors. For this reason the contradiction with the above trends is very evident, for a Government has not ever shown such as contrasting attitude towards its built and natural heritage as this one. The need for immediate returns to finance improbable tax reduction programs and absurd new infrastructure projects such as the bridge on the Messina Strait is guiding the the present Government's financial strategy.

The case of Italy shows that heritage can be at risk from its own governing bodies, if only economic values are taken into consideration when shaping policies of heritage protection and *mise en valeur*.

Gaetano Palumbo (ICOMOS UK)
Andrea Baldioli
Marco Acri

References

Dezzi Bardeschi, M 2003, Restauro: punto e da capo. Frammenti per una (impossibile) teoria. Milano: Franco Angeli

English Heritage 2002, *The State of the Historic Environment Report 2002*. Accessed at http://www.english-heritage.org.uk/sher/report.htm

Hassler, U, G Algreen-Ussing, N Kohler 2002, Cultural heritage and sustainable development in SUIT. Accessed at http://www.lema.ulg.ac.be/research/suit/Reports/Public/SUIT5.2c_PPaper.pdf

Klamer, A, and P Zuidhof 1999, The Values of Cultural Heritage: Merging Economic and Cultural Appraisals, pp. 23-61 in *Economics and Heritage Conservation*. Los Angeles: Getty

Masse-Stamberger, B, and T Richard 2004, A vendre, cause réforme de l'Etat...in *L'Express* March 15, 2004. Accessed at http://www.lexpress.fr/info/economie/dossier/etatargent/dossier.asp

Myerscough, J 2001, *Transversal reviews of National Cultural Policies: National Institutions in Transition: Desetatisation and privatisation. Final report*. Strasbourg: Council of Europe, Council of Cultural Co-operation. CC-CULT (2001)10, accessed at http://www.coe.int/T/E/Cultural_Co-operation/Culture/Resources/Publications/CC-CULT(2001)10_EN.pdf

Settis, S 2002, *Italia SpA. L'assalto al patrimonio culturale*. Torino: Einaudi.

Throsby, D 2002, Cultural Capital and Sustainability Concepts in the Economics of Cultural Heritage, pp. 101-118 in M de la Torre (ed) *Assessing the Values of Cultural Heritage*. Los Angeles: Getty Conservation Institute

Emiliani, V 2004, Osservazioni al Codice, in www.patrimoniosos.it

Citadel of Alessandria

Historic Giant: a symbol of Italian and European military history

To understand the military fortress of Alessandria and the problem that it represents today, we need to see one of the few available aerial images, because although this enormous military architecture site is among the best in Europe for its integrity and its originality, paradoxically, most people, even 'specialists', do not seem to know of it.

Begun by Savoy in 1728 and finished in 1745 (by Ignazio Bertola and Francesco de Willencourt), the citadel takes in and has replaced a entire fortified town of Alessandria, Bergoglio, that has been on the left bank of the Tanaro river since the 13th century. Thousands of inhabitants had to be evacuated during those years, as the construction of the enormous elliptical-shaped hexagon continued to have houses, churches and convents within its enclosure until 1749.

Today it is an authentic Italian historic site, as its fortifications are still perfectly preserved, made up of six impressive ramparts with redoubts, that are still fully standing even on the inside, its ditches and buildings with several storeys laid out around the vast treed parade ground. In spite of a five-month siege in 1745–6, the Citadel was not ever stormed, but in 1799 it was occupied by the Austrians, and later by the French. After the victory of 14th June 1800 at Marengo Napoleon Bonaparte had it substantially modified to make it into a huge warehouse (by François de Chasseloup-Laubat).

In the 19th century, the Citadel was a witness and protagonist of national history. Revolutionary riots took place here in 1821, important figures such as Vochieri and Garibaldi were imprisoned here in the cells in the Palace of the Governor, but the citadel was also a logistic base of great importance throughout the three wars of independence and during World War I. At times of maximum use, the citadel was able to accommodate thousands of soldiers and horses, but also military schools, lodges, laboratories and other structures of which we have evidence today.

Finally, during World War II, bombing on the city caused serious damage in the citadel which became a prison for deportees and partisans, (six of whom were shot in front of the Santa Barbara bastion). It even housed the expeditionary Brazilian corps in Italy for a short time at the end of the war.

The Citadel today

A risky situation

For quite a few years already, the citadel has been in a situation of increasing deterioration. It is no longer a strategic structure for the Army, neither from a military standpoint, nor a logistical one. It is no longer operating as a barracks and its maintenance has been reduced over time so that it is now practically non-existent. Vegetation has long attacked the exterior fortification system, certain buildings are likely to collapse and have already been abandoned and contained by 'transennas' by the military. A historic palace had already been destroyed years ago, while there have been recent new constructions in concrete, and asphalt installations.

The disastrous flood of 6th November 1994, with 11 deaths in Alessandria, enormous damage, tens of victims in Piedmont, completely flooded and seriously damaged the large site by exacerbating its already precarious situation, by increasing the level of humidity inside the lower ground floors, the cannon-gun openings, and galleries, and infilling the huge bastion areas with mud and rubbish. This tragedy for the citadel nonetheless saved the town centre, as it escaped the powerful floodwaters which unfortunately hit the nearby villages and the town's northern districts.

For centuries, the town of Alessandria has paid a heavy fine for the restrictions of this military presence. Near the citadel there is now as there was in the past, the military district with important barracks and the big military hospital. The town is gradually being freed of these limitations, but left with the responsibility for these huge structures at the heart of the urban infrastructure and its immediate fringe. This has contributed to identifying a cultural and town-planning gap in the city, that it has tried to manage these last few years by confronting the challenge of the reuse of these large buildings from a technical, architectural and managerial, perspective. The area's size, about 80 hectares, and the difficulty of finding functions everyone agrees on, are making the citadel's situation even more serious.

The first actions

In 1997, in order not to be caught unawares when the Army abandoned the citadel, the local authorities put the Turin Polytechnic Institute in charge of doing preliminary study. This has yet to take place, and it seems that it will remain a mere idea for a while. The local institutions have started the *Committee for the enhancement of the Citadel of Alessandria* with the active participation by the Prefecture, Piedmont Surveyors, and from the State and Defence property agencies.

The work of the Polytechnic Institute, namely the Department Casa-Città in the Faculty of Architecture, developed a first *study of the metaproject* . The length and methodologies of the research, and the then lack of will from the authorities, did not allow a complete technical plan and an in-depth study of the problem still being prepared, and that still does not have a program direction for property's difficulties and its availability as a site. The most contentious course is still however to attempt to reconcile the conservation of historic and military structures with the idea of 'second historic centre' with museums, services and offices, as well as a large furnished park which the city lacks.

The study was presented to the public in May 1999 and displayed at an exhibition installed in the citadel's Bastion S Antonio under the title 'Re-inhabit the fortress' (Umberto Allemandi & Co, Turin 2002). The research received a favourable reception from the Minister for Cultural Properties and Activities who, via surveyors, ensures institutional and technical attention and collaboration. In 1999 the site's inscription on the World Heritage List was officially requested. This is most unlikely, given the current length of the Italian 'waiting list', but it is useful to try and raise the awareness of the Institutions, public opinion and experts at the national level, linking it to the neighbouring Residences of the House of Savoy and the numerous other Piedmont fortresses (Exilles, Fenestrelle, Vinadio, Gavi, and so on).

The same year, the Ministry for Cultural Properties declared its preparedness to include the citadel, already a declared National Monument for years, in the Property of the Historic and Artistic State to take on its improvement, once demilitarisation took place, in close collaboration with the Region, the local authorities and, if possible, with the other private and public cultural institutions interested in using the spaces in the citadel, preferably for cultural purposes. One of the rare points agreed for discussion, the future use of the Citadel of Alessandria – this grandiose and scenographic site, is of absolute importance in the context of the most significant historic phase of our region and of our country. That is why in 1998, the Province of Alessandria considered appropriate to propose as a priority the creation of a large ground-breaking Army History Museum, devoting a conference in February 1999 to this idea.

In between this time the Ministry of Public Works started the restoration works of one of the buildings to make it into one of its offices, likewise the National Archives of Alessandria asked to be transferred in the citadel, proposing to restore the Firearms Room.

A future for the Citadel

Perspectives for the „Citadel-Marengo" system

In autumn 2002, the State allocated considerable funding to the Province of Alessandria for the project, 'Renewal of the Military Citadel of Alessandria'. Ensuing meetings with the Army and the other responsible institutions have permitted an understanding that the military presence will continue in the citadel at least a few more years, and that the Army can and must take on again the maintenance of buildings that are still in use, in a new framework of sustainable management, whilst agreeing to proceed to the partial freeing up of redundant areas and buildings. The citadel improvement must begin right away with the military, and can no longer wait for their departure. Cases like Perpignan and Copenhagen can serve as examples.

An international project rehabilitation competition, open to technical teams able to make integrated, affordable and credible proposals for the site's restoration and reuse according to its historic importance, must guarantee at the same time a strong drive for the entire city's tourist and cultural development. The project must not limit itself to only the citadel's internal structures, but solutions are needed to draw attention to all the fortifications and link them with the unique system of the three forts that surround

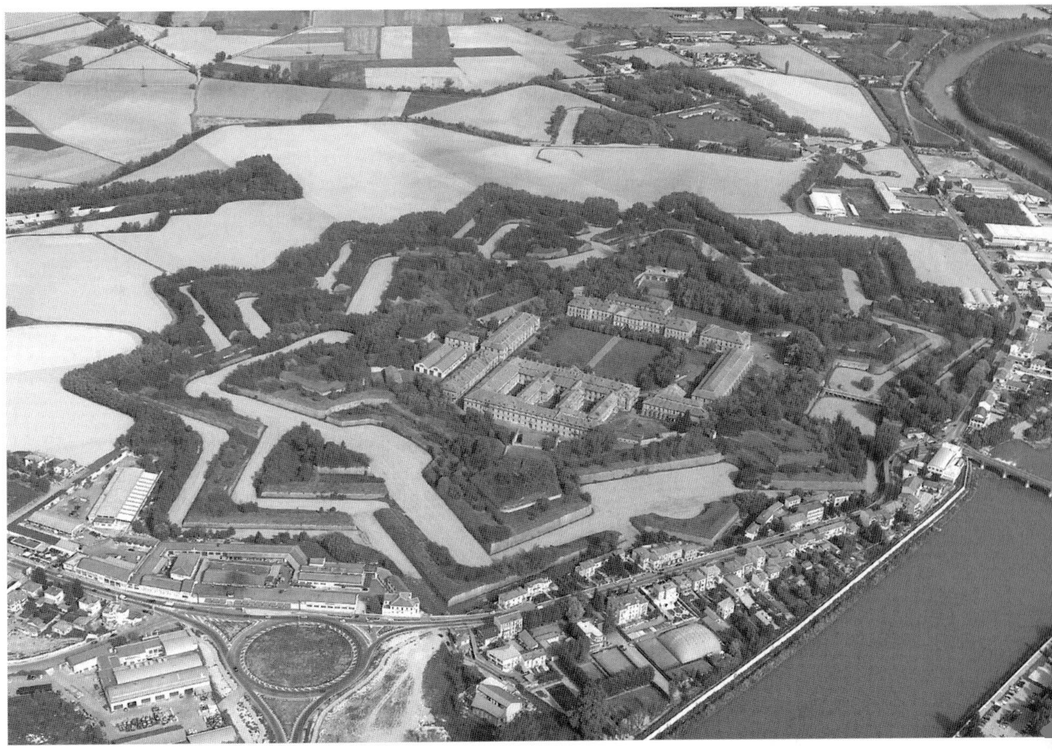

Aerial view of the Citadel of Alessandria

Vue aérienne de la Citadelle d'Alessandria

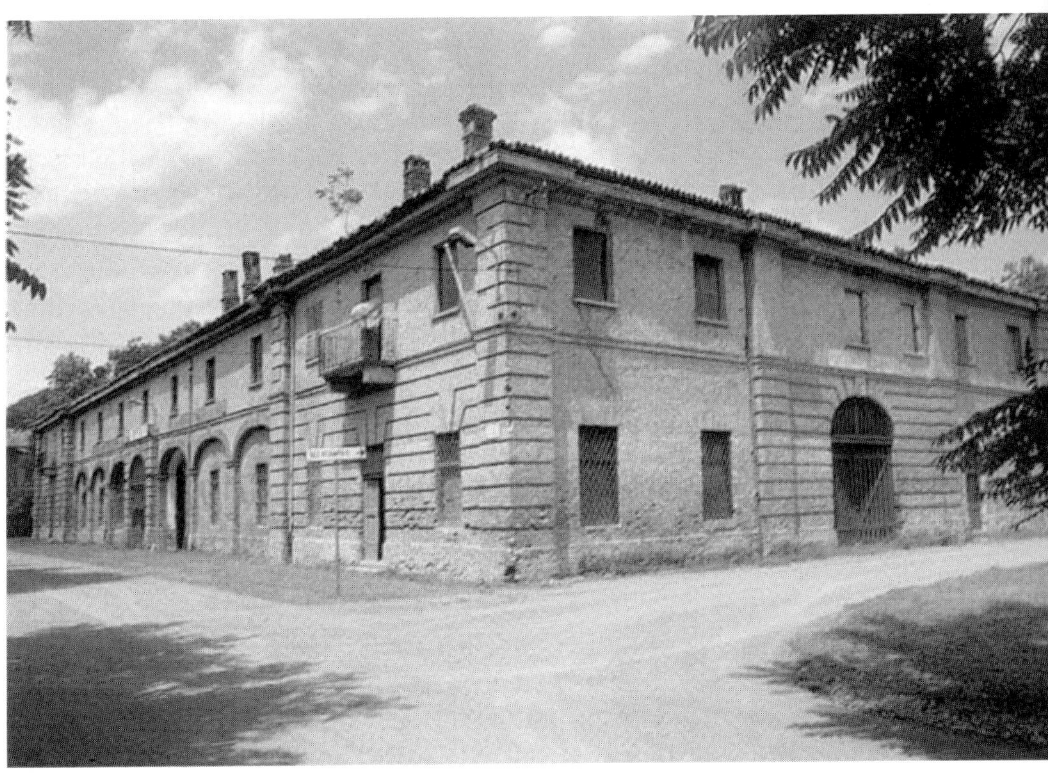

Alessandria, Sapper Magazine – first half 19th century

Alessandria, le Magazin du Génie de la première moitié du XIXème siècle

the city to the south and also in Marengo with the proposed museum and the battle site.

At the same time, the reports of the collaboration and of 'shared life' already installed years ago on the occasion of shows, conferences and exhibitions, must be formalised with the military personnel. A program agreement will have to be set without waiting for the closure of the military depot, to put into operation the various ideas that are already definite.

The problem of the reuse must be faced from the very beginning, with a need to identify who can take possession of the structures that the Armed Forces no longer use and which are already risking abandonment and collapse. These are all the fortification systems, the outer and inner galleries of the cavaliers and bastions, the upper floors of the Governor's Palace, the powder magazines, the Cavallerizza at risk of collapsing, the beautiful and valuable Baroque hospital church rich in stucco, but in a very bad conservation condition.

Conservation Proposals

While waiting for the creation of the Foundation that may in future have responsibility for the management of the citadel, the local authorities must try to avoid irreparable damage and at least foster the most urgent maintenance and restoration of the bastions, the Cavalerizza and the North entrance.

The opening to the public of the fortifications system, with walks and space for athletic activities, the Parade Ground, of at least one bastion and the huge Armory, an ideal location for big exhibitions and fairs, could ensure the possibility of public recognition of the citadel even with the presence of the military. That way it would keep their historic defence and protective function by using the spaces still appropriate, about two-thirds, as a depot for material that is not war related.

To achieve these ideas, the Administrations must make clear and unequivocal choices on the overall goal for the citadel and the area on which it is located:

- Preserve at least to the north the original view of the fortifications and rehabilitate for tourists the historic city entrance through the Soccorso Gate;
- Rehabilitate the zone that surrounds the site, by reconsidering accessibility and resolving the serious parking problem;
- Separate the zone that is still military from the zone that could be allocated for public use or as a park in an intelligent and aesthetically appropriate way;
- Increase the quality of activities and public events hosted by the citadel (exhibitions, concerts, theatrical performances, conferences, fairs, and so on);
- Clarify the feasibility of the proposals for more immediate goals with a museological nature or a cultural nature, such as the National Archives for a start, the large exhibition / conference space that the city lacks, as well as the military museum and potential university structures.

In any case, it is particularly vital to successfully complete in the anticipated time the competition to establish the project, to undertake the works after that as soon as the considerable required resources, about 100 million euros, are found, without neglecting the issue of future management and the corresponding costs.

Massimo Carcione
ICOMOS Italy

La Citadelle d'Alessandria, géant historique à sauver

Un symbole de l'histoire militaire italienne et européenne

Pour comprendre la citadelle militaire d'Alessandria et le problème qu'elle représente aujourd'hui, il est indispensable d'en voir une des rares images aériennes disponibles: cet énorme monument à l'architecture militaire, parmi les meilleurs en Europe pour son intégrité et son originalité, est aussi paradoxalement très peu visible et la majorité des personnes, même parmi les « spécialistes », semble ne pas le connaître.

Commencée par les Savoie en 1728 et terminée en 1745 (projet de Ignazio Bertola et Francesco de Willencourt), la Citadelle a englobé et remplacé tout un bourg fortifié d' Alessandria, Bergoglio, sur la rive gauche du Tanaro depuis le XIIIème siècle. Pour la construction de l'immense hexagone de forme elliptique, il a fallu évacuer des milliers d'habitants pendant ces années; jusqu'en 1749 la Citadelle a conservé dans son enceinte maisons, églises et couvents. Aujourd'hui encore le parfait état de conservation de ses fortifications (composées de six remparts grandioses « à oreillons », tout à fait intègres même à l'intérieur), des fossés et des bâtiments à plusieurs étages disposés autour de l'immense place d'armes plantée d'arbres, font de la citadelle un monument authentique de l'histoire d'Italie. Malgré 5 mois de siège en 1745–6, elle ne fut jamais emportée d'assaut, mais fut occupée par les Autrichiens (1799), puis par les Français suite à la grande victoire remportée le 14 juin 1800 à Marengo – petit bourg aux portes d'Alessandria – Napoléon Bonaparte la fit profondément modifier (projet de François de Chasse-loup-Laubat) pour en faire un immense entrepôt.

Au XIXème siècle, la citadelle fut témoin et protagoniste de l'histoire nationale : ici se déroulèrent les émeutes révolutionnaires de 1821, ici trouva place la prison de personnages du Risorgimento comme Vochieri et Garibaldi (les cellules sont dans le Palais du Gouverneur), mais la citadelle fut aussi base logistique de grande importance au cours des trois guerres d'indépendance et de la première guerre mondiale : dans les moments d'utilisation maximale, la Citadelle réussit à accueillir des milliers de soldats et de chevaux, mais aussi des écoles militaires, des ateliers, des laboratoires et autres structures dont nous gardons aujourd'hui d'importants témoignages.

Enfin, pendant la deuxième guerre mondiale, les bombardements sur la ville provoquèrent de sérieux dommages à la Citadelle qui devint prison pour déportés et partisans (six d'entre eux furent fusillés devant le bastion Santa Barbara) et accueillit même, pendant une courte période à la fin de la guerre, le Corps expéditionnaire brésilien en Italie.

La Citadelle aujourd'hui

La situation en danger

Depuis plusieurs années déjà la Citadelle vit une situation de dégradation croissante, car elle ne constitue plus pour l'Armée une structure stratégique, ni du point de vue militaire, ni logistique ; ayant cessé d'exister en tant que caserne opérationnelle, son entretien a diminué dans le temps jusqu'à devenir aujourd'hui pratiquement nul. La végétation a agressé depuis longtemps le système des fortifications extérieures, certains édifices sont à risque d'effondrement et ont déjà été abandonnés et renfermés par des transennes par les militaires ; il y a des années déjà un palais historique a été détruit, tandis que récemment de nouvelles constructions en béton, des installations et des asphaltages ont été réalisés.

L'inondation catastrophique du 6 novembre 1994 (11 morts à Alessandria seulement, des dégâts énormes et des dizaines de victimes dans tout le Piémont) a complètement envahi et sérieusement endommagé l'ensemble monumental en aggravant des situations déjà précaires, augmentant le taux d'humidité à l'intérieur des sous-sols, des cannonières et des galeries, et remplissant de boue et de détritus les immenses locaux des bastions ; cette tragédie pour la citadelle a néanmoins sauvé le centre ville, qui a évité ainsi la violente montée des eaux qui a malheureusement frappé les hameaux et les quartiers au nord.

La ville d'Alessandria paie depuis des siècles un lourd tribut aux « servitudes militaires » : à côté de la citadelle le district militaire rassemble d'importantes casernes et le grand hôpital militaire; ces servitudes sont en train de la libérer graduellement, abandonnant d'immenses structures au cœur du tissu urbain et dans la périphérie immédiate. Ceci a contribué à déterminer une sorte de fossé culturel et urbanistique pour la ville, qui ces dernières années essaie de s'en sortir en affrontant – sous un angle technique (architectural et de gestion) le défi de la réutilisation de ces grands édifices : les dimensions (environ 80 hectares) et la difficulté de trouver des affectations partagées par tout le monde rendent la situation de la citadelle encore plus grave.

Les premières interventions

En 1997, pour ne pas être pris au dépourvu au moment de l'abandon de la citadelle par l'Armée, les organismes locaux avaient chargé l'Ecole Polytechnique de Turin de la réalisation d'une étude préliminaire; cet événement qui semblait alors imminent n'a pas encore eu lieu jusqu'à présent et, semble-t-il, restera pour quelque temps à l'état de projet. Les institutions locales ont donné vie au *Comité pour la Mise en Valeur de la Citadelle d'Alessandria* avec la participation active de la Préfecture, des Surintendances du Piémont, de l 'Agence du Domaine de l'Etat et des Commandements Militaires mêmes.

Le travail de l'Ecole Polytechnique (précisément le Département Casa-Città de la faculté d'Architecture) a permis de développer une première *étude de métaprojet* : la durée et les modalités de la recherche n'ont pas permis (il n'y avait alors aucune volonté de la part des organismes) d'effectuer des relevés techniques complets et d'approfondir l'étude d'un problème encore *in fieri*, qui n'a pas encore d'orientation de programme quant à la difficile situation de la propriété et de la disponibilité du site : l'orientation la plus partagée reste toutefois la tentative de concilier la conservation des structures historiques et militaires et le projet d'un « deuxième centre historique » avec musées, services et bureaux, maisons et boutiques, ainsi qu'un grand parc équipé dont la cité est presque dépourvue.

L'étude a été présentée au public en mai 1999 et illustrée par une exposition aménagée dans le Bastion S. Antonio de la Citadelle; récemment publiée sous le titre « Réhabiter la forteresse », éditions Umberto Allemandi & C. (Turin 2002), l'étude a été favorablement accueillie par le Ministère pour les Biens et les Activités culturelles qui, par le biais des Surintendances, assure attention et collaboration institutionnelle et technique. En 1999 l'inscription du monument dans la Liste du Patrimoine Mondial de l'UNESCO a été formellement demandée: chose improbable, vu la longueur actuelle de la « Liste d'attente » italienne, mais utile pour essayer de sensibiliser les institutions, l'opinion publique et les experts au niveau national, reliés aux résidences voisines de la Maison de Savoie et aux nombreuses autres forteresses du Piémont (Exilles, Fenestrelle, Vinadio, Gavi, etc).

La même année le Ministère pour les Biens Culturels a déclaré sa propre disponibilité à insérer la citadelle (déclarée Monument National depuis des années) dans le Domaine de l'Etat historique et artistique pour entreprendre sa mise en valeur, une fois la démilitarisation concrétisée, en collaboration étroite avec la Région, les organismes locaux et si possible avec les autres institutions culturelles publiques et privées intéressées à utiliser les espaces de la citadelle, pour des buts culturels de préférence. Un des rares points fermes des discussions, l'utilisation future de la citadelle d'Alessandria, est en fait l'importance absolue, dans le cadre de la phase historique la plus significative de notre Région et de notre Pays, de ce site grandiose et scénographique; c'est pourquoi la Province d'Alessandria a considéré opportun proposer en 1998 comme priorité la création d'un grand et innovatif Musée de l'Histoire de l'Armée en consacrant à ce projet un congrès en février 1999.

Entretemps le Ministère des Travaux Publics a commencé les travaux de restauration de l'un des édifices pour y réaliser un de ses sièges ; de plus les Archives Nationales d'Alessandria ont demandé à se transférer en Citadelle, en proposant de restaurer la Salle d'Artifice.

Un avenir pour la Citadelle

Perspectives pour le système « Citadelle – Marengo »

En automne 2002 l'Etat a attribué à la Province d'Alessandria un financement considérable pour le projet de « Recouvrement de la Citadelle militaire d'Alessandria » ; les réunions qui ont suivi avec l'Armée et les autres Institutions responsables ont permis de comprendre qu'une présence militaire persistera dans la citadelle au moins quelques années; l'Armée peut et doit donc reprendre, dans un nouveau cadre de gestion durable, l'entretien des immeubles qui sont encore en son utilisation, en acceptant en même temps de procéder à la libération partielle de zones et d'édifices hors d'usage. Il faut donc commencer tout de suite à mettre en valeur la citadelle avec les militaires, et ne plus se borner à attendre leur départ : des cas comme Perpignan ou Copenhagen peuvent servir d'exemple.

Le concours international de projets de réhabilitation, ouvert à des équipes techniques en mesure de proposer des hypothèses intégrées, finançables et crédibles de restauration et réutilisation dans le respect de l'importance historique du site, doit garantir en même temps une forte impulsion au développement touristique et culturel de la ville entière ; le projet ne doit donc pas se limiter aux seules structures internes de la citadelle, mais des solutions sont nécessaires pour mettre en valeur toutes les fortifications et réunir, dans un système unique les trois forts qui entouraient la ville au sud ainsi que Marengo, avec le musée et les lieux de la bataille.

Parallèlement, les rapports de collaboration et de « vie en commun » déjà instaurés depuis des années à l'occasion de spectacles, congrès et expositions, doivent être formalisés avec le personnel militaire: un « accord de programme » devra être stipulé, pour rendre opérationnelles les différentes idées déjà explicitées, sans attendre la fermeture du dépôt militaire.

Le problème de la réutilisation doit être affronté dès le début : il faut donc identifier qui peut prendre possession des structures que les Forces Armées n'utilisent plus et qui risquent déjà l'abandon ou l'effondrement : tout le système des fortifications, l'extérieur et les galeries internes des cavaliers et des bastions, les étages supérieurs du Palais du Gouverneur, les poudrières, la Cavallerizza qui menace de s'effondrer, la belle église baroque de l'Hôpital riche en stucs de valeur, mais en très mauvais état de conservation…

Propositions d'intervention

En attendant la constitution de la Fondation qui s'occupera peut être à l'avenir de la gestion de toute la Citadelle, les organismes locaux doivent essayer, pour éviter des dommages irréparables, de promouvoir au moins les interventions les plus urgentes de entretien et restauration des bastions, de la Cavallerizza et de l'entrée au Nord.

L'ouverture au public du système des fortifications, avec des promenades et des espaces pour les activités sportives, de la Place d'Armes, d'un bastion au moins et de l'immense Armurerie (siège idéal pour de grandes expositions et foires) pourrait assurer la possibilité de mise en valeur publique de la Citadelle même en présence de militaires, qui garderaient ainsi leur fonction historique de défense et de protection en utilisant les espaces encore appropriés (2/3 de l'ensemble environ) comme dépôt pour le matériel à l'exclusion des armes.

Pour réunir ces circonstances, les Administrations doivent effectuer des choix clairs et univoques sur la destination globale de la Citadelle et de la zone sur laquelle elle se trouve

- préserver au moins au nord la vue originale sur les fortifications et réhabiliter du point de vue touristique l'entrée historique à la ville à travers la « porte du Soccorso »;
- réhabiliter la zone qui entoure le monument, en reconsidérant la viabilité en fonction de la facilité d'accès et en résolvant le problème grave des parkings;
- séparer de façon intelligente et esthétiquement correcte la zone encore militaire de la zone pouvant être affectée à des utilisations civiles ou à parc;
- augmenter qualitativement les activités et les manifestations publiques accueillies dans la Citadelle (expositions, concerts et spectacles de théâtre, congrès, foires, etc..);
- préciser la faisabilité des hypothèses de destination plus immédiates ayant un caractère muséographique et culturel : les Archives Nationales in primis, le grand espace pour expositions et congrès qui manque à la ville, ainsi que le musée militaire et les structures universitaires éventuelles.

Il est surtout indispensable d' achever à terme dans les temps prévus, le concours de mise en projet, pour entreprendre par la suite les travaux dès que les ressources considérables nécessaires (environ 100 millions d'euros) auront été trouvées, sans délaisser le problème de la future gestion et des coûts correspondants.

Massimo Carcione
ICOMOS Italie

Sardinia's Vernacular Earthen Architecture

Courtyard houses

Sardinian earthen heritage is the most extensive in Italy and recognised formally as one of the richest of the Mediterranean basin because it embodies functional, structural, rural, and urban characteristics that are missing in other regions. Also, the importance of Sardinia's earthen buildings lies in the impressive number of surviving mudbrick villages. A rough calculation shows that more than one third of all island villages' historic centres are made of earth.

Until 1950, mudbrick and stone were the most frequently used building materials in Sardinia, but today their quality has deteriorated considerably because relevant skills have been forgotten or are lacking. The island can be divided into two main areas: the north, where mountain houses of stone with several storeys are more widespread, and the south, where mud-brick courtyard houses are more common. The main entrance of this latter type usually faces the street through a large gateway that gives the building a monumental impression. The residential area of the house is usually characterised by a long arcaded loggia that acts as climatic buffer and where housework took place and onto which the rooms opened. Also, town growth by adding courtyard houses resulted in shared shading, but also in an internal and private lifestyle.

Sun-dried clay bricks, locally called *làdiri* (from the Latin word *later*, brick), were made using thick malleable mud with added straw. Houses were built under the supervision of the *maistru de muru* (the Sardinian expression for master craftsman), a very experienced and senior mason who was skilled with every material involved in the construction process.

Having virtually only two main seasons – winter and summer – both characterised by extremes, made the use of earth as a building material necessary and led to the development of features such as the arcaded loggia together with shared shading and inward-looking spaces in order to cope with climate swings. The use of earth as a building material is also because it was the only locally available material in the alluvial area and because of the constant winds so essential for the drying process. Another important influence in the closed-in nature, particularly of the farmhouses, is related to the area's agricultural economy. In fact, the evolution of this form of vernacular housing cannot be understood properly without being set within the context of the farming systems in use before the start of the 20th century. Such architecture is the expression of Sardinian tradition and culture and it needs to be conserved in order to check the loss of cultural identity to contemporary living standards. Another important and practical reason for the conservation of this heritage is the demand for sustainable housing. Also, the fact that Sardinia's endangered heritage requires immediate attention was stressed by the 2000 *Heritage at Risk* report where it was stated that '...this entire heritage will be gradually destroyed as soon as the houses are abandoned or replaced by horrible constructions in concrete and plastic'.

Survey of Threats

Although it is a common opinion that 20th century housing policies have failed, at the moment mudbrick structures are very deteriorated and sometimes they have not been repaired since the day they were built. In fact, nowadays a courtyard house owner either builds a concrete house on the site of the old one, or builds it on the outskirts of the village. This incongruous occurrence of a lack of awareness of environment conservation is slowly changing, but there is still a need for proper guidelines and practice when conserving earthen buildings.

In order to understand the most common symptoms of decay that affect inhabited mudbrick buildings, a questionnaire was designed. The overall number of completed questionnaires was 288 and this population size was considered to be adequate for the area being examined. The aim of this study, stimulated by the distinct lack of literature on the main symptoms and problems of such buildings, is to survey the main threats and mechanisms of deterioration. The work is a general survey of the area under examination, and not a detailed analysis of the peculiarities of single buildings.

Mudbrick construction in Sardinia reached a peak between the end of the 19th century and the start of World War II. This is demonstrated by the survey which shows that 9.1% of the buildings involved were built before 1900, 31.5% were built between 1901 and 1960, whilst the remaining 59.4% of the respondents answered that the date was unknown. The popularity of modern building materials for repair purposes can be quantified according to questionnaire responses, showing that 59.7% of the total number of buildings included in the questionnaire have been repaired with modern materials, whilst only 14.9% are repaired with traditional materials, the remaining percentage was not repaired since construction or was unknown.

At this point, it is relevant to understand the proportion of these buildings located in historic centres. The total number of buildings in historic centres included in the questionnaire is 137, of the 288. It can be therefore demonstrated through a cross-query that only 18.2% of the buildings located in historic centres have been conserved with traditional materials. This survey paints a gloomy picture of the region's landscape, giving evidence of the complexity of this phenomenon. Moreover, today owners and practitioners still tend to replace traditional porous coats with a combination of hard cement-based renders and chicken mesh as a binding agent. Today this is causing more damage to the historic fabric than any other misrepair. The main disadvantage of using cement-based coats is their high alkalinity and also the migration of salts towards the inner face of the render where they can crystallise and make the softer and more porous fabric lose cohesion, in this case the mudbrick. The questionnaire results on coating systems are lime plaster (42.7%), cement plaster (39.9%), mud plaster (6.6%), tile cladding (0.4%), and not available (10.4%).

If common sense was the key of conservation regulations in protecting earthen architecture prior to the cement era (pre-1950), by contrast what subsequently followed seems to deny local building cultures. It appears likely that since then, cement lobbies have played a role in the way mudbrick was perceived as a building material on the island, with a consequence that demolition and rebuilding with reinforced concrete increased rapidly. A lack of consideration for the historic fabric can be read in recent conservation regulations where PVC windows, cement plinths, and other inadequate materials are imposed for repair work by heritage regulations.

Modern building materials still play a relevant role in the repair and maintenance of mudbrick buildings. This is not only because of a lack of awareness of building users, but also of professionals. Since the mid-20th century, new construction is with modern materials and therefore the repair and maintenance of Sardinian vernacular heritage has relied on inadequate techniques and alien materials. It can be speculated therefore that such deterioration is more the result of a cultural problem and, in this respect, regulation and craftsmanship play their proper roles.

The main obstacle against the acceptance and the conservation of such buildings is the lack of awareness and pride in the build-

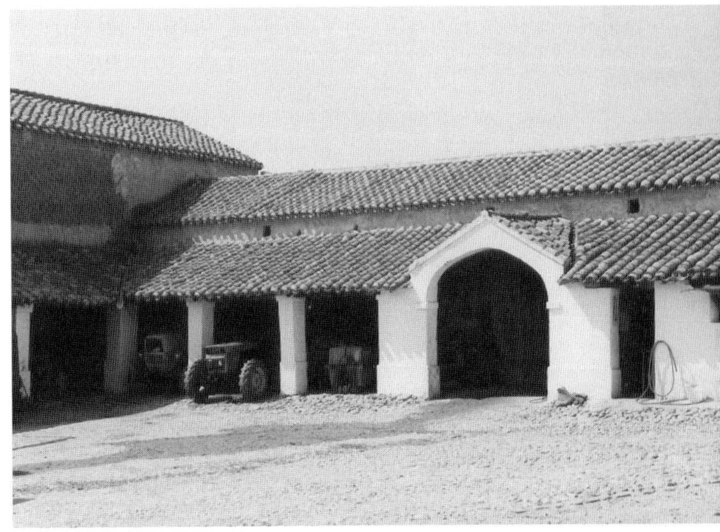

Courtyard house in Ussana, Sardinia

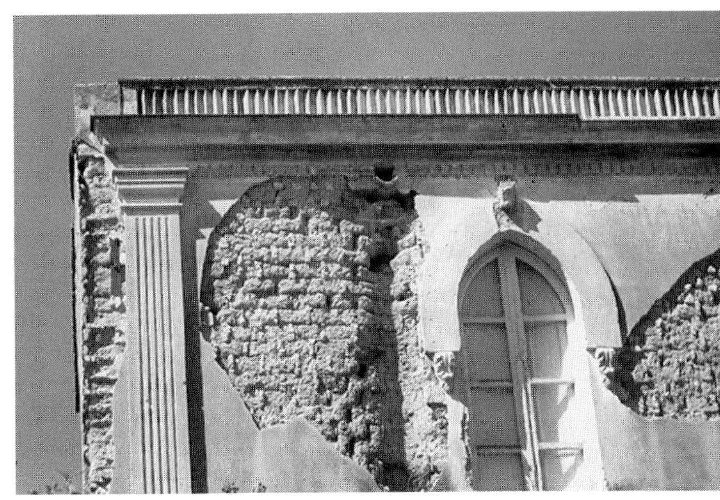

Erosion of mudbrick caused by neglect and lack of maintenance of downpipes and gutters (Samatzai, Sardinia)

Misrepair of an earthen wall by means of cement blocks (Ussana, Sardinia)

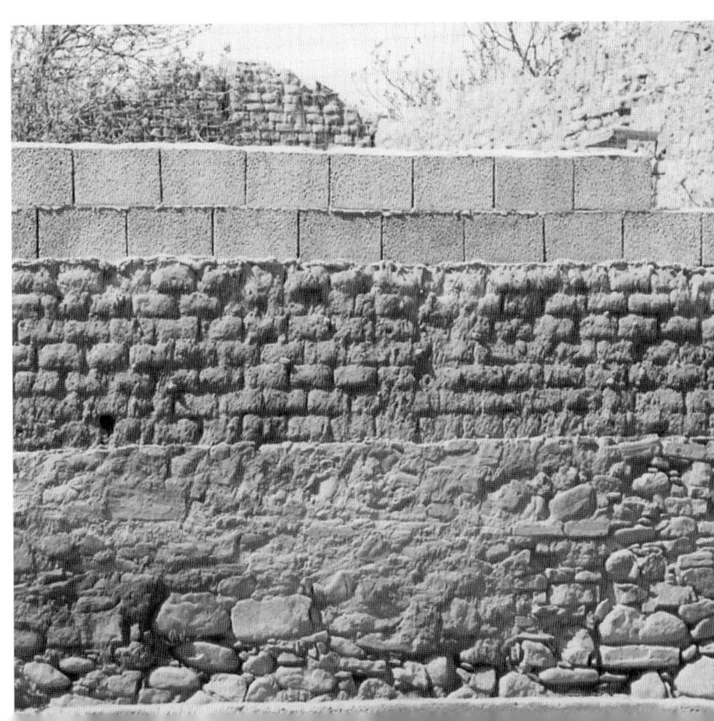

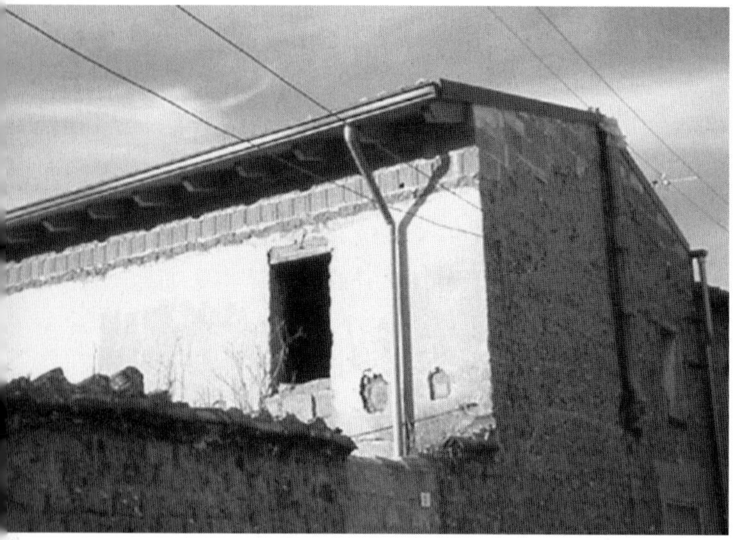

The top part of this earthen building shows repair with cement blocks (Terralba, Sardinia)

ings on the part of their owners and users, and this is confirmed by direct observation. The aesthetics of vernacular buildings in Sardinia do not correspond to the portrayals existing in today's media. It seems that there is a need to show that one does not have to live in modern buildings to be able to enjoy the comforts of modern life.

The main reasons for abandoning vernacular architecture and the resultant heavy introduction of unfinished architecture can be identified in the social changes that have occurred on the island:

The sense of shame associated with the material is still strong in the island because, as noted earlier, mudbrick is considered as a peculiar resource of the poor.

- A further reason is related to the traditional construction system. Dwellings were traditionally built by the addition of cells or units, according to the financial situation and to the need of more rooms. Such cells were called *domus* (houses), so that there was no distinction between the terms 'room' and 'house'. This organic growth of such dwellings was characterised by the use of traditional materials and unchanging architectural codes. During the second half of the 20th century this traditional building with incremental parts was applied with catastrophic consequences to modern materials and design.
- Another reason can be related to the improvement of transportation facilities and a consequent drop in the costs of building materials. The construction industry has a strong motivation to keep modern materials and methods in the market because they are more profitable.
- Another important reason for abandoning earthen buildings involved the continuous complaints about the need for their constant maintenance.
- A lack of scientific research on building cultures and materials.
- Building a new house in the outskirts of villages is preferred to repairing a historic building in the village centre where regulation is considered to be too conservative and restrictive.

During the last fifty years, the conservation of earthen buildings of Sardinia has too often relied on the use of non-porous materials. This is principally due to the fact that practitioners tend to apply those skills and methods employed in new construction to historic buildings. Another cause is due to the conventional and simplistic idea that 'strong' materials should be used, with the result that mortars are often rich in cement, if not made entirely of cement. Such material is commonly used in Sardinia in the shape of blocks for the replacement of deteriorated sections of earthen walls.

Recommendations for Conserving Sardinia's Mudbrick Buildings

A series of themes on how conservation and public awareness can be improved have been identified, and are listed below. These are by no means intended as firm practical proposals, but simply as an outline of where and how improvement can occur:

- Reversibility and minimum intervention into the historic fabric.
- Traditional, local, and recycled materials in contemporary repair. Employing local materials has several advantages, not least being that the sources for the original materials are close to the site. The recycling of building materials is especially applicable to the earthen buildings of Sardinia. Soil was often traditionally recycled and reconstituted in the form of mudbricks for replacement purposes, but also in the form of mortar, dry packing, and less frequently in the form of mud render.
- Repair 'like with like' (mud with mud, lime with lime, and so on).
- Repairs guided by building traditions and by past craftsmen, and the role of training. The lack of specialised craftsmen in the repair of earthen buildings, together with the issue of training needs, is constantly deplored in the literature on Sardinian earthen heritage. Buildings are conserved with inappropriate modern materials and methods and this is due to the fact that the workmanship necessary for using traditional materials requires more skill, sensitivity and grounding in traditional culture than does that required for using modern materials. The suggestion advanced here is that the role of the master craftsman and his knowledge of traditional repair methods should be re-instituted by on-site training of young apprentices including the involvement of older craftsmen. This would be in keeping with traditional practice in Sardinia, where young apprentices were trained at different levels before reaching the status of master craftsman.
- Maintenance after repair. Annual maintenance and the renewal of sacrificial layers are essential tools for the conservation of earthen buildings. The key to maintenance is that if a fault is not repaired, instant failures will occur. Regular and cyclical maintenance was historically undertaken in Sardinia. However, in today's world, building regulations do not ever provide any recommendations on post-construction maintenance and repair. This absurd lack of interest in maintenance is also shared by building users who have certain preconceptions against maintenance, often owing to the frequent work that its adoption usually implies. The suggestion given here is that building regulations should be more explicit about requiring the use of traditional building materials and methods.

Dr Enrico Fodde
ICOMOS Italy

Tuscan archipelago – Island of Pianosa

Pianosa, the ancient *Planasia*, one of the seven islands of the Tuscan Archipelago, located 15 km south west of the Island of Elbe, is the jurisdiction of the Commune of Campo nell'Elba. The Commune of Campo has become the owner of four buildings, a new management building, accommodation for foreigners, the refectory for former agents, and Caserne Biano Quirico, as well as a big part of the agricultural land. This follows the dissolution of the then municipal use determined by Decree of the Tuscan region 2887 of the 30/5/2001, although seized at the last minute by the State of Libourne's Property Agency and currently still *sub iudice*. Its dimensions,10 km^2, and even the presence of the penitentiary have protected the island until now from the destructive property development that has totally ruined the other Tyrrhenian islands.

Archaeological evidence on the island covers a time span from the Palaeolithic to the present day.

The availability of freshwater and a few points to beach small boats favoured interaction with the mainland as well as the other Tyrrhenian islands. It is no coincidence that Pianosa is mentioned in the works of Classical Greek and Roman writers.

We find numerous remains from Roman times, when Pianosa, like the other islands in the archipelago, became a place of rest and recreation. A luxurious villa, with its remains on the east coast, housed Agrippa Postumo, grandson of Augustus, during his exile and he was assassinated there in the year 14.

There are cement structures along the northern coastline of Punta Teglia and upstream, traces of huts linked to cisterns for wine production, also referring to Villa Agrippa, known as 'Bagno'. Remains of walls and basins dug into the rock in the northwest bay indicate the existence of an ancient anchorage point.

Between the 4th and 6th centuries, Pianosa, just as the other islands of the archipelago, offered refuge to the first monastics. It is probably in this epoch that behind the promontory of the Teglia, at the junction of several underground caves a big catacomb was formed, the second biggest in Italy north of Rome, after that in Chiusi. Altered in the 19th century by a cellar being installed, the catacomb was only recently freed from its use as the prison sewer and dump by the Pontifical Commission for Sacred Archaeology.

Implicated from the 10th to 14th centuries in the struggles between the maritime republics of Pisa and Genoa for the control of the High Tyrrhenian Sea, in 1399 Pianosa went under the domination of the Appianin lords of the Piombino.

The Appiani domain lasted until 1554, with only a brief interruption in 1501 by Cesare Borgia. Then the island was dispossessed by Admiral Dragut's Franco-Turks in the war between France and Charles V, delivering its inhabitants to slavery and leaving it deserted. Afterwards, it was only visited seasonally by shepherds and farmers from the Island of Elbe. Pianosa became the property of the princes of Boncompagni Ludovisi.

In 1814, the island was conceded along with Montecristo to Napoleon, who was confined to Elbe. The Congress of Vienna assigned it to the Grand Duchy of Tuscany, which tried to restore agriculture and animal husbandry, by providing it with a coast guard detachment and by housing the few inhabitants and garrison in its grottoes. From that moment on, the island depended administratively on the municipality of S. Piero in Campo (Elbe).

In 1846, the building began of the church dedicated to S. Gaudenzio. It still stands today on the esplanade in front of the prison entrance, the prison dating to the first half of the 20th century.

Finally, in 1856, the Grand Duchy of Tuscany implemented a project of Napoleon's, by establishing an experimental reformatory for young delinquents. Later from 1858, the agricultural penitentiary colony remained in use, even after Italy's unification.

The first director of the prison was Leopoldo Ponticelli of Reggio Emilia who built almost all the buildings that we see on the island today, using convicts as labour and the local tufa as building material, in a project that followed the then dominant neo-Gothic in a provincial yet ingenious style. These include the castellated walls behind the port's small jetty, Fort Teglia in place of one of the Appiani forts, the Observatory, the Punta del Marchese convalescence home for the detainees convalescing from tuberculosis. It is thanks to him that we owe that section of the street that links the 19th-century structures of the little port to the rest of the island. The house built for the agronomist hired for the island by the Grand Duchy also goes back to the second half of the 19th century.

The first archaeological research in Pianosa goes back to those years. The research was led by Don Gaetano Chierici, pioneer of the old stone age research in Emilia, and promoter and first director of the municipal Museums of Reggio Emilia. Invited to Pianosa in 1874 by his fellow citizen Ponticelli, Chierici, guided by the discoveries made a few years previously by R. Foresi, investigated prehistoric sites, but also undertook the first excavations and uncovering of the Villa Agrippa as well as the first description of the catacomb. In 1875, he published the results of the enquiries in *Gli antichi monumenti della Pianosa* ('The ancient monuments of Pianosa'), the first and only monograph on the antiquities of the island. The remains and artefacts found during the excavations are preserved at the Archaeological Municipal Museum of Reggio Emilia.

Entrance to the esplanade of the church (IGM, s.50, f.328-341)

Entrée à l'esplanade de l'église (IGM, s.50, f.328-341)

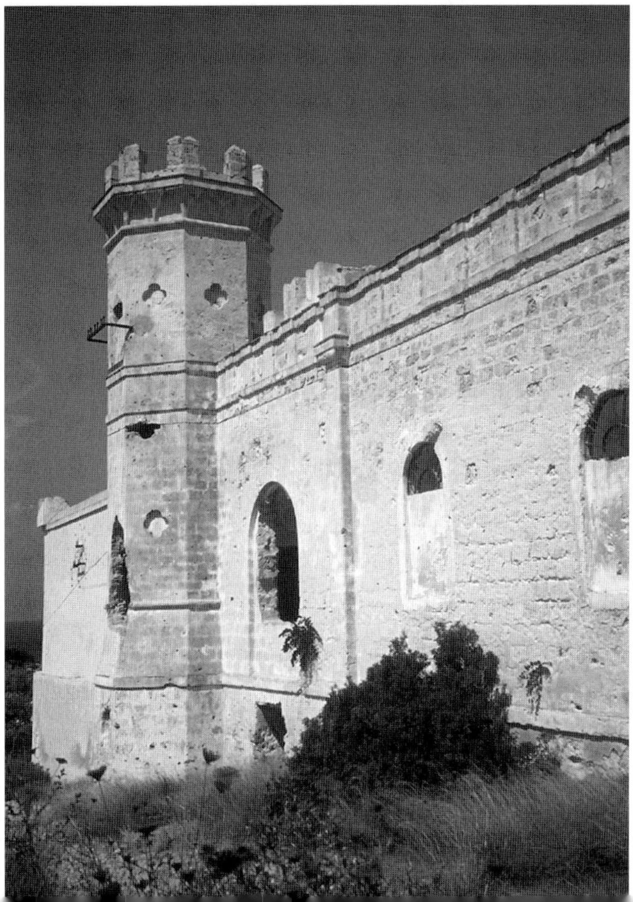

During the 20th century, the penitentiary colony was transformed into a tight security prison, with barracks and other security structures. This construction was wanted by General Dalla Chiesa and led to the building of a high wall in reinforced concrete through the remains of Villa Agrippa.

Once the prison was demolished, the island was included in the Natural Park of the Tuscan Archipelago on 31 October 1997. A protection area up to 1000 m off the coast had already been established in 1989 around the island. In 1995 an association was founded for the protection of Pianosa. The island is the object of a research program by the University Institutes and the CNR, and the Tuscan Surveyor of Archaeological Property has undertaken research and restoration there on several occasions.

However, without any maintenance the buildings of the 19th century are abandoned and certainly risk collapsing. Moreover, Pianosa is included on the lists of the society Patrimonio dello Stato S.p.A which means that as a result it is likely to be sold.

Mirella Marini Calvani
ICOMOS Italy

References

Barbara SASSI, *Il „Bagno" di Agrippa e le ricerhe di Gaetano Chierici nell'isola di Pianosa*, Pagine di Archeologia 4, Reggio Emilia, 1999
Marco BAZZINI, *Materiali dall'isola di Pianosa presenti nelle collezioni dei Musei Civici di Reggio Emilia,* Pagine di Archeologia 2, Reggio Emilia, 1999
Fausto A. FORESI, *Il porto di Pianosa,* Pise, 1999
and verbal communications with the lawyer Lorenzo Calvani

Archipel Toscan – Ile de Pianosa

Pianosa, l'ancienne *Planasia,* une des sept îles de l'Archipel Toscan, située à 15 km au sud-ouest de l'Ile d'Elbe, se trouve dans la juridiction de la Commune de Campo nell'Elba. Suite à la liquidation des utilisations municipales disposée par Décret de la région Toscane 2887 du 30/5/2001 (tardivement saisi par l'Agence du Domaine de l'Etat de Livourne actuellement encore *sub iudice*), la Commune de Campo est devenue propriétaire de quatre immeubles (nouvelle Direction, hébergement pour étrangers, Réfectoire des anciens Agents, Caserne Biano Quirico), ainsi que de grande partie des terrains agricoles.

Ses dimensions (10 km^2) et la présence même du pénitencier l'ont préservée jusqu'à présent de la destruction immobilière qui a massacré les autres îles tyrrhéniennes.

Les témoignages archéologiques sur l'île couvrent un arc chronologique qui va du Paléolithique à nos jours.

La disponibilité d'eau sur place et quelques points d'accostage pour bateaux de petites dimensions favorisent les échanges avec la terre ferme ainsi qu'avec les autres îles tyrrhéniennes. Ce n'est pas un cas si Pianosa est citée dans les ouvrages des auteurs anciens, grecs et latins.

On y retrouve, plutôt nombreux, des vestiges de l'époque romaine, période où Pianosa, tout comme les autres îles de l'archipel, devient lieu de repos et de divertissement. Une villa luxueuse, dont on peut voir les restes sur la côte orientale, y accueillera l'exil de Agrippa Postumo, petit-fils d'Auguste, qui y fut assassiné en 14 après J.C.

Des structures en ciment le long de la ligne de côte au nord de punta Teglia et, en amont, des traces de cabanes associées à des vasques pour la production de vin se réfèrent, elles aussi, à la villa d'Agrippa (dénommée »Bagno«).

Des restes de murs et de bassins creusés dans le roc signalent dans la baie à nord-ouest l'existence d'une ancienne escale.

Entre le IVème et le VIème siècle Pianosa, tout comme les autres îles de l'Archipel, offre refuge au premier monachisme. C'est probablement à cette époque que derrière le promontoire de la Teglia, de l'union de plusieurs hypogées, se forme une grande catacombe, la deuxième pour ses dimensions dans l'Italie au nord de Rome, après celle de Chiusi. Altérée dès le XIXème siècle par l'installation d'une cave, la catacombe n'a été affranchie de son utilisation comme égout et décharge à laquelle la prison l'avait affectée que récemment par la Commission Pontificale pour l'Archéologie Sacrée.

Impliquée du Xème au XIVème siècle dans les luttes entre les républiques maritimes de Pise et de Gênes pour le contrôle de la Haute Mer Tyrrhénienne, Pianosa passe en 1399 sous la domination des Appiani, seigneurs de Piombino.

La seigneurie des Appiani, qui n'a subi qu'une brève interruption en 1501 par Cesare Borgia, durera jusqu'en 1554, époque où, dans la guerre entre la France et Charles V, elle sera dépouillée par les Francs-Turcs de l'amiral Dragut, qui réduira ses habitants en esclavage, en laissant l'île déserte.

Fréquentée par la suite uniquement de façon saisonnière par des bergers et des agriculteurs de l'Elbe, Pianosa passera en propriété des princes Boncompagni Ludovisi.

L'île sera concédée, avec Montecristo, à Napoléon, confiné à l'Elbe, en 1814.

Le Congrès de Vienne l'attribuera au Grand - duché de Toscane, qui essaiera d'y rétablir l'agriculture et l'élevage, en la dotant d'un détachement de garde-côtes et en accueillant dans ses grottes

Map of the island of Pianosa

Plan de l' île de Pianosa

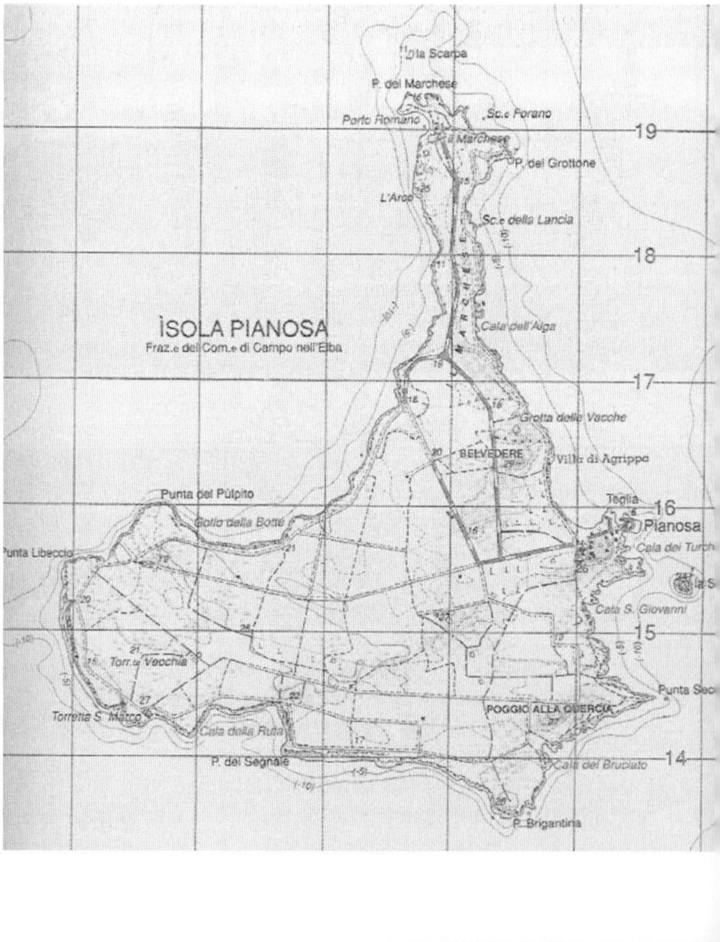

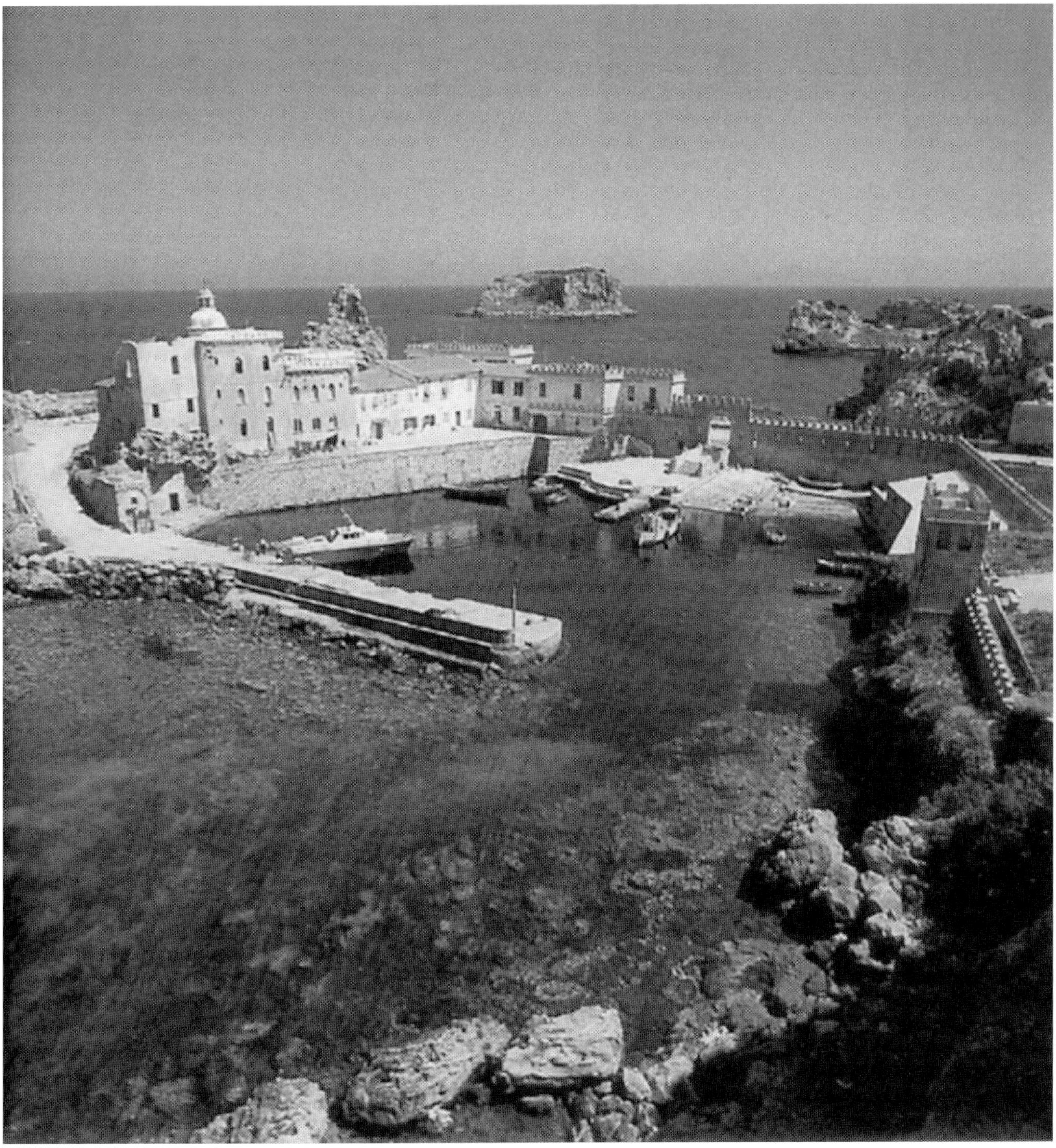

View of the island of Pianosa (photo: Mirella Marini Calvani)

Vue de l' île de Pianosa

les rares habitants et la garnison. A partir de ce moment, l'île dépendra du point de vue administratif de la municipalité de S.Piero in Campo (Elbe).

En 1846 commencera la construction de l'église consacrée à S.Gaudenzio – qui existe encore aujourd'hui sur l'esplanade devant l'entrée au pénitencier – qui sera complétée dans la première moitié du XXème siècle.

Enfin, en 1856, le Grand-duché de Toscane réalisera un projet de Napoléon, en y instituant, en voie expérimentale, une colonie de jeunes délinquants à corriger; par la suite, à partir de 1858, la colonie pénitentiaire agricole est restée en fonction même après l'unité d'Italie.

Le premier directeur de la prison est Leopoldo Ponticelli de Reggio Emilia qui, en utilisant comme main d'oeuvre les forçats et comme matériel le tuf local, fait construire presque tous les bâtiments que l'on peut voir aujourd'hui sur l' île, les murs crénelés derrière le petit môle du port; le Fort Teglia à la place d'un fort des Appiani; l'Observatoire; la maison de convalescence pour détenus guéris de la phtisie de Punta del Marchese, avec un projet qui adhère de manière provincialement ingénue au langage néogothique, à l'époque dominante. C'est à lui que nous devons le tronçon de rue qui relie les constructions du petit port du XIXème siècle au reste de l'île. La maison construite pour l'agronome engagé pour l' île par le Grand-duché remonte elle aussi à la deuxième moitié du XIXème siècle.

Les premières recherches archéologiques à Pianosa remontent à ces années-là. Les recherches sont menées par don Gaetano Chierici, pionnier de la recherche palethnologique en Emilie, promoteur et premier directeur du Cabinet delle Antichità Patrie, premier noyau des Musées Municipaux de Reggio Emilia. Invité à Pianosa en 1874 par son concitoyen Ponticelli, Chierici, guidé par les découvertes faites une dizaine d'années auparavant par R. Foresi, entreprend des recherches sur les sites préhistoriques, mais effectue aussi les premières fouilles et le premier relevé de la villa d'Agrippa; la première description de la catacombe. En 1875, il publie les résultats de ses explorations dans *"Gli antichi monumenti della Pianosa" (« Les anciens monuments de la Pianosa »)*, première et unique monographie existant sur les antiquités de l'île. Les vestiges retrouvés lors de ses fouilles sont conservés au Musée Archéologique Municipal de Reggio Emilia.

Au cours du XXème siècle, la colonie pénitentiaire a été transformée en prison de toute sécurité, avec des casernes et autres structures de surveillance; la construction voulue par le général Dalla Chiesa à travers les vestiges de la villa d'Agrippa d'un haut mur en béton armé.

Une fois le pénitencier supprimé, l'île a été insérée le 31 octobre 1997 dans le Parc Naturel de l'Archipel Toscan.

Une ceinture de protection jusqu'à un mille de la côte avait déjà été instituée en 1989 autour de l'île.

- En 1995 une Association est née pour la sauvegarde de Pianosa.
- L' île est l'objet de programmes de recherche de la part d'Instituts universitaires et du C.N.R.
- La Surintendance aux Biens Archéologiques de la Toscane y a effectué des recherches et des restaurations à plusieurs reprises.
- Mais les édifices du XIXème siècle, privés de manutention, sont en état d'abandon, certains à risque d'effondrement.
- Pianosa est, de plus, insérée dans les listes de la société Patrimonio dello Stato S.p.A. et, par conséquent, susceptible d'être vendue.

Mirella Marini Calvani
ICOMOS Italie

Références

Barbara SASSI, *Il "Bagno" di Agrippa e le ricerche di Gaetano Chierici nell'isola di Pianosa*, Pagine di Archeologia 4, Reggio Emilia,1999
Marco BAZZINI, *Materiali dall'isola di Pianosa presenti nelle collezioni dei Musei Civici di Reggio Emilia*, Pagine di Archeologia 2, Reggio Emilia,1999
Fausto A.FORESI, *Il porto di Pianosa*, Pise, 1999
et les communications verbales avec l'avocat Lorenzo CALVANI

Protection of the Baia Underwater Park

The uniqueness of the archaeological evidence of Baia, be it on land, be it underwater, has made this site famous worldwide. Also, thanks to the pioneering experience of underwater investigations by Nino Lambroglia in 1959[11] and to the first underwater stratigraphic excavation campaigns between 1981 and 1982,[12] Baia has come to hold a significant role in the history of underwater archaeology.[13]

In 1998, the admirable and far-sighted work of the Naples Archaeological Management Agency[14] favoured the conception and the creation of an archaeological underwater pathway inside an extensive expanse of water in front of Punta dell'Epitaffio,[15] where sailing, anchorage and fishing has been prohibited. A temporary association of businesses has however been granted a concession for this area.

On the basis of Article 114[16] of Law no. 388,[17] the Ministry of Environment and Land Protection, under its own legislation,[18] has established the Baia Underwater Park, with the following objectives (Article 3):

- *The environmental and archaeological protection of the area of interest;*
- *The improvement, also for social and occupational scopes, of the environmental, historical, archaeological and cultural resources in the area;*
- *The dissemination of knowledge of marine ecology, of biology of marine and coastal environments and of the underwater archaeological heritage in the area;*

Baia, Punta dell'Epitaffio, archaeological underwater pathway

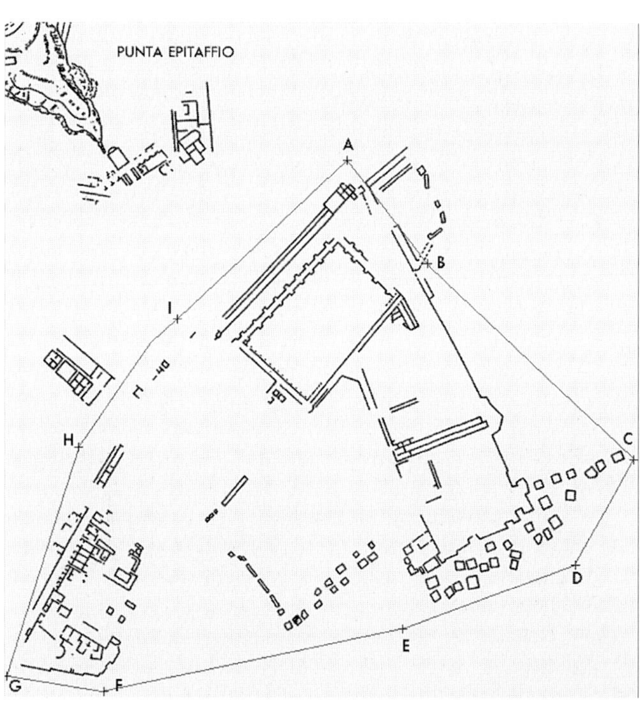

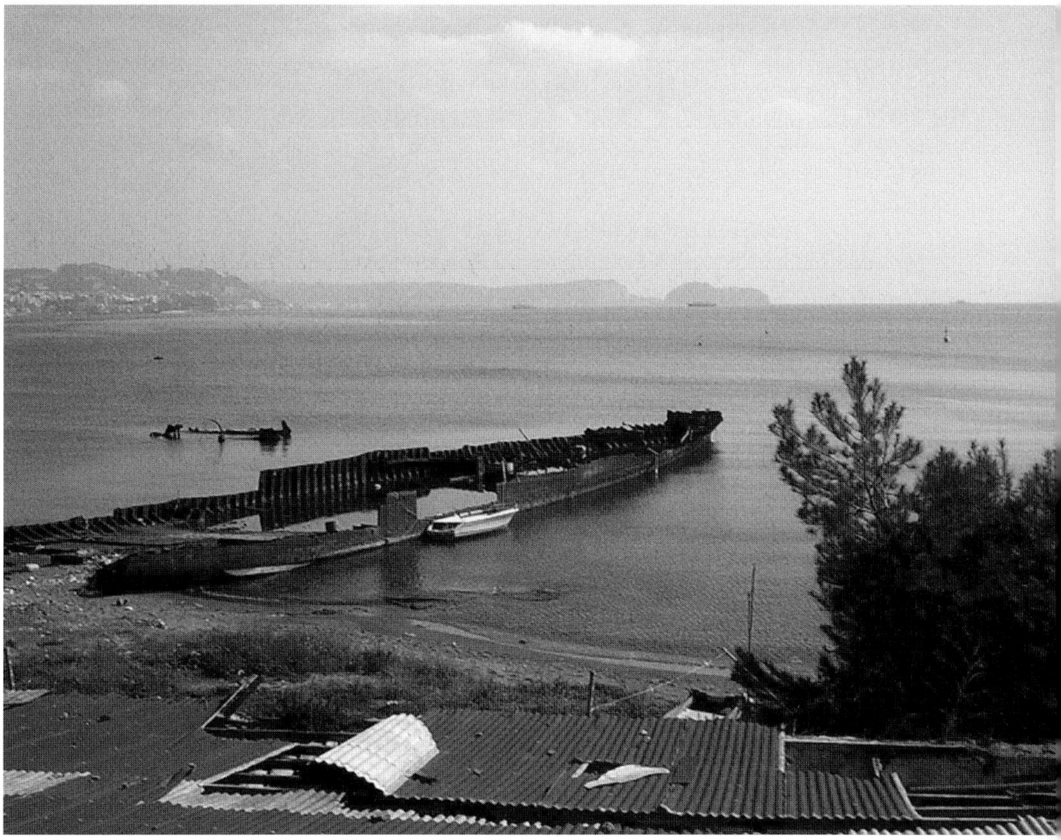

Baia, hulks near the zone A of the Underwater Park

- *The implementation of educational programs for the improvement of common knowledge in the field of ecology, marine biology and archaeology;*
- *The realisation of educational and scientific research programs in the sectors of ecology, marine biology, environmental protection and archaeology with the scope of assuring a systematic knowledge of the area;*
- *The promotion of socio-economic development compatible with the historical, natural, environmental realities in the area, also privileging traditional local activities already present.*

The Park, extending itself from the southern pier of the port of Baia, that coincides with OMLIN pier and the head of the pier at the Lido of Augusto in the Municipality of Pozzuoli,[19] is divided into three sections, each one having its own separate protection regime:

- Zone A includes the tract of the sea in front of Punta dell'Epitaffio.[20] It is completely protected. Swimming, all diving, sailing, access and mooring of all vessels, anchorage, mooring and all forms of fishing are prohibited. A lessening of these prohibitions is foreseen for the previous authorisation and supervision of the management body for vessels that carry scientific research programs and for visitors, on condition that it has a draught less than 2.50 m. This will also apply to guided underwater visits compatible with the underwater heritage protection requirements for underwater objects archaeological find. Exceptions are also made for recreational fishing with rods or fishing-lines, although exclusively for local residents.
- Zone B includes the tract of the sea between the pier of 'Lido di Augusto' and the land stretch of Lido Montenuovo.[21] It is under general conservation; therefore free navigation, anchorage, mooring and all other types of fishing are prohibited. On the other hand, bathing and snorkelling are allowed. Also granted with the management agency's prior consent and control by the managing body are the navigation of recreational boats, fishing by local residents and the local fishing corporations based in the municipality.
- Zone C includes the remaining tract of sea inside the Park boundary. It is under partial protection and within its boundaries it is permitted to anchor, to moor in the areas designated by the management agency and compatible with the requirements of protection of deep water. With a prior permit and the management agency's monitoring the sailing of recreational crafts and fishing are allowed.

In the three sectors, it is nevertheless prohibited, based on article 4, comma 1, of D.M. of 7 August 2002, to carry out any kind of activity that could alter the current state of the places and that could impact on the protection of the environmental and archaeological heritage. In particular, the following is prohibited:

- The removal, illegal search and damage (also partial) to archaeological objects and of geological and mineral formations.
- Hunting, capturing, picking, damaging and all other activity that could endanger or perturb the vegetal species and animals, including the introduction of alien species.
- The alteration to any degree, direct or indirect, of the geophysical environment and of the biochemical characteristics of the water, the discharge of solid or liquid waste. In general, the introduction of discharges not in rule with the most restrictive prescriptions foreseen by the current norms which could alter, even only temporarily, the characteristics of the marine environment and the archaeological submerged objects.
- The introduction of arms, explosives, all means of destruction or capturing, as well as toxic or polluting substances.
- Activities that could do harm, hinder or upset the accomplishment of the educational and research programs in the area.

After almost two years of the formation of the park, with the exception of some isolated works of conservation, no real working plan for the improvement or sustainable development of tourism have been worked out and there are still many problems linked to its protection.

In the first place, the persistent issue remains of abusive mooring. This disregards the most basic norms of security put forward by the code of navigators and the obligations established by the Ministry of Cultural Heritage, by continuing to position mooring buoys, and so on, over archaeological structures. Also, it could be correct to infer that organised crime has been infiltrated in this sector, reporting considerable gains despite the modest risks inherent to this type of activity.

Also, the lack of daily monitoring favours illegal fishers who use explosive materials to recover entire colonies of fish – dories, basses and maigres – that are particularly abundant within the archaeological structures in the Park. This happens without considering the risk of deterioration of the mosaics along the underwater trails, which are left deprived of their covering often during guided tours. An additional risk is the consecutive development of the marine vegetation among the individual small elements, and the danger of being damaged later on by violent sea storms.

In the light of what has come from this short analysis of problems connected to protecting the first Italian archaeological underwater park, it is desirable that some concrete operational strategies are decided on soon for the protection and the improvement. Likewise, above all, universities and/or public research centres should be involved in its management.

Actually, this author thinks that in whichever sector, including the no-profit one, the 'private person' tends inevitably to stick exclusively to his own interests, which do not always coincide with those of the public good. Also, the private individual tends to want the maximum practical benefit with the minimum investment possible.

Instead, the management by one or more associated universities together could offer major guarantees of transparency and integrity, in scientific, technical, operational and administrative terms. It would also ensure the involvement of the many who have been operating in the area over past years.

Fabio Maniscalco
ICOMOS Italy

References

AA.VV., *La prima campagna di rilevamento della città sommersa di* Baia, in 'Forma Maris Antiqui', 2, 'Rivista di Studi Liguri', 25, 3-4, 1959, pp. 302-309.

AA.VV., *La seconda campagna di scavo e rilievo a* Baia, in 'Forma Maris Antiqui', 3, 'Rivista di Studi Liguri', 26, 1-4, 1960, pp. 361-364.

AA.VV., *Baia. Il ninfeo imperiale sommerso di Punta Epitaffio*, Napoli 1983.

B. Andreae, F. Zevi, *Gli scavi sottomarini di Baia*, in 'La Parola del Passato', 37, 1982, pp. 114-156.

G. Di Fraia, N. Lombardo, E. Scognamiglio, *Contributi alla topografia di Baia sommersa*, in 'Puteoli', 9-10, 1985-1986, pp. 211-299.

P.A. Gianfrotta, F. Maniscalco (eds.), *Forma Maris. Forum internazionale di archaeologia subacquea, Pozzuoli, 22-24 settembre 1998*, Napoli 2001.

N. Lamboglia, *Inizio dell'esplorazione di Baia sommersa (1959-1960)*, in AA.VV., *Atti del III Congresso internazionale di archaeologia sottomarina, Barcellona 1961*, Bordighera 1971, pp. 225-252.

F. Maniscalco, *Un ninfeo severiano dalle acque del porto di Baia*, in 'Ostraka', 4, 2, 1995, pp. 257-271.

F. Maniscalco, *Ninfei ed edifici marittimi severiani del Palatium imperiale di Baia*, Napoli 1997.

F. Maniscalco (ed.), *Tutela, conservazione e valorizzazione del patrimonio culturale subacqueo,* 'Mediterraneum. Tutela e valorizzazione dei beni culturali ed ambientali', vol. 4, Napoli 2004.

F. Maniscalco, N. Severino, *Recenti ipotesi sulla conformazione del Lacus Baianus*, in 'Ostraka', 11, 1, 2002, pp. 167-176.

P. Miniero, *Baia: dallo scavo subacqueo, al Museo, al parco archaeologico sottomarino... e le prospettive di tutela?*, in P.A. Gianfrotta, F. Maniscalco (eds.), *Forma Maris. Forum internazionale di archaeologia subacquea, Pozzuoli, 22-24 settembre 1998*, Napoli 2001, pp. 29-35.

F. Pallarés, *Quelle prime ricerche*, in P.A. Gianfrotta, F. Maniscalco (eds.), *Forma Maris. Forum internazionale di archaeologia subacquea, Pozzuoli, 22-24 settembre 1998*, Napoli 2001, pp. 13-28.

1 Laws 1089 on the Preservation of Artistic and Historic Heritage and 1497 on the Protection of Natural Beauties.

2 An exceptional example of this trend during the 1960s is the urban and industrial sprawl of the Venice region, with the urban explosion of the city of Mestre and the Chemical Industrial Quarter of Porto-Marghera, which still represents one of the major threats for the conservation of the Lagoon and the historic city centre.

3 Law 28/2/1985 n° 47.

4 On the contrary an increase of illegal constructions was registered in the biennium 1983-1984, after the announcement of the measure, and the number of estimated cases was 230,000.

5 Law 724 of 23.12.1994.

6 Law 326 of 24.11.2003.

7 Association Bianchi Bandinelli, Comitato per la Bellezza, FAI, Greenpeace, INU, Italia Nostra, LAC, LAV, Legambiente, LIPU, Marevivo, VAS, WWF.

Baia Underwater Park, mosaics with their covering removed by unknown divers (photo: F. Rastrelli)

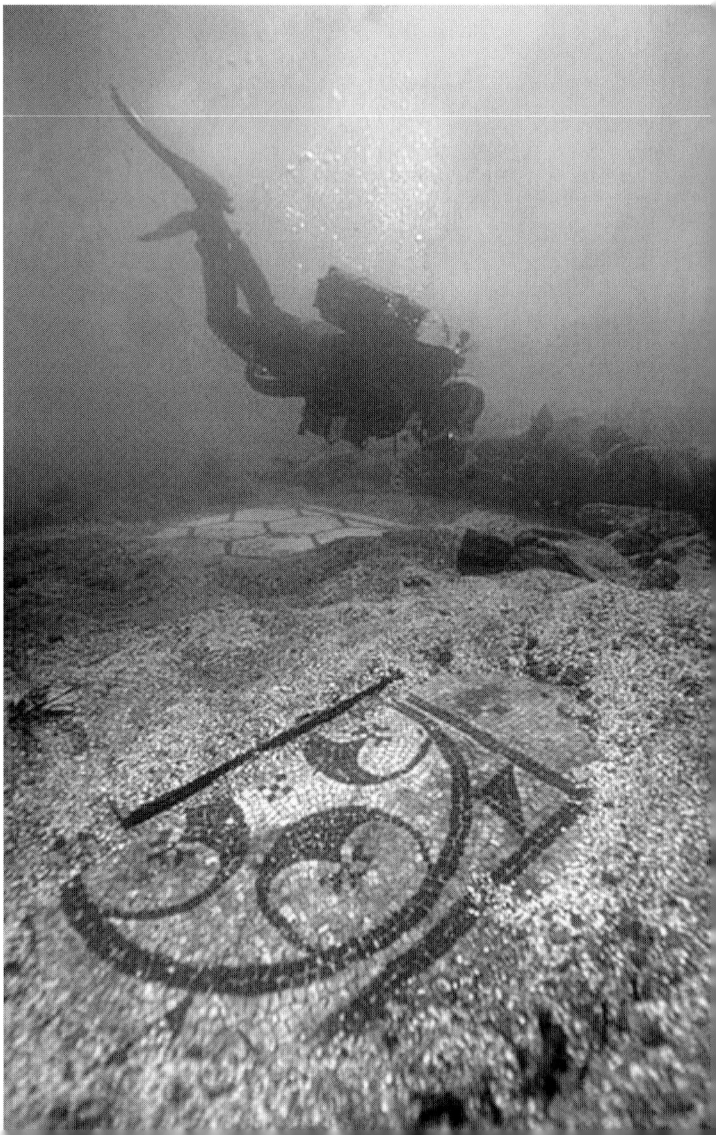

8 Unfortunately comprehensive data referring to the previous experiences are missing. However the case of Rome for the remissions of 1985 and 1994 can be mentioned when, gaining a total amount of 477 millions euros, an impressive 2992 million euros has been paid for infrastructure supply and related matters.

9 art. 27 law 326, 2003

10 Decreto Legislativo 22 gennaio 2004, n.41: Codice dei Beni Culturali e del Paesaggio (expanding the law 29 ottobre 1999, n. 490, the so-called Testo Unico dei Beni Culturali e Ambientali)

11 See N. Lamboglia, *La prima campagna di rilevamento della città sommersa di* Baia, in 'Forma Maris Antiqui', 2, 'Rivista di Studi Liguri', 25, 3-4, 1959, pp. 302-309; AA.VV., *La seconda campagna di scavo e rilievo a* Baia, in 'Forma Maris Antiqui', 3, 'Rivista di Studi Liguri', 26, 1-4, 1960, pp. 361-364; N. Lamboglia, *Inizio dell'esplorazione di Baia sommersa (1959-1960)*, in AA.VV., *Atti del III Congresso internazionale di archaeologia sottomarina, Barcellona 1961*, Bordighera 1971, pp. 225-252; F. Pallarés, *Quelle prime ricerche*, in P.A. Gianfrotta, F. Maniscalco (eds.), *Forma Maris. Forum internazionale di archaeologia subacquea, Pozzuoli, 22-24 settembre 1998*, Napoli 2001, pp. 13-28.

12 Cfr. B. Andreae, F. Zevi, *Gli scavi sottomarini di Baia*, in 'La Parola del Passato', 37, 1982, pp. 114-156; AA.VV., *Baia. Il ninfeo imperiale sommerso di Punta Epitaffio*, Napoli 1983.

13 On the recent searches in the field of underwater archaeology at Baia, see: G. Di Fraia, N. Lombardo, E. Scognamiglio, *Contributi alla topografia di Baia sommersa*, in 'Puteoli', 9-10, 1985-1986, pp. 211-299; F. Maniscalco, *Un ninfeo severiano dalle acque del porto di Baia*, in 'Ostraka', 4, 2, 1995, pp. 257-271; F. Maniscalco, *Ninfei ed edifici marittimi severiani del Palatium imperiale di Baia*, Napoli 1997; P.A. Gianfrotta, F. Maniscalco (a cura di), *Forma Maris. Forum internazionale di archaeologia subacquea, Pozzuoli 22-24 settembre 1998*, Napoli 2001; F. Maniscalco, N. Severino, *Recenti ipotesi sulla conformazione del Lacus Baianus*, in 'Ostraka', 11, 1, 2002, pp. 167-176; F. Maniscalco (ed.), *Tutela, conservazione e valorizzazione del patrimonio culturale subacqueo*, 'Mediterraneum. Tutela e valorizzazione dei beni culturali ed ambientali', vol. 4, Napoli 2004, *passim*.

14 Cfr. P. Miniero, *Baia: dallo scavo subacqueo, al Museo, al parco archaeologico sottomarino... e le prospettive di tutela?*, in P.A. Gianfrotta, F. Maniscalco (eds.), *Forma Maris. Forum internazionale di archaeologia subacquea, Pozzuoli, 22-24 settembre 1998*, Napoli 2001, pp. 29-35.

15 Situated between Punta dell'Epitaffo and the northern shore of the antique access canal *lacus Baianus*.

16 Especially comma 10, that recognises the importance to guarantee protection, knowledge and improvement (also for social and occupational purposes) of underwater parks and museums with relevant environmental, historical, archaeological and cultural importance. It foresees the conception of the submerged Park in the waters of Baia in the gulf of Pozzuoli.

17 Dated 23 December 2000 and published in the 'Gazzetta Ufficiale della Repubblica Italiana', no. 302 of 29 December 2000.

18 Dated 7 August 2002 and published in the 'Gazzetta Ufficiale della Repubblica Italiana', no. 288 of 9 December 2002. The decree is agreed between the Ministers of Cultural Property and Activities, Infrastructure and Transport, Agricultural and Forestry Policies and with the agreement of Campania Region, the Ministry of Environment and Land Protection.

19 Art. 2, comma 1, of the Ministerial Decree of 7th August 2002 also defines the limiting coordinates for the Park :

Point	Latitude	Longitude
A 1	*40° 49'.91 N*	*014° 05'.94 E*
B	*40° 49'.60 N*	*014° 05'.94 E*
I 1	*40° 49'.07 N*	*014° 04'.61 E*

20 According to Art. 4, comma 2, of the Ministerial Decree of 7th August 2002, zone A also consists of the stretch of sea limited by the following co-ordinates:

Point	Latitude	Longitude
E 1	*40° 49'.49 N*	*014° 04'.70 E*
F	*40° 49'.24 N*	*014° 05'.05 E*
G	*40° 49'.20 N*	*014° 04'.60 E*
H 1	*40° 49'.40 N*	*014° 04'.53 E*

21 In the cartography enclosed to the Ministerial Decree of 7 August 2002, zone B is limited by following co-ordinates :

Point	Latitude	Longitude
A 1	*40° 49'.91 N*	*014° 05'.94 E*
B	*40° 49'.60 N*	*014° 05'.94 E*
C	*40° 49'.60 N*	*014° 05'.62 E*
D 1	*40° 49'.91 N*	*014° 05'.62 E*

Highway or Heritage?

The construction of the Autostrada A 31 Valdastico Sud via Vicenca to Rovigo threatens the surroundings of Palladio's famous villas in the Veneto. ICOMOS – unfortunately in vain – joined the protests of several environmentally concerned organisations, as Italia Nostra, WWF Italia and British Landmark Trust (owner of Palladio's Villa Saraceno). In the following, we are quoting in parts from the abundantly illustrated report of SAVE Europe's Heritage (e-mail: save@btinternet.com):

Italy's Assault on a World Heritage Site

The Villas of Palladio were inscribed on the World Heritage List in 1996. This was a worthy and fitting tribute to the most influential architect of the Western World, agreed unanimously by the World Heritage Committee.

Now this remarkable landscape is under horrific assault. The threat comes first from relentless unchecked building in open country, initially around the towns, but rapidly spreading across fields well away from any village. The second threat comes with the proposal to build 54 km of motorway, the Valdastico Sud, south of Palladio's home town Vicenza.

This motorway will have a devastating effect for the following reasons. First there will be 7 exits in just 54 km, each one with a major roundabout raised above the flat plain as well as exit tollgates. Second, the new road passes within hundreds of metres of dozens of fine and beautiful villas and farms, splitting up the fields of one farm after another. With it will come a perpetual spear of noise that will destroy the tranquillity of centuries.

Third, the motorway will bring industrialisation on a colossal scale. The Motorway Company has already called for 400 hectares (1000 acres) of development land to be provided along the new road to make it viable. Even before the road has been put out to tender, the march of the giant capannoni continues at an accelerating pace. These capannoni –"brutes" of concrete warehouses - are spreading down the main road south of Vicenza (ironically named the Riviera Berica) obscuring the views of villas and church campanili on neighbouring hills. Still worse they spring up randomly in open fields like dragons' teeth in the Argonaut legend, blighting whole stretches of hitherto unspoilt landscape.

The Italian Government stands condemned of utter neglect of what was (and in parts still is) one of the richest and most beautiful and historic lowland landscapes in western Europe. This is an area shaped by man over two millennia – a landscape moulded by engineers and far-sighted statesmen which is now to be destroyed by engineers and short-sighted politicians who are too blind or ignorant to appreciate the achievement of their predecessors. It is lamentable that the striking beauty and harmony of this country, whether seen from the valley floor or the surrounding hills has never been deemed worthy of official classification and protection.

The success of the Italian national monument service – the Soprintendenze – in preserving the centres of cities has been the admiration of the whole world. The regional Soprintendenze of both Verona and Venezia have objected to the proposal as well as the Soprintendenza Archeologica. So has the Minister of Heritage – the Ministero per i beni e le attivita' culturali – through its directorate for architecture and the landscape. All this has been swept aside.

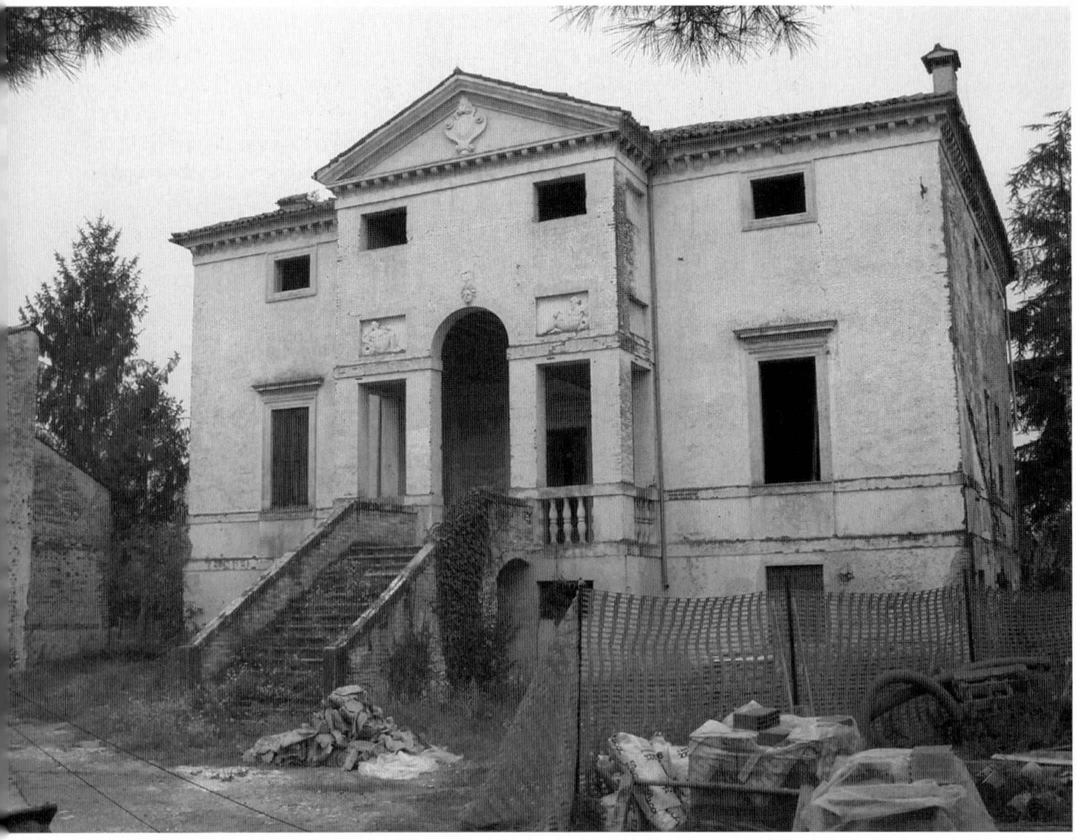

Villa Forni-Cerato in Montecchio Precalcino near Vicenza, a building by Andrea Palladio (1541-2). A piece of World Heritage in an increasing state of decay (leaking roof, no windows, the dilapidated interior with endangered wall paintings).

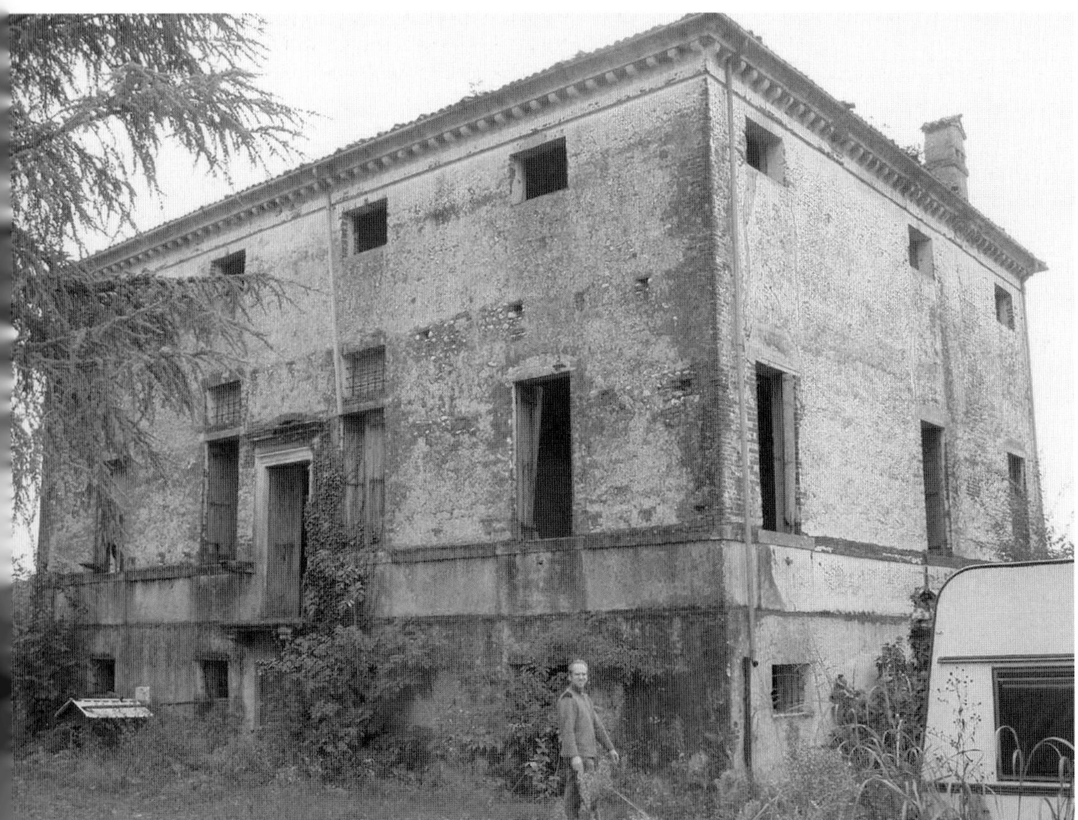

Rear of the Villa Forni-Cerato

The Villa Landscape

The villas by Andrea Palladio on the World Heritage List comprise just 16 out of more than 3000 historic villas in the Veneto. Most of these have been listed or classified by the Soprintendenza but a considerable number remain without protection. In the province of Vicenza alone there are 480 villas. The most famous is the Villa Rotonda immediately south of Vicenza; other Palladio villas are the Villa Pojana, Villa Pisani Placco (Montagnana), Villa Pisani Bonetti Bedeschi (Bagnolo di Lonigo) and the Villa Saraceno nursed back to life with exceptional sensitivity by the British Landmark Trust.

An Engineer's Landscape

More than 2000 years have contributed to assemble the elements of a unique European region, where technological as well as artistic features compliment each other in an enlightening manner that allows the traveller to form an impression of one of the continent's cultural heartlands. Bad enough, that the villas as artistic abbreviations of a way of life since the 16th century are threatened by the gross dimensions of a new motorway, its environmental damage and subsequent deterioration of the land that surrounds them - even more damage would ensue for the tightly knitted web of rivers, rivulets, canals and ditches that shows how innumerable generations made the land safe and fit for a thriving agriculture that still today serves the market.

The scandal of the Environment Commission

Italy like all EU countries is required by law to obtain an assessment of the environmental impact of major infrastructure projects. On 8 November, 2001, the Environment Commission rejected the proposals for the Valdastico Sud as too damaging. The Motorway Company then withdrew the proposals which the Government was thereby obliged to reject. Subsequently by decree of 19 September, 2002, 23 out of 36 members of the Commission were replaced. Surprise, surprise, the new Commission promptly approved the route of the road, with only minor modifications, on 18 December 2002. Few of the modifications significantly mitigated the damage of the road. Some actually increased them.

The Failure of the System

No less serious is the failure of the Regione Veneta to carry out the landscape plans which it is obliged to undertake as a preliminary to protection of landscapes of special beauty or interest, and indeed to act as a basis for properly planned development. The failure to carry out such plans has led to some of the worst clogged and polluted roads in Europe.

At the same time the Regione Veneto continues to promote the Veneta as an attractive tourist destination, ignoring the fact that recent intense industrialisation will increasingly damage its appeal. It also ignores the high priority many Italians now place on Nature and nature conservation, reflected in the growing activity of the Worldwide Fund for Nature and the Fondazione per Ambiente Italiano.

The Italian Government should intervene, as it is empowered to do, to carry out the necessary landscape plans itself. This is not a local matter - it concerns a World Heritage site, with a setting that is already badly damaged and likely to be extensively destroyed.

If the Italian Government is unwilling to meet its responsibilities a serious effort needs to be made to place the Villas of the Veneto on the list of World Heritage in Danger. While the villas are not under direct physical threat to their fabric, the all-essential frame, the landscape which they were built to enjoy and which is integral to their beauty and history, is under sustained assault. [If development is not checked, the beauty of the villas south of Vicenza will be severely compromised and in some cases fine historic buildings will be abandoned or left empty because the noise and intrusion of industry and roads makes them uninhabitable and renders them valueless.]

For years, Italy has set an inspiring example to the world in the protection of its great buildings and monuments. The Soprintendenze for monuments and archaeology are among the most professional, knowledgeable and respected bodies of their kind in Europe. Yet the Italian Government brushes aside their advice and legitimate concerns. Italy is thus failing the whole world by allowing crude devastation of one of the cradles of European architecture and landscape beauty.

What can be done

1. *Urgent action must be taken to protect the tranquil fenland landscape south of Vicenza from further despoliation. New development must be contained within strictly limited areas near towns. These areas must be sited to ensure minimal damage to views across the landscape. New capannoni must be screened by trees, not dense conifers but lines of trees typical of the landscape. These will soften the impact of the capannoni without being an intrusion themselves as conifers would be. The height of new commercial and industrial buildings should not be higher than the average tree line.*
2. *New landscape regulations must prevent further random building in open country. 'Clandestine' buildings - edifici abusivi - erected without permission must be demolished. No building should be allowed along the motorway or near motorway exits to ensure the rural character of the landscape remains.*
3. *If it is to be built, the motorway should be screened by high earthen banks like those along canals and rivers. This has been done successfully along a section of the Valdastico Nord and is proposed for a section near the Villa Saraceno.*
4. *Tax concessions encouraging the construction of capennoni in sensitive landscape areas should be discontinued.*
5. *Instead tax incentives (Tremonti bis) should be provided to encourage the repair of historic buildings, particularly empty ones.*
6. *Urgent steps should be taken to ensure all historic villas, farms and other buildings of historic interest and their historic settings are protected by the Soprintendenza.*
7. *Protection of the setting of Veneto villas must be strengthened. This means protection only of immediately adjacent land, the 'vincolo di rispetto' but longer views to and from villas. For Palladio villas which are inscribed on the World Heritage List this is a matter of major importance.*

Report prepared by:
Marcus Binney
Franziska Bollerey
Alexander Creswell
Axel Fohl
Adam Wilkinson
Antonio Verlato

JAPAN
Protection of Wooden Cultural Heritage from Earthquake Disaster

National treasures and important wooden cultural heritage places of Japan are mostly concentrated in Kyoto, Nara and Tokyo. Particularly in Kyoto, cultural heritage places are scattered with high density in the relatively small basin, which is incomparable with any other city and/or town. Case studies have been conducted to develop a protection system from post-earthquake fire for the oldest wooden temple structure in the Kyoto basin, making use of a water curtain. A fire extinguishing system is also proposed for the historic conservation area covering the hillsides of the Kyoto basin. The results are to be adopted in a project of the Japanese government to establish a post-earthquake fire protection system.

The vulnerability of Kyoto cultural heritage places at risk from the Nankai and Tonankai earthquakes

Earthquake disaster management of the Japanese Government

The Japanese Government reformed the administrative system in January 2001 and new ministries and agencies have been established. The Cabinet Office is one and given a relatively higher status than the other ministries. The Office has four major councils to advise the Prime Minister on important issues. The Councils are on Economy and Fiscal Policy, Science and Technology Policy, Central Disaster Management Council, and Gender Equality, respectively.

As indicated above, earthquake disaster is one of the most important issues for the Japanese Government. Therefore, after the revision of the administrative system of the central government, the Cabinet Office began to establish technical committees to discuss important issues regarding earthquake disasters. One of them is the Committee for the Tonankai and Nankai earthquakes which are inter-plate earthquakes in the subduction zone along the Pacific Ocean. This committee, however, deals with not only inter-plate earthquakes but also intra-plate earthquakes occurring on the inland zone of [the] Japanese islands.

Figure 1 shows the distribution of active faults around the Japanese archipelago. As shown in the figure, inland active faults are concentrated with a high density in the central part of the main islands of the Japanese archipelago, namely the central mountain area and the Kinki district which include old capital cities such as Kyoto and Nara.

Kyoto, Nara, Osaka and Kobe are major cities designated as Government Ordinance and these cities are relatively separate from the major subduction earthquake zone. On the other hand, these major cities are surrounded by inland active faults. The Japanese Government started a research project on 98 active faults in 1995 and will finish in 2004. This research revealed many scientific facts about the active faults by excavating trenches across the faults, namely the period of every fault's past activities, the amount of dislocation and so on.

Cultural heritage in the Kyoto basin

Nara was the capital of the first centralised government of Japan in the 8th century. After that, Kyoto was the capital of Japan from 794 until the capital was transferred to Tokyo in 1869. During these periods, many temples and shrines were built and lost, mostly from post-war fires in Nara and Kyoto. Still today however, the density of cultural heritage places in Nara and Kyoto is very high compared to other areas as shown in Figure 2.

As shown in the figure, more than 70% of national heritage places are concentrated in the Kinki district which unfortunately coincides with the location of the surrounding inland active faults as shown in Figure 1. This is the reason why we are anticipating that the cultural heritage places in the Kinki district will suffer from the next major earthquake, probably caused by the inland active fault.

The total number of national treasures in Nara is almost the same as that of Kyoto but the density of that in Kyoto is quite high compared with that of Nara. This is because important cultural assets and national treasures in Nara are dispersed among villages and towns and the density per unit area is not as high as in Kyoto. On the other hand, the number of National Treasures per 100,000 people in Kyoto is 135 and this is much larger than that of 30 in

Active faults around the Japanese archipelago

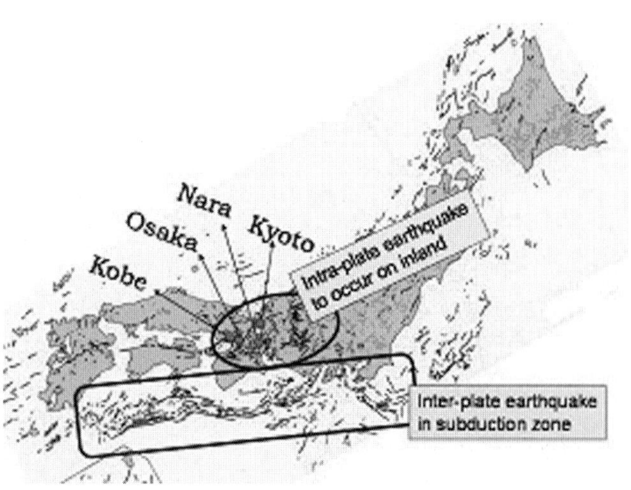

Distribution of National Treasures and important cultural assets

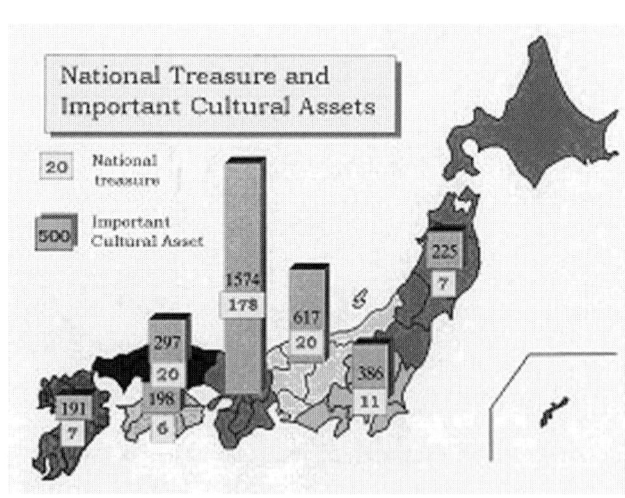

Tokyo. This implies that Kyoto is the most endangered city in terms of the vulnerability of its cultural assets against earthquake risk.

Kyoto was the capital of Japan for eleven hundred years before it moved to Tokyo 130 years ago. Therefore there are many cultural heritage items, not only built structures but also movable artistic assets. More than twenty percent of the national treasures of Japan are concentrated in the Kyoto basin, a relatively small area of 12 km by 15 km. Considering that the occurrence of strong earthquakes due to inland active faults surrounding the Kyoto basin is anticipated within the next few decades, analysis of the risk of cultural heritage places in the Kyoto basin burning down should be assessed for all the wooden buildings that are designated national treasures.

Lessons Learnt by the Kobe Earthquake in 1995

The vulnerability of existing fire extinguishing systems of temples and shrines in Kyoto

During the 1995 Kobe earthquake, the fire-extinguishing systems of two temples with high status in Kyoto broke down due to a break in the pipe connecting the water gun to the reservoir. Kyoto is about 50–60 km away from the epicentre of the Kobe earthquake and this fact made us aware of the vulnerability of the temples' and shrines' buried water pipe systems. Once a strong earthquake hits Kyoto, the Kyoto basin will be extensively shaken and most fire-extinguishing systems will be disrupted.

On the other hand, after the main shock of the Kobe earthquake, the post-earthquake fires occurred simultaneously in many places in Kobe and more than 7,000 houses were burned down. More than 10% of casualties lost their lives to fire. The percentage of wooden houses older than 50 years in Kobe was about 6.9% but that of Kyoto is 15.9%. This means that Kyoto is much more vulnerable to fire than Kobe.

These facts imply that many fires will take place and the fire-extinguishing systems of the temples and shrines will be disrupted when a major earthquake hits Kyoto.

The difficulty of restoring community heritage places damaged by earthquake

Many cultural heritage places were damaged by the Kobe earthquake in 1995. In Japan, cultural heritage places are categorised according to historical value. Many historic properties exist in Japan, from national treasures to local buildings of community heritage importance. Generally, the buildings listed by the nation are considered to be in the most important category according to public esteem. In this category, buildings with the highest authority are called National Treasures. Buildings listed at the prefecture level are in the second-highest rank, and those approved by the municipality are in third position, and those not approved by any group are in the lowest rank of public standing.

Today, detailed research makes clear the number of cultural heritage places damaged by the 1995 Kobe earthquake. The number of nationally listed damaged buildings is 33, listed by prefectures is 44, and approved for listing by municipalities is 22. The number of nationally listed reconstructed buildings is 33, those prefecture listed is 42, and municipality listed is 19. Most buildings listed by some level of government survived. At the same

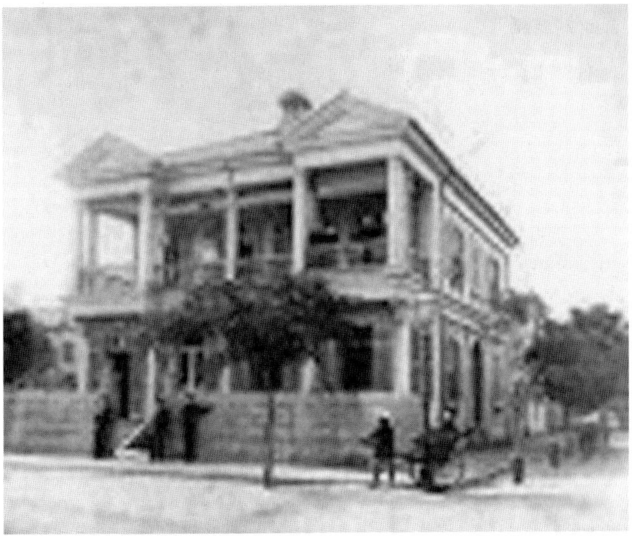

Kyokyoryuti 15 banken before destruction

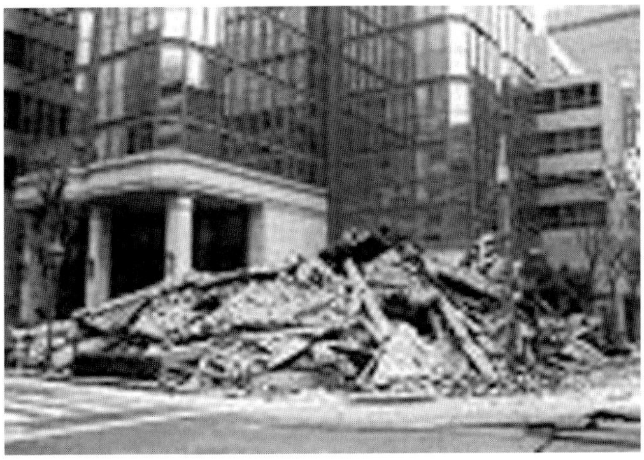

Kyokyoryuti 15 banken, destroyed by earthquake

Kyokyoryuti 15 banken, in process of reconstruction

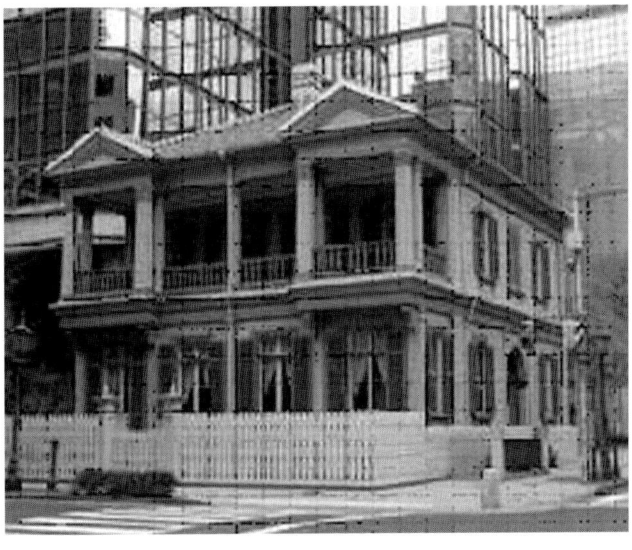

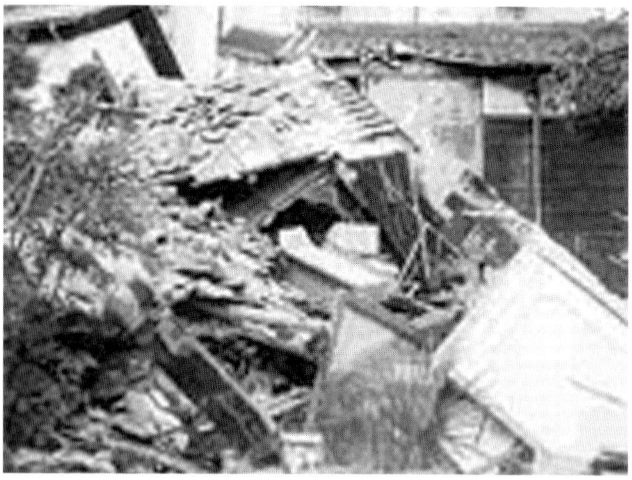

Lost community heritage (Sarankaku)

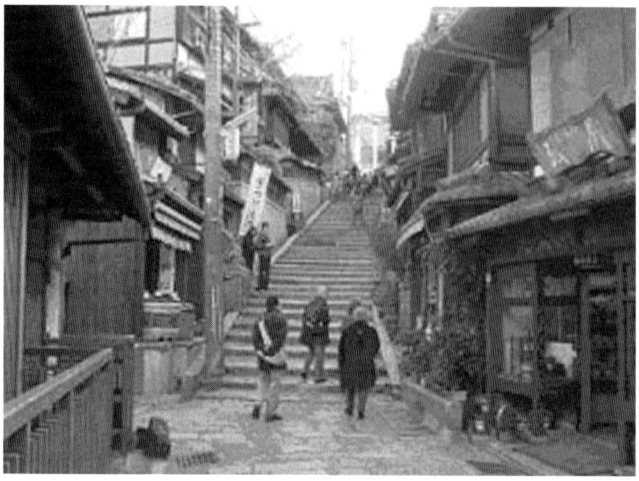

The Kiyomizu temple, World Heritage area

time, it is clear that many local community heritage buildings not listed by any government body disappeared in the Kobe earthquake. From the AIJ (Architectural Institute of Japan) survey we know that about 30% of the buildings disappeared that were not listed at any government level.

Kyukyoryuti 15 bankan was nationally listed in 1989 and used as a Chinese restaurant. This heritage place was completely destroyed by the Kobe earthquake in 1995. The owner needed a large amount of funds for reconstruction, approaching 860 million yen. But as this building is nationally listed, the owner got a large subsidy from the national government. In addition, because the Kobe earthquake caused serious damage, the grant level was raised by the national government. In the end, the owner bore 5% of the reconstruction costs.

Sarankaku, in which Junichiro Tnizaki, a great Japanese literary figure, lived for 3 years, was completely destroyed by the Kobe earthquake in 1995. Ninety million yen were needed to reconstruct the building. It had not been listed by any level of government and the owner did not get any great subsidy from any group. The committee for the reconstruction of *Sarankaku* gained the cooperation of the mass media and asked for donations. But the committee got less than one tenth of the necessary funds to reconstruct the building.

In comparing *Kyukyoryuti 15 bankan* to *Sarankaku*, it is clear that there are great differences in terms of funding. Local buildings of community heritage, not listed by any assembly, could not get enough money, and they are doomed to be condemned in a great earthquake. Against that fact we must keep buildings that are important to local community heritage.

Risk Finance to prepare for disaster risk

It is useful to think of preparedness funds on a routine basis for ruins. Using earthquake insurance is one of the best solutions to get sufficient funds for reconstruction. Insurance is a system which is sympathetic to the weak. Even if someone has little financial credit, those signing up to insurance can provide for an emergency, just by paying a fixed insurance fee a year. But Japanese earthquake insurance has in essence three problems. One is that the contract amount is limited to between 30% to 50% of fire insurance which is under contract with an insurance company. The other is that signatories cannot gain insurance money at a rate proportional to the amount of damage. Another is that the insurance money is capped at 50 million yen. It is difficult to solve these problems, because earthquakes are a disaster risk. It makes designing an insurance system difficult. But if these problems are solved, accession to earthquake insurance provides an excellent way of Risk Finance to prepare for the risk of disaster.

Increasing the number of Inscribed Heritage Buildings is another solution to preserve buildings such as community heritage places. In Japan, the Government established the Inscribed Heritage system in 1996. The owner inscribes local community heritage buildings that are not approved by listing by any other bodies on the list of Inscribed Heritage Buildings. When the inscribed building is badly damaged, the owner gets a subsidy which is less than for a listed building. But in the case of inscribed buildings, it is permitted to change the appearance and the interior flexibly for constructive use. This system is useful not only to get a subsidy but also to motivate the owner and supporters to increase their awareness about preserving heritage. The number of buildings appearing on the list in Japan is far less than in the United States of America. It is important to increase the number of Inscribed Heritage Buildings.

The value of heritage depends on individual beliefs. Some people think *Kyukyoryuti 15 bankan* is more important than *Sarankaku*. But some people think *Sarankaku* is more important than *Kyukyoryuti 15 bankan*. Whether a cultural heritage building is approved or not, citizens' motivation for heritage preservation is the most important factor.

Risk Control with a Safe Environment

Proposal for an Environmental Water Supply System in Kyoto

It is true that the risk finance to prepare for disaster risks is important, but risk control to reduce the level of damage is also essential. Regional resources such as natural water and citizen participation provide a great potential for risk control in the case of earthquake fire.

During the Kobe earthquake, serious damage to modern infrastructure was caused by the lack of water for fire-fighting, and at that time, natural water within the neighbourhoods was used. It is important to improve this potential for urban natural water and citizens' participation as 'Environmental Water Supply System (EWSS) for Disaster Prevention' which is maintained and protects wooden cultural cities from fire and preserves urban water.

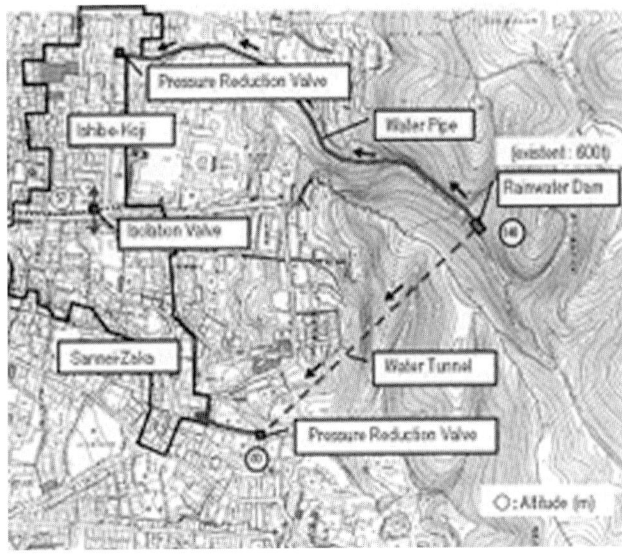

Water route planning for water pressure

Concepts of Environmental Water Supply System

The concepts of EWSS were found in the experiences of the Kobe earthquake. These systems need to be built by various kinds of water resources to maintain a water supply at any time, and the right amount of water to enable fire-fighting at multiple levels from small fires to spreading fires.

An Estimation of the Earthquake Fire Hazard Area in Kyoto

Kyoto City, one of the historical cities in Japan with many wooden cultural heritage places, is selected as a case study district for planning an EWSS. The characteristics of the city area are analysed according to the percentage of elderly and the average number of persons in each family as the index of fire risk, and the amount of wooden structures as the index of the risk of the fire spreading.

In addition, the risk from earthquakes in being able to isolate fires is analysed from the width of roads around the area. The possibility of a fire spreading from a neighbourhood to cultural heritage places is checked also by simulating the spread of such a fire.

The results show that The Sannei-zaka Historical Preservation District in the World Heritage Area is one of the most endangered areas of all the nationally listed heritage conservation districts in Kyoto.

Hydrants and sprinklers

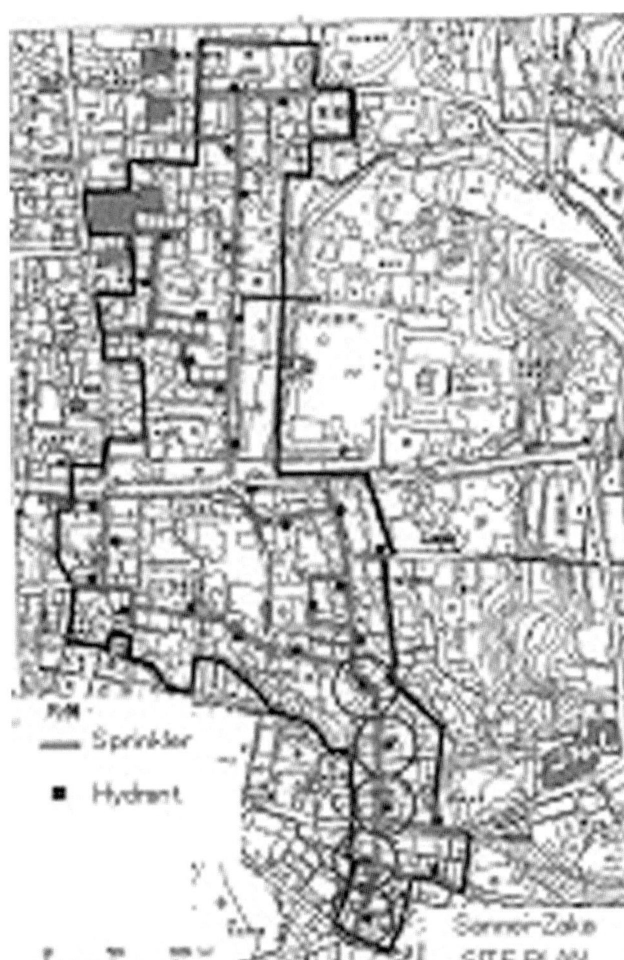

Case Study Planning of EWSS in the Sannei-zaka Historical District

Achievable plans for EWSS in Sannei-zaka Historical Preservation District are designed by researching the geographical characteristics around this area.

It uses existing natural water as the resource from a small dam 80 m higher using gravity for water pressure. The easily operated hydrants and the sprinkler nozzles are placed to deliver functional fire fighting water to citizens in this district, and also, some cisterns beside the river are added as a back up for this system. The dam will be able to keep sufficient water for at least one hour of fire-fighting by this EWSS.

It is important for us to regain the natural water environment in urban areas. We should create a safe and pleasant environment that preserves wooden cultural heritage structures in communities as well as modern structures. The concept of EWSS emphasises the necessity of a sustainable water environment and the restoration of the historical atmosphere with its aesthetic values and safety from natural hazards. The outcome of this research can be readily applied to similar problems in developing countries by making use of their skills and low cost technology. It is our obligation to preserve and pass irreplaceable cultural treasures to future generations, without damage caused by natural disasters.

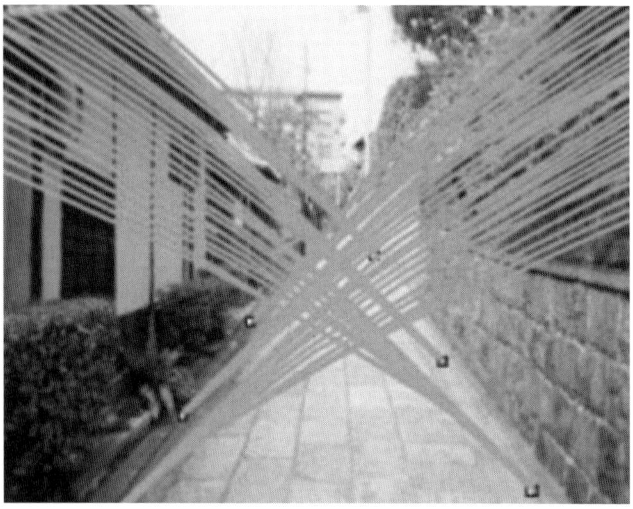

Sprinkler system for a narrow street

Local and Government Initiative

One of the authors recognised the importance of protecting cultural heritage from post-earthquake fires after the 1995 Kobe earthquake and the Council for the Protection of Cultural Heritage from Post Earthquake Fire was established in 1997, collecting influential people from relevant fields. Two years later, a non-governmental body 'The Organisation for the Protection of Cultural Heritage from Natural Disasters' was established. In August 2001, Metropolitan Tokyo approved this organisation as a non-profit organisation.

The government of Japan organised a committee to explore the feasibility of establishing actual fire protection systems for cultural heritage from post-earthquake risks in June 2003 and this committee will make public the basic concept of protecting cultural heritage places from natural hazards. On the other hand, the local government of Kyoto examined the safety of infrastructure in the Kyoto basin against strong ground movement triggered by an inland active fault which passes through the city.

Thus, the activities in relevant fields for the protection of cultural heritage places have been gradually activated and some realistic proposals for a protection system are expected. Within the situation described above, the authors conducted case studies to develop a protection system for historic conservation areas. The results are to be adopted in a Japanese government project to establish a post-earthquake fire protection system in the near future.

In March 2001, the Council for Science and Technology Policy, mentioned in the beginning of this paper, made public the Science and Technology Basic Plan 2001–2005. This plan proposed emphasising major four fields such as life science, information technology, nano-technology and environmental issues. The Council identified the next four topics to be promoted and natural disaster issues were included in the suggested fields. In the Plan, the importance of protecting cultural heritage places from natural disasters is recognised for the first time in the central government's official documents.

In conjunction with this Council's report, the Ministry of Land, Infrastructure and Transport began a research and development program in the field of construction technology and three proposals were adopted. The authors proposed a project concerning the protection of historical cities from post-earthquake fires. This project will be the first research project supported by the Japanese government in the field of the protection of cultural heritage and old towns themselves.

Takeyuki OKUBO[1], Kenzo TOKI[2] and Masami KOBAYASHI[3]
ICOMOS Japan

Acknowledgments
The authors have collaborated with the Kyoto City Fire Department and the members of the technical committee of the NPO for the Protection of Cultural Heritage from Disaster, in conducting the case studies. We would like to express our deepest gratitude for their co-operation.

1 Associate Professor, Kyoto University, Kyoto, Japan, Email:okubo@archi.kyoto-u.ac.jp

2 Professor, Ritsumeikan University, Kyoto, Japan, Email:toki-k@se.ritsumei.ac.jp

3 Professor, Kyoto University, Kyoto, Japan, Email:mkoba@archi.kyoto-u.ac.jp

JORDAN
Petra

In 1985 the ancient town of Petra with its almost 4000 individual heritage sites was declared a World Heritage site. Petra is particularly famous for its hundreds of façades cut from the bedrock. The other sites are caves without projecting façades, so-called sanctuaries, sacrificial sites and altars, inscriptions and votive tablets, stairs and streets, statues and reliefs as well as temples, houses and villas. From around 400 BC to the 4th century the rock town of Petra in the south of Jordan was the capital of the Nabataeans and had up to 30–40.000 inhabitants. With the end of their territorial independence the Nabataeans also lost their economic and political influence so that Petra became increasingly unimportant in the course of the 4th century.

Today, the rock-cut architectural heritage, as well as the buildings erected of ashlar masonry, are at risk because of weathering, decay, insufficient care and lack of conservation.[1] There are three main causes for the weathering and destruction:

- collapse due to static cracks, gaps and crevasses and falling loose fragments,
- erosion caused by uncontrolled rainwater drainage and floods,
- weathering from salt contamination.

Ashlar Stone Buildings

Especially at risk are the buildings made of stone masonry. Many of the ruins from the Neolithic, Nabataean, Roman and Byzantine periods threaten to collapse. These ruins were perfectly preserved in the sandy soil of the desert, but after their rediscovery via excavation they were left to their fate and are now increasingly deteriorating. Many of the sites and buildings excavated in Petra in the past decades are now in a critical state. This applies for instance to the main temple Qasr al-Bint, the Winged Lions Temple, the excavated remains above Zipp Fir'awn, the fortifications on the al Habis Medieval, Jabal al Madhbah and Al Wu'ayra, north-east of Petra, as well as to the great number of dam walls and rock-carved cisterns. Remains of buildings in the centre of the town, such as the ruins of the so-called Royal Palace, the Nymphaeum, the 'Roman House' and the Small Temple all require urgent conservation.

Apart from these buildings, there are also certain sections of the rock-cut façades which were made of ashlar masonry. According to recent investigations, 14% of all structural elements of these façades are either completely or partly made of cut stone.[2] In most cases these areas are seriously at risk of falling off. Not only is the natural stone severely weathered, but also the remains of the once rich decoration. During a survey of 211 tomb façades, traces of plaster, colour and stucco could be found on nearly 24% of these façades. Apart from the once coloured and plainly stuccoed rock façades the few remains of the original lavish stucco decoration at Qasr al-Bint and the finely stuccoed back walls of caves on the eastern wall of el-Habis also show signs of gradual loss.

The rock-cut façades

The rock massif of Cambrian sandstone is affected by alveolar and tafoni weathering. Holes and hollows of a few centimetres up to several metres are characteristic of this form of weathering, which in Petra is caused by salt weathering. The damaging salt is rock salt (NaCl), which is a mineral component found in the rock.

There are serious floods every February and March caused by heavy seasonal rainfall rushing through the narrow wadis. This must be considered as the greatest threat to the heritage sites.[3] Water diffuses through the normally coarse-porous sandstone and dissolves part of the salt inside the stone. This leads to salt deposits on the stone surface and to damage. As a result, almost all experts agree that the main problem for the heritage sites is uncontrolled rainwater runoff.[4]

The builders of Petra, the Nabataeans, were very aware of the destructive force of the water. For this reason the majority of structures were equipped with drainage systems. Nowadays, most of them have either filled up or are partly destroyed, which in many places leads to damage to the façades.[5]

Recent examinations on 14 sites of the so-called King's Wall show that the degree of weathering is on average about 50%. About 30% of all rock-cut facades are threatened by tectonic cracks and clefts.

Incorrect restoration and shortcomings

In the last 30 years extensive restoration was carried out on Qasr al-Bint and on the Temenos gate. In all these processes, mortar

Al-Khazna at the end of the Siq

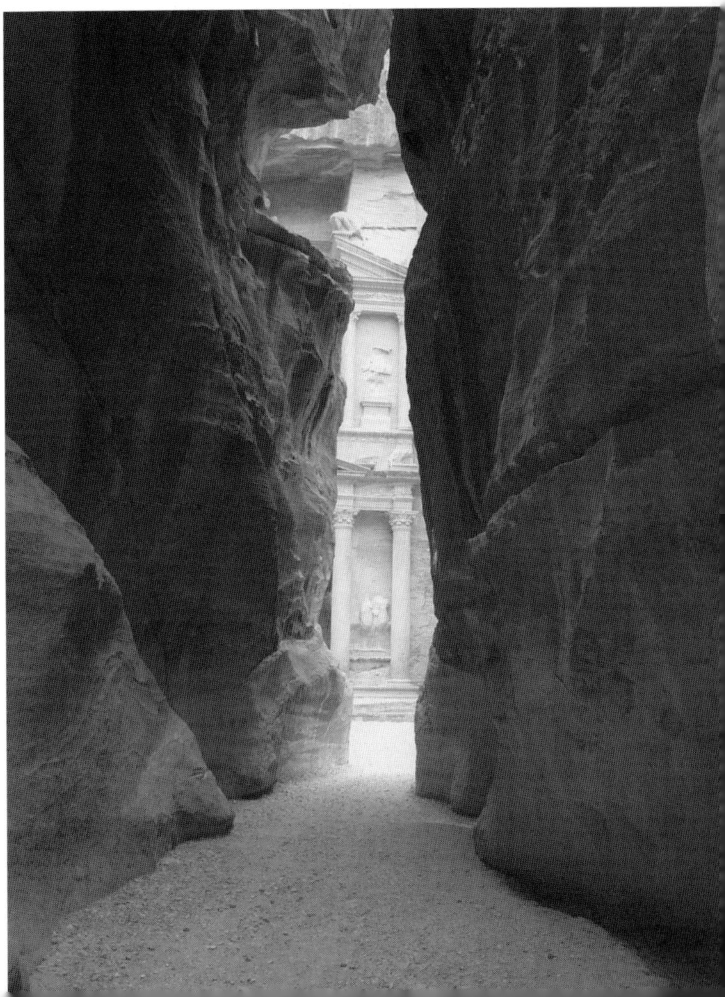

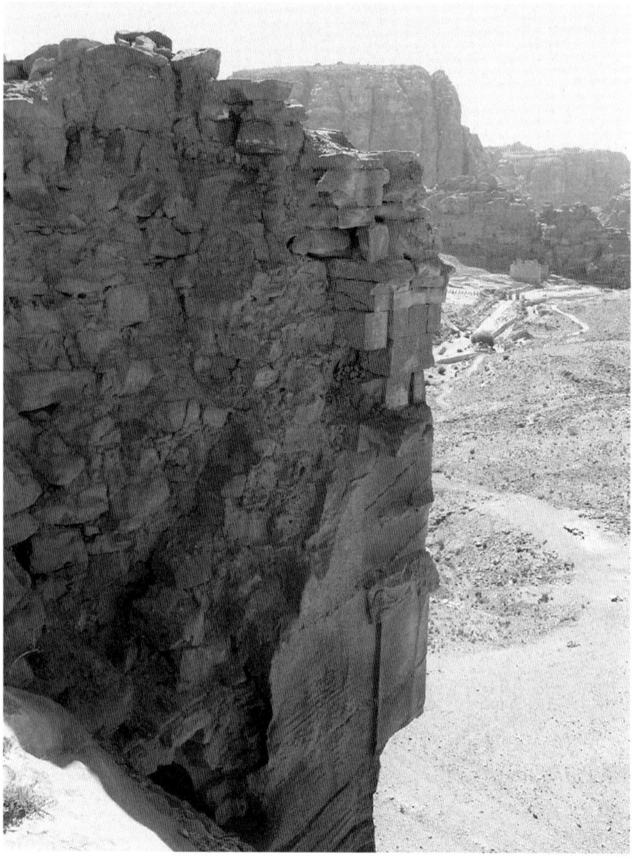

Palace Tomb, left corner

containing cement was used. This very hard and dense building material leads to an acceleration of the weathering processes of the original material and has resulted in further damage. Until now, there is no stone workshop for the large number of decorative elements, such as ornamented and partly stuccoed and painted capitals, friezes and waste fragments. Many of these pieces remain largely unprotected against weathering.

Outlook

Taking into account the large quantity of tasks, the number of heritage sites, and the size of the entire complex, effective protection is extremely difficult. In order to achieve a lasting conservation management of Petra a joint effort by an association of counties is necessary. This is why a German-Jordan project established a conservation and restoration centre in Petra (CARCIP) between 1993 and 2002. Undertaken as part of this project were a model restoration of the 14 Tombs site (Monument 825), a number of emergency stabilisations on buildings and façades and the conservation of Tomb No 826.

Apart from CARCIP's restoration work, various other teams of archaeologists are involved in restoration projects. In 2000, the altar construction of Qasr al-Bint was restored with the help of UNESCO. Currently, a casing is being erected for the wall paintings of the excavated villa on Ed-Zantur hill and the paintings are being conserved.

A strategy needs to be developed for the future which takes account of the conditions, competence and available capacities in order to achieve a lasting protection of the monuments in Petra.

Wanja Wedekind

1 D Bumbaru, S Burke, M Petzet, M Truscott, and J Ziesemer 2000, Jor-

Palace Tomb 765, measurement results ►

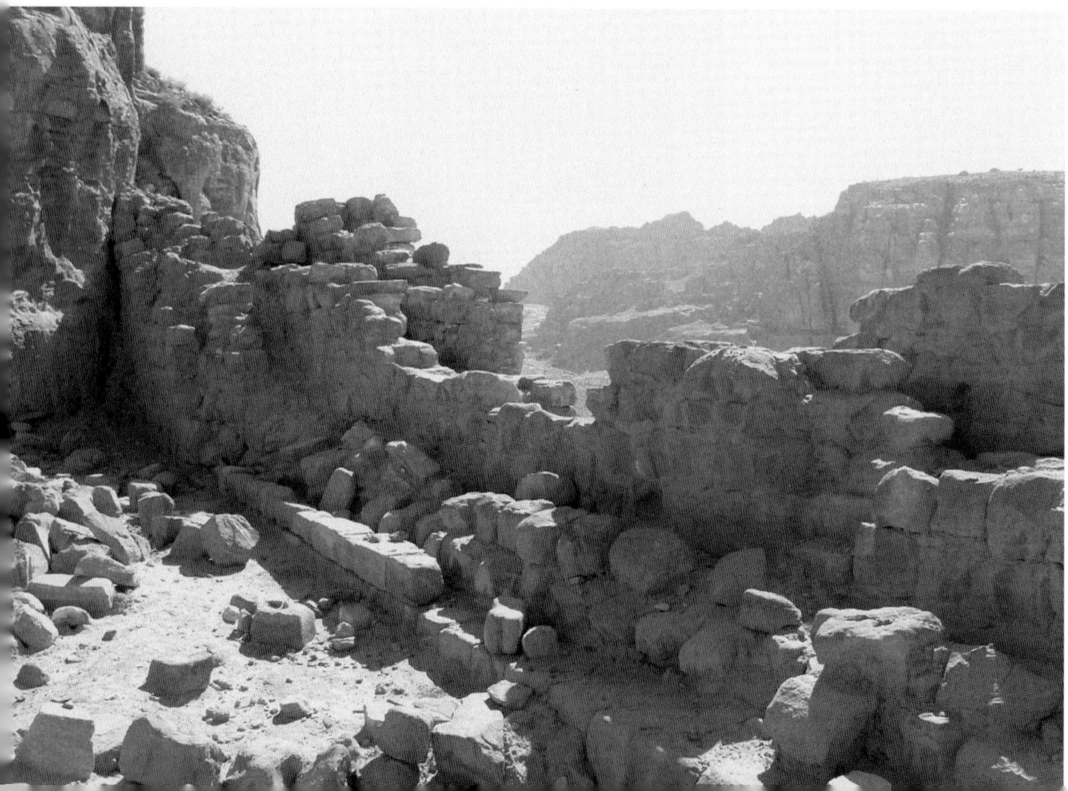

Palace Tomb: Elements, which have been masoned, not cut from the rock

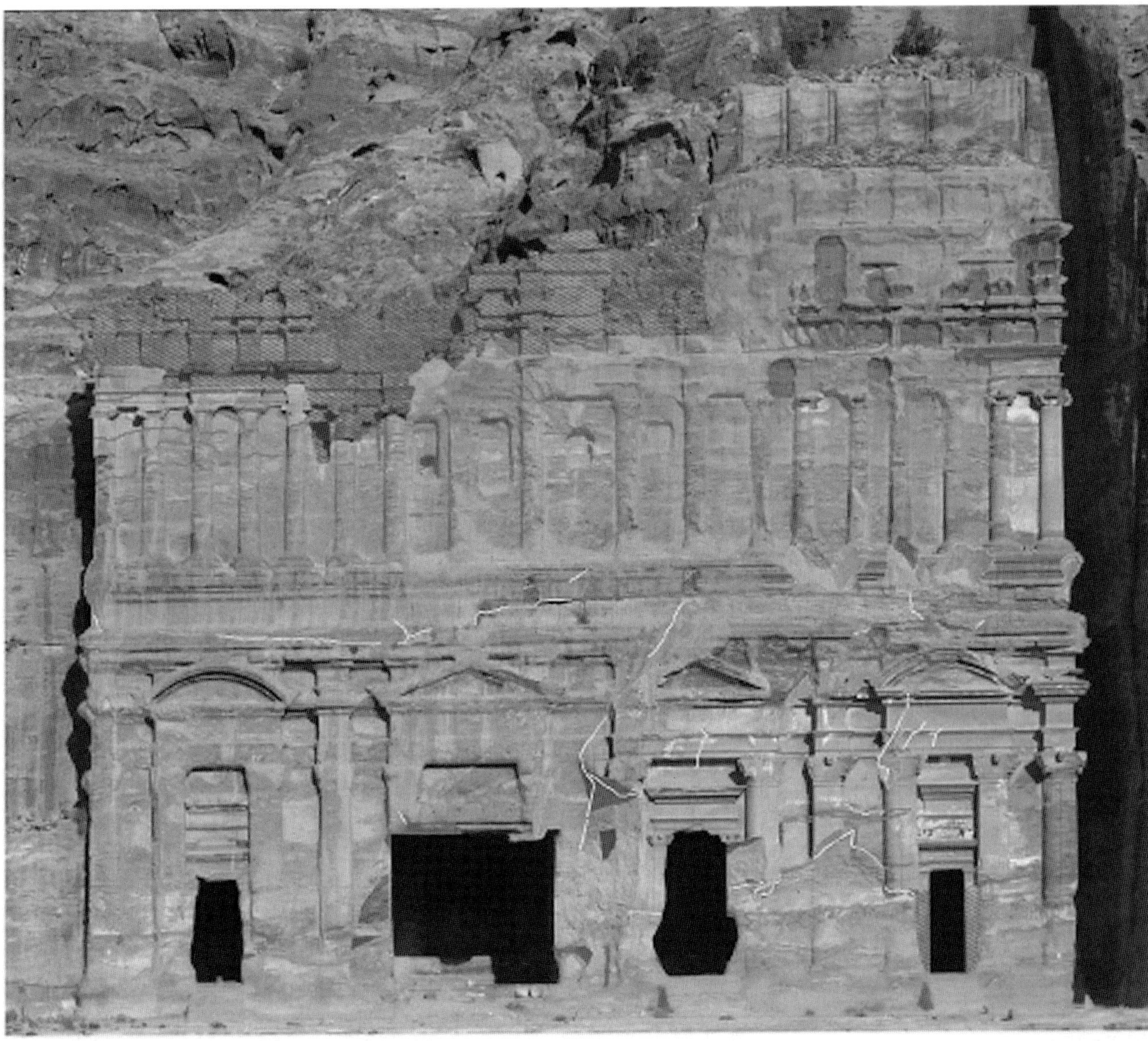

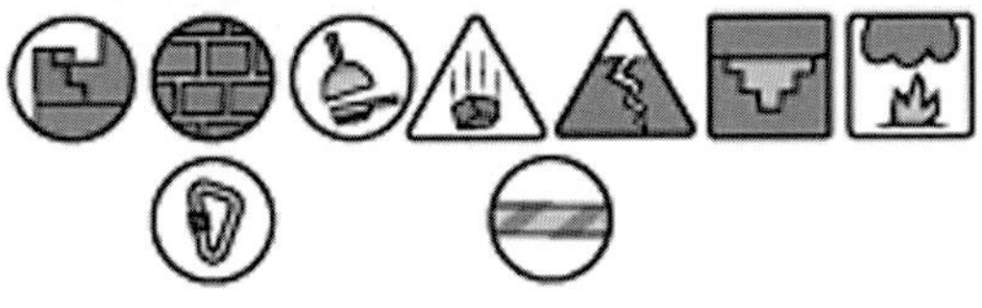

CARCIP

Conservation And Restoration Center In Petra

measurement results

	85,5% conserved shape
	53,3 % weathering rate
	47,4 % weathering
	2,5 % alveolar / tafoni weathering
	116,9 m weathered limonit
	57,7 m cracks
	3,5 % broken area
	7,7 % stonewalled part

monument type :	Roman temple tomb
date of erection :	first century AD
monument location :	G5
monument name :	Palace tomb
monument orientation :	297°
façade size (h,w) :	47,5 x 43,9 m
tomb room size (h,w,d) :	5,3 x 8,2 x 7,7 m
	8,9 x 7,8 x 12,2 m
	8,5 x 9,3 x 8,8 m
	5,6 x 12,4 x 14,9 m

notes : first room sealing unfinished

dan – Heritage @ Risk!, in *Heritage at Risk, ICOMOS World Report 2000 on Monuments and Sites in Danger*, München, pp. 123–124.

2 *Ein Pflege- und Konservierungsplan der antiken Entwässerungssysteme zum Schutz der Felsfassaden in Petra, Jordanien*, Diplomarbeit, Hochschule für angewandte Wissenschaft und Kunst Hildesheim/Holzminden/Göttingen 2003, p. 66.

3 Lane; Bousquet 1994, *Petra National Park Management Plan*, Main Report, UNESCO Paris, p. 111.

4 This applies to the 'Petra Archaeological Park Operating Plan' (2000, p. 4), the 'Petra National Park Management Plan, Main Report' for UNESCO by Barry Lane and Bernard Bousquet (1994, p. 111 und p. 116) after Kühlenthal, Fischer, Petra. Die Restaurierung der Grabfassaden (ICOMOS - Hefte des Deutschen Nationalkomitees XXXIV), München 2000, pp. 71–74.

5 B Fitzner and K Heinrichs 1994, Damage diagnosis at monuments carved from bedrocks in Petra, Jordan, in: *The conservation of monuments in the Mediterranean Basin, Stone and monuments: methodologies for the analyses of weathering and conservation*, Proceedings of the 3rd International Symposium Venice, 22–25 June 1994 (Scientific editors: V Fassina, H Ott, F Zezza), Venice 1994, p. 670.

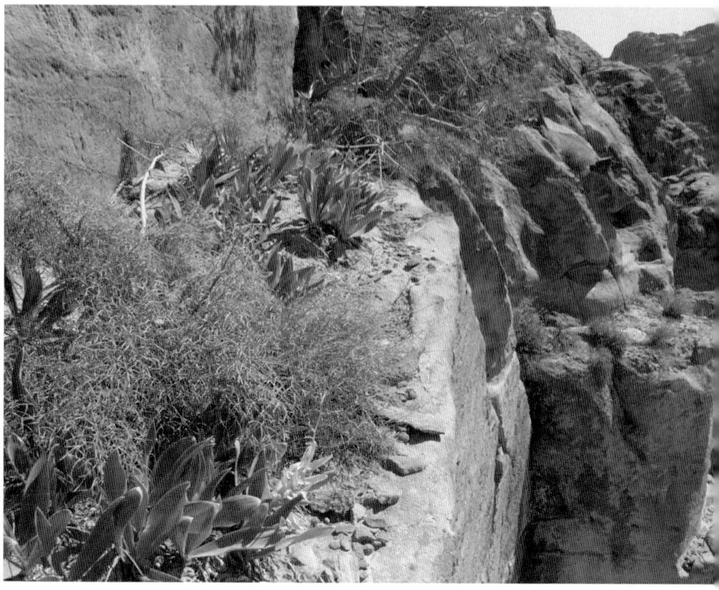

Corinthian Tomb, verdure

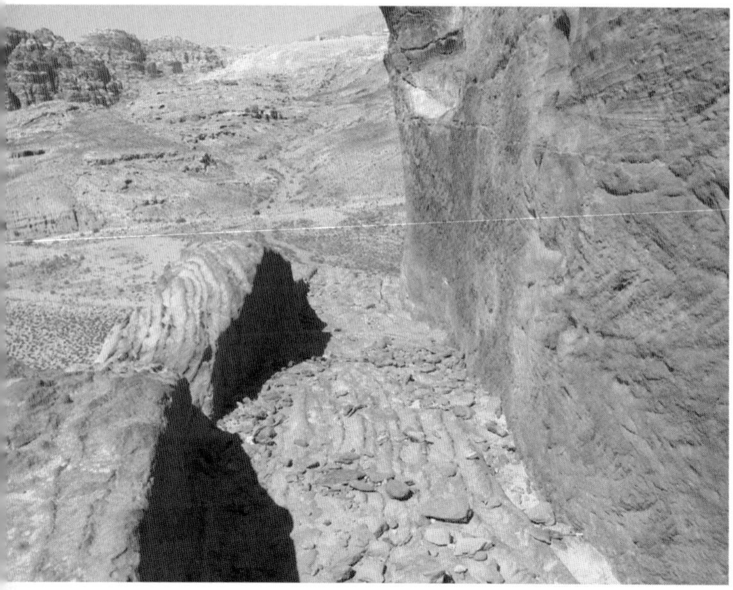

Corinthian Tomb, drainage

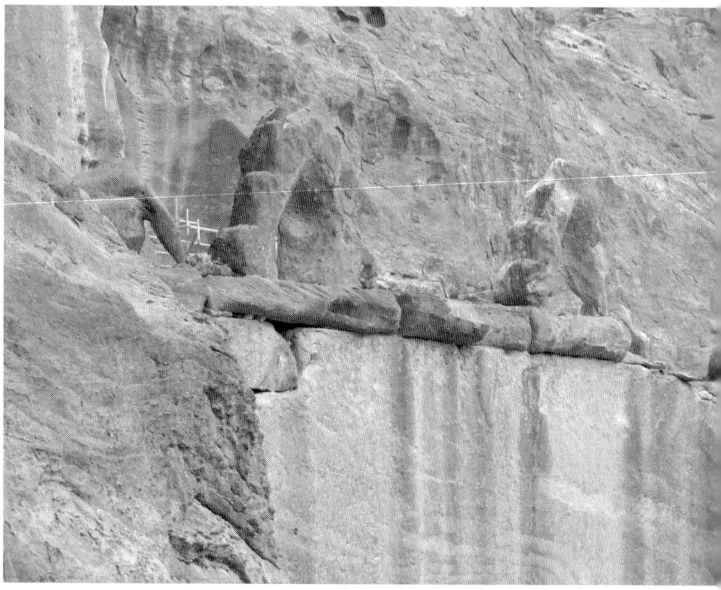

Tomb 824, endangered architectural elements

Weathered stucco decoration from the capital of the Great Temple

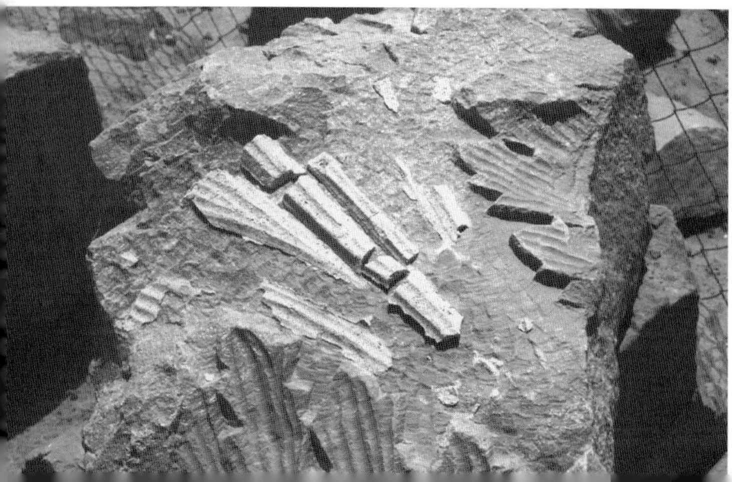

Wadi Mousa, wall remains

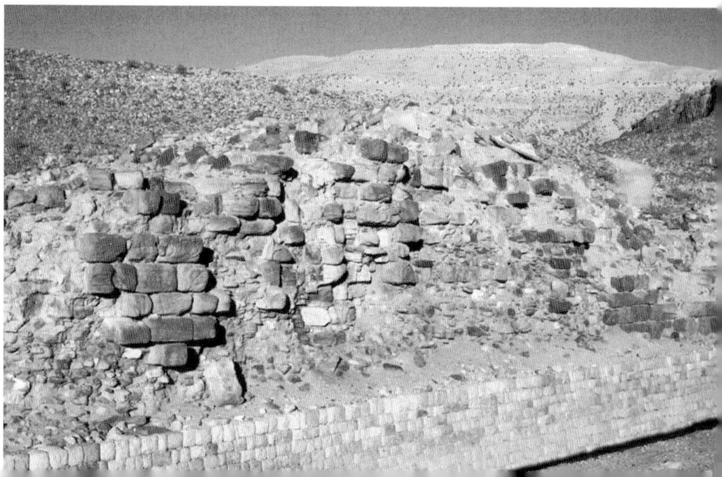

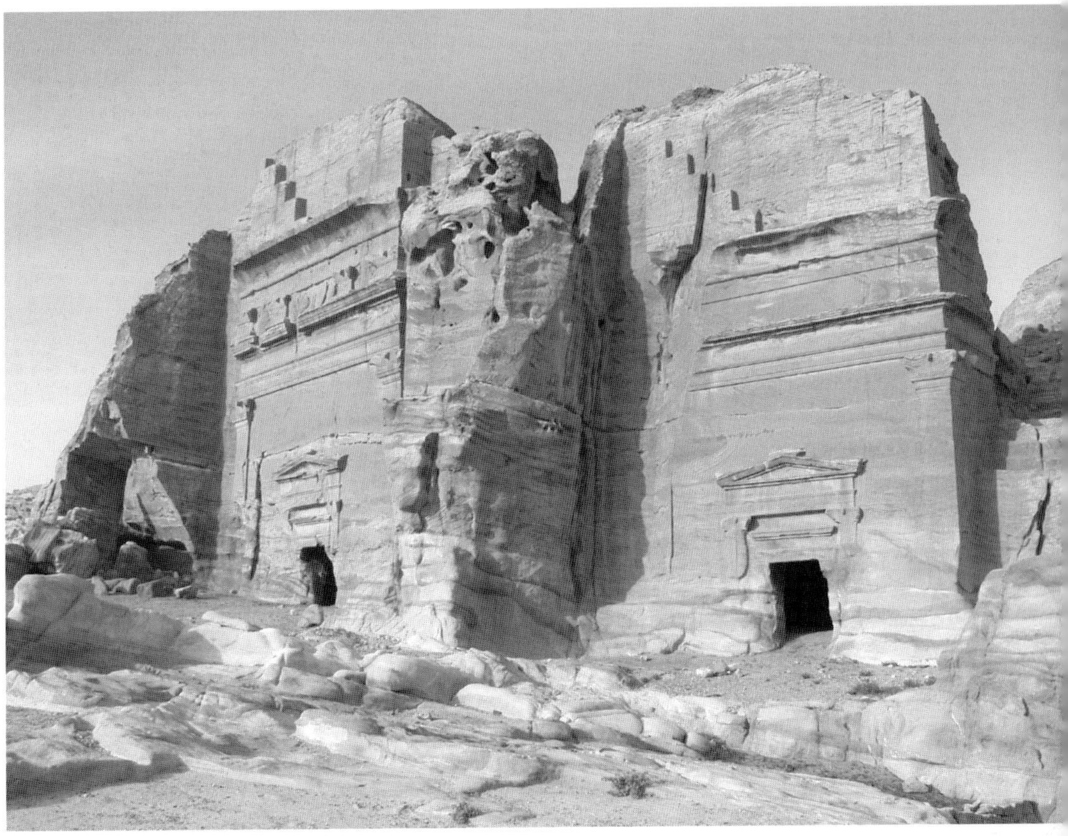

Tombs 649 and 650

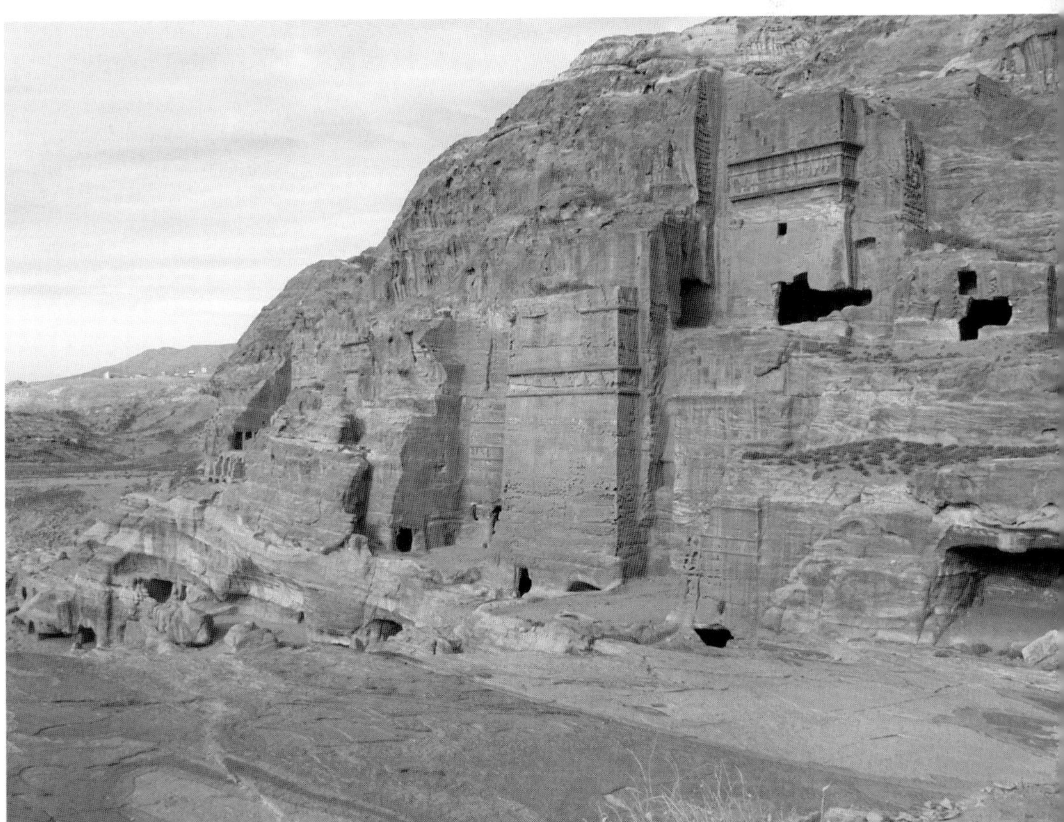

Tombs 779–803

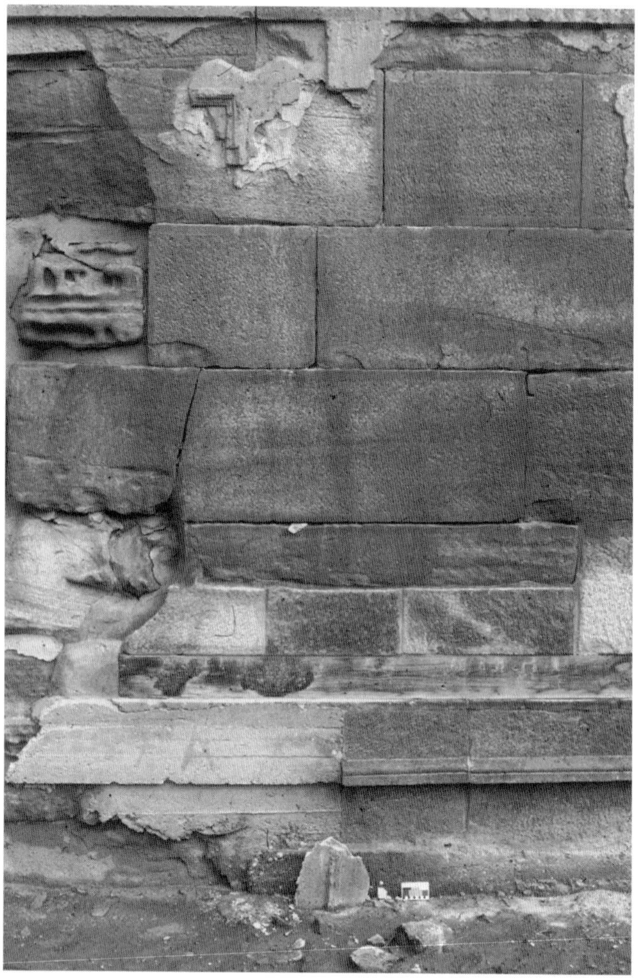

Qasr al Bint, condition of stucco decoration

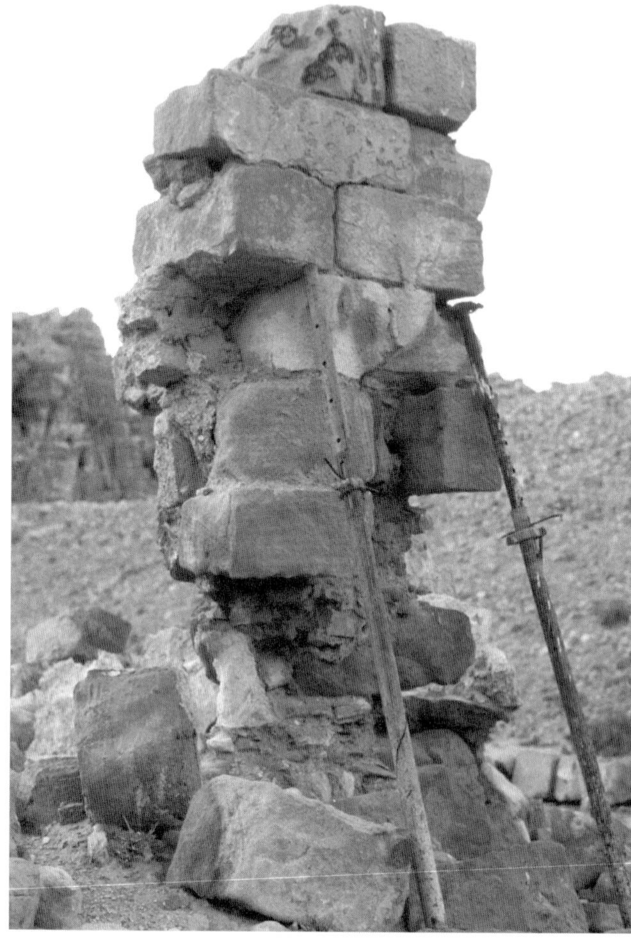

King's Palace, masoned corner

Temenos Gate, cement mortar

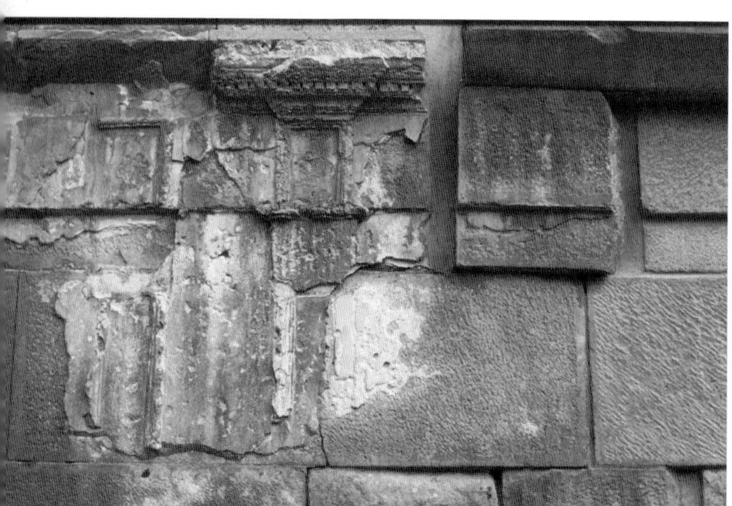

Qasr al Bint, recent rupture on stucco decoration

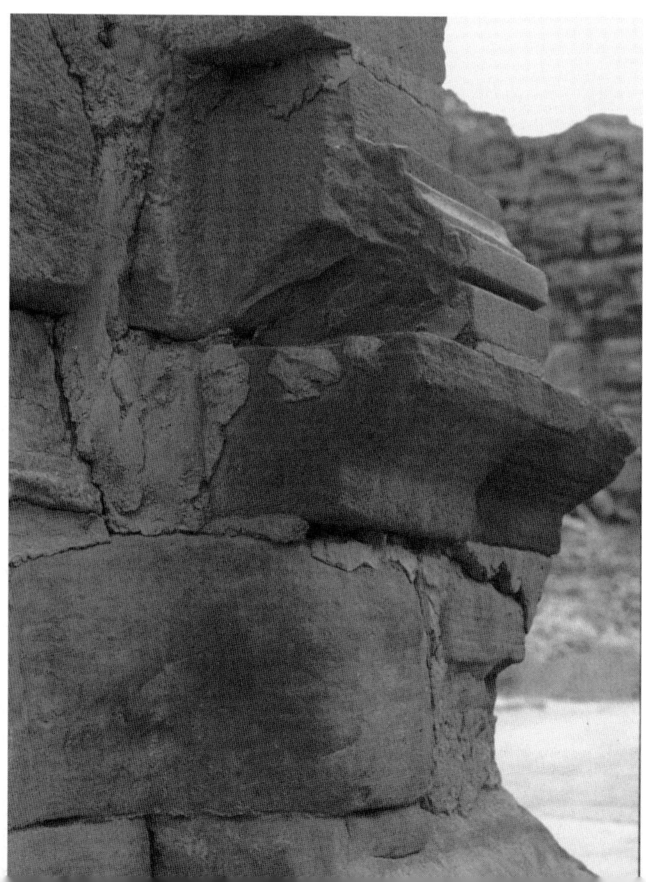

KAZAKHSTAN
The Petroglyph Site of Tamgaly-Tas

The petroglyph (rock engravings) site of Tamgaly-Tas is located 25 km north of Lake Kapchigai, along the cliffs of a gorge on the right bank of the Ili river in an arid landscape. It consists of three main engraved rocks supporting five images of Tantric deities of the Buddhist Lamaist pantheon, and few inscriptions in Tibetan, Mongol-Djungar and Manchu scripts. Some images and inscriptions are engraved within an area of 50 m x 50 m on the southern and south-east surface of some of the largest rocks. Three main stone blocks, 30 m from each other, are covered by large-size images of Buddhist deities and inscriptions in Tibetan, Mongol-Djungar and Manchu. Also a few other rock surfaces in the immediate surroundings have some inscriptions. All the images can be recognised by their attributes as Tantric deities belonging to the Buddhist Lamaist pantheon:

- 3 Buddhas (fully enlightened beings): 1 historical Buddha (Sakyamuni) and 2 self-born transcendental Buddhas (Akshobya and Man-la),
- 1 Bodhisattva (re-embodied ancient Buddha or helpful future Buddha): Chenrezig-Avalokitesvara,
- 1 enlightened patriarch: Nagarjuna.

All the inscriptions, either beneath or near the images, are religious invocations.

The first study and documentation of the Tamgaly-Tas gorge was by the ethnographer Chokan Valikanov who visited the site in 1856 and made some watercolour sketches of the rocks' Buddha images and inscriptions. In 1856 and 1857, the historian Z Semenov visited the site, reporting that the gorge of Tamgaly-Tas was crossed by the main caravan road between Tashkent and Kulja and

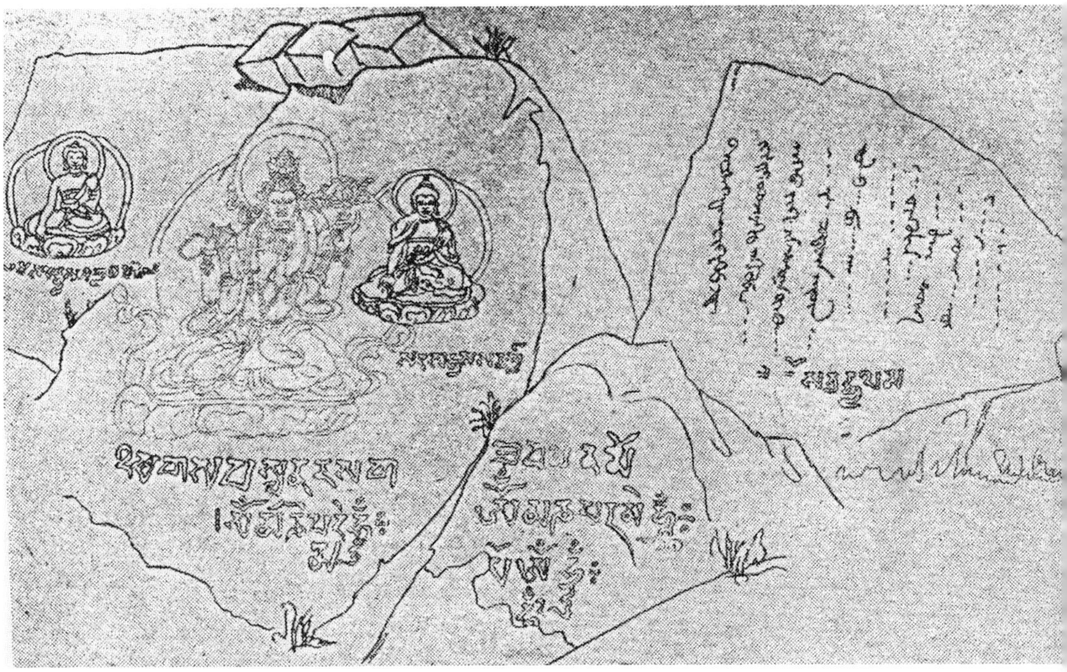

Tamgaly-Tas, Buddha images and inscriptions (drawing by Chokan Valikanov, 1856)

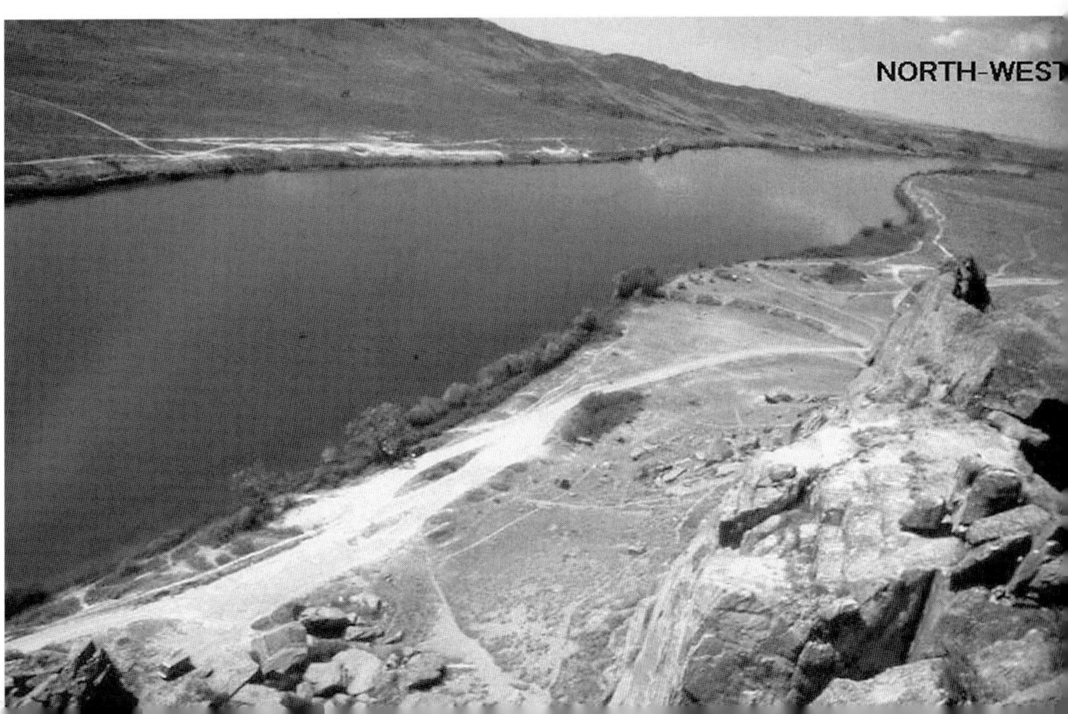

View of the area of Tamgaly-Tas with the petroglyph site on the right bank of the Ili river

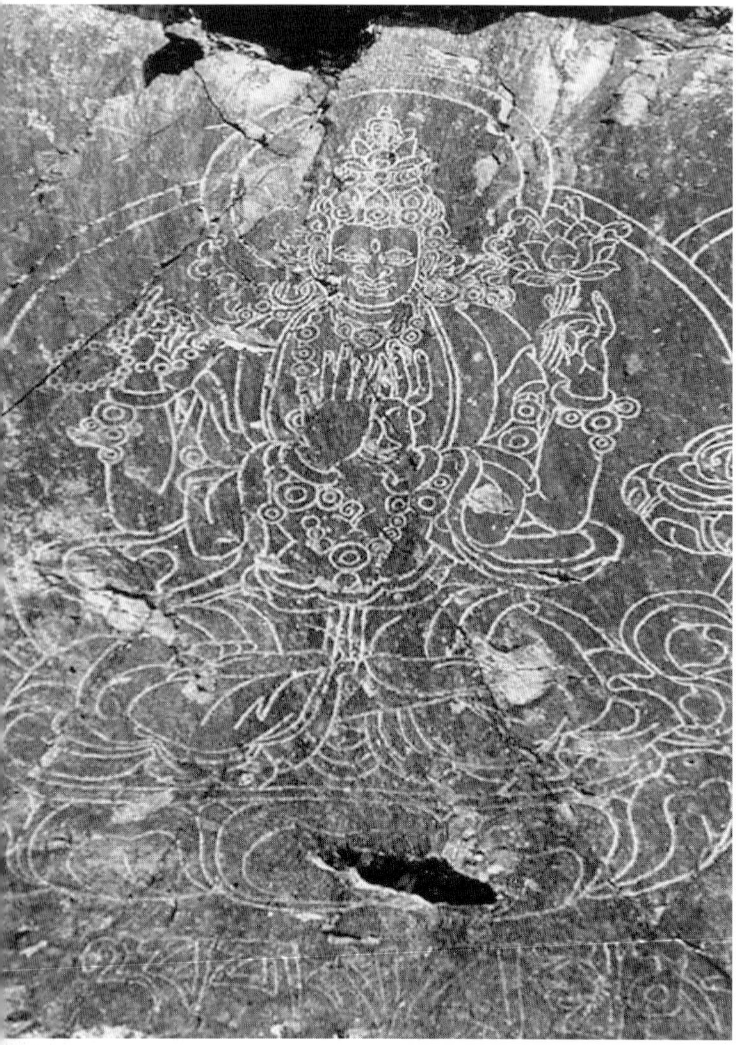

Tamgaly-Tas, stone 1

Semipalatinsk, and making some sketches of the rock engraving (by the painter Pavlov Kosharov). The most complete description and photographic documentation of the site was carried out in only 1897 by orientalist and local historian, H H Pantusov. He presented the material to the academic A A Posdniev who partially translated the Tibetan inscriptions.

During the Soviet period the site was mentioned in many publications on Kazakhstan petroglyphs, but no additional research was carried out. In 1981, the Alma-Ata Regional Council of National Deputies decided to nationally recognise and protect the late medieval petroglyphs of the Tamgaly-Tas gorge (Decision of the Executive Committee of 27 February 1981, No 4–91). However, nothing has been done: the area of the heritage protection zone for the site has not been determined and no interpretation boards about the site's value have been put up. Recent surveys of the site by members of the Laboratory of Geo-Archaeology discovered remains of Neolithic camps, Bronze Age settlements and other rock engravings in the area surrounding the Buddhist monument.

To our knowledge, the stones of Tamgaly-Tas were engraved by the Oirat-Djungar (or Kalmyk) people who were Western Mongol tribes converted to Tibetan Lamaist Tantric Buddhism in the 16th century. Under the rule of Galdan, they built the new and last of the steppe empires in conflict with the Manchu, Russian and Kazakh powers. During the early 18th century, the Djungar conquered East Semirechie and moved their headquarter from Semipalatinsk to Kulja. It was at that time that Tamgaly-Tas was built (1705–1710?). The Oirat-Djungar were defeated by the Russian, Kazakh and Chinese armies several times, the final defeat being in 1755–1758 in Djungaria resulting in their massacre and deportation.

The Tamgaly-Tas petroglyph site, built on an important river crossing of the Silk Road, shows all the characteristics of a temple. On one side its construction follows the general many-millennia long tradition of rock engravings always signifying places endowed with spiritual powers and ceremonial functions. On the other side, it follows the specific Buddhist tradition of open-air ritual sites, of which parallels can be found in the Himalayas, Zanskar, Tibet, Pamir, Tienshan (Issyk-Ata in Kyrgyzstan), Mongolia, no doubt quite common among nomadic peoples. The Buddhist

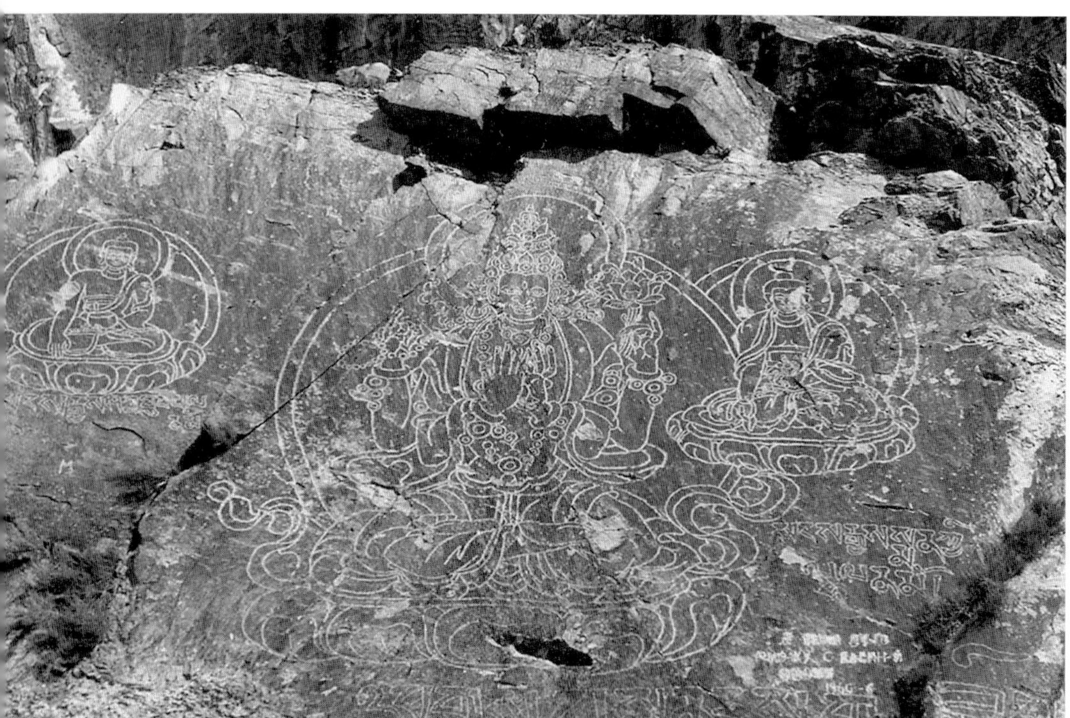

Petroglyphs of Tamgaly-Tas, stone 1

petroglyphs of Tamgaly-Tas represent the most westerly and northerly example of such ritual sites, and, when compared with the traditional Tibetan compositions, show some particular Central Asian traits, because of the presence of the Buddha of Medicine.

In recent decades, easier access to the area and increased visitor numbers were enabled by a road running along the river's right bank in the immediate proximity of the rock art. As a result during weekends and festivities the site is now a destination for picnics, fishing and also rock climbing activities on the steep cliffs a few metres behind the site. In 2003, a caravanserai was constructed on the left bank of the river to shoot a film, a fact that increased the tourist attraction of the area. Due to the natural and artistic beauty of the site, its cultural uniqueness and proximity to Lake Kapchigay and to the town of Almaty, the number of national and international visitors is increasing annually, making Tamgaly-Tas one of the main tourist attractions in Kazakhstan.

When comparing the drawings and photos of the site of the 19th century with its condition up to five years ago, the images and inscriptions are seen to be in quite a satisfactory conservation state. But the present increase of the social use of the site demonstrates on the one hand the site's growing popularity, its prospects as a tourist destination and its importance as cultural heritage. On the other hand, it indicates the beginnings of site pollution, disturbance to its magnificence, and threats to its safety. Over the last four to five years, modern names have been engraved next to most of the old petroglyphs. But the most serious threat of all is that all three groups of figures have been vandalised by throwing stones or deliberately shooting at some symbolic parts of the figures, such as the hands and eyes.

The Laboratory of Geo-Archaeology has developed a detailed work program to protect the Tamgaly-Tas petroglyph site, which will hopefully be put into action soon with NIPI PMK (State Institute for Scientific Research and Planning on Monuments of Material Culture) and the Municipality of the town of Kapchigai.

Jean-Marc Deom

historian, ISP - Laboratory of Geo-Archaeology A Medoev, Inst of Geology, Acd of Sciences, Almaty KZ: ispkz@nursatkz

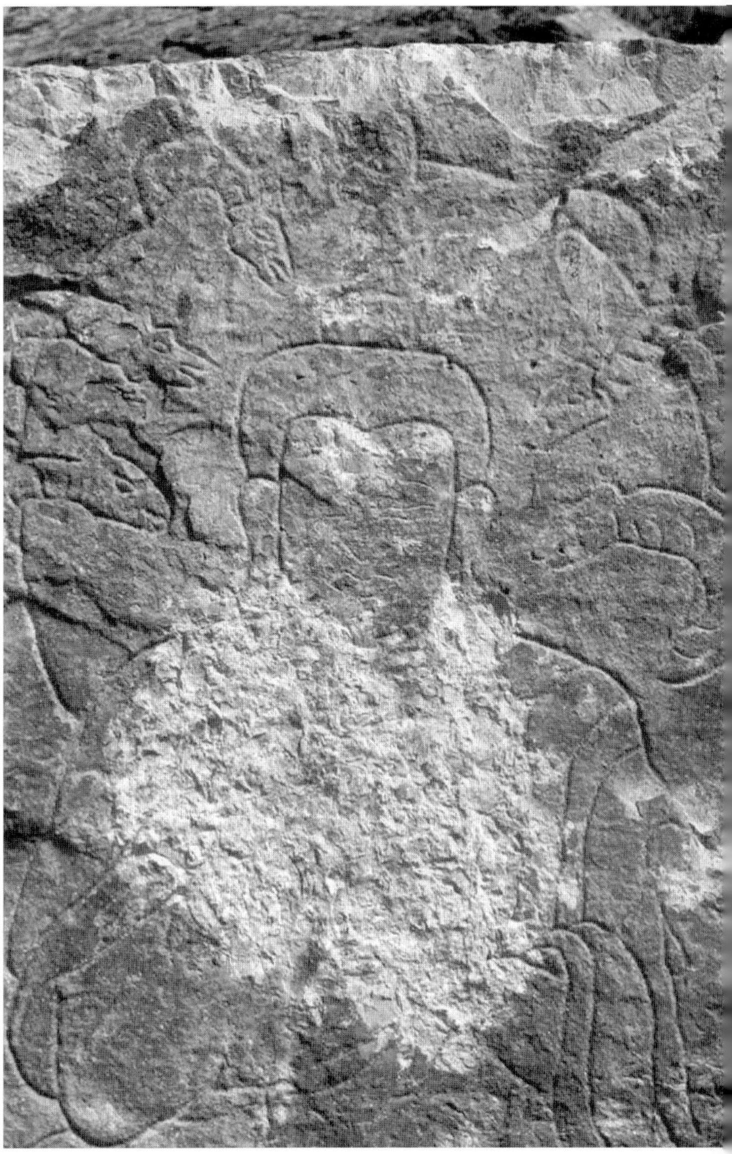

Tamgaly-Tas, stone 2, detail

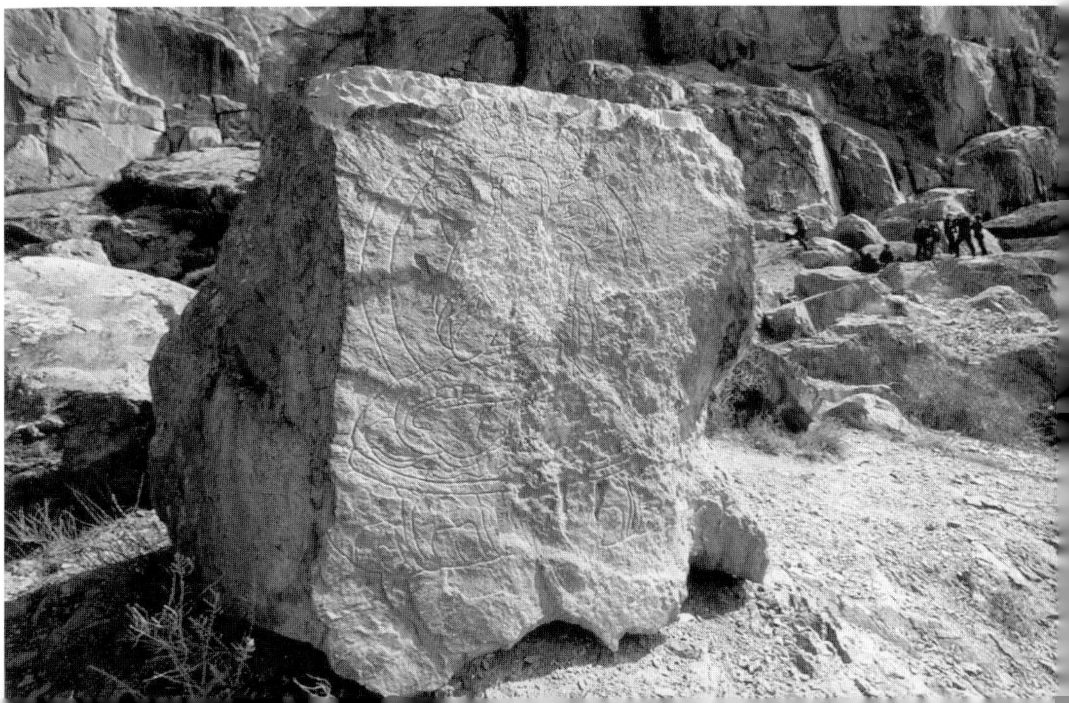

Petroglyphs of Tamgaly-Tas, stone 2

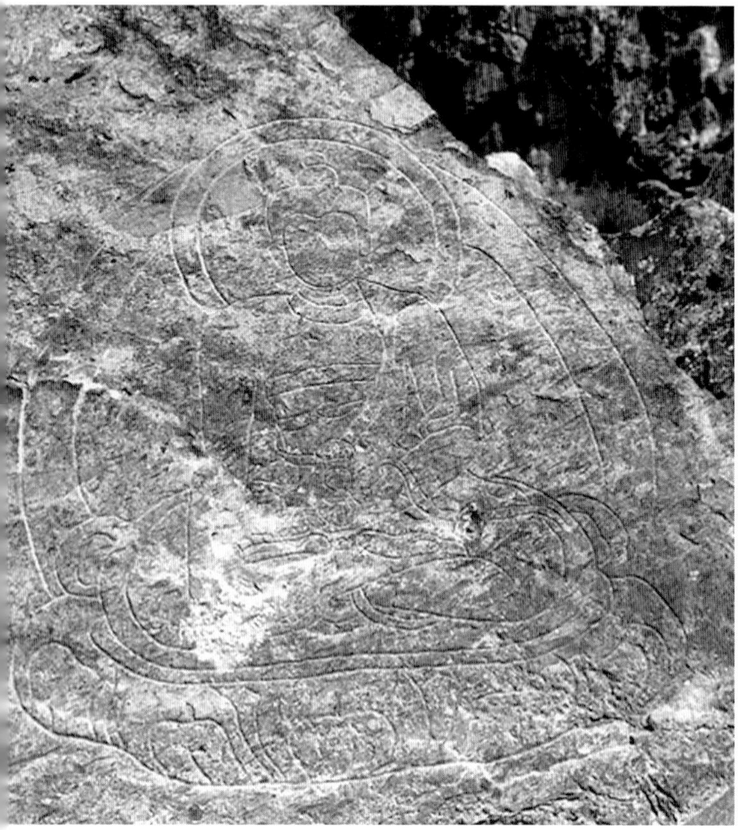

Tamgaly-Tas, stone 3

Tamgaly-Tas, Tibetan inscription

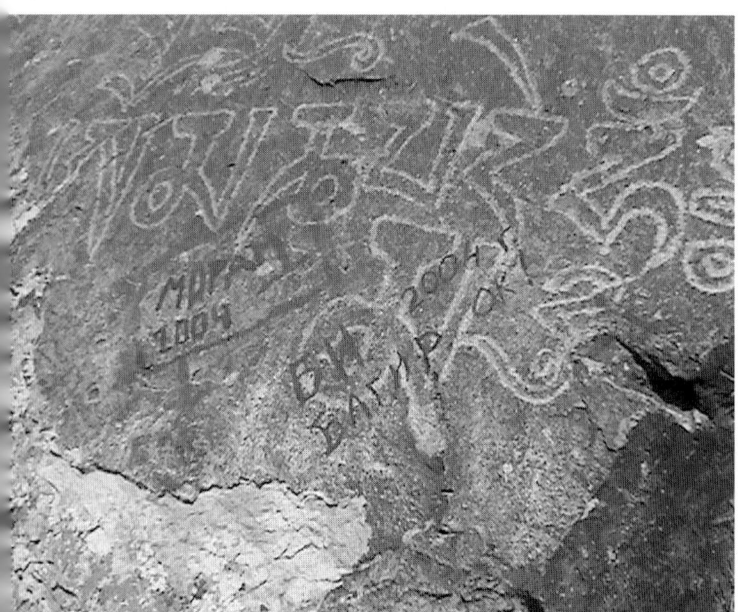

Tamgaly-Tas, litter at the foot of the petroglyphs

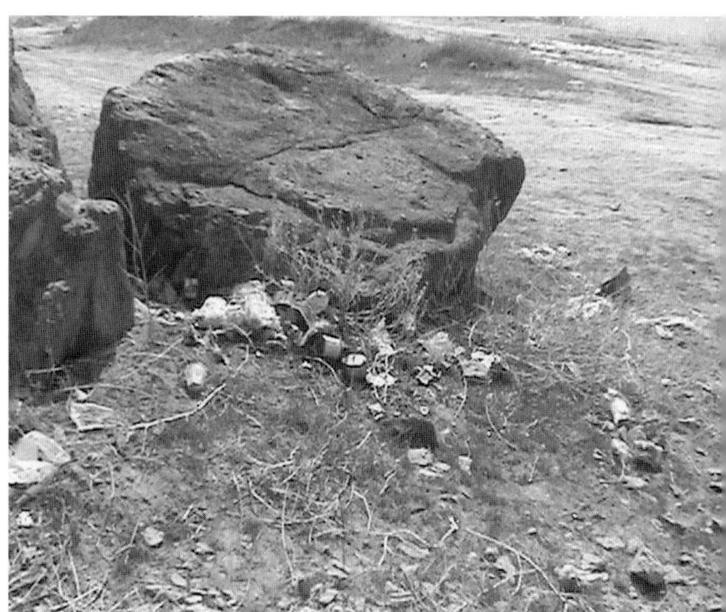

KOSOVO

Introduction

This article is primarily focused on the effects of the March 2004 riots, when over two days Kosovo-Albanian crowds attacked the Serbian minority and Orthodox and Serbian heritage in almost every municipality in Kosovo.

The fate of cultural heritage is revealed as a burning topic in the Balkans. As a sign of the long traditions of all the region's cultures, it has been a target of destruction but also of use and misuse. In countries where different groups are fighting on the basis of ethnicity, heritage can become a weapon and a provocation. Many of the region's museums, libraries, religious buildings, archaeological sites, and the like, have been destroyed in the former Yugoslavia during the last fifteen years to oppress these cultures and people connected to them.

In the case of Kosovo, I believe it is also quite important to mention that the Kosovo-Albanian people, who have been present in the area for centuries alongside Serbians and Turks, have three different religions. The majority of Albanians are Muslims but there are also quite a number of Roman Catholic Albanians and some Orthodox Christians, a fact that is rarely mentioned in international publications. As elsewhere in Europe, many people in Kosovo, especially in the cities, are not religiously observant. The March riots were not religiously motivated.

Background

A large number of Orthodox and Serbian buildings were destroyed during the riots. While most of the attacked buildings were modern structures, there was also damage to some invaluable Byzantine churches. The riots seem to have been well organised and focused on symbols of the Serbian presence in Kosovo, no matter the historic value. It is unlikely that the rabble, nor perhaps even its organisers, could see the difference between a 14th–century church, which has escaped destruction for centuries and is a part of their own history, and a 20th–century copy built in large numbers primarily as signs of the Serbian presence in Kosovo.

Approximately 35 churches, chapels and monasteries in seventeen municipalities were destroyed or damaged in only two days. For most of both Kosovo-Albanians and international watchers, the riots and its brutality came as a shock. It was not obvious that the strong frustration towards the UN Mission in Kosovo (UNMIK) for not being able to solve the everyday problems of the people and the Kosovo's status with respect to Serbia, would turn into violence against the Serbian minority and their symbols.

The international military forces (KFOR), whose task it was to protect both Kosovo's peoples and their heritage, did not seem to know how to react in such a fierce situation. Much of the destruction could have been avoided if the soldiers had been better prepared. In many cases the mob even returned a day or two later to continue their violence.

During the following weeks there were determined and strong efforts to collect information about the situation for heritage from Serbia and from international heritage organisations, such as UNESCO, the Council of Europe and Cultural Heritage without Borders, but also from local Kosovar authorities and UNMIK.[1]

In response to strong pressure by the European Union and the United Nations on the Kosovar parliament to financially support

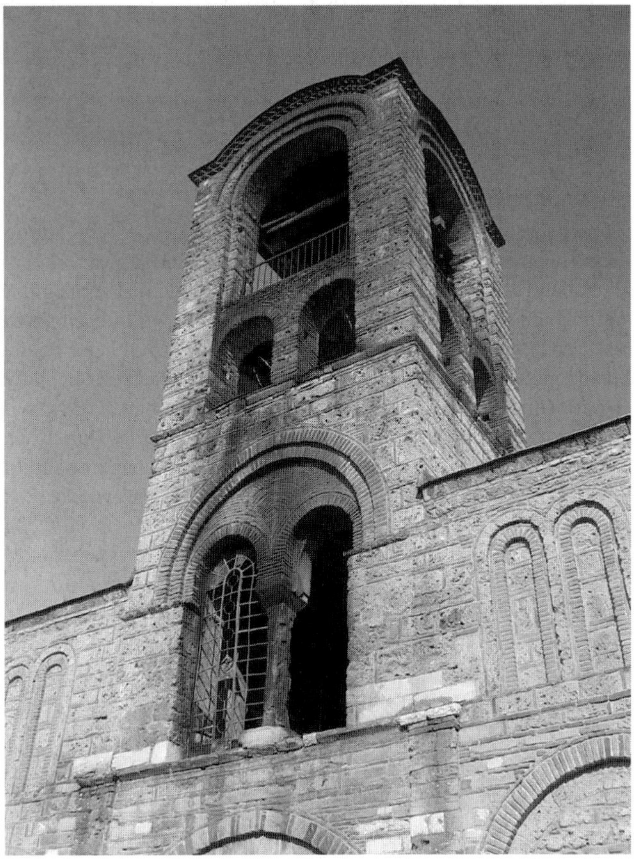

The clock tower of Ljeviska church after the March 2004 riots

the reconstruction, the parliament decided in June to earmark 3.5 million Euros to repair the damaged Orthodox heritage. This funding will most likely be concentrated on the most significant buildings, as the total cost for restoration and reconstruction is at least ten times higher. Many priceless frescoes and iconostases (painted altar screens) are lost forever.

Analysis and overview of threats to heritage

There are a number of reasons why heritage is in danger in Kosovo. Some of it is of a political nature, such as the relations between Serbia and Kosovo. Another reason is the unemployment among young men, who are readily affected by extremist propaganda. Both factors are beyond the scope of this article, for more information the International Crisis Group's report 'Collapse in Kosovo'[2] is recommended.

Another reason is that the wars in Yugoslavia during the 1990s largely destroyed the existing infrastructure to preserve heritage. The exodus of Serb specialists from the heritage institutions, who withdrew along with the Yugoslav troops in June 1999 taking institutional records with them, has left Kosovo with largely dysfunctional institutions and museums.

A third reason is that many heritage places have yet to be restored, including hundreds of mosques and other Kosovo-Albanian heritage as well as Orthodox churches, that were damaged or

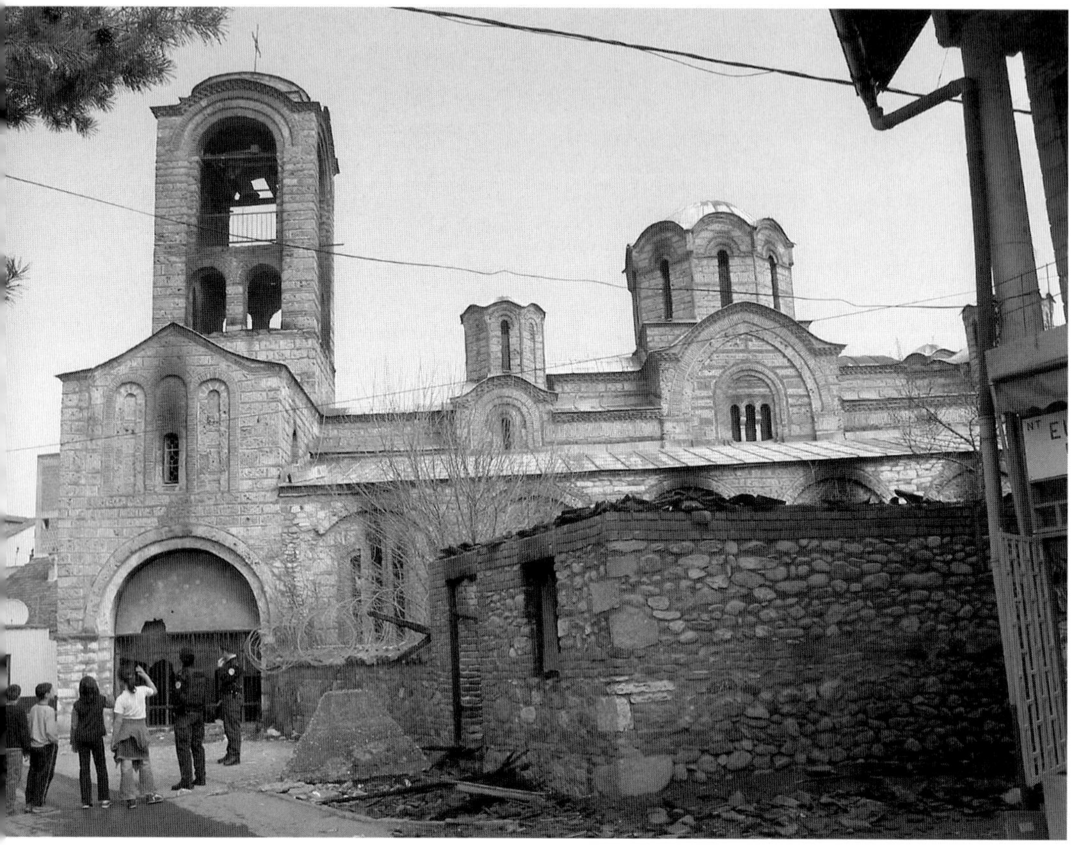

Ljeviska church in Prizren after the March 2004 riots

destroyed in the 1998–99 conflict. There are also a very limited number of international donors.

Case studies – three examples

Ljeviska church in Prizren

A Byzantine church of invaluable international importance, it has existed for centuries side by side 16th century mosques, such as that of Sinan Pasha, and Prizren's Roman Catholic cathedral, as a brilliant example of the different cultural influences along one of the important Balkan trading routes. The violence against it in March 2004, as if it were merely a building representing the contemporary Serbian presence, was a shock not only for Serbian and international experts, but for most Kosovo-Albanians as well. Until March 2004, the Ljeviska church had been protected through time by the local Kosovo-Albanian population, and seen as also representing their heritage. But now there is no guarantee that it will not happen again, if nothing radical is done to change people's awareness, including that of refugees from the countryside who have flooded into Prizren and other cities. The restoration of the Ljeviska church and other damaged Byzantine churches is the highest priority for Kosovo heritage authorities, UNESCO and the Council of Europe.

Kalaja district in Prizren

The Kalaja (Potkaljaja) district, a historic urban quarter of old houses located on the slopes leading up to the ancient fortress, was more or less burnt down during the March riots. It used to be inhabited by a mixed, mostly Serbian population and many houses were already abandoned after 1999. Apart from this, the area is a strong symbol for Prizren, almost as much as the different religious buildings, as well as representing Serbs' right to be present in Kosovo beside other ethnic groups. It is of enormous importance that the area be reconstructed and that the former owners be able to regain their properties and that they feel safe to return.

New Serbian Orthodox Cathedral of the Holy Trinity in Gjakova

This is a 20th century church that represents the torture and horror of the 1998–99 war to the local Kosovo-Albanian population. Many Gjakovar families say they lost their loved ones in that church. Built in 1998 with municipal funds as a memorial to Serbian troops, it was already badly damaged after the 1999 war. Now it has been totally demolished. For most people in Gjakova it was just a relief to be rid of what they see as a symbol of terror. It is not very likely that it will ever be reconstructed.

Solutions to these threats, ideas that are emerging

The importance of preserving heritage that represents the presence of many different cultures is still obvious in the region. All the strength of this sector may and should be used towards positive developments - to unite instead of separating. A knowledgeable and professional handling of different aspects of this heritage is an important aspect of peaceful and democratic development. Capacity-building has to focus both on the institutions and the players in the free market. With a regional approach both a higher standard can be reached, because of the actual expertise available in the region, and at the same time a network of competent professionals in the heritage sector can be rebuilt. Here the museums, archives and libraries have an important role to play.

But it is not enough! There have to be strong efforts to achieve public awareness. Public understanding of the significance of heritage is an important tool for understanding other cultures. It is also essential for the day-to-day protection of heritage places. There are different options that must be worked on in parallel:

- The European Heritage Days, a Council of Europe initiative that has been running for almost fifteen years in most European countries, have not yet been tried in Kosovo. The concept has proven to be most effective in drawing the media's and public's attention to cultural heritage.
- Local NGOs have a key-role to play in making cultural heritage seen and understood by the community, especially those who might be very difficult to reach by authorities or through ordinary channels. If people feel that their shared cultural heritage is worth protecting, we have achieved much towards a more peaceful society.
- Restoration and awareness campaigns directly connected to restoration projects can energise local communities to create a platform for local development. In Kosovo, as in other places in the Balkans, the key word has been tourism, not mass tourism, but a small-scale sustainable tourism based on a rich heritage of diverse ethnic origins, such as Prizren town, the Decani monastery (added in June 2004 to the World Heritage list by UNESCO), the Orthodox Patriarchate complex in Pec/Peja and many others, in combination with an exciting natural heritage. This should create awareness among everyday people of the economic benefits of preserving all the different symbols of their dynamic past.

The privately owned, traditional vernacular architecture in Kosovo, much of which was damaged in the 1998-1999 war, is also in danger, but for other reasons - the desire to become 'modern' and difficulties in maintaining buildings properly.

In this case, target groups for capacity building are, apart from private owners, also craftsmen, architects, ethnologists and suppliers of materials who will gain expertise from practical repair works. Private owners of built heritage need a change in attitude, to be proud of this link to their ancestors, but also needed are different financial solutions to enable them to restore or maintain their buildings, if and when the interest is there. Heritage restoration, including not only major heritage sites but also traditional residences and historic urban centres, also has to be tied to economic development and tourism. This can provide a continuing incentive for the community to use, value and preserve the rich but endangered cultural legacy of this historic European region.

Dick Sandberg, Architect SAR/MSA,
CHwB (Cultural Heritage without Borders),
Sweden, member of ICOMOS,
with thanks to András Riedlmayer, Harvard University

1 See CHwB local office in Kosovo website: http://www.chwb.org/-kosovo

2 International Crisis Group website: http://www.crisisweb.org/home/index.cfm?id=1243&l=1

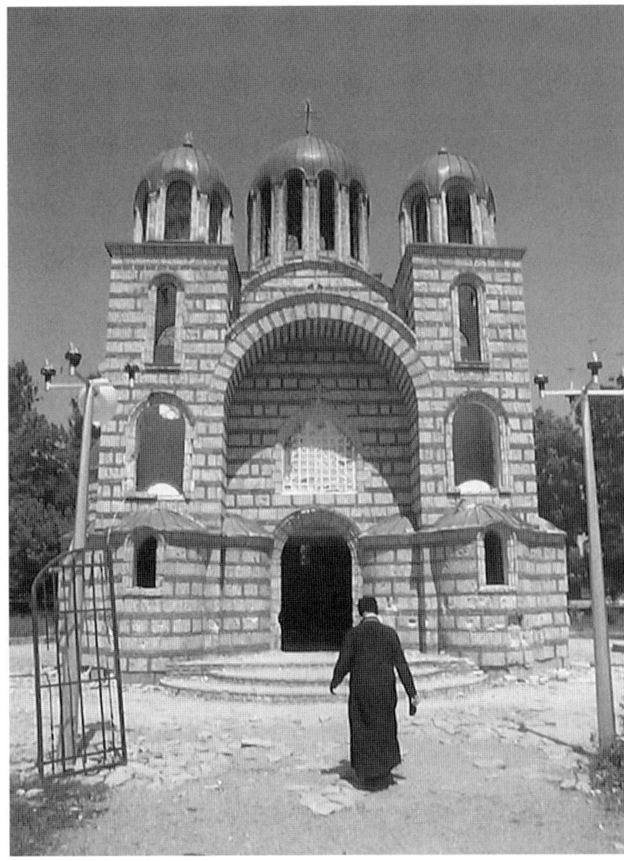

The New orthodox cathedral in Gjakova in 1999

The New orthodox cathedral after the March 2004 riots

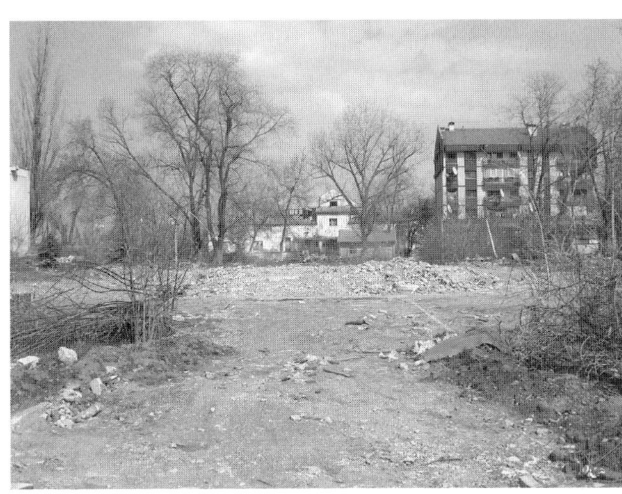

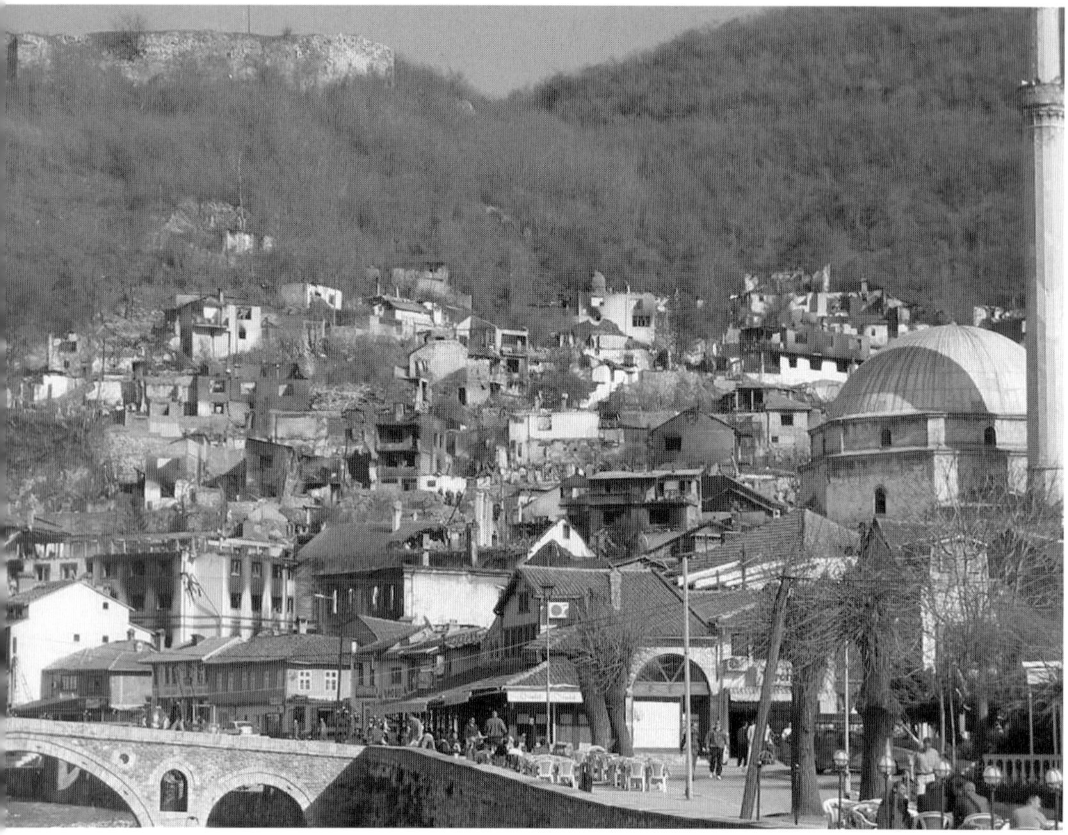

Prizren Potkalaja district after the March 2004 riots

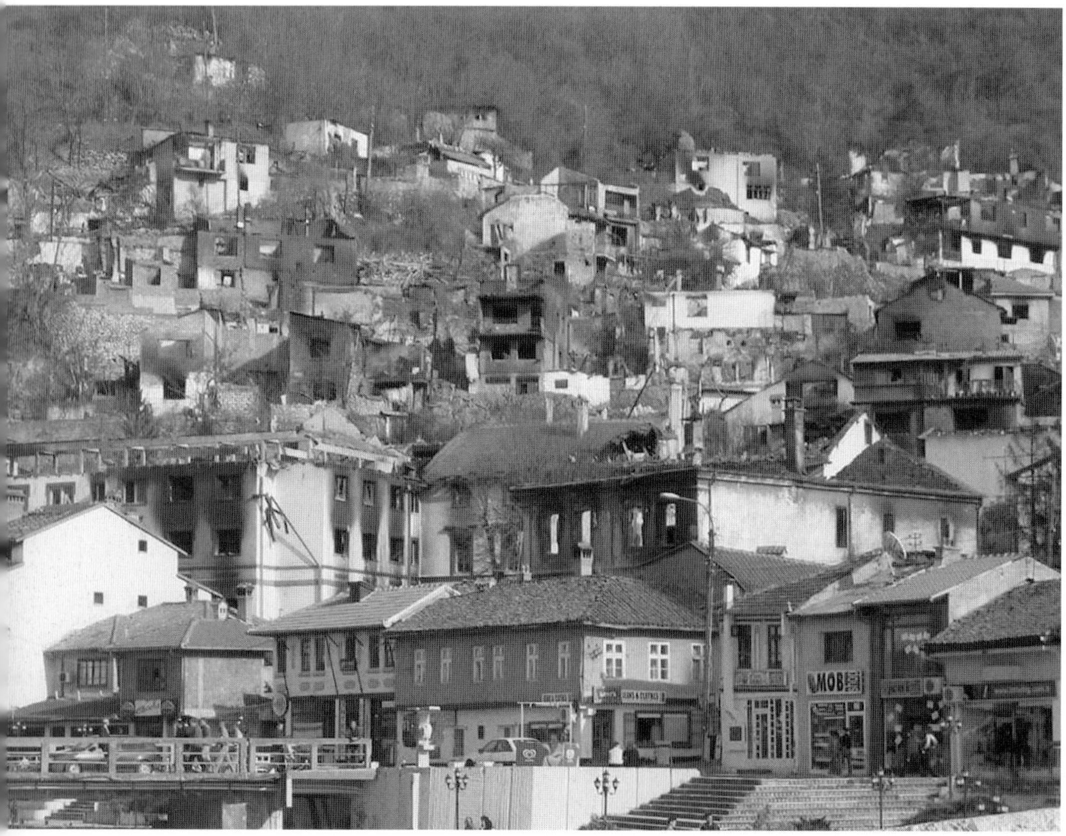

Prizren Potkalaja district after the March 2004 riots

KYRGYZSTAN
Krasnaya Rechka

Under the Western Turkic and Turgesh *Khanates* from 560 to 760, the section of the Chu Valley between Bishkek (40 km east of Bishkek, Chu Valley) and Lake Issyk-kul became one of the main political, economic and military centres in Eurasia, connected with Byzantium and China by the Northern Silk Roads. Archaeological excavations carried out in the Chu Valley between 1940 and 2000 revealed towns and monumental structures dating from the 5th to 12th centuries that reflected the cultural and artistic traditions of many countries and peoples, from Byzantium in the west to India in the south and China in the east.

The main towns of the valley, Navikat (today Krasnaya Rechka), Suyab (Ak Beshim) and Balasagyn (Burana), were founded during the 6th century, later developing significantly and becoming unique centres of symbiosis between Indian, Chinese, Sogdian and Turkic cultures, as well as a connecting link between these cultures.

The archaeological sites of the Chuy Valley represent a unique mixture of urban settlements and religious buildings of different cultures. Throughout the Soviet period excavated ruins and remains of earthen architecture were not protected properly. Deterioration has therefore already taken place, and if urgent conservation measures are not carried out the remains will be lost forever, representing an irreplaceable loss of this unique heritage of the medieval cities in Kyrgyzstan.

A UNESCO/Japan Trust Fund Project has currently started to document and conserve some of the most important structures. One is the so-called Temple II at Navikat, dated to about the 8th century.

The temple covers 17 m x 17 m and consists of a sanctuary room of 6 m x 5 m with a domed roof and a roofed corridor. The remains of an 8 m long reclining clay statue of Buddha have been uncovered in the rear corridor, and Bodhisattvas were discovered in the southern corridor and on both sides of the sanctuary gates. These are now in the Hermitage Museum, St Petersburg. Fragments of wall paintings, a Chinese stela with carvings and inscriptions, fragments of a manuscript on birch-bark in Brahmin script and Sanscrit language, have also been found with gilded bronze statuettes of Bodhisattvas and deities of Sogdian and Indian origin. In 1961, the temple's 10.4 m long western corridor was excavated. The walls of this corridor are plastered and covered with frescos, the traces of which are still visible. An incomplete clay statue of the reclining Buddha was discovered, measuring about 8 m in length and about 1.5 m in height. The entire sculpture was originally painted red, as were the surfaces of the pedestal. Fragments of frescoes were also found.

Navikat is only one of many examples of extensive expressions of urbanism of which we have scarcely any knowledge and which need urgent assistance and further protection.

Michael Jansen
ICOMOS Germany

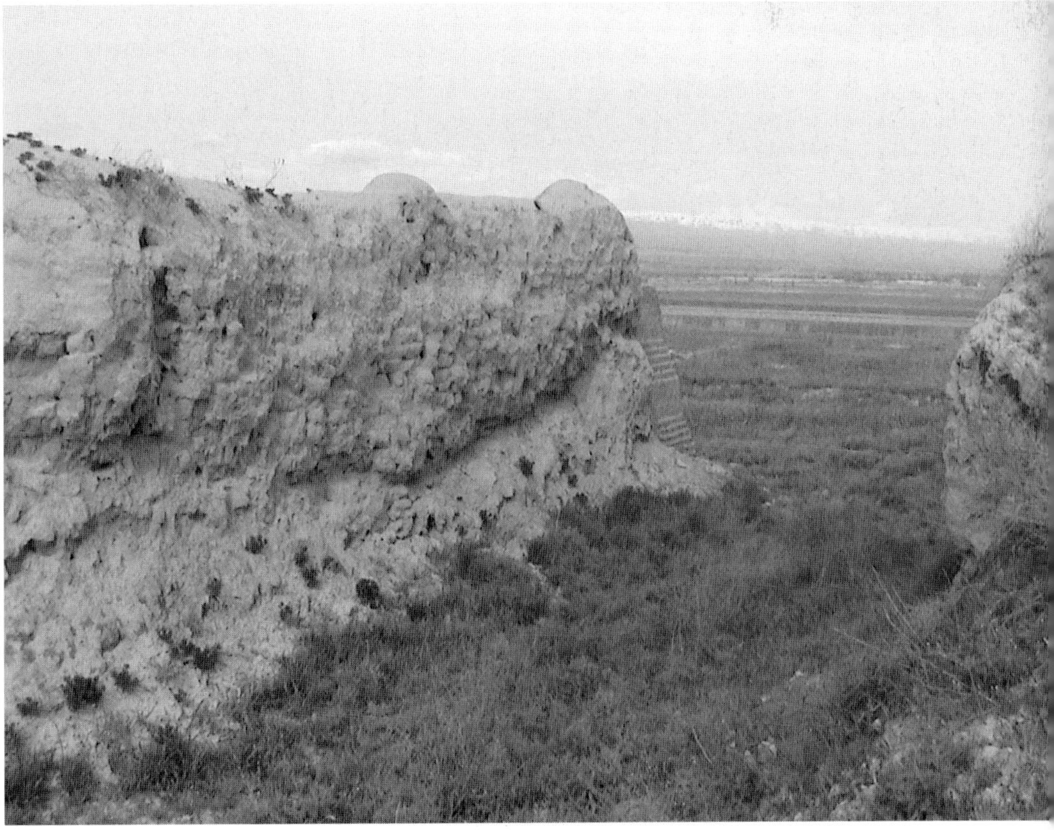

The mudbrick cella wall from south

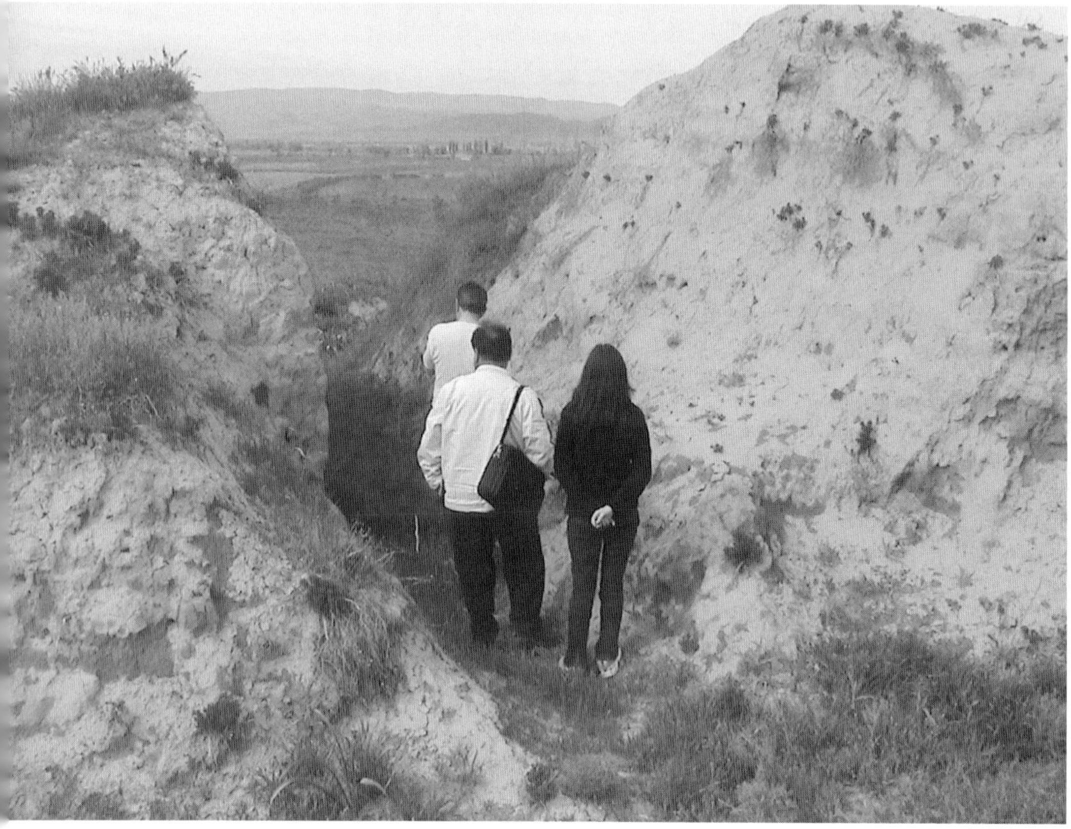

A part of the *pradakshina patha* with the highly threatened mudbrick structures of the cella (left) and the outer wall

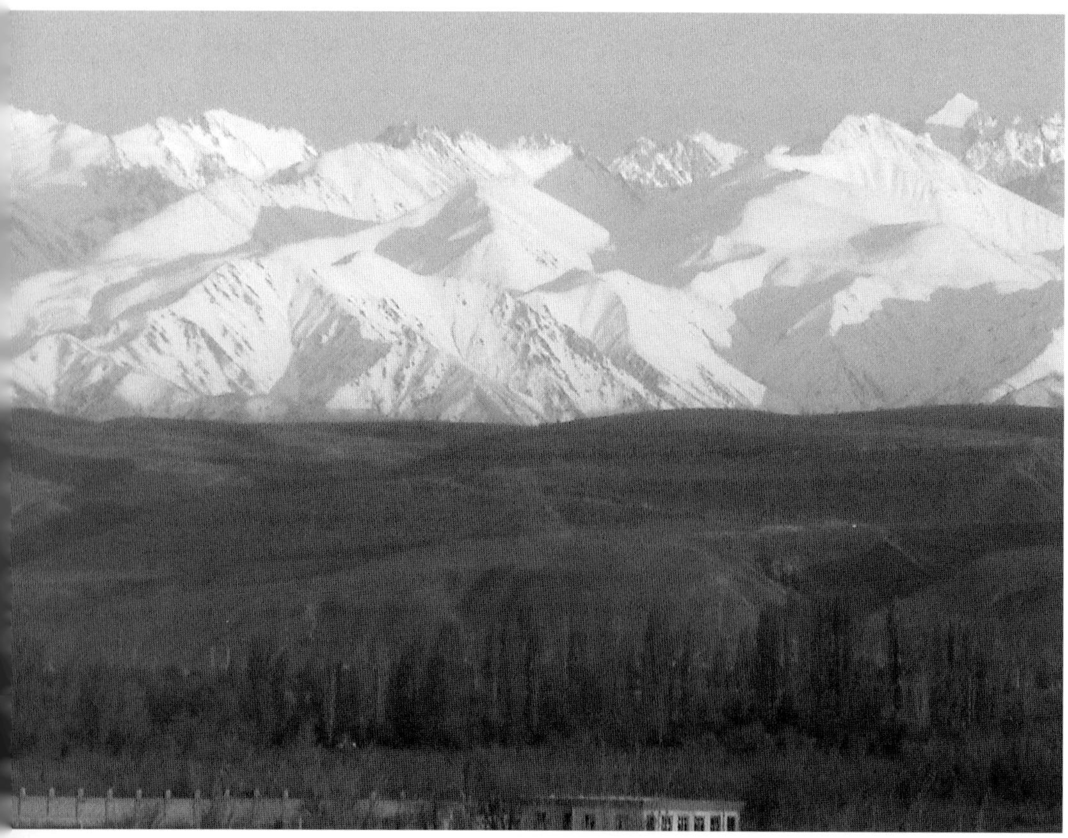

The nearby mountains of the Tien Schan, over 4000 m high

LITHUANIA
Wooden Architecture of Vilnius Historic Suburbs

In the 2001-2002 edition of *Heritage at Risk*, the Lithuanian National Committee of ICOMOS mentioned wooden architecture in historic suburbs as the most endangered of several groups of cultural heritage items in Lithuania.

The historic centre of Vilnius – Old Town – is inscribed on the World Heritage List, but the survival of the wooden architecture of the historic suburbs of Vilnius remains problematic. For the Vilnius historic suburbs – Užupis, Žvėrynas, Antakalnis, Šnipiškės, Markučiai – have grown as separate residential areas in the configuration of the town's centre. Wooden architecture has survived there unevenly. Old wooden buildings still dominate in large areas of Žvėrynas, Šnipiškės and Markučiai. In Užupis and Antakalnis, groups of wooden buildings or individual ones are interwoven with brick buildings surrounded by a new urban environment.

The wooden architecture in Vilnius has survived from the 19th and the beginning of the 20th centuries, but it is very diverse typologically as well as stylistically. We possess a broad spectrum of historical architectural trends and influences which have been reflected in the architecture of the wooden buildings. In the suburbs domestic residences were built among abundant vegetation. The architecture of the houses was unusual: there are elements of vernacular architecture, Russian *dacha* (summer-cottages), Swiss resort or Polish Zakopan styles. Modest, functional homes for one or two families predominate. There are quite a few more sumptuous villas, rental properties for some families and some complexes of wooden manors. In the Vilnius suburbs, the character of wooden architecture varied because of different developments, the cost of land and the wealth of that area's inhabitants.

For some centuries, Žvėrynas and Markučiai have been recreational places for the inhabitants of Vilnius. Summer residences, villas, and restaurants were built. In the middle of the 19th and the beginning of the 20th centuries wooden residential areas were built. In Žvėrynas, members of the rich and middle class built more sumptuous and rental houses. Buildings in Žvėrynas distinguish themselves by their abundance in décor and architectural elements - turrets, verandas, mezzanines, and gable dormers. After the St Petersburg-Warsaw railway was built, Markučiai became a residential area for poor people. There are few old villas left, but the newly built houses, being small and of modest architecture fit well into the vivid, hilly landscape. Single and unique wooden buildings have survived in Užupis and Antakalnis.

Wooden architecture is the oldest in Šnipiškės. Unfortunately, it is in very poor condition and finds itself in the most intensive development zone of the town centre. The Šnipiškės quarters are part of that area's cultural heritage. It is a significant historic suburb dating to the second part of the 19th and the beginning of the 20th centuries. The suburb possesses a characteristic urban plan of streets and narrow quarters where low-storeyed wooden houses predominate. Most houses have vernacular traits; an unusual cultural building type is characteristic of this suburb, reminiscent of buildings in small towns or villages. It is a residential area where poor people lived.

In recent years development processes have been very active in Vilnius, the capital of Lithuania. The political, social, and economic situation encouraged development by new investments, an increased cost of land in the town centre and the council's ambitious plans. Possibilities are sought to make more intensive use of the area in the town centre. One or two storey wooden buildings in poor condition have become an obstacle to new construction and there are attempts to destroy them. But these areas are very close to the Vilnius Old Town World Heritage area and its environment falls under the visual protection zone of Vilnius urban heritage. New construction is regulated by the cultural heritage laws. Unfortunately, in reality only unique buildings are protected.

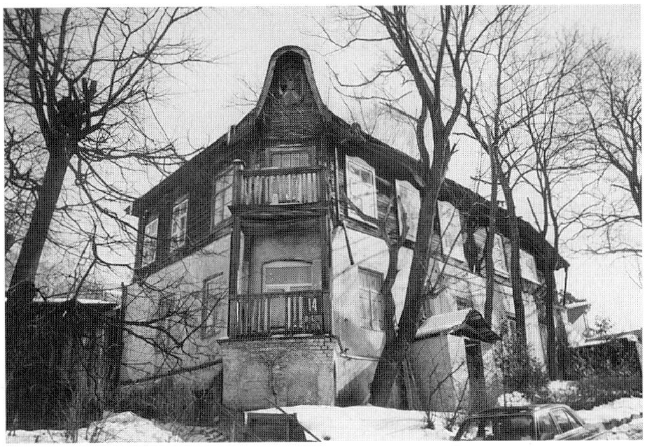

House in Pavasario Street

For example, the Šnipiškės area is an unusual complex of Vilnius historic urban suburb and architecture. The cultural value of this complex is obvious, but the buildings are in a poor physical state. There are sub-standard sanitary conditions, which do not correspond to present requirements. In addition, on the right bank of the Neris river, south of Šnipiškės, a new Vilnius centre has grown up, possessing the potential to develop further. Twenty to thirty-three storey buildings make up this new centre. We are therefore faced with evident contradictions. On the one hand, the area's obvious cultural heritage which has poor physical condition and poor living standards, on the other hand there is the rapidly growing contemporary town centre.

Taking account of the area's location and its problems, it is necessary to carry out an entire review of existing buildings from a cultural heritage perspective. The area's protected zone, established twelve years ago, must be revised and could be reduced. The selected portion of the area for further preservation should be the most characteristic one as cultural heritage is involved. This part should be suitable for not only restoration but also for its future integrity, survival and use.

Wooden architecture is gradually being lost to natural timber decay, fires, incompetent repair or building renewal. Wooden houses that are covered by bricks and contemporary additions grow in number. Old decorative details, authentic elements of buildings, doors, window frames, the patterns of the boards are gradually being lost. Society and house owners do not value the wooden buildings sufficiently; they do not know how to maintain them. It would be useful to have an exemplary restoration of one house. It might be organised with the help of restorers from other countries. It could be an effective example and stimulus in the right direction to save this wooden architecture. It goes without saying, a special program, supported financially by the state or municipality, would be of great help. It would be better if such programs were worked out for every Vilnius historic suburb. Of course, today the proper restoration of a wooden house is very expensive for most owners. State support could be expected only for the most unique buildings.

Due to the reality of this problem, the Vilnius council is initiating the development of a 'Strategy to protect the wooden architectural heritage in the central area of Vilnius' and an inventory of wooden buildings. The aim of the strategy is to present concrete proposals, having evaluated the present range of wooden architectural heritage and their physical situation. Many wooden buildings are in a critical state now, but unfortunately, developing and implementing strategic plans are a long process.

G.Mikneviciene, J.Glemza
ICOMOS Lithuania

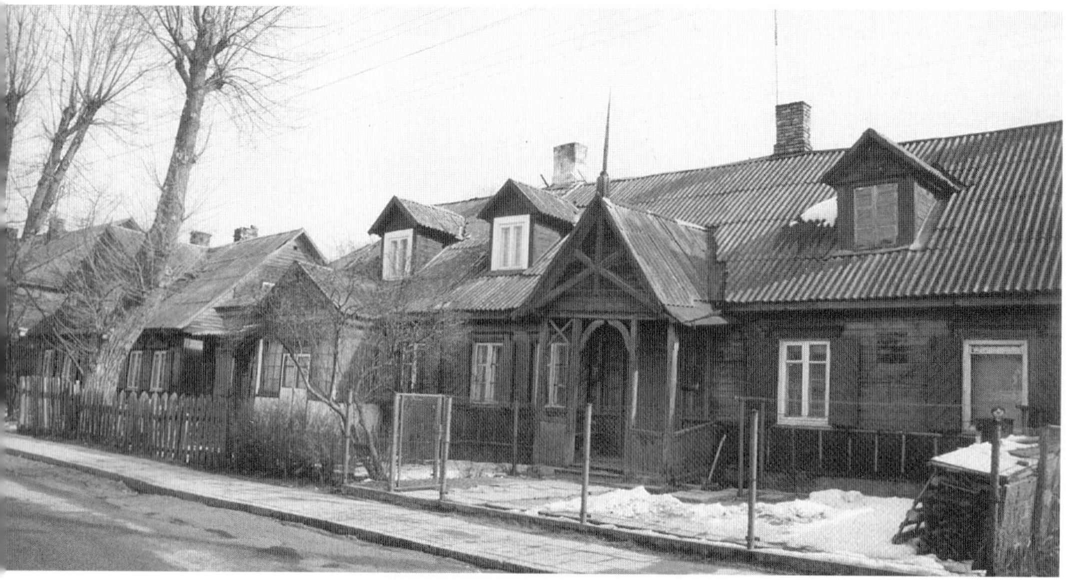

Wooden houses in Giedraièiu Street

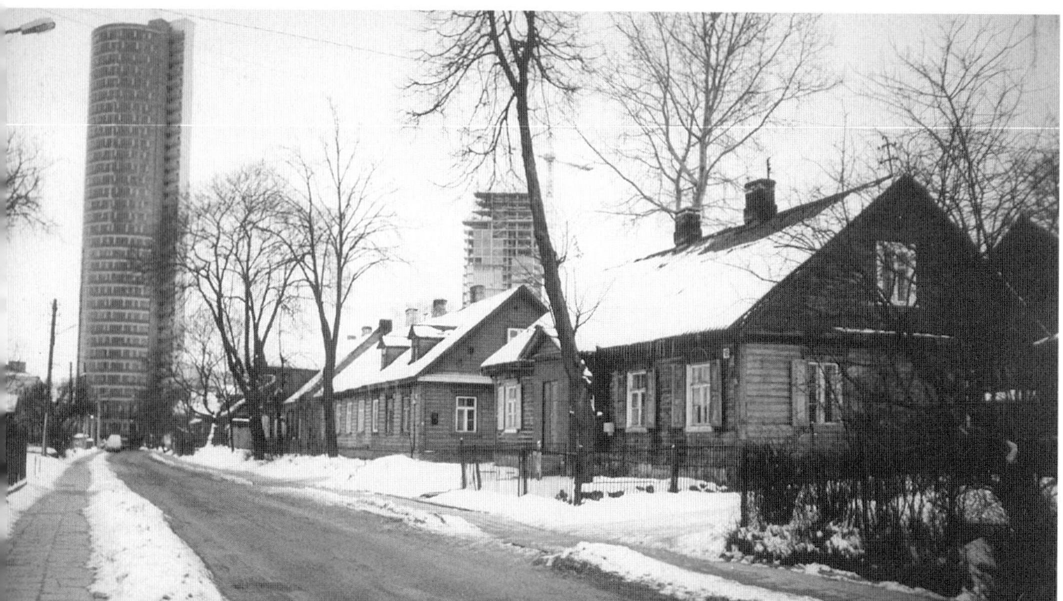

Another view of Giedraièiu Street

Wooden house in Antakalnis suburb

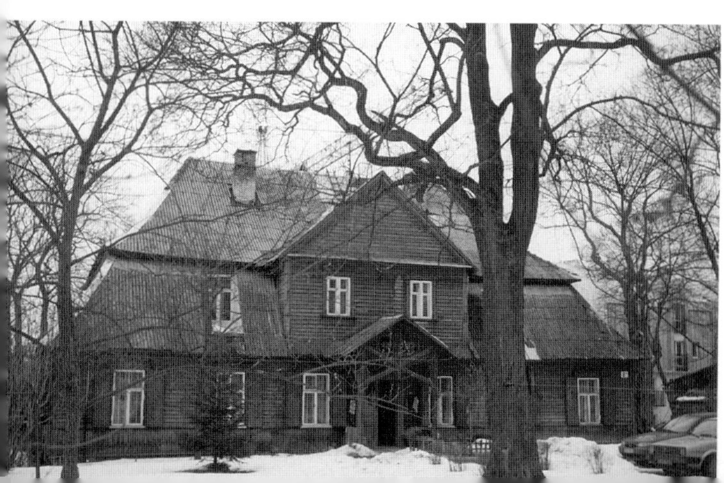

Old wooden house and modern constructions in the background

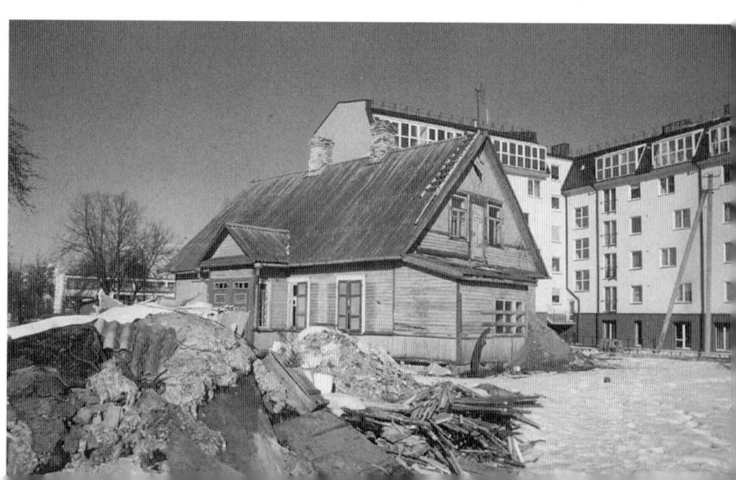

MEXICO
San Juan Cuauhtinchan, Puebla

Pre-hispanic Cuauhtinchan

The Cuauhtinchan culture is much older than those of the Toltecs and Aztecs. It goes back to the formative epoch, when small groups of gatherers and incipient farmers settled at the site to form small villages, around 1200 BC; even before this the Olmecs had spread from the coast of the Gulf towards Puebla, Morelos and the Cuenca del Mexico between 1500 and 1200 BC. The earliest historical references to Cuauhtinchan are mostly in the Chichimeca Toltec History, the annals of Cuauhtinchan, and the Cuauhtinchan maps, documents written and painted by the 'tlacuilos', which preserve the cultural traditions of this area.

Colonial Cuauhtinchan

The Spanish Conquest took place at the end of July 1520, before that of Tenochtitlan. The religious conversion of the population was carried out from 1527 to 1528. Several buildings were constructed to house the Franciscans, until, in 1554, the construction of the present church began, as part of an assemblage consisting of a porch, the church, the monastery, the pilgrims' gate, the vegetable garden and the churchyard.

The church consisits of a single nave divided into five sections, with a semi-circular apse containing the high altar.

The high altar of the church of San Juan Bautista, Cuauhtinchan

In Latin America there are three wall-mounted altarpieces that are complete and datable to the 16th century: Huejotzingo, San Bernardino de Xochimilco, and San Juan de Cuauhtinchan, Puebla. The Cuauhtinchan altarpiece is probably the oldest wall-mounted one in America that preserves all of its integral elements. Its maker is unknown, although in 1597 Juan de Arrue was contracted to replace the altarpiece of San Francisco de Puebla, renovated and with a new sacrarium. The artist stamps it, to a high degree, with the Italianate style of the age, but does not omit the strong Flemish touch that characterises much Spanish painting of the time.

It must be noted that the Cuauhtinchan altarpiece is the oldest still existing in Mexico. It is a large triptych, which gives it an archaic appearance. It consists of three main sections and three rows, despite the ornamentation of its surround. It is of reticular composition based on ionic columns, these being fluted in the first section and balustraded in the others, with the timber boarding decorated with charming cherubs.' The subjects illustrated in the eleven paintings of the altarpiece are the central themes of the Christian doctrine, which are found, with some variations, in the Renaissance altarpieces of New Spain.

According to the studies made to determine the state of conservation of the principal altarpiece of the 16th century church of San Juan Bautista Cuauhtinchan, part of the monastic grouping at the site in the state of Puebla, the chief threats to the altarpiece are the following:

Changes in Humidity

- Parts of the structure are seen to be out of place, preventing the paintings from being properly fixed in place, with gaps of up to 3 or 4 cm from the frames;
- Joints between sections have been separated by the accumulation of dust, which attracts damp, causing movements in the timber and growth of micro-organisms;
- Absence of mouldings and coats of pictorial paint;
- Cracks in the timber and coats of pictorial paint;
- Fissures in the undercoat and pictorial paint;
- Cracks, ridges, cracking and flaking in the pictorial paint;
- Inconsistencies in the restoration work of 1986;
- The column on the left of the crucifixion has come away at the top and is fastened to the body of the altarpiece with plastic cable;
- Changes in humidity cause the severe shrinking of the painted panels and the animal-fibre fabric that covers the panels, which, on reducing in size, are insufficient for the area covered by the pictorial paint and the undercoat, materials which are not as drastically affected as timber and fibre;
- It can be seen that all the boards placed as an emergency measure in 2000 no longer have the required effect, having broken away from the pictorial coating;
- The absence or loss of undercoat and pictorial coating;
- Bulging or hollowing, consistent with the separation of the undercoat from the supporting structure over fairly large areas, forming bubbles up to 40 cm across. This threat is not visible to the naked eye, and cannot be seen in the photographs;
- Fissures, splits in the undercoat and pictorial paint;
- Cracks, ridges and flaking in the pictorial paint.

Dirt

- Accumulation of dust and bird droppings.

Presence of woodworm

- During the restoration of 1986 the altarpiece was fumigated, which aided in its conservation. At present the beginning of an infestation can be seen in the boards of the first section.

ICOMOS Mexico

References

'Restoration work at the Monastery of San Juan Cuauhtinchan', Office of Urban development and Ecology. April 25th 1987

Tovar de Teresa, Guillermo 'The Altarpieces of Cuauhtinchan', Ediciones Luis Lagarto, Mexico 1988.

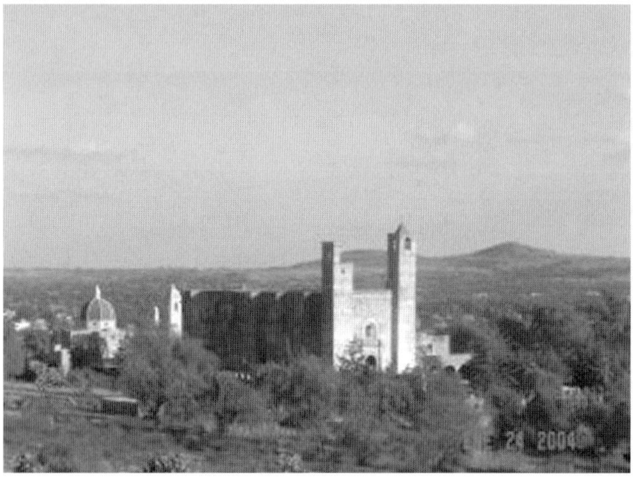

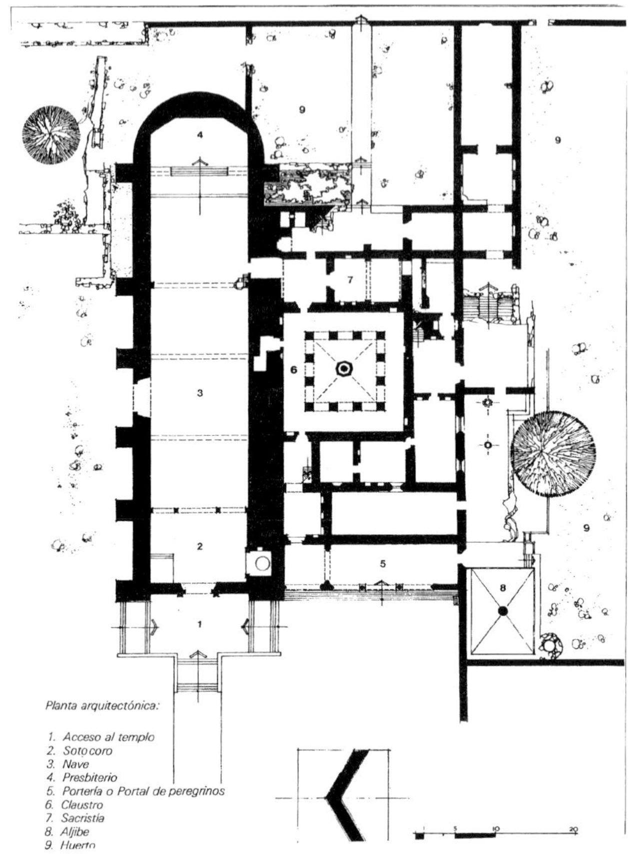

General view and ground-plan of San Juan Cuauhtinchan ▲ ►

Major retable of San Juan Bautista Cuauhtinchan after the restoration in 1986

Retablo mayor de San Juan Bautista Cuauhtinchan, Puebla después de la restauración de 1986

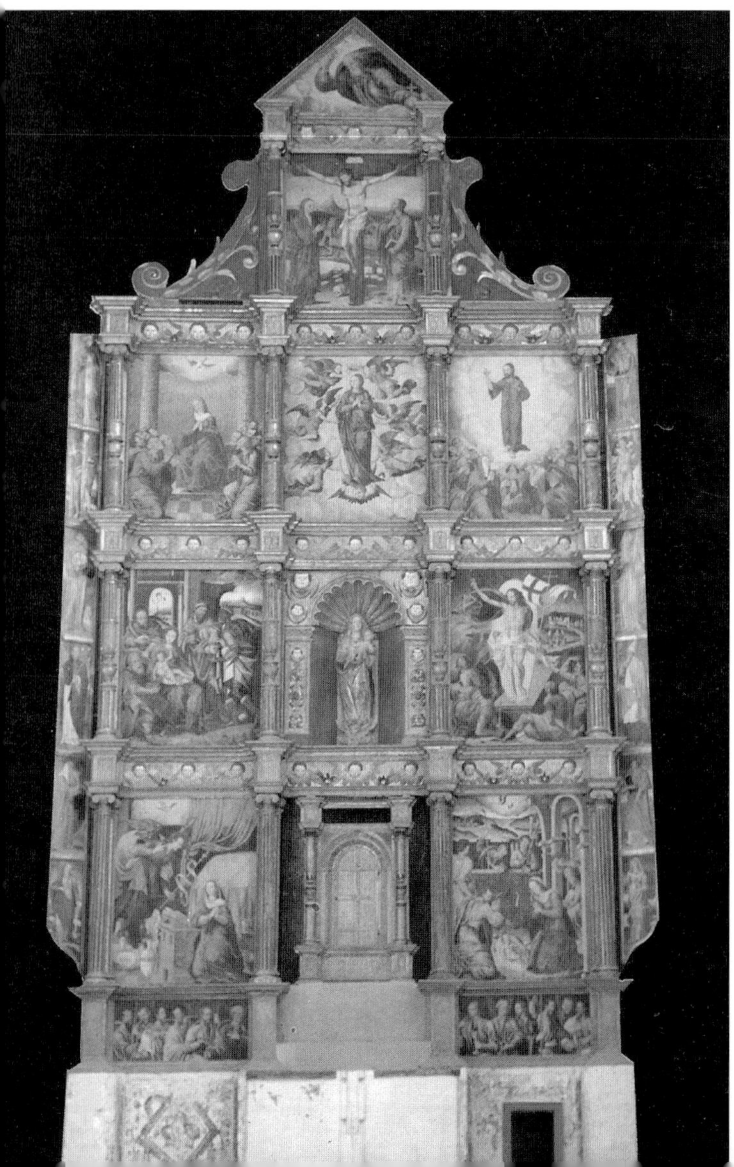

Structural cracks caused by changing humidity

Grietas en estructura por cambios de humedad

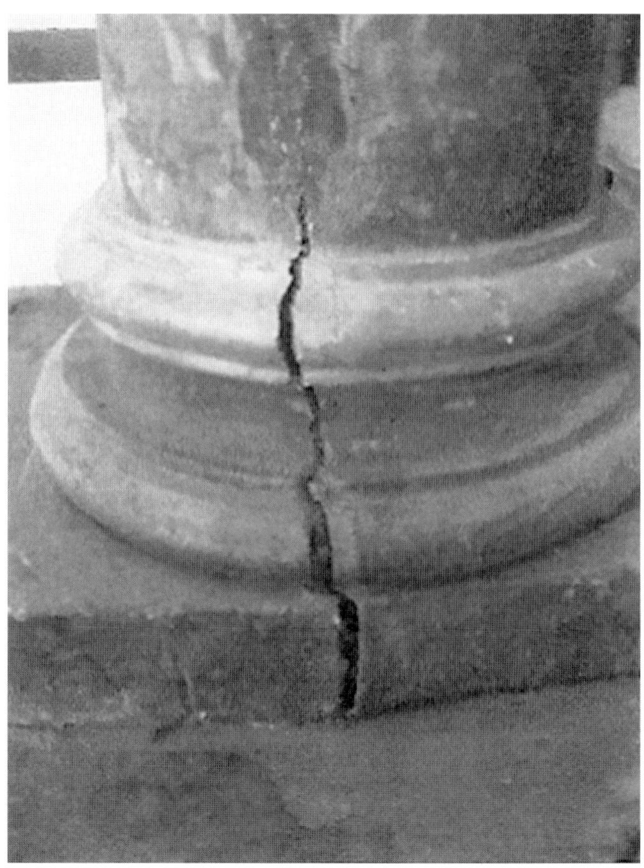

MEXICO
San Juan Cuauhtinchan, Puebla

Cuauhtinchan Pre Hispánico

"La cultura de Cuauhtinchán precede en milenios a la Tolteca y Azteca. Se remonta a la época formativa, en que pequeños grupos de recolectores y agricultores incipientes se establecen en el sitio para formar pequeñas aldeas, hacia 1200 AC, y aún antes los Olmecas se dispersaron de la costa del Golfo hacia Puebla, Morelos y la Cuenca de México entre 1500 y 1200 AC. Las noticias históricas más lejanas referentes a Cuauhtinchán proceden en su mayoría de la *Historia Tolteca Chichimeca* de los anales de Cuauhtinchan y finalmente de los *Mapas de Cuauhtinchán*, documentos que conservan la tradición cultural de esta zona y que fueron escritos y pintados por los *tlacuilos*.[1]"

Cuauhtinchan Colonial

La conquista española se realizó en finales de julio de 1520, incluso antes de Tenochtitlan. La conversión religiosa de la población se llevó a cabo entre 1527 y 1528. Se construyeron diversas edificaciones para albergar a los Franciscanos hasta que en 1554 se inició la construcción de la actual Iglesia parte del conjunto compuesto por un atrio, el templo, el convento, el portal de peregrinos, la huerta y el camposanto.

El templo se compone de una sola nave dividida en cinco tramos de un ábside de planta semicircular que aloja al altar mayor.

Retablo Testero del Altar Mayor en el Templo de San Juan Bautista de Cuauhtinchan: Patrimonio en Peligro

"En América Latina existen tres retablos de testero, completos y datables del siglo XVI: Huejotzingo, San Bernardino de Xochimilco y San Juan de Cuauhtinchan, Puebla[2]". Probablemente el de Cuauhtinchan es el más antiguo retablo de testero de América que conserva todos sus elementos integrantes. Se desconoce quien fue el autor del retablo aunque "en 1597 Juan de Arrúe celebró un contrato para colocar, remozado y con un sagrario nuevo, el retablo que estuvo en San Francisco de Puebla...[3]". El autor "imprime en grado sumo el arte italianizante de la época, sin embargo, no por ello deja de lado el fuerte acento flamenco que caracteriza a mucha de la pintura española de esa época[4]".

"... es preciso señalar que el retablo de Cuauhtinchan es el más antiguo que aún se conserva en México. ... es un gran tríptico, lo cual le confiere un aspecto más arcaizante. Constituido por tres cuerpos y tres hileras, su aspecto es muy sobrio, a pesar de los grandes rizos del remate. Su arquitectura ofrece una composición reticular a base de columnas jónicas estriadas las del primer cuerpo, abalaustradas las del resto del conjunto, y entablamentos decorados con simpáticos querubines.[5]"

Según los dictámenes realizados para determinar el estado de conservación del retablo principal del templo de San Juan Bautista Cuauhtinchan, correspondiente al siglo XVI y perteneciente al conjunto conventual de la localidad en el estado de Puebla, las principales amenazas al retablo son:

Cambios de humedad

En la estructura:
- se han observado elementos de la estructura que están fuera de lugar y que no permite que las pinturas estén fijas en el lugar que les corresponde, con separaciones hasta de 3 ó 4 cms de su marco;
- uniones entre elementos, separadas con la acumulación de polvo lo cual atrae la humedad provocando movimientos en la madera, así como la proliferación de micro organismos;
- faltantes de molduras y capa pictórica;
- grietas en la madera y capa pictórica;
- fisuras de la base de preparación y capa pictórica;
- grietas, caballetes, craqueladuras y escamas en la capa pictórica;
- resanes de la intervención de 1986 con poca consistencia;
- columna del lado izquierdo de la Crucifixión separada del extremo superior y amarrada con cable de plástico al cuerpo del retablo;
- Los cambios en la humedad causan el encogimiento severo de los paneles pintados y de las fibras animales que cubren los paneles que al disminuir su tamaño resultan insuficientes para las dimensiones de la capa pictórica y base de preparación, materiales que no son tan drásticamente afectados como la madera y las fibras;
- velados en todas las tablas que se colocaron como medida de emergencia en el 2000 y que han perdido su efecto ya que se han roto junto con la capa pictórica;
- faltantes o pérdidas de base de preparación y capa pictórica;
- abombamiento u oquedades, consistentes en la separación de la base de preparación al soporte en áreas relativamente grandes, formándose bolsas de aire de hasta 40 cms. Esta amenaza no es perceptible a simple vista por lo que en las fotografías no se puede apreciar;
- fisuras de la base de preparación y la capa pictórica;
- grietas, caballetes y escamas en la capa pictórica.

Suciedad

En la estructura y pinturas:
- Acumulación de polvo y excrementos de aves.

Presencia de xilófagos

- En la restauración de 1986 se fumigó el retablo lo cual ha ayudado su conservación. En la actualidad se detectó un incipiente ataque en las tablas del primer cuerpo.

ICOMOS Mexico

[1] *"San Juan Bautista Cuauhtinchán. Restauración 1987"*. Jorge Olvera. Secretaría de Desarrollo Urbano y Ecología, 1988.
[2] *"Obras de Restauración al Convento de San Juan Cuauhtinchan"* Secretaría de Desarrollo Urbano y Ecología. Abril 25, 1987
[3] Tovar de Teresa, Guillermo *"Los Retablos de Cuauhtinchán"*, Ediciones Luis Lagarto. México, 1988
[4] Ídem.
[5] Ídem.

MEXICO
Vernacular Mexican Architecture in Danger

Mexican vernacular architecture is among one of the types of built cultural heritage in danger and its destruction is accelerating the most. Vernacular buildings are found either scattered in the countryside, beside villages that had a rural character only a few decades ago, or else are forming groups of houses in some historic cities.

Today unlike twenty years ago, these buildings represent very poor value both to owners and local authorities. They are often destroyed or severely altered for several reasons. One reason lies in the federal government's indifference and ignorance, especially that of the department responsible for national heritage. Users and builders of vernacular architecture have a mistaken notion of progress and modernity that considerably influences the loss of this cultural architectural heritage throughout the country. On the other hand, the excessive introduction of industrial building materials, such as cement blocks, zinc and asbestos sheets or asphalt cardboard, has contributed to the radical alteration of areas. Because people feel they are climbing the socio-economic scale, they use these materials as a substitute to traditional elements in their houses.

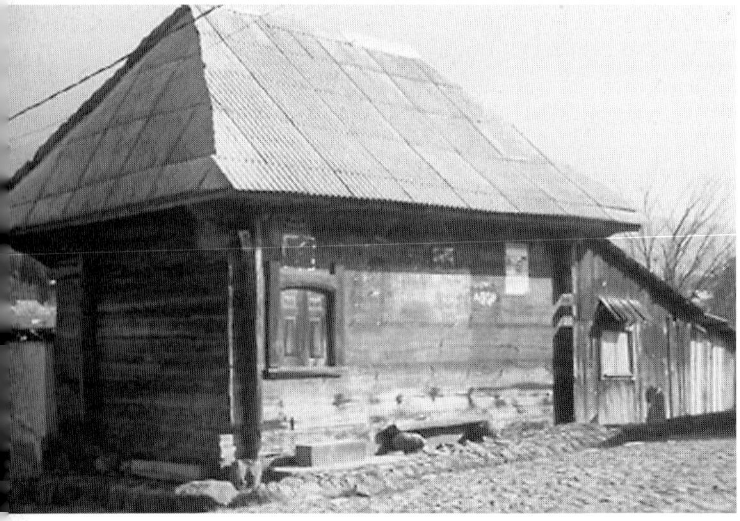

Wooden construction in Angahuan (Michoacan)

Destruction of adobe buildings in Hueyapan (Morelos)

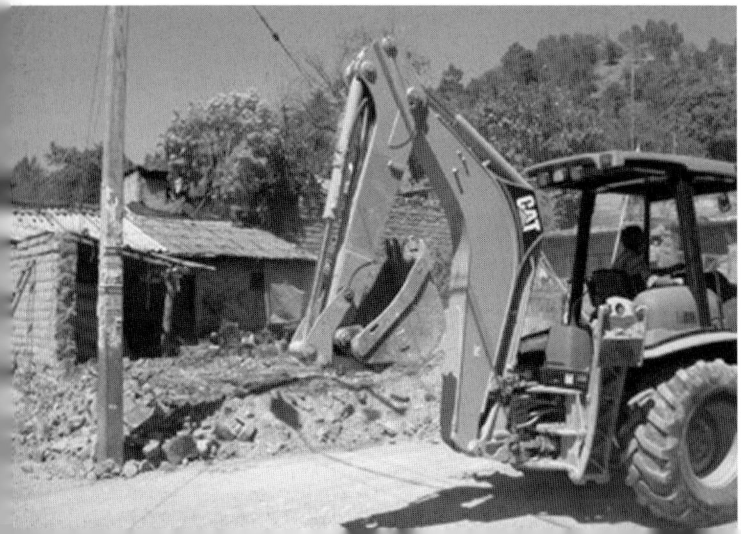

One way to support the preservation of the existing most representative examples is to denounce what is happening. This must be at the highest international level relevant to threatened built heritage until Mexican authorities understand that they should undertake educational campaigns to promote such values both in the local as well as the academic and government spheres.

With this aim in mind, two case studies follow:

Angahuan, Michoacan

Angahuan is located on the foothills of Paricutin Volcano, on the Purepecha Plateau in the state of Michoacan. It is a group of villages founded by Vasco de Quiroga, a Spanish priest who in the 16th century became known for his defence of the Indians and for teaching them several arts and crafts, that until now remain a precious heritage for the entire state of Michoacan. Quiroga was inspired by the *Utopia* of Thomas More based on establishing 'hospital-villages' called *huataperas* in *Purepecha* language.

Local people, who call themselves *purepechas* and who have an indigenous origin, kept their building tradition until several years ago. Their houses are built completely in wood, once abundant in the surroundings, although nowadays it is a scarce resource. Wood construction in Michoacan is one of the techniques that goes back several years as a craft taught to the Indians by Vasco de Quiroga. It consists of wooden joints without any nails, the buildings being based on a plank and beam system. The roof is covered with tiles and pronounced, strongly sloping eaves, with an attic built into it and used as grain storage as well as helping to insulate the house against the winter cold and the rainy season. This type of traditional house is known as *troje,* meaning grain storage.

Recently, traditional *trojes* have been destroyed in Angahuan. The demolition has several causes, among which the increasing number of visitors attracted to Angahuan's great sixteenth-century temple has had a considerable economic impact because of the impossibility of planned and ordered development. *Trojes* are being replaced by buildings that not only force an improvement in the inhabitants' quality of life but also devastate the landscape and the harmony present in the natural surroundings of the village because of the new buildings' incongruous and exceedingly inferior quality.

Currently, Mexico ICOMOS, headed by their Scientific Committee of Vernacular Architecture, Michoacan ICOMOS and the Universidad Michoacana de San Nicolás de Hidalgo, are uniting their efforts to rescue two or three areas on the Purepecha Plateau, hoping that these first experiences are taken as examples in the future for sites such as Angahuan that need rescuing.

Hueyapan, Morelos

Similar situations are occurring throughout the country. The small town of Hueyapan, on the foothills of the Popocatepetl Volcano, is

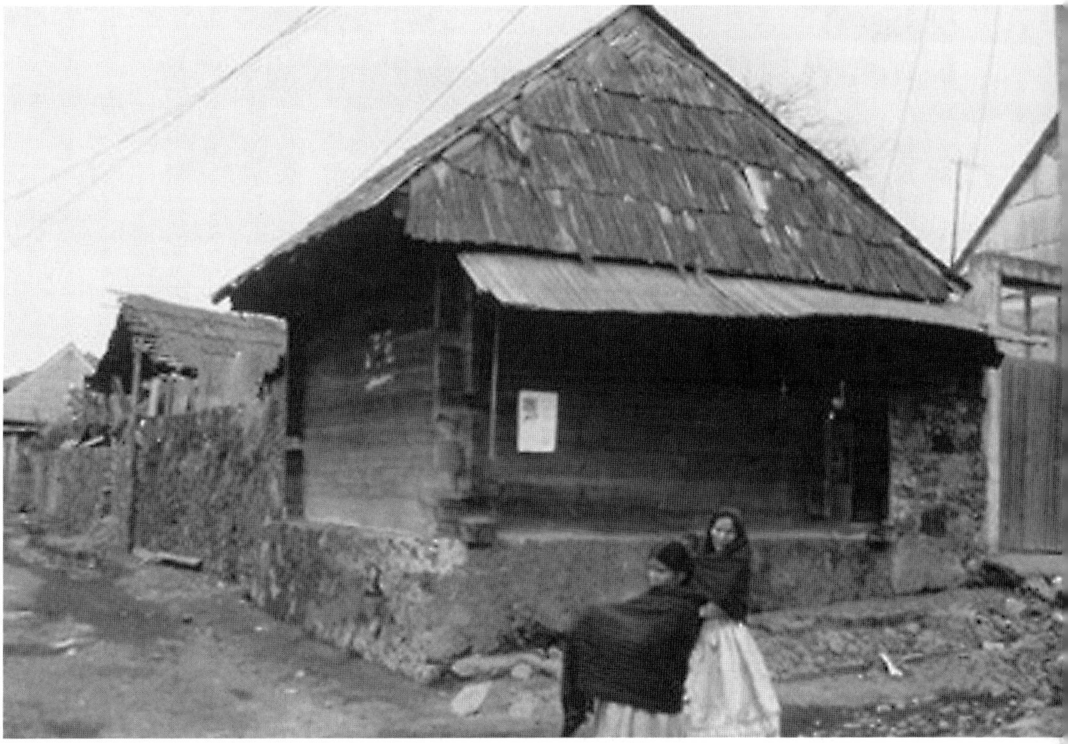

Houses in Angahuan (Michoacan)

mentioned as it represents an extraordinary example of two and three storey adobe buildings in Mexico. These are tiled-roof houses that include a grain storage attic as does the *troje*. They are well adapted to the uneven terrain of the area. Built from a very good quality of clay naturally improved with volcanic ash, as well as using the expertise of local craftsmen, these houses have lasted in fairly good condition for about a hundred years. In vernacular architecture they represent a good response to the need for shelter against winter cold and the long rainy season.

As in the above case of the *troje*, the reasons relating to the destruction of this built heritage have a cultural background. They are also a result of the impact of the influence of the cement industry, poor housing programs and an absence of policy on preserving and improving the traditional vernacular houses of rural communities.

In fact, only 30% of the houses that existed ten years ago survive. They are quickly being replaced. Yet while local people accept that their adobe houses are much more comfortable to insulate against extreme temperatures, they claim: "But we need to feel modern".

A program carried out by a professor of the Faculty of Architecture at the National Independent University of Mexico focuses on offering the community the possibility of having modern, comfortable, clean and inexpensive houses built in adobe. This is a genuine challenge with strong forces against it, but it is certainly an effort worth making on behalf of this significant adobe heritage and of this local community.

Valeria Prieto
Scientific Committee of Vernacular Architecture
ICOMOS Mexico

Adobe buildings in Hueyapan (Morelos)

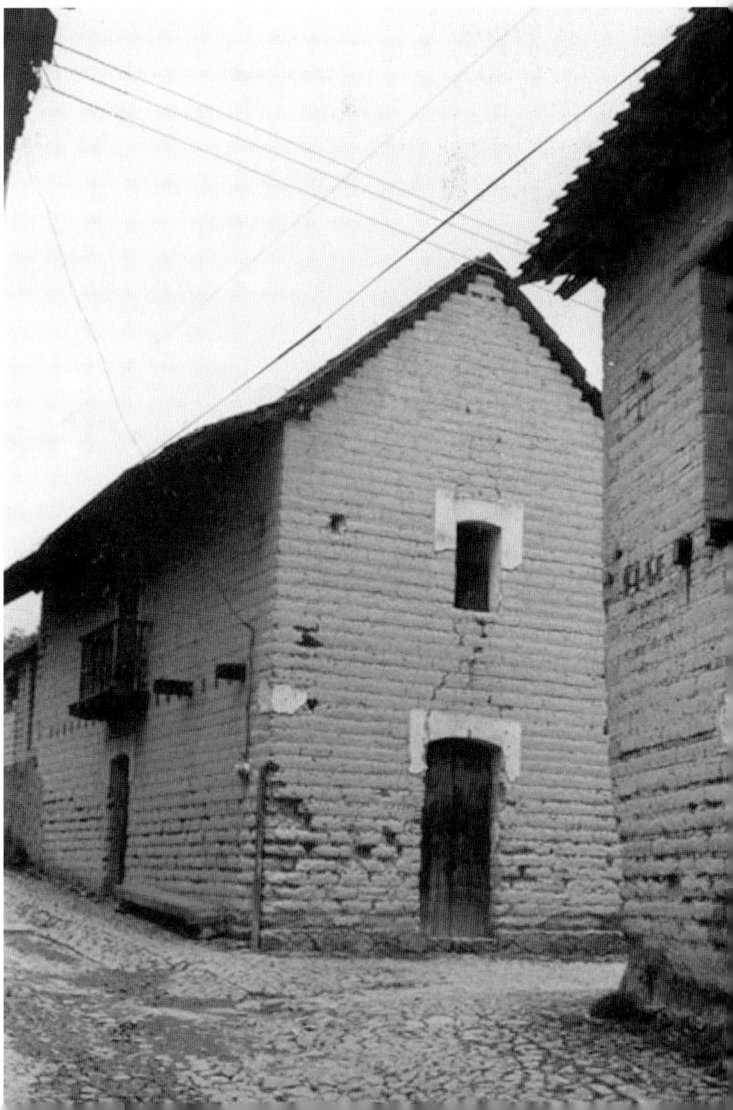

MOROCCO
Fort of Villa Cisneros (fort de Dakhla)

In July 2004 Moroccan authorities began demolishing parts of the Fort of Villa Cisneros (fort de Dakhla). This fortification, erected by the Spaniards, goes back to the 1880s and is an important witness of the historical evolution of the Western Sahara. ICOMOS' attention was drawn to the ongoing demolition by the *Grupo de cultura saharani 'Suerte Mulana'*.

In the meantime ICOMOS Morocco has informed us that the Moroccan Ministry of Culture has a great interest in this building and is planning to initiate the process of listing the fort as a historic monument. The Director of Cultural Heritage stated that: "Steps are currently being taken to restore the fort and to convert it into a 'maison de culture'".

After the printing deadline we received news that „the authorities started the last phase of the Fort destruction on 13 December 2004" – unfortunately, this could not be verified anymore. We can only hope that this important historic building will be saved after all.

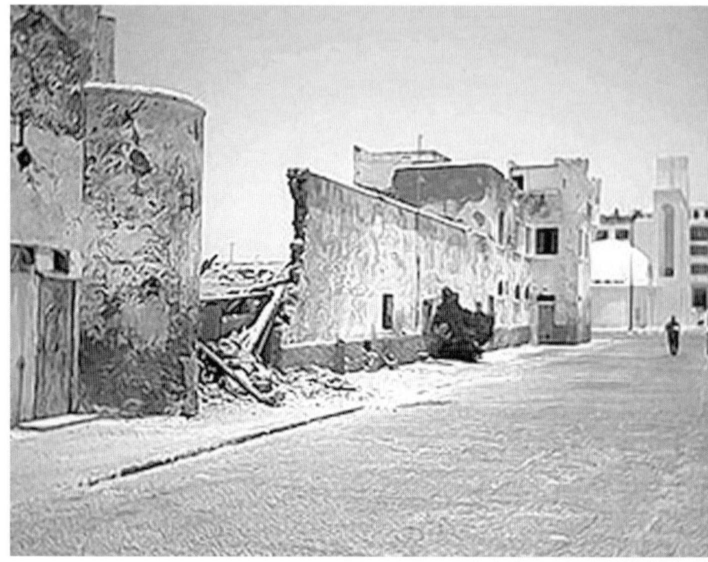

Demolition of a wall of the fort

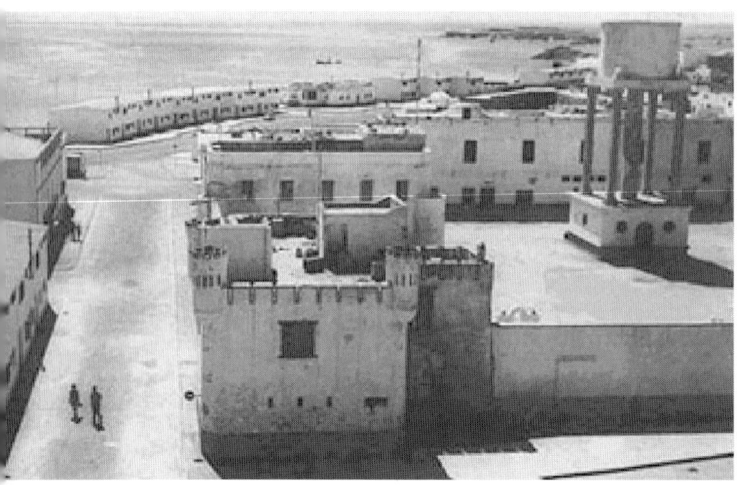

Aerial view of the fort

Historic view of the fort from 1916

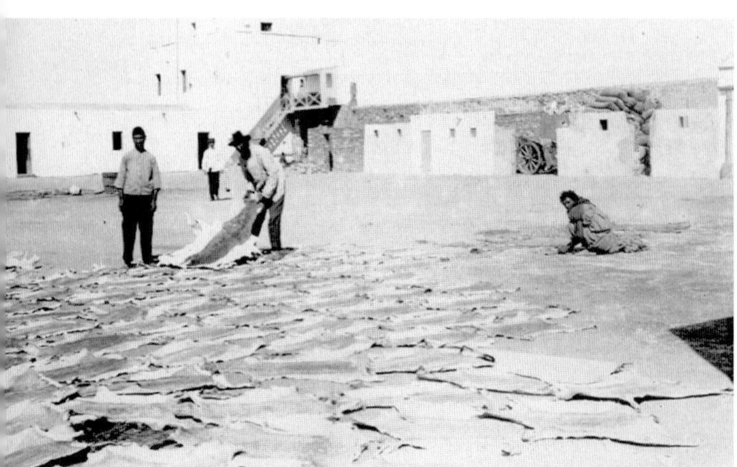

Historic view of the fort from 1916

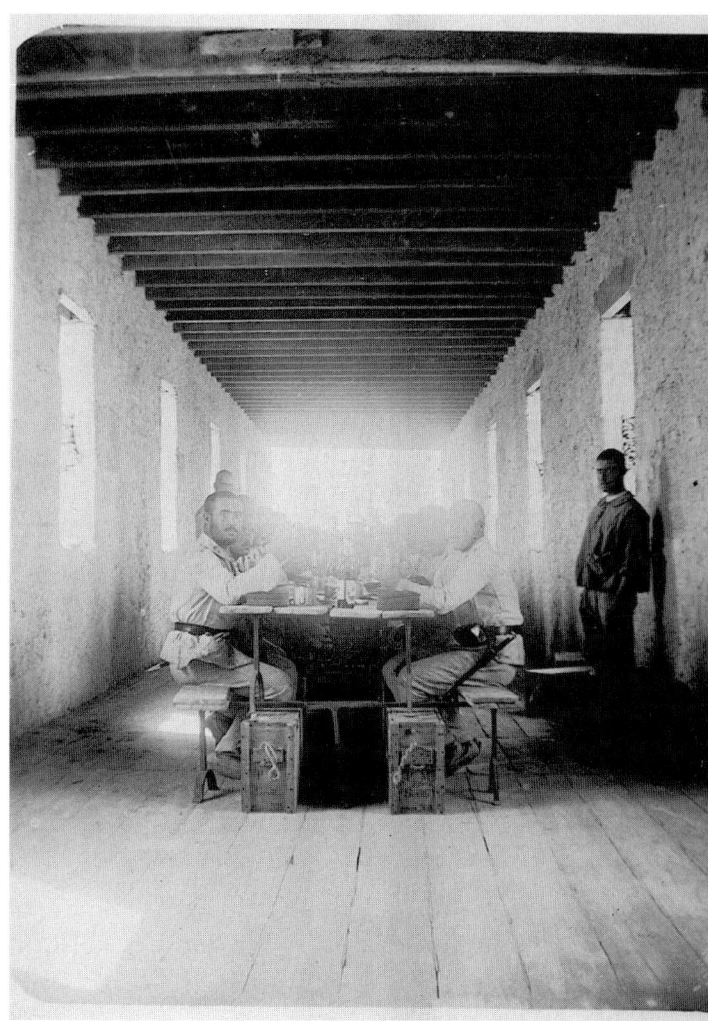

THE NETHERLANDS
Historic farmhouses at risk

Historic farmhouses play a significant role in our cultural heritage, particularly in an open and flat landscape like that of The Netherlands. However, these cultural landscapes are an aspect of our heritage which is now at risk. Alarming figures highlight this problem: of the approximately 200,000 farmhouses that existed in the Netherlands in 1940, over 50% have been demolished. Consecutive inventories of historically interesting farmhouses in 1988 and 2000 indicate that 18% of these disappeared in just twelve years. Every day eleven farmers close down their businesses.

Year of the Historic Farmhouse

In order to raise awareness, The Netherlands celebrated in 2003 the 'Year of the Historic Farmhouse' (*Jaar van de Boerderij*). A special project agency, The Year of the Historic Farmhouse Foundation, was set up by representatives from cultural heritage organisations, farmers' associations and organisations for the preservation of farmhouses. This foundation received financial support and encouragement from three government departments, the regional governments, cultural funds and sponsors.

Already five years in advance, the Foundation started its work in order to involve and to inform relevant parties such as the national and regional governments, local authorities, public servants, architects, private organisations, and so on. In that period the Foundation has organised a wide range of activities like courses, workshops, expert meetings, publications and publicity.

Publications

The Foundation took the initiative in three publications which were important to illustrate various aspects of the preservation of historic farmhouses.

The first report was published in 2001. It was an inventory by SHBO (Dutch Institute for Historic Farm Research) of the number of existing farmhouses, how old they are, whether listed or not, their agricultural use or other functions, their condition and deterioration etc.

The second report (2002) was an inventory of governmental policies, laws and regulations, problem areas and recommendations for the improvement of policy. Quite often, the policies and regulations of the various authorities are in contradistinction and do not always serve historic farmhouse preservation.

The third publication was an illustrated book for owners of historic farms with best practice on how to alter their buildings for new functions in respect towards heritage values. It is important to find new uses for the farmhouses that lose their original agricultural one. At this time it is a critical moment in the life of the farmhouse. Architectural solutions to serve re-use can destroy the values and appearance of the historic farmhouse in a severe and decisive way.

In addition to these publications 150 others were published in the framework of the year, varying from scientific studies to walking or cycling itineraries.

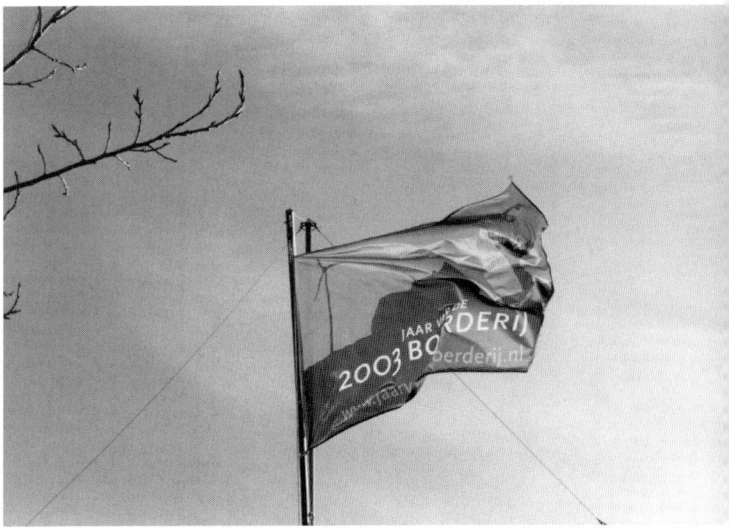

The flag of the theme-year

Public events

In the year 2003 itself, a large number of events attracted general public participation. In total about 600 activities and events were organised by the Foundation and various other parties:

- In all twelve provinces of The Netherlands there were committees with their own programs focussed on their region's typical agricultural heritage;
- During twelve weekends from May to July, the Foundation offered activities all over the country which took place at historic farmsteads. The themes of these weekends included architecture, literature, music, visual arts, film, regional cooking and youth;
- A number of yearly events like the Dutch Heritage Days and the Week of the Countryside incorporated the topic of the threat to historic farmhouses in their program;
- As well as this there were also many exhibitions, conferences and workshops, and there was a competition to choose a 'Farm of the Year'.

International scientific conference

In co-operation with the ICOMOS International Scientific Committee on Vernacular Architecture (CIAV), a conference was held from 21 to 25 October 2003 in the city of Amersfoort. There were interesting lectures from various parts of the world, workshops and excursions. The results of the conference were presented at the closing conference of the Year.

Evaluation

The Year of the Historic Farmhouse aimed to increase interest in the historic farm in the Netherlands. This must lead to:

- An increased knowledge of the historic farm in its regional differentiation and its context within history, agriculture, architecture and the landscape;
- A greater involvement of owners and others who might contribute to a better preservation of historic farms;
- A wider public support base for the conservation of historic farms.

The results of the year are especially encouraging. The public and governments are now certainly more aware of the historic farm. There was an impressive interest by the media during the year, about 1,500 articles being published in newspapers and periodicals.

It is hoped that fewer historic farms will be destroyed out of ignorance or by a lag in information or effective policies. A number of private organisations working in the cultural heritage field are encouraged to continue their work. However, given the developments in agriculture, the historic farm is still at risk!

Emil van Brederode
secretary of the Year of the Historic Farmhouse Foundation
secretary of ICOMOS Netherlands
The Netherlands ICOMOS

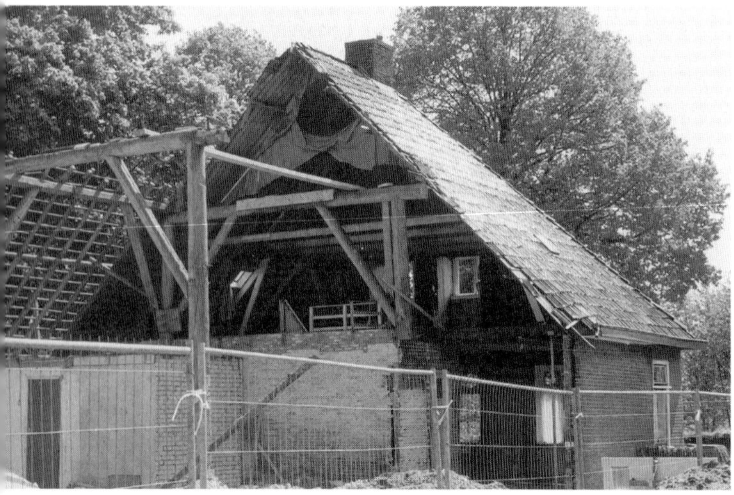

A farm in reconstruction, showing the traditional structure. Will the result of this building activity meet the standards of the Venice Charter?

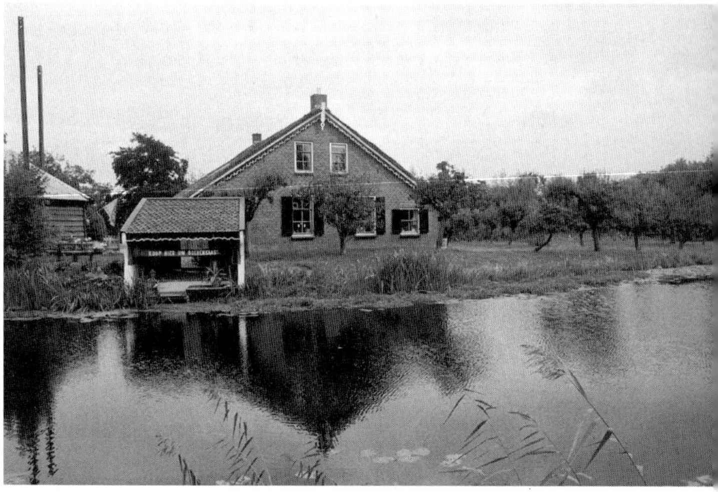

A traditional Dutch farm in its natural environment

NEW ZEALAND

Introduction

This 2004 report continues to highlight significant New Zealand heritage at risk and supplements previous reports from ICOMOS New Zealand / Te Mana O Nga Pouwhenua O Te Ao. It discusses heritage protection mechanisms in New Zealand and recent legislative changes which have included heritage as a matter of national importance.

Statutory protection of Heritage in New Zealand

The Resource Management Amendment Act 2003 (RMA), Historic Places Act 1993 (HPA) and the Conservation Act 1987 are the three main legislative tools that govern the management and protection of historic heritage within New Zealand.

The New Zealand Historic Places Trust / Pouhere Taonga (NZHPT) is a charitable trust established by an Act of Parliament in 1954. It administers the HPA and its mission is to promote the identification, protection, preservation and conservation of the historical and cultural heritage of New Zealand. The Trust also manages over 60 historic places as museums open to the public. The NZHPT is one of several statutory bodies in the cultural sector funded by the Government. This funding is administered by the Ministry of Arts and Culture.

Identifying significant heritage

The NZHPT maintains a register of over 6,000 historic places, historic areas, *wahi tapu*, and *wahi tapu* areas. *Historic Places* in the Register include archaeological sites, buildings, trees, cemeteries, gardens, shipwrecks, landscapes and many other types of places. *Historic Areas* are groups of related historic places such as precincts of buildings and sites. Emphasis is on the significance of the group. *Wahi Tapu* are defined as places sacred to Maori (the indigenous people of New Zealand). *Wahi Tapu Areas* are groups of *wahi tapu.*

Historic places are considered to have significance because they possess aesthetic, archaeological, architectural, cultural, historical, scientific, social, spiritual, technological or traditional significance or value. *Category I* status is given to registered places of 'special or outstanding historical or cultural heritage significance or value'. *Category 2* status is given to places of 'historical or cultural heritage significance or value'.

Legal Protection of Archaeological Sites

The Historic Places Act 1993 regulates activity that would modify archaeological sites in New Zealand. The Act makes it unlawful for any person to destroy, damage or modify the whole or any part of an archaeological site without the prior authority of the New Zealand Historic Places Trust. This is the case regardless of whether the land on which the site is located is designated, or the activity is permitted under the District or Regional Plan or a resource or building consent has been granted. The Act also provides for substantial penalties for unauthorised destruction, damage or modification. Archaeological sites are defined as places associated with pre-1900 human activity, where there may be evidence relating to the history of New Zealand.

Indigenous heritage

Indigenous heritage, the heritage of Maori and Moriori people, is recognised in the ICOMOS New Zealand Charter for the Conservation of Places of Cultural Heritage Significance (The New Zealand Charter) as a special case where decision-making should rest with the indigenous people at the tribal (*iwi*), sub-tribal (*hapu*) and family (*whanau*) level. Because of the particular associations of such heritage with ancestral figures, ranking systems, such as are used in the NZHPT Register and in district plan schedules, are not considered to be appropriate mechanisms to be applied to Maori and Moriori heritage places.

Conservation Lands

The Department of Conservation (DoC) is the central government organisation that has responsibility for the conservation of natural and historic heritage, principally on Crown conservation lands managed by the Department, for the benefit of present and future generations of New Zealanders. The Department works to restore, maintain, protect and interpret sites of historic and cultural importance on public conservation land. Nearly 8 million hectares, some 30% of New Zealand's total area, are managed by the Department.

Other organisations maintain lists or registers of significant heritage

Of particular importance is the New Zealand Archaeological Association (NZAA) Site Recording Scheme which is the national system for recording information on archaeological sites. This contains over 55,000 records.

The Institute of Professional Engineers of New Zealand (IPENZ) identifies and registers sites, projects and structures with characteristics that make them worthy of notice as important features of the nation's engineering heritage.

A number of local councils maintain heritage inventories. One example is the Auckland Regional Council's Cultural Heritage Inventory (CHI). This is a GIS-linked database containing 8,000 recorded archaeological sites, 1,000 sites with historic maritime associations within the coastal environment, 2,100 historic buildings and structures of significance to the local and regional community, and over 600 botanical heritage sites (trees and other plantings).

Heritage at the local level

City, District and Regional councils have a significant responsibility for the protection and management of historic heritage under the Resource Management Act 2003, through the formulation of district plans and by managing the process of granting resource consents. Councils are also responsible for managing the effects on heritage that arise out of the planning and resource consent process. District Plans, reviewed every 10 years, contain Schedules of Heritage Places of value to the community, which are protected through district plan rules.

The performance of local authorities in heritage protection varies widely throughout the country. These differences may come more into focus over the next year following changes made to the Resource Management Act, which raised cultural heritage to the same level of national importance as natural heritage.

Heritage orders and heritage protection authorities

A Heritage Order is a provision in a district plan to protect the heritage characteristics of a particular place. A Heritage Protection Authority is able to give notice to a local council of a requirement for a heritage order to protect the special heritage characteristics of a place or structure of special cultural, architectural, historical, scientific, ecological, or other interest, as well as its surrounding land. All Ministers of the Crown, local authorities, and the Historic Places Trust are automatically a heritage protection authority under the Resource Management Act 2003, and a number of other bodies are eligible to apply to the Minister for the Environment to become a heritage protection authority. Where a heritage order is included in a district plan, no one without the prior consent of the heritage protection authority can do anything that would compromise the effect of the heritage order.

Guiding documents for heritage conservation

The ICOMOS New Zealand Charter for the Conservation of Places of Cultural Heritage Significance (The New Zealand Charter) is increasingly becoming recognised as the standard document that guides conservation practice in New Zealand. ICOMOS New Zealand is now reviewing the Charter, which first came into use in 1993.

Conservation planning is also a widely accepted practice in New Zealand with some councils including requirements for the preparation of conservation plans as condition for the granting of resource consents for the adaptation of places of high heritage significance. This process is guided by both *The Conservation Plan* by Australian James Semple Kerr (1992), and the NZHPT's *Guidelines for Preparing Conservation Plans* (2000).

Other protection mechanisms

The *Reserves Act* 1977, the *Building Act* 1991, and the *Antiquities Act* 1975 are also relevant to the protection and management of historic heritage. The *Antiquities Act*, which is administered by the Ministry for Culture and Heritage, provides for the protection of antiquities. The Act controls the sale and disposal of artefacts, and provides for the ownership of Maori artefacts to be established and recorded. The *Reserves Act* contains provisions which allow for the establishment and management of Historic Reserves, which are typically managed by the Department of Conservation, the New Zealand Historic Places Trust, local government and in some cases community groups, City, District and Regional Councils.

New Zealand Heritage at Risk

ICOMOS New Zealand's past contributions to *Heritage at Risk* have focussed on specific places of risk, including the Auckland volcanic landscape and the Cook Landing Site National Historic Reserve. We have also listed types of heritage or themes at risk, including:

- New Zealand's archaeological heritage and associated cultural landscapes impacted by urbanisation and subdivision in the northern North Island;
- New Zealand's earliest colonial heritage and associated cultural landscapes threatened by encroaching incompatible development;
- New Zealand's modern (post-1940s) buildings;
- maritime heritage;
- historic heritage in conflict with natural heritage values;
- 'humble' heritage. (see *Heritage at Risk* 2000).

These places and issues still largely remain at risk. The only significant legislative change that gives hope for increased security and recognition of heritage has been an amendment to the *Resource Management* Act in 2003 that adds to Section 6 - Matters of National Importance - 'the protection of historic heritage from inappropriate subdivision, use and development'. This brings with it an expectation from heritage professionals that the amendment will see increased activity on the part of Regional and District councils in assessing, reviewing and identifying historic heritage in their areas and making better provision for its protection in planning documents. Whether or not this proves to be the case will be a matter for future reports. Members of the New Zealand heritage sector note the following places and themes at risk in New Zealand:

Archaeological sites under threat from rural farming

Sites representative of New Zealand's first Polynesian and European settlers.

Threats

Farming is a major part of New Zealand's economy: internal resources and external exports rely heavily on the farming industry. In addition, New Zealand has a strong ethos of private property rights, and many landowners resist the perception that their land and everything on it is not theirs to do with what they will. There is a common misconception in the farming industry that the presence of archaeological sites will prevent the economic use or development of the land.

Possible Solutions

Educating landowners as to the nature and implications of the archaeological resource, and especially of its value and significance. Co-ordinating better with local government management systems and rules in district plans.

Coastal archaeological sites susceptible to sea erosion

A high percentage of pre-European sites are located along the coast. They are significant not only because they relate to New Zealand's first people but also because so many of them are sensitive to development.

Threats

These include a rising sea level, apparent increasing storminess, and the destabilisation of dunes by recreational vehicles.

Possible Solutions

Surveying to assess damage and set priorities, either for remedial action or, failing that, urgent excavation (preservation by record). Participation of all key stakeholders is required (Maori tribal groups, New Zealand Historic Places Trust, territorial and regional authorities, Department of Conservation).

New Zealand's railway heritage

The industrial and cultural heritage including structures, archaeological sites, cultural landscapes (urban and rural) and railway settlements, sites and wider communities such as Frankton Junction, Raurimu and Taihape.

Over the last 15 years, since the restructuring of New Zealand's national railway system, all 19th and 20th century railway properties have been sold into private ownership and there are now very few railway workers. This is leading to the loss of railway communities, their social structures and buildings. Of the ten 20th century planned settlements based on garden suburb ideals, two have been lost (Newmarket and Taihape) while the remaining settlements are under the increasing threat of urbanism, subdivision and infill housing (in both urban and rural areas), and building removal (in rural areas). Substantial removal of rural railway houses has taken place. The New Zealand railway 'row' settlement of the 1920s is also under increased threat as people seek houses for relocation, and because the railway settlement has yet to be recognised officially as heritage.

Threatened along with the housing communities are the railway lines, the stations and associated buildings, both urban and rural, and associated buildings such as shops and halls. Many lines have been removed and a number of stations closed, sold off and/or removed including buildings built up to the 1950s. Modernisation of the Auckland rail network currently underway has brought with it increased expectations (by the planners at least) of modern facilities with the result that little emphasis is being placed on the incorporation of the older timber-built stations as network facilities for rail passengers.

Threats

These include urbanism, house removal, vandalism, removal of 'redundant' stations from their railside context.

Possible solutions

Strengthening education on the historical context of railway in the development of New Zealand at school and community levels. Undertaking national heritage survey of railway places and the degree of risk and solutions identified. Detailed recording of places where removal or demolition cannot be prevented.

Historic Towns

New Zealand's historic settlements have developed in different ways. Prior to the major phase of European settlement, Kororareka (now Russell), grew in the early 1800s as a provisioning port for European and American whaling ships. Some were established under planned settlement schemes such as those founded by the Bohemians at Puhoi, the French in Akaroa, the Albertlanders on Northland's Kaipara Harbour or the English Wakefield settlement of Canterbury. Other towns were established in response to such factors as the availability of land for pastoralism, and opportunities for commerce and tourism, or grew with the development of transport and communication. Some have been eclipsed by such events as natural disasters (as at Te Wairoa), or by the decline in the railways industry (as at Taihape) or timber milling (as at Dargaville and Kohukohu).

Historic towns are distinctive in their expression of the diversity of those who created them. Their continued attraction rests in such things as their distinctive street patterns, the relationship of the urban area to its landscape setting, and such elements as materials, scale, size, construction and colour of its buildings.

Threats

These include:

- 'Mainstreeting', the introduction of reconstructed and often historically absent features such as extensive paving, bollards, imported English cast iron lamp posts and other street furniture in downtown areas, in an attempt to promote economic revival in declining towns.
- Lack of consultation with the residents on the qualities that make towns distinctive.
- 'Heritage as a designer style', such as the recent boulevarding, in a quasi Franglais style, of the predominantly English part of the historic town of Akaroa on Banks Peninsula, in order to meet the perceived needs of local tourism.
- Lack of conservation planning preceding urban design exercises aimed at enhancing townscapes.

Possible solutions

- Preparation of regional inventories of historic towns at risk, followed by education programs to inform district councils of their significance.
- Evaluation of the cultural heritage significance of historic towns and development of conservation plans prior to extensive maintenance, urban design or economic recovery-led enhancement proposals.
- Full consultation with residents and other interest groups who value the place and have a comprehensive understanding of what gives the place its distinctive character.

Public and Commercial interiors of the early 20th century

- A significant record of the built environment, of 'going to town' when New Zealand was still predominantly rural, and other social and commercial activity.
- A record of interior design by both private people/architects and government architects.
- Increased rarity value due to extensiveness of loss of original interiors.
- The loss of the use of many significant buildings such as Post Offices and large department stores in the last ten years from restructuring has led to many interiors being stripped of decorative and sometimes structural materials. In some major towns such as Hamilton, only one or two interiors from pre-1950s remain intact - none have protection at regional or local level.

Threats

Redevelopment, façadism, café development, 'adaptive re-use' that promotes external appearance over internal integrity, unwillingness of authorities to intervene in spaces perceived as 'private'.

Possible solutions

Protecting at regional and local government level through District Schemes/rules. Educating on early 20th century heritage and the value of interiors. Providing more for the interpretative recording of existing interiors to promote greater understanding and education about their significance.

Loss of domestic heritage in growing urban/city centres

These places are significant in telling the story of the growth of towns/cities. They reflect earlier patterns of living, including the frequently close historical interconnection between places of dwelling, work and other activities, including recreation and religious worship.

Threats

High developmental pressure as land prices increase.

Possible solutions

Zoning areas of cities/towns as residential and removing the expectation of being able to develop. Protecting the historic heritage by listing as heritage items on district plans.

Historic cemeteries

These are representative of early religious beliefs and social mores. Grave furniture such as headstones reflect aspects like craft traditions and levels of infant mortality, as well as personalise the past. Genealogy is a growing interest. Many cemeteries incorporate evidence of past botanical landscapes.

Threats

These include neglect, lack of funds to conserve, and a general lack of appreciation by New Zealanders of their significance as an historic record and resource. High operating costs are reflected in either lack of essential maintenance by local councils or church trustees, or by conversion to lawn cemeteries with loss of monumental stonework.

Possible solutions

These include the education, adoption by local community groups, and research as to wider significance. Integrating the recording of grave sites, furniture, associated structures and landscape features (including botanical remnants) can raise their profile within the community and improve understanding of their historical importance.

ICOMOS New Zealand / *Te Mana O Nga Pouwhenua O Te Ao*

NORWAY

World Heritage sites

Norway has five sites inscribed on the World Heritage List: Bryggen (1979), Urnes Stave Church (1979), Alta Rock Drawings (1985), Røros (1980) and the Vega Archipelago (2004). Risk-assessments are currently being made, but none of the World Heritage sites are considered Heritage at Risk. Periodic reporting conducted for the sites of Bryggen (2000) and Røros (2003) emphasise the importance of safeguarding the authenticity, integrity and significance of the sites.

The construction of the wharf of Bryggen is threatened by new use and by damage to the built structures caused by passing traffic. This results in vibrations which can result in a shift of deposits and archaeological layers. Measures to mitigate this impact have been taken by moving vehicles out towards the front of the quay area. A management plan prescribes actions for permitted adaptive reuse of the wharf structure.

Røros World Heritage Town is a living historic environment, and the integrity of its historic urban structure is threatened by modern urban development and general town expansion or encroachment. Measures are being taken with building surveys, urban design and planning, and extensive fire protection programs.

For the Alta Rock Art site the need for an appropriate tourism management strategy should be addressed urgently.

For the Urnes Stave Church, the main management challenges are the protection of its authentic wooden structure as well as the issue of fire protection.

Churches

Legislation protects all churches in Norway built before 1850. Many of these suffer from decades of a lack of maintenance. The cost of repair for these churches is calculated to exceed 1 billion Euros. Today, many parishes are experiencing a radical decline in their active congregations. The parish is the owner of the churches, but the county is responsible for the maintenance of the buildings. The National Council of Bishops has recently agreed that it will be acceptable to demolish churches. The lack of funds at the county level, a decreased will for regular upkeep and the approval to demolish churches, come together to constitute a serious threat to churches in Norway. In these circumstances, the Norwegian Church Council (the highest institution within the Norwegian Church) recently concluded that it is not possible to maintain all churches. The Council would like guidelines on how to sell and demolish churches that are no longer in active use.

Fire constitutes the most serious threat to Norwegian churches, sadly assisted by isolated fringe Satanic movements. Considerable efforts are being made to provide churches with fire protection systems. Many of them, however, still lack even an adequate fire warning system.

Cultural landscapes

The cultural landscape in Norway is undergoing rapid change. Two main reasons are the decrease in the number of farms, especially hill or 'mountain' farms, and the diminishing extent of cattle grazing in the higher altitude and rough grazing areas. Today, forests are reaching higher altitudes, low timber prices making harvesting unprofitable. The stone fences, grave mounds, ruins, and meadows [denoting former landuse] are overgrown and increasingly invisible. Farm closures are not only a threat to cultural heritage but also to biological diversity, as 50% of all threatened plants in Norway are to be found on grazing land.

The number of working farms decreased from 155,000 to 71,000 between 1969 and 2000. Thirteen per cent of all houses on agricultural properties were not in use at the beginning of 2000, and about fifty per cent of all residential buildings on agricultural properties were located on farms where the land on which they are situated is not cultivated. The total number of farm buildings where people still live is about 900,000, with more than 210,000 abandoned (certainly not all of them should be protected). The landscape at higher altitudes was traditionally maintained by cattle, but the number of farms in these areas has fallen from 26,437 in 1939 to 2,742 in 1999.

A major threat to cultural landscapes also comes from the expansion of local communities that surround larger towns, for example the communities neighbouring Oslo that are under great pressure to develop housing and industrial areas on agricultural land.

ICOMOS Norway

PALESTINE

Destruction of Mamluk-era houses for settlers' road through Hebron's Old City

August 9, 2004 – After almost two years of legal delays and a court-ordered reduction in the number of historic buildings slated for destruction from 22 to 3, Israeli bulldozers flattened three centuries-old building complexes and damaged five others in Hebron, West Bank.

The area lies between Kiryat Arba settlement where 6,000 Israelis reside on the outskirts of Hebron, and Ibrahimi Mosque. Many families have vacated the area since 1990 due to harassment from settlers and military forces, but 30 families still live on al-Haram street. Israeli Prime Minister Ariel Sharon first proposed in 1996 that a settlers' corridor of 1,000 housing units be built in the historic Arab area to connect sprawling Kiryat Arba with the micro-settlements of militant settlers in the midst of Hebron.

Following a military attack in the area on twelve Israeli soldiers in November 2002, Sharon told army commanders that Israel would "take advantage of the opportunity" to "minimize the number of Palestinians living among the Jewish settlers." A settlement strip, six to twelve meters wide, 730 meters long, and fortified by a two-meter-high concrete wall, was proposed by Israel at the time, for "security." 61 parcels of family-owned land and 22 houses – 3 Mamluk, 13 Ottoman, 4 Mandate era, and 2 modern – were targeted for demolition, but due to the nature of old city construction, the projected collateral damage threatened 150 historic houses. The Hebron Rehabilitation Committee (HRC), which implements an international award-winning restoration program in Hebron's Old City, appealed to the Israeli High Court to stop the order, with the support of residents and Palestinian, international and Israeli experts, including Bimkom, an Israeli planning-rights NGO, which compared the architectural importance of Hebron's Old City to that of Acre, a World Heritage Site.

An initiative in 2000 by HRC to rehabilitate the neglected area had earlier been stopped by Israeli military orders. In their official statement against the 2002 proposed demolitions, the HRC argued for the historical, civilizational value of the Old City: "These historic buildings in the Jaber neighborhood and the adjoining cross-vaulted alley ... comprise an integral part of the architectural fabric of the old town as well as an intrinsic part of the historic surroundings of the Ibrahimi Mosque." The High Court recommended that the army "reconsider" or adjust the order, citing the diplomatic harm to Israel that might ensue, and eventually approved the demolition of three of the buildings. Hebron residents expect more demolitions in future.

This experience demonstrates that international concern should be expressed and can be effective in protecting cultural heritage wherever it is endangered and whatever the pretexts used for its destruction. The Palestine National Committee of ICOMOS urges you to be alert to the ongoing destruction of World Heritage in Palestine that Israel claims is necessary for specious reasons of security.
Contact: icomos@icomos-palestine.org
Website: www.icomos-palestine.org.

ICOMOS Palestine

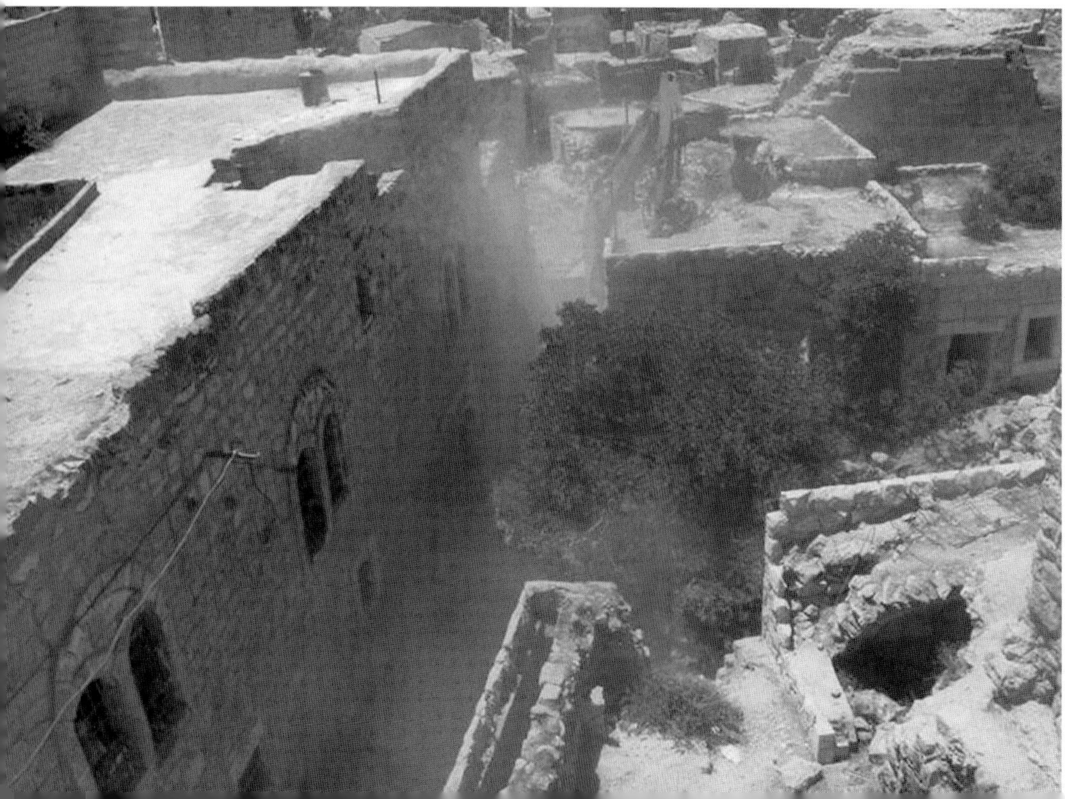

Destruction of Mamluk-era houses for settlers' road through Hebron's Old City

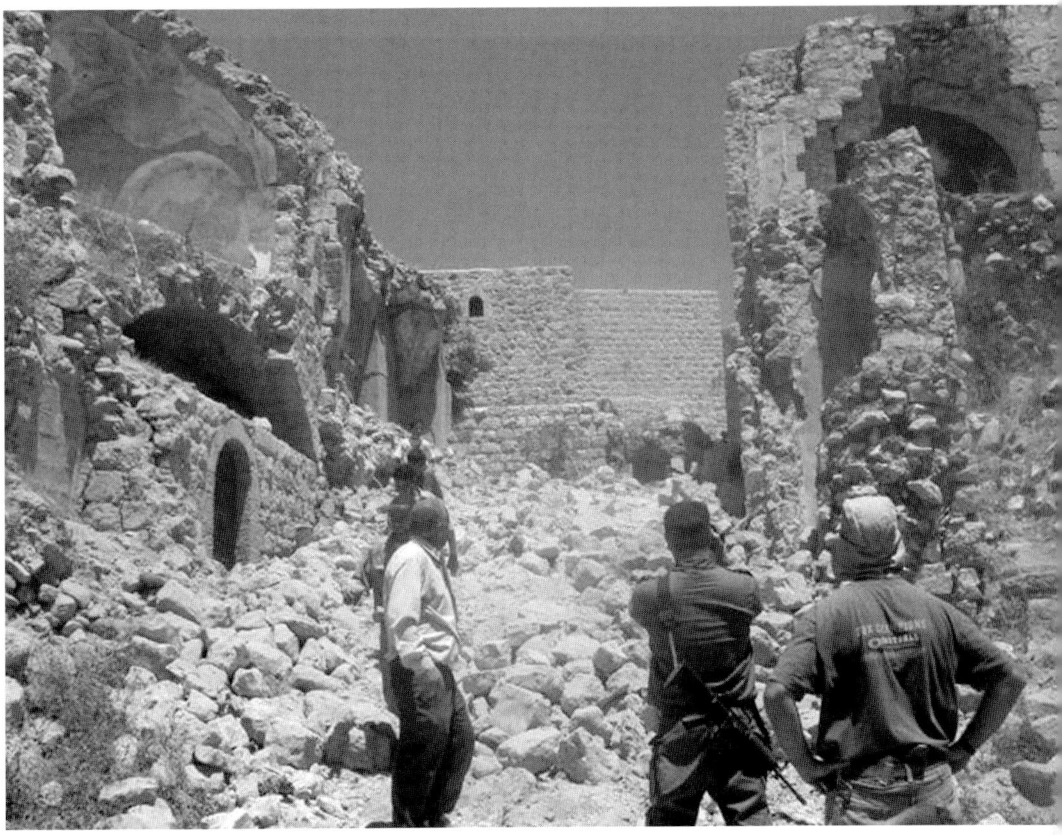

Destruction of Mamluk-era houses for settlers' road through Hebron's Old City

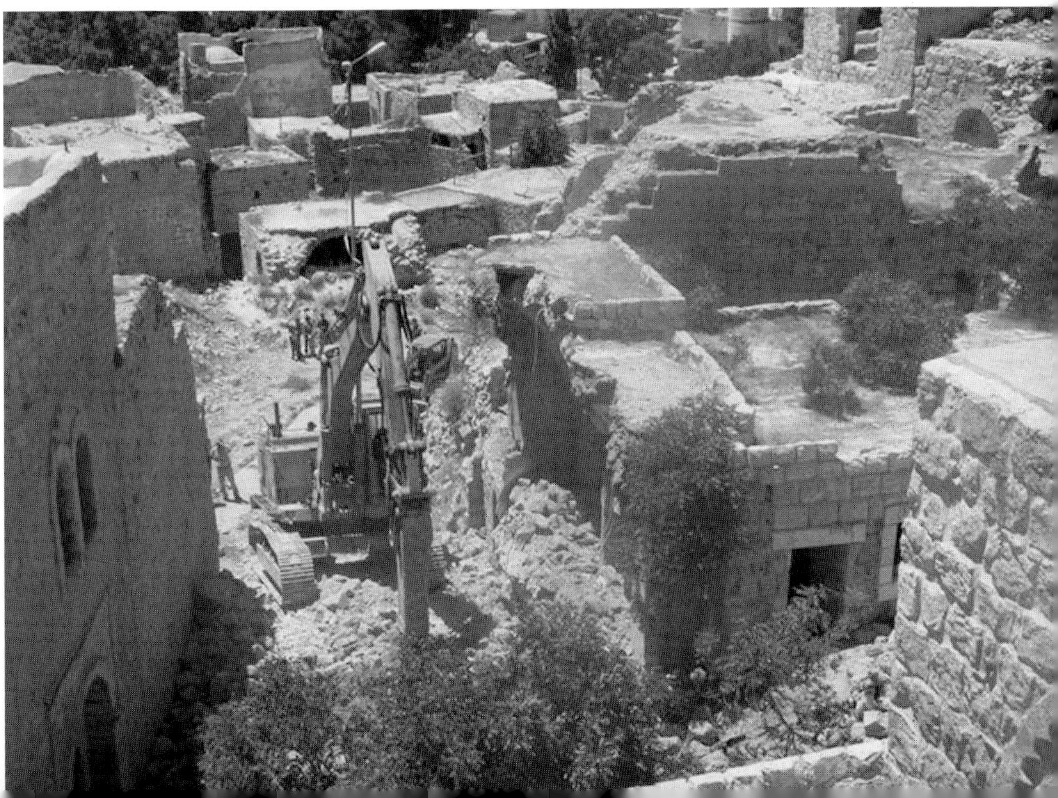

Destruction of Mamluk-era houses for settlers' road through Hebron's Old City

Destruction of Nablus cultural heritage continues

In ICOMOS' last *Heritage at Risk* report for 2002–2003, ICOMOS Palestine reported extensively on the damage to the cultural heritage of the Old City of Nablus. The online report in particular (http://www.international.icomos.org/risk/2002/palestine2002.htm) shows photographs of the destruction to several heritage sites. This took place during 2002 and created an international outcry, that included a statement by UNESCO:

...grave concern for the continuing loss of all innocent lives and at the destruction and damage caused to the cultural heritage in Palestinian territories in particular the reported damage caused to the Basilica of the Nativity in Bethlehem Birth Place of Jesus Christ and one of the most significant historic sites on earth; the historic centre of Nablus including its mosques and the old City of Hebron. (UNESCO 2002)

In April 2002, UNESCO declared that the historic city of Nablus was of 'outstanding universal value according to article 12 of the 1972 World Heritage Convention and urged Israel to ensure the protection of all heritage in the Palestinian territories in its multicultural diversity'. (UNESCO 2002)

In January 2004, several institutions concerned with cultural heritage met to condemn further Israeli military acts that inflicted damage on Palestinian heritage sites. Again Nablus' heritage suffered severely. ICOMOS presents a press release by the Palestinian Department of Antiquities and Cultural Heritage, Department of Tourism and Antiquities:

Press Release – Intentional Destruction of the Historic City of Nablus

At the time when the world was celebrating the advent of the New Year 2004, the Israeli military was busy demolishing the remaining part of the historic town in Nablus. During a week of continued military siege imposed on the city, a series of historic buildings were demolished by the Israeli forces, including the Abdelhadi Palace in the Qaryoun quarter. The palace, which was built in the 17th century, is regarded as a major cultural heritage site in the old city of Nablus. Archaeological tunnels and more than five other major buildings were also demolished.

We recall the great damage that has been inflicted on cultural heritage sites in the Palestinian areas since October 2000. These sites have suffered military bombing and shelling, causing partial or even total destruction. The attack on cultural heritage sites has intensified since the major incursion in April 2002, causing irreparable damage, especially in the historic towns and cities, including Bethlehem, Hebron, Gaza, Beit Jala, Tulkarem, Salfit, Jenin and Nablus. Sieges, curfews, roadblocks and military closures imposed on Palestinian cities and villages have prevented the Palestinian Department of Antiquities from attending to its task of protecting its cultural heritage. Many archaeological sites, historical buildings, public and religious buildings have been the target of the Israeli military aggression. But the old city of Nablus represents the most severe case. The damage in Nablus is spread all over the old city, including private dwellings, religious buildings (churches, mosques and sanctuaries), traditional soap factories, old markets, historical bathhouses, water tunnels and the city's infrastructure. The damage in the historic core is estimated at more than 70% of the city's fabric and includes Al-Khadra Mamluk Mosque, the Greek Orthodox Church, and the Sheikh Musallam Sanctuary. Six traditional soap factories, including Al-Nabulsi and Canaan factories in Al-Yasmina quarter, and the Caravansarei of Khan Et-Tujjar were demolished. More than one hundred private dwellings are estimated to have suffered partial or complete damage, including the damage to the infrastructure such as roads, electricity supply and sewage.

The name of Nablus is identified with the Roman city of Neapolis founded in 72 AD by the Flavian emperors and it has been continuously inhabited since then. It is the political and economic capital of the northern districts of Palestine. The city, famed for its history, handicrafts and sweets, looks now as though it was devastated by a severe earthquake. The collapsed buildings have created a situation of great danger to public safety. In addition to the many people who were killed and wounded, hundreds of families were obliged to leave their homes forever.

The old city of Nablus is an important component of the cultural identity of the Palestinian people and an integral part of its heritage. Its intentional destruction has an adverse consequence on the human dignity and the human rights of the Palestinian people. At the same time its destruction is a great loss for humanity.

The renewed attack on the old city of Nablus is a clear violation of the UNESCO declaration against intentional destruction of cultural heritage. The Palestinian Ministry of Tourism and Antiquities appeals to the international community, especially the UNESCO World Heritage Committee and other international organizations to condemn Israel for its continuous violations of international law and its targeting of cultural heritage sites. The Ministry urges the member states of UNESCO and its Director General to take immediate measures to stop the intentional destruction of cultural heritage in the old city of Nablus.

Ministry of Tourism and Antiquities
Department of Antiquities and Cultural Heritage
(www.thisweekinpalestine.com)

References

UNESCO 2002 Report of the Rapporteur, UNESCO Convention concerning the Protection of the Cultural and Natural Heritage, Bureau of the World Heritage Committee, 26th session, 2-13 April 2002 (http://whc.unesco.org/archive/repbur02.htm.#sec16).

PANAMA
Demolition of Historic Façades in Casco Antiguo World Heritage Site

Historic Context

The Isthmus of Panama was first discovered by Europeans in 1501. Shortly after, Panama City, the American continent´s first city on the Pacific Ocean side, was founded on 1519. During 1671, British corsair Sir Henry Morgan sacked and burned the city. As a consequence, in 1673 the new Panama City, this time a fortified ramparted Spanish colonial *recint,* had to be built on an entirely new peninsula, following the tradition of military engineers working for the Crown. The Casco Antiguo de Panamá, as it is now called, became a national historic district in 1976. In 1997 and more recently with extensions in 2003, it was included in the World Heritage List by UNESCO, primarily for its universal and exceptional significance and value.

Local Legal Context

Panama's historic landmarks (MH – *Monumentos Históricos*) and national historic districts (CMH – *Conjuntos Monumentales Históricos*) are legally protected and ruled by the following local historic preservation laws: No. 91 Law of 1976, No. 14 Law of 1982, and the No. 9 Law of 1997.

The local official body that, among other capacities, has the legal power and authority to preserve, protect, promote for rehabilitation/restoration, safeguard, inspect during construction, and classify, is the Dirección Nacional de Patrimonio Histórico (DNPH). This body, however, is always advised by the Comisión Nacional de Arqueología y Monumentos Históricos (CONAMOH – the national commission of archaeology and historic buildings

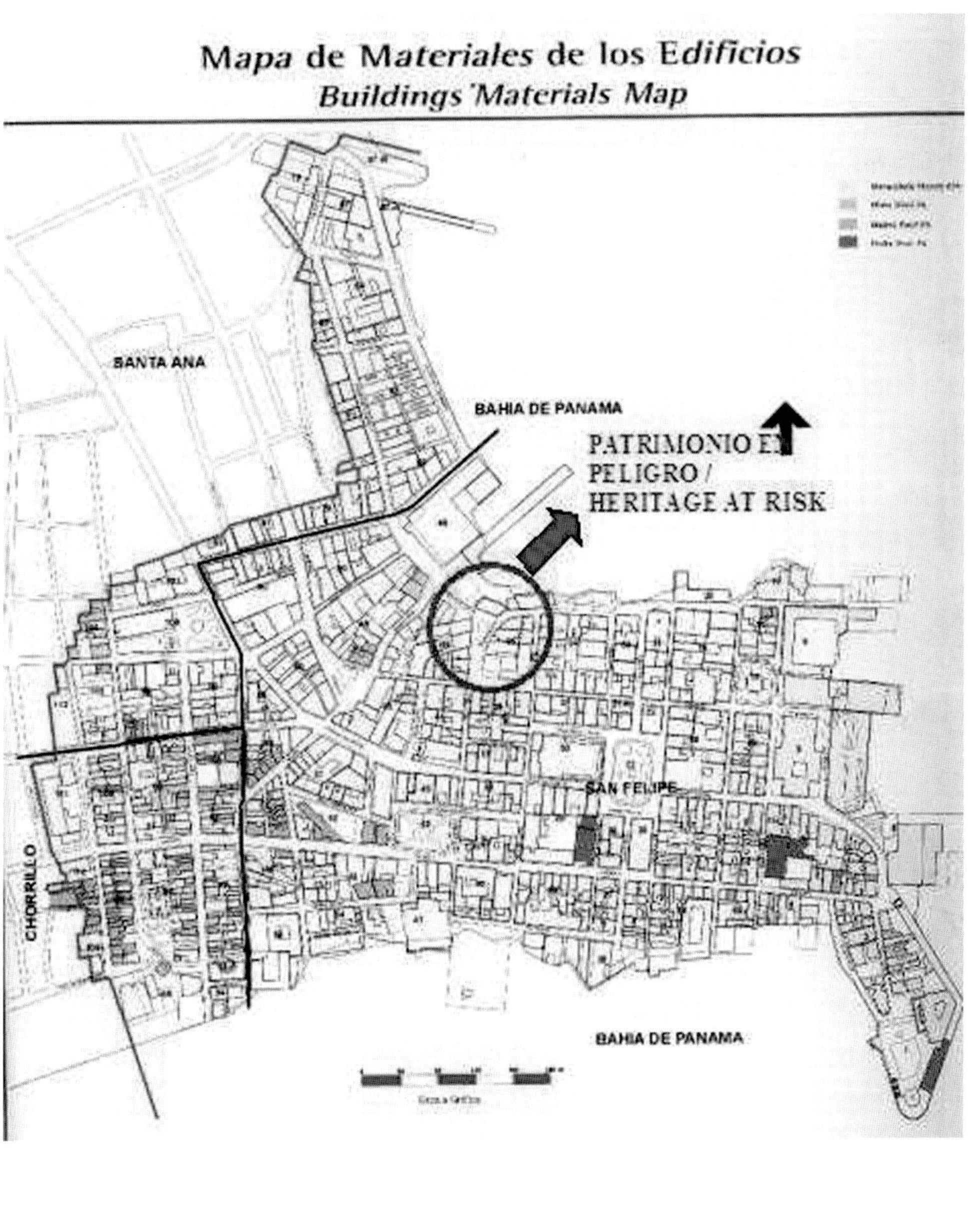

Project location in Panama City old quarter

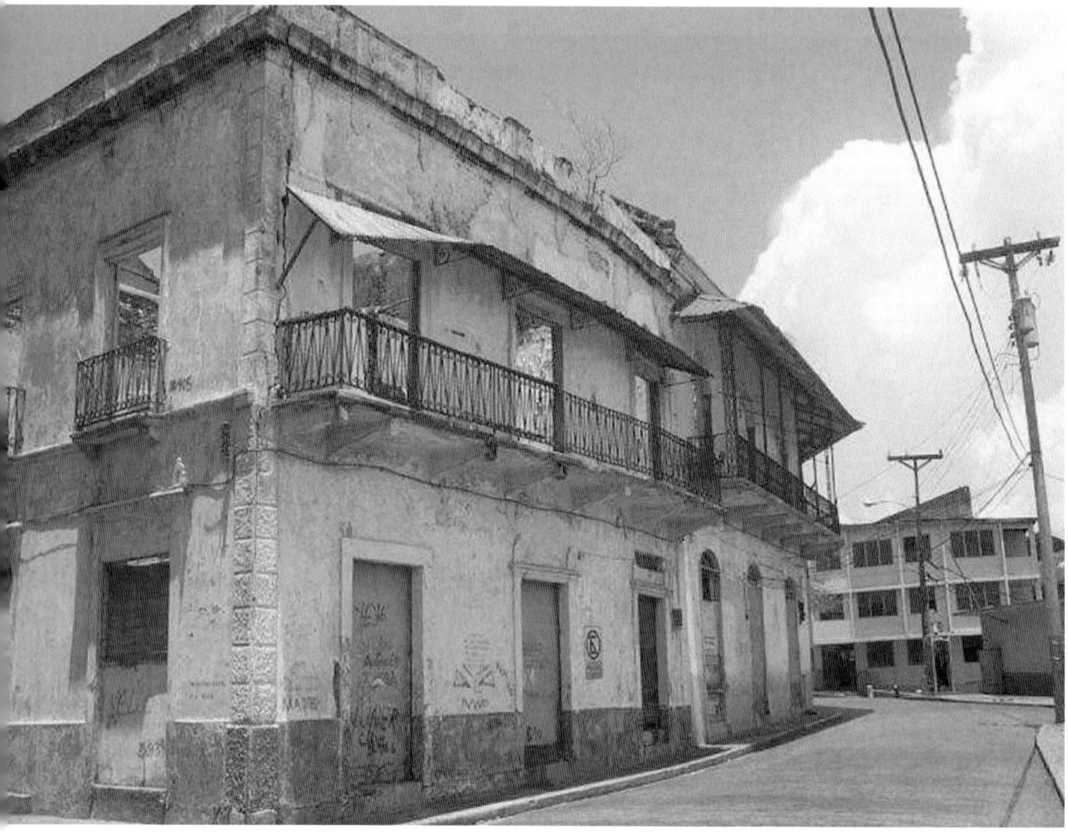

Ave. Eloy Alfaro, facade (demolished)

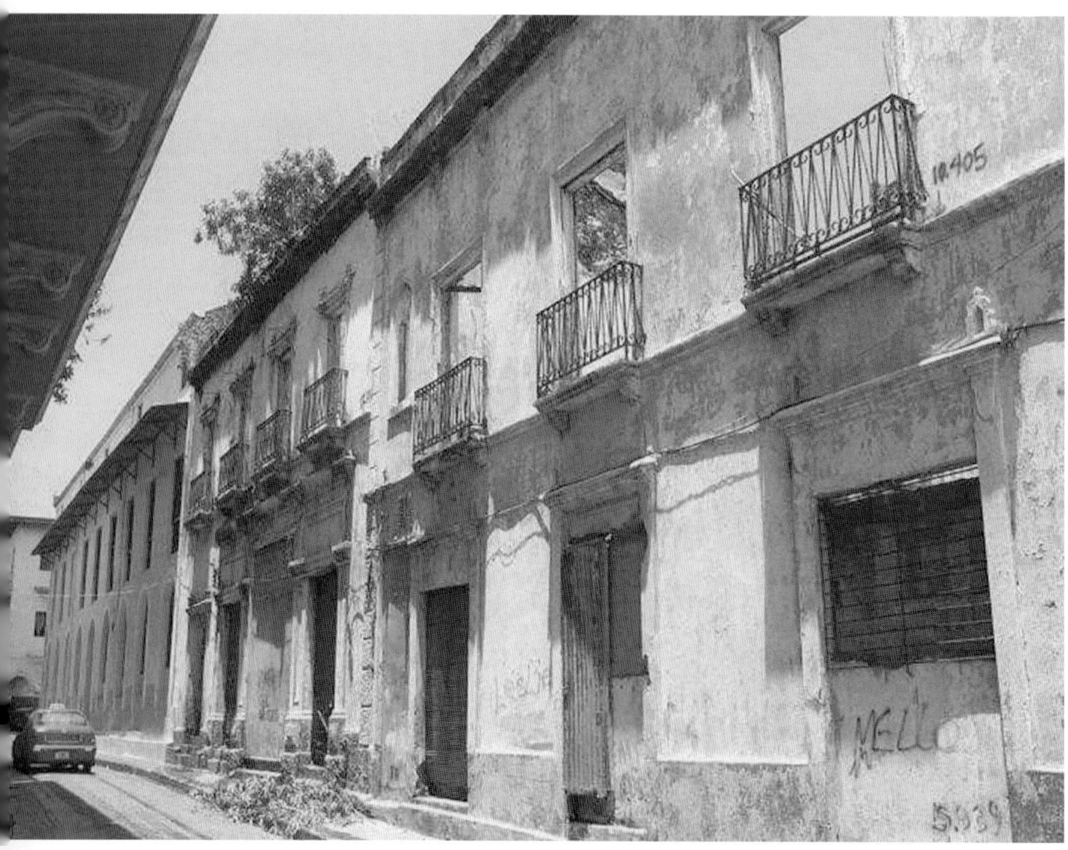

8th Street, facade (demolished)

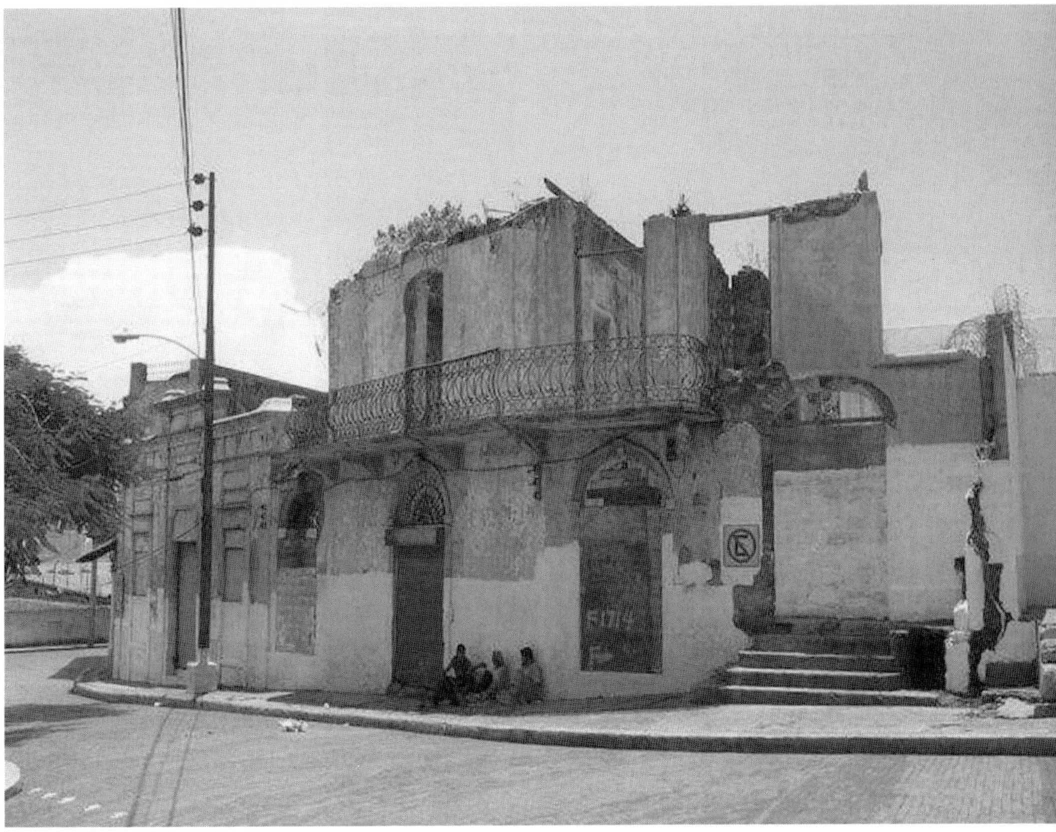

9th Street, facade (demolished)

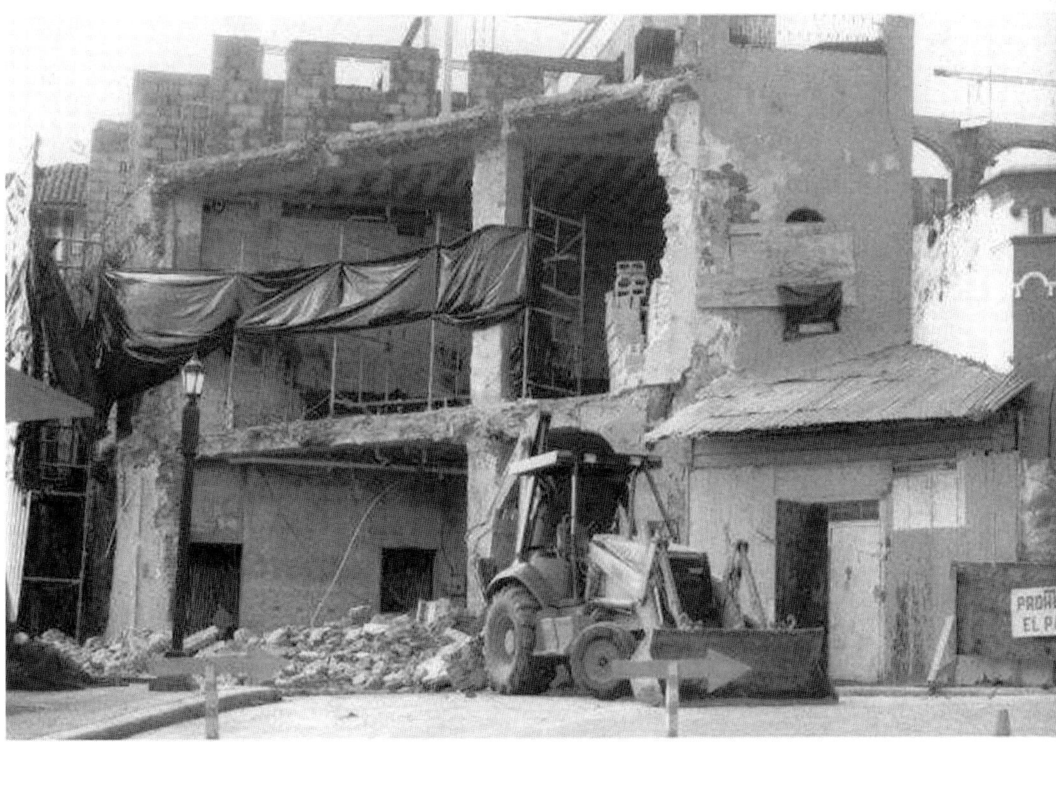

The demolished facades covered in plastic

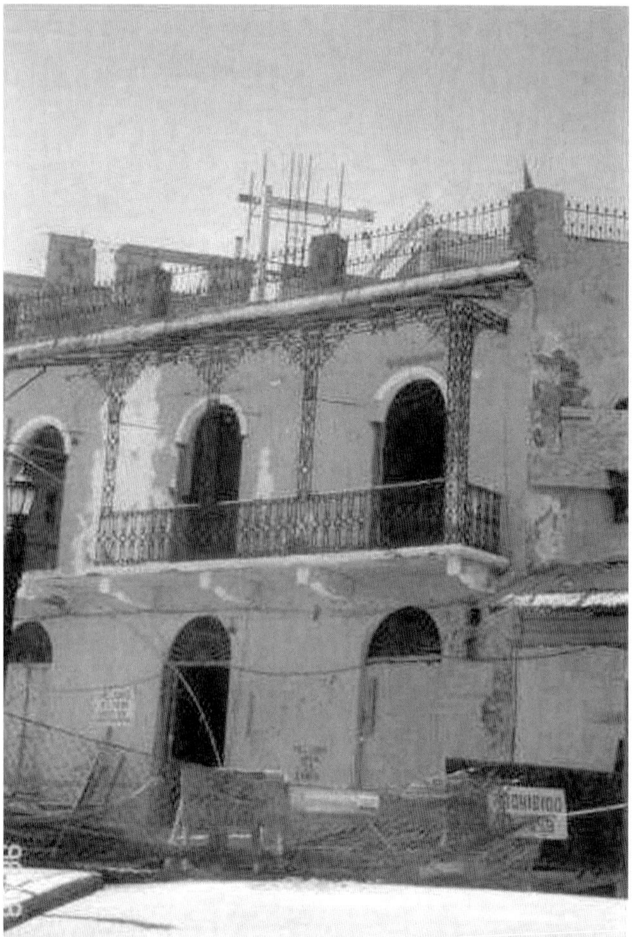

Demolition process

Demolition completed

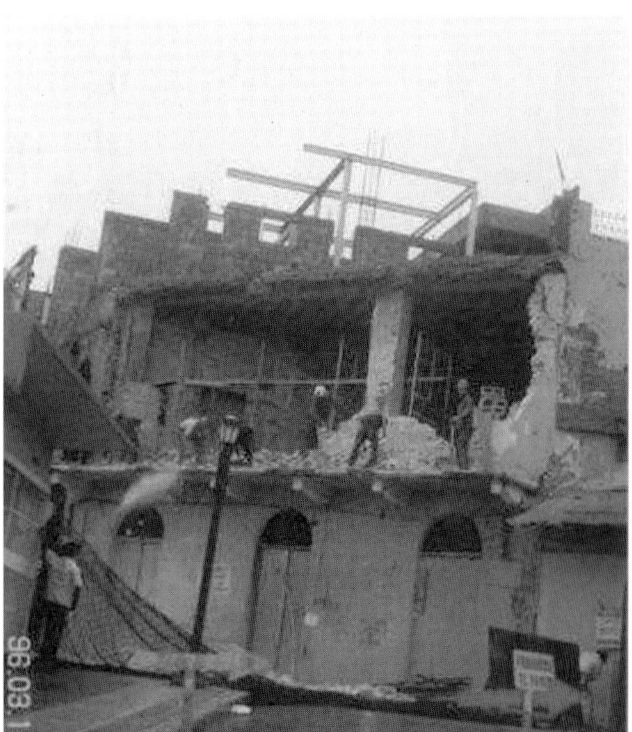

and sites). This interdisciplinary commission representing several cultural institutions, basically oversees, technically recommends, and approves or rejects any rehabilitation/restoration project on any historic landmark (MH) and historic district (CMH).

Report on Recent Demolition

The ICOMOS National Committee of Panama urgently calls for international attention and support because of a recent case of the demolition of a historic building that took place in the Casco Viejo, which is the result of the lack of commitment, significance and responsibility of the local heritage authorities.

On 27 February 2004, a historic building located on the corner of 4th Street and A Avenue partially collapsed due to the owner's lack of maintenance. However, a substantial part of the structure survived. Unexpectedly, during the clean-up of the collapsed material, the entire property was razed to ground level. Immediately, the ICOMOS National Committee approached the authorities to call their attention to this matter and remind them of scientific shoring and structural support techniques and to give them a copy of the recent report 'Recommendations of the Analysis, Conservation and Structural Restoration of Architectural Heritage'.

In spite of our calls for consideration, an unfortunate situation recently took place. In a current 'rehabilitation' project, consisting of four historic buildings located in and formerly part of the Hospital and Convent of San Juan de Dios, demolition took place of the historic façades and a new internal structure was built that considerably altered the scale and size of the original buildings as well as being visible externally. This sensitive project is located right in the block between 8th and 9th Streets and Eloy Alvaro Avenue, that is right on one of Casco Antiguo´s only two entrances, encompassing a group of buildings that once formed a unique historical complex that was an important part of the site.

During our research into the case, our committee was informed that this project had fully approved plans. However, the demolition of façades and the alteration of the building scale was not considered in these plans, and apparently took place during construction without undergoing necessary previous approval procedures. It is our understanding that the DNPH authority gave permissions for the demolition without previously consulting the CONAMOH commission. Moreover, it is clear that there were no appropriate supervision controls to prevent and avoid the alteration of scale.

As we write this report, the demolished façades have been covered in plastic and are in the process of reconstruction, giving way to a possible historically false record. The obvious scale and size alteration has been submitted for approval, yet the construction has not been stopped nor stayed.

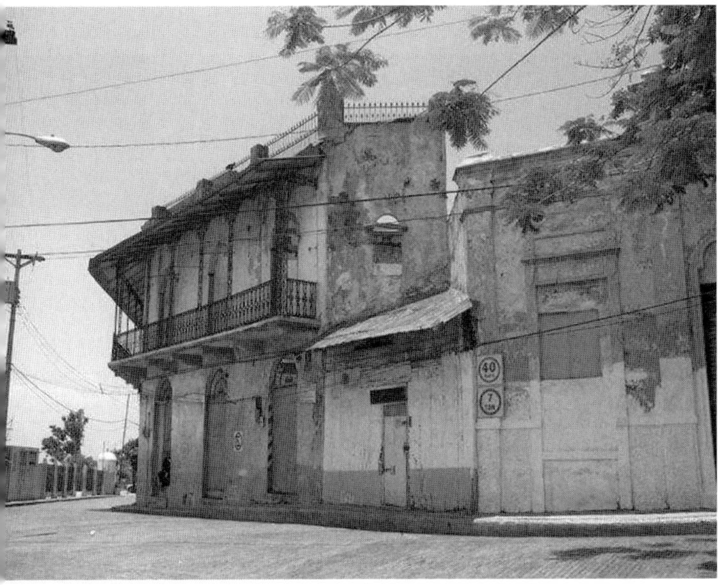

9th Street and Eloy Alfaro (demolished)

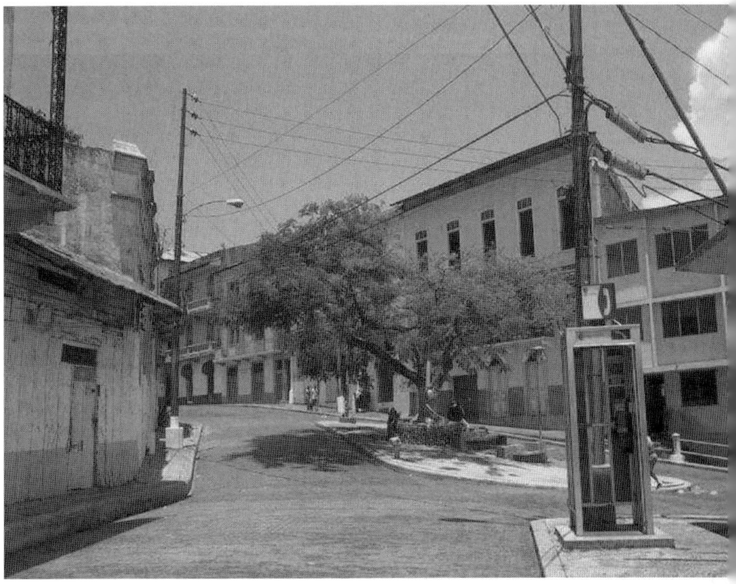

9th Street, facade (demolished)

The demolished facades covered in plastic

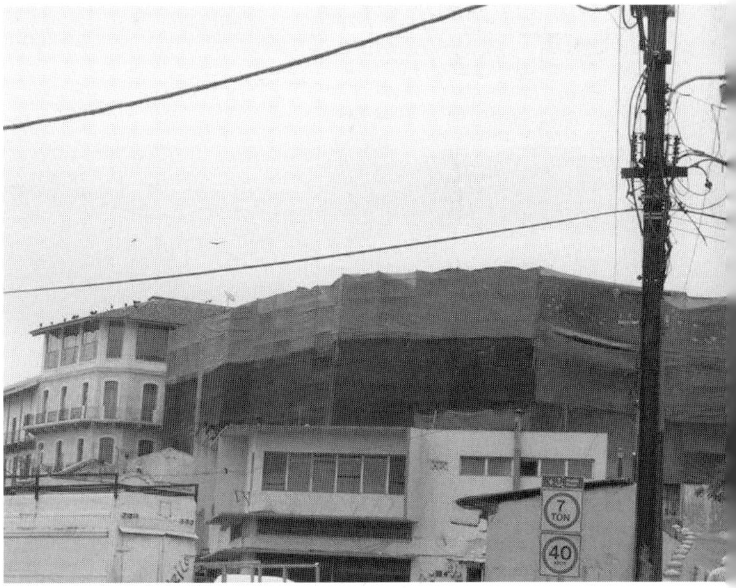

Call for International Support

We therefore urgently call for international support so that these sad cases do not happen again and proper measures and action may be taken against local conservation authorities that permit these activities and against developers that propose such procedures.

Our committee has protested publicly to local newspapers, television news and in written reports sent to both the DNPH authority and CONAMOH commission. However, we still have not been informed of what will happen further on this case. We will continue to do all we can to safeguard and supervise these and other situations, but we cannot achieve any success if we are left alone by the international heritage conservation community.

ICOMOS Panama

PERU

With regard to the 2004 Annual Report on *Heritage at Risk*, we must report that the greatest threat to the cultural heritage of Peru arises mainly from the deficiencies of a national cultural policy. It gives no attention to the preservation of the nation's cultural property, either by suitable legislation and provisions or by budget allocations to allow for the appropriate direction and management of cultural heritage.

Statute 24047 requires that sites and monuments are declared to be such by the government in order for it to be able to protect them, which is almost impossible in a country such as Peru where there is not even a complete and up-to-date inventory of cultural property. Furthermore, the National Institute of Culture is very much a second-ranking organisation; it has neither the power nor the fund to attend to the defence of the national cultural heritage.

To demonstrate the constant threats to our cultural heritage, we attach some reports to show how an important archaeological site at Trujillo has been destroyed, despite having been previously declared a Protected Zone by the National Institute of Culture. It is in the north of the country and only 5 km from the site of Huaca de la Luna y el Sol, an internationally renowned monument.

Those directly responsible are the Chavimochic Project and the local municipal construction engineers, who have levelled the site and subdivided it with no regard for the important remains dating from 5000 BC to 600 that they were destroying.

Quebrada de Santo Domingo, destruction of archaeological zone

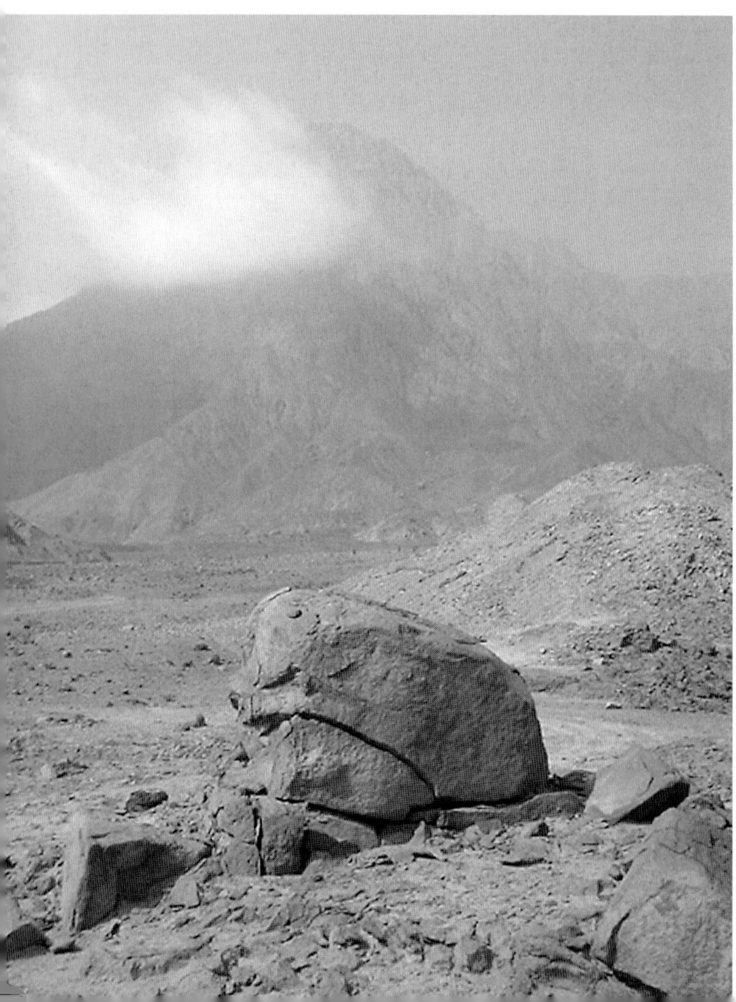

We suggest to call the attention of Peruvian government authorities to the need to strengthen the National Institute of Culture by providing the budgets, legislation and standards necessary to ensure the protection, defence and preservation of the cultural heritage of Peru.

ICOMOS Peru

The following reports by Melissa Massat have appeared on an international website, TRACCE Online Rock Art Bulletin: http://rupestre.net/tracce/ with another appearing in the local newspaper near the site.

Save Santo Domingo

by Melissa Massat

In the far north of Peru, about 20 km east of the city of Trujillo is a highly endangered archaeological site located in the Quebrada de Santo Domingo, a very historical and scenic 32 km² dry river valley, just west of Alto de la Guitarra. Opening onto the Moche River Valley and cradled by the colourful Cerro Colorado mountain range, it is strategically located between the archaeological complexes of Cerro Oreja (Galinazo Period) and Cerro Arena (Salinar Period), and faces north across an impressive series of Saharan style sand dunes towards the Caballo Muerto/Galindo Complex. Located about 5 km from the well-known Moche Huaca de la Luna and just south of the Chavimochic irrigation canal, the area was designated intangible by the Peruvian Institute of Culture.

The archaeological evidence in this valley indicates human ritual activity from the Lithic Period to Intermedio Tardio Period (10,000 BC - 1400) and includes shelters, platforms, canals, ceremonial paths (one very long one of 10 m width), as well as many stone point and tool workshops.

Most impressive and most endangered is a dense distribution of geoglyphs dating from 5000 BC to 600 depicting zoomorphs, anthropomorphs, hunting scenes and complex spirals.

The archaeological structures, as well as the varied flora and fauna, were up until now very well preserved because of their inaccessibility. However, in the past two years the local Chavimochic Irrigation Canal authorities have clandestinely organised the quarrying, bulldozing, and distribution – even sale – of lots of land in this so-called intangible zone.

Strangely enough the inventory, photos or articles relating to this vast archaeological zone have never been published and the INC has turned a blind eye to the illegal exploitation by the Chavimochic and municipal engineers, for lack of funds or political power to protect it. Obviously, once the entire zone is bulldozed, there will be no need to protect it.

A local guide, Victor Corcuera, is leading an active campaign with limited resources to alert authorities and the press – but the Trujillo area is already dominated by the Huaca de La Luna (research funded by private donations and foreign scientific organizations) and Chan Chan, an endangered World Heritage monument managed by the INC. The local archaeologists are reticent to protest too loudly the destruction of the zone, because the INC controls their activity and careers, and every archaeologist has many 'tales of woe' to lament. The local public is so accustomed to living on old tombs and finding pre-Hispanic pottery on their land that one more archaeological site in their back yard is hardly a surprise.

I do believe that anyone who has the slightest interest in early human settlements and Rock Art will agree that this particular site is worth saving. Its strategic and well defined geographical position at the crossroads of a large span of pre-Hispanic and colonial settlements so precariously close to uncontrolled urban and agricultural development; its precious treasures of geoglyphs, lithic structures, stone workshops; its wildlife and breathtakingly beautiful scenery which have survived centuries of El Nino's, winds and pillage make it a most valuable natural and prehistoric landscape and thus an important research base for archaeologists, ecologists, geologists, and anthropologists concerned with urban development and the environment.

Peru is a signatory to the UNESCO Convention Concerning the Protection of the World Cultural and Natural Heritage and should be bound to preserve all its archaeological sites. My request for help presumes that international pressure may lead the local people and authorities to realize the treasure they are destroying and includes organizing a petition to send to Peruvian authorities, writing heads-up to international press, mobilising the international community of archaeological professionals and amateurs to learn about and research this spectacular site, and seeking aid and development organisations' help to solve the urban-growth problem which so menaces the historical and natural environment.

While Ulf Bertilsson, President of the ICOMOS International Rock Art Committee, has pointed out 'the crucial issue' of the risk of destruction of Rock Art by tourism, it is imperative to honour the UNESCO Recommendation Concerning the Preservation of Cultural Property Endangered by Public or Private Works which considers „...that cultural property is the product and witness of the different traditions and of the spiritual achievements of the past and thus is an essential element in the personality of the peoples of the world..."

6 December 2003

Quebrada de Santo Domingo – Save Geoglyphs in Northern Peru

by Melissa Massat

Response is dismay, but also amazement and admiration for the rich archaeological heritage of Peru.

From UNESCO Lima, I have received word that my concerns have been transmitted to the World Heritage Centre in Paris. Another Internet Site has joined the campaign to Save the Quebrada de Santo Domingo: About.com /thanks to Kris Hirst http://archaeology.about.com/b/a/065997.htm

But the printed press remains silent.

In a meeting yesterday with the regional directrice of the Instituto Nacional de Cultura, Victor Corcuera was told that Lima is 'buzzing about the Quebrada de Santo Domingo' and that she offers 'carte blanche' or an open invitation to any archaeologist or institution which can come to investigate the site. You probably know that Peru has hardly any funds for research. The local INC doesn't even have the funds to block the entrance or pay a guardian. And it is most doubtful that it will consider undertaking a lengthy judicial process to claim damages from responsible parties. Does anyone know of an organization that has emergency funds at least to help the INC block entrance to the site?

Secondly, the head of the school of Archaeology at the National University in Trujillo has just extended his offer of support to Victor in his campaign to save the site. The site, so close to the city, offers an incredible opportunity for the students to study the evolution of pre-Hispanic civilisation, with vestiges spanning from the lithic to Chimu periods. (Again, support does not mean financing by strapped University authorities.) University staff is mainly involved in the Huaca de la Luna project which receives all its funding from private and foreign academic participation and the University maintains the city's Archaeological Museum with collaboration from foreign governments. Students do their internships guiding at the Huaca and in the Museum.

So in the context of tight competition for funding and recognition, the head of the Archaeological school has offered his support of efforts to save Santo Domingo, which is a positive step – but destruction is rapid.

Scientific and Academic Institutions have the means and influence to generate investigation of this site and possibilities of collaboration with the University there would be so motivating for the Peruvian students and local public. Therefore, developing a program to investigate and protect the Quebrada de Santo Domingo needs to be urgently promoted.

Recommendations appreciated. It seems incredible to have to mention or hear so many times 'lack of funds' when it comes to saving priceless heritage.

Quebrada de Santo Domingo, destruction of archaeological zone

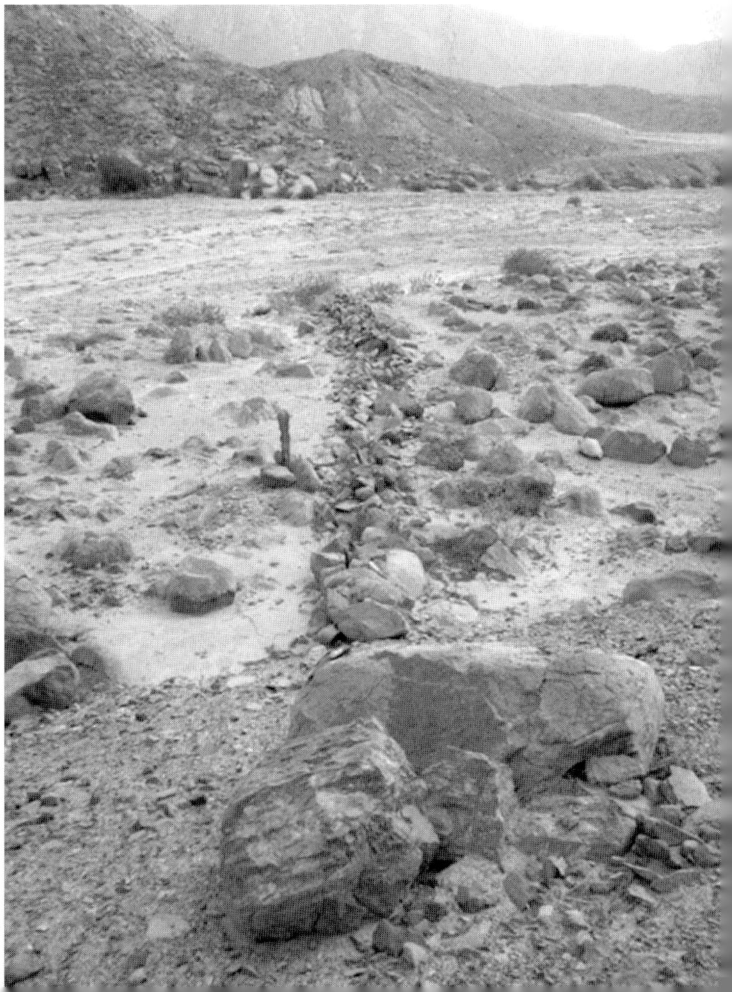

As Ulf Bertillson, President of ICOMOS Rock Art committee, has said „Such events should be prevented and can be prevented". I remember Bamiyan.

21 February 2004

Destruction of archaeological zone at Quebrada de Santo Domingo

INC staff and Tourism Administration have confirmed this week that heavy machinery from the Chavimochic project had entered the protected zone at Quebrada de Santo Domingo, Laredo, endangering the area while extracting soil for construction work.

On the morning of Wednesday, 3rd of March, the official tourist guide, Victor Corcuera, went by bicycle to Quebrada de Santo Domingo to look for conclusive proof of the destruction of national heritage by dump trucks and power shovels.

INC is concerned – Barriers have been erected

The director of Conservation and Cultural Heritage at the National Institute of Culture, Cesar Galvez Mora, noted that this institution has not neglected to provide protection for the Quebrada de Santo Domingo area (near Ochiputur Hill at Laredo), and confirmed that heavy machinery had been seen there at the time of the most recent inspection.

He maintained that various 'problems' had arisen during the last week, and that the head of the INC Department of Archaeological Monuments, Jesus Briceno, had gone to the area after receiving a telephone call to report these events.

Local, Trujillo, 6 March 2004

Quebrada de Santo Domingo, double spiral web

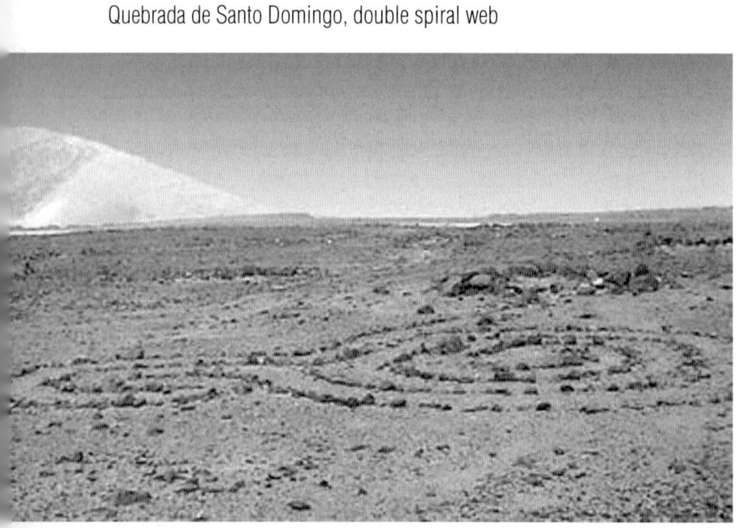

PERU

Con respecto al Reporte Anual 2004 de Patrimonio en Peligro debemos informar que la mayor amenaza contra el Patrimonio Cultural del Perú deriva principalmente de una inadecuada política cultural del Estado, que no pone atención a la preservación de los bienes culturales de la Nación, ya sea con leyes y dispositivos adecuados o con la asignación de presupuestos que permitan un adecuado manejo y gestión del patrimonio cultural.

La ley 24047 requiere que los sitios y monumentos hayan estado declarados como tales por el Estado para que este pueda protegerlos, lo que es casi imposible en un país como el Perú donde ni siquiera se tiene un inventario completo actualizado de los bienes culturales. Por otro lado, el Instituto Nacional de Cultura de segundo orden; no tiene el poder ni el Presupuesto para intervenir en defensa del Patrimonio Cultural Nacional.

Para ilustrar el constante peligro en el que se encuentra nuestro Patrimonio Cultural, les estamos enviando un CD por correo postal, donde ustedes podrán apreciar como un importante sitio arqueológico, ubicado en Trujillo, al Norte de nuestro país y a solo 5 Kilometros del Sitio arqueológico Huaca de la Luna y el Sol, monumento de prestigio Internacional, ha sido destruido a pesar que fue previamente declarado como Zona Intangible por el Instituto Nacional de Cultura.

Los directos responsables son el Proyecto Chavimochic y los ingenieros de la Municipalidad de la zona, los cuales han nivelado el terreno, y lo han lotizado sin importarles los importantes vestigios que destruyeron, los cuales datan desde los 5000 años antes de Cristo hasta los 600 años después de Cristo.

Les sugerimos hacer una llamada de atención a las autoridades del Gobierno Peruano para fortalecer al Instituto Nacional de Cultura, que se den los presupuestos, leyes y normas necesarias que permitan garantizar la Protección, defensa y conservación del Patrimonio Cultural del Peru.

(un articulo en español con fotos se encuentra al http://www.unitru.edu.pe/revistas/espacios/turprinc.htm)

ICOMOS Péru

Destruyen zona arqueológica en Quebrada de Santo Domingo

El personal del INC y la Policía de Turismo verificó, esta semana, que maquinaria pesada, del proyecto Chavimochic, ingresó a la zona intangible de la Quebrada de Santo Domingo, Laredo, poniendo en peligro el área al extraer la tierra como material de construcción.

En la mañana del miércoles 3 de marzo, el guía oficial de Turismo, Víctor Corcuera Cueva, se desplazaba en su bicicleta hasta la Quebrada de Santo Domingo, buscando una prueba contundente de la destrucción del patrimonio cultural con volquetes y palas mecánicas.

INC no es indiferente – Se colocarán barreras

El director de Conservación y Patrimonio Cultural del Instituto Nacional de Cultura, César Gálvez Mora, anotó que su institución no se ha cruzado de brazos en la protección del área de la Quebrada Santo Domingo (en las cercanías del cerro Ochiputur de Laredo) y confirmó que en la última inspección se verificó la presencia de vehículos pesados en la zona.

Sostuvo que durante la última semana se constataron algunos „problemas" y el jefe del departamento de Monumentos Arqueológicos del INC, Jesús Briceño, acudió a la zona en respuesta a una llamada telefónica que denunciaba el hecho.

Local, Trujillo 6 de Marzo del 2004

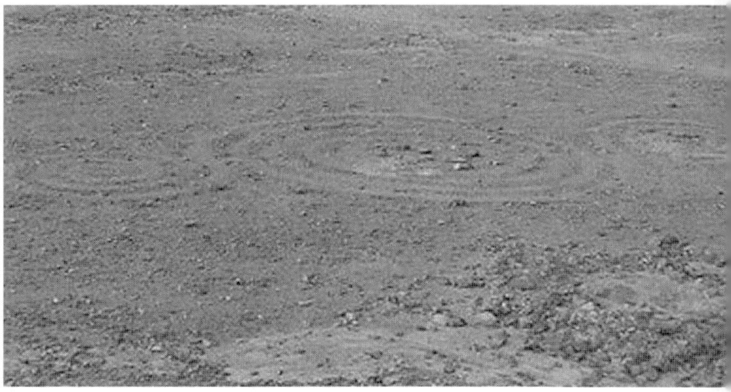

Quebrada de Santo Domingo, triple spiral

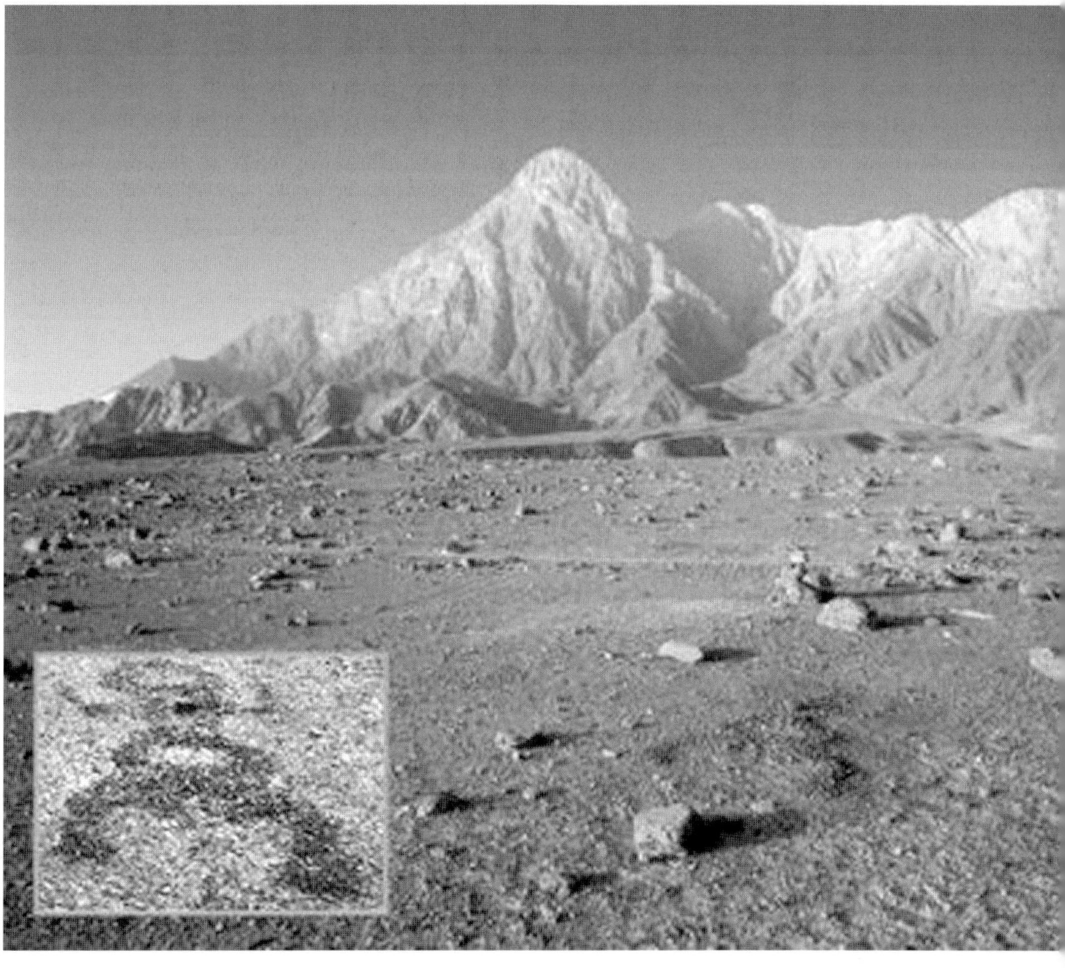

Quebrada de Santo Domingo, mujer view

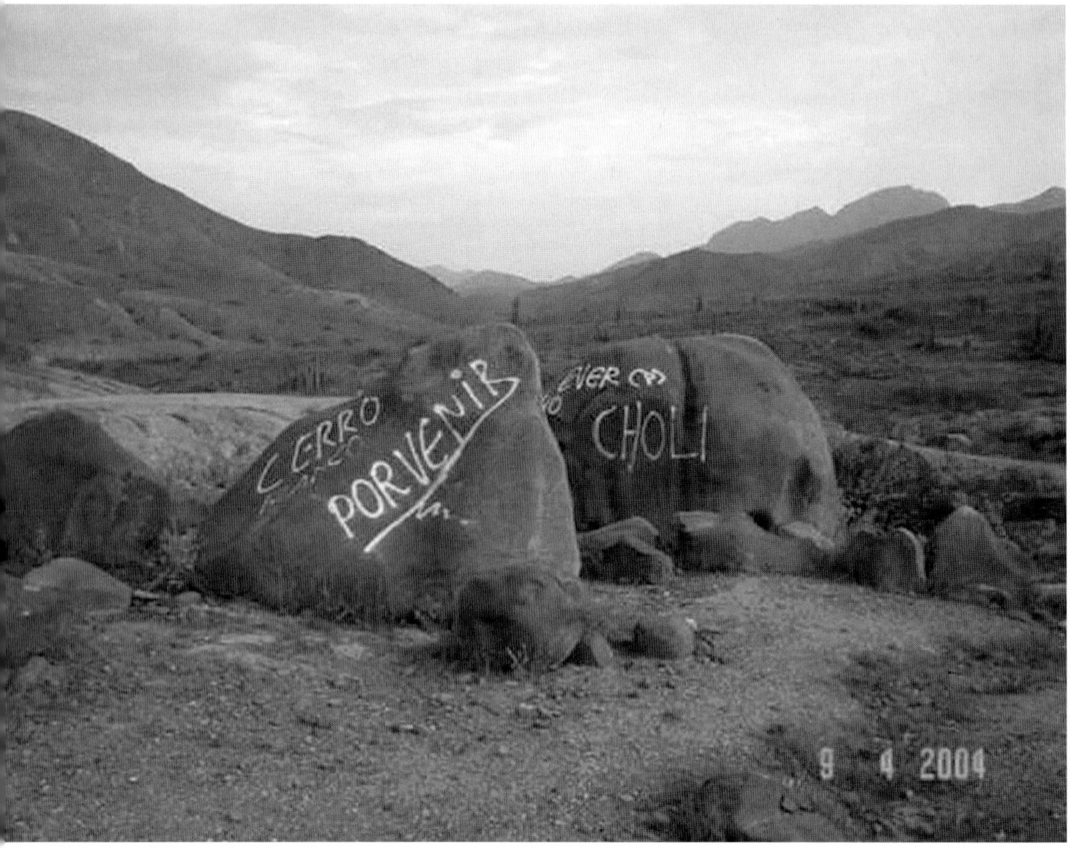

Quebrada de Santo Domingo, destruction of archaeological zone

What will be the outcome of this destruction?

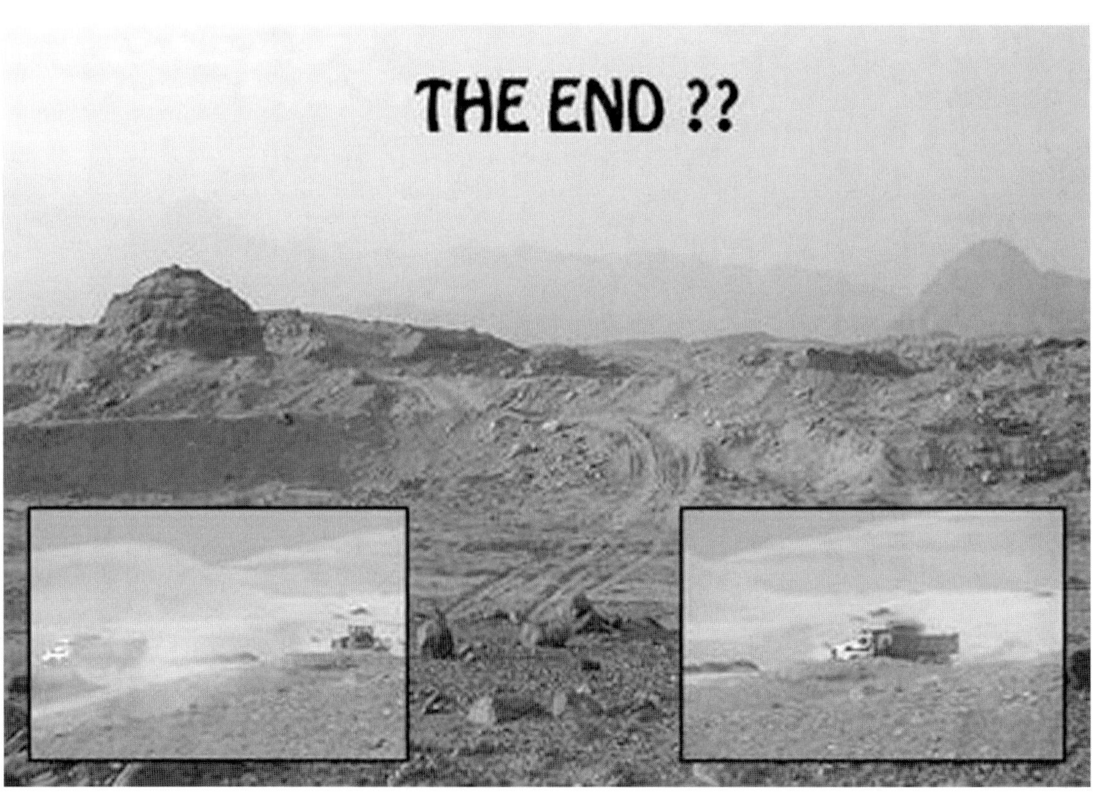

POLAND
Military heritage places at risk

Introduction

Poland is very interesting for its variety of different fortifications. It is connected with our history full of battles and preparation against different invasions. This was caused by the geographical location of Poland in Europe, on the lowland between the Atlantic Ocean and the Ural Mountains. These geo-historical factors are the reasons that the art of fortification developed in Poland through time.

It is possible to study the characteristic elements of different types of fortification in Poland – the medieval, Renaissance and modern. Polish defence architecture is characteristic of various schools of fortifications, such as the Italian, Dutch, French, Polish, Prussian, Russian, Austrian, German and Soviet systems. That all these different types of fortresses are found in the area of one country is unique in Europe.

The Polish State Heritage Conservation body also pays attention to fortifications. The most recent heritage legislation of July 2003 mentions defence structures as a new category. In so doing, one of its most important threats disappeared. This parliamentary decision is very important for the future preservation and restoration of this type of heritage.

There are many types of defence structures under Polish State protection. From a total of 60,042 declared cultural heritage places, 1173 are listed as fortifications. Of these, 829 are medieval and 344 are more modern fortifications (from 17th to 20th centuries). Of these latter, 33 date to the 20th century.

There is a wide range in scale among these fortifications, including large defensive areas of the 19th century fortification systems and very small structures of the 20th century, such as World War II shelters.

The most significant in Poland are modern fortresses from the end of the 19th century and beginning of the 20th century built by the invaders of Poland, Russia, Austria and Prussia. The characteristic features of this type of heritage are the large fortified areas with individual cores of masked forts consisting of rings, concealed roads and different types of green spaces.

There are also very interesting Polish, German and Soviet 20th century military systems connected with World War II, and built during the Cold War under the Warsaw Pact. Again, it is very rare for European countries to have so many examples of 20th century defence systems. These structures have become more interesting not only to scientific research but also as tourist attractions since the 1989 political changes in Poland and since Poland joined NATO in 1999.

The number of identified fortifications has increased during the last few years. It is connected with the ongoing process of change and rationalisation that is taking place in our army. After joining NATO, the Polish military forces have been reorganised and reduced. For this reason, many former camps and some training fields are redundant. Secret features lose their special military value and are being opened up. They have not been renovated or rebuilt but simply left alone. It is difficult to find new functions for these heritage sites. Because of this, defence structures are finally destroyed. Some of the historic fortifications, which were army property for many years, are now in State or municipal ownership, some of them are privately owned. Many, because of their previous clandestine character, are not listed in the heritage register; their legal protection is more difficult.

Fortifications were already identified as threatened in the Polish report of the 2000 *ICOMOS World Report on Monuments and Sites in Danger*. The situation has not changed very much since then. Defence heritage is still in danger in Poland.

Causes of risk

Threats to military cultural heritage places are caused by many factors. The reasons for being at risk vary. Most of them are connected to legislation, management problems and education.

Legislation issues

Incompleteness of the heritage registration of defence structures for many reasons:

- A lack of knowledge of the full defence resources,
- Incorrect entries in register decisions,
- Ongoing use by the Polish military forces, in regard to the secret nature of some military cultural heritage place,
- A lack of monitoring, control and insufficient legal provision for reuse and reconstruction,
- Property legislation problems.

Use and maintenance problems

- A lack of political will and the mismanagement of conservation by authorities, both central and local;
- A lack of interest, civic initiative and care on behalf of local communities;
- Long-term non-use of defence structures, causing a lack of maintenance and lack of heating, resulting in the deterioration of the site;
- Difficulties in finding new functions for redundant military cultural heritage places;
- Conflict between the new use and original function;
- Threats created as a consequence of modernisation as well as the change in ownership of military cultural heritage places;
- Inappropriate use by the owners, lack of proper maintenance, insufficient or inadequate maintenance;
- Neglect of routine repairs;
- The large costs of maintenance, adaptations and conservation works at the fort, which are very often much greater than at other heritage sites;
- A lack of sufficient conservation funds, both government budgets and private funds;
- A lack of funds to manage and maintain spatially very large military structures and fortifications;
- A lack of funds for capital repairs and even routine repairs;
- Errors committed during renovation and restoration work;
- Risk from natural disasters due to atmospheric effects, vegetation and human factors. The most destructive to the earth, brick and stone structures is water erosion and uncontrolled vegetation growth and expansion;
- The transfer of military cultural heritage places from the Department of National Defence, caused by losing their strategic values, resulting in a lack of management for these sites;

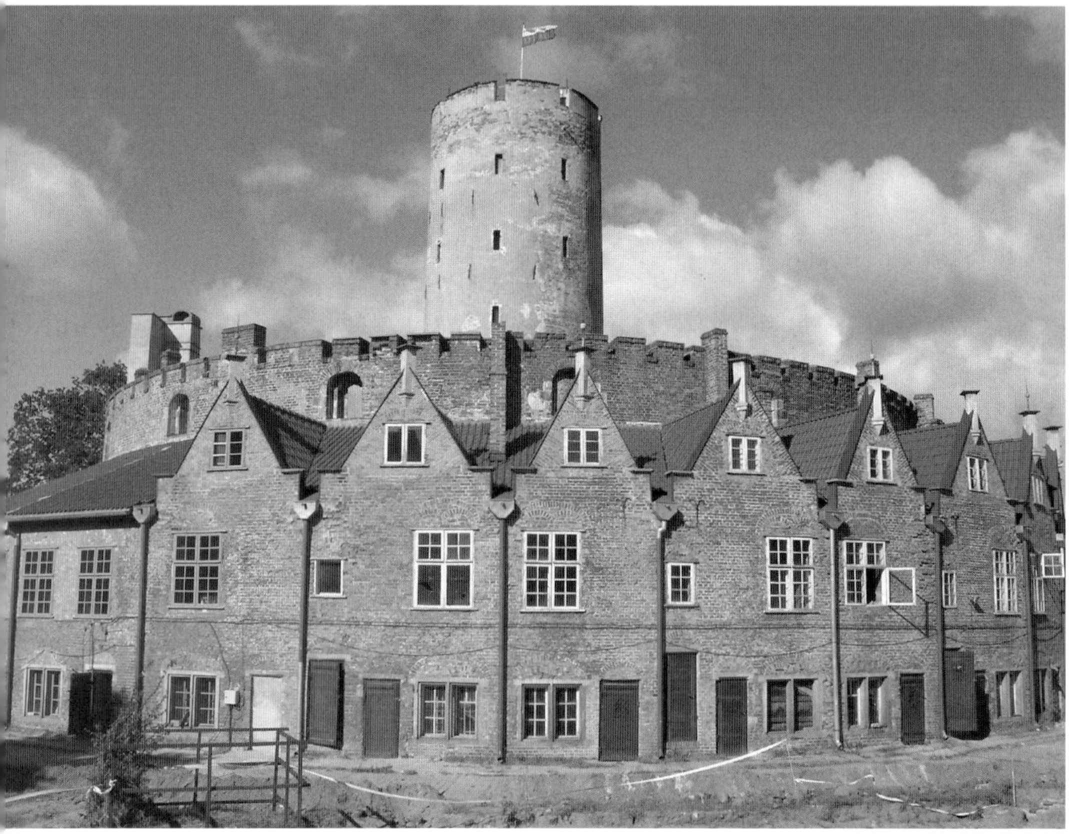

Vistulamouth Fortress in Gdansk is a unique example of the coastal defensive architecture of the 17th and 18th centuries

Vistulamouth Fortress in Gdansk, view to the still existing "Siarkopol", the area of gathering sulphur, which is the cause for a strong presence of sulphuric dust

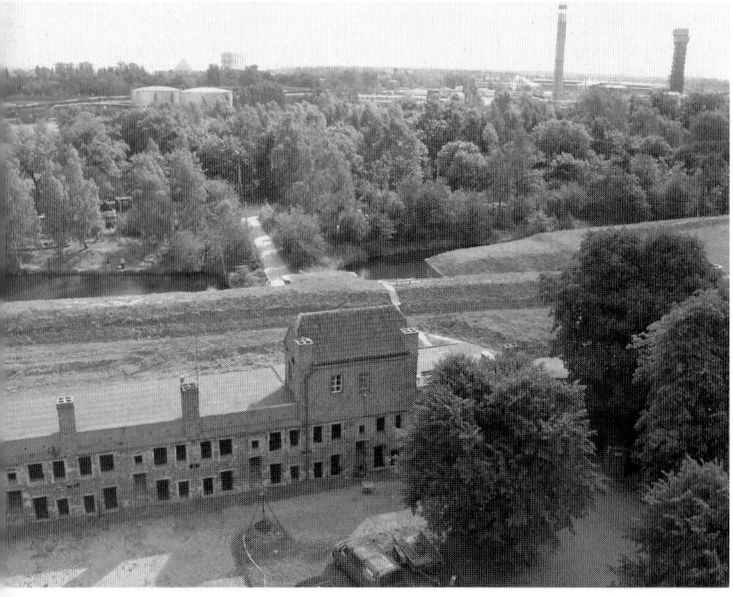

Vistulamouth Fortress in Gdansk, view on to the damages of the bastion's bricks caused by water

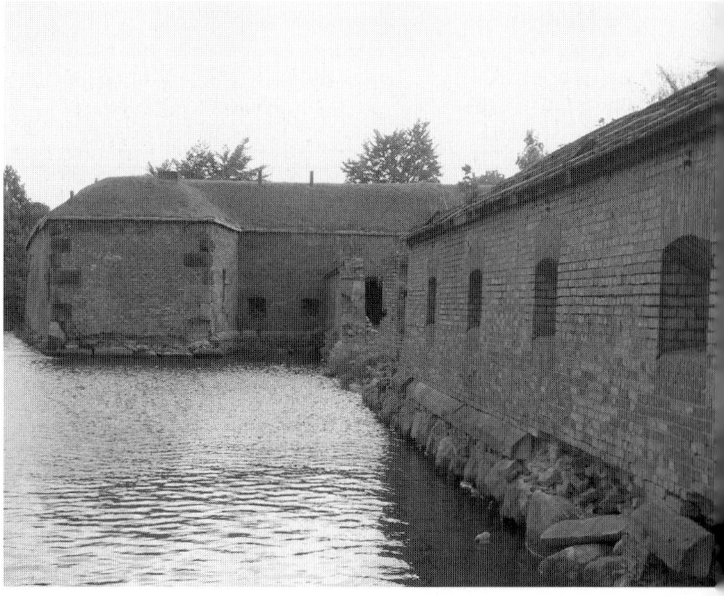

- New cadastral divisions for new owners of the historic military properties that cause a deterioration of their significance;
- Looting of the original armour-plated defence parts to seel them as salvage and, in smaller scale, bricks robbing for cheap building materials;
- Vandalism;
- A lack of structural assistance programs dedicated to preparing management plans and restoring military cultural heritage places;
- The threat of possible military use of significant historic forts during military conflicts.

Research and education

- Insufficient knowledge of the scientific, historic and artistic values of military cultural heritage places and fortifications;
- A lack of education and awareness by individuals of the heritage values of fortifications and their preservation;
- A lack of understanding of the need to protect 19th and 20th century fortresses built by the invaders of Poland, Russia, Austria and Prussia, Nazi Germany and the Soviet Union;
- The lack of a complete effective inventory;
- Secrecy of some military cultural heritage places which makes research impossible;
- The lack of research programs;
- The lack of a strategic approach to heritage conservation management;
- Insufficient specialist training;
- The lack of recognition of 20th century forts, particularly post-World War II, built during the Cold War and under the Warsaw Treaty.

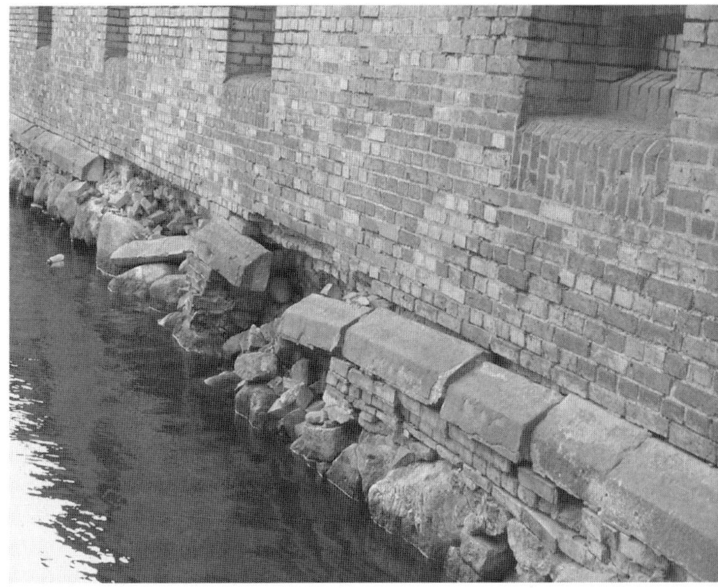

Vistulamouth Fortress in Gdansk, the brick bastions in need of conservation work

Emerging solutions

Activities connected with the protection of military cultural heritage places could vary because of the different risks. Work should focus on legislation problems, education and research, inventories, and appropriate use and maintenance, and developing protocols for the transfer of ownership and management of the military cultural heritage places which are redundant to the military.

The most important activities are:
- The verification of heritage registers regarding their accuracy, especially of the boundaries of legally protected areas;
- The compilation of fortifications and the military cultural heritage resources on the heritage register;
- Include defence landscapes in legally protected items because of cultural and natural values in such landscapes. Because of their particular character fortress landscapes could be treated as a prototype for the integrated protection of cultural and natural values;
- Include provincial conservators in the process of transfer of secret military cultural heritage places, which are redundant to the army;
- Education on different levels about the range of heritage values, preservation and management of historic forts and military cultural heritage places;
- Include the problems of the conservation and management of fortifications and military cultural places in national, regional and local strategies.

Vistulamouth Fortress in Gdansk, conservation of the earthworks on the bastions

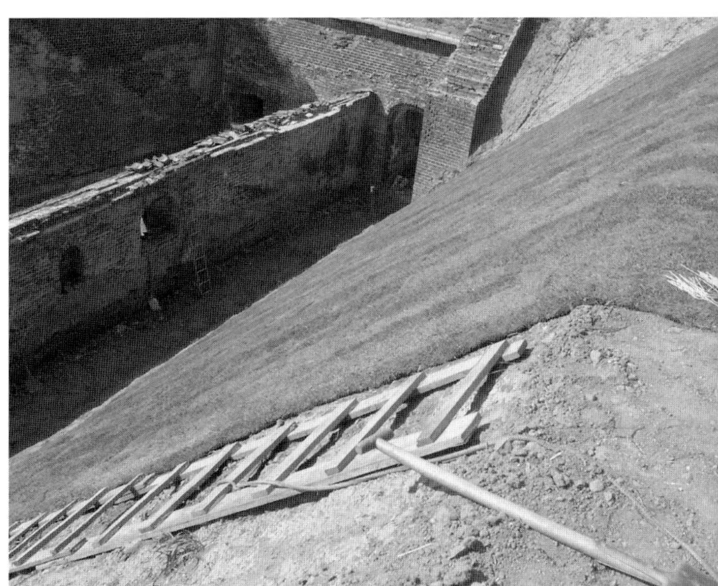

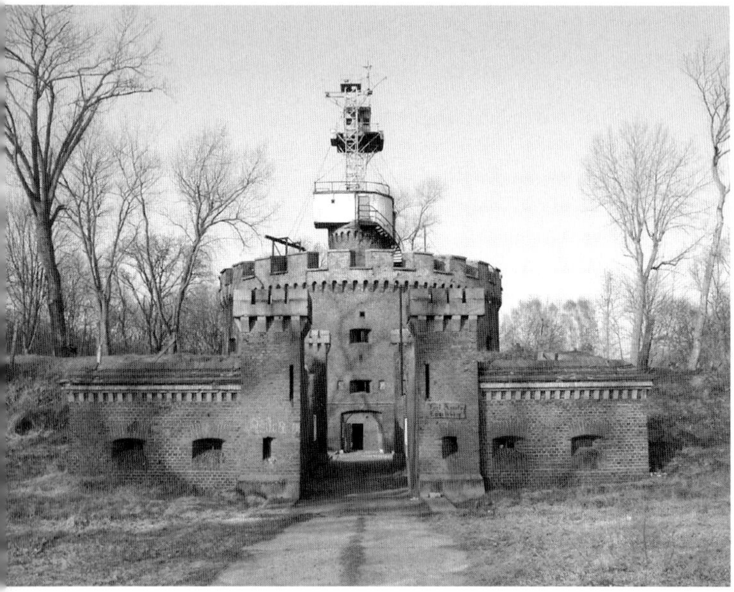

Swinoujscie, 19th-century Prussian fort "Saint Angel"

Examples of activities

'Conservation and development of defence structures' - conservation program of the Ministry of Culture

Numerous activities have been undertaken to study, plan and launch a revival process for Polish fortifications. The Ministry of Culture provided a special program for the identification and preservation of historic fortresses in 1997–1999, which was administered by the Fortification Society. As a result of this program, many new items and fortified areas have been investigated and some of them have been entered in the heritage register. A few conservation and management projects have been established. They are connected with 16th, 17th and 18th century fortresses in Kostrzyn, Klodzko, Srebrna Gora, 19th century Prussian fortifications, such as the Boyen fortress in Gizycko, fortifications of Torun, Poznan, Russian fortifications in Modlin, Osowiec and Deblin, the Austrian fortresses in Krakow and Przemysl and 20th century Polish, Soviet and German military defence areas of Hel, the Biebrza wetlands and the Festungsfront of Oder-Warther-Bogen.

The Vistulamouth Fortress in Gdansk

The revitalisation of a fortress requires significant technical and financial resources, which is very difficult to obtain. One of the possibilities is to find money for restoration from different private or government founds. This was achieved by the Gdansk History for the renovation of the Vistulamouth Fortress, which is a branch of the museum. Assistance came from the World Monuments Fund, which inscribed the Vistulamouth Fortress in Gdansk, one of the most significant fortresses in Poland, in the World Monuments Watch List of 100 Most Endangered Sites, being listed in 1996, 1998 and again in 2000.

The Vistulamouth Fortress in Gdansk is a unique example of coastal defence architecture of the 17th and 18th centuries with legible layers of the following fortification systems. The first brickwork fortification in Vistulamouth was built at the end of the 15th century. It was a brick tower known as the Lighthouse which acted as a traditional guardhouse and lighthouse. This fortification was rebuilt in the 16th century when a powerful brick three-floor bastion with casemates for heavy guns was erected round the Lighthouse, and a four-bastion brick and earthwork fortress was built. Works continued in the 17th century when the right river bank fortifications of the fortress were shielded by the earthen five-bastion Eastern Bulwark and then a smaller Western Bulwark was constructed on the left bank of the Vistula river. Work on the Vistulamouth Fortress fortifications continued in the 18th century, when the stone shelters were constructed. The fortress lost its military importance in the 19th century and it was partially damaged. The Vistulamouth Fortress was not used after World War II because of serious obstacles. One was atmospheric pollution at the site caused by Gdansk Phosphorous Fertilizer Plant and the strong presence of sulphuric dust caused by 'Siaropol'. The second obstacle is the partition of the site between the Treasury and the local councils. The World Monuments Fund nomination helped to obtain financial support for the Vistulamouth Fortress protection, for a pilot conservation project on the Artillery Bastion at the fortress and for initial restoration work.

Pomiechowek, 19th-century Russian fort, one of the Modlin stronghold military objects, still used by the army

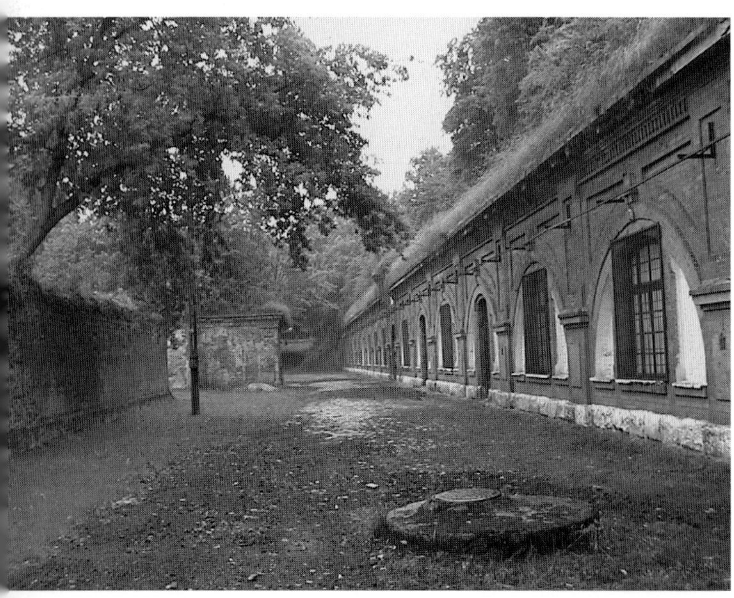

Directions for activity

The significance of historic defence systems and fortress landscapes has become more accepted in Poland. They are beginning to be treated as a shared European heritage. There are, however, still many problems regarding their proper preservation and management, noting that many significant fortresses have still not been renovated. Problems relate to the large size of military areas, the lack of management or bad management, result from today's restructure of the Polish army, legal imperfections and the deficiency of our education, as well as various other reasons. These problems have to be solved quickly if we want to keep fortresses in Poland for future generations and find new uses related to culture, education and tourism. The same, or very similar problems occur in various other countries, not only in Europe but also around the world.

Lidia Klupsz. ICOMOS Working Group on Fortifications
ICOMOS Poland

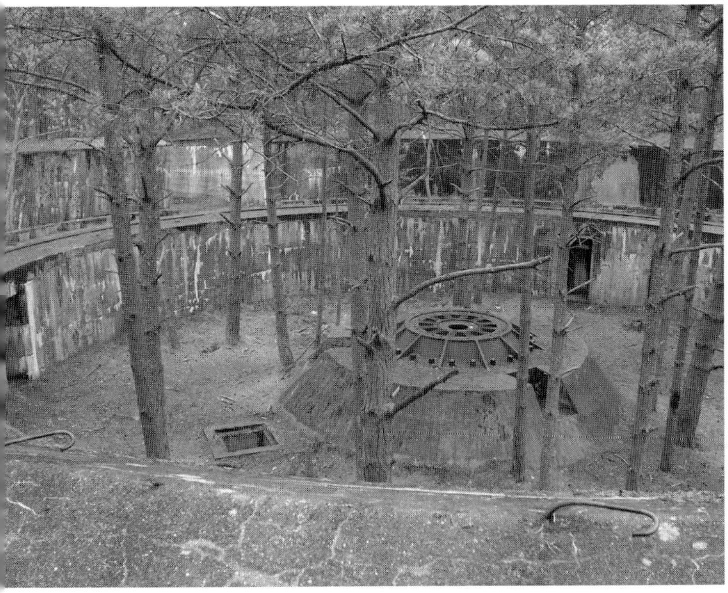

Schleswig Holstein Battery on Hel Peninsula, an example of a German military structure from World War II

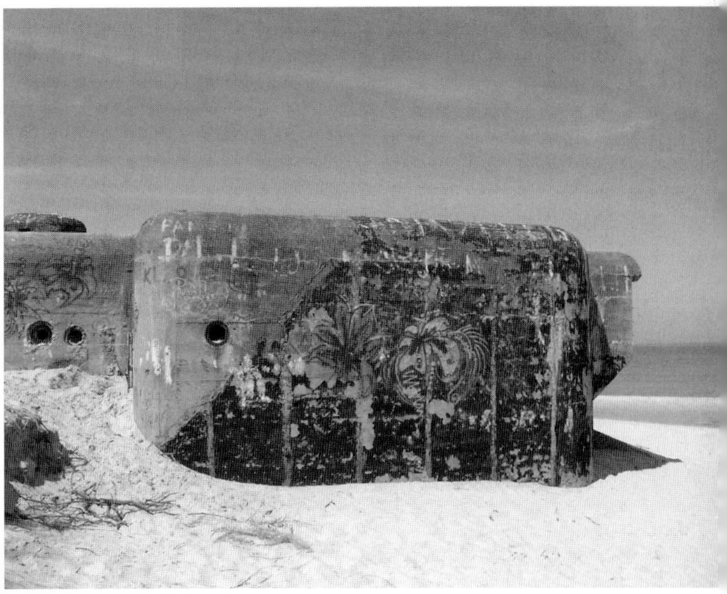

Jastarnia, an example of a Polish shelter from 1939 on Hel Peninsula

Buszno, west-Poland, example of a Soviet military structure from the Cold War

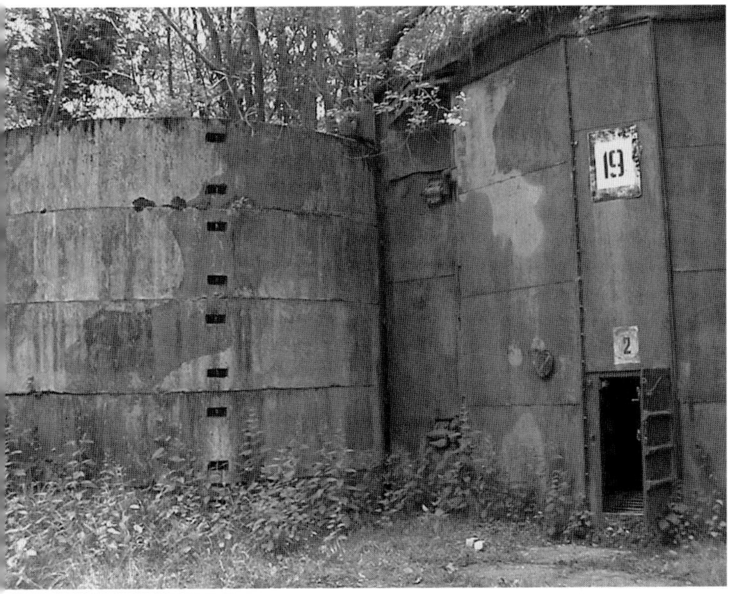

Brzeznica, near Borne Sulinowo, example of a Soviet military structure for missiles from the Cold War

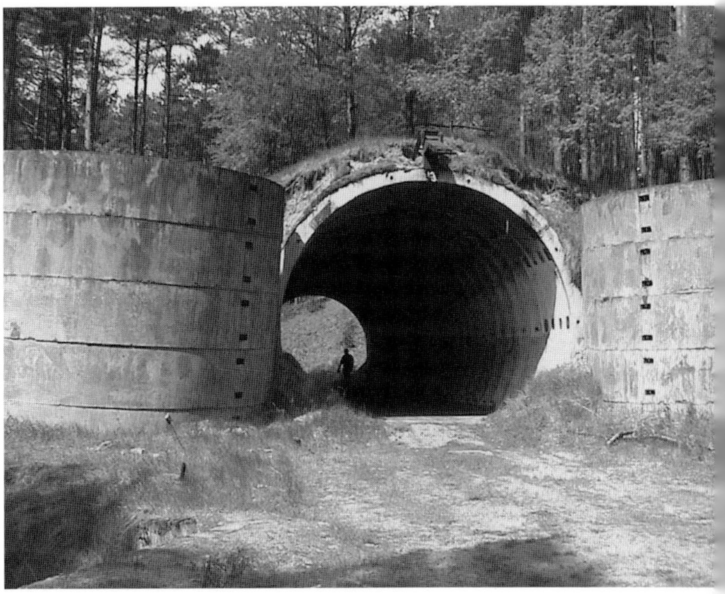

Wildenbruch Palace, Swobnica

If a building is no longer used adequately and lacks necessary maintenance, it will fall into disrepair very quickly. An example is Wildenbruch Palace in Swobnica, which survived Word War II undamaged, but is now seriously at risk. The Palace, that belonged to the Margravate of Brandenburg-Schwedt, was built from 1680 by the Prussian Electress Dorothea, second wife of the Great Elector. Its central projection originally was crowned by a pediment, and the palace integrated the round tower as well as other parts of the original medieval castle of the Order of St John. It is likely that the architect was the Dutchman Cornelis Rijkwaert, who worked in North Germany in the late 17th century and also built the Electress' residence in nearby Schwedt on the other side of the river Oder.

Many buildings by Rijkwaert, who was also the architect of Oranienbaum Palace near Dessau, were destroyed after 1945, for instance the palaces in Schwedt and Hohenfinow-an-der-Oder. In all the rooms of the three-storeyed Wildenbruch Palace, richly ornamented stucco ceilings can be found, though these are mostly in a deplorable state. These ceilings are presumed to be the work of Giovanni Battista, Jean Bellon and Giovanni Simonetti, all three stucco artists who also worked in another building by Rijkwaert, the recently restored Junkerhaus in Frankfurt-an-der-Oder.

The side wings of Wildenbruch Palace were subsequently added to the *corps de logis* by Johann Friedrich Nering. He was the chief architect for the Great Elector and worked for the Electress after Rijkwaert's death.

We can only hope that reporting on this forgotten example of European architectural history in this edition of *Heritage at Risk* will result in an initiative to save this outstanding building.

Klaus Merten

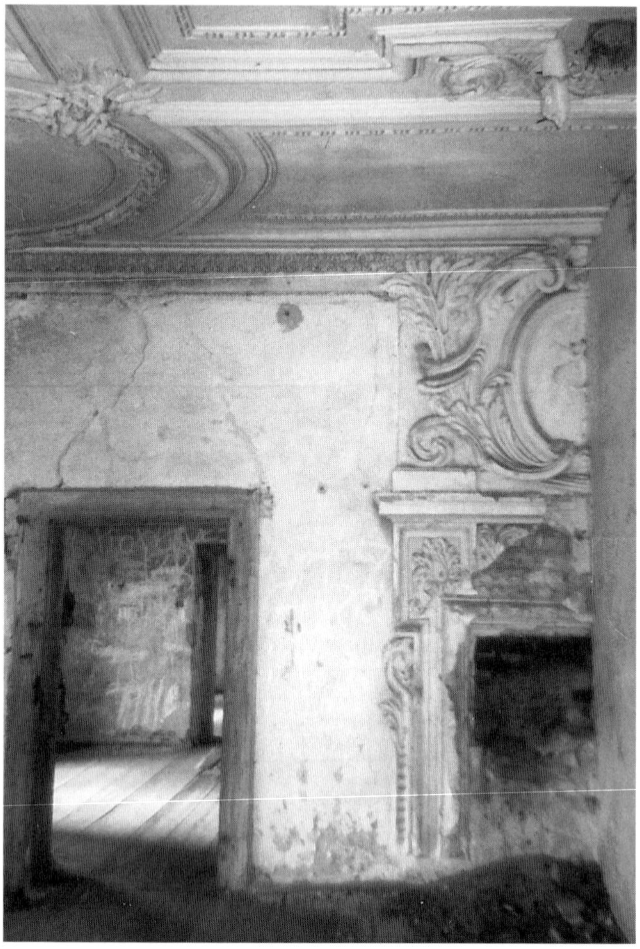

Wildenbruch Palace, interior with stucco work

Wildenbruch Palace in Swobnica

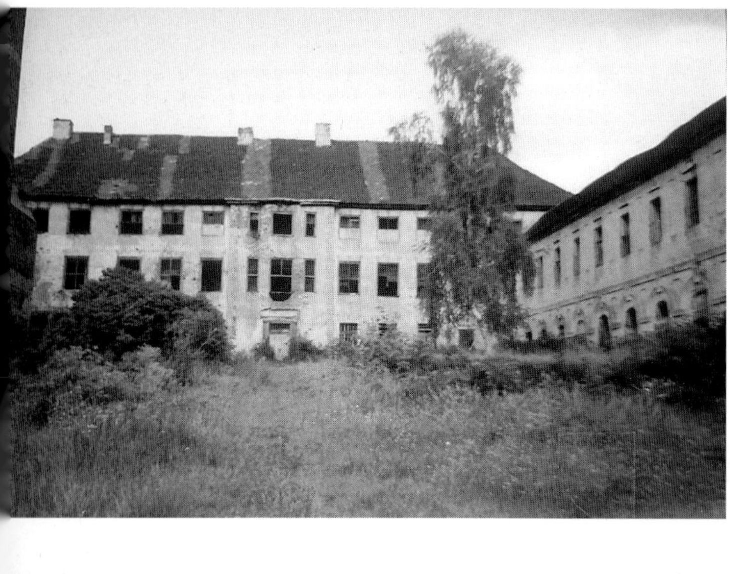

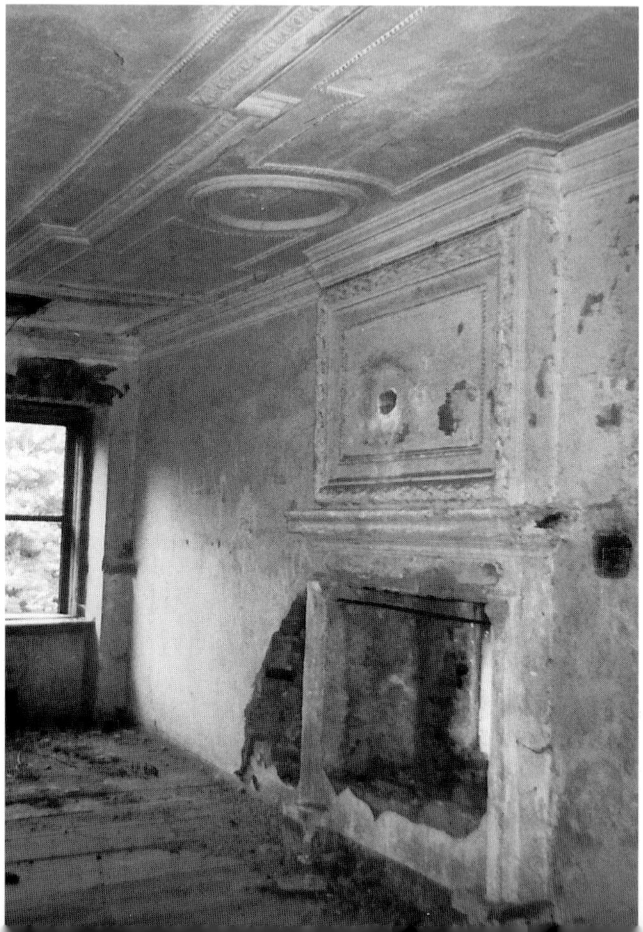

ROMANIA
Heritage at Risk in Roşia Montana

In spite of all protests (see *Heritage at Risk* 2002/2003, pp. 175/176) the cultural heritage in Roşia Montana is still very much at risk.

According to the plans of Roşia Montana Gold Corporation 331 tons of gold and 1600 tons of silver are meant to be exploited in the region of Roşia Montana in the next 17 years. The open-air mining process would destroy the greatest part of the town as well as several cultural monuments. The Roman and medieval mining galleries of several kilometres length are of outstanding value. Only the medieval centre of Roşia Montana (Hungarian name Verespatak) with its three churches and some buildings from the 18th century or earlier would remain on the shore of a 180 m deep artificial lake filled with cyanides, which threaten the valley of the Maros and the Tisza. The new settlement for the people of Roşia Montana would be situated above the Roman mining settlement Alburnus Maior. The archaeological excavations of the previous years could not bring everything to the light. On the contrary, they proved the extraordinary richness of the site, which would perish completely.

ICOMOS issued two resolutions about the case of Roşia Montana at its General Assemblies in Madrid 2002 and Victoria Falls 2003. These emphasised the responsibility of the decision-makers for the dangerous situation. The ICOMOS congress in Pécs (40 Years of the Venice Charter, 22–27 May 2004) reiterated its concerns about this matter and called upon all authorities to take further steps in order to save both the cultural and the natural heritage in Roşia Montana:

ICOMOS rejects the investment of the new gold mine of Roşia Montana (Romania). This dangerous technology threatens the natural heritage of the site and the fauna and flora of the rivers Maros and Tisza, as well as the cultural heritage of the old mines used from Prehistoric through Roman and Middle Ages, endangers equipment of the old mining technology as well as 18th-century architectural heritage of the small mining town. The new residential area offered for the inhabitants of the old town would annihilate the remains of the original Roman settlement, Alburnus Maior.

Despite two resolutions of ICOMOS about this case, preparations for the investment are still going on. ICOMOS demands to stop the investment immediately.

Pécs, 27 May 2004

Roşia Montana, 17th-century stone breaking mill

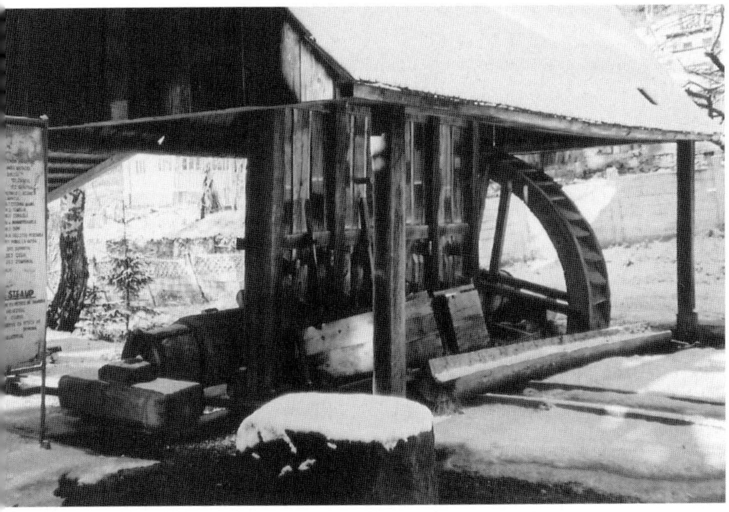

Roşia Montana, Catholic church

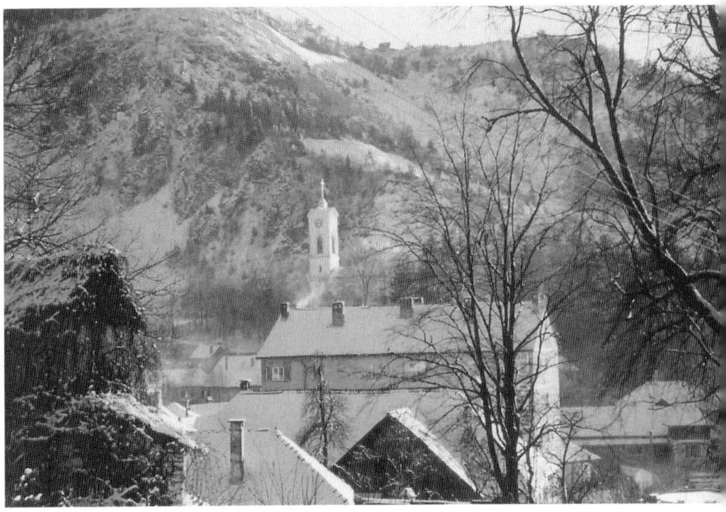

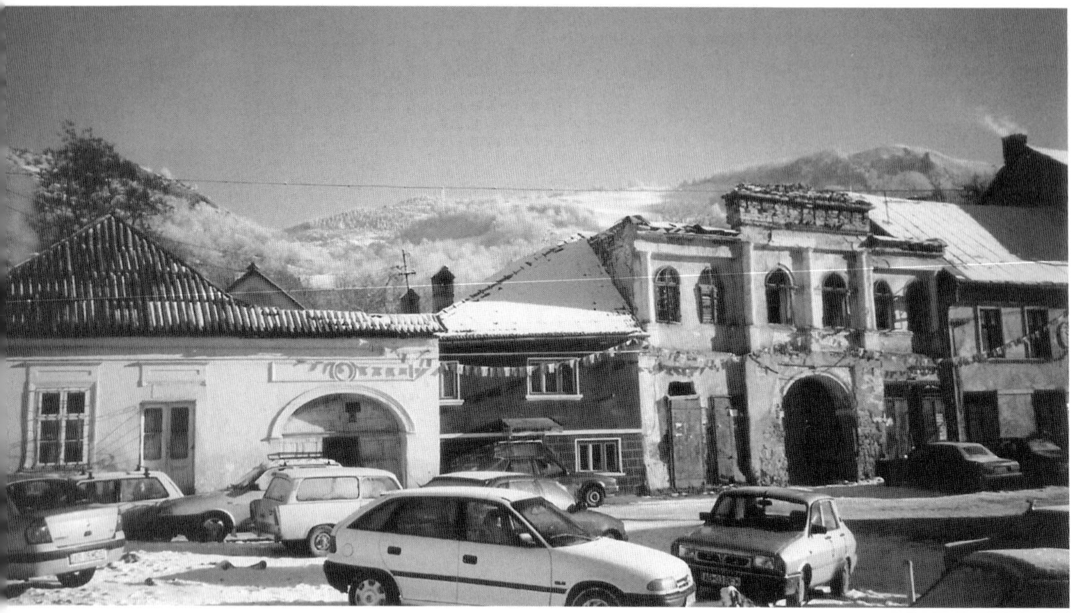

Roşia Montana, main square

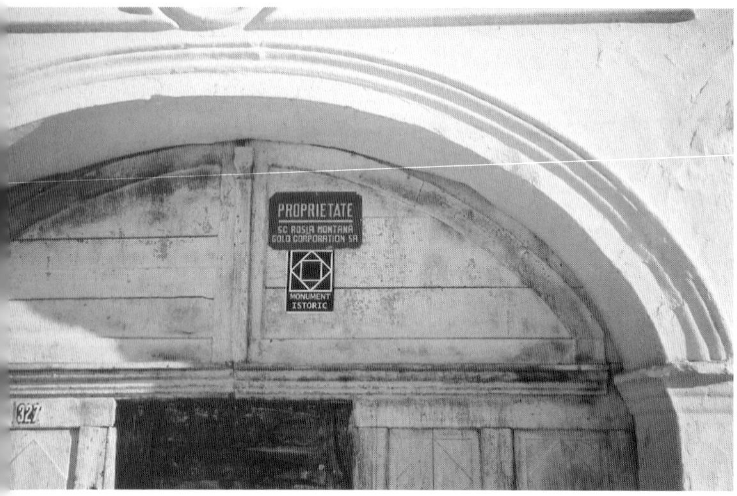

Roşia Montana, historic monument, property of Roşia Montana Gold Corporation

Roşia Montana, old crucifix

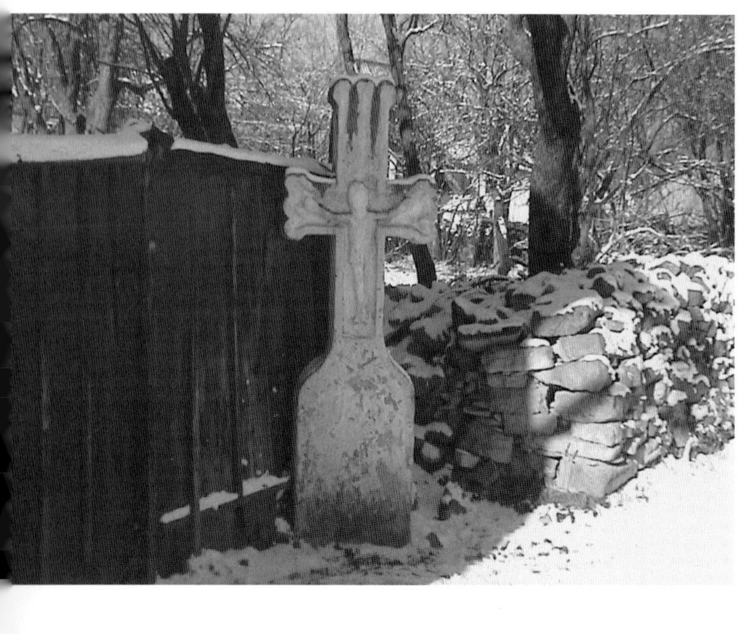

Roşia Montana, Roman gallery

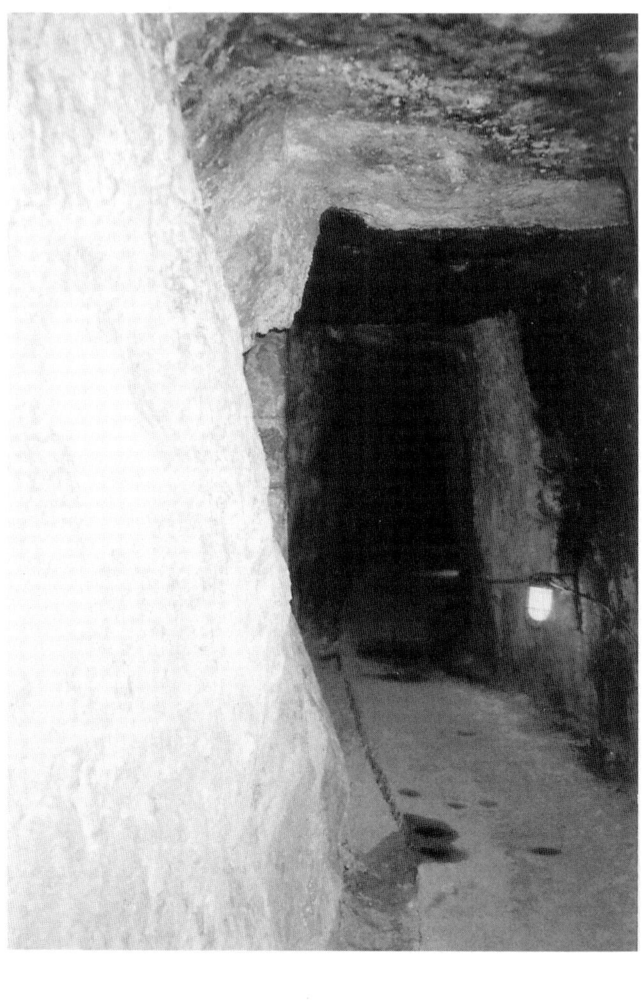

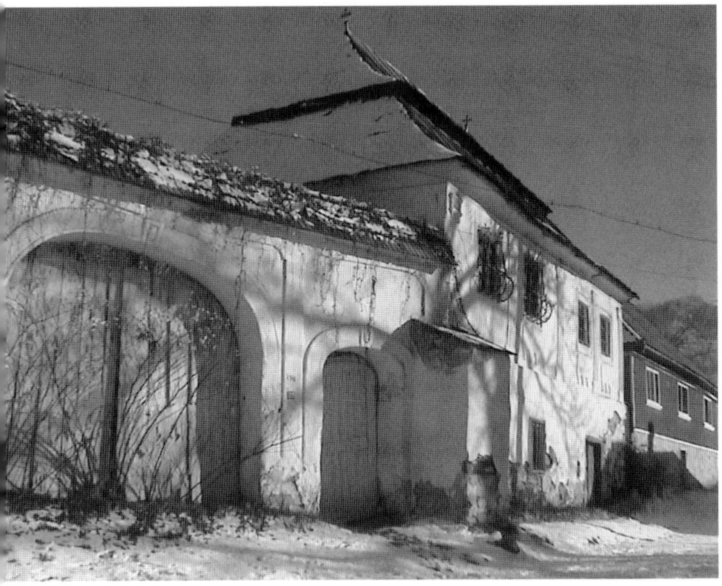

Roşia Montana, old house

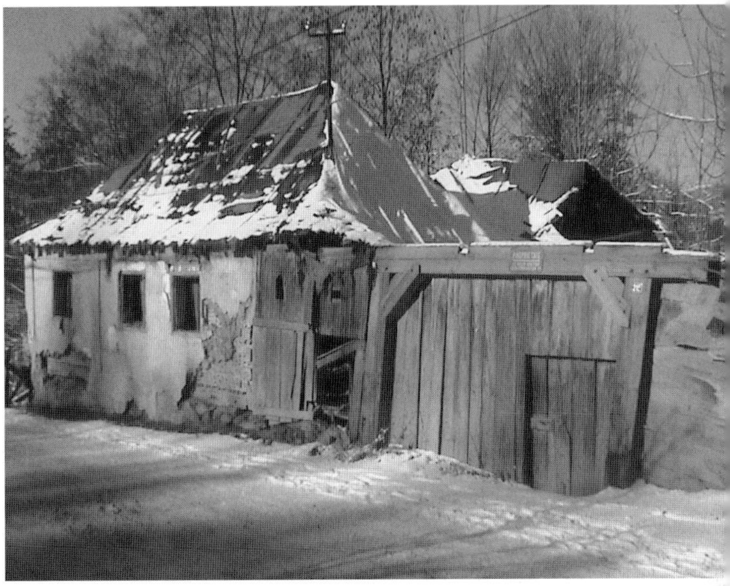

Roşia Montana, property of Gabriel Resources

Roşia Montana, Roman gallery

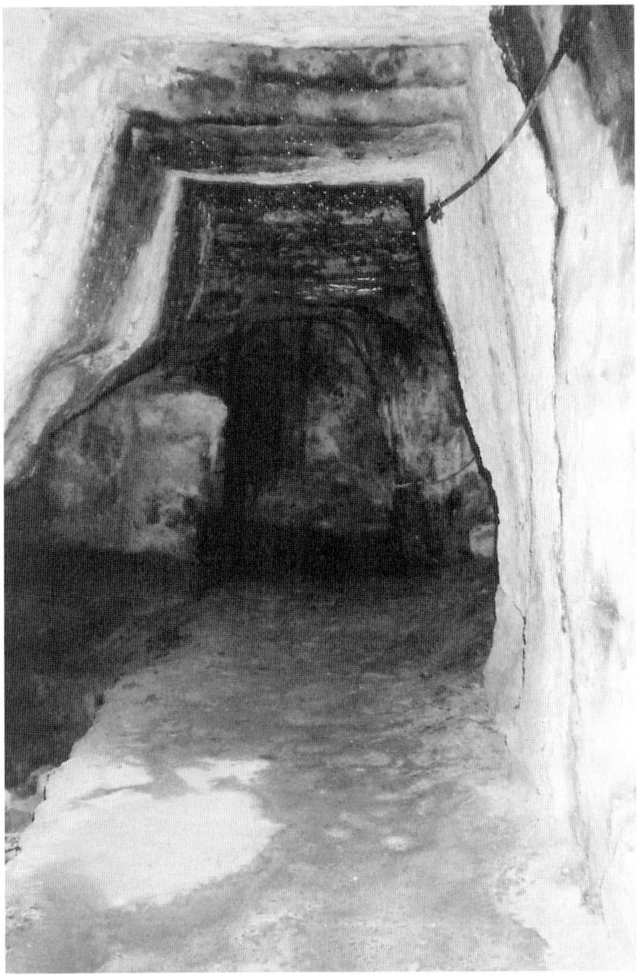

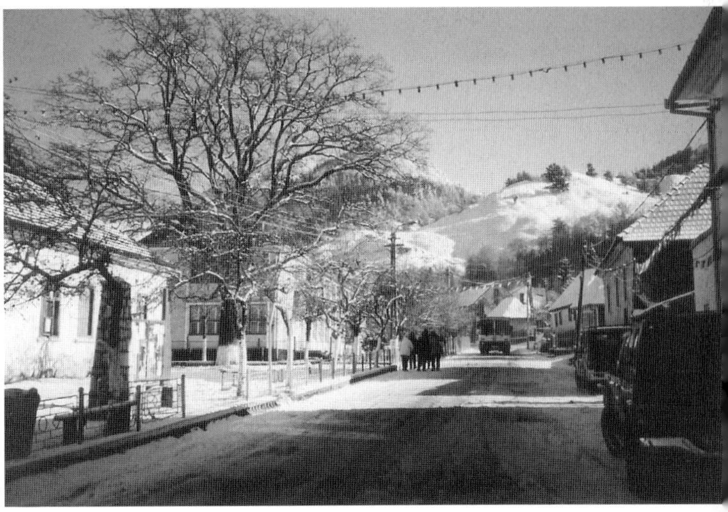

Roşia Montana, main street

Roşia Montana, mine entrance

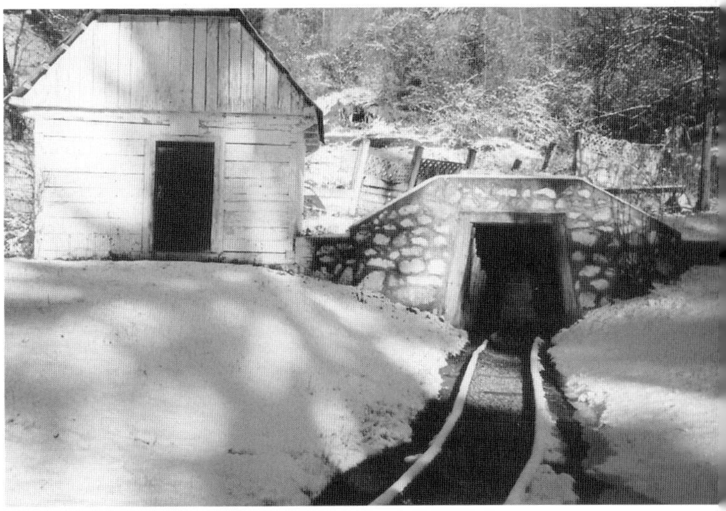

RUSSIA
Perspectives on privatisation

The media often influences how the general public perceives issues in cultural heritage conservation. The following two examples about the possibility of privatising part of Russia's heritage show this clearly. The articles also highlight a major issue in all countries but particularly in those moving towards capitalist systems – how to fund heritage protection and conservation. Here issues regarding the selling of state-owned heritage buildings to private owners are fully canvassed.

Privatising Is the Only Way to Save Many Historic Monuments

Governor Valentina Matviyenko's initiative to privatise historical buildings has caused a stir in Russia. Many have a sinking feeling in the pit of their stomach. Yet how should the matter be dealt with? The idea of handing them over is upsetting, yet not letting them go will be their ruin.

The authorities are consoling those who fear what might happen to these monuments. The matter is nothing to do with well-known establishments like the Hermitage, Peterhof, or the Russian Museum. Moreover, the establishments likely to be privatised are those which are in an unsatisfactory condition and lack efficient users (criteria which, truthfully speaking, have been seriously eroded.) Representatives of the Culture Ministry emphasise that if they are privatised, use of monuments will be strictly controlled.

The idea of privatising monuments was quickly opposed by one influential figure Mikhail Piotrovsky, director of the State Hermitage Museum. His arguments are as follows: „Cultural monuments cannot be fully owned by anyone – neither by private individuals nor by the state. We received our cultural heritage to pass it on to the next generation, not to do with it as we please".

Critics of Matviyenko's idea point to two basic risks – unsatisfactory restoration, and the use of monuments for unsuitable purposes. „For example, to serve as a restaurant" writes someone from the ranks of the conservatives. In theory, the state can easily control both these issues. All the same, it is well known how bureaucrats control businessmen. The effectiveness of such control is distinctly dubious.

On the other hand, even a cursory study of the situation concerning so-called „second-class" monuments reveals two things. Firstly, they are in a horrific condition. Secondly, there is an obvious lack of state funds for restoration, and an absence of a notable number of businessmen willing to put their money into restoration under any conditions. The recent story of the private residence on the English Embankment being leased to LUKoil clearly demonstrates the reason for the stalemate – the price of the matter, that is to say the cost of restoration, is huge. It amounts to tens of millions of dollars. Serious businessmen don't want to invest that kind of money without firm guarantees that the building won't be seized back after reparation. And in our country even right of ownership does not give a 100-percent guarantee. Thus entrepreneurs prefer not to take the risk.

Entrepreneurs are one thing. Yet even the Russian Orthodox church – an institution treated so well in every way by the authorities – is not exactly bursting to take back the churches once nationalised by the Communists. Why, for example, did the church choose Kazan Cathedral as its pulpit? Why not the spiritual St Isaac's? As far as we know, the main argument in favour of Kazan Cathedral was its better preservation and compactness.

City Hall's committee for the conservation of monuments has published a list of monuments that could be first in line to be auctioned off. The present state of some of them is no better than the Konstantin Palace before restoration, which cost, as we recall, more than $300 million. Only the walls remain of stables belonging to the Znamenka estate. The Samoilovoi Palace with its park not far from Pavlosk is, without the slightest exaggeration, a pile of bricks. The Sheremetyev private residence on Shpalernaya is the left-over ashes of the former Union of Writers. The palace of Grand Duke Alexei Alexandrovich on the Moika is somehow still standing. But opposite stands the monstrosity of the Admiralty shipyards. This is the view from the windows. I don't think there will be many volunteers wanting to privatise and restore these monuments back to their original state.

But this is St Petersburg. Go a few kilometres away from the centre into the depths of the Leningrad region, and how many cultural monuments will we find there? And in what condition!

I believe the main argument of those opposed to privatisation is rooted on an emotional level. The truth is that the degradation of stables and their 'use for unsuitable purposes' did not begin under the Bolsheviks. From the middle of the 19th century stables were sold and used as factories.

Our decisive governor Matviyenko is offering a radical solution - to privatise. And it seems she has the right idea. Privatisation is the only way to preserve monuments - not only in a material sense but in a legal one too. Yet after all this, they say that Piotrovsky has succeeded in raising doubts at the very highest level about the expediency of privatisation, and thus a final solution is being delayed. What a century we live in ...

Vladimir Gryaznevich
St Petersburg Times, Opinion
News from Russia in English
18 May 2004

Oligarchs line up to buy listed buildings...

The governor of St Petersburg has proposed legislation that will allow the sale of palaces for half their estimated value – but to be restored

The St Petersburg city government has announced plans to privatise more than 2,000 listed buildings over the next few years, including several dozen important Czarist-era palaces. Several of Russia's oil barons have already expressed strong interest in acquiring grand historic residences in the city.

While the city currently rents [out], but does not sell, listed buildings to private companies, St Petersburg governor, Valentina Matvienko, said last month that privatisation is the only way to save the city's dilapidated historical centre from total ruin because the government does not have the funds to maintain these buildings properly.

"Businessmen say that if they owned the palaces they rent, they wouldn't be afraid to invest in renovation," said Ms Matvienko. "We need to be careful that the city's architectural style isn't altered but, at the same time, we can't allow our architectural heritage to crumble." It is not yet known whether the proposed new law would allow foreigners to purchase property in St Petersburg, a subject on which Ms Matvienko will not be drawn. Such a liberalisation would certainly provoke a strong response from Russian nationalists.

Ms Matvienko said that a list of the first group of buildings to be sold is still being compiled, but local media have reported that these include the suburban Znamenka Palace near Peterhof, the Kochubei Palace in Pushkin, and the Sheremetev Palace in the city centre, part of which houses a branch of the State Museum of Theatre and Music.

Ms Matvienko, who is close to President Putin, has asked city legislators to prepare a law allowing for the privatisation of listed buildings. It is expected to be ready later this year.

She has also said that she will ask the State Duma, which is currently controlled by the pro-Putin political party, United Russia, to amend a 2001 federal law forbidding the privatisation of federally protected sites.

According to preliminary plans, the city plans to sell listed buildings for half their market value, but the new owners must agree to undertake full renovation in consultation with specialists from St Petersburg's Landmarks Preservation Committee (KGIOP). The new owners of the listed buildings must also provide public access several times a year.

"This will be ownership with serious obligations and under strict State control," said Vera Dementieva, head of the KGIOP: "Owners will be required to repair listed buildings, or they will forfeit ownership".

Privatisation may have already begun. Last month the local media revealed that Russia's second richest man, oil magnate Roman Abramovich, who currently resides in England, is spending $5 to $10 million on renovations to the Tenishev Palace on the English Embankment, next to the State Historic Archives, which President Putin has taken over for his own administration.

A few hundred metres down the embankment, Russia's largest oil company, Lukoil, is preparing to purchase the Baron Stieglitz Palace, on which it currently has a 49-year lease. The company said it will spend $30 million on renovating its palace and gardens over the next two years.

John Varoli

9 June 2004

SERBIA AND MONTENEGRO

The risks facing the cultural and natural heritage of Serbia and Montenegro are still marked by the delayed societal transitions. Economic crises and political instability exert a great influence on the working conditions in which the heritage conservation service operates. Significant efforts have been made during the past three years towards improving the organisation of this service, linking with international institutions, improving knowledge, upgrading methodologies, supporting strategic planning, and determining the priority of involvement on the basis of the type and degree of threat to heritage. Despite this, insufficient financial resources still cripple or hinder the realisation of most of the planned conservation projects. These circumstances greatly impede professional activities, as well as prompt expert, preventive and operational involvement in tasks to protect and conserve cultural heritage. This is the reason why annual programs and urgent interventions still take precedence over long-term programs, which strive for a more complex understanding of cultural properties and are the only ones which can guarantee any continuity for conservation.

Case Study 1 – Protection of archaeological excavation along the route of the future Niš – Macedonia highway

Systematic expert surveys, carried out during 2002 along the route of the future highway between Niš and the Macedonian border, have recorded 22 archaeological sites which would be destroyed by this road construction. Salvage archaeological excavations were carried out for the Institute for the Protection of Cultural Monuments of Serbia on nine of these archaeological sites between February and September 2003.

The excavation results indicate long periods of occupation in the Vranje and Preševo basins, from prehistoric (settlements from 5000 BC up to the 10th century BC) and Classical times (necropolis, thermae, *villa rustica*, *vicus* 4th–5th century), to the medieval (*necropolis*, sacral buildings 14th–16th centuries). Until now, these sites were unknown to experts, and they indicate intensive settlement in the Vranje and Preševo basins, primarily thanks to their natural resources and strategic location. This area was also part of the natural communication route connecting the southern Balkan Peninsula with Central Europe.

The newly discovered archaeological sites are located directly on the route of the new highway, or in its immediate vicinity. Subsequent research indicated that only some of these sites will be endangered by construction work. The risk of damage to the partly excavated sites is multiplied by illicit excavations and treasure hunters. There is also an extremely negative attitude to medieval Orthodox sacred buildings and *necropoli* on the part of the local community in this part of southern Serbia. The risks of further damage to these heritage sites could perhaps be reduced if the archaeological sites were fully investigated, not only the area threatened by the highway construction, and if surviving architectural remains were appropriately displayed to the public.

Case Study 2 – Smederevo fortress

The medieval fortress on the right bank of the Danube, situated on today's pan-European corridor, 45 km from Belgrade, was built in the Byzantine tradition of fortifications. It has its original architectural body of a fortification complex dating from late medieval

Archaeological site Crkvište, remains of sacred building (14th – 15th century)

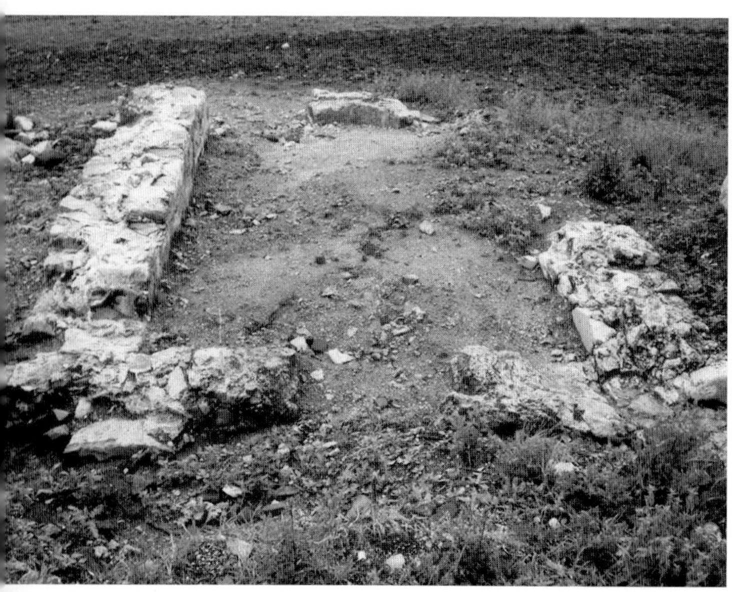

Old cemetery, Grave no. 1, necropolis (14th – 16th century)

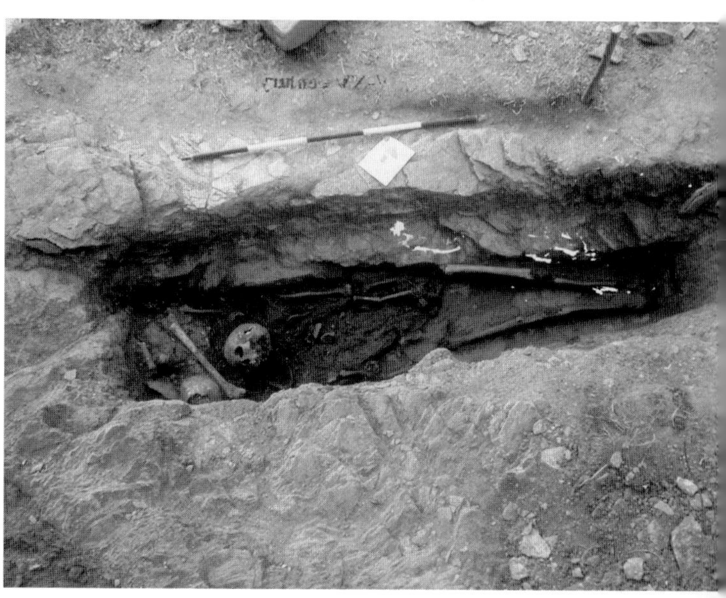

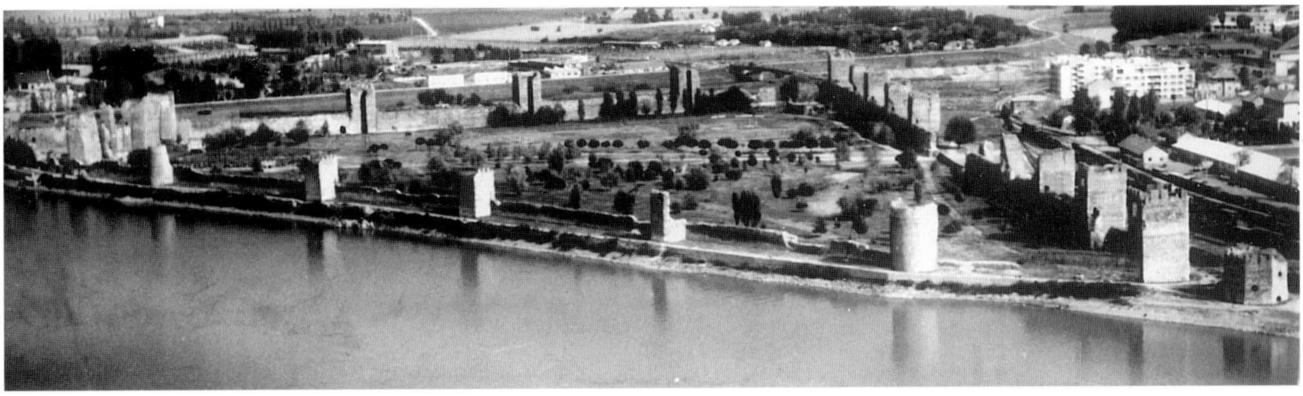

Smederevo fortress, fortification complex

times. During the period of its most intensive occupation, in the first half of the 15th century, the city of Smederevo was the main political, religious, economic and trade centre in this part of Europe, and a link between the Balkans and Central Europe. The fortress surrounds an inner area of 11 hectares, while its outer area extends to the surrounding urban structures. The grandeur of this fortress is manifested by 25 massive towers about 25 m high, connected by ramparts over 2 m thick. The total length of the ramparts amounts to 1.5 km. The city park is located inside the fortress, and is used occasionally for cultural gatherings, concerts, and fairs. The immediate surroundings of the fortress are used as a boat marina, the area along the river-bank as a river port, and the fort is also partly encircled by railway tracks.

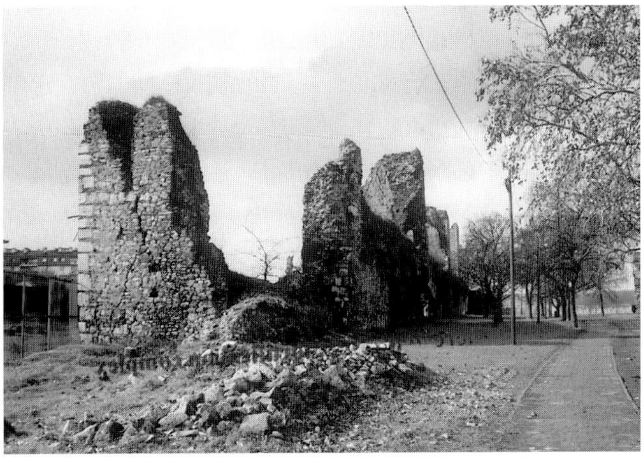

Smederevo fortress, detail

Different natural and unnatural factors currently affect the general state of this monument complex. The fortress suffered considerable damage during both World Wars. It was bombed several times. During World War II, the explosion of a munitions dump located inside the fort demolished a large section of the ramparts facing the city, while certain parts of the walls were loosened and dislodged. This situation remains unchanged up to the present day. During construction of the Danube hydro-electric plant in the Đerdap Gorge in the 1970s, a high water level defence system was erected. Before this, the fortress was flooded several times. Nevertheless, after the construction of the hydro-electric plant, problems appeared with high levels of ground water and ground instability on the plateau between the two rivers where the fortress stands. They caused a permanent risk of the walls and towers subsiding, and resulted in a serious disturbance to the stability of the entire complex. The railway station with its associated buildings is a particular problem, endangering the fortress and its satisfactory use given its location and function. There is also the ever-present danger of inappropriate structures being built around the complex, in the fort's immediate surroundings.

On the whole, all these factors have worked together over time to cause the slow deterioration of the Smederevo Fortress, primarily due to current existing renovation plans not being carried out.

Smederevo fortress, detail

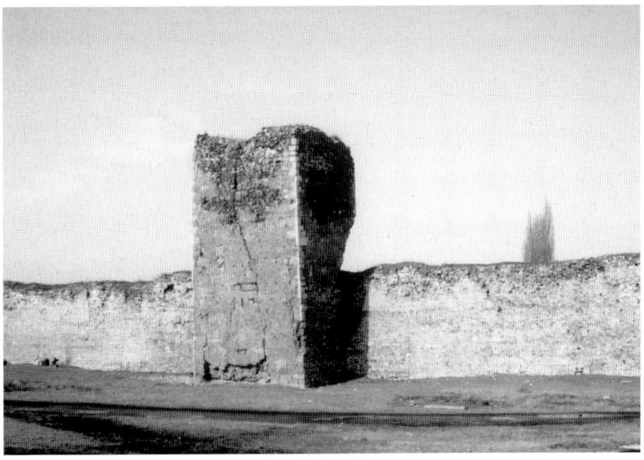

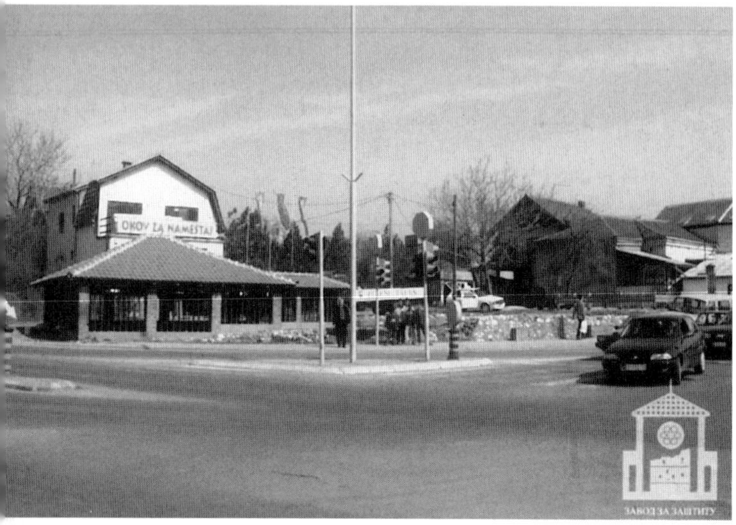

Niš, Basilica with martirium

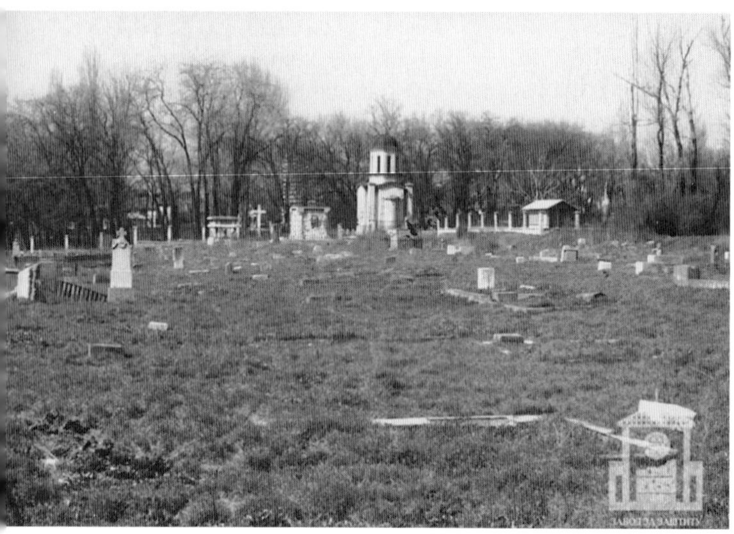

Niš, St. Panteleimon Cemetery

Niš, Old Cemetery

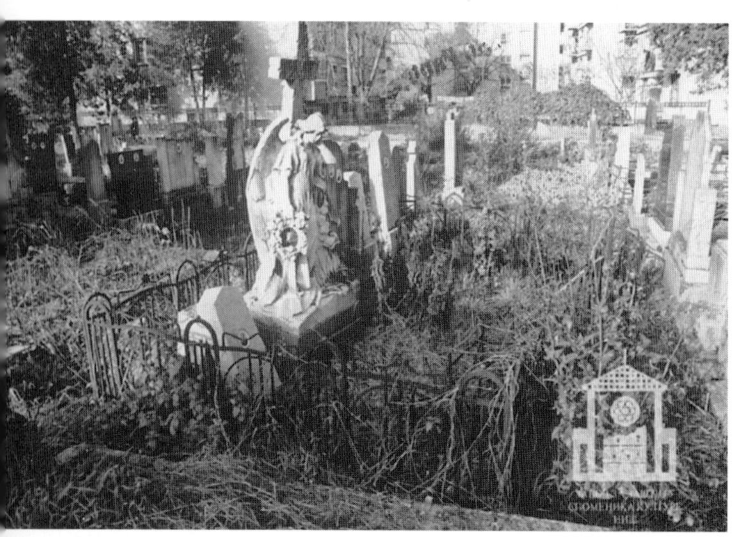

Case Study 3 – Old cemeteries in Niš

Jagodin-mala, a late Classical and early Christian *necropolis,* extends to the north-east of the fortress, the area on which ancient and medieval Niš was located. It represents an extremely significant archaeological site because it was used for burial from the 4th up to the 12th century. Beside individual graves, there are built and group crypts. The most significant is an early Christian crypt decorated with frescoes (from the end of the 4th century), while the foundations of a *basilica* with *martirium* are located on the very edge of the *necropolis.*

Urban development and the construction of new residences threaten all these items, as well as the *necropolis* as a whole. Indeed, a settlement was first established here towards the end of the 19th century, and subsequent urban development has led to intense construction which continues unabated, although without city planning or control of what is happening at the site. Many crypts have been demolished as a result or used as foundations, cellars, or even septic tanks.

Panteleimon Cemetery was formed at the end of the 19th century, next to the Church of St Panteleimon on the north-eastern outskirts of the city, as an extension to an existing medieval and early Christian *necropolis.* Burials took place until the end of the 1940s. For many years since then, the cemetery was used as a children's playground, for grazing cattle, and for rubble and rubbish disposal. This resulted in most of the gravestones being pulled down, taken away, or covered over, while a number of graves were moved to other cemeteries. Today, only two family chapels and several gravestones remain visible. Part of the cemetery has been usurped by the construction of houses, while the remaining area is being considered as a possible city park.

Old Cemetery (cemetery below the *Gorica*): the Old Cemetery of Niš is stretched out in the southern part of the city, on the edges of the old city nucleus. Although it is impossible to confidently determine this cemetery's date of origin, it is certain that it was used as a burial ground as far back as the 18th century. The oldest preserved graves date back to the beginning of the 19th century. Burials were ended in 1971, and thanks to this, many heritage sites from different periods of the last two centuries are still preserved in this cemetery.

Today, it is completely surrounded by the city. It contains several thousand graves, crypts, and family chapels. Its artistic and historic value can be attributed to some 200 heritage sites, eight of which are heritage listed. The entire cemetery was registered in 1991 as a cultural and historic complex.

The problem with this graveyard, as with most old graveyards in Serbia, basically stems from general negligence by the community as well as the cemetery services responsible for their care and maintenance. This is why the graveyard is quite neglected, covered with weeds, hounded by bands of stray dogs, and turned into a dump. The council's care amounts to trimming the bushes each spring. As always, an excuse for such neglect is found in the lack of permanent funding for maintenance. The graveyard is still disorganised in the urban sense, with no structured paths (except for the main one), and with no lighting or guards; some areas present a very ugly picture.

In the past, this state of affairs led to occasional vandalism of individual sites, even to looting chapels and breaking into crypts. Many graves have been desecrated. Nevertheless, there was hardly any concern for this state of affairs. During the 1970s and early 1980s, there was even a proposal to move this cemetery and build an apartment complex in its place.

The situation became alarming when, towards the end of 2003, a large number of tombs were damaged during a very short period of time (maybe even during one single night). On this occasion of extreme vandalism, some 200 tombstones were damaged - pulled down, broken, or covered in graffiti. This event further violated the already quite degraded heritage values of the Old Cemetery.

In order to protect and preserve this cultural and historical complex, two models have been proposed. One is to turn the cemetery into a memorial park, and place it under permanent city care, the other to reactivate certain parts of the cemetery for burials, in which case the cemetery could rely on its own sources of funding. If the latter solution is adopted, strict criteria for burials, grave memorials, usage and maintenance must be adopted, because old cemeteries are quite often damaged by new burials and tombstones, that are incompatible with existing aesthetic and landscape values.

The Jewish Cemetery is located on the north-western city outskirts, near the former Cattle Market. According to the stories of Jews living in Niš, there are some 1000 Jews buried here, mainly Sephardim from Niš and Prokuplje. The tombstones are mostly in the form of stone sarcophagi (mainly monolithic), or horizontal plates with different stylised decorations of a symbolic character, connected to the Kabala. These tombstones are unique in appearance and artistic treatment. The oldest ones probably date to the 18th century. Besides its artistic and memorial value, this complex also represents an important record of several centuries of Jewish presence in Niš. This cemetery is currently under interim heritage protection.

Many years of general indifference brought this cemetery to a very bad state; it is neglected and has deteriorated, but it has also been overtaken by illegal construction. In fact, a dense illegal Rom [Gipsy] settlement has appeared and grown in the northern part of the cemetery, with house foundations often being built into gravestones, which are used to pave passages and yards, or even as furniture inside the houses. On the opposite side of the graveyard, an illegally erected four-metre-high wall took over part of the cemetery and destroyed a large number of tombstones. A few months ago, someone dumped a large quantity of rubble and covered part of the cemetery. On this occasion, both the public and the responsible institutions showed some interest in the condition of this graveyard.

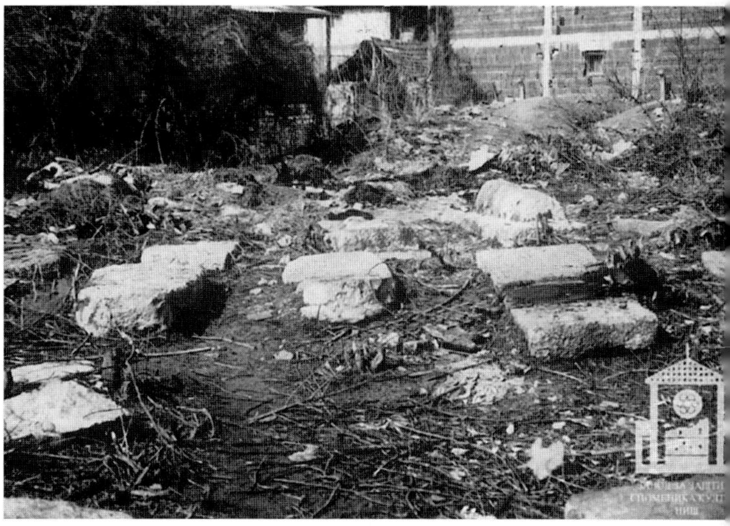

Niš, Jewish Cemetery

Because there are hardly any Jews living in Niš today, the impossibility of quickly and easily removing the illegally constructed buildings, and the lack of necessary financial resources, it is currently difficult to see a solution to save, restore and interpret this important cultural property.

ICOMOS Serbia and Montenegro

SPAIN

Avila – Alterations and construction of a parking lot and new housing in the Plaza de Santa Teresa (the Mercado Grande of Avila)

(abridged translated version of report by ICOMOS Spain)

General frame of reference for this report

The alterations and construction of parking and housing in the Mercado Grande of Avila have been systematically revised in the light of the criteria set out in international documents, on which the judgements of the National Committee of ICOMOS Spain are based, as well as national and regional documents. The basic texts are:

- Venice Charter, 1964
- Convention on Natural and Cultural World Heritage, 1972
- Operational Guidelines for the above Convention
- Statute of Historic Spanish heritage, 1985
- Charter on the Conservation of Historic Towns and Urban Areas, 1987
- International Charter on Cultural Tourism, 1999
- Statute of Cultural Heritage of Castilla and León

Background and development of the project

The project for the construction of a parking area and housing in the Mercado Grande of Avila is complex and has been in development for more than ten years, and is connected to a whole series of town-planning changes being carried out in the city.

Extract chronology:
1993: Architect engaged to make a volumetric study of the property owned by the Caja de Ahorros de Avila (Savings Bank of Avila) at one side of the Plaza de Santa Teresa, and a proposal for new paving.
1994: Two proposals made, including a new street from the Plaza, maintaining traffic in the Plaza, and a parking area for 293 vehicles.
1995: Third proposal, including removal of vehicular traffic from the Plaza by means of an underpass, confirmed as technically possible. The proposal is accepted by the Town Council and the Avila Caja de Ahorros Bank, which so far had taken the initiative. It becomes increasingly clear that the project must be incorporated into the process of review and development of the General Plan and the Specific Plan for the Historic Complex.
1996: The new Mayor gives orders, as suitable, for the inclusion of the alterations to the Plaza de Santa Teresa and the Mercado in the General Plan.
1997–1998: Both of the above plans (1995), with modifications, approved by the Town Council, after study of the legislative framework.
1999: Project for the Plaza del Mercado Grande taken up again, architect chosen for construction of underground parking area. One contrary vote from a Councillor of the United Left Party, who requests an ICOMOS report on the project.
2000: The Municipal Commission approves the project, but at the general session of July the United Left Party warns that it will inform UNESCO, as is obligatory, given the scope of the projected work.
2001–2002: Permit for works granted, with some alterations.
2003: Municipal quantity surveyor approves work, which has now begun, but problems are noted in the Cultural Heritage Report. The architect himself informs members of the Cultural Heritage Commission that he has observed in the plans changes to façades that go beyond the issues considered, and votes against these. He states that professionals in different areas have noted the criteria applicable to work in the area, but no attention has been paid to them. It must be made clear that the modifications to the basic project of 2001 were not sanctioned by any competent public body. Public debate on various parts of the project begins.

A group of six university professors sends a report to the World Heritage Centre of UNESCO, denouncing the project as unsuitable for a site so central to the history of Avila. The United Left and Socialist Workers' parties call for the work to be halted.

UNESCO demands that the project be altered and made suitable for the historic centre of Avila, particularly with regard to the height of surrounding buildings.

Reflections on the Project

The most general consideration is that the authenticity of the Plaza de Santa Teresa and its surrounding area has been very much compromised. This is particularly serious in that the area and its buildings form part of the zone lying between two sites specifically included in the World Heritage Listing – the city wall and the church of San Pedro – with which the Plaza forms a conceptual historic unit. The Plaza is necessarily part of the 'zone of respect' required in the delimitation of all World Heritage sites, as it forms an area essential to the integrity and authenticity of both of the above sites. The Plaza de Santa Teresa (known as the 'Mercado Grande') is a site of the highest value in the traditional environment of Avila for its inhabitants, as there is no other to be compared with it as the true urban focus of the city.

The process:

- According to the Directions for the Application of the World Heritage Convention, in all member nations where World Heritage Sites are registered it is obligatory to announce any project of importance (either new work or restoration) which may noticeably affect the values which were the original cause of the listing as soon as it is under consideration and before any decisions are taken that will be difficult to reverse.
- According to the above, there have been serious irregularities in the legal proceedings, not only in the approval of this substantial and now controversial project, but also in the approval of the establishment of norms by the managing body of Avila, such as the General Plan for Urban Planning and the Special Plan for Protection of the Historic Complex of Avila. These include measures relative to the project, which was already in progress before the approval of the said plans.
- The World Heritage Committee of UNESCO was not informed of the project, which, if done, would have avoided all the problems arising from its development.

The architect:

We cannot ignore the responsibility of Mr José Rafael Moneo Vallés in the inadequacy of the project for the area in question. Any architect must be fully aware of the regulations applying to the site of proposed work. Mr Rafael Moneo is a trained architect, and one of the best known and most reputable Spanish architects, with a great deal of work both within Spain and abroad. For this reason, and the fact of having staff who no doubt assist him, it is unjustifiable that he should make alterations in such basic and unarguable matters as volume, sunlight exposure, arbitrary interpretation of a historic site as a place of memory, respect for environmental values, consideration of sites, the value of the urban landscape, or new constructions in historic cities or the surroundings of monuments - all issues clearly and explicitly discussed in many international charters, as well as in documents produced or accepted by UNESCO.

Formal considerations:

- In this project, and regarding the results, Mr Moneo seems to have shown himself to be completely unaware of the background to his project, despite his efforts to establish the contrary in his statement.
- Given the chronology of the project of reform and construction of parking areas and new buildings in the Plaza de Santa Teresa, it may be seen that both the General and Special Plans were adjusted to the project while taking form, rather than the contrary, with incoherent and illogical results. This process, unethical and unsuitable in urban planning, indicates the inflexibility of the operation. It must be emphasised that from the initial stages there was a marked violation of instructions in that the World Heritage Committee was not informed of the changes to the General and Special Plans, as respectively drafted.
- The most serious aspect from the heritage point of view has to do with the loss of central position for the real landmarks of the area: the wall and church of San Pedro, both declared as World Heritage sites. With the construction of the building marked as 'A', the form, the character of the urban landscape and the traditional atmosphere of this basic enclave have been radically changed. There is now a marked imbalance in favour of the new construction and to the detriment of the monuments.
- Apart from its great importance as a monumental site, the Plaza de Santa Teresa undeniably formed part of the environmental values of the area, and of the 'zone of consideration', without which none of the sites can be properly protected, although they were also guaranteed international protection.
- The completely inappropriate typology of building 'A' is totally foreign to the pre-existing urban landscape, and in open contrast to the wall and church of San Pedro and their surrounding constructions. There is a marked visual impact and distortion of the historic surroundings, minimising the scale of the monuments and weakening the powerful visual relationship between San Pedro and the entrance in the wall, with its parapets. The new construction typology is foreign not only to the adjoining buildings, but also to those of the North side of the Plaza, with its architectural rhythm and 19th-century arcades, and its restrained eclecticism. These considerations do not judge or question the quality of the building in isolation, but its unsuitable placement, out of context, in this part of the city of Avila.
- The total height of the building is to be 5 storeys for building 'A' and 3 for the smaller building 'B'. Building 'A' is to be one storey higher than the taller buildings that were demolished.
- The linkage of building plots has been changed without having provided any adequate solution for urban problems.
- Buildings have been demolished, some of undoubted value, at

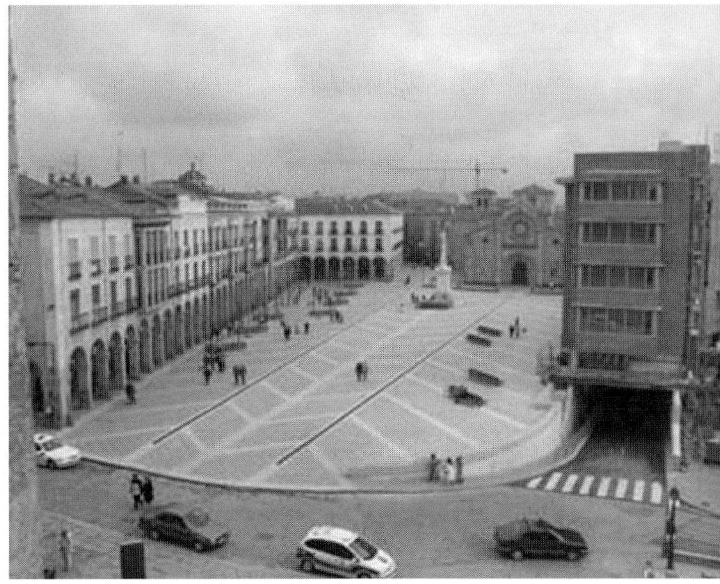

Avila, Plaza de Santa Teresa (Mercado Grande), on the right new building 'A' with entrance to the parking area

Avila, Plaza de Santa Teresa (Mercado Grande), on the right new building 'A' with entrance to the parking area

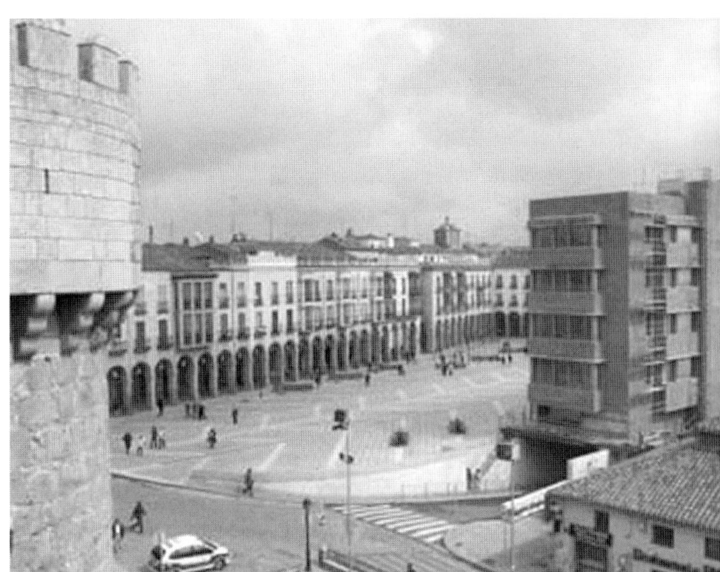

least in the general built environment; these were not included in the General Plan of 1986 or in the Special Plan for Protection of the Historic Complex of Avila, but stand between two sites on the World Heritage List and are within the historic complex of Avila defined as a Cultural Interest Site under Spanish legislation. Therefore, being under international protection, they had a degree of protection higher than that to be granted by any national legislation. In such cases the lack of a specific listing does not mean that the individual sites are not protected, as they form part of an environment, the radical change of which, as caused by the construction in the Plaza de Santa Teresa, is inadmissible. The demolition of the buildings, although local or regional legislation appeared to have been observed, constitutes a flagrant violation of the World Heritage Convention and its Operational Guidelines, which, in such a case as this, are standards of a higher rank than internal laws and other legal dispositions.

- The pre-existing slope of surfaces in the surrounding area has been altered. The slope is also a witness to the process of shaping the Plaza, and does not impede the traditional accessibility to it.
- The surface of the Plaza has been uniformly treated, which, combined with the lack of decorative elements, converts it into a 'hard' area, further emphasising the presence of building 'A'. This, according to a considerable number of residents, has caused a loss of 'atmosphere', and does not encourage its use as a place for walking and relaxation.
- The unsuitability of building 'A' is even greater with regard to the convent and parish church of la Magdalena. This stands on a lower level, and seems almost completely overwhelmed by the volume of the new construction, which in this sector becomes not a 'backdrop', but a complete new façade which seeks to strengthen its presence as the principal element from whichever angle one looks at the Plaza, to be seen at street level and, above all, from the parapet of the wall.
- The materials used on the outside of the new buildings are not adapted in texture or colour to those used around them, and furthermore they are brightly coloured, in contrast with the surrounding buildings.
- The tunnel, which has allowed the Plaza to be made a pedestrian precinct, and gives access to the new parking area and the bypass road, is an aggressive intervention, especially from the area of the wall and La Magdalena, although it also stands out when seen from the Plaza de D Claudio Sánchez Albornoz.
- The shadow thrown over the Plaza, particularly by building 'A', is considerably larger than that of the original buildings, because it has absorbed into a single block the variety of previous buildings, and is higher than any of these.
- This has caused a significant public reaction in the city, as during the long cold winters of Avila the Plaza now receives less sunlight and is less comfortable for use.

Regarding proposed uses:
The presence of parking in a public space should never have arisen for this Plaza for the following reasons:

- Its position in a very important area of the historic complex. Although the Plaza is outside the walls, it is in the centre of the historic framework of Avila, forming part of, and structuring, the suburban fabric. The name 'Mercado Grande' itself shows clearly the significance of this space in the urban environs of Avila.
- It was a place very much involved from an archaeological point of view, as shown by later excavations and the publication of these by the Town Council.
- It is a highly symbolic site, and held in great affection by the town population, not only for its use and the public perception of it, but also in its very name. A comment on its popular name, 'Mercado Grande', has already been made; the official name refers to the best-known figure of the city, Santa Teresa de Avila.
- There is a parking area close by, less than 300 m away, and there is no contention in any document that it is over-used; on the contrary, some commentaries and reports presented in town council meetings speak of under-utilisation.

Other issues:
Although the authors of this report have not carried out an exhaustive inquiry among the town population about the project, during the fieldwork many residents gave on opinion expressly opposed to the construction of building 'A', and none were in favour of it.

Recommendations

- To urge the Town Council of Avila, the Assembly of Castilla and León, and the Government of Spain, in the future, to inform UNESCO, in the manner required, of all projects relevant to any site on the World Heritage List, and in turn to apply strictly the principles of the Agreement and the Instructions of UNESCO at the time of giving permission for any type of town-planning project.
- To begin a process of thorough revision of the town-planning legislation for the management and conservation of the City of Avila, putting special emphasis on the strict fulfilment of the legislation applicable to the area declared as World Heritage and its zone of consideration. This revision must follow the procedures for consultation of the World Heritage Committee of UNESCO.
- To revise, within the previous process, the cataloguing of the Avila Special Plan, as, in the absence of catalogue listing of properties which should have this, there are signs that the listing was incorrectly carried out, leaving aside important categories, particularly regarding properties which form the urban landscape and traditional environment of Avila (the architecture of surrounding monumental sites, as important for the fabric of the city as the sites themselves, the Plaza de Santa Teresa being a principal example in this regard).
- To revise in detail the approval process for the project dealt with in this report, contrasting its content with regard to the basic project or projects.
- To inform the project architect, D José Rafael Moneo Vallés, of the advisability and relevance of a thorough knowledge of the heritage stipulations that affect a site such as the Plaza de Santa Teresa of Avila, which, as has been mentioned, is the historic zone lying between two monumental sites included in the World Heritage List.
- To call for liability, and assume it on behalf on the relevant bodies, regarding the alteration of alignments, building sites and volumetric measurements of historic sites. It is important to realise that the 19th-century configuration of a square may be of the highest socio-urban value in the history of Spanish cities, and a basic element in the understanding and interpretation of the process of shaping a city, and this even though we refer to a city which is substantially valued for its medieval heritage.
- To establish a new project for the reform of the Plaza de Santa Teresa, and buildings 'A' and 'B', which recovers alignments, the arrangement of urban lots, historic volume measurements, typology, texture and colouring of façades, all in harmony with

the character, atmosphere, authenticity and proportions of the square.

- The fact that modifications have been made to part of a historic city at various times, as is the case of the Plaza de Santa Teresa/Mercado Grande, does not imply that carte blanche is given to make any change, and to continue transforming it because its previous state was not, or did not seem to us, good enough, or because of the well-worn demands of architects today to be allowed to insert contemporary constructions into historic complexes, destroying their traditional buildings and spaces. The logical and correct move is to establish, from a specific point which is necessarily the time of inscription in the World Heritage listing that experiments shall no longer be made on a site as significant as the Plaza, above all, those which involve new work which will do no more than reopen the city's wounds. This applies especially as today there exist principles and international standards which, as has been adequately explained, try to avoid this continuing in a historic city which has been declared World Heritage, and in the sites affected by this declaration, and their immediate surroundings.
- With this formula the customary level of sun exposure can be restored to the square, an aspect which deeply concerns many residents who use this public space, beyond the questions directly related to heritage issues.
- The new project, as well as restoring to the façades the rhythm of traditional urban building lots, must vary the treatment of the openings in the façade, principally in the wall of building 'A' that faces the square, introducing another design to reduce the excessive number of openings that it now has (144), and restoring the dimensions and proportions of window spaces in the façade of the previous typology the sum of various architectural styles in harmony with the Plaza as a whole, without falling into mimicry or historical pastiche.
- The system of facing the building with red panels is considered entirely inappropriate in relation to its neighbouring monumental environment, and it should be emphasised that there is no precedent of such a colour treatment. The best solution would be to find a material close in texture and colour range to those of the adjacent monuments and the buildings of the area.
- The pedestrian system of the Plaza should also be restructured, eliminating the 'transparency' of design, and promoting the customary routes for stopping and walking on. The program of plantings is poor and not fully integrated, and should also be improved.
- The passage and access to the parking lot and the underground road from the Plaza itself and in front of the wall, should also be eliminated, reorganising the traffic in this sector, so that access to the parking lot will be in the opposite direction, (for both entering and leaving, through the exit) and in one direction, for the safety of the pedestrians at the front of the Plaza and the access to the historic centre, so as to recuperate a more dignified façade to face the wall. The present entrance to the street and the parking lot must be eliminated by means of a planned integration with the surrounding area.
- A traffic study must be made to analyse other possible parking areas, and to evaluate demand and average traffic density at the perimeter of the historic centre.
- The Avila Town Council is strongly advised to show more sensitivity towards all aspects of conservation, restoration and intervention in the architectural and cultural heritage of the city, and particularly towards the opinion of citizens and legally recognised associations regarding the state of conservation and possible operations to be carried out in their heritage.

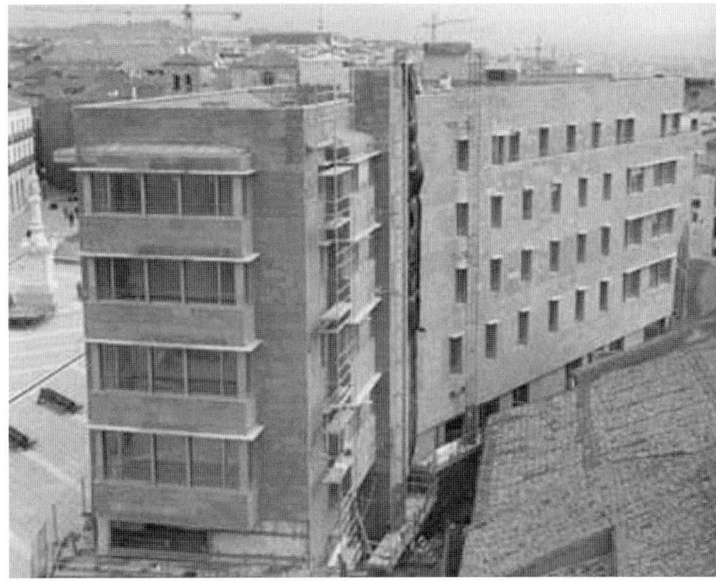

Avila, building 'A' by Rafael Moneo, rear side

Avila, Plaza de Santa Teresa (Mercado Grande), seen from the town wall

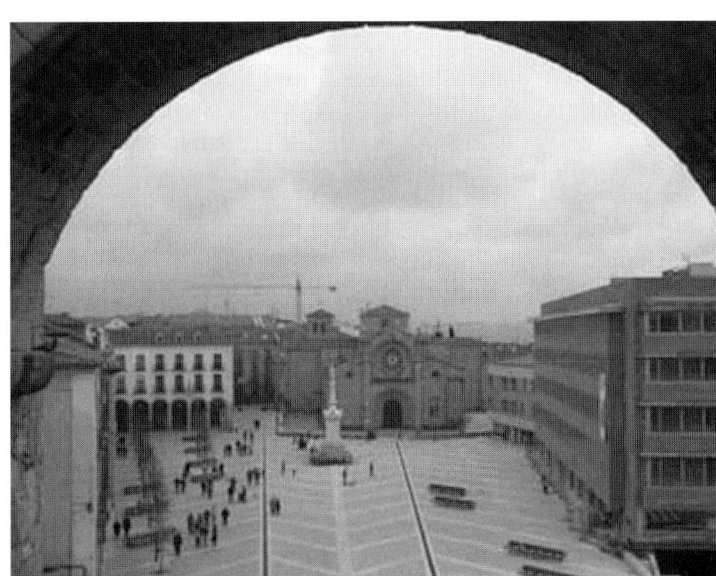

Long term recommendations

- Ensure that all applications that take part in the development and control of projects with World Heritage effect, are fully understood, and UNESCO standards are applied, most importantly the text of the Agreement, and the instructions for application. This must be particularly taken into account by the Department of Culture and regional and local institutions.
- We cannot begin on a project and then 'try to make the work fit the standard or standards'.
- It is essential that new architecture is integrated, and harmonises with the monumental surroundings and with the constructed urban landscape, and that the residents understand, and accept any intervention in their most significant heritage area.
- The residents' perception of the monumental heritage as their own is as important as the management of their maintenance and conservation by elected authorities.
- In the case of historic cities and other kinds of sites listed as World Heritage, it is necessary that citizens are informed of the values that motivated the listing, and the necessity of conserving them, making them conscious of these values, and thus promoting a public awareness which will allow projects to be carried out in accord with the values of authenticity and integrity of the site in question.

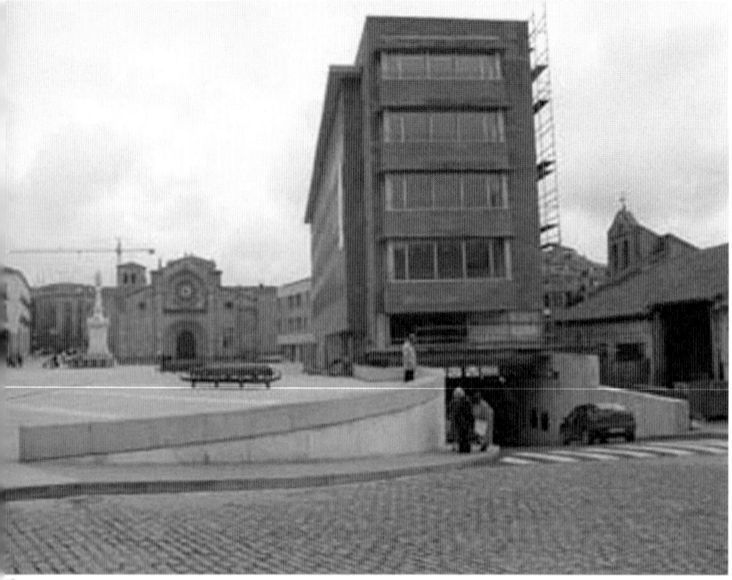

Avila, Plaza de Santa Teresa (Mercado Grande), on the right new building 'A' with entrance to the parking area

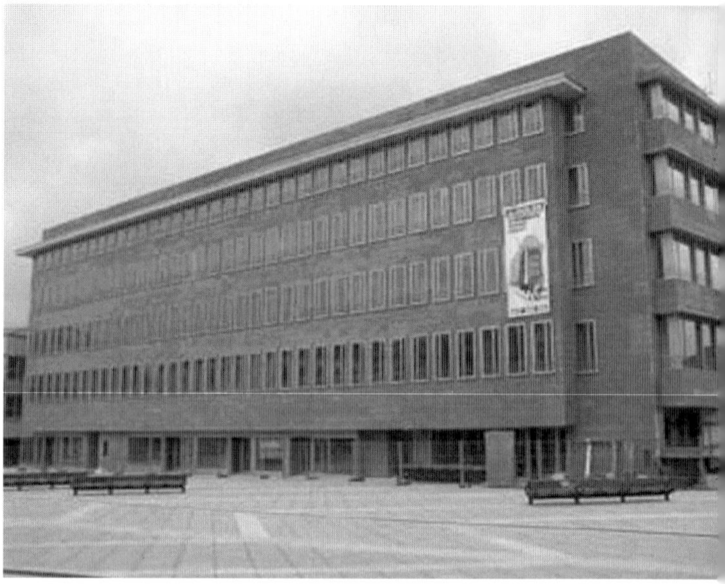

Avila, building 'A' by Rafael Moneo, front

Avila, Plaza de Santa Teresa (Mercado Grande) with town wall and arcaded houses, the visual integrity destroyed by the inappropriate scale and typology of building 'A'

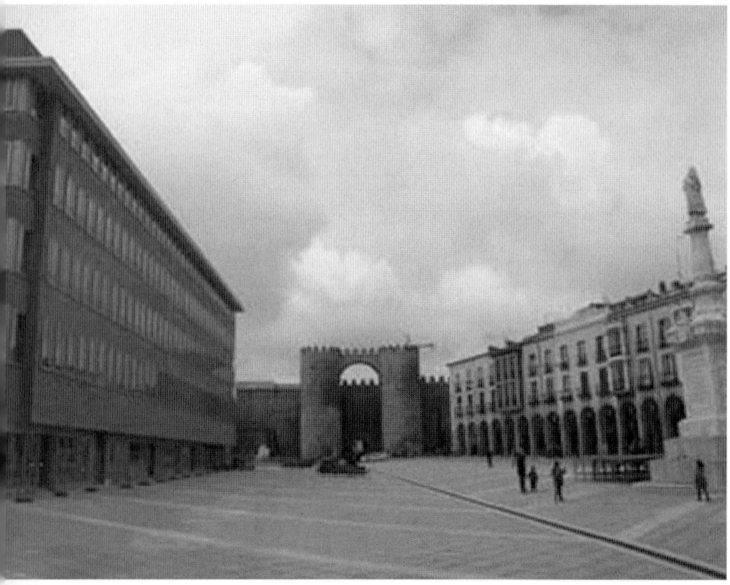

Avila, Plaza de Santa Teresa (Mercado Grande), now dominated by building 'A'

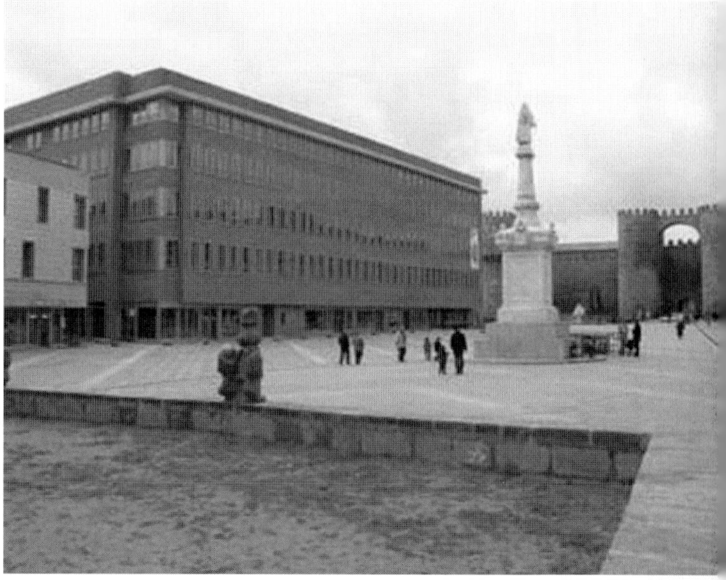

Avila – Reforma y construcción de un aparcamiento y nuevos edificios en la Plaza de Santa Teresa (el 'Mercado Grande')

Marco General de referencia para esta informe

La reforma y construcción de aparcamientos y viviendas en el Mercado Grande de Ávila ha sido objeto de una revisión sistemática a la luz de los criterios de documentos internacionales -que son los que motivan la opinión del Comité Nacional de ICOMOS España- y también nacionales y autonómicos. Los textos fundamentales son:

- Carta de Venecia, 1964
- Convención sobre el Patrimonio Mundial Natural y Cultural, 1972
- Directrices para la aplicación de la antedicha Convención
- Ley de Patrimonio Histórico Español, 1985
- Carta de las Poblaciones y Áreas Históricas, 1986
- Carta Internacional sobre el Turismo Cultural, 1999
- Ley de Patrimonio Cultural de Castilla y León, de 2002.

El artículo 6 de la citada Convención dispone que los Estados parte reconocen que el Patrimonio Mundial situado en el territorio de cualquiera de ellos constituye un patrimonio universal en cuya protección la comunidad internacional entera tiene el deber de cooperar.

En coherencia con lo anterior, los Estados Parte están obligados a reconocer que el patrimonio natural y cultural situado dentro del territorio de cualquiera de ellos constituye un patrimonio mundial en cuya protección la comunidad internacional en su conjunto está obligada a cooperar. Cuando un Estado soberano propone la inscripción de un bien situado en su territorio en la Lista del Patrimonio Mundial y la obtiene, somete libremente dicho bien al régimen de un tratado y, consiguientemente, reconoce la necesidad de salvaguardar sus valores, incluso mediante la acción internacional si ello resulta necesario. En caso contrario, se quebraría la garantía internacional que supone la existencia de un sistema imparcial de protección colectiva, derivado del acuerdo de los Estados firmantes de la Convención.

Avila Plaza de Santa Teresa (Mercado Grande), San Pedro and building 'B'

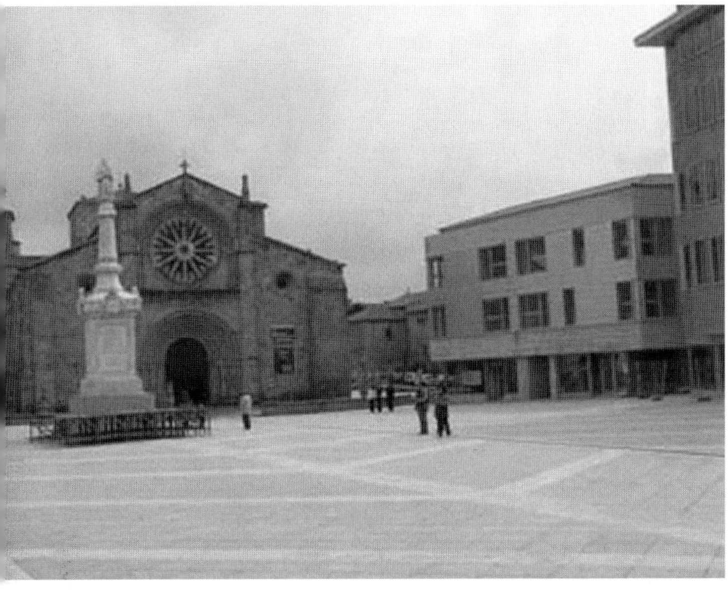

Una Convención es un Tratado, en virtud del cual los Estados soberanos prestan su consentimiento para que determinadas materias sean reguladas conforme a lo estipulado en el propio Tratado, cediendo, así, una parte de su soberanía en pro de un beneficio colectivo que estiman superior al que podrían conseguir por sus propios medios.

Todas las obligaciones que los Estados han decidido asumir a través de su capacidad soberana como partes de la *Convención del Patrimonio Mundial* son fruto de una lógica basada en el interés común o general. Por tanto, las obligaciones derivadas de la Convención son obligaciones *erga omnes* (es decir, frente a todos). Obligaciones cuya violación supone no sólo una ofensa respecto al Estado directamente afectado, sino contra todos los miembros de la comunidad internacional que pueden exigir su cumplimiento.

La inscripción de bienes en la Lista del Patrimonio Mundial no responde a ninguna obligación. Son los Estados Parte, como se ha señalado anteriormente, los que la solicitan libremente y, con ello, se someten voluntariamente a lo estipulado en el Tratado que han firmado, es decir, en este caso a la *Convención del Patrimonio Mundial.*

La Convención de Viena, de 1969, sobre interpretación de los Tratados es un instrumento de derecho internacional que estipula claramente que ningún Estado puede invocar las normas de su derecho interno para incumplir lo estipulado en un Tratado internacional que ha suscrito.

Por tanto, a la luz de lo expuesto en el párrafo anterior, es preciso tener en cuenta que las **Directrices** para la Aplicación de Convención del Patrimonio Mundial establecen lo siguiente con relación a la solicitud de inscripción de bienes en la Lista del Patrimonio Mundial:

v) La inscripción de un bien (requiere por parte del)... Estado del que emana la propuesta ... su ***compromiso*** *de protegerlo.*

vi) Cuando un bien haya sufrido un deterioro que suponga la ***pérdida de las características*** *que habían determinado su inscripción en la Lista del Patrimonio Mundial, se aplicará el procedimiento relativo a la* ***exclusión*** *eventual del bien* ***de la Lista****...* Exclusión ésta, que puede llegar a ser definitiva.

Tales valores o características que, inexcusablemente, debe ofrecer todo bien, tanto para ser inscrito como para permanecer incluido en la Lista del Patrimonio Mundial, son: poseer un **valor universal excepcional** y respetar las condiciones de **autenticidad e integridad** en las que se basó su inscripción.

La inscripción de un bien en la Lista del Patrimonio Mundial requiere que dicho bien responda al criterio de autenticidad en lo relativo a su concepción, sus materiales, su ejecución o su entorno. Una de las causas que pueden determinar la inclusión del bien en la Lista en Peligro es la 'pérdida significativa de la autenticidad histórica', y los planes urbanísticos que pudieran hacer peligrar sus características esenciales.

Refiriéndose a las ciudades históricas, las Directrices agregan que, a causa de la fragilidad del tejido urbano y de la urbanización galopante de las periferias, no podrán considerarse solamente desde un punto de vista abstracto en función del papel que puedan haber desempeñado en el pasado o como símbolos históricos. La organización del espacio, la estructura, los materiales, las formas y, de ser posible, las funciones del conjunto deben testimoniar esencialmente la civilización o sucesión de civilizaciones en las que se basa su inscripción en la Lista del Patrimonio Mundial.

Las mismas Directrices, señalan la necesidad de contar con disposiciones legislativas y administrativas que garanticen la protección del conjunto y la de su entorno, previendo incluso un tratamiento apropiado de éste último.

Se exige también que los conjuntos gocen no sólo de una protección jurídica nacional, autonómica -en el caso de España-, provincial y municipal, sino también de mecanismos de gestión adecuados, y de mecanismos de control de la planificación. Se piden igualmente garantías de una aplicación eficaz de esas leyes, así como de esos mecanismos de gestión.

En la sección **'Gestión'**... se determina que los Estados Parte deberán presentar, además de los textos jurídicos que protegen el bien, un **análisis explicativo sobre la manera en que dichas leyes funcionan**.

Por lo que se refiere a la llamada **'zona de respeto'** que debe figurar en el expediente que dio lugar a la inscripción, y que se concibe como un espacio alrededor del bien cuyo uso es restringido a fin de reforzar su protección, no es suficiente que exista un mapa en el que se delimiten sus límites exactos, sino que se hace preciso definir con detalle **las características y la utilización autorizada de dicha zona.**

Por otra parte, ha de tenerse en cuenta que el Consejo Internacional de Monumentos y Sitios (ICOMOS) es el Organismo encargado por la UNESCO para asesorar a ésta en las cuestiones relativas al Patrimonio Mundial. Y ello, tanto en lo que se refiere al informe de evaluación sobre su posible inscripción en la Lista de bienes de tal categoría, como en los posteriores informes sobre su estado de conservación y gestión cuando los valores que determinaron su inscripción se encuentran amenazados. Por tanto, resulta necesario destacar la importancia que reviste el hecho de que las Cartas y Recomendaciones de ICOMOS sean tenidas en cuenta por los Estados Parte de la Convención.

La Carta de Venecia, documento al que obedece la constitución de ICOMOS, y cuyos postulados se mantienen hoy en día, amplió notablemente la noción de patrimonio en su momento, abarcando en su definición y objetivos tanto al monumento como al conjunto histórico: Así, su artículo 1° dice que: 'La noción de monumento histórico comprende la creación arquitectónica aislada así como el conjunto urbano o rural que da testimonio de una civilización particular, de una evolución significativa, o de un acontecimiento histórico. Se refiere no sólo a las grandes creaciones sino también a las obras modestas que han adquirido con el tiempo una significación cultural'. No cabe, por tanto, entender que los postulados de la Carta de Venecia se refieren sólo a los monumentos aislados y no a las ciudades históricas. Es decir, no se refieren únicamente a criterios de intervención en la restauración de un monumento. El artículo 3° añade que: 'La conservación y restauración de monumentos tiende a salvaguardar tanto la obra de arte como el testimonio histórico', destacando así la importancia de éste último y sentando la base para entender que lo contrario no es una práctica admisible. En su artículo 6° dispone que: 'La conservación de un monumento implica la de un marco a su escala. Cuando el marco tradicional subsiste, éste será conservado, y toda construcción nueva, toda destrucción y cualquier arreglo que pudiera alterar las relaciones entre los volúmenes y los colores, será desechada'. Son criterios de conservación, donde el valor de conjunto queda reflejado en la expresión oficial del artículo 6° 'marco tradicional'. Todo el proceso de gestión del bien, incluyendo su conservación y posible restauración, debe respetar ese marco.

Por lo que se refiere a los usos, el artículo 5ª de la misma Carta dice que: 'La conservación de monumentos siempre resulta favorecida por su dedicación a una función útil a la sociedad; tal dedicación es por supuesto deseable pero no puede alterar la ordenación o decoración de los edificios. Dentro de estos límites es donde se debe concebir y autorizar los acondicionamientos exigidos por la evolución de los usos y costumbres'. Es decir, la Carta no es inmovilista, sino que reconoce claramente que la dedicación de los monumentos y conjuntos históricos a una función útil a la sociedad es deseable, pero añade que los acondicionamientos exigidos por la evolución de los usos y costumbres deben respetar los límites marcados en el propio artículo.

Otros artículos de la Carta de Venecia hacen también referencia a la autenticidad y a la importancia de conservar los valores no sólo estéticos, sino también históricos, y no se opone en modo alguno a que las obras de restauración, cuando un trabajo de complemento resulte indispensable, lleven el sello de nuestro tiempo, pero naturalmente esto no podrá ser interpretado de forma aislada, es decir, sin tener en cuenta lo dispuesto en los anteriores artículos. Así pues, el *artículo 9º* dice que: 'La restauración es una operación que debe tener un carácter excepcional. Tiene como fin conservar y revelar los valores estéticos e históricos del monumento y se fundamenta en el respeto a la esencia antigua y a los documentos auténticos. Su límite está allí donde comienza la hipótesis: en el plano de las reconstituciones basadas en conjeturas, todo trabajo de complemento reconocido como indispensable por razones estéticas o técnicas aflora de la composición arquitectónica y llevará la marca de nuestro tiempo. La restauración estará siempre precedida y acompañada de un estudio arqueológico e histórico del monumento'. Lo que quiere decir que la restauración se debe basar sobre datos científicos claros, evitando el falso histórico, pero no es de manera alguna 'carta blanca' para destruir todo aquello que se haya añadido al bien en el transcurso de la historia. Por eso, el *artículo 11* de la propia Carta, dice: 'Las valiosas aportaciones de todas las épocas en la edificación de un monumento deben ser respetadas, puesto que la unidad de estilo no es un fin a conseguir en una obra de restauración. Cuando un edificio presenta varios estilos superpuestos, la desaparición de un estadio subyacente no se justifica más que excepcionalmente y bajo la condición de que los elementos eliminados no tengan apenas interés, que el conjunto puesto al descubierto constituya un testimonio de alto valor histórico, arqueológico o estético, y que su estado de conservación se juzgue suficiente. El juicio sobre el valor de los elementos en cuestión y la decisión de las eliminaciones a efectuar no pueden depender únicamente del autor del proyecto'. Cuando se habla del respeto a todas las épocas, ello no implica de modo alguno que en nuestro tiempo seamos libres de alterar los bienes libremente. Menos aún en casos de bienes inscritos en la Lista del Patrimonio Mundial. La inscripción se hace al reconocer que un determinado bien, en el estado de integridad y autenticidad en que se halla en el momento de su inscripción, reúne valores universales sobresalientes. Cualquier alteración posterior del bien puede constituir un grave atentado contra dichos valores y conllevar la desclasificación del bien como Patrimonio Mundial.

En clara coincidencia con *La Carta de Venecia y otros documentos internacionales citados en este informe*, los valores que determinan la inscripción de un bien en la Lista del Patrimonio Mundial, así como la lectura que ofrecen como documentos históricos, deben ser respetados, y las intervenciones sobre los mismos no deben alterar sus materiales, sus volúmenes y formas, ni las incorporaciones realizadas en todas las épocas. La adaptación a nuevos usos no podrá atentar contra los valores que determinaron la inscripción del bien en la Lista del Patrimonio Mundial, debiendo ceñirse al 'criterio de autenticidad en lo relativo a su concepción, sus materiales y su ejecución', como tal testimonio histórico, sin que quepan interpretaciones subjetivas respecto al valor de las obras incorporadas en uno u otro período de la historia. Lo contrario representaría vulnerar el compromiso adquirido por el Estado Parte al acreditar, no solo la autenticidad e integridad del bien en el momento de proponer su inscripción, sino su deber de conservar estos valores una vez alcanzada ésta.

En consonancia con lo anterior, ha de tenerse también en cuenta que, según disponen las Directrices para la aplicación de la Convención del Patrimonio Mundial se debe informar a la UNESCO sobre el propósito de 'iniciar o autorizar, en una zona protegida por la Convención, considerables obras de restauración o nuevas edificaciones que pudieran modificar el valor del bien como parte del patrimonio mundial'. Del tenor de las antedichas Directrices se desprende la obligación de informar a la UNESCO del propósito de elaborar un Plan urbanístico en una ciudad inscrita en la Lista del Patrimonio Mundial, como es el caso del proyecto de aparcamientos y viviendas en la plaza de Santa Teresa de Ávila, que puede dar cobertura jurídica a transformaciones de sustantiva y gran envergadura.

Según disponen las Directrices, tal información, destinada a evitar que el valor mundial del bien pueda sufrir modificaciones, debe efectuarse 'lo antes posible, (por ejemplo, antes de redactar los documentos básicos para proyectos específicos)' y - en cualquier caso - 'antes de que se tomen decisiones difícilmente reversibles'.

La Carta Internacional para la Conservación de Poblaciones y Áreas Urbanas Históricas de ICOMOS, tras reconocer, en total sintonía con la *Convención del Patrimonio Mundial y sus Directrices*, el grave problema que supone el hecho de que los núcleos históricos de población se hallen amenazados por la degradación, el deterioro y, a veces, por la destrucción provocada por el desarrollo urbano, establece los siguiente:

Artículo 1. La conservación de las poblaciones o áreas urbanas históricas sólo puede ser eficaz si se integra en una política coherente de desarrollo económico y social, y si es tomada en consideración en el planeamiento territorial y urbanístico a todos los niveles.

Evidentemente, el artículo 1 resalta la importancia de la dimensión 'económica y social' de la conservación del patrimonio. Pero debe pensarse en el desarrollo a largo plazo, hoy entendido como desarrollo duradero o sostenible. Este criterio trasciende a los intereses inmediatos y busca la conservación de todo recurso en función de los derechos de las generaciones futuras a su uso y disfrute. Esto es especialmente importante cuando se trata de bienes del patrimonio mundial.

'Revitalizar' es un término jurídica y técnicamente indeterminado, por lo que no cabe utilizarlo como elemento de justificación de intervenciones contrarias a la protección, porque el sentido de la revitalización, en todo caso, debe guardar relación con las garantías de la conservación. Las actuaciones innovadoras que se sustentan sobre la destrucción de los espacios e inmuebles tradicionales de una ciudad histórica están consideradas como contrarias al concepto más recientemente incorporado a los documentos internacionales, que reclaman la 'sostenibilidad' de las decisiones relacionadas con la conservación y la revitalización. Así, ciertas actuaciones contemporáneas representan la dilapidación de unos bienes comunes en un momento determinado de la historia de una comunidad. Estos conceptos están reflejados en los ocho principios de la conservación de las ciudades históricas Patrimonio Mundial adoptados por la OCPM, como fruto de los trabajos realizados en años recientes. Y cabe recordar que la ciudad de Ávila pertenece a dicha organización.

Lamentablemente, el afán de arquitectos de nuestros días de realizar intervenciones de nuevo cuño, o 'de contraste' que deje su impronta en centros históricos y espacios monumentales ha dado lugar a muchos más ejemplos negativos que positivos. La nueva arquitectura en las ciudades históricas tiene que respetar la tradicional. Y su introducción en los centros históricos no se puede considerar un valor positivo cuando supone la eliminación de los valores que los definen como tales. Especialmente en el caso de bienes que, como Ávila, han sido inscritos en la Lista del Patrimonio Mundial, no se pueden permitir obras que muy bien pueden ubicarse en espacios nuevos en los que nadie podrá discutir ni su valor como obra en sí misma ni su efecto en el entorno, aspectos que sólo el paso del tiempo podrá juzgar en justos términos. El respeto a los valores y la tipología, sin caer en el falso histórico, es fundamental e ICOMOS lo defiende como un principio no opinable.

Las Directrices de la Convención del Patrimonio Mundial, al establecer las características de las ciudades que pueden optar a su consideración como Patrimonio Mundial, dicen: Es difícil evaluar la calidad de las ciudades actuales; sólo la historia permitirá distinguir aquellas que tienen un valor ejemplar para el urbanismo contemporáneo.

Si bien la globalización inunda el planeta con arquitectura contemporánea, cada vez más abundante y homogénea, cabe preguntarse si los países que se sitúan en la verdadera vanguardia de la misma y con los que la competición resultará también cada vez más dura, destruirían la fisonomía tradicional de una ciudad como Ávila si la tuvieran. Las ciudades históricas que conservan su valor característico, su peculiar y distintiva personalidad, van siendo cada vez más escasas y, por tanto, más y más valiosas y apreciadas con el paso del tiempo. Su valor se deriva, no de las inserciones que pueden realizarse en nuevos espacios, sino de la conservación de la integridad y autenticidad propias de un conjunto que se quiere consolidado para su comprensión cultural.

Ante ese tipo de intervenciones, se debe considerar lo que dispone la citada Carta Internacional para la Conservación de Poblaciones y Áreas Urbanas Históricas en los siguientes artículos:

Artículo 2. Los valores a conservar son el carácter histórico de la población o del área urbana y todos aquellos elementos materiales y espirituales que determinan su imagen, especialmente:

la forma urbana definida por la trama y el parcelario;

la relación entre los diversos espacios urbanos, edificios, espacios verdes y libres;

a. *la forma y el aspecto de los edificios (interior y exterior), definidos a través de su estructura, volumen, estilo, escala, materiales, color y decoración;*
b. *las relaciones entre población o área urbana y su entorno, bien sea natural o creado por el hombre;*
c. *las diversas funciones adquiridas por la población o el área urbana en el curso de la historia.*

Y añade que:

Cualquier amenaza a estos valores comprometería la autenticidad de la población o área urbana histórica'.

Está claro que es fundamental que se cumpla el principio del respeto al parcelario y la trama, a las relaciones entre los diversos elementos y los de éstos con el entorno, a la forma y el aspecto exterior e interior de los edificios (estructura, volumen, escala, materiales, color, etc.), y a las funciones adquiridas a lo largo de la historia . Los elementos de carácter contemporáneo han de ser excepcionales y su introducción no debe alterar los antedichos aspectos. Sin embargo, los autores y auspiciadores del proyecto en discusión parecen defender con más ahínco la introducción de elementos nuevos que la conservación, lo que no se corresponde con el mantenimiento de la autenticidad de los valores universales del bien y, por lo tanto, es contradictorio con lo dispuesto por la Convención del Patrimonio Mundial y sus Directrices. Como se indica más arriba, éstas últimas señalan la importancia que conceden a la organización del espacio, la estructura, los materiales, las formas.

En ese mismo sentido, el *artículo 10* de la misma Carta dispone: En el caso de ser necesaria la transformación de los edificios o la construcción de otros nuevos, toda agregación deberá respetar la organización espacial existente, particularmente su parcelario, volumen y escala, así como el carácter general impuesto por la calidad y el valor del conjunto de construcciones existentes'.

Guarda relación con lo anterior, y con la obra llevada a cabo en Ávila que es objeto de este informe, el *artículo 12* que establece: 'La circulación de vehículos debe ser estrictamente regulada en el interior de las poblaciones y áreas urbanas históricas, y las zonas de estacionamiento deberán planearse de modo que no degraden su aspecto ni su entorno'.

En su *artículo 9* dice que: 'La mejora del 'hábitat' debe ser uno de los objetivos básicos de la conservación'.

Ciertamente, este artículo es también muy importante, ya que la mejora del hábitat es clave para la conservación. Ese es uno de los grandes retos para todo especialista que realiza intervenciones en un centro histórico: hacer compatible la conservación con la calidad de vida, lo que supone tener en cuenta que la población tiene derecho a conservar aquello con lo que se identifica y siente como suyo.

Finalmente, el *artículo 6* de la misma Carta dice que: 'En caso de que se careciera de un plan de conservación o éste estuviera en estudio, antes de la adopción del plan todas las actividades necesarias para la conservación deberán ajustarse a los principios y métodos de la presente Carta y de la de Venecia'.

La Carta Internacional sobre Turismo Cultural de ICOMOS, al hacer mención del espíritu que la inspira, pone de manifiesto que el concepto de Patrimonio incluye sus entornos, tanto naturales como culturales. Y, tras confirmar que un objetivo fundamental de la gestión del Patrimonio consiste en comunicar su significado, expone que esto implica la responsabilidad de respetar los valores del Patrimonio..., así como los paisajes y las culturas a partir de las cuales se ha desarrollado el Patrimonio.

Al sentar los Principios relativos a la necesidad de que los programas para la protección y conservación del patrimonio faciliten a la comunidad local y al visitante la comprensión y el aprecio de los significados del Patrimonio, especifica, más concretamente, que los programas de interpretación deberían presentar información sobre el entorno físico. Y determina que la protección y conservación de su integridad física y ecológica y de su contexto medioambiental deberían ser un componente esencial en el desarrollo de las políticas sociales, económicas, culturales y turísticas.

Respecto a la infraestructura y los proyectos, especialmente los de desarrollo turístico, la Carta es también muy clara al manifestar que deberían tomar en cuenta... los paisajes naturales y culturales, las características de su biodiversidad, así como los amplios contextos visuales de los sitios con Patrimonio. Deberían utilizarse preferentemente – añade – los materiales propios de cada localidad, y tomar en cuenta los estilos de la arquitectura local y de la tradición vernácula.

Las llamadas a la necesidad de conservar y proteger la autenticidad en el entorno de los monumentos y los conjuntos urbanos, están igualmente presentes en los documentos doctrinales más recientes de ICOMOS, como son los ***Principios para el Análisis, Conservación y Restauración de las Estructuras del Patrimonio Arquitectónico***.

Por lo que se refiere a las construcciones tradicionales consistentes en elementos que no posean un valor sobresaliente dentro de un conjunto, como la arquitectura en la que se inscribirían alguno de los edificios tradicionales o decimonónicos desaparecidos en la operación, ya se ha señalado anteriormente que la *Carta de Venecia* dispone en su artículo 1 que: *La noción de conjunto urbano se refiere no sólo a las grandes creaciones sino también a las obras modestas que han adquirido con el tiempo una significación cultural.*

Por último, cabe reseñar que el proyecto de Carta sobre la Interpretación de los Lugares con Patrimonio Cultural (en última fase de estudio para ser aprobada por la Asamblea General de ICOMOS en 2005), recoge los criterios ya establecidos en los documentos anteriormente reseñados. Es interesante destacar que en él se observa la importancia, cada vez mayor, que se concede a la protección y conservación de todos los aspectos que contribuyen a la correcta interpretación de los monumentos y los sitios como parte sustantiva de su integridad y autenticidad, como elementos indispensables para comprender sus valores. El Principio 3.1, relativo al '*Contexto y Ubicación*', establece lo siguiente:... *Deben tenerse en cuenta todos los aspectos relacionados con el significado cultural y natural del lugar y sus valores, sin resaltar el valor de cualquiera de ellos hasta el punto de excluir a los demás...*

Fuentes del Informe

Entrevistas y contactos:

Excmo. Ayuntamiento de Ávila (Excmo. alcalde; secretario municipal; concejal de Urbanismo; Mª Rosa López Sanchidrián; Grupo de Izquierda Unida).

D. José Rafael Moneo Vallés, arquitecto autor del proyecto, quien contestó a un cuestionario de preguntas por carta y además facilitó, por correo, la Memoria del Proyecto y con posterioridad cinco contactos de fotografía aérea en color (30 x 40) del conjunto, una vez finalizada la obra.

D. Miguel Ángel Vázquez Herrero, arquitecto de la Ponencia Técnica de la Comisión Territorial de Patrimonio de Ávila durante la fase de tramitación administrativa del proyecto.

Asociación Ciudadanos por el Patrimonio Ávila.

Bibliografía facilitada por el Excmo. Ayuntamiento:

Mercado Grande de Ávila. Excavación arqueológica y aproximación cultural a una plaza. VV.AA.Excmo. Ayuntamiento de Ávila. Área de Urbanismo. 223 pp. Ávila, 2003.

Información administrativa:

De la Consejería de Cultura y Turismo de la Junta de Castilla y León: Informe sobre construcciones de edificios de viviendas y locales comerciales en la plaza del Mercado Grande de Ávila según proyecto de D. José Rafael Moneo (30 de diciembre de 2003), solicitado en su día por el Comité del Patrimonio Mundial. Está firmado por el Director General de Patrimonio y Bienes Culturales, D. Enrique Saíz Martín y el Alcalde-Presidente del Excmo. Ayuntamiento de Ávila D. Miguel Ángel García Nieto. Con él se adjunta una publicación sobre el Mercado Grande de Ávila y una serie de anexos:

- Anexo 1: Evolución del Mercado Grande.
- Anexo 2: Estudios previos.

- Anexo 3: Propuesta final.
- Anexo 4: Fotografías.
- Anexo 5: Plano de sombras.
- Anexo 6: Publicación en el Boletín Oficial de la Provincia de Ávila.

Información sobre la plaza del Mercado Grande requerida al Excmo. Ayuntamiento por los representantes del Comité Nacional de ICOMOS España (extracto de la Memoria del proyecto de D. José Rafael Moneo Vallés – julio 2001). Al texto se le adjuntó otro extracto sobre exposiciones públicas del proyecto para el conocimiento de los ciudadanos – artículos publicados entre enero de 2001 a septiembre de 2002 – y un plano acotado de los perfiles de la plaza en el proyecto – julio 2001 –.

Informe de la Comisión Territorial de Urbanismo sancionando el proyecto -28 de junio de 2000-.

Fichas de Seguimiento Administrativo de la Ponencia Técnica de la Comisión Territorial de Patrimonio (del 24 de abril de 2001 a 24 de marzo de 2003, Expdte. OT-74/ 1998-12; Expdte. MU-98/2000-4; Expdte. NP-47/2001-2) y de la Comisión Territorial de Patrimonio, desde el 7 de mayo de 2001 al 29 de abril de 2003.

Otras fuentes

Información variada – sobre el contenido del proyecto y accionesdel grupo de defensa del patrimonio *Ciudadanos por el Patrimonio, Ávila*. Es de destacar la riqueza de documentación cartográfica y fotográfica y el dossier de prensa – de mayo de 2001 a febrero 2004 –. También aportan información sobre otros casos que creen denunciables en la ciudad (destrucción de una villa romana, destrucción del cementerio musulmán medieval, y actuación sobre la casa-palacio de Gaspar Bullón).

Información y transcripción de Actas de Órganos colegiados del Ayuntamiento de Ávila facilitada por el Grupo de Izquierda Unida. A su vez, se facilitó un extenso dossier de prensa.

Trabajo de campo realizado en dos visitas a la ciudad de Ávila. Además de las anotaciones pertinentes se generó un dossier fotográfico de los autores de este informe, de unas 100 fotografías, que también se aporta en formato CD-ROM.

Antecedentes y desarrollo del proyecto

El proyecto de construcción de un aparcamiento y viviendas en el Mercado Grande de Ávila es un proyecto complejo y cuyo desarrollo, prolongado durante más de diez años, se entronca con toda una serie de cambios urbanísticos que se dan en la ciudad.

A continuación se ofrece un extracto del proceso

1993 – A finales de este año, D. Jesús Terciado, a la sazón, presidente de la Caja de Ahorros de Ávila -que es propietaria de las casas nº 12, 13 y 14 de la plaza de Santa Teresa o Mercado Grande- encarga al arquitecto D. José Rafael Moneo Vallés un estudio que completase la volumetría de las propiedades que la Caja poseía en el flanco sur de la plaza, así como una propuesta de nuevo pavimento. En dicho año, la ciudad cuenta como instrumento urbanístico su Plan General de Ordenación Urbana de 1986.

1994 – En febrero se presenta la primera propuesta: una plaza que, manteniendo el tráfico rodado en superficie, eliminaba el desnivel del sector meridional de la plaza y aspiraba a dar más importancia a la iglesia de San Pedro. Se pretende también abrir una nueva calle desde la plaza hasta el llamado 'Pilón de las Bestias', fragmentando así los volúmenes. El tráfico rodado en la plaza se mantiene.

Ante esta propuesta, el entonces alcalde, D. Ángel Acebes, sugiere a Caja Ávila que amplíe el ámbito de la propuesta, incluyendo en ésta el resto de parcelas que componen el flanco sur de la plaza, y proyectando un aparcamiento que resolviese, en opinión del ex alcalde, una de las demandas del centro de la ciudad. De esta forma, se presenta una segunda propuesta que, manteniendo el tráfico rodado sobre la plaza, propone un aparcamiento para 293 vehículos con entrada y salida por la Cuesta de Nuestra Señora de Sonsoles.

Es preciso mencionar que durante este período se inicia una importante labor de reflexión y proyección urbanística basada en dos documentos: la revisión del Plan General de Ordenación Urbana de Ávila, y la elaboración del Plan Especial de protección del conjunto histórico; documentos que, como se comentará, se concluirán años después aunque la Exposición Pública en fase de Avance se hace de forma conjunta para los dos planes en diciembre de este año.

1995 - En febrero se presenta un nuevo estudio ya más pormenorizado, tercera propuesta, para atender la sugerencia del alcalde del año anterior, ampliada a otros aspectos. Así, en este estudio se elimina el tránsito rodado en la plaza mediante un paso inferior que, utilizando la misma vía de acceso del aparcamiento desde la Cuesta de Nuestra Señora de Sonsoles tuviera salida a la plazuela de Don Claudio Sánchez Albornoz. Un mes más tarde se presentan los planos de este proyecto que confirman la posibilidad técnica de este paso, teniendo en cuenta las condiciones topográficas.

En abril, el Ayuntamiento acuerda suspender de forma cautelar el otorgamiento de licencias de edificación y demolición en una serie de enclaves del término municipal mientras se resolvía el proyecto de revisión del Plan General, y en junio se presenta una versión ya más completa de la llamada en este informe *tercera propuesta*. En ella se ajustan superficies, se establecen las entradas y salidas de peatones y se definen con mayor precisión los volúmenes. El proyecto fue aceptado por la Corporación Municipal y por la Caja de Ahorros de Ávila, institución que hasta entonces había llevado la iniciativa. A partir de este momento se hace cada vez más patente la necesidad de incorporar el proyecto al proceso de revisión y elaboración del Plan General y el Plan Especial del Conjunto Histórico (PGOUAV y PEPCHAV respectivamente).

1996 – A mediados de 1996 se renueva la corporación municipal, al frente de la cual se sitúa la alcaldesa Dª Dolores Ruiz Ayúcar. Ésta da las órdenes oportunas para que el Plan General incluyese la reforma de la Plaza de Santa Teresa o del Mercado Grande.

1997 – El Ayuntamiento de Ávila aprueba inicialmente el 7 de marzo el Plan General de Ordenación Urbana – PGOUAV – y el Plan Especial de Protección del Conjunto Histórico de Ávila – PEPCHAV-, y los somete a información pública. No obstante, muy poco después, a la vista de la Sentencia del Tribunal Constitucional de 20 de marzo de 1997, que declaró inconstitucional gran parte del Texto Refundido de la Ley sobre el Régimen del Suelo y Ordenación Urbana, el Ayuntamiento acuerda, con fecha 14 de abril de 1997, suspender el acuerdo de aprobación inicial para analizar el nuevo marco legislativo.

A los pocos meses, tras introducir una seria de modificaciones para adaptar el Plan a la legislación urbanística en vigor, se acuerda, de nuevo, la aprobación inicial de los documentos urbanísticos antes reseñados y la celebración del trámite de información pública en el pleno municipal de 9 de junio. Al final del verano, el 20 de septiembre, se produce la suspensión de licencias en todo el término municipal.

1998 – El 2 de febrero, PGOUAV y PEPCHAV se aprueban provisionalmente por el Ayuntamiento, y el 30 de abril la misma institución acuerda la aprobación de los textos refundidos de ambos documentos en los que se recogen las prescripciones de todos los informes y alegaciones que había suscitado. Ya en junio, se recibe en la Delegación Territorial de la Consejería de Medio Ambiente y Ordenación del Territorio de la Junta de Castilla y León, el expediente completo de la Revisión del Plan General de Ordenación Urbana de Ávila, del que se separa el Plan Especial de Protección del Conjunto Histórico, toda vez que su aprobación definitiva compete al Ayuntamiento de Ávila (de conformidad con el artículo 35.2.a) de la Ley del Suelo de 1976, en relación con el artículo 5 del Real Decreto Ley 16/1981).

Reunidas la Ponencia Técnica de la Comisión de Urbanismo de Castilla y León (20 de julio de 1998) y la Comisión de Urbanismo de Castilla y León (29 de julio de 1998), se acordó informar favorablemente la aprobación definitiva de la Revisión del Plan General de Ordenación Urbana de Ávila, con una serie de modificaciones. Solventados todos los obstáculos, la Consejería de Medio Ambiente y Ordenación del Territorio aprueba el PGOUAV el 19 de octubre (BOCYL, 27-X-98). Por su parte, el PEPCHAV recibe la aprobación definitiva el 9 de noviembre (BOCYL, 3-XII-98).

1999 – En julio toma posesión de la nueva alcaldía D. Agustín Díaz de Mera y García Consuegra. Se retoma el proyecto de la plaza del Mercado Grande y convoca un concurso para la construcción de un aparcamiento subterráneo y la remodelación de la Plaza de Santa Teresa. El concurso se resuelve a favor del arquitecto D. José Rafael Moneo Vallés, quien procedió a poner al día los estudios realizados desde 1993, redactando un Plan Especial de Reforma Interior (para la UE 76/1 del PGOUAV) y un Estudio de Detalle (para el ARI nº 9 del PEPCHA). Así, esta que puede ser denominada cuarta propuesta se enmarca ya en el contexto de la legalidad urbanística reciente de la ciudad aunque, no obstante, tanto PGOUAV como PEPCHA ya habían sido redactados con el pie forzado de esta intervención.

En septiembre, al explicarse el '*Contrato de asistencia y consultoría para la redacción del proyecto y dirección facultativa de la obra de remodelación y construcción de un aparcamiento subterráneo en la Plaza de Santa Teresa (El Grande) de Ávila*', el concejal de Izquierda Unida Sr. González Suárez manifiesta su voto contrario al mismo en la Comisión de Gobierno del día 8 del mes antedicho, solicitando un informe de ICOMOS sobre el proyecto.

2000 – El 6 de abril de 2000 la Comisión Municipal de Gobierno acuerda aprobar inicialmente los trámites del proyecto para la plaza, pidiendo el preceptivo informe vinculante de la Comisión Territorial de Urbanismo y la Comisión Territorial de Patrimonio Cultural. Poco después de dos meses, el 14 de junio de 2000, la Comisión Territorial de Patrimonio Cultural informa favorablemente y dos semanas más tarde, el 28 de junio de 2000, la Comisión Territorial de Urbanismo hace lo propio.

El 28 de julio de 2000, el Pleno Corporativo del ayuntamiento aprueba definitivamente el PERI y el Estudio de Detalle del Mercado Grande, promovidos a iniciativa municipal, siendo alcalde-presidente D. Agustín Díaz de Mera y García Consuegra. En este pleno se produce de nuevo una importante disensión del grupo municipal de Izquierda Unida, especialmente en lo referente a la construcción del aparcamiento, y desde este grupo se conmina a enviar el proyecto a UNESCO dada la envergadura del mismo y la obligación de comunicar a dicho Organismo cualquier intervención de cierto calibre.

2001 – El 1 de marzo la Junta de Compensación del Mercado Grande solicita licencia para realizar las obras y se remite el proyecto (en fase de Proyecto Básico) para su aprobación por la Comisión Territorial de Patrimonio Cultural; ya que, aunque aprobado el PEPCHA, se trata de un espacio afectado por los entornos de dos Bienes de Interés Cultural (la muralla y la iglesia de San Pedro). El 20 de marzo el propio D. Rafael Moneo explica, en conferencia-exposición pública, los contenidos del proyecto, y el 7 de mayo de 2001 la Comisión Territorial de Patrimonio Cultural de la Junta de Castilla y León acuerda aprobar el proyecto básico en todos su extremos salvo en algunas cuestiones relativas exclusivamente a los materiales. El dictamen de esta Comisión entra en el Ayuntamiento el 1 de junio.

El 16 de agosto se presenta el proyecto de ejecución por los promotores, visado por el Colegio Oficial de Arquitectos de Castilla y León el 31 de julio de 2001.

El 22 de octubre de 2001 la Ponencia Técnica de Medio Ambiente y Urbanismo del Ayuntamiento de Ávila informa favorablemente la solicitud de licencia de obras. Al mes siguiente, el 15 de noviembre de 2001, y tras realizar una modificación sugerida por su Ponencia Técnica en relación con la eliminación del casetón de los ascensores, la Comisión Territorial de Urbanismo de la Junta de Castilla y León da su visto bueno al proyecto y el día 30 del mismo mes de noviembre, mediante Decreto de Tenencia de Alcaldía, se concede la licencia de obras.

2002 – Durante este año se aprueba un proyecto reformado en dos ocasiones (27 de junio y 21 de noviembre) en lo que respecta a construcción del aparcamiento y la reforma de la plaza de Santa Teresa y se debaten las condiciones de adjudicación de la concesión del aparcamiento.

2003 – Las obras obtienen el 27 de enero de 2003 el visto bueno del aparejador municipal quien emite informe de inspección, haciendo constar que la obra, ya muy avanzada, se ajusta a lo reflejado en el proyecto.

No obstante, los problemas en relación con el conjunto del proyecto se recrudecen en varias instancias a partir de ese momento.

Problemas registrados en la Ponencia y Comisión Territorial de Patrimonio Cultural

El 22 de enero, la Ponencia Técnica de la Comisión Territorial de Patrimonio Cultural eleva a la Comisión Territorial de Patrimonio Cultural un informe en el que señala cómo la mayoría de sus miembros considera la propuesta presentada por el equipo redactor del proyecto de viviendas y aparcamientos como inadecuada en relación con los materiales; cuestión que estaba sin resolver desde hacía casi dos años.

Ante este informe de la Ponencia Técnica, la Comisión Territorial de Patrimonio Cultural acuerda el día 30 girar visita a las obras y tras la recepción de nueva documentación el día 18 de febrero cita a D. Rafael Moneo, por petición de este arquitecto, para la explicación de la propuesta el día 24 de marzo. Una vez que éste realiza su exposición, el presidente de la Ponencia Técnica defiende que se utilicen materiales no considerados en el Plan Especial atendiendo a su *carácter singular*.

Es particularmente interesante la intervención del arquitecto Ponente en esta reunión, ya que, sin consentimiento del presidente, lo que ya indica un ambiente enrarecido, entrega documentación a los restantes miembros de la ponencia e informa sobre los siguientes puntos:

- Información variada sobre la ficha de seguimiento administrativo del proyecto, listado cronológico de las últimas actuaciones del expediente, copia de la memoria y carátulas de los planos de la propuesta, fotografías en color del estado actual de la obra y su propio informe.
- Señala que se han observado en el proyecto cambios que van más allá de los materiales cuestionados. Así, hay diferencias entre el proyecto básico autorizado por la Comisión Territorial de Patrimonio Cultural el 7 de mayo de 2001 y la documentación presentada a nivel informativo el 18 de febrero. Los cam-

bios afectan a las fachadas en el número de huecos, dimensiones y emplazamiento; aumento de volumen en los vuelos cerrados y variaciones en cornisas. Además, y eso parece aún más grave – con lo que sería de gran interés contrastar fuentes- señala que hay diferencias entre el proyecto básico original presentado el 7 de mayo de 2001 y el aportado al Servicio que está a su cargo con fecha 14 de febrero de 2003. Las diferencias, inexplicables en un proceso correcto por cuanto que no se había aceptado ningún reformado sobre el proyecto básico original, se establecen en relación con el número de huecos, dimensiones, emplazamiento, volumen de vuelos cerrados, variaciones en cornisas y en las alturas y volúmenes de las cubiertas.

- Por otro lado, también considera inadecuada la propuesta de acabados del edificio A – el que tiene una mayor altura.

A pesar de estas cuestiones, y a instancias del presidente de la Ponencia, que señala que el único objeto a debatir se centra en los elementos exteriores en razón de lo que en su día – 7 de mayo de 2001 – prescribió la Comisión, la Ponencia aprueba autorizar la propuesta con el **único voto en contra** del arquitecto Ponente. Éste realiza un voto particular que se reproduce a continuación ya que expresa de forma clara que a lo largo del proceso existieron profesionales de distinta responsabilidad – concejales, técnicos urbanísticos...– que recordaron los criterios con los que debía intervenirse en el sector y, a pesar de ello, no se les escuchó:

Existen dos elementos arquitectónicos que son fundamentales y del mayor valor en la conformación de la Plaza: La Iglesia de San Pedro y la Muralla, debiendo estar supeditada toda actuación dentro de la Plaza a la preservación de estos dos elementos, en sí mismos y en su entorno, con su percepción visual, evitando competencias con nuevos edificios, tanto en colores, materiales, texturas y escala comparativa. Todo ello es con el fin de que no resulten alterados sus valores, pues se consideran obras en sí mismas acabadas, depuradas por el paso de los siglos, que no necesitan alteraciones intrínsecas, ni en su entorno y que únicamente es necesario conservarlas. Partiendo de estas premisas y analizando el impacto visual de la Propuesta presentada, acentuada al estar desarrollada en el lado mayor que une los dos Monumentos dentro del conjunto, se produce un fuerte desequilibrio en la Plaza a favor de la Propuesta y en perjuicio de los dos Monumentos, con repercusiones de minimizar en escala con los nuevos edificios, alteración en la percepción de sus colores, materiales y textura actuales, producido todo ello por la fuerte competencia de los edificios de la Propuesta, pasando a ocupar los dos Monumentos una escala inferior y la percepción, secundaria, en el conjunto de la Plaza a favor de los edificios de la Propuesta. Por todo lo expuesto se considera que no es adecuada la propuesta con las modificaciones producidas en relación al proyecto básico autorizado, ni en los acabados exteriores.

Es importante insistir en que las modificaciones producidas en relación con el proyecto básico autorizado en mayo de 2001, caso de ser ciertas las palabras del arquitecto Ponente – y no hay indicios que las pongan en duda – no han sido sancionadas por ningún Órgano competente ni antes ni después de esta reunión de la Ponencia Técnica.

La Comisión Territorial de Patrimonio Cultural asumió el informe de la Ponencia Técnica y, sin hacer ninguna alusión a las cuestiones del arquitecto Ponente acordó, el 29 de abril, autorizar la propuesta presentada con las variaciones que recogía con dos pequeñas intervenciones relacionadas con la eliminación de una escalera y un trastero y la división de un ventanal en varios huecos, y, dado que la consideran una 'actuación singular', y basándose en lo que permiten el Plan Especial de Reforma Interior y el Estudio de Detalle, se resuelven y especifican los acabados exteriores de los inmuebles respecto al tipo y textura del granito y los materiales de carpintería.

Repercusiones del proyecto en el cabildo municipal abulense y en la vida de la ciudad

A principios de 2003, con las obras de los nuevos edificios muy avanzadas, próximas a alcanzar el nivel máximo de cumbrera -cinco alturas –, entre la opinión pública de Ávila se desata la polémica sobre su adecuación al entorno, y ésta es asumida por la oposición política del Ayuntamiento, y no sólo por el grupo de Izquierda Unida como había sucedido hasta entonces, y otras iniciativas ciudadanas, incluida las de dos sindicatos. Además, surgen también en la ciudad algunas críticas respecto al deterioro de los materiales utilizados en el pavimento de la plaza, que era ya accesible a los ciudadanos desde el verano anterior.

Una de las iniciativas más importantes, por las repercusiones que tendrá pocos meses después, es la de un grupo de seis profesores universitarios liderada por D. Serafín de Tapia que se dirigen por escrito fechado el 28 de enero al director del *Centro del Patrimonio Mundial* de UNESCO, y en el que denuncian la inadecuación del proyecto a un lugar tan sensible dentro del entramado histórico abulense.

Los grupos de *Izquierda Unida* y del *Partido Socialista Obrero Español* llevan al pleno municipal de 31 de enero, como asunto de urgencia, la presentación de una moción conjunta sobre los edificios en construcción. Se acepta la inclusión del asunto, pero la moción es rechazada. Es de interés destacar que en la moción se recuerda la necesidad de aplicar el texto de la *Convención* y otros documentos, como la *Carta Internacional para la Conservación de Poblaciones y Áreas Urbanas Históricas*. Se trata de una moción argumentada y bien basada, en la que se propone paralizar las obras del edificio más alto de los proyectados por D. José Rafael Moneo Vallés (edificio A), solicitar informes – entre ellos de ICOMOS – y rebajar la altura del edificio construido aplicando para ello soluciones de valoración y permuta.

A principios de febrero, y tras unirse los dos sindicatos más representativos de España – Comisiones Obreras CC.OO. y la Unión General de Trabajadores UGT –, se produce una manifestación ciudadana contraria a la construcción del inmueble – día 3 – que reunió entre 1.000 y 2.000 personas según la prensa local, cifra considerable para una población como Ávila.

Ante la dimensión urbana que adquiere el asunto, se presenta de nuevo en el pleno municipal de 25 de abril como asunto de urgencia una nueva moción, a la que acompañan de un número no especificado en las actas de firmas de ciudadanos, de los partidos *Izquierda Unida* y *Partido Socialista Obrero Español*; aunque en este caso se limitan a pedir un acuerdo sobre paralización de las obras y rebajar la altura del edificio A. En esta ocasión se desestima incluso la incorporación del asunto por vía de urgencia.

La escala de repercusiones sigue en aumento cuando en la reunión del Comité del Patrimonio Mundial, celebrada en París entre el 30 de junio y el 5 de julio, surge, y se recoge en su acta la preocupación por el impacto del proyecto y su repercusión en la autenticidad de Ávila como integrante de la Lista del Patrimonio Mundial. UNESCO exige que se corrija el proyecto, se adecue al centro histórico de Ávila, y que se remita documentación pertinente antes del 1 de febrero de 2004.

El asunto se lleva a un pleno municipal extraordinario el 11 de septiembre en el que se tratan varios temas sobre el patrimonio abulense, especialmente el de la plaza de Santa Teresa. Se trata de un debate largo y de fuerte enfrentamiento y que no termina con ningún acuerdo, sino que es una mera muestra ante el pleno de la posición de los distintos grupos municipales sobre el asunto. En el mismo, el concejal de *Izquierda Unida* Sr. González Suárez se hace eco del debate suscitado en todas las escalas (municipal, regional, estatal e internacional) y pide al pleno que considere la necesidad de llevar a cabo lo solicitado por UNESCO paralizando cautelarmente la obra; que se negocie la reducción de alturas y que se difunda esta actuación, para que en los ámbitos local y nacional se reponga la imagen de Ávila. El concejal Sr. Blanco Rubio del *Partido Socialista Obrero Español* se pronuncia en la misma línea, aunque este partido nunca se opuso a la construcción del aparcamiento subterráneo. El concejal Sr. Monforte, entre otras consideraciones, declara que el *Partido Popular* enviará todos los informes que requiera UNESCO, de hecho refiere que ya se está trabajando en él, y que cumplirá lo que desde esa institución se exija, aunque *reseña 'que estamos ante algo tan subjetivo -ante la valoración del proyecto- como puede ser el gusto y la estética, si el edificio es alto o bajo, si los volúmenes se ajustan a esa concepción estética o no'*.

En diciembre se termina el informe de la Consejería de Cultura y Turismo de la Junta de Castilla y León sobre las construcciones de edificios de viviendas y locales comerciales en la plaza del Mercado Grande de Ávila solicitado por el Comité del Patrimonio Mundial.

Consideraciones sobre el proyecto

La consideración más general es la de que la autenticidad de la plaza de Santa Teresa, y también su entorno – especialmente en la aledaña parroquia de la Magdalena – ha sido muy alterada. Esto es especialmente grave por cuanto este ambiente y sus inmuebles forman parte de un espacio comprendido entre dos bienes específicamente inscritos en la Lista del Patrimonio Mundial como son la muralla de la ciudad y la iglesia de San Pedro. Por lo que respecta al primero de ellos, dicho espacio afecta precisamente a una parte tan importante del mismo como es la *Puerta del Alcázar* que es la más emblemática de cuantas posee la muralla-. Además, la Plaza de Santa Teresa constituye una unidad conceptual histórica con ambos bienes, en especial la *Puerta del Alcázar*, siendo no sólo un espacio abierto para la contemplación de la muralla y su grandiosidad, sino también la antesala de ingreso a la antigua ciudad. Necesariamente la Plaza de Santa Teresa está incluida en la 'zona de respeto' exigida en la delimitación de todos los bienes del Patrimonio Mundial, superando en este caso cualquier connotación despectiva que pretenda atribuirle un valor secundario, puesto que constituye un espacio de carácter esencial para la integridad y autenticidad de los dos bienes.

Por otra parte, también desde el punto de vista tradicional, la Plaza de Santa Teresa, conocida como el 'Mercado Grande', es un espacio del más alto valor ambiental para los habitantes de Ávila. Incluso puede considerarse que esta plaza cumple, de forma consuetudinaria a lo largo de los tiempos, las funciones de plaza mayor en Ávila por cuanto que no existe ninguna otra que pueda equipararsele, ni siquiera en el interior de las murallas, como verdadero foro urbano desde el punto de vista morfológico, funcional o social.

Respecto al proceso:

- De acuerdo con las Directrices para la Aplicación de la Convención del Patrimonio Mundial, es obligación preceptiva de todo Estado Parte en cuyo territorio se hallan bienes inscritos en la Lista del Patrimonio Mundial, informar sobre todo proyecto importante (sea obra nueva o de restauración) que pueda afectar sensiblemente a los valores que motivaron la inscripción, desde que se halle en fase de idea. Tal información, como se ha señalado en la primera parte de este informe, debe efectuarse lo antes posible, por ejemplo, antes de redactar los documentos básicos y, en cualquier caso, antes de que se tomen decisiones difícilmente reversibles.
- Por lo antes dicho, existe una grave irregularidad en el procedimiento legal seguido no sólo para la aprobación que está ahora en controversia de esta obra sustantiva, aunque circunscrita a un escenario urbano concreto, sino para la aprobación de los instrumentos normativos de la gestión de Ávila, como son el Plan General de Ordenación Urbana – PGOUAV – y el Plan Especial de Protección del Conjunto Histórico de Ávila – PEP-CHAV – , más aún cuando en ellos se incluyen medidas relativas a hacer viable el proyecto, que ya estaba siendo impulsado aún con anterioridad a la aprobación de los citados planes (desde el año 1993, tal como se deduce del propio informe facilitado por la Junta de Castilla y León y otros documentos administrativos consultados).
- Tampoco se envió al Comité del Patrimonio Mundial de la UNESCO el proyecto, paso que habría ahorrado todos los problemas derivados de su desarrollo.
- Existen algunas dudas no fácilmente identificables a partir de la documentación disponible que señalan la alteración de algunos elementos del proyecto a lo largo de su proceso de aprobación que convendría estudiar más en profundidad en lo que respecta a la aprobación del proyecto de ejecución básico – o básicos – presentado.

Respecto al autor del proyecto:

- No se puede obviar la responsabilidad de D. José Rafael Moneo Vallés en la inadecuación del proyecto al espacio en cuestión. Cualquier arquitecto ha de conocer perfectamente las reglas que rigen en el espacio sobre el que se realiza una propuesta. La normativa que desarrollan los planes generales, planes especiales de reforma interior y estudios de detalle – entre otras figuras – es básica, pero también lo es el conocimiento de las obligaciones derivadas de la pertenencia de un espacio a ámbitos especiales, como la propia Lista del Patrimonio Mundial.
- D. Rafael Moneo no es un arquitecto sin formación, al contrario, se trata de uno de los más reconocidos y prestigiosos arquitectos españoles; con una profusa obra dentro y fuera de España. Por este motivo, y por la presencia de un estudio que sin duda respalda al arquitecto, no es justificable que ontroduzca modificaciones en cuestiones tan básicas – y no opinables – como cambios de volumetría, soleamiento, interpretación arbitraria del espacio histórico como lugar de la memoria, respeto de los valores ambientales, contemplación de los bienes, el valor del paisaje urbano, o cómo intervenir en nuevas edificaciones en ciudades históricas o en entornos de monumentos, cuestiones todas ellas presentes, de forma clara y explícita, en numerosas cartas internacionales, además de en los textos propios o aceptados por UNESCO.

Respecto a los aspectos formales:

En este proyecto, y a tenor de los resultados, el Sr. Moneo parece haberse manifestado, como arquitecto, completamente ajeno al entorno donde se inscribe su proyecto, a pesar de sus esfuerzos por convencer de lo contrario en la redacción de la Memoria.

Dada la cronología de realización del proyecto de reforma y construcción de aparcamiento y nuevos edificios en la plaza de santa Teresa, se observa que tanto el Plan General como el Plan Especial se han ajustado al mismo a medida que ambos tomaban forma proyectual y no al contrario, lo que resulta incoherente e ilógico. Esta actuación, carente de ética e inapropiada en el desarrollo del planeamiento urbano, indica la naturaleza perentoria de la obra. Las nuevas obras, en cualquier ciudad, deben adecuarse a la normativa urbanística existente y no que ésta se reforme o se redacte *ex novo* para adaptarse a las características de la obra a construir, como es el caso que nos ocupa. Cabe reiterar que desde las etapas iniciales se estaba cometiendo *otra notable irregularidad al* no informar debidamente al Comité del Patrimonio Mundial sobre las modificaciones del Plan General y del Plan Especial, en sus redacciones respectivas.

El aspecto más grave, desde el punto de vista patrimonial, tiene que ver con la pérdida de protagonismo de los verdaderos hitos monumentales del ámbito: la muralla y la iglesia de San Pedro, ambos declarados Patrimonio Mundial. Actualmente, el único elemento que sobresale en la plaza es el edificio denominado 'A' y no precisamente por su adecuación arquitectónica al entorno. Con su construcción, tanto la forma, como el carácter del paisaje urbano y la atmósfera tradicional de este enclave básico del entramado histórico de Ávila, que constituye el marco histórico de emplazamiento de ambos monumentos así como el nexo de unión física y eje visual entre los mismos, han sido radicalmente transformados. Se ha producido un grave desequilibrio, en el conjunto de la plaza, a favor de la nueva edificación y en perjuicio de los monumentos que, con la nueva solución, se minimizan, empequeñeciendo su impronta histórica. Esto constituye un daño ingente a los valores de autenticidad e integridad, fundamentales para acreditar los méritos necesarios del bien a la hora de solicitar su inscripción en la Lista del Patrimonio Mundial e, igualmente, a la hora de mantenerla.

Además, y con independencia de la mayor relevancia monumental, tanto de la muralla como de la iglesia de San Pedro, la Plaza de Santa Teresa, con su configuración en el momento de producirse la declaración como Patrimonio Mundial y los edificios que existían en el área afectada, formaba necesariamente parte indiscutible de los valores ambientales propios y de la 'zona de respeto', sin la cual ambos bienes directamente afectados por tal declaración no se pueden proteger adecuadamente; y, por lo tanto, gozaban también de unas garantías de protección internacional en cuanto a su ulterior tratamiento y conservación, respaldadas por el compromiso adquirido por el Estado Parte.

La tipología, absolutamente inapropiada, de la nueva edificación 'A', por su excesivo volumen, traza de fachada unitaria frente al ritmo fraccionado del parcelario anterior, dimensionado y distribución de huecos (144 vanos en una fachada de 53 m), cubierta plana, textura, cromatismo, etc. resulta totalmente extraña al paisaje urbano preexistente, y en abierto contraste con los monumentos de la muralla y de la iglesia de san Pedro, así como con su entorno edificado. El nuevo diseño y configuración de la plaza ayudan también a la potenciación de la imagen del nuevo edificio proporcionando así un fuerte impacto visual y una distorsión del entorno histórico, minimizando la escala de los monumentos y atenuando, con ello, el imponente diálogo visual entre San Pedro y la Puerta de la muralla, con su adarve. La nueva tipología edificatoria planteada, nada tiene que ver con la arquitectura a la que ha sustituido, ni con la del resto de la ciudad histórica y resulta ajena, no solo respecto a los monumentos colindantes, sino también a los edificios situados en el flanco Norte de la plaza con su ritmo arquitectónico y sus soportales decimonónicos, con su eclecticismo contenido. El nuevo edificio, intempestivo en su volumen, forma y cromatismo, al minimizar los monumentos proporciona una fuerte distorsión visual en su entorno histórico y difícilmente puede dialogar nunca armónicamente con ellos en ese contexto, ni en escala ni por historia, si no es estableciendo una competencia arquitectónica desigual. Con estas reflexiones no se juzga ni se cuestiona la calidad del edificio como pieza o ejercicio arquitectónico aislado, sino su ubicación inadecuada, fuera de contexto en este sector de la ciudad de Ávila.

La altura máxima de la edificación se decide que sea de cinco plantas para el edificio mayor – 'A' – y de tres para el más pequeño – 'B' –. En este sentido, el edificio 'A' viene a tener una planta más que los edificios más altos que fueron derribados. De hecho, la cubierta horizontal del nuevo edificio parece coincidir con la cumbrera de los antiguos, de tejado a cuatro aguas, pero aprovechando y macizando el hueco ofrecido por el desnivel que existía entre dicha cumbrera y las cornisas. En todo caso, se ha producido un aumento de altura en la fachada que da a la plaza, donde la elevación de rasantes del suelo en el borde meridional ha provocado también una sustancial alteración de su histórico desnivel topográfico.

Las alineaciones han sido modificadas para dar una pretendida mayor monumentalidad a la relación entre la muralla y la iglesia de San Pedro, retranqueando en algo más de cuatro metros el edificio 'B'. Esta alineación es injustificada, ya que la relación entre esos dos monumentos no necesitaba de ninguna intervención, la nueva calle que sesga la única parcela en dos programas arquitectónicos bien diferentes no resuelve ningún problema de accesibilidad a la plaza, y la panorámica geográfica del valle Amblés a que se refiere la Memoria es una utopía naturalista hiperbolizada. Contrariamente a lo pretendido, la monumentalidad de la muralla y la iglesia de San Pedro se han visto afectadas. La muralla tenía un protagonismo mayor que las edificaciones antes existentes y, sin embargo, ahora presenta una imagen referencial considerablemente disminuida por la presencia del nuevo edificio 'A' que, como se ha dicho, ha aminorado las posibilidades de apreciación de este bien en su auténtica escala y sabor ambiental.

La trama parcelaria histórica se ha alterado, sin que el resultado haya servido para solucionar de forma adecuada ningún problema perentorio o urgente de la ciudad.. Y se ha hecho agrupando, mediante el sistema administrativo de la ejecución urbanística en una Junta de Compensación, cinco parcelas distintas, consiguiendo, así, incrementar, tanto la superficie útil final, como el volumen, dado que en el contexto abulense, el PGOU permite unos increíbles e inaceptables '3,5 m^2/m^2' de edificabilidad.

- El objetivo de las actuaciones era abordar la intervención de un área dividida en dos formas de ordenación-intervención. La primera, calificada como Área de Rehabilitación Integrada (ARI nº 9), incluida en el Plan Especial, y la Unidad de Ejecución UE 76/1, incluida en el Plan General y en el Especial.
- Los objetivos descritos para la ARI 9 eran: mejorar la imagen de la fachada Sur de la Plaza de Mercado Grande; reactivar los usos comerciales, institucionales y residenciales de la manzana; dotar de aparcamiento al área del 'Mercado Grande'; reducir el impacto negativo del tráfico en superficie, con la creación de un paso subterráneo; estudiar la reordenación visual del eje San Pedro-Puerta del Alcázar.
- Los objetivos del la UE 76/1: reordenar la fachada Sur de la Plaza del 'Mercado Grande', *sustituyendo ruinas y edificación poco adecuada al entorno*; creación de una vía pública que conectara la plaza con la calle Pilón de las Bestias.
- La manzana nº 6 estaba formada por cinco edificaciones de distintos uso (fincas 12, 13, 14 (EDIFECA S.L.), y 15–16 (parti-

culares), con una superficie real privada de 1.938 m² (red viaria municipal de 110 m²) y construida de 6.394 m².

- Las superficies de cesiones eran, sobre rasante, de 356,72 m² (258,31 m² de privada y 98,41 m² de pública) y bajo rasante – parking – de 1.510,70 m².
- Según reza en la propia Memoria facilitada por el arquitecto, la planta del edificio de la parcela 1 sería el resultado de unir las parcelas nº 2, 3 y 4 del *Proyecto de Actuación Mercado Grande* con superficies 674 m², 226 m² y 140 m², respectivamente. La superficie de construcción es de 1.040 m² para dicha parcela 1, y de 652 m² para la nº 2. El frente abierto es de 54 m de longitud. Frente a las Murallas aparece una fachada de 9 m sobre la rampa de acceso al paso; una fachada de 53 m en la calle de bajada al Pilón y otra de 28 m sobre el nuevo. En realidad las dos parcelas mencionadas son sólo una, que al estar fracturada por una nueva calle, introduce una confusión en la apariencia externa del proyecto (dos edificios).
- El proyecto contempla la apertura de una nueva calle, fragmentando el cosido de la nueva parcela en dos piezas. El bloque más pequeño, junto a San Pedro se retranquea 4 m.

Con respecto a la superficie máxima edificable:

- La superficie máxima edificable para el conjunto formado por las dos parcelas se obtiene aplicando un desproporcionado aprovechamiento tipo de 3,5 m²/m² (fijado por el planeamiento general también para este entorno monumental, lo cual es inaceptable, carente de lógica y un grave error urbanístico en ciudades monumentales como Ávila) a la superficie total de 2.048 m², tras la suma de las parcelas, resultando un valor final de 7.168 m².
- Además, la ocupación **es del 100 %** sobre la superficie neta definida.

Se han derribado edificios, algunos – según el archivo fotográfico histórico – de indudable valor, al menos, ambiental; arquitecturas todas que no estaban incluidas en ningún catálogo (ni en el Plan General de 1986, ni en el Plan Especial de Protección del Conjunto Histórico de Ávila – PEPCHA) pero que, encontrándose en el espacio comprendido entre dos bienes inscritos en la Lista del Patrimonio Mundial (además de estar incluidos en el conjunto histórico de Ávila declarado Bien de Interés Cultural según la legislación española), y formar conceptualmente parte de una unidad ambiental con éstos, queda sumamente claro que estaban protegidos como zona de su entorno. Por lo tanto, gozaban de un grado de protección superior al que le pueda otorgar cualquier norma interna, al estar protegidos internacionalmente. En esos casos, la falta de catalogación singularizada no significa que los bienes en sí mismos no estén protegidos, pues forman parte de un ambiente cuya alteración radical, como es la provocada por las obras de la Plaza de Santa Teresa, es inadmisible. Y, en todo caso, si se piensa realizar cualquier tipo de intervención en ellos es preceptivo informar '*antes de redactar los documentos básicos*', como ya se ha indicado, al Comité del Patrimonio Mundial de tal proyecto. El derribo de los edificios, aun cuando aparentemente se hayan cumplido normas locales o autonómicas, constituye una violación flagrante de la Convención del Patrimonio Mundial y sus Directrices, que en el caso de este tipo de bienes son normas de mayor rango que las leyes y demás disposiciones de carácter interno.

Se han alterado las rasantes existentes en el ámbito. La rasante es también un testigo histórico del proceso de conformación de la plaza y no constituía un obstáculo para la tradicional accesibilidad a la plaza.

La plaza ha sido objeto de un tratamiento uniforme de su superficie, lo que, unido al hecho de que se encuentra casi totalmente falta de elementos decorativos, la convierte en una plaza 'dura', resaltando aún más la presencia del edificio 'A'. Esto, a juicio de un importante número de ciudadanos, le hace perder calidad ambiental y no favorece su uso como lugar de paseo y de solaz descanso.

Aunque las críticas ciudadanas siempre enfatizan sobre la influencia del edificio 'A' en la plaza de Santa Teresa, conviene destacar que la inadecuación del mismo es mucho mayor en todos los sentidos sobre el vecino convento y parroquia de la Magdalena, justo en el flanco sur. Éste, en una cota inferior aparece completamente asfixiado por el volumen de la nueva construcción, que en este sector se comporta no como 'trasera' sino como una auténtica nueva fachada, buscando reforzar el protagonismo de su presencia, desde cualquier ángulo en que se aborde la contemplación de la plaza, circunstancia ésta que se aprecia tanto al nivel de la calle como, sobre todo, desde el adarve de la muralla.

Los materiales utilizados en el exterior de los nuevos edificios no se adecuan, en textura y color, a los utilizados en el entorno, adoptando, además, una coloración llamativa que contrasta con la de los inmuebles que los rodean. La argumentación utilizada para su elección, basada en el carácter singular del proyecto, tampoco justifica su inclusión, máxime si se tiene en cuenta que se está proyectando sobre un conjunto histórico en el que tiene que actuarse con visión global armonizadora.

El túnel, que ha permitido la peatonalización de la plaza, el acceso al nuevo aparcamiento y el paso circunvalatorio de los vehículos, es una intervención agresiva, especialmente desde el entorno de la muralla y la Magdalena, aunque también resulta importante, si se analiza desde la plaza de D. Claudio Sánchez Albornoz.

La sombra proyectada sobre la plaza, especialmente por el edificio 'A', es considerablemente superior a la que proyectaban los edificios originales, a causa de que la fachada de dicho edificio 'A' - que ha absorbido en un solo bloque la diversidad de edificaciones antes existentes y procedido a homogeneizar la altura- es superior, en ese frente sur, a la que tenían cualquiera de las fachadas de los edificios a los que ha sustituido, tal como se desprende del esquema planimétrico que se nos ha facilitado. La condición de soleamiento de la Plaza a lo largo de los meses de un año, donde la inclinación sobre el plano de la eclíptica de 23 1/2º (solsticios de invierno y verano, y equinoccios de primavera y otoño), marca ángulos de soleamiento bien distintos, según estaciones, es una característica climática que no se resuelve en absoluto con la información mínima de planimetría del ángulo de radiación facilitada (Anexo V de la Memoria, cálculo de sombras para el 21 de septiembre, situada la altura del sol a las doce).

Este aspecto ha creado un importante estado de opinión en la ciudad por cuanto que el clima de Ávila, de inviernos largos y fríos, impone unas condiciones de uso menos confortables de la plaza al menguar la insolación que recibe.

Respecto a los usos propuestos:

El uso de aparcamiento en un espacio público es una cuestión que nunca debió de plantearse en esta plaza por:

- Situarse en un espacio muy significativo del conjunto histórico. Aunque se trate de una plaza extramuros, se encuentra localizada en el centro del entramado histórico de Ávila, formando parte, y estructurando, el tejido de arrabal. La propia denominación de *Mercado Grande* da buena cuenta del significado de este espacio en el entorno urbano abulense.
- Era un lugar muy comprometido desde el punto de vista arqueológico, tal y como demostraron las excavaciones posteriores y

la publicación realizada por el Excmo. Ayuntamiento, a tal efecto.

- Es un espacio simbólicamente muy notable y querido para la población. No sólo por su uso y percepción, sino también por la propia denominación. La popular, *Mercado Grande*, ya se ha comentado; la oficial se corresponde con el personaje más reconocido original de la población: *Santa Teresa de Ávila.*
- Existe un aparcamiento muy próximo, a menos de 300 metros y no se argumenta en ningún documento que esté sobrecargado; al contrario, algunos comentarios e informes presentados en los plenos municipales hablan más bien de infrautilización.

Otras cuestiones

Aunque los autores de este informe no han realizado una encuesta exhaustiva entre la población sobre el proyecto, sí que han conocido durante la elaboración de los trabajos de campo la opinión expresa de muchos ciudadanos contraria a la construcción del edificio 'A' – y ninguna a favor –.

Recomendaciones

Básicas:

- Instar al Ayuntamiento de Ávila, a la Junta de Castilla y León y al Gobierno Español para que, en lo sucesivo, se remita a UNESCO en la forma que prescribe la normativa todo proyecto de relevancia en cualquier bien inscrito en la Lista del Patrimonio Mundial; y, a su vez, para que apliquen con rigor los principios de la *Convención* y las *Directrices* de UNESCO a la hora de sancionar cualquier tipo de proyecto urbanístico.
- Iniciar un proceso de revisión profunda de los instrumentos de planificación de la gestión y conservación de la Ciudad de Ávila, poniendo especial énfasis en el estricto cumplimiento de las normas aplicables al área correspondiente al bien declarado Patrimonio Mundial y su zona de respeto. Esta revisión deberá realizarse cumpliendo los procedimientos de consulta al Comité del Patrimonio Mundial de la UNESCO.
- Revisar, dentro del proceso anterior, la catalogación del Plan Especial de Ávila, por cuanto que, a la vista de la ausencia de catalogación de inmuebles que debieron contar con ella, hay indicios de que la catalogación se ha hecho de forma incorrecta, dejando al margen categorías importantes, especialmente en lo que respecta a inmuebles en los que descansa el paisaje urbano y el ambiente tradicional de Ávila (arquitecturas de entornos monumentales, tan importantes para el tejido de la ciudad como las propias piezas de relevancia histórica monumental, siendo la plaza de Santa Teresa paradigmática en ese sentido).
- Revisar detalladamente el proceso de aprobación del proyecto de ejecución de la obra objeto de este informe, contrastando su contenido respecto al proyecto básico – o proyectos básicos –.
- Informar al autor del proyecto, D. José Rafael Moneo Vallés, sobre la conveniencia y aplicación de un buen conocimiento de los condicionantes patrimoniales que afectan a un espacio como la plaza de Santa Teresa de Ávila que, como se ha dicho, es el entorno histórico consolidado entre dos monumentos incluidos en la *Lista del Patrimonio Mundial.*
- Pedir responsabilidades, y asumirlas por parte de los Órganos pertinentes, respecto a la alteración de alineaciones, parcelas y volúmenes históricos, así como por la desaparición de algunos de los inmuebles originales. Es importante asumir que la configuración decimonónica de una plaza puede ser un valor sociourbano de primera categoría en la historia de las ciudades españolas, y una parte básica en la lectura e interpretación del proceso de conformación de la ciudad, y esto aunque estemos en una ciudad en la que se valora de forma sustancial su patrimonio medieval.
- Establecer un proyecto nuevo de reforma de la plaza de santa Teresa y de los edificios ('A' y 'B') que recupere alineaciones, ritmo parcelario, volúmenes históricos, tipología, materiales, textura y cromatismo de fachadas acorde todo ello con el carácter, atmósfera, autenticidad y proporciones que históricamente ha tenido la plaza. Al mismo tiempo, se cuidarán los entornos de la muralla e iglesia de San Pedro, y se prestará especial atención al flanco sur de la Magdalena. Para su realización, se tomarán todas las medidas correctivas aplicables al caso, con el fin de restituir los volúmenes históricos, demolición de estructuras y cualquier otra necesaria para recuperar, en la medida posible, la espacialidad, las proporciones y el ambiente tradicionales. De esta manera se podrá demostrar, al menos, un interés por acercarse al nivel de autenticidad e integridad que, dentro de su evolución histórica, tenía el bien en el momento de su consagración internacional, que es cuando tal autenticidad se define.
- El hecho de que se hayan dado modificaciones a lo largo de diversos períodos de la historia en parte de una ciudad histórica, como es el caso de la Plaza de Santa Teresa o del Mercado Grande, no implica que por ello se dé carta blanca para hacer cualquier tipo de intervención en ella y seguir transformándola porque lo anterior no fuera – o así nos lo parezca – suficientemente bueno. O por esa manida demanda del arquitecto contemporáneo para que se le permita incrustar, a toda costa, obra actual en entornos históricos destruyendo sus edificios y espacios tradicionales. Lo lógico y correcto es establecer que a partir de un determinado momento – que tiene que ser necesariamente el de la inscripción en la Lista del Patrimonio Mundial –, se dejen de hacer experimentos en un espacio tan significativo como la plaza, sobre todo aquellos que implican nuevas obras que no hacen sino abrir y revivir las heridas que tiene la ciudad. Especialmente cuando hoy en día existen unos principios y una normativa internacional que, como se ha explicado suficientemente, tratan de evitar que esto siga sucediendo en una ciudad histórica que ha sido declarada Patrimonio Mundial y, más aún, en los bienes afectados por tal declaración y su entorno inmediato.
- Con esta fórmula se recuperarán, además, los niveles de insolación habituales en la plaza: un aspecto que, más allá de las cuestiones directamente relacionadas con el patrimonio, preocupa profundamente a muchos ciudadanos en la vivencia de ese espacio común.
- En el nuevo proyecto, junto a la recuperación en las fachadas del ritmo de la parcelación tradicional, debería variarse el tratamiento de los huecos – principalmente en el lienzo del edificio 'A' que mira a la plaza – introduciendo otro programa que mitigara el excesivo número de vanos existentes (144) y recuperara las dimensiones y proporción de huecos de la tipología anterior – suma de varias arquitecturas diferentes –, en armonía con el conjunto de la plaza, en su frente, sin entrar en mimetismos y falsos históricos.
- El sistema de revestimiento con aplacados en color rojo se considera del todo inapropiado con relación al entorno monumental más próximo, y cabe destacar que no existe ningún antecedente de semejante programa cromático en el mismo. La solución más adecuada sería buscar un material más acorde con la textura y con la paleta de colores de los monumentos adyacentes y de los edificios de dicho entorno.

- Reestructurar el sistema de peatonalización de la plaza, eliminando el diseño diáfano de espacios y fomentando los recorridos de estancia y paseo – y no sólo de paso – por ella. Del mismo modo, el programa de manchas de vegetación establecido es pobre y no proporciona una adecuada integración. Debe enriquecerse.
- Eliminar el paso y acceso al parking y a la calle subterránea desde la propia plaza y por delante de la muralla, reorganizando el tráfico en este sector, de forma que el acceso al aparcamiento sea en sentido contrario (de entrada y salida, por la propia salida) y de una sola dirección, para salvaguardar del tráfico deambulatorio frente a la Plaza y el acceso al centro histórico, y así recuperar una fachada más digna hacia la muralla. El acceso actual a la calle y al aparcamiento deberá eliminarse, realizando un tratamiento urbanístico de integración con el entorno.
- Que se plantee un estudio de tráfico que analice otros posibles aparcamientos disuasorios y evalúe demandas e Intensidad Media de Tráfico de los perímetros del Centro histórico.
- Se recomienda muy vivamente al Ayuntamiento de Ávila ser más sensible con todos los aspectos que se refieren a la conservación, restauración e intervención en el patrimonio arquitectónico y cultural de la ciudad y, en especial, con la opinión de los ciudadanos y asociaciones legalmente reconocidas, respecto al estado de conservación y a las posibles intervenciones a realizar o que se hacen en su patrimonio.

De fondo:

- Instar a todas las instancias que participan en la elaboración y sanción de proyectos con influencia en el Patrimonio Mundial para que conozcan y desarrollen la normativa de UNESCO, fundamentalmente el texto de la *Convención* y de las *Directrices* para su aplicación. Esto debe ser especialmente tenido en cuenta por el Ministerio de Cultura, pero también, y no con menos importancia, por las instituciones autonómicas y locales competentes en materia de cultura – consejerías, delegaciones provinciales, comisiones de patrimonio, gerencias de urbanismo… – , alcanzando también a todos los responsables en la elaboración de proyectos, especialmente a los arquitectos. No se puede proyectar y luego 'tratar de adecuar la obra a las normas o las normas a la obra'. Para conseguir y desarrollar un buen proyecto es necesario que exista un buen conocimiento previo de toda la normativa aplicable (incluida, naturalmente, la internacional) y que ésta se cumpla.
- Los proyectos en centros históricos no pueden ser entendidos como propuestas arquitectónicas aisladas o piezas al margen del conjunto urbano y del contexto social en el que se desarrollan. Es esencial que las nuevas arquitecturas se integren y armonicen con los entornos monumentales y con el conjunto urbano construido y que la población entienda, acepte y asuma cualquier intervención que se produzca en sus ámbitos patrimoniales más significativos. Intervenir con proyectos pretendidamente buenos, o que se presume que se valorarán mucho en el futuro por el perfil de su autor, pero que el grueso de la población actual no entiende – y este proyecto es a todas luces paradigmático de eso –, resulta una fórmula harto extendida hoy en día pero realmente antidemocrática de gestionar las ciudades históricas. Ese tipo de conducta no puede justificarse con el renombre de un determinado autor.
- Que los ciudadanos sientan como propio el patrimonio monumental y sus entornos es tan importante como pueda serlo la propia gestión de su mantenimiento y conservación por parte de los gestores políticos.
- Es necesario que en el caso de las ciudades históricas y de otro tipo de bienes inscritos en la Lista del Patrimonio Mundial se informe debidamente a los ciudadanos sobre los valores que motivaron dicha inscripción y la necesidad de conservarlos, sensibilizándoles para ello, y fomentando así una conciencia pública que haga viable la realización de proyectos acordes con los valores de autenticidad e integridad del bien del que se trate.

The Special Protection Plan for Laguna as a very serious threat

The Special Protection Plan for La Laguna was provisionally approved by decree of the municipal council of this city, with a view to its final approval in December 2004. Its implementation represents a very serious threat and the elimination of the heritage features that were the basis for the outstanding universal value leading to inclusion of La Laguna on the World Heritage List.

General considerations on the protected area

It is necessary to comply strictly with the commitment acquired before the UNESCO with regard to the delimitation of the 'zone of respect' (buffer zone surrounding or contiguous to the core zone) included in the dossier submitted for inscription of La Laguna on the World Heritage List, which cannot be altered, and much less reduced, unilaterally by the Special Protection Plan (SPP). It would be necessary to submit such a proposal for consideration by UNESCO and run the risk of it losing its status as World Heritage.

An adequate plan for conservation and management of the landscape is lacking. Neither the General Urban Development Plan approved after inscription nor the Special Protection Plan include regulations on the conditions for the buffer zone that take into account the needs of the heritage city which has seen both its internal and external landscape context altered. This is especially grave in a city that is an example of a 'city-territory', whose boundaries encompassed the entire valley reaching as far as the nearby mountains.

Considerations on the historic urban design of La Laguna – volumes, lot division, town houses

Starting from an erroneous prior analysis of the population data and the application of standards specific to a newly created urban development area, a method was devised for applying construction coefficients (a method unrelated to special urban planning criteria used in the field of conservation) that results in a generalised increase in the maximum construction area by means of the expression 'movement of building area'. The new plan allows an increase in building volume to a much larger volume than that currently existing (changing from a coefficient of usable building area of 1.3 to 1.7, or a 30% increase), permitting a 24% increase in the number of housing units. This represents a grave alteration of the historic building volumes as well as an unacceptable overbuilding of the area declared World Heritage.

As a result of the above, building heights above those of currently existing buildings are allowed, virtually condemning single-storey buildings, which still have a certain presence in some parts of the historic city of La Laguna, to disappear. Furthermore, the Plan also allows generalised encroachment of courtyards and gardens, covering the former and occupying the latter with newly created volumes described as a new building type.

The Plan permits certain alignments and changes in ground levels and, above all, a grave alteration in the historic lot division of La Laguna by means of a complex system based on unacceptable criteria which would permit aggregations of lots and, more importantly, segregations of lots in practically all blocks of the historic city. The team drafting the Special Plan aims for their ideal lot division to prevail over the currently existing lot division, which is the one that is actually obligatory to protect.

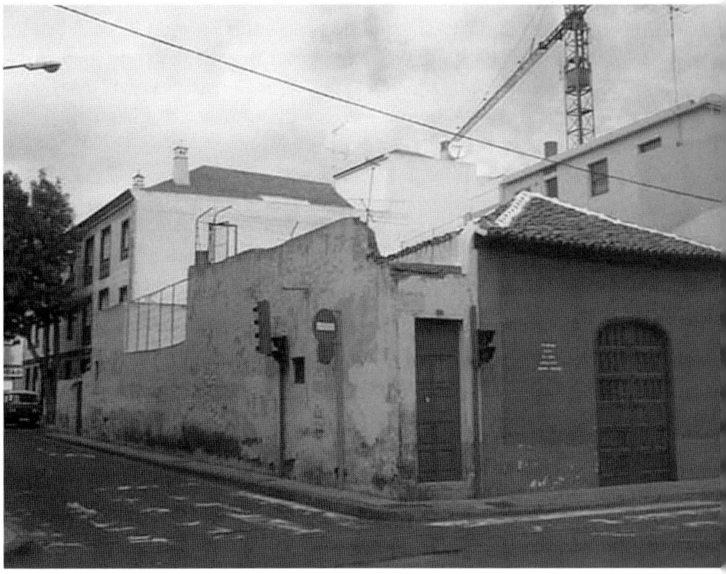

Capilla de la Cruz de los Plateros, C/San Juan (10-03-2002), Antes de modificación de la manzana en el ámbito del Bien Cultural.

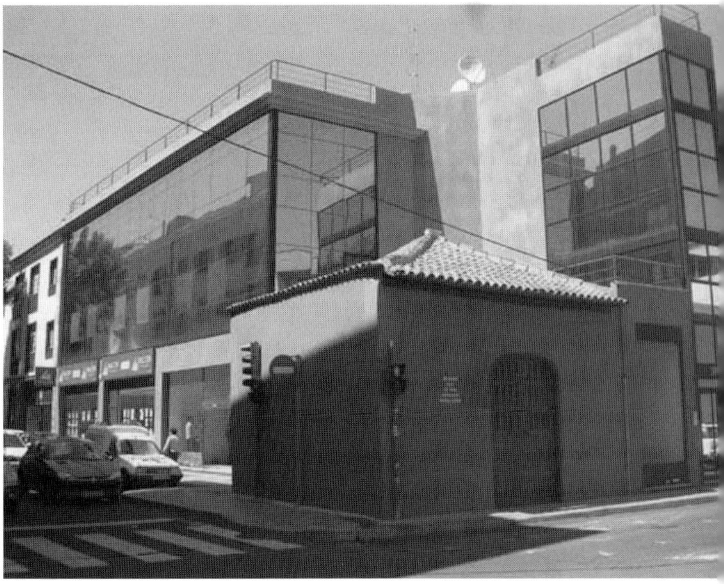

Capilla de la Cruz de los Plateros. C/San Juan (03-11-2002), Modificación de la manzana en el ámbito del Bien Cultural.

Calle de San Juan (10-03-2002), Antes de modificación de la manzana en el ámbito del Bien Cultural.

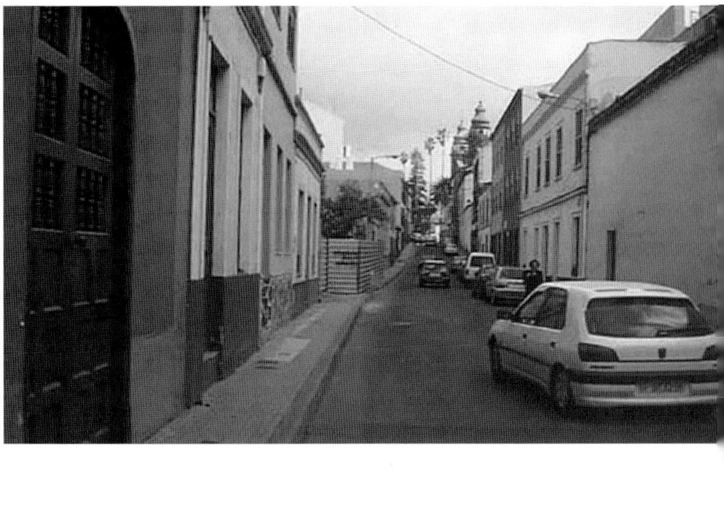

The list of protected buildings is precarious and there are abundant contradictions in the lists of buildings that should be protected. It does not respect the commitments to protect outstanding buildings acquired before the UNESCO in the dossier attached to the request for inscription of La Laguna on the List of World Heritage Sites (see attached document for a description of the notable reductions in protection proposed in the PEPRI – Special Plan for Protection and Inner City Renovation). Neither is protection afforded for the numerous houses – '*casas terreras*' dating from the late 19th and early 20th centuries – which should be preserved not only as simple atmosphere-lending elements, but also as genuine exponents of the traditional vernacular architecture of La Laguna.

Based on the above, it can be concluded that:

- There are multiple repetitions among the 591 buildings included on the list of protected buildings (they are listed on their respective streets as different from those occupying corners);
- There are 8 proposals for deletion of listed buildings whose justification is highly inadequate;
- There are 117 deletions of listed buildings which are not cited;
- There are 33 buildings listed as 'Atmosphere Level 2', which are operations of facadism;
- There are 498 buildings listed as 'Atmosphere Level 1', which have not been assigned a building type according to the dossier.

The plan does not provide adequate guarantees concerning some of the traditional unchanging features of the town house, particularly with regard to the use of two and four-sided pitched roofs and maintenance of the open courtyard. It should also reinforce the obligation to use traditional materials and prevent the use of improper cladding materials, as well as revealing the original stonework as a decorative element of the facade. It also fails to mention the necessary preparation of a colour chart for La Laguna.

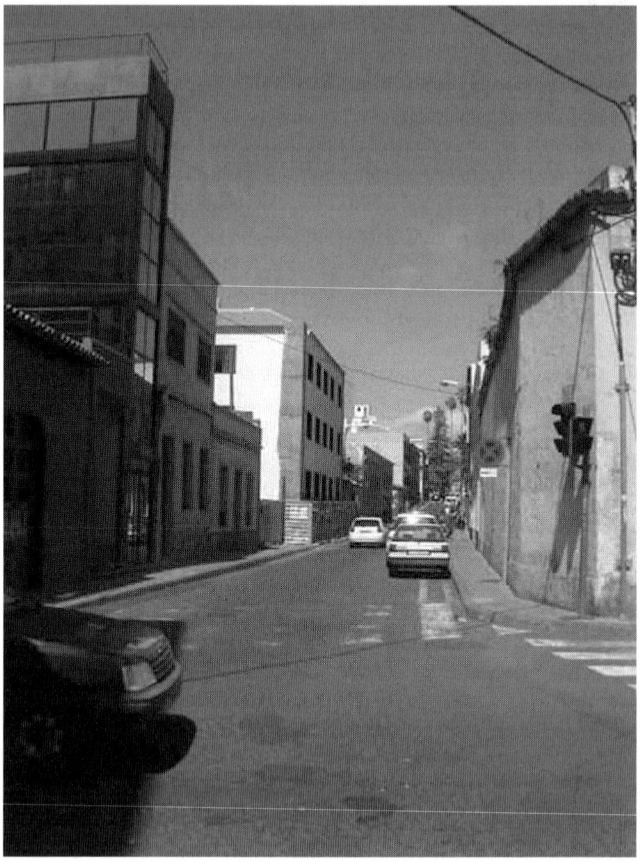

Calle de San Juan (03-11-2002), Modificación de la manzana en el ámbito del Bien Cultural.

Considerations on permitted uses

The term 'revitalisation' is used as a justification for a series of actions that only represent the support of the public institutions for urban development operations which in a later phase will result in the sale of residential building types inappropriate to historic city centres (semi-detached houses, apartments, studios…). This, judged by previous studies, will lead in all certainty to unjustified over-development and transformation of the historic city centre, as has already occurred in other Spanish cities, into an area better suited for obtaining high returns on real estate investments than for serving as a place of high heritage quality.

The special plan does not establish effective measures to curtail a foreseeable disproportionate development of commercial activities and other types of services in the historic centre.

Considerations on public spaces, accessibility and parking areas

Several of the most representative public spaces of the city are redesigned, modifying their shape, structure and character.

The policy for creating pedestrian networks and setting the boundaries for non-motorised private traffic is highly deficient and very far from the approaches and achievements of other European and Spanish cities.

The minimum requirements for parking areas are inadequate for dwellings, offices and business premises and the potential impact of uncontrolled construction of underground parking garages in the area of the old town houses of the city is especially worrying, owing to the geotectonic conditions of the site on which they are built.

Considerations on management of urban planning in the historic centre of La Laguna during the process of drafting of the Special Protection Plan

For the duration of the period of administrative processing of the Special Protection Plan, it was agreed that the drafting team would report on all municipal licenses that are later submitted for their approval by the Canary Island Heritage Commission (as indicated in the contract signed with this team). Although the city council assures the contrary, and according to said agreement a real and necessary suspension of licenses has not occurred during the period of drafting of the Special Protection Plan, numerous urban development actions subject to approval under the scope of the plan have been authorised.

A considerable number of buildings included in the dossier have been hollowed out and some have been demolished. Alignments have also been modified in some cases.

El Plan Especial de Protección de la Laguna como amenaza muy grave

El Plan Especial de La Laguna ha sido aprobado provisionalmente por decreto de la Alcaldía de esa ciudad, con vistas a su aprobación definitiva el diciembre 2004. Su puesta en vigor representa una amenaza muy grave y la desaparición de los rasgos patrimoniales que se acreditaron como fundamento de su valor universal excepcional y a los valores por los que La Laguna fue incluida en la Lista del Patrimonio Mundial.

Consideraciones generales respecto al área protegida

Es preciso observar escrupulosamente el compromiso adquirido ante la UNESCO en lo que se refiere a la delimitación de la "zona de respeto" (zona tampón o poligonal de respeto) incluida en el expediente de solicitud de inscripción de La Laguna en la Lista del Patrimonio Mundial, que no puede ser alterada, y mucho menos disminuida, unilateralmente por el Plan Especial de Protección (PEP). Sería necesario someter tal propuesta a consideración de la UNESCO y arriesgarse a perder la condición de Patrimonio Mundial.

Falta planificar la adecuada conservación y el tratamiento del paisaje. Ni en el Plan General aprobado después de la inscripción, ni en el Plan Especial de Protección se regulan condiciones para el área de respeto que tengan en cuenta las necesidades de la ciudad patrimonial, que ha visto modificado su contexto paisajístico tanto exterior como interior. Esto es especialmente grave en una población ejemplo de ciudad-territorio cuyos límites alcanzaban todo el valle hasta alcanzar las montañas próximas.

Consideraciones respecto al entramado histórico de La Laguna – volúmenes, parcelario, caserío

De un análisis previo erróneo de datos de población y de la aplicación de unos estándares propios de un polígono de actuación de nueva creación, se deduce el método de aplicar unos coeficientes de edificabilidad (técnica ajena al planeamiento especial en la materia de la conservación) que provocan un incremento generalizado de la edificabilidad mediante la expresión „movimiento de la edificación". El nuevo plan admite un aumento de volumetría mucho mayor que la existente (pasa del 1,3 de aprovechamiento al 1,7, lo que supone un 30 % más), permitiendo incrementar en un 24 % el número de viviendas. Esto supone una grave alteración de los volúmenes históricos, así como macizar de forma inaceptable la zona declarada Patrimonio Mundial.

Como consecuencia de lo anterior, se permiten unos aumentos en las alturas de los inmuebles y que condenan prácticamente a la desaparición a los edificios de una sola planta, todavía con cierta presencia en algunas zonas de la ciudad histórica de La Laguna. Además, el Plan también permite de forma muy generalizada la invasión de patios y huertas, cubiertos los primeros y ocupadas las segundas mediante volúmenes de nueva creación descritos como una nueva tipología

El plan permite alterar algunas alineaciones, rasantes y, sobre todo, admite una grave alteración del parcelario histórico de La Laguna mediante un sistema complejo y con criterios inadmisibles que permitirían las agregaciones – sobre todo-y-también – las segregaciones en prácticamente todas las manzanas de la ciudad histórica. Se pretende que el parcelario ideal del equipo redactor del Plan Especial prevalezca sobre el parcelario real, que no es otro que el que realmente es obligado proteger.

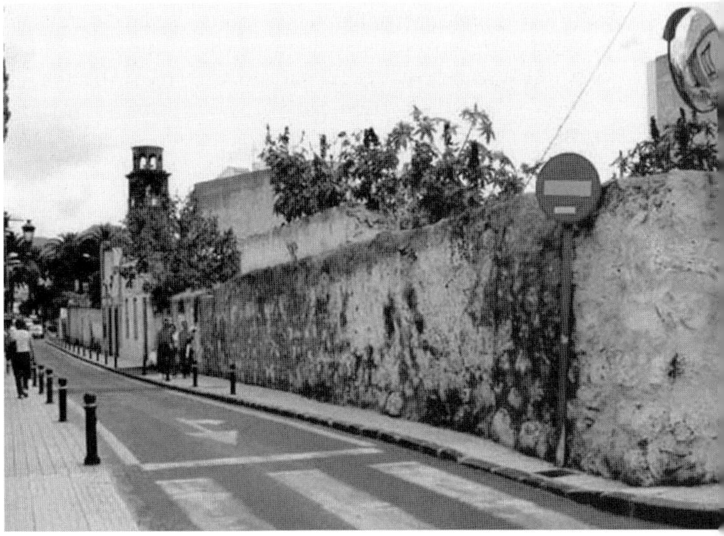

Modificación de alineación prevista en PEP y ya aprobada por el Cabildo Insular, C/San Antonio, Situación actual (julio 2004).

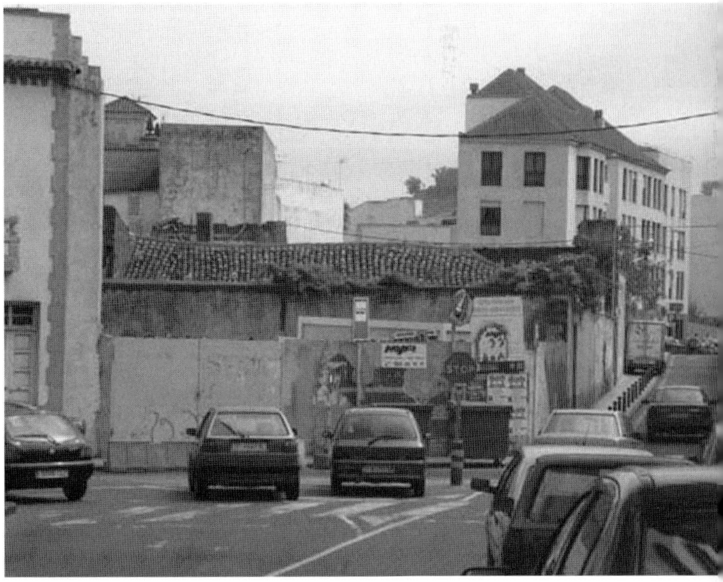

Modificación de alineación prevista en PEP y ya aprobada por el Cabildo Insular, C/San Antonio (julio 2004), Vista desde la Plaza de la Concepción (Plaza del Dr. Olivera).

Propuesta de proyecto-tipo según el PEP, C/Herradores (19-03-2004).

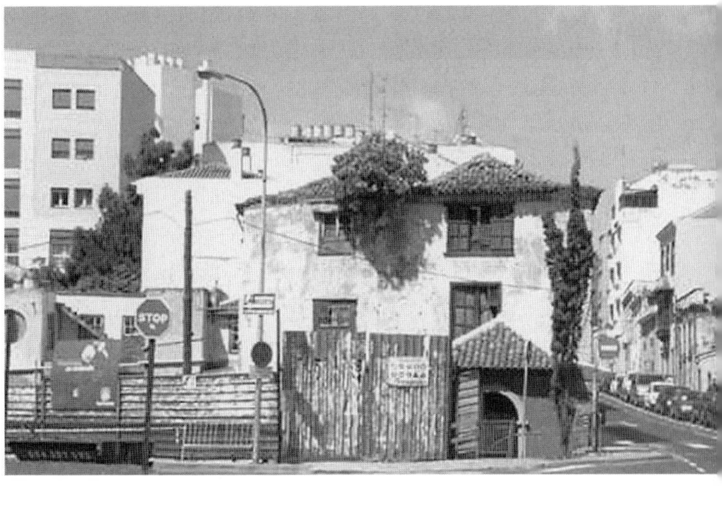

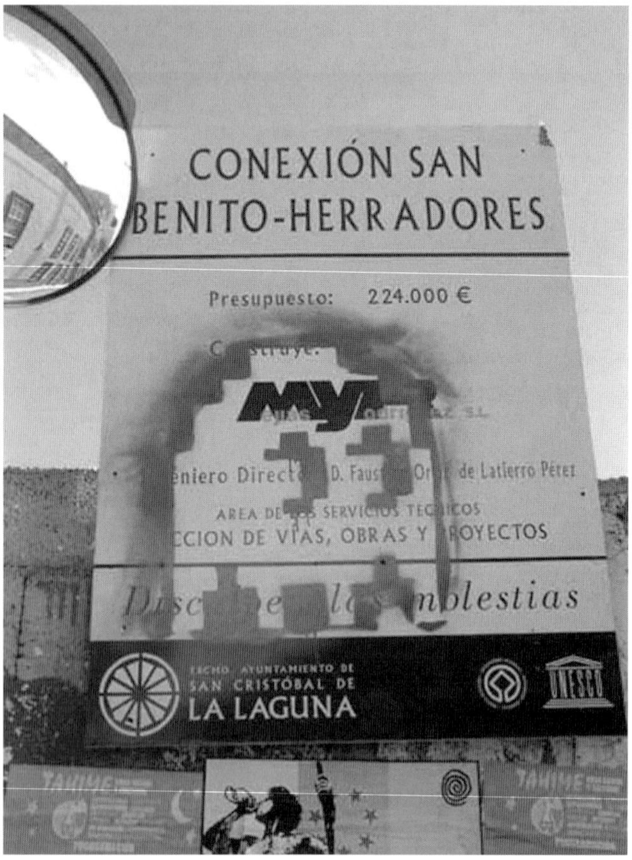

Modificación de alineación prevista en PEP y ya aprobada por el Cabildo Insular, C/San Antonio, Cartel anunciador del Ayuntamiento (julio 2004).

Destrucción de galería y eliminación de patio del Colegio de los Jesuitas (después Universidad de San Fernando, hoy Real Sociedad Económica de Amigos del País (16-09-2004).

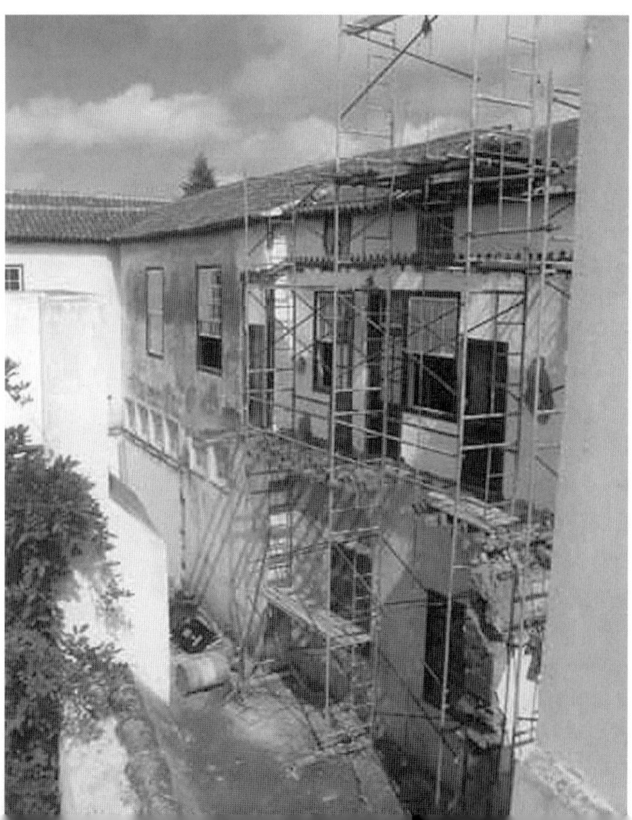

El catálogo de edificios protegidos es precario y surgen abundantes contradicciones en los listados de inmuebles que deben ser protegidos. No respeta los compromisos de protección de edificios singulares adquiridos ante la UNESCO en el expediente que acompañó a la solicitud de inscripción de La Laguna en la Lista del Patrimonio Mundial (ver documento anexo en el que se detallan las notables reducciones en la protección propuestos en el PEPRI). Tampoco protege las numerosas casas terreras de finales del siglo XIX y primeros decenios del XX, que deben ser conservadas no como simples elementos ambientales, sino como exponentes genuinos de la arquitectura vernácula tradicional de La Laguna.

De todo lo anterior se deduce que:

Entre los 591 inmuebles incluidos en listado de edificios a proteger hay múltiples repeticiones (se citan en sus respectivas calles como diferentes de los que ocupan esquinas)

- Hay 8 propuestas de descatalogación cuya justificación es muy deficiente;
- Se producen 117 descatalogaciones reales no citadas;
- Se admiten 33 catalogados en nivel "Ambiental 2", que son operaciones de fachadismo;
- Hay 498 catalogados en nivel "Ambiental 1" sin asignación de tipología conforme al Expediente.

El plan no asegura convenientemente el respeto a algunas de las invariantes tradicionales en el caserío, especialmente en lo que respecta al uso de cubiertas a cuatro y dos aguas y el mantenimiento del patio abierto. También debería reforzar la obligación de utilizar materiales tradicionales e impedir la presencia de aplacados inadecuados, así como el descubrimiento de la piedra como elemento decorativo de la fachada. Tampoco hace alusión a la necesaria elaboración de una carta de color para La Laguna.

Consideraciones respecto a los usos permitidos

La palabra „revitalización" se utiliza como justificación de un conjunto de actuaciones que solamente representa el apoyo de las instituciones públicas a operaciones inmobiliarias de las que se desprenderá una fase ulterior de venta de tipologías residenciales no propias de centros históricos (adosados, apartamentos, estudios…). Esto, a juzgar por los estudios previos, conducirá con toda seguridad a su injustificada masificación y a su conversión, como

Destrucción de galería y eliminación de patio del Colegio de los Jesuitas, después Universidad de San Fernando, hoy Real Sociedad Económica de Amigos del País (21-11-2004).

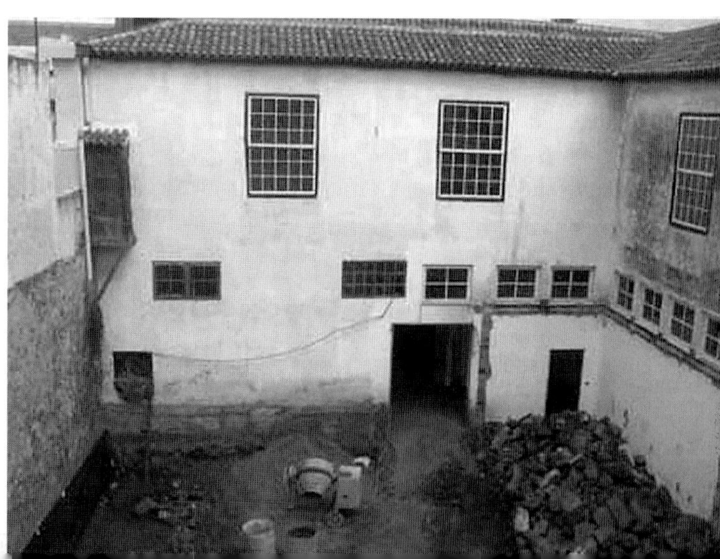

ya ha sucedido en otros centros históricos españoles, en espacios más preparados para rescatar altas plusvalías de las inversiones inmobiliarias que para servir de lugares de calidad patrimonial.

El plan especial no establece medidas efectivas que acoten el desarrollo previsiblemente desmesurado de las actividades comerciales y de otro tipo de servicios en el centro histórico.

Consideraciones respecto a los espacios públicos, la accesibilidad y los aparcamientos

Varios de los espacios públicos más representativos de la ciudad son reproyectados modificando su forma, su estructura y su carácter.

La política de crear redes peatonales y acotar el tráfico privado no motorizado es muy deficiente y se encuentra muy lejos de los planteamientos y logros de otras ciudades europeas y españolas.

No son adecuadas las obligaciones mínimas de aparcamientos para viviendas, oficinas y locales comerciales y, sobre todo, es muy preocupante el posible impacto de la construcción desmedida de aparcamientos subterráneos en el conjunto del caserío de la ciudad dadas las condiciones geotectónicas del emplazamiento sobre el que ésta se asienta.

Consideraciones respecto a la gestión urbanística del centro histórico de La Laguna durante el proceso de redacción del Plan Especial de Protección

Durante el período que ha durado la tramitación del Plan Especial de Protección se ha convenido que el equipo redactor contratado sea el que informe a nivel municipal todas las licencias que después son remitidas para su aprobación por la Comisión Insular de Patrimonio (según consta en el contrato firmado con dicho equipo). Aunque desde el Ayuntamiento se asegura lo contrario, y de conformidad con dicho acuerdo no se ha producido una real y necesaria suspensión de licencias durante el período de redacción del Plan Especial de Protección, sino que se han autorizado numerosas actuaciones sujetas a aprobación en el ámbito del plan

Se ha procedido a llevar a cabo un buen número de vaciados en edificios incluidos en el expediente presentado para la inclusión de La Laguna en la Lista del Patrimonio Mundial y a algunos derribos, así como a modificar las alineaciones en algún caso.

Propuesta de proyecto-tipo según el PEP, C/Herradores (19-03-2004).

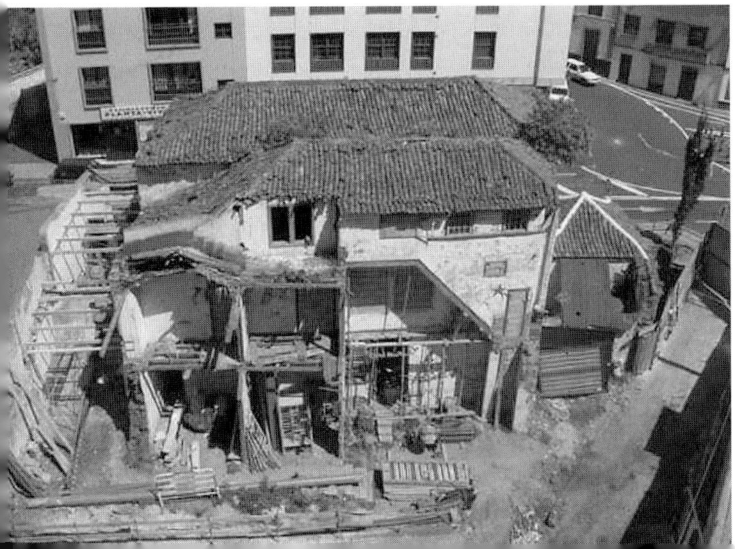

Report on town-planning intervention in the Historic Town Complex of Cáceres, World Heritage City

Cáceres was declared a Historic-Artistic Town Complex by decree on 21 January 1949, ratified by the orders of the General Board of Fine Arts in 1965, extended from its previous limits by resolution of the National Administration on 18 November 1982 (Official Bulletin of State 26 November) and adopted as the protection perimeter according to the Special Plan for the Protection and Restoration of the Architectural Heritage of the City of Cáceres (1990), now in force.

The Ribera del Marco is the tectonic trench which defines the southern frontage of the historic-artistic town complex: Old City, World Heritage (1986) and the extramural quarters of the Historic Centre (Fuente Concejo – XIV, Mira al Rio, San Roque and San Francisco). These were identifiably urban from the 13th century, with the presence of kitchen gardens in use, a watercourse from the Marco, proceeding from the Calerizo water-storage, old tanneries, and wash-houses for wool.

Despite the deposit of heritage material, juxtaposed and superimposed, the Marco riverbank area has been considered by municipal agencies from the 16th century onwards as the poor, dirty and neglected 'backroom' of Cáceres, in contrast with the splendid western facade of the Plaza Mayor.

The first attempt at integrated management was proposed in 1981 by the editors of the Special Plan for the Interior Restoration of the Ribera del Marco (Sector CCH-30-1; this was in development of the General Town Planning Project of 1975), in which I took part as a member of the G-2 team, without any administrative involvement regarding the integrated restoration, included in the planning process by subsequent Councils, with the inevitable result of deterioration in material, social aspects, function and environment.

In December 2003 an editorial team under my direction produced for the Ministry of the Arts the Report on the State of Conservation of the Old City of Cáceres, World Heritage, (Edition 2), making use of the protection policies formulated from 1986 to 2003, according to the instructions issued by the World Heritage Convention. For the protection of the Ribera del Marco, we consider it necessary to propose to ICOMOS the establishment of a non-urbanised surrounding zone, to include all of the symmetrical slopes of the Sierra de la Mosca (northern, eastern and western sides), as far as the Virgen de la Montana Sanctuary, the vantage point for panoramic views towards the historic centre, so as to be included in the new Special Plan for Protection of the Historic Site, which is to be revised.

Ignoring the previous determinations, the Cáceres Town Council has decided to introduce, in the framework of revision of the present general urban plan, the Ronda Este Interior project, a road of 10 metres in width and high traffic capacity to direct the flow of vehicles (15,000 vehicles per day) between the east and west of the city along the Ribera del Marco tectonic trench (Fuente Concejo-Mira al Rio-San Francisco).This would involve the demolition of the San Francisco bridge, to be replaced by a roundabout, the encroachment upon and restriction of the protection perimeter of the Historic Complex, by means of the expropiation and destruction of 12 residential buildings which are introduced into the complex with a degree of environmental protection in the technical index of the Special Plan, as well as the considerably increased impact on, and contamination of all kinds, of the area proposed for protection: the destruction of kitchen gardens, the modification of

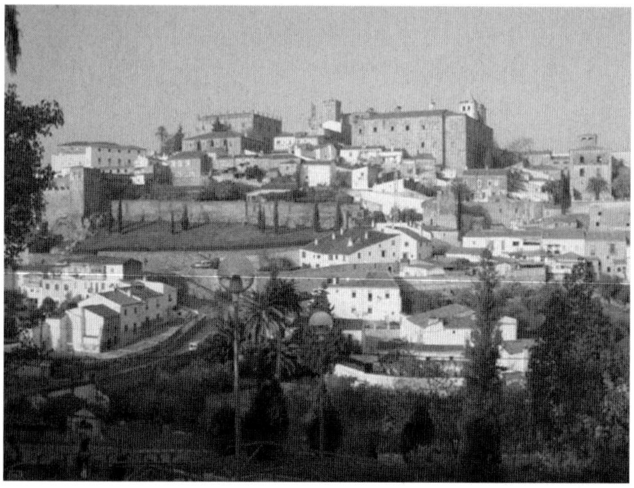

Ribera del Marco, Cáceres, with the World Heritage Old City in the background

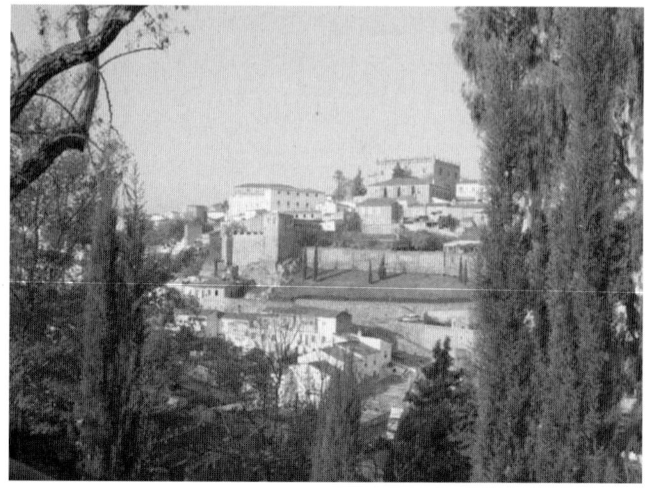

Ribera del Marco, Cáceres, with the World Heritage Old City in the background

water courses and overflow channels at the side, reducing the amount of space for pedestrians, playing fields and tourist routes.

To carry out the said project, which affects the decisions of the Special Protection Plan for Heritage Protection, now in force, the Town Council modifies them exactly as it wants. This is without accepting that very probably a professional archaeological study made beforehand would bring to light the route of the Roman Via de la Plata in dealing with the Ribera del Marco area of Cáceres.

Once again the Municipal Corporation has ignored the instructions of the World Heritage Convention regarding the heritage area of Old Cáceres, as given in the ICOMOS Assessment report of December 2003. This allowed the interests of concrete construction to prevail, to the detriment of the legitimate interests of the residents and the urban community.

If the town-planning contradictions were not enough, the Ronda Este Interior project, to be financed by European Union funding under the pretext of the rehabilitation and enlargement project for the garden of the old Jewish quarter, will eventually turn into an operation of traffic reform and access, in a city which hopes to be a European Cultural Capital in 2016.

In August 2004 the political majority in the Town Council approved, in plenary session, the Fuente Concejo-Mira al Rio-San Francisco project, fixing the imminent commencement of public works and demolition for the month of October 2004.

Confronted by this threat to our heritage, I informed the Board of Management of ICOMOS Spain of this (Madrid, general session of 16 July 2004). At the end of July 2004 I sent to María Rosa Súarez-Inclán Ducassi, President of ICOMOS Spain, a detailed report including the Ronda Este Interior Project, allegations, photographs, media reactions to the alarm arising among the Ribera del Marco neighbourhood associations and professionals in Cáceres involved in heritage matters, grouped in the citizens' association 'Save the Ribera del Marco'.

For all the reasons given, as a resident of the city of Cáceres, as a professor of the University of Extremadura, and as Vice-President of ICOMOS Spain, with the approval of the Presidency of the National Spanish Committee of ICOMOS, I wish to request from the international directive bodies of ICOMOS urgent protection. This in the face of imminent danger, for the heritage city of Old Cáceres (World Heritage), for its historic and artistic town complex and for the surrounding protective area of Ribera Del Marco.

Professor Antonio-J. Campesino Fernández
Vice-President, ICOMOS Spain

Municipal project – Ronda Este Interior along the Ribera del Marco (Cáceres)

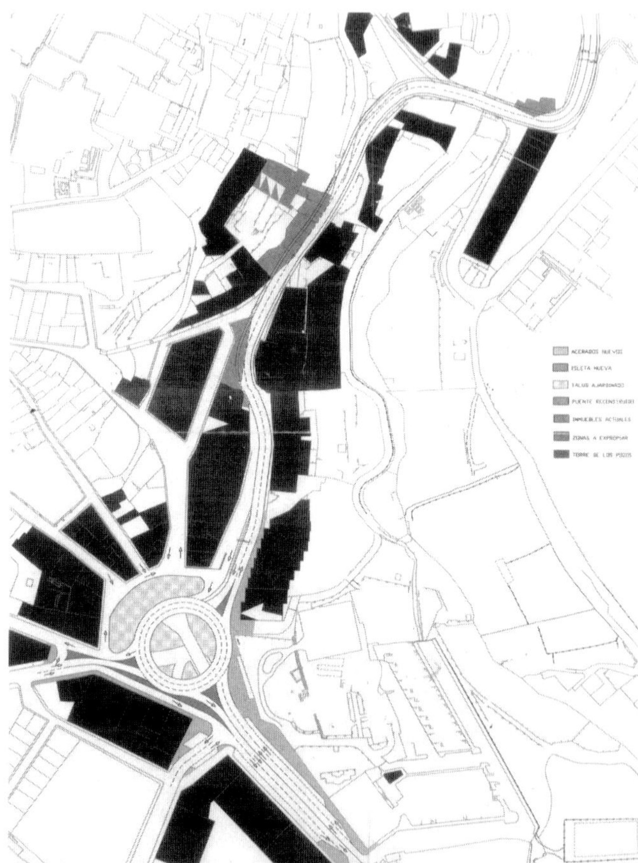

Informe sobre Intervención Urbanística en el Conjunto Histórico de Cáceres, cuidad del Patrimonio Mundial

Que el Conjunto Histórico-Artístico de Cáceres fue declarado por Decreto de 21 de enero de 1949, ratificado por las Instrucciones de la Dirección General de Bellas Artes de 1965, ampliado en sus límites preexistentes por Resolución de la Administración estatal de 18 de noviembre de 1982 (BOE de 26 de noviembre) y asumido como perímetro de protección del vigente *Plan Especial de Protección y Rehabilitación del Patrimonio Arquitectónico de la Ciudad de Cáceres* (1990).

Que la Ribera del Marco es la fosa tectónica que define la fachada de mediodía y delimita el perímetro oriental del Conjunto Histórico-Artístico: Ciudad Vieja, Patrimonio Mundial (1986) y barrios extramuros del Centro Histórico (Fuente Concejo – XIV –, Mira al Río, San Roque y San Francisco) que contienen las señas urbanas de identidad desde el siglo XIII, con presencia de huertas en explotación, curso de agua del Marco procedente de la cubeta cárstica del Calerizo, antiguas tenerías, lavaderos de lana...

Que, pese al depósito de contenidos patrimoniales, yuxtapuestos y superpuestos, la Ribera del Marco viene siendo interpretada por los gestores municipales desde el siglo XVI como la trastienda pobre, sucia y abandonada de Cáceres, en contraste con la fachada noble occidental de la Plaza Mayor.

Que el primer intento de ordenación integral fue propuesto en 1981 por los redactores del *Plan Especial de Reforma Interior de la Ribera del Marco* (Sector CCH-30-I, en desarrollo del Plan General de Ordenación Urbana de 1975), de cuyo equipo G-2 formé parte, sin materialización política alguna de los contenidos de rehabilitación integrada, insertos en el planeamiento, por parte de las sucesivas Corporaciones con el lógico resultado de deterioro morfológico, social, funcional y ambiental.

Que en diciembre de 2003, un equipo redactor bajo mi dirección, elaboró para el Ministerio de Cultura un *Informe sobre el Estado de Conservación de la Ciudad Vieja de Cáceres, Patrimonio Mundial* (Formulario II), valorando las políticas de protección arbitradas desde 1986 hasta 2003, en aplicación de las Directrices de la Convención del Patrimonio Mundial. Para la protección de la Ribera del Marco, entendimos necesario proponer a ICOMOS el establecimiento de un entorno sin urbanizar, que abarcara toda la vertiente simétrica de la Sierra de la Mosca (laderas norte, este y oeste) hasta el Santuario de la Virgen de la Montaña, mirador obligado de protección de vistas y perspectivas hacia la Ciudad Monumental, al objeto de que fuera asumido por el nuevo Plan Especial de Protección del Centro Histórico, a punto de revisión.

Que el Ayuntamiento de Cáceres, haciendo caso omiso a las determinaciones anteriores, decide en el marco de revisión del vigente Plan General de Ordenación Urbana, introducir el Proyecto de Ronda Este Interior, un víal de 10 metros de anchura y alta capacidad de tráfico para la canalización del flujo de vehículos (15.000 veh./día), entre el oeste y este de la ciudad por el fondo de la fosa tectónica de la Ribera del Marco (Fuente Concejo-Mira

Aerial view of the eastern edge of the Historic-artistic Town Complex, closely associated with the Almohad fortification which delimits the intramural area of the Old City of Cáceres (World Heritage, 1986), in the urban sector of Ribera del Marco. The intention of the Ronda Este Interior project, as conceived by the municipal government, is based on the destructive cutting of this medieval ring-road by a ten metre wide road. This breaks into the historic town-complex and takes land at the perimeter, demolishing the small modest dwellings at the edge, under environmental protection, and risks the precarious stability of the 12th century Almohad outer wall and the olive grove of the old Jewish quarter. It also destroys the necessary surrounding protection area of the Ribera del Marco with a highly polluting traffic route.

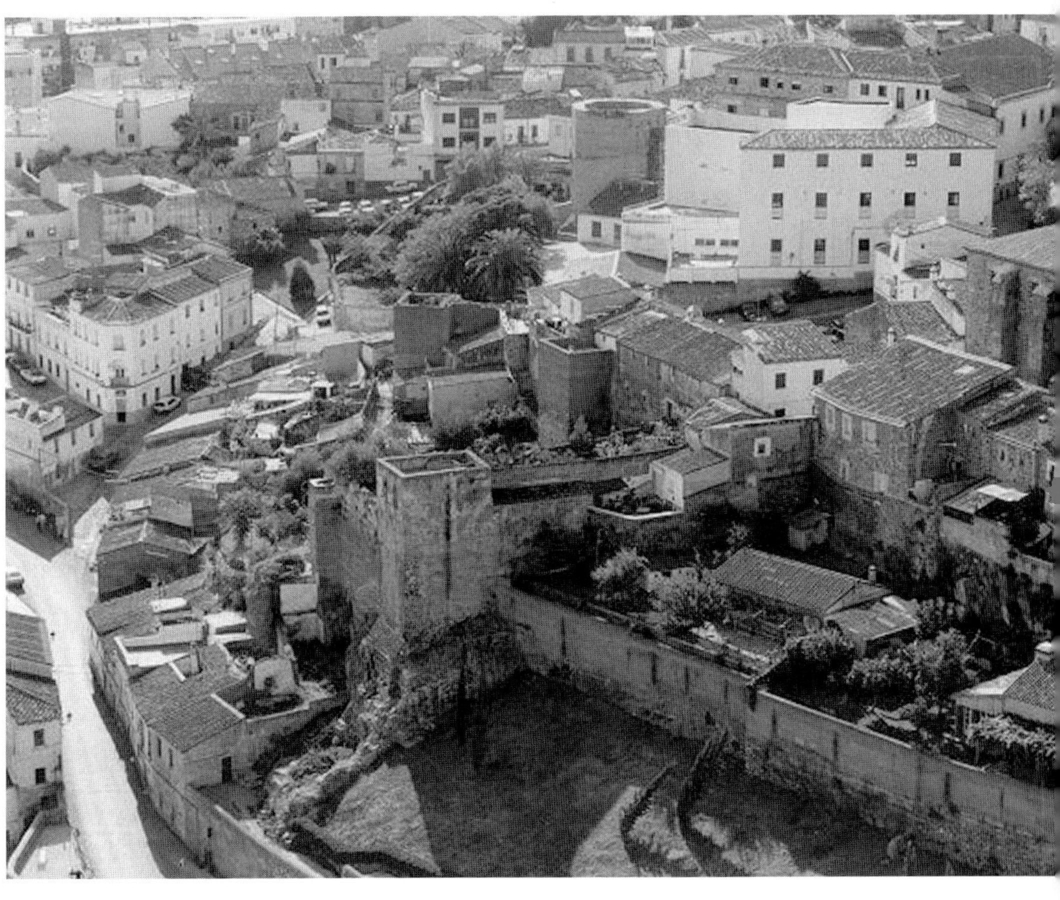

al Río-San Francisco), lo que implicará la destrucción del puente de San Francisco, sustituido por una rotonda, la invasión y restricción del perímetro de protección del Conjunto Histórico, mediante la expropiación y derribo de 12 viviendas de borde, insertas dentro del Conjunto con grado de protección ambiental en las fichas técnicas del Plan Especial, así como la multiplicación de impactos y agresiones contaminantes de todo tipo sobre el entorno previsto de protección: arrasamiento de huertas, modificación de acuíferos y escorrentías de ladera…, en detrimento del espacio peatonal, de ocio lúdico y paseo turístico.

Que para la ejecución del citado Proyecto, que afecta a las determinaciones del vigente Plan Especial de Protección del Patrimonio, el Ayuntamiento las modifica puntualmente a su antojo, sin querer aceptar que, muy probablemente, un estudio arqueológico profesional previo sacará a la luz el trazado de la Vía de la Plata romana en su discurso cacereño por la Ribera del Marco.

Que, una vez más, la Corporación Municipal hace caso omiso a las Directrices de la Convención del Patrimonio Mundial, relativas al respeto del entorno patrimonial de la Ciudad Vieja de Cáceres, contenido en el Informe de Evaluación de ICOMOS, de diciembre de 2003, haciendo prevalecer los intereses de los agentes del hormigón en detrimento de los legítimos de los residentes y de la colectividad urbana.

Que, por si las contradicciones urbanísticas no fueran suficientes, el Proyecto de Ronda Este Interior, que se financia con Fondos Europeos bajo el pretexto de Proyecto de Rehabilitación y Ampliación del jardín de la Judería Vieja, acabará desarrollándose como operación de Reforma de Tráfico y Accesibilidad, en una ciudad que aspira a ser Capital Cultural Europea en 2016.

Que la mayoría política que gobierna el Ayuntamiento ha procedido a la aprobación en Pleno, durante el mes de agosto de 2004, del Proyecto de Fuente Concejo-Mira al Río-San Francisco, fijando el inminente comienzo de obras y derribos para el próximo mes de octubre de 2004.

Ante la agresión patrimonial antedicha, procedí a informar a la Junta Directiva de Icomos-España (Madrid, Junta Ordinaria de 16 de julio de 2004) y a enviar, a finales del mes de julio de 2004, a Dñª. María Rosa Suárez-Inclán Ducassi, Presidenta de ICOMOS-España, un profuso dossier con el *Proyecto de la Ronda Este Interior*, alegaciones, imágenes y repercusiones periodísticas de la alarma social desencadenada entre las Asociaciones de Vecinos de la Ribera del Marco y entre los profesionales carereños comprometidos con el patrimonio, agrupados en el Foro y Plataforma Ciudadana "Salvemos la Ribera del Marco".

Por todo lo expuesto, como ciudadano cacereño, como Catedrático de la Universidad de Extremadura y como Vicepresidente de ICOMOS-España, con el Visto Bueno de la Presidencia del Comité Nacional Español de ICOMOS, tengo a bien SOLICITAR, de los directivos internacionales de ICOMOS el amparo urgente ante la inmediata agresión al patrimonio de la Ciudad Vieja de Cáceres (Patrimonio Mundial), a su Conjunto Histórico-Artístico y al entorno de protección de la Ribera del Marco.

Prof. Dr. Antonio-J. Campesino Fernández
(N.I.F. 11682881-P)
Vicepresidente de ICOMOS-España

SRI LANKA

Shortly before this *Heritage at Risk* publication was printed we received first news from the areas affected by the great tsunami disaster of 26 December 2004, especially from Sri Lanka concerning the World Heritage site of Galle. The Fort itself is intact. The water went inside and damaged some of the buildings superficially, such as the doors being ripped off the hinges. The 16th-century sewer lines along the roads have given way in some places. Most of the old buildings in Galle town but outside the Fort have been reduced to debris. A historic church in Matara has suffered, too. The talking point is that all along the coastal belt no Buddhist statue or Stupa has been damaged. In some areas the statues stand amongst piles of debris.

Three days after the disaster ICOMOS Sri Lanka sent the following statement:

26/12: Reconstruction, conservation and the preservation of memory

Three days after the great tsunami disaster of 26 December the Sri Lanka National Committee of ICOMOS (the International Council on Monuments and Sites) met and issued a statement which 'mourned the death of thousands of fellow Sri Lankans and peoples of neighbouring countries as well as visitors from far off lands'. ICOMOS SL commiserated with the hundreds of thousands who are bereaved, displaced, whose lives have been disrupted and homes and work places destroyed. Although in various ways ICOMOS SL members in their individual capacities were involved in assisting the bereaved and the dislocated, and discussed how to systematize or concentrate efforts, the meeting mainly focussed on the little discussed socio-psychological and socio-cultural dimensions of the situation.

The human scale of this disaster was one of unprecedented magnitude. Within minutes, hundreds of thousands were killed, injured or displaced, lives disrupted, homes and work places destroyed. Clearly the pressing need of the hour was the burial of the dead, the search for the missing, the consolation of the bereaved and continuing and intensified assistance to all those who have been made homeless or otherwise adversely affected by the tragedy. But it was also necessary to look to the future — to the aftermath of the tragedy, the continuing effects of it on the lives of millions, where people and local communities have to rebuild their lives, restore their living and working environments and undertake the million tasks of reconstruction.

Human tragedy and physical environment

There are, first of all, the human costs of the tragedy which need to be confronted: death and bereavement, the nightmare of the missing, trauma, injury, the possibility of disease, the longer term effects on individual health, the emerging economic consequences on occupations, employment, loss of property, living conditions ...the list is long and endless. And there is not only the rebuilding of lives but also the reconstruction of the physical environment.

It is this latter task which the planning sector of government has already begun to think about. ICOMOS SL draws attention to the deepest implications of this work. As the forward planning for reconstruction begins, it is also vital that the preservationist

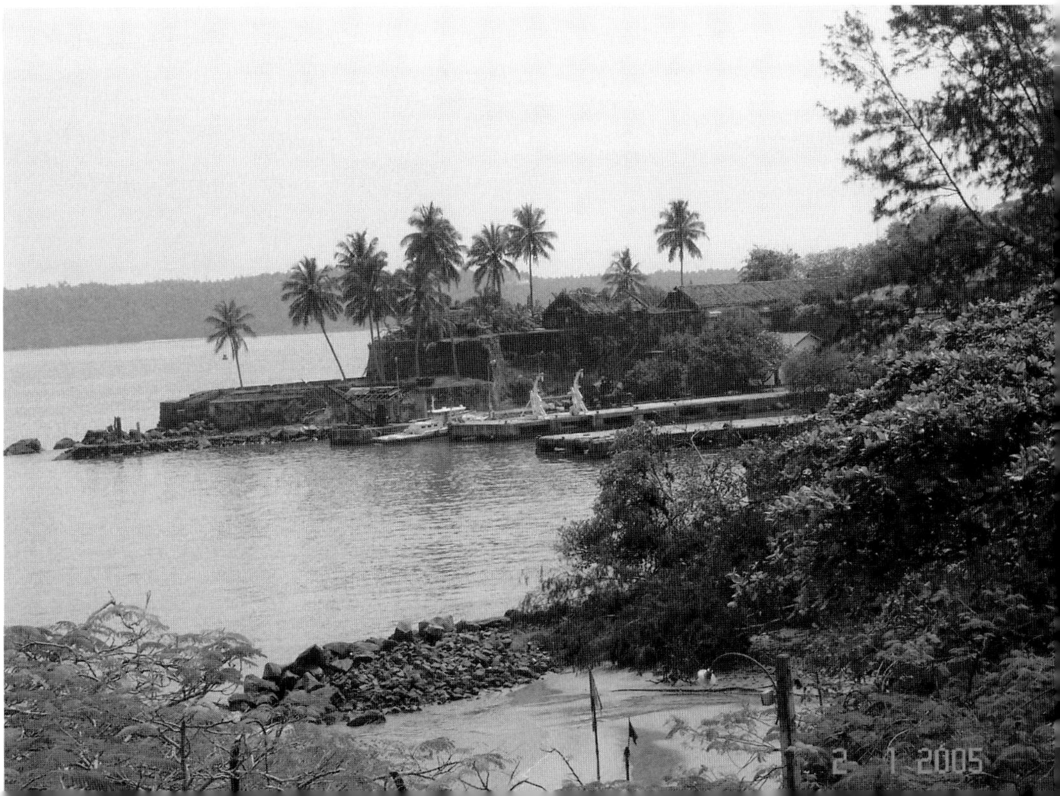

Without the unauthorized buildings dotting the coastline outside the historic fort, the Zwartz bastion of the Galle Fort is now clearly visible. The lower terrace is the Portuguese section from the 15th century.

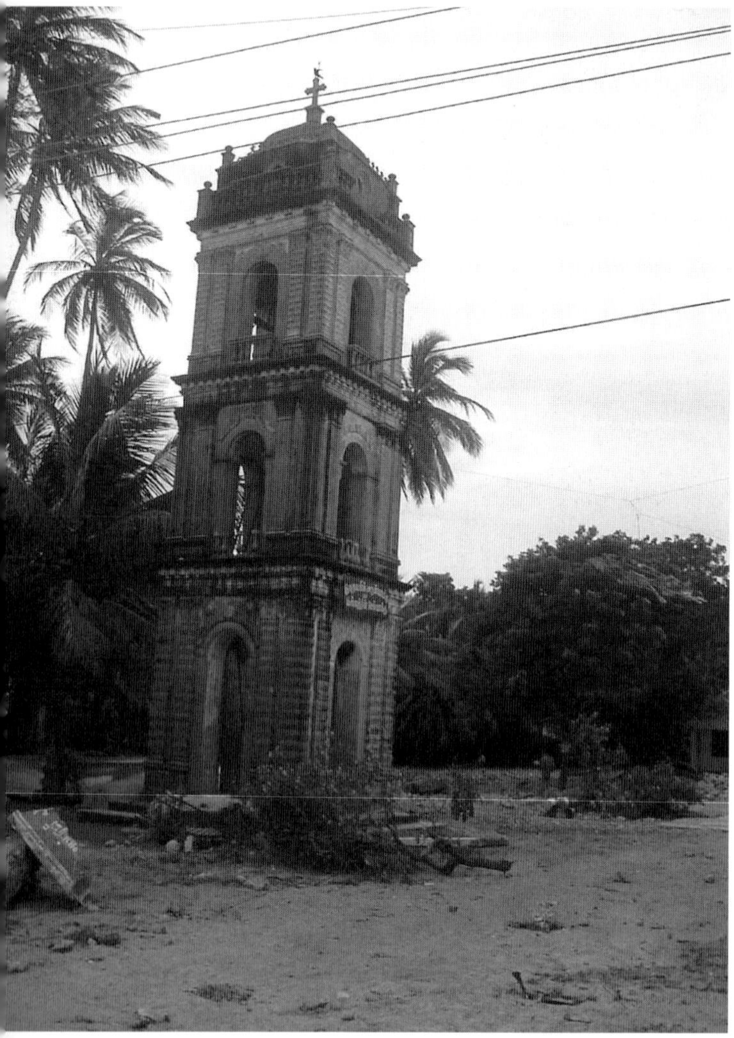

Church in pt. Pedro that has survived the tsunami

dimension is built into the national vision that is being formulated and the national tasks that are envisaged.

- *It is important therefore that the preservation or restoration of heritage buildings and other cultural monuments, environments and landscapes are incorporated as an important aspect of the rebuilding plans.*
- *From an economic point of view, conserving and restoring an old building or buildings is often more cost effective than tearing it down and building anew, however much clearing and new construction may seem to be the easier option – although exercising that option would need a conservationist perspective, skills and experience.*
- *In catastrophes of this nature, there is an important socio-psychological and socio-cultural need for local communities and individuals to see and feel that the familiar environments with which they identify are not totally wiped out.*
- *Conservation and restoration is a very special contribution towards preserving and carrying the memory of the past into the rebuilding of the future.*
- *'Maintaining the familiar' is one of the most valuable components of the entire restorative process, helping to 'keep one's moorings', to retain identity, to engender and strengthen a psychology of survival and recovery in the face of great destruction.*
- *In another sense, a country's coastline is part of its fundamental memory – the palaeoclimatic and archaeological remains found here are a vital and subtle source of information about its relations with the world beyond its shores in geological and historical time.*
- *Preserving, conserving and restoring the remains that have survived this disaster is a fitting monument to those affected by the tragedy.*

Coast conservation and damage assessment

No doubt in some instances entire urban centres and rural and suburban settlements have been entirely wiped out, but in others enough is left for conservation or restoration. It is precisely for this reason that it is important a program should begin at once to assess the damage and plan the protection and preservation of heritage buildings and environments as an integral part of the reconstruction master plan. In order to do this the University Departments of Archaeology, Architecture, and Historical and Cultural Studies are being invited by ICOMOS SL to establish small teams to undertake a rapid survey program of the coastal region. The survey will be based on the Protected Sites and Monuments scheduled under the Antiquities Ordinance and also the Report on the Inventory of Places of Religious and Cultural Significance and Areas of Scenic and Recreationmal Value within the Coastal Zone of Sri Lanka (P.L. Prematilleke, 1989) published by the Coast Conservation Department (1989). The preliminary situation survey is positioned to commence in the second week of January and will be completed before the end of the month.

Archt. Plnr. Pali Wijeratne
(President SL ICOMOS National Committee)

Dr. Roland Silva
(Honorary President, ICOMOS)

Prof. Senake Bandaranayake
(Past President SL ICOMOS Com.)

Prof. Nimal de Silva
(Past President SL ICOMOS Nat. Com.)

Archt. Veranjan Kurukulasuriya
(Joint Secretary, SL ICOMOS Nat. Com.)

29 December 2004

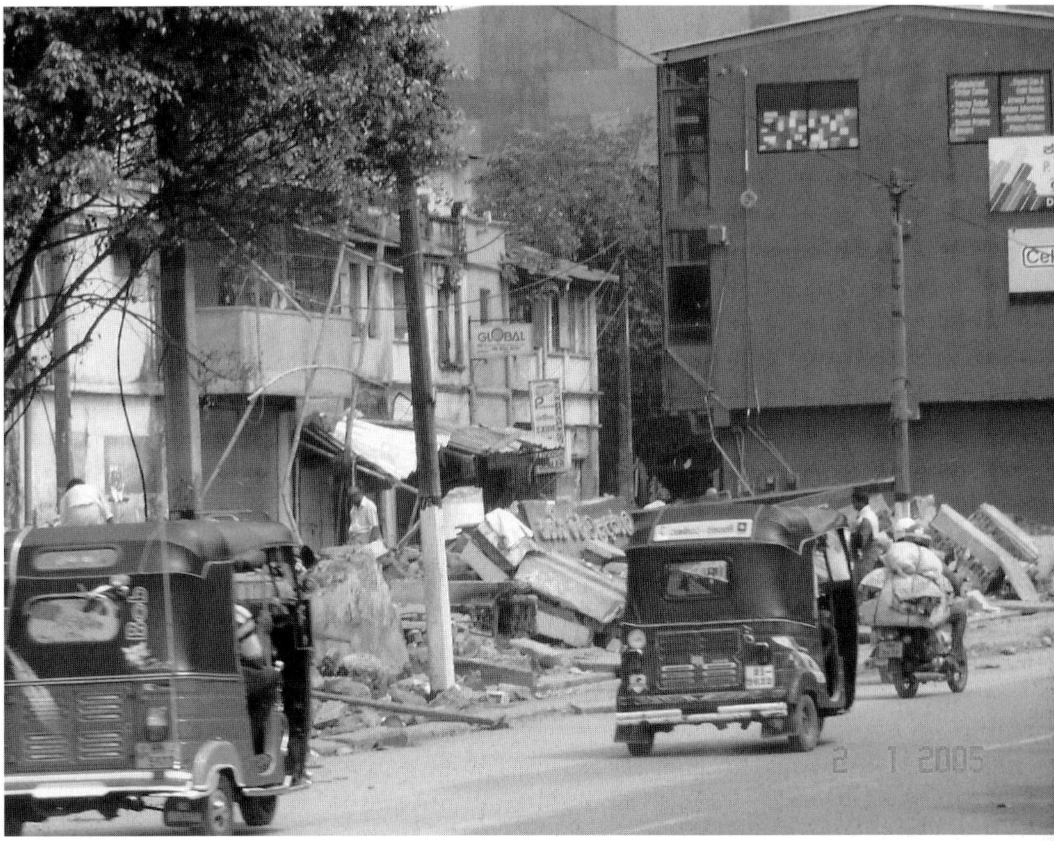

The 17th-century fish market of Galle town was totally destroyed on 26th December 2004

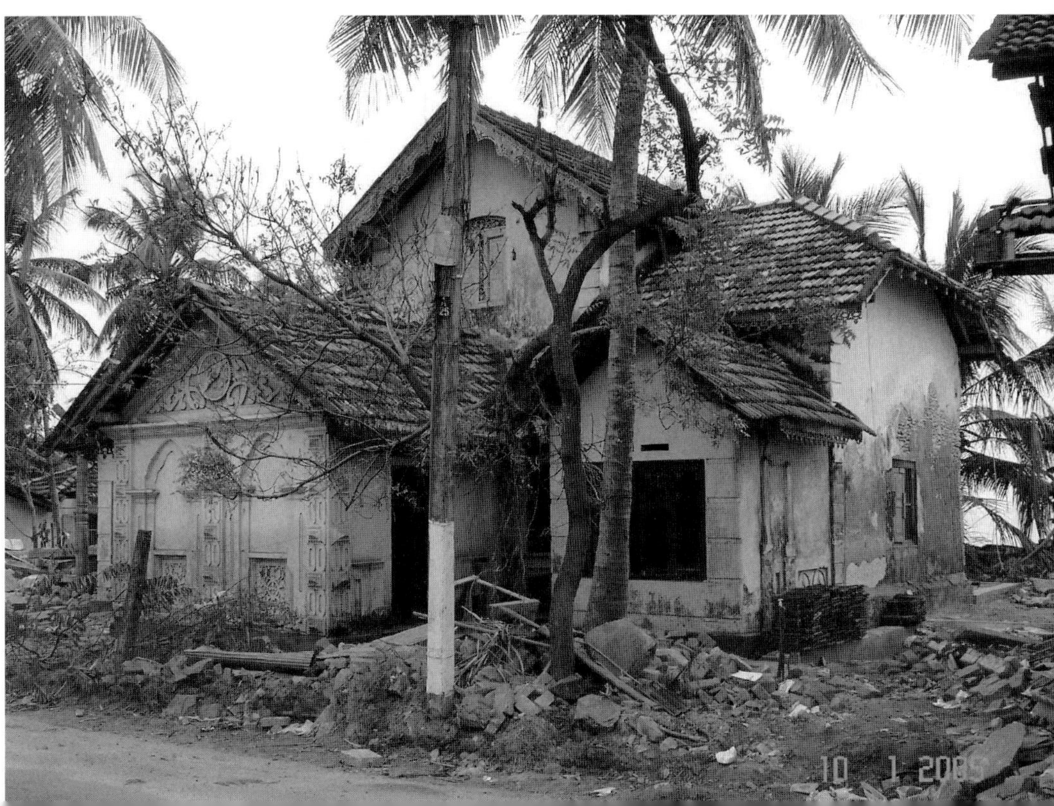

Just outside Galle some historic houses have escaped with minor damages

SWEDEN
Historic Gardens

The last five years show a rising trend of both academic and popular interest in historic gardens and their conservation. Today institutions give courses in garden history, seminars are arranged regularly and research is in progress at different levels in different disciplines, as well as field surveys.

We are seriously concerned that this current promising development might lose its momentum. Our concern is based on the Swedish National Heritage Board discontinuing their only appointment of a specialist on historic gardens last [northern] summer. As a result, no person has responsibility for the general supervision or support for the assessment and conservation of historic gardens and parks. At a time when economic cut-backs are forced on regional and local authorities, this reduction in expertise at the national level is an even more serious loss.

Right now there is an urgent need for further action in the following areas:

- Inventories for a national register of the different types of historic gardens and parks, including their contents of decorations and plants (for National Collections).
- Strategies to protect the most significant gardens, including historic research, survey, conservation programs, conservation measures and maintenance by expert and skilled gardeners.
- Evaluation of methods and results of finished projects.
- Information on the most useful methods and recommendations by available experts at regional and local levels.

This work needs to be systematically organised for the most efficient use of the limited resources at our disposal.

Maria Flinck, garden conservationist
Dr Catharina Nolin, garden historian

TAJIKISTAN
A view from outside

Tajikistan is a wonderful mountainous country with prosperous valleys, that attracted people to live there from the earliest times in human history. Its territory was always on the crossroads of the main trade and cultural routes between the largest civilisations of the Eurasian continent and throughout history it was part of the greatest states of Central Asia: Bactria and Soghd, Achaemenid empire, Greek Bactria, the kingdoms of Kushan, Gaznovids, Samanids, Karakhanids and Timurids. A rich cultural heritage is evidence of that and has the highest universal value.

Since the collapse of the Soviet Union in 1991, the country has passed through a series of severe tests of economical and political change, followed by the civil war. But since the very outset of recovery from this difficult time, the government of the new Republic of Tajikistan has been paying considerable attention to cultural heritage preservation. The Inspectorate for Heritage Protection, Historical and Cultural Reserves, the State organisation for heritage restoration, under the Ministry of Culture has started functioning again. The country has a List of Properties of National Significance protected at the government level, and sites of universal value are already entered on a World Heritage Tentative List, with work begun preparing the nominations.

But all this is just a beginning and the amount of heritage in danger is vast, but the team of experienced professionals dealing with cultural properties is too few. Old conservation methods and technologies from the 1970s–80s continue to be in use in the country, with insufficient inauthentic materials and with restoration prevailing over conservation, despite the results of such works being visible on numerous medieval architectural monuments all over the country. And when one threat is from improper conservation, another is a total absence of conservation, while many archaeological sites of exceptional value were excavated many decades ago, or are under continuous archaeological study. When comparing the results of the effect of these two main threats, it is difficult to judge which is the more dangerous for Tajikistan's heritage: conservation or its absence.

Mohammad Basharo Mausoleum (11th –14th centuries)

The Mausoleum was erected over the grave of the prominent Sufi saint Mohammad Bosharo, highly esteemed in the region, who lived in the 8th–9th centuries. It is situated in a small village (*kishlak*), Mazary Sharif, 25 km from the town of Penjikent. The building was erected on a small platform at the foot of a mountain with an ancient necropolis, which started to develop as far back as pre-Islamic times. A picturesque mountainous landscape with beautiful and worshipped places of nature, not affected much by human activity, together with the unhurried traditional village life nearby is an excellent setting for the monument with its preserved original architectural appearance, formed as a result of the building's harmonious evolution over several centuries (11-12th–14th centuries) in the Middle Ages.

Today the building is not large but has extended symmetric planning, with burial chambers by the sides of the main worship hall (*ziarat-hana*), covered with domes and vaults of varied styles, traditional for the region in different periods. But originally, it was a small mosque (11th–12th centuries) erected near the holy grave, which being a place of great spiritual value was enlarged at least once later. One of the most significant construction periods is in the 14th century (1342–43), when a beautifully decorated portal was erected. It is faced with beautiful Islamic motives and inscriptions as well as using non-glazed carved terracotta and polychrome glazed carved terracotta, combined with various types of majolica and its incrustations into terracotta. It shows the early stage of transmission from monochrome decoration to polychrome, and is a rare or unique example in the whole of Central Asia. The portal design follows a decoration of painted clay *michrab nishe* (11th–12th centuries) of the building, also a rare or unique preserved example in the region. The original carved wooden portal door as well as carved gravestones are also among exceptional preserved examples. As has been already stated by most researchers, the mausoleum is of high artistic, historical and architectural significance and ranks among the best samples of medieval Central Asian architecture.

The most recent technical examination of the building shows that its condition on the whole is stable for the moment, but despite there being no cracks and other visual damage, it is overall inadequate. Restoration works with inauthentic materials, such as concrete and bitumen, insufficient water insulation and damp reduction, done in the 1980s, have brought many problems to the building. Original brickwork is highly affected by water and salts moving and excreting. There are many signs of recent plaster falls,

Mohammad Basharo Mausoleum

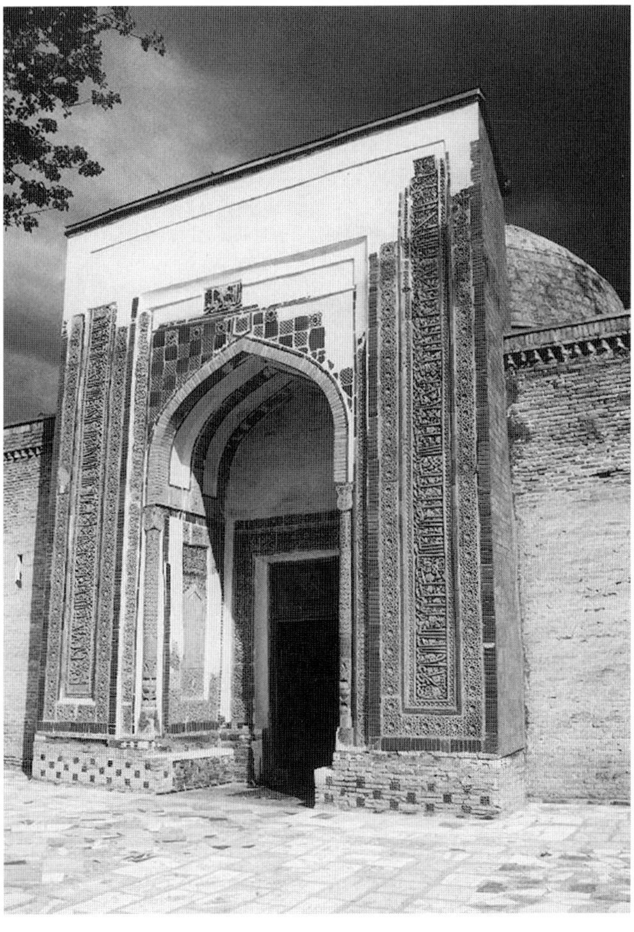

new leaks are appearing and condensation areas in spite of annual maintenance. Permanently very high humidity inside the building is not suitable for its wooden and clay items and paintings, as well as for visitors. Emergency works should be done as soon as possible, which could correct restoration mistakes and stop the monument's deterioration processes.

Hissar Fortress (1000 BC–20th century)

Situated approximately 20 km from the city of Dushanbe, it is a former eastern capital of the Bukhara khanate. The first settlement was established here in the first centuries BC, from the Greek-Bactrian and Kushan periods, as administrative centre of Hissar valley, the area being known as Shuman in the early Middle Ages. According to Suan Tzin this name was first mentioned in the 7th century, he wrote, it took four days to cover the territory of the khanate Su-man from the West to the East and one day from the South to the North. One of the most significant caravan routes, described in detail by most travellers, passed here, and until the 20th century, it was a prosperous city beloved by its powerful rulers. Only at the time of the Russian invasion into Central Asia, the Bukhara emir, supported by the Tsar's troops, succeeded in conquering Hissar in 1870. It later happened that he took his last refuge in its fortress before leaving his lands for Afghanistan in 1924 when the Red Army came to Bukhara and it was announced as the People's Republic of Bukhara.

After establishing Soviet power on the territory of the Bukhara khanate, the administrative centre moved to Dushanbe, and Hassar city was neglected. Left by their inhabitants, Bek's Residence and other buildings at the fortress were destroyed by earthquakes and people in few decades. The fortress has turned into a wonderful archaeological site with many well preserved layers from the 1st millennium BC until contemporary times. Only the fortress' earthen wall still reminds us of its former glory.

Life in the fortress' surroundings with *rabads* and markets, mosques, caravanserais and *madrasas* also has gone and the city has became a conservation site, which with all its monuments shows the history of the beginning and evolution of urban structural development since the 1st millennium BC until the 20th century. The monuments exist successfully within the modern, yet very traditional village, which often reuses the old city fabric.

The fortress area with its surroundings is inscribed in the List of Properties of National Significance of the Republic of Tajikistan and was announced as a State Historical and Cultural reserve. Hissar Fortress itself is included in the World Heritage Tentative List. Much work was done in the 1980s with the aim of heritage conservation, but unfortunately, the works on all the medieval building remains were done according to the at the time popular restoration methodology of using modern materials instead of authentic ones, without anticipating proper damp insulation and water reduction and drainage. Now all of them - the Fortress gateways, Kuhna madrasah (14th–16th centuries), Nav madrasah (18th century), Sangin Mosque (10th–16th centuries), Mahdumy Azam Mausoleum (10th–16th centuries), are suffering from the major effect of all this, causing damp with salts rising in the brickwork, condensations and high humidity in the interiors. Destruction by restoration is here close to destruction resulting from an absence of any conservation: the ruins of the Fortress' earthen walls are standing without having had any maintenance for about 70 years, disappearing beneath the rain, winds and pressures from animals and people. In former times, as eye-witnesses say and old photos prove, they had a height of about 7 m with a width of 3 m.

Ajina Tepa Buddhist Monastery (5th–8th centuries)

Among the best-known and studied examples of Buddhist heritage sites in Central Asia are the remains of the monastery now known as Ajina Tepa. It is situated in the Vahsh river valley not far from the city of Kurgan-Tube. The ruins are the remains of an earthen rectangular building complex, of approximately 50 m x 100 m. Its regular plan represents the remains of a building complex, consisting of two parts, one of which was monastic and another a temple. Each part had an internal square courtyard at its centre, standing on the common main symmetric axis. All the halls and premises of the complex were arrayed around these courts in a regular order, connected by a system of vaulted corridors, open to the courts. A cross-system of *aivans* (traditional Central Asian open premises) provided the appearance of a double mandala to the building plan, and reflected many times in numerous large and small stupas, found during archaeological excavations at the site. This composition of the building plan with a 4-*aivan* courtyard in the centre, as at the Ajina Tepa monastery, became the most popular plan for all types of public buildings (madrasas, mosques, and so on) as well as rulers' palaces, some centuries later in the Islamic period. The Buddhist site of Ajina Tepa is among those rare examples clearly demonstrating a succession of cultural traditions reflected in architecture.

Excavations of the remains were undertaken in the late 1960s, when the whole monastery complex was unearthed. Many artefacts of exceptional artistic value were found, and the most of them made of mudbrick: a reclining Buddha in Nirvana (12 m long), and many fragments of painting and sculpture on Buddhist themes. All of them have already found their conservators and places in the best museums, but the site itself with its tangible and intangible values, unique to the whole of Central Asia and to the world, was left without any conservation works until recently. This in spite of the fact that it is inscribed in the List of Properties of National Significance of the Republic of Tajikistan and even in the World Heritage Tentative List. Until now, these were all merely declarations.

The earthen structures are melting and disappearing being exposed to rain and winds. Cotton fields cut through with irrigation channels have come close up to the foot of the monastery platform, which rises above the flat landscape. These channels bring salts in the sub-surface water even up to its top, contributing much to the destruction of the wall remains, as do domestic and wild animals, attracted to this site for the shade of its earthen shelters. Comparing the survey materials from excavations in the late 1960s, it is easy to realise that some parts of the site may disappear in the nearest several years, if no attempt for its conservation is made. Not tomorrow – but right now.

Ancient Penjikent (5th–8th centuries)

The remains of this mudbrick city, 1.5 km from the modern city of Penjikent, are recognised worldwide as the best example of a medieval pre-Islamic town in Central Asia. It is a fact, that it is the rarest medieval city site in the region, at which archaeological research is going in all directions, studying urban life as an integral structure and source of knowledge: palaces and everyday dwellings, public buildings and burials, urban networks, monumental and decorative arts, all reflecting early medieval Central Asian culture, all being of interest to researchers.

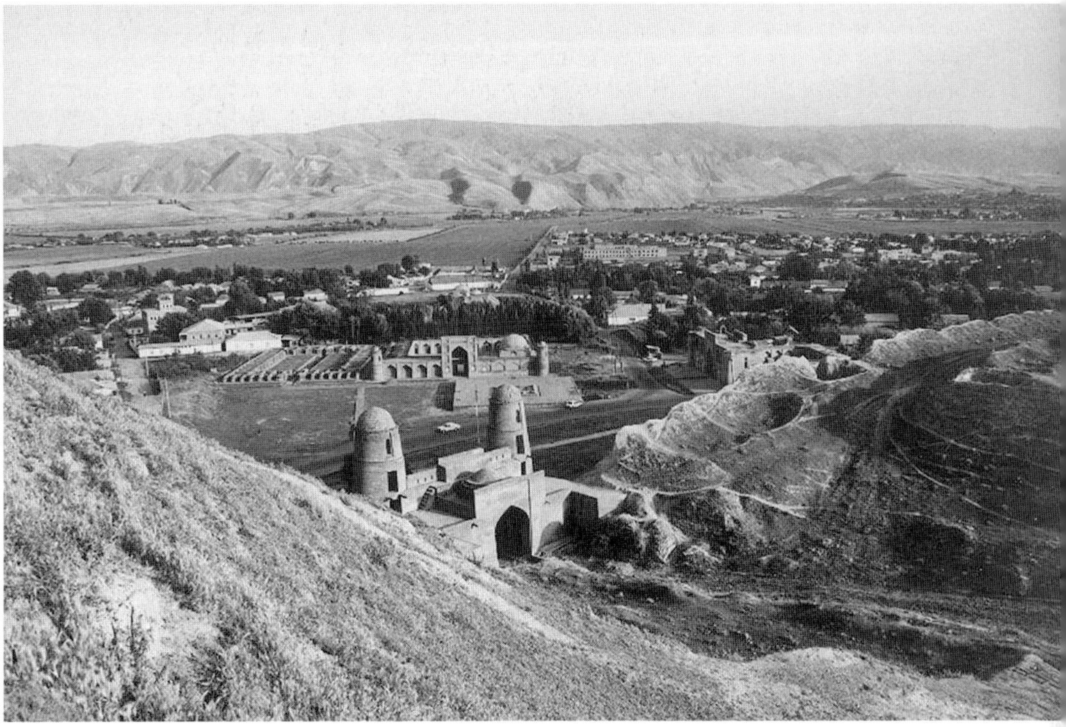

View from Hissar Fortress Citadel

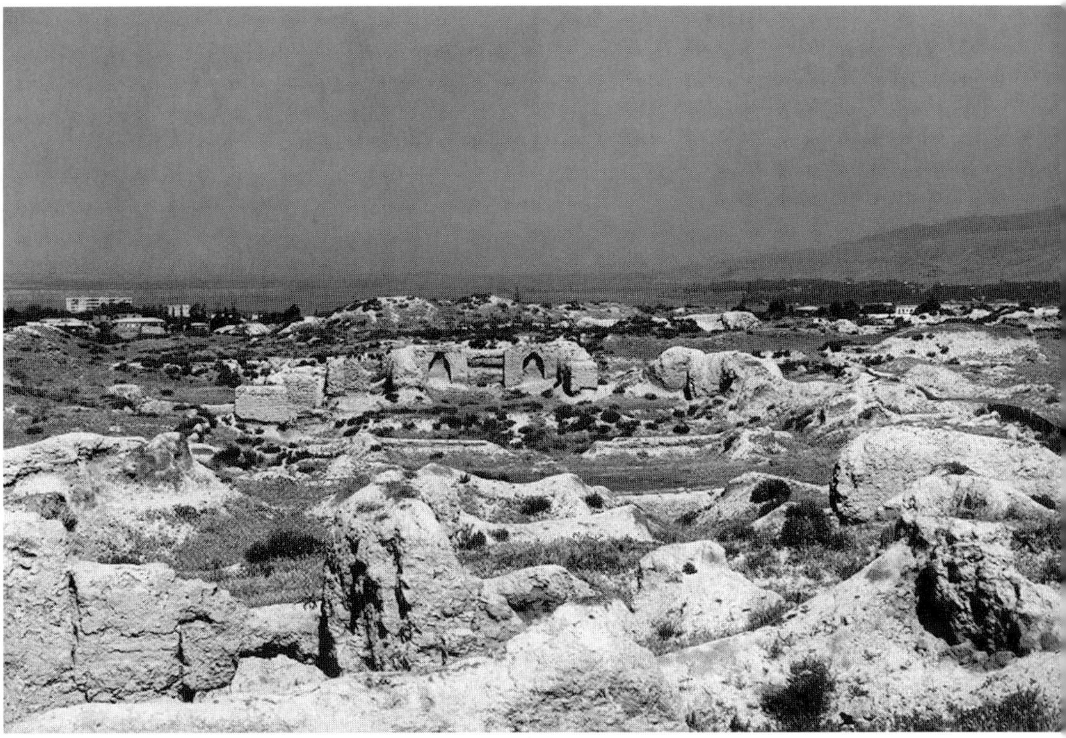

Ancient Penjikent

The city was established in the 5th century 60 km to the east of Samarkand as a separate estate, which was sometimes independent and sometimes a tributary possession of this powerful neighbour. It was built on the edge of a plateau with a precipice, forming its northern and western borders and was surrounded by mudbrick fortified walls with city gates on the other sides. A large palace for the ruler stood on a separate hill under the protection of the citadel and fortified castle. The city fabric was developed over four centuries following a regular rectangular network of streets on the area of about 35 ha. Archaeological excavations have been going on in this area permanently since 1946 and about two-thirds of it is already unearthed.

The Penjikent city site is included in the List of Properties of National Significance of the Republic of Tajikistan and in the World Heritage Tentative List, but archaeological excavations are still going on there continuously without anticipating any conservation works to protect the monument. Mudbrick building remains are under an intensive process of erosion and destruction, melting from year to year, turning into dust.

Khulbuk (9th–12th centuries)

The archaeological site of Khulbuk is located in a picturesque place near the famous mountain with the world's largest deposit of salt. There are beautiful caves and oases with springs here, attracting many people all year round. In early medieval times Khulbuk was the capital of a large Khuttal region. The city citadel was erected on a platform of about 7 m–10 m in height, its buildings were made of adobe, mud and fired bricks, and even the platform slopes and defensive walls were faced with fired bricks. The palace area of the citadel was excavated in the 1980s. As many scholars agree, it is one of the rarest studied palace complexes of the early Moslem Middle Ages in the region, and its architecture is an outstanding example of the same type. Besides that, a lot of unique discoveries have been made here in the process of excavations. For example, unique finds include found fragments of the main gates' portal decoration, and impressive decoration of excavated building interiors, made of carved ganch/gypsum, as well as fragments of wall painting.

Some conservation has been done at the site by back-filling with earth. Artefacts are stored and displayed in the nearby Khulbuk Museum and in other state museums of the republic. The site is included in the List of Properties of National Significance of the Republic of Tajikistan and in the World Heritage Tentative List. In 2002 a National historical and cultural reserve of Khulbuk was established aiming for the site's protection, conservation and presentation for public. In the near future, it is planned to remove all modern dwellings from the territory of the monument's protection zone and this work has already started. The site itself is included in the program of the 2005 celebrations devoted to the 2500th jubilee of the city of Kulyab, near which it is located.

All this seems good, but such jubilees often become a serious threat to heritage sites, because usually large financial allocations have to be used in a very short time, often not enough to follow world recognised heritage conservation standards. And as usual, the tasks, coming from the highest governmental level are directed mainly on making high impression on the public of the grandeur of cultural properties, without regarding such things as authenticity and the site's real needs, and restoration in such cases often takes a dominating role. We won't try to judge here the project of reconstruction/restoration of the portal and the walls of Khulbuk citadel, on which the restoration works have been already started, but we are appealing to our colleagues in Tajikistan not to use inauthentic materials, and not to hurry to restore the ruins.

Natalia Turekulova
Timur Turekulov
ICOMOS/Kazakhstan

Khulbuk Citadel

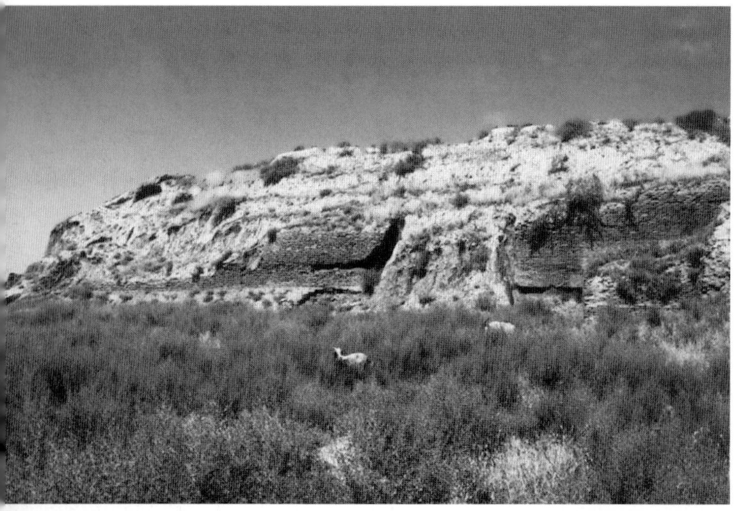

Adjina Tepe, Buddhist monastery

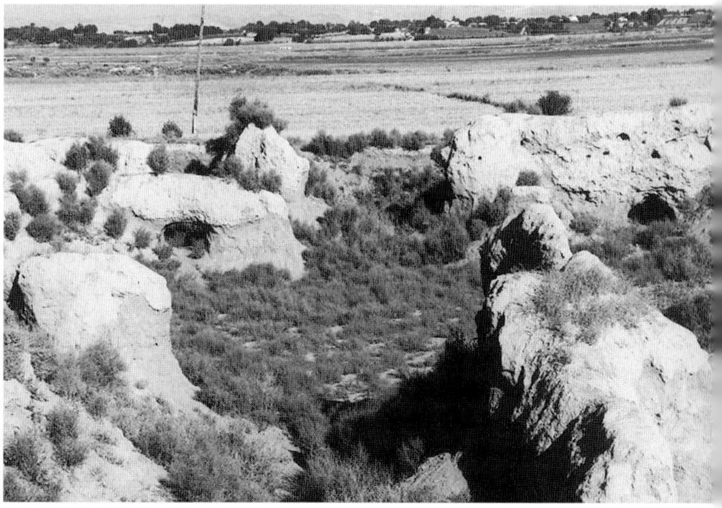

THAILAND
New Measures for Heritage at Risk

ICOMOS Thailand has support to report on heritage under threat from the Fine Arts Commission and the Royal Association of Siamese Architects, which is responsible for the Architectural Conservation Awards. The awards have been given annually since 1982, presided over by Her Royal Highness, Princess Maha Chakri Sirindhorn.

This year the Commission has improved the award criteria by adding another category, namely the Award for Significant Architecture for Conservation, in order to compile a list of buildings at risk. The objective of this award category is to promote and encourage an awareness of the value of heritage conservation, and to give future assistance to owners for conservation and maintenance. This issue has been publicly announced to invite nominations of buildings for this new award.

In this first year, there are 21 eligible nominations which can be categorised as:
- 4 Palaces and government buildings,
- 10 Private properties,
- 7 Religious buildings.

The nominations have a variety of histories and aspects of heritage value, yet they mostly have a similar level of risk. There are three sites which are representatives of the group as follows:
- Bang Rak Old Customs House,
- Ratchakarun School, Thon Buri,
- Samsen Filter Plant.

These buildings were all built from the reign of King Rama V to King Rama VII (1868–1934), when Thailand was highly influenced by Western European nations in terms of economic, social, and, inclusively, art and architecture.

Bang Rak Old Customs House: Trade and communications with European countries led to agreements via business contracts, which greatly affected the economic and tax system of Thailand. A customs house was built for the first time in the country, and this building was designed by an Italian architect and built in 1888 on the Chao Phraya river bank. It was once a large and stately building but it is now used as the Bang Rak Police Fire Brigade Residence. Its condition is as seen today.

Ratchakarun School: Originally a nobleman's house, the building was bought by the Muslim Krungthep Witthayathan Foundation and converted to a school. The architecture indicates European influences applied to local domestic architecture. Its date was understood to be later than the customs house, that is from 1897 onwards. The style was popular amongst wealthy people, or was chosen for public buildings because of its favourable features such as the beautiful and stately appearance and fine decorative craftsmanship which added to the value of the architecture. Unfortunately, the school has been redundant since 1978 and so abandoned. Its location by the river-bank has also increased natural risks and worsened problems.

Samsen Filter Plant: This site represents a page in the history of water and sewerage works in Siam, and also a turning point of construction technology imported from foreign countries. Modern architecture with reinforced concrete construction makes this building a pioneering example of 20th-century architecture in Thailand, although to some scholars this kind of building is not worth conserving because it lacks elaborate decorative elements similar to former times. Waterworks have since been so highly developed that this filter plant has today become a redundant structure.

Today, the historic and spiritual values of these buildings have been neglected. The owners may not care for their maintenance, or their function may have been changed until they are left in a ruinous state. They are at risk of physical deterioration from temperature change, moisture, and use. Another kind of risk ranges from the change of use that leads to the application of inappropriate building materials which reduce the value of and cause damage to the beauty of an architectural heritage site.

Another problem facing old buildings are economic developments and a preference for new buildings, which may result from the rapid increases in land prices. The above examples include buildings which are redundant, but there has been very little thought about rehabilitation and rather more on demolishing buildings to be replaced by new ones. The historic and aesthetic values of these heritage places have not been involved.

ICOMOS Thailand has joined this activity to consider the award giving initiated by the Association of Siamese Architects, and intends to continue to support this activity in the coming years. We hope that this will be another means to encourage the public to be aware of the value of heritage places, to watch over them, and to help conserve their values for the future.

ICOMOS Thailand

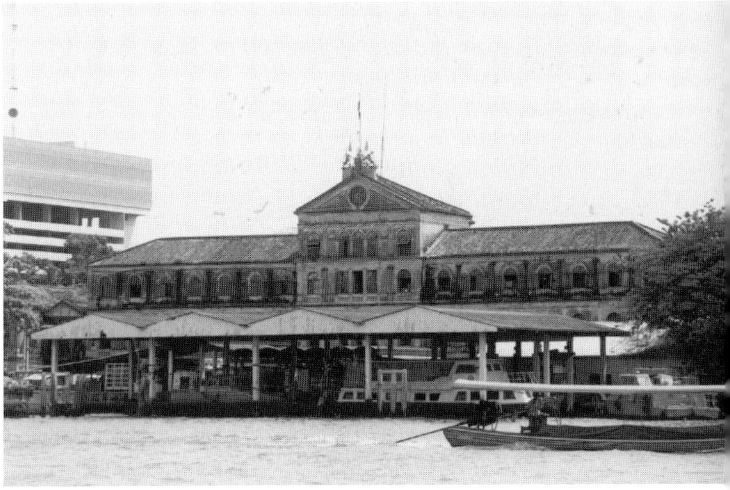

Bang Rak Old Customs House, river front

Bang Rak Old Customs House

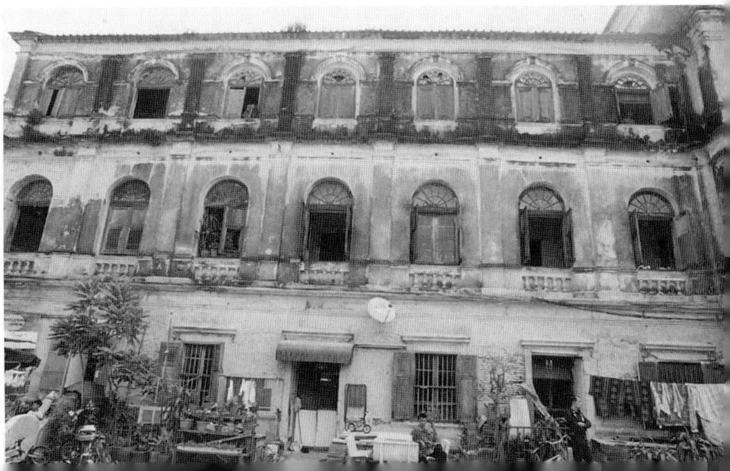

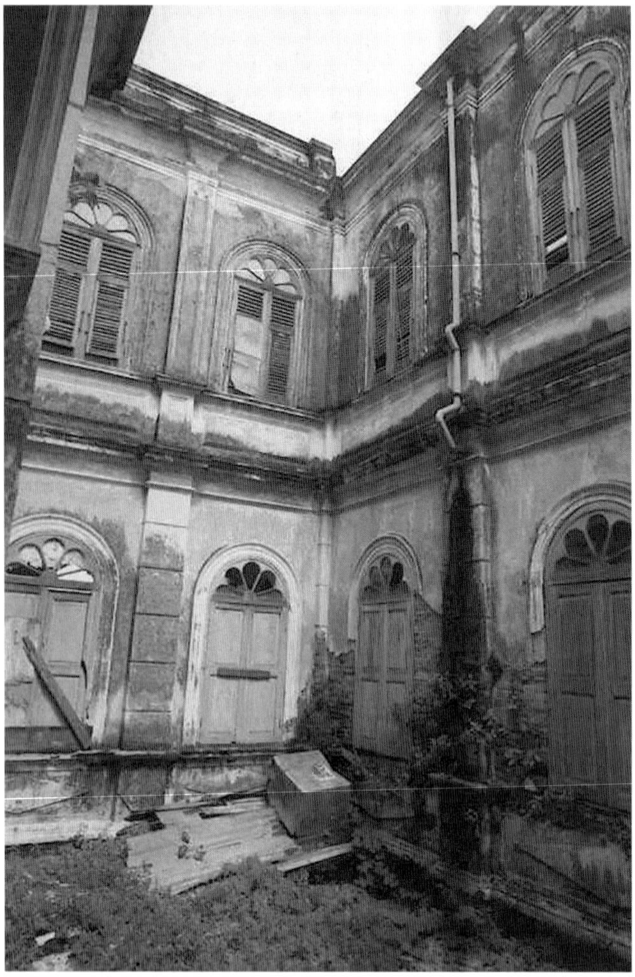

Ratchakarun school

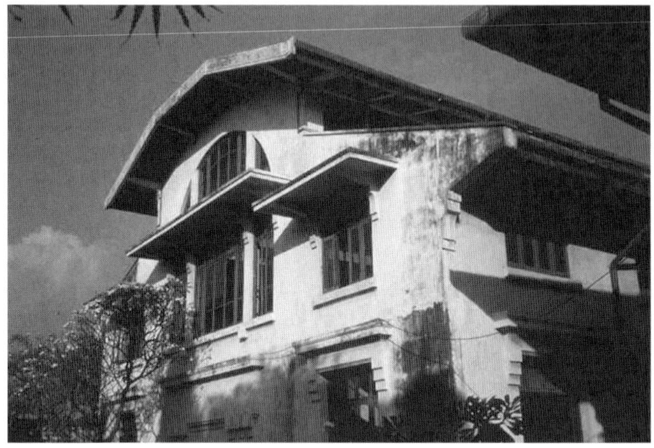

Samsen filter plant

Ratchakarun school

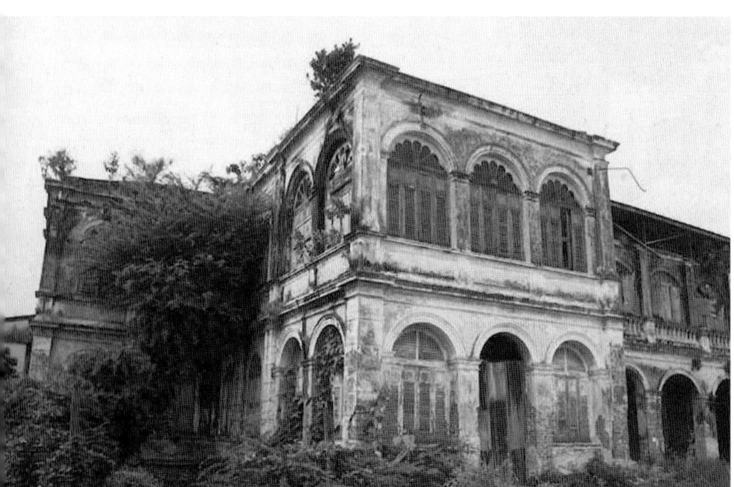

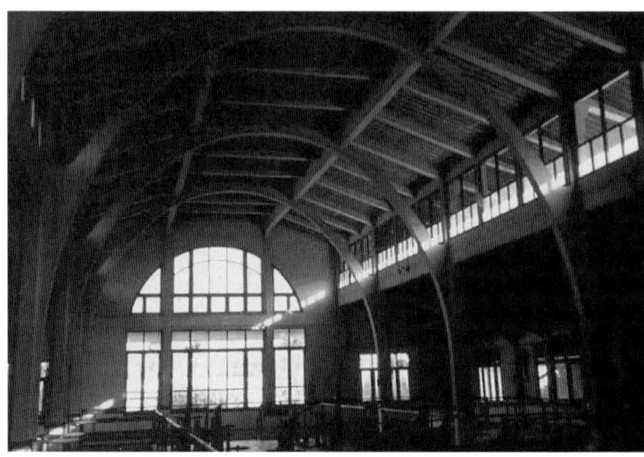

Samsen filter plant

TURKEY
Churches built in Ottoman times

In the later Ottoman centuries Christian minorities, such as the Greeks and Armenians, were again able to build their own schools and churches, which had long been restricted. Ottoman rulers slowly realised the impossibility of a total Islamicisation and decided to give their non-Moslem citizens more freedom to have and keep their own cultural identity. If we look at the outlying Ottoman border provinces in the Balkans and in Armenia, it now seems that we can trace as far back as the 17th and 18th centuries a greater and rather earlier phase of Christian activity there than on the Empire's mainland. The climax of the Christian regeneration and advance was reached in the 19th century and corresponds with the political liberalisation of the Ottoman Empire, the so-called *Tanzimat* (reform) era, under the rule of Sultan Abdülmecit I (1839-1861). Now perhaps for the first time in Ottoman history, fitting literary attributes for this period might be the term *Pax Ottomanica* which indeed benefited Christian communities in the 19th century, or Lord Kinross' perceptive and apt book title in 1956 considering modern Turkey not as 'Asia' but instead as 'Europa Minor'. At that time, on occasion extremely large churches were erected all over Anatolia in the centres of Greek and Armenian settlement – in East Anatolia, Cappadocia, the Trebizont (Trabzon) region and on the West Coast. These were built, not only in a neo-Byzantine, neo-Gothic, Classical or historical style, but also in a convincing Christian-Ottoman architectural style.

However, dramatic historical events at the beginning of the 20th century ended forever this last fortunate and flourishing period of Anatolian Christianity. The Armenian genocide reached its climax in 1915 and the mistake of the Kingdom of Greece to launch a military attack on Anatolia, the remaining central body of the collapsed Ottoman Empire, after it lost in World War I, ended in an unbelievable disaster. The last acts of this drama were the burning of Smyrna (Izmir) in September 1922 and the complete expulsion of the Anatolian Greek population (with the exception of Constantinople and some islands), ratified in 1923. This brought an end to Christianity in areas which had been Christianised since the time of the apostles, but equally also ended traditional Turkish settlement and culture in Greece and on the Balkans.

The present state of some of the surviving monuments

Both the post-Byzantine churches and their late classical and Byzantine predecessors are in roughly the same situation. In fact many post-Byzantine churches were built on or in the ruins of medieval ones (for the state of these earlier heritage sites see *H@R* 2002–2003). The main problem is until now that most of the Christian heritage places built during the Ottoman period, just as their earlier counterparts, are not scientifically recorded and therefore, up to now have not been as eligible for heritage protection by even European let alone by Turkish art-historians and archaeologists.

In Anatolia we face the same problems as those we found and are finding in the Balkans and in Greece. In some cases an Anatolian Christian church is now used as a mosque which ensures its survival as a building. Other examples verify a secular use of churches. For example in 1982, it was discovered that an 18th century village basilica was being used as a farm-house in the village of Çakıl (Greek: Michania), Bithynia, on the far eastern Kyziko peninsula on the shores of the Sea of Marmora. Astonishingly two oval canvas paintings, of Christ and an Evangelist, which originally hung between the wooden columns of its *naos*, were at the time still being kept at the site by the farmers.

Anatolian churches were and are being blown up, destroyed and are still being used inappropriately. For example, the impressive cathedral-church of Hagios Gregorios of Nyssa built in 1863, that dominated the silhouette and skyline of Trebizont, was blown up in the 1930s to permit modern city development.

The problems in protecting and caring for heritage places are many and widespread. Many churches do not possess an attractive outer or inner appearance, or no longer do, because at times the building materials used were quite plain. This also leads to an inappropriate management assessment and evaluation, because a building might be ranked as not aesthetic enough to be protected at all. It is precisely this that has caused and is causing the loss of many heritage buildings in many rural areas, as well as the strong interest to readily getting cheap building materials for modern structures.

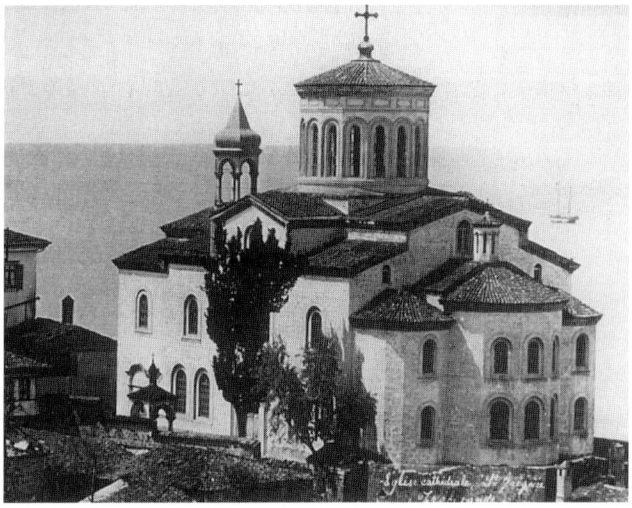

Trebizont, church 'Hagios Gregorios of Nyssa (1863), blown up in the 1930s

Yayla Köyü, area of Muğla (Caria), village church (19th c.): View from the north

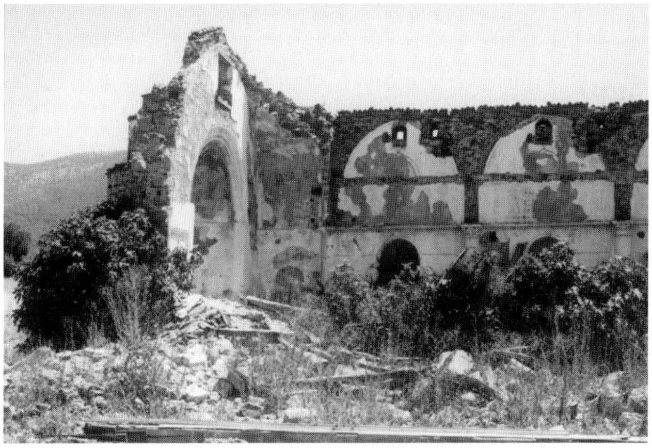

Other reasons also lead to the total destruction of the often empty and ruined buildings: the destruction of the south-western Anatolian one-aisled 19th century village church of Yayla Köyü (the former Greek village of Hagios Antonios), near Muğla in the historical landscape of Caria, was caused by the collapse of its rotten wooden roof construction reported in 1998. It is mostly the domes and vaults of these churches that are structurally at risk, and such cracked masonry can clearly be seen in the village of Cunda on Cunda Adası (Greek: Moscho–Nisi) near Ayvalık (Greek: Kydonia) on the West coast. The triconch cross-domed church of this village is in definite danger of collapsing. Cracks in the building's brickwork are undeniably threatening the pillars and the vaults, and this might lead to a total collapse of the building in the near future. As well as this, we still find remains of the church furnishing, such as the iconostases, which often were constructed of wood, and bishop's thrones and chancels, in a ruined state, for example inside the church of Hagios Archangelos Michael in Sille near Konya in Phrygo-Lycaonia. In addition, stucco decorations

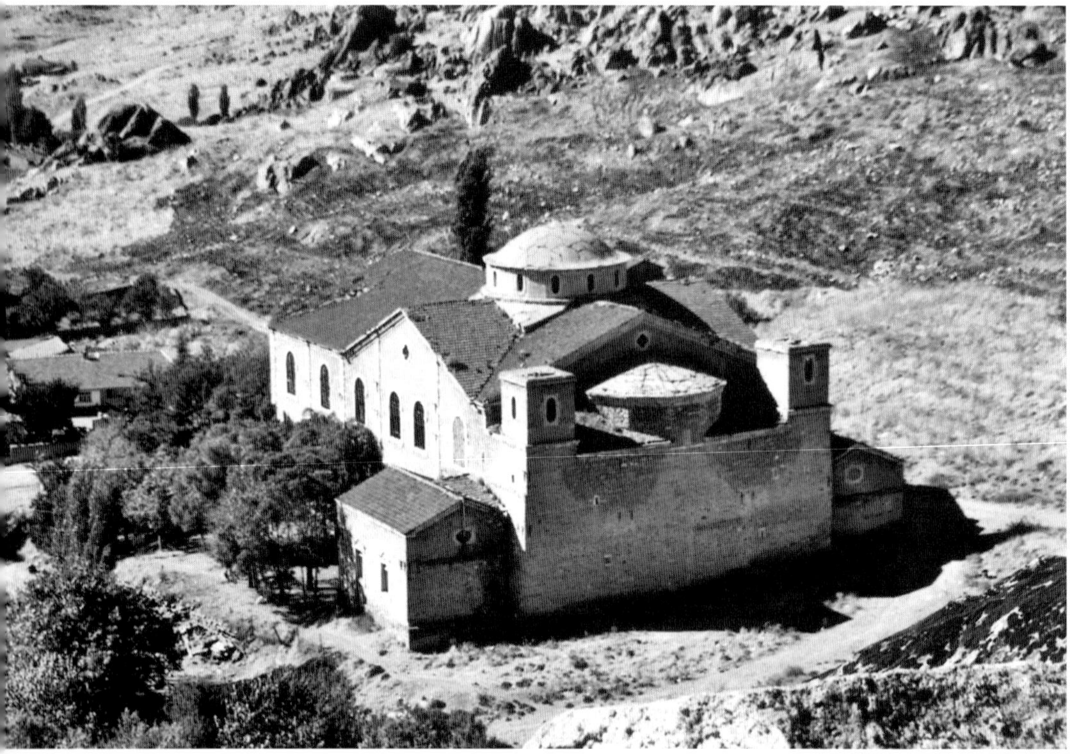

Sivrihissar, large Armenian domed basilica built in 1881 (2003)

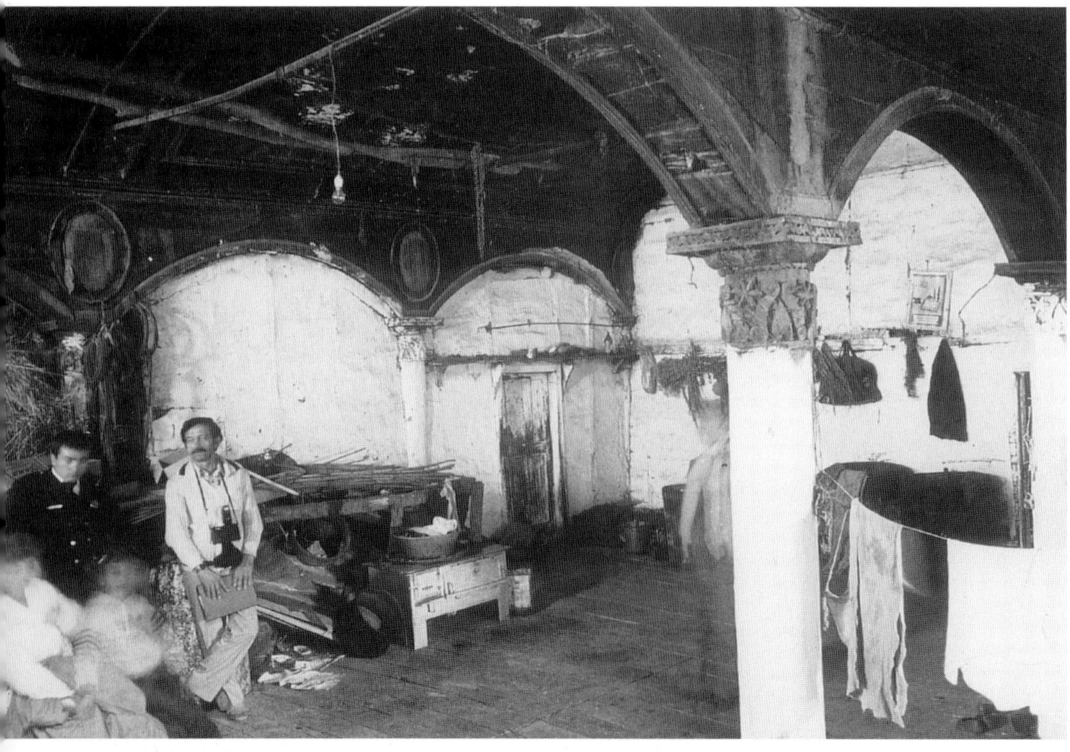

Çakıl – Michania, basilica inside, building used as a farm-house as seen in 1982

and wall-paintings of the churches are particularly at great risk of total loss and destruction, mostly because of vandalism to the lower parts of the unused buildings. Consider for example the 19th century painting 'Baptism of Christ' in a niche on the south of the eastern apse of the domed triconch church in Cunda, Cunda-Island off the coast of Ayvalık–Kydonia. Another risk is water, which can pour through leaking vaults and roof constructions and cause the loss of painted and decorated plaster.

The basic practical problem for the municipalities, especially of small villages, can be summarised in frequently heard questions: "How do we cope and what do we do with buildings like this?", and if interest is aroused: "Who helps us financially?"

Also architectural changes to buildings can be demonstrated and are causing damage to the original structure. The large Armenian domed basilica of Sivrihissar, built in 1881 some 120 km south-west of Ankara, was used as a factory for a long time and it was decided to add walls in the western interior, so destroying the concept and sense of its original architecture. The building now stands empty. Also the large basilica of Misti, built 1844 in southern Cappadocia, is now used as a storehouse for building materials such as sand, wood and stones. There is finally the non-religious use of a church as a farm-house as mentioned above.

Conclusions

Some Anatolian municipalities have good ideas about what to do with their historical Christian architectural heritage, which is mostly located in town and village centres. The consciousness and awareness of historical events help in a better treatment of the heritage places and this is the main key in solving their poor conservation state, and the fragile condition the buildings are mostly in currently.

The use of churches as local museums, concert halls or art-galleries, or as other places for general public cultural use, are perhaps a good way to protect them as heritage places. Plans to transform churches into mosques can be connected with considerable interference. For example, the municipality of the Euphrates small town Nizip banned continuing the transformation of the town's Byzantine church into a *Camii* (mosque) during the 1990s; it was recently planned to change the unused building into a museum. In this case, the erection of a planned minaret was stopped. To ensure a long-term success of such ideas financial support, international and European involvement are urgently needed.

Alexander Zäh
ICOMOS Germany

References

Kiel, M 2001 Modern Electronics in the Study of Turkish Architecture, *Electronic Journal of Oriental Studies* IV1-8, (M. Kie, N. Landman, H. Theunissen (eds), Proceedings of the 11th Congress of Turkish Art, Utrecht, The Netherlands, August 23-28, 1999) No. 25:1-8. (see http://www2.let.uu.nl/Solis/anpt/ejos/pdf4/25Kiel.pdf)

İlter, F 1994 *Bazı Örneklerle Osmanlı Dönemi Mimarlı_nda* XIX. Yüzyıl Ege Bölgesi Kiliseleri: Gökçeada (İmroz) – Ayvalık – Selçuk 'Şirince (Kırkıca) Köyü', XI. Türk Tarih Kongresi, Ankara, 1987-2000, Planlar, Resimler.

Zäh, A 2002 Die Basilika von Misti. Eine unbekannte Kirche des 19. Jhs. im südlichen Kappadokien, *Wiener Zeitschrift für die Kunde des Morgenlandes* 92: 205-216.

Zäh, A 2003 *Zur Typologie kirchlicher Architektur im südwestlichen Kleinasien*, Maintal.

Zäh, A 2004 (in print) Aspekte der anatolischen Kirchenkunst im Osmanischen Reich. Ein Beitrag zur kunsthistorischen Grundlagenforschung, *Wiener Zeitschrift für die Kunde des Morgenlandes* 94.

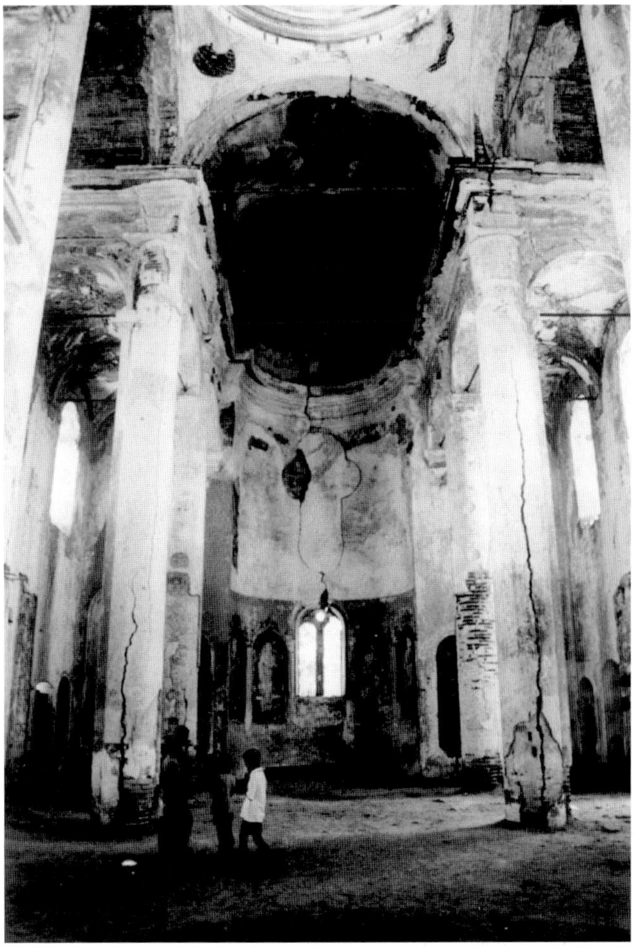

Cunda Adası, near Ayvalık, domed church, cracked brick-pillars and vaults

Cunda Adası, domed church, vandalised niche painting 'Baptism of Christ'

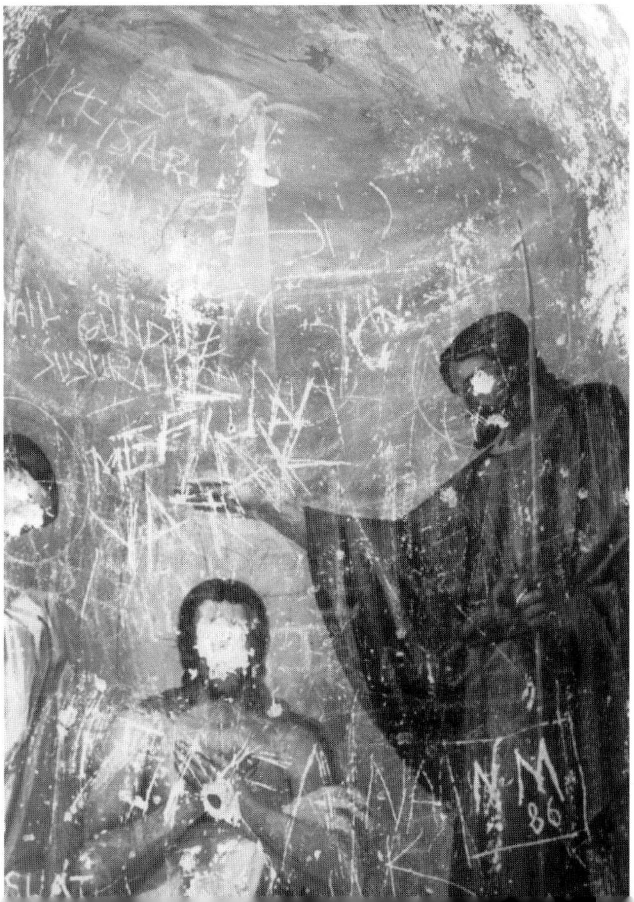

UKRAINE

In its long historical development, Ukraine has always been at the epicentre of events determining the historical and political map of Europe. Since the great movements of peoples, Ukraine situated in the geographical centre of Europe, has found itself on the migratory routes of large ethnic groups, and therefore has confidently held a leading position in commercial, economic, cultural, and political relations between West and East.

This has set preconditions for Ukraine's specific character as a multi-ethnic state with influences assimilated from different cultures and an extraordinarily diverse architectural and urban heritage.

Eastern region

Ukrainian Frontier (1731-1739)

The Ukrainian frontier extends along the eastern part of Ukraine, south of Kharkiv. In the 17th-18th centuries, this region was the scene of the Government's implementation of its plan to develop, step by step, unoccupied lands adjacent to Ukraine-Turkish borders. On the basis of pilot projects, a re-settlement system involving people from other Ukrainian regions, was created there for the first time in European town-planning. This system was to become a shield to protect the metropolis against invasions by Crimean Tatars, vassals of Turkey. The system's structure was formed by lengthy chains (many hundred kilometres) of town-fortresses connected by various fortifications into linked defensive lines.

The extension of the Ukrainian frontier spanning the watershed between the Dnipro and Siversky Donets rivers is some 285 km long. This border represents a continuous moated rampart with 16 fortresses and two hundred redoubts and blockhouses mounted along it. The area of each fortress' inner court is about 1.2 ha, the perimeter of its ramparts 980 m. The fortifications were designed and their construction supervised by French fortification engineers G M de Brigny and D I de Bosquet, under the guidance of Kyiv Governor General A I Tarakanov. In building the borderline, 20,000 Cossacks and 10,000 peasants were employed under Cossack Colonel Halahan.

Today this line of border is in critical state. Saving this unique monument to the art of fortification and town-planning is one of the most urgent tasks, and presents serious organisational as well as methodological problems.

Central region

Church of the Transfiguration of the Saviour, village of Polichyntsi, Kazatyn district, Vinnytsia Region (1661)

The Church is situated at the end of the village, on a hill above a small river. This place of worship is tripartite, two-tiered, with three cupolas. The first storey is built of stone, the second tier and the drums are of brick.

The architecture of this Orthodox church is unique and represents a combination of fortifications with tripartite churches of wooden vernacular architecture. This heritage place is a very rare example of the 17th century stone church in Ukraine with well-preserved bright vernacular features of wooden architecture combined with defensive elements.

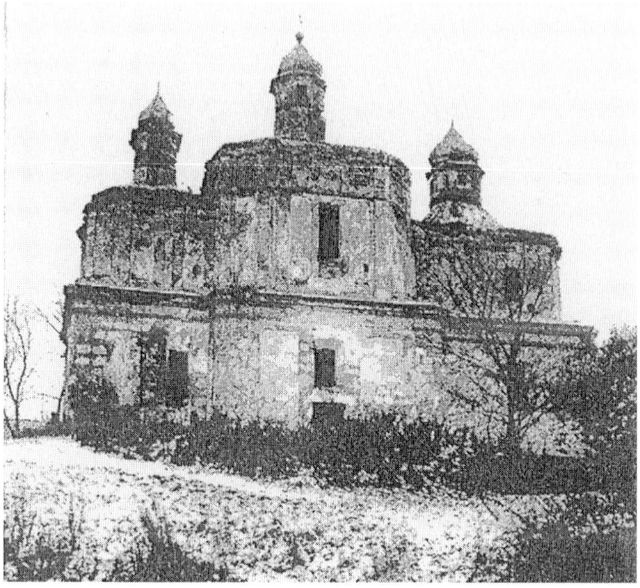

Church of the Transfiguration of the Saviour, village of Polichyntsi

The heritage place is in a critical state. It is in urgent need of help to prevent its collapse and begin conservation works, but lack of funds prevents an immediate start.

Southern region

Caravanserai in the town of Bilogorsk, Independent Republic of Crimea (1654)

The Caravanserai in Bilogorsk is a unique monument of Islamic medieval architecture in the Crimean region. It is situated in the Old Town at the crossroads of the old caravan route from Ghezlev (Evpatoria) to Kafa (Pheodosia). There were eight caravanserais at that time, but only one of them, the largest, Upper Tash-Khan, has survived to the present day. Built on a rectangular plan, the Caravanserai was a fortified building surrounded by high walls with watchtowers at the corners. The external lower part of the wall was blank, the upper part housed vertical embrasures. There were two gateways with metal gates. There were a well and a mosque in the spacious courtyard, and around its perimeter 120 rooms were arranged in two levels with semicircular tunnel vaults (*ayvans*). The lower level was for goods storage, the upper for lodging and defence.

Until the mid-1950s, the western wall survived relatively well-preserved with its inner buildings (about 42 m lengthwise, 1.5 m in thickness). Now less than 18 m of the wall survives, with a maximum height of 4.7 m. To the left of its façade there is a semicircular arch of the gateway, above which there is a rectangular window with metal grating. There are two embrasures to the right on the second level. On the side of the courtyard, three semicircular tunnel vaults have survived – a gateway and two rooms (about 4 m x 4 m), one room with a fireplace. The gateway and entrances to the rooms have been conserved, walled-up with cut Inkerman stone. A layer of deposit at the walls is no less than 1.5 m deep.

At this place, heritage conservation problems come into collision with the town's poor budget.

Western region

Castle of the Synavskys, in the town of Berezhany, the Ternopil Region (1554)

The Castle in Berezhany is an outstanding monument to the 16th–17th centuries' defence architecture in Ukraine. It was built in 1534–1554 by Russian *voivode* Mykola Synyavsky. This fortified castle was not ever conquered by enemies and its ruin is due to the World Wars, natural forces and time. The Castle began to deteriorate from the beginning of the 19th century. For a long time it was used as a barracks, then its stonework served as a source for building materials. The Castle was already in ruins before the beginning of the 20th century, and all its interiors, collections and decoration had been lost.

Today, only two levels of the Castle walls survive. The polygonal towers also survive two-storeys high, yet without floors. The semicircular south tower is still four-storeyed. All the towers have well-preserved embrasure systems including those with 2–3 side passages. The buildings surrounding the Castle courtyard consist of four two-storeyed wings and a three-storeyed main palace building; all are ruined. The palace is the only building with extant fragments of a decorative Attic band with a blank arcature with key embrasures in the recesses.

The entire complex, consisting of the Castle, the Holy Trinity Catholic Chapel and remnants of the 17th century fortifications, is one of the largest and most successful castles in Ukraine. Its rich history and high significance require its immediate restoration.

The ruined state of the Castle complex has not passed unnoticed in public opinion. Attempts at saving and conserving this great structure give no way to indifference. There have been attempts to create trust funds and start-up projects, research and educational activities aimed at saving the Castle. A State Historic and Architectural Preservation Trust has been created in the town. Businesses, organisations and establishments take part in cleaning and tidying up the Castle grounds. Unfortunately, the town's financially deficient budget cannot afford urgent conservation works on the buildings which see an ever greater collapse each year.

ICOMOS Ukraine

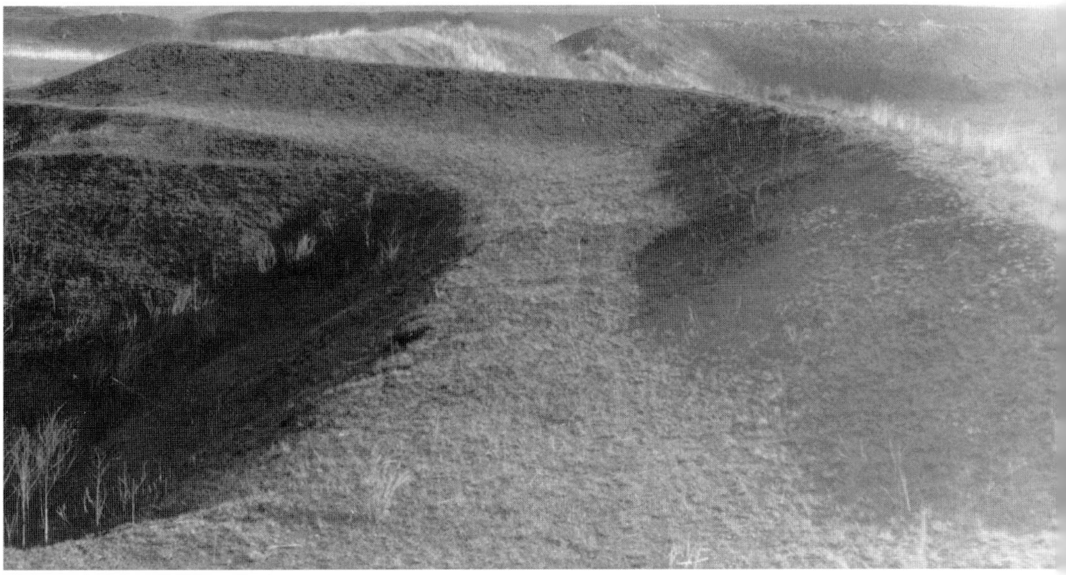

Ukrainian frontier

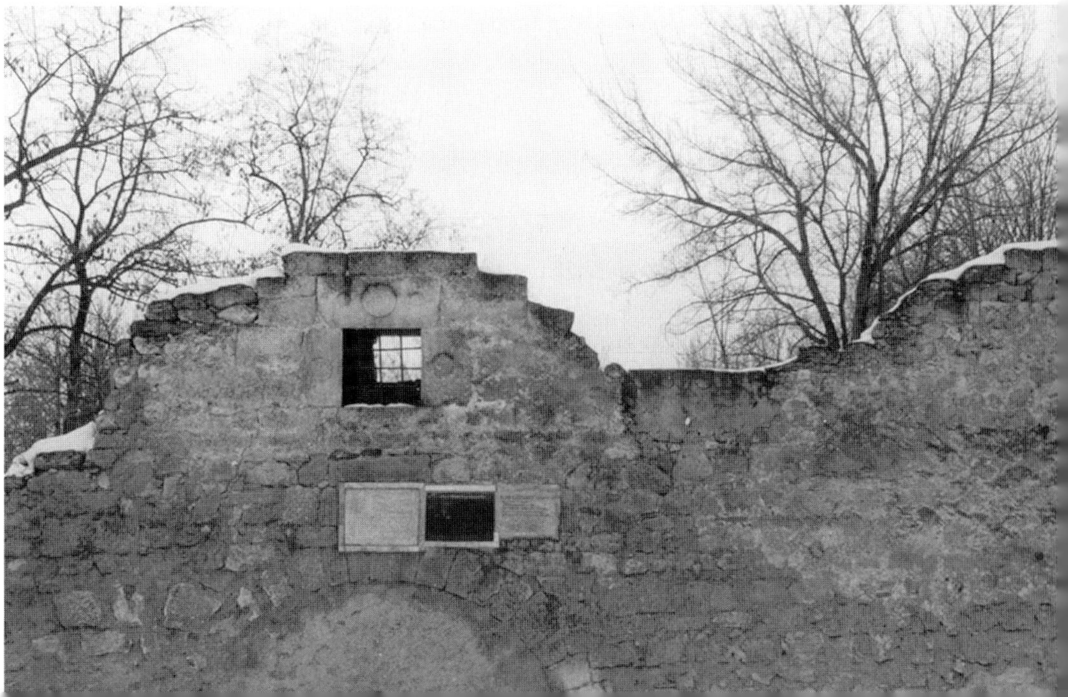

Caravanserai in Bilogorsk, Independent Republic of Crimea

UNITED STATES OF AMERICA
11 Most Endangered Places in 2004

Since 1988, the 11 Most Endangered Historic Places list produced by the USA National Trust for Historic Preservation has been one of the most effective tools in the fight to save the irreplaceable architectural, cultural, and natural heritage of the United States. US/ICOMOS refers to this program as a useful tool for the USA to highlight the nation's heritage issues.

The 11 sites chosen each year are threatened by neglect, insufficient funds, inappropriate development or insensitive public policy. Some are well-known, such as the Vieux Carré in New Orleans or Ellis Island in New York Harbor. Others, like the Kennecott Copper Mines in Alaska or the village of East Aurora, New York, are less famous but just as important, because they too represent preservation challenges facing thousands of communities. Each site raises awareness about the dangers to specific parts of America's heritage and about preservation generally.

The list has now brought national attention to more than 140 significant buildings, sites and landscapes. At times, that attention has galvanized public support to rescue a treasured landmark, while in others it has been an opening salvo in a long battle to save an important piece of our history. 11 Most has been so successful at educating the public that now more than 20 states and numerous cities and towns publish their own lists of endangered places.

The following list for 2004 shows the range of endangered places in the USA, as well as possible solutions:

Nine Mile Canyon, Carbon and Duchesne Counties, Utah

Located in a remote part of Utah, Nine Mile Canyon is often called "the world's longest art gallery" as it contains more than 10,000 images carved onto canyon walls by Native Americans. The canyon also contains many historic sites – including stagecoach stations, settlers' cabins, ranches, and iron telegraph poles installed by the famed 19th-century Buffalo Soldiers – that stand as reminders of the area's pioneer history. Now this historic canyon is under increasing pressure from tourism, recreation, and energy development that threaten its significant prehistoric and historic resources.

Nine Mile Canyon, Rock Art

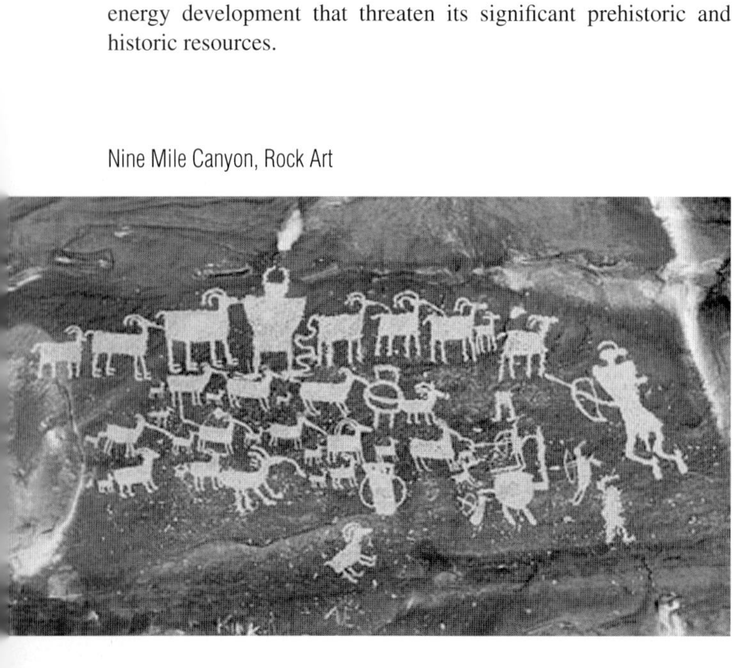

History

The Native American cultures that inhabited Nine Mile Canyon starting over 1700 years ago left a legacy of rock shelters, granaries and rock art throughout the canyon area. Held in a patchwork of federal, state, county and private ownership, the canyon is said to contain the highest concentration of monochromatic prehistoric rock art in North America. These petroglyphs and pictographs are attributed to the Archaic, Fremont and Ute people. Nine Mile Canyon is also an area with many diverse historic sites from the days of pioneer settlement, such as stagecoach stops, ranch buildings and settler's cabins.

Threat

This renowned area is now threatened by increased tourism, recreation and demands for domestic energy production. Although previously developed for oil and gas, the area is under increasing pressure by burgeoning demands for energy which could transform the historic landscape into an industrial zone with heavy industrial trucks rumbling through the narrow canyons in close proximity to fragile Native American rock art. Currently proposed projects for energy development and exploration would result in tens of thousands of trips by these trucks, in addition to numerous wells being drilled. Without a thorough inventory of the cultural resource sites at risk and adequate measures for protection, these activities could result in the destruction of irreplaceable cultural sites. This stretch of desert landscape, much larger than its name implies, is patrolled by a single ranger who seeks to protect the petroglyphs from well-meaning, but often destructive, tourists and recreational enthusiasts. A sustainable balance between increased tourism, energy development and cultural-resource protection must be found or these irreplaceable cultural and historic resources will be lost forever.

Solution

Nine Mile Canyon's best hope for remaining a world and national treasure rests on raising public awareness, planning and increased program funding. Nearly ten years ago BLM developed a plan for management and interpretation of the canyon, but it has never been implemented. Implementation of this plan, cooperative efforts between federal, state, local and private landowners, additional funding for cultural resource protection and tourism services are all steps needed to preserve its significant and irreplaceable treasures. BLM needs to ensure that energy exploration and development, as well as recreational management, complies strictly with federal laws that protect cultural resources from the harmful consequences associated with those activities.

Ridgewook Ranch, Home of Seabiscuit, Willits, California

Far away, in the oak and redwood-studded ranchlands of northern California, Ridgewood Ranch, Home of Seabiscuit, is in jeopardy, its former thoroughbred glory dulled by deterioration.

Nestled in the oak and redwood-studded ranchlands and mountains of Northern California is the home of a great American legend, Seabiscuit. It was here in 1939 at Ridgewood Ranch that an improbable winning trio – owner Charles Howard, jockey Red Pollard and trainer Tom Smith – nursed the ailing racehorse back to health after a serious injury. Seabiscuit's recuperation set the stage for an electrifying blaze-of-glory career finish at Santa Anita Racetrack that captured Depression-era America's imagination. Recently, a new generation has been introduced to the Seabiscuit tale through Laura Hillenbrand's book *Seabiscuit: An American Legend* and an Academy Award-nominated movie. Now, Seabiscuit's home and final resting place is in jeopardy, its former thoroughbred glory dulled by deterioration due to inadequate funding for maintenance.

History

Seabiscuit's owner, Charles Howard, a self-made millionaire auto dealer, purchased 16,000 acres in rural Mendocino County in 1919 as a cattle ranch and country home. Howard transformed the ranch into a thoroughbred facility unparalleled in California, building two large mare barns, a breeding barn, feed barns, paddocks, a half-track, and many other structures. It was here that Seabiscuit recuperated from injury in 1939, and enjoyed his retirement after his renowned victory at Santa Anita in a custom-built stud barn within view of the family home. From 1940 until being laid to rest on the ranch in 1947, Seabicuit became a major tourist attraction, with thousands of visitors passing under the gate proudly proclaiming "Ridgewood Ranch, Home of Seabiscuit."

Threat

Still a working ranch, the property is owned by the Golden Rule Church Association, which has endeavored to be a model steward of the ranch. The church has kept developers at bay, but lacks the resources to protect the structures and landscape that comprise Seabiscuit's legacy. Many of the property's sites have been inadequately maintained over a period of several decades. Without urgent attention and funds for stabilization, restoration and maintenance of the historic ranch, Seabiscuit's home won't survive.

The Golden Rule Church Association has been actively working with the Mendocino Land Trust and the newly-formed Seabiscuit Heritage Foundation to develop strategies for the long-term protection of Ridgewood Ranch. A conservation easement is being developed that would protect 4,600 acres (7 square miles) of the ranch. The California Department of Conservation has already committed up to $1,000,000 to purchase a farmland easement on the property, and the Church has agreed to donate a substantial portion of the easement value and to provide public access.

Solution

Additionally, historic preservation planning for the historic ranch core is underway. Solutions being discussed are: development of preservation easements to protect the ranch's significant historic sites in perpetuity; assistance with long-range planning, including conditions assessments and studies of the cultural heritage resources on the property; and community education programs, including workshops and publications with special attention to tourism and marketing. Although all of these solutions are viable, funding is in short supply.

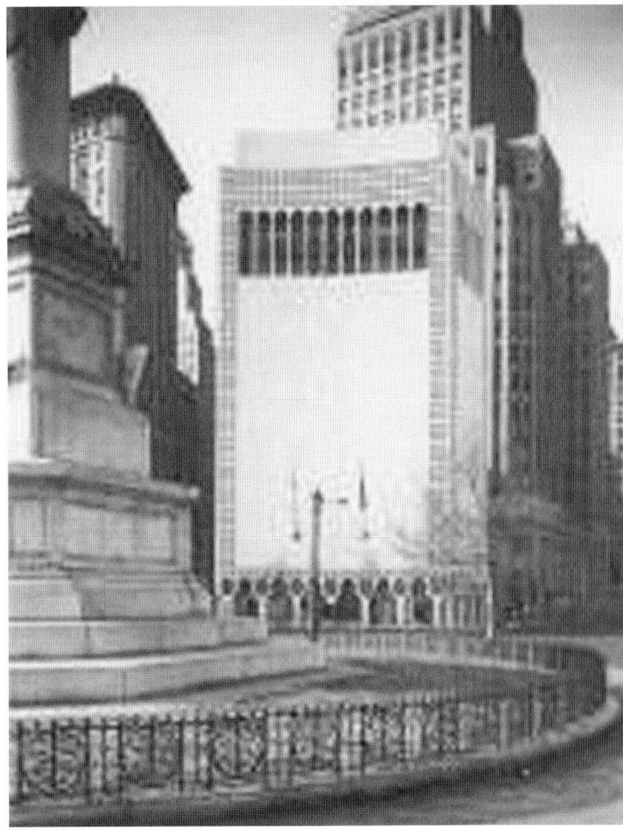

Columbus Circle, New York

2 Columbus Circle, New York, N. Y.

In New York City, an unorthodox and controversial icon of the recent past, 2 Columbus Circle, located on the south-west corner of Central Park, may soon be stripped of its architectural integrity.

Created by architect Edward Durell Stone, who also designed Washington's famed Kennedy Center for the Performing Arts, 2 Columbus Circle is a nationally recognized – albeit controversial – icon of the Modern Movement. Sporting a marble skin, porthole windows and a street-level arcade that critics have likened to a row of lollipops, the unorthodox building is radically different from the glass-and-steel boxes typical of its era.

Now it is slated to be sold and renovated as a permanent home for the Museum of Arts and Design. That's the good news; the bad news is that the design proposed for the new use would strip 2 Columbus Circle of its architectural integrity, and since it is not protected by New York's preservation ordinance, these changes could be made without any kind of preservation review. This means that unless the new owner can be persuaded of the building's significance, sweeping architectural changes could rob 2 Columbus Circle of its distinctive character and rob America of an engagingly quirky icon of the recent past.

History

Located at the southwest corner of Central Park, 2 Columbus Circle has been controversial ever since its completion in 1964. Originally designed to showcase the modern-art collection of supermarket heir Huntington Hartford, the building housed New York City offices during the 1980s and 1990s but is now vacant, pending transfer to the private Museum of Arts and Design. The building was listed on the Preservation League of New York State's "Seven to Save" this year in recognition of its architectural and historical significance to the citizens of New York.

Threat

The new design for the building by Brad Cloepfil, although not finalized, includes extensive alterations that would destroy major elements of Edward Durell Stone's design. The destruction of 2 Columbus Circle's original façade would mean the loss of a unique chapter of America's story.

Solution

The National Trust urges the owners of 2 Columbus Circle, currently the City of New York, but soon to be the Museum of Arts and Design, to develop a restoration plan for the building that respects its integrity as a modernist masterpiece and celebrates its unique form and design. Listing in the State and National Registers of Historic Places and public hearings by the New York Landmarks Preservation Commission for landmark designation of 2 Columbus Circle will give the building added protection and ensure that all possible measures are taken to protect this important resource.

State of Vermont

With historic villages and downtowns, working farms, winding back roads, forest-wrapped lakes, spectacular mountain vistas and a strong sense of community, Vermont has a special magic that led National Geographic Traveler magazine to name the state one of „the World's Greatest Destinations.“ Yet in recent years, this small slice of America has come under tremendous pressure from the onslaught of big-box retail development. The seriousness of this threat led the National Trust to name the state to its list of America's 11 Most Endangered Historic Places in 1993. Back then, Vermont was the only state without a Wal-Mart. Today it has four – and it now faces an invasion of behemoth stores that could destroy much of what makes Vermont Vermont.

To highlight the threat to this vital piece of America's heritage, the National Trust for Historic Preservation named the state of Vermont to its 2004 list of America's 11 Most Endangered Historic Places.

During the 1990s Wal-Mart located three of its four Vermont stores in existing buildings and kept them relatively modest in size. Now, however, the world's largest company is planning to saturate the state – which has only 600,000 residents – with seven new mammoth mega-stores, each with a minimum of 150,000 square feet. Theses potential new stores may be located in St. Albans, Morrisville, Newport/Derby, St. Johnsbury, Bennington, Rutland, and Middlebury. Wal-Mart's plans are sure to attract an influx of other big-box retailers. The likely result: degradation of the Green Mountain State's unique sense of place, economic disinvestment in historic downtowns, loss of locally-owned businesses, and an erosion of the sense of community that seems an inevitable by-product of big-box sprawl. With deep regret, the National Trust takes the rare step of re-listing Vermont as one of America's 11 Most Endangered Historic Places.

History

Big-box development typically occurs on the outskirts of town, consuming farmland and open space, fueling sprawl and other problems associated with insensitive expansion. Communities often welcome these large stores in the hope that they will bring economic benefits. Too often, however, the stores bring hidden costs and cause significant economic and social harm.

Threat

The distinctive characteristics that define Vermont – historic towns, villages and rural landscapes – could be lost if sprawl-type development is allowed to occur in a haphazard, out-of-scale, land-consuming manner. The one-size-fits-all big-box "template" has proven to be detrimental to communities across the United States because of its negative economic and environmental impact on historic downtowns and local businesses. The size and design of these stores often overwhelm their surroundings, and impersonal corporate identity too often trumps community character.

Solution

The arrival of big-box sprawl often fostered by retailers such as Wal-Mart has been resisted by increasing numbers of communities that are determined to prevent or minimize the loss of their open space and the erosion of the economic vitality of their traditional business districts. People want and should have easy access to basic goods at low prices – but they also have the right to determine how their communities should grow and what they want to preserve and protect. At the very least, communities should accept big-box development with their eyes open and understand its long-term costs. Some big-box stores have adapted to local standards and worked to fit in gracefully with existing commercial districts. Some have even located in recycled vacant properties in existing downtowns. Vermonters should learn from what has happened elsewhere and persuade Wal-Mart and other large retailers to adapt the way they do business so as to enhance existing communities. Wal-Mart should change to accommodate Vermont, not the other way around.

Tobacco Farms, Southern Maryland

For almost 400 years, wood-frame tobacco barns have dotted the rolling fields of Southern Maryland, their shapes defining the character of the area's rural landscapes and their simple construction echoing traditional timber-framing methods used in England for centuries. Once essential to the process of air-curing tobacco, a mainstay crop of Maryland's agriculture since the 17th century, historic tobacco barns are now being lost at an alarming rate as the region's agricultural land is consumed by the spread of the D.C. metropolitan commuter-shed. Pressure from residential sprawl has only been aggravated by the unintended consequences of Maryland's 2001 „tobacco buy-out“ state policy, which encouraged farmers to stop cultivating tobacco. Scores of tobacco barns now have no productive purpose, and stand unused and deteriorating.

History

For many generations, these tobacco barns have been central to the economy of Maryland and a defining architectural characteristic of the region's rural landscape. First built by English settlers in the 17th century, these air-cure tobacco barns are unique to Maryland and provide a glimpse into four hundred years of the area's complex agricultural and economic history.

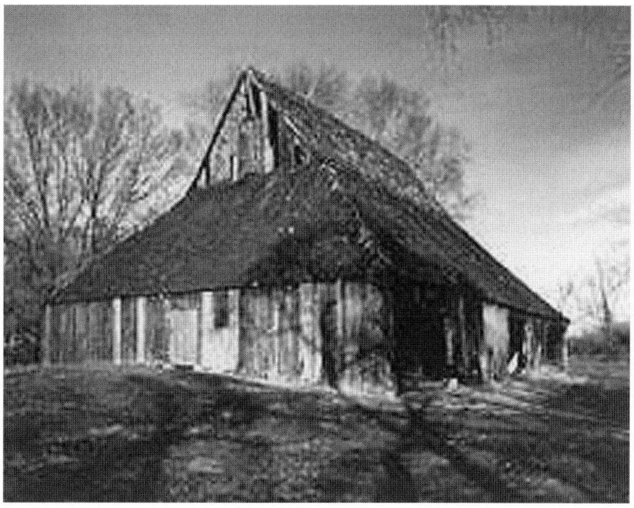

Tobacco barn, Southern Maryland

Threat

Southern Maryland is rapidly changing, and residential subdivisions and shopping centers replace tobacco fields. In 2001, a state-sponsored program to discourage tobacco cultivation offered farmers a substantial payment if they stopped growing tobacco. Almost all of Maryland's approximately 1,000 tobacco farmers accepted the buy-out and no longer cultivate what was once Maryland's primary „money crop." The buy-out made hundreds of tobacco barns instantly obsolete. Unless viable alternative uses can be found, these modest landmarks will fall to development pressure, deferred maintenance, and weather.

Solution

Congress created the Historic Barn Preservation Program in 2002 to identify and promote practical solutions for the continued agricultural use of older and historic barns but has yet to appropriate funding for this program, which is administered by the U.S. Department of Agriculture's Rural Development program. Additionally, supporting the hard work of farmers in their on-going effort to develop and implement productive new agricultural uses for the barns, as an alternative to tobacco cultivation. Preservationists can help by contributing to a special fund established by Preservation Maryland, the National Trust's statewide nonprofit partner, to promote continued agricultural use. The National Trust's BARN AGAIN! Program encourages preservation and provides technical and financial assistance for adapting historic barns for agricultural uses. This program may also help save these important buildings.

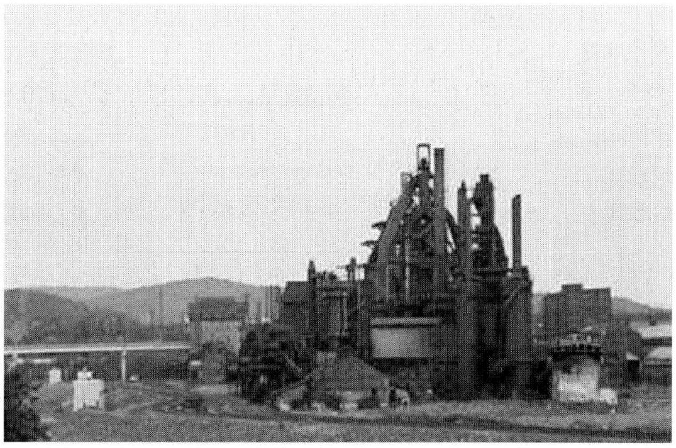

Bethlehem Steel Plants, Bethlehem, Pennsylvania

Bethlehem Steel Plants, Bethlehem, Pennsylvania

One of the nation's most important steel plants, the Bethlehem Works in Pennsylvania played a pioneering role in the development of America's steel and defense industries. Steel from the Bethlehem Works was used to build the Empire State Building, the Golden Gate Bridge and the Lincoln and Holland Tunnels, and to reconstruct the White House in the Truman era. Today, the sprawling mill lies dormant, in danger of being cleared for a retail complex or industrial park. Unless preservationists succeed in saving the birthplace of integrated steel-making, there might not be a single blast furnace, machine shop, foundry or crucible building left on the site of one of America's – and the world's – greatest industrial triumphs.

Bethlehem Steel Plants, historic view

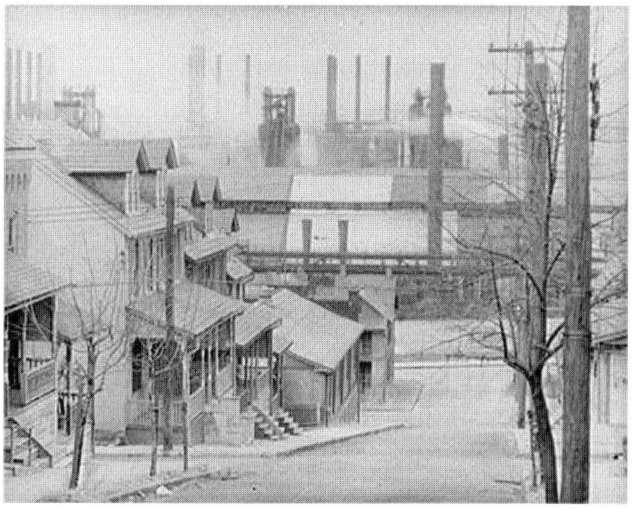

History

As the birthplace of the modern American defense industry, the plant manufactured the first modern battle fleet for the U.S. Navy in 1885 and remained the nation's largest shipbuilder and military supplier for generations. Some of steel-making's most significant technological innovations – including the fully integrated Bessemer process, heavy steel forging, and the production of continuously wide flange structural beams and columns – were developed or perfected here. The site is unique because it possesses the greatest number of buildings, structures and equipment remaining of any shut-down steelmaking facility in the country.

Threat

Now known as Bethlehem Works, the former plant, which closed in the mid-1990s, encompasses about 100 acres with more than 25 buildings and other structures dating from as early as 1863. Despite some basic infrastructure investment, virtually nothing has been done to protect the buildings, which have begun to experience deterioration and vandalism. Roofs are leaking and, in some cases, have blown off, and windows and doors have been broken and interior contents damaged. Because future ownership and development plans are in question, no significant steps are being taken to prevent further damage and deterioration. Despite vandalism and weather, the greatest threat lies in the probability of demolition.

Solution

While it still owned the site, Bethlehem Steel Corporation developed a comprehensive master plan for the plant that would have retained key buildings and structures. This included investing approximately $13 million into new infrastructure for half of the site with new roads, utilities and streetscape improvements. However, when Bethlehem Steel lost the property in 2003 due to bankruptcy, the site's future became uncertain. Currently there are several options for adaptive reuse, including a mixed-use plan anchored by a proposed National Museum of Industrial History, with other portions of the complex converted to new retail or industrial purposes. The site deserves an innovative redevelopment approach that retains the key aspects of the plant while integrating new, compatible infill construction.

Endangered List Program

These are just six of 11 sites the National Trust for Historic Preservation named this year for its 2004 list of America's 11 Most Endangered Historic Places. The other five places can be read about online at www.nationaltrust.org/11most/2004/index.html. The State of Vermont, which was also listed in 1993, makes a rare and regrettable reappearance.

As Richard Moe, president of the National Trust, points out the List includes places:

From factories that defined a nation to the home of a racehorse that inspired generations, from rural archaeological sites to big-city high rises, from individual landmarks to entire neighborhoods, historic places tell us who we are as a nation. They constitute an epic cultural narrative whose chapters include not only world-famous icons but hidden treasures. Unless all of us become aware of the importance of our heritage and take action to preserve it, America's past won't have a future. That's the real message of the 11 Most Endangered list.

In 2003, The History Channel broadcast the 'Save Our History' program, focussing on two sites that were on the National Trust for Historic Preservation's list of America's 11 Most Endangered Historic Places and are now being restored. From May 2004, The History Channel will also run a series of public service announcements that highlight the 2004 list.

US/ICOMOS

Reference

This report is almost verbatim from the National Trust for Historic Preservation website www.nationaltrust.org/11most/

Archaeological Heritage

Introduction

In this issue of *Heritage at Risk* the ICOMOS International Committee on Archaeological Heritage Management presents some issues for archaeological heritage around the world. Three regions were selected as the focus of this report – Eastern Europe, East Asia, and North America. Each of these ICAHM regions has presented different issues. Japan reports on the accelerating rate of site 'salvage', that is removal of the site, in the face of development. In Eastern Europe, there are a raft of issues, many related to the speed of change in heritage systems in societies in transition, and in the USA and Canada, a focus on central urban development pressures on below-ground cultural remains.

None of these risks to archaeological heritage are unique to that country or that region. They draw our attention to some key problems for archaeological heritage, primarily in terms of general misunderstandings about archaeological heritage by other heritage practitioners. ICAHM takes this opportunity to hopefully shift perceptions and remind ICOMOS and others dealing with heritage places and sites that:

- archaeological heritage is NOT only sub-surface; this notion has an effect of causing it to be invisible in development processes, such as in Japan with its horrifying rate of site salvage in the face of development, when sites are fully removed. 'Rescuing' such sites is in fact destroying them, as removing the entire site provides no opportunity for later analysis by more modern techniques of evidence remaining *in situ* – this way we lose our past;
- archaeological heritage is NOT simply individual sites, they are interconnected with each other, both representing a past landscape of human interconnectedness. They are also inextricably linked to the environment; the draining of peat bogs in Eastern Europe, for example, not only destroys many individual smaller archaeological sites, but a past landuse – this way we lose our link to the land;
- archaeological heritage is NOT simply artefacts for museum display, whether in a hotel lobby in the location of the former site, or in an actual museum, as is often the case in central business districts where sub-surface heritage is removed for carparks; it is evidence of past lifestyles and who we have been – this way we lose our story.

Archaeological heritage includes all physical manifestations of past ways of life, and includes many 'monumental' items of heritage around the world. Very visible sites, such as Roman temples, ruined medieval castles, temples in South East Asia, or magnificent rock art, all are surrounded by an extensive associated cultural landscape. But they are frequently treated as stand-alone 'monuments', for their stylistic and built characteristics, not as holders of past meanings, as 'archaeological heritage'.

Conserving such large archaeological monuments as individual sites means they are too rarely approached in their full cultural context, that includes both the monumental and the 'invisible'. This is a network of meaning, a cultural landscape, too often invisible to those making heritage conservation and development decisions limited to the 'visible' past. Fragmented approaches, both site-by-site, and by dividing 'below-ground' and 'monumental' heritage, risk ignoring the fullest evidence of former societies – the villages and economic resources, the trade-routes, the layerings of time, and the associated stories lasting through to the present in the local community, usually the descendants of such former cultures.

ICAHM urges its ICOMOS colleagues to look at the examples below and realise that much can be done in our heritage community to improve our approach to the heritage of the past, by having a wider understanding of what is actually our archaeological heritage.

Whilst these remarks may merely seem to be those of a 'Cinderella' in heritage conservation, at a time when ICOMOS sees landscape and setting as worthy of the next General Assembly's scientific focus, there is an opportunity to approach all heritage places in a more integrated and holistic way.

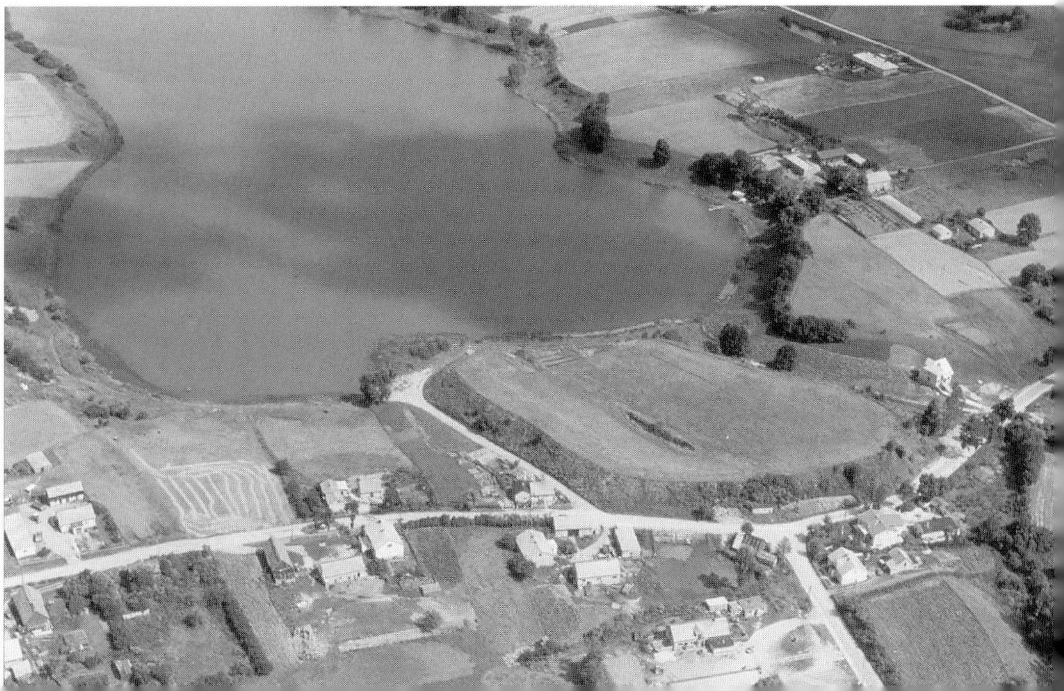

Zale – early medieval stronghold at Zale in northern Poland, systematically destroyed by ploughing (photo: Zbigniew Kobylinski)

Eastern Europe

The most serious threats to the archaeological heritage in Central and Eastern Europe, based on information collected from the Czech Republic, Latvia, Poland and Russia are seen to be:

Illegal excavation

The looting of archaeological sites and illicit trafficking of archaeological finds seems to be growing and is a common problem in this part of Europe. The uncontrolled use of electronic metal detectors is part of this activity (for example in Poland, Latvia and the Czech Republic), while in Russia it frequently takes the form of bulldozing burial mounds. The reasons vary and range from use of the mound material for other purposes, to a wrongly conceived interest in archaeology. Even if the law theoretically protects archaeological sites it is very difficult to protect them physically from such destruction. In Poland, additionally there is no consensus among archaeologists about how to deal with this problem, and some scholars even advocate cooperation with those wielding metal detectors.

Development

As all countries of the post-Soviet bloc are developing rapidly, a common threat for archaeological sites comes from various council and industrial developments. Obsolete laws sometimes do not demand the inclusion of the protection of archaeological sites in planning documents at an early stage (for example in the Czech Republic). In other cases, the process of spatial development can be too fast to be controlled (for example, in Latvia the rapid development of areas surrounding towns).

Agricultural activities

Systematic ploughing destroys most archaeological sites (for example, in Poland some 400,000 sites were recorded on agricultural lands, most of them regularly ploughed), but it is not a readi-

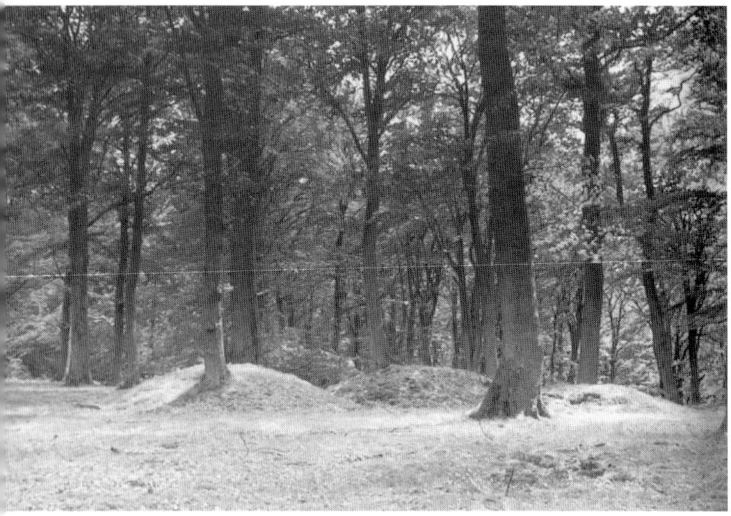

Runowo – early medieval barrows at Runowo in northern Poland – example of archaeological and nature protection area (landscape park) (photo: Zbigniew Kobylinski)

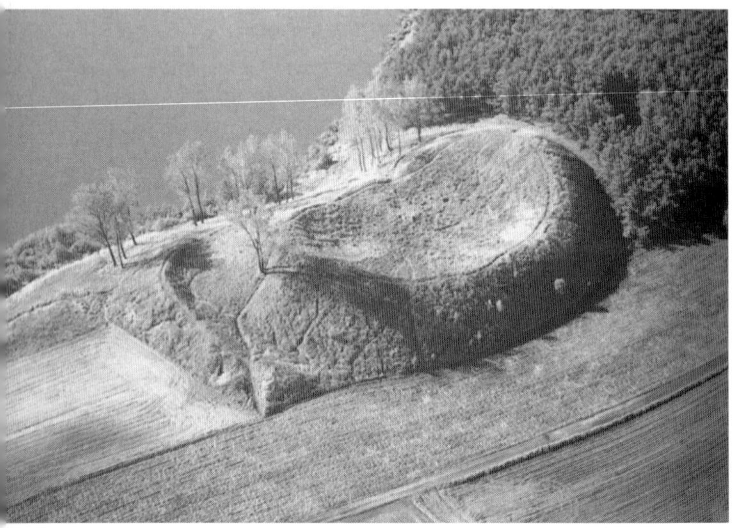

Napole – early medieval stronghold at Napole in northern Poland – the site is in good condition and not ploughed, but the neighbouring area is destroyed – so the site is not part of a historical landscape, but an isolated monument (photo: Zbigniew Kobylinski)

Prehistoric barrows in the south-eastern part of Poland, totally destroyed by ploughing and visible only as soilmarks (photo: Zbigniew Kobylinski)

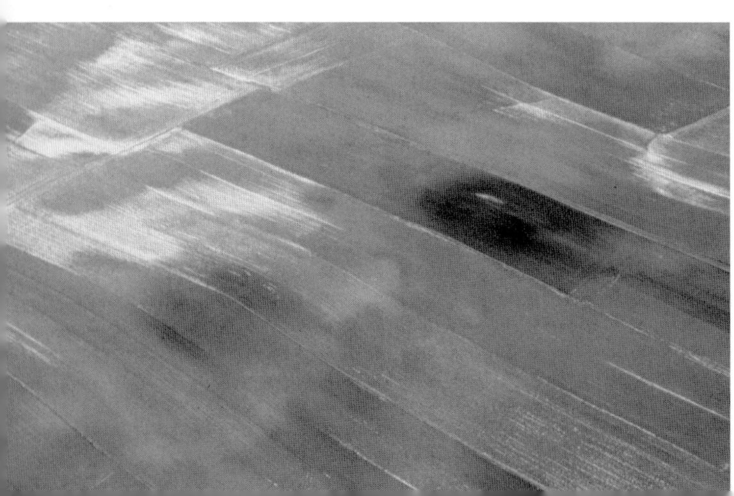

Prehistoric barrows in the south-eastern part of Poland, totally destroyed by ploughing and visible only as soilmarks (photo: Zbigniew Kobylinski)

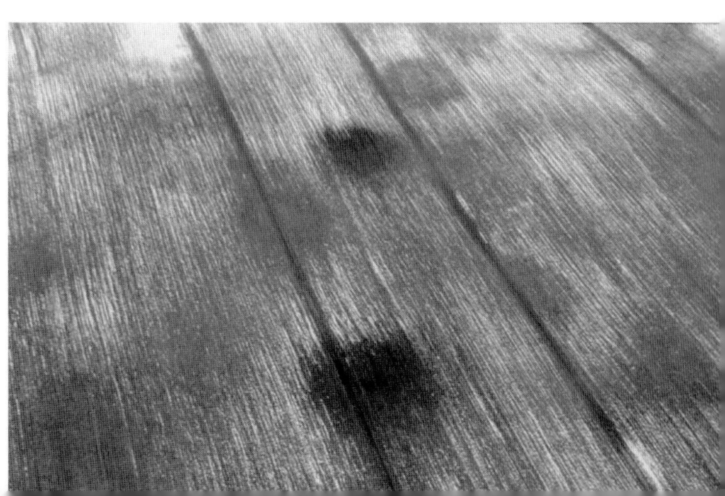

ly visible problem, and difficult to control by conservation services. Also, while the developer might be legally forced to pay for rescue excavation, this is not possible in case of farmers.

Changes in water systems

Large-scale changes to hydrological systems such as in Latvia, where the government supports the building of hydro-electric power stations on small rivers, cause the flooding of some archaeological sites and the destruction of others during the construction of dams. In Poland, by contrast, archaeological sites located in wetlands and peat bogs are destroyed by their drainage and development projects, which cause the lowering of the water-table and the dying out of sites.

Ineffectual agencies

Weak archaeological protective services seem to be a common phenomenon in all these countries. Even in cases where the law is good, conservation services are not able to provide effective protection to archaeological sites for purely practical reasons - too few people employed in conservation services, a lack of vehicles, low salaries, and so on. In addition there is lack of public education about the significance of archaeological heritage and the need for its protection. As a result, conservation activities are reactive rather than proactive in character.

East Asia

Case Study – Japanese rescue excavation

There are many aspects regarding heritage at risk in Japan as well as in other parts of East Asia. We limit the geographical area to the Japanese islands and review recent trends and arrangements for this report on archaeological heritage at risk.

In 1973, the total number of excavations carried out in a year was only 1244; of these excavations, 204 were conducted for academic research by universities, institutions and museums. The other 1040 excavations were rescue excavations carried out mostly by local administrative organisations, such as prefectural or boards of education. Rescue excavations have gone on increasing year after year, and in 1997 they had reached 11,738. On the other hand, academic research excavations stayed much the same as before, being 325. Total excavation numbers in the past six years have decreased a little, and according to the new data the total in 2004 numbered 8604, although the year had yet to end.

During the past three decades, the archaeological heritage management system in Japan has developed both in excavation logistics and administrative management. Most of all archaeological sites have been excavated before a development project. Today, it is very rare in Japan to have destruction without any kind of archaeological excavation. This is a positive feature of Japan's archaeological heritage management, as a basic treatment through the 'beneficiary payment principle', that is that the developer or other body that will benefit for the proposed development pays for such costs as site excavation.

On the other hand, ironically, this positive archaeological heritage management system now functions as one aspect in rationalising site destruction or as an indulgence of a 'necessary evil', for a great many archaeological sites have disappeared as a result of rescue excavation. It is in only a few cases, that there is opportunity for the site to be preserved as a 'historic site', designated as heritage by the national or local government.

North America – Urban development

Background

The approach to archaeological resource management in major urban centres throughout North America varies considerably. Although archaeological heritage management is typically the responsibility of Provincial / State, or Federal agencies, city planners often have considerable influence in determining when, or if, archaeological assessments occur prior to development projects proceeding. This is problematic for at least two reasons:

- most planners lack knowledge of the applicable heritage legislation and
- many planners assume that because a location has been developed to some degree in the past, that these areas no longer have archaeological potential.

While this latter point is true to some degree, a knowledge of locations that tend to correlate with archaeological sites, property development history, and construction methods are required before a true assessment of archaeological potential may be made with any level of confidence. Given the pace of development in many North American cities (for example, Vancouver) this problem has become acute and the impact upon archaeological heritage resources is a growing problem. In this latter scenario, the response to potential impacts to archaeological heritage resources is reactionary.

Twenty-five years ago, urban archaeology in the United States burst into the limelight with imaginative and well-organised programs in major metropolitan areas like Baltimore, New York, and Phoenix, along with energetic programs in smaller cities like Alexandria (Virginia) and Annapolis (Maryland). The last of these, under the direction of Mark Leone, did much to nurture not only public interest, but also academic vitality, in the field. Thanks to such pioneering work, urban archaeology in the United States is well established today.

Yet much about urban archaeology remains problematic. As is the case in Canada, urban archaeology programs are often located in city or county departments of planning. This is somewhat ironic, since essential aspects of conducting archaeological research are frequently not well envisioned. Urban areas are often thought of as the province of architectural treasures, not archaeological ones. To be successful, urban archaeologists must typically be as proficient in advocacy as in archaeology.

Trends

Approaches to archaeological heritage management in urban centres throughout North America are as diverse as the communities they represent. In some cities such as Seattle, policies exist that require archaeological resources to be considered in the development planning process. In other jurisdictions, such as Vancouver, the approach to archaeological heritage resource management is passive and lacking vision. One growing trend, noted in the Canadian province of Ontario, has cities and municipalities developing and implementing archaeological master plans which use archaeological, historical, and environmental data to develop predictive models that identify areas requiring archaeological assessment prior to development. Ontario jurisdictions with these master plans include: Halton, Waterloo, London, Ottawa-Carleton, Niagara-on-the-Lake, Richmond Hill, Vaughan, and Kingston (Dieterman and Williamson 2001). Currently the City of Toronto, Canada's largest city, is in the process of developing a comprehensive archaeological heritage master plan that considers both pre-contact aboriginal and post-contact archaeological resources within its jurisdiction.

Given the emphasis on above-ground cultural resources in cities, the first hurdle faced by archaeologists is to convey the possibility that there is valuable material below ground that might be damaged during rehabilitation of urban landscapes. Even when the archaeologist is successful in transmitting this message, it is not unusual that project boosters, no matter how adept they have been at raising funds for construction, will balk at providing funds needed for even minimal cataloguing and analysis of finds, and preparation of professional reports.

The sheer volume of material that is recovered at an urban site is usually daunting. Any archaeologist who has excavated both prehistoric and historic sites knows that the latter often yield more artefacts than do the former. While prehistoric artefacts are frequently created from organic materials that do not last long enough to be recovered by archaeologists, artefacts made in historic times are more likely to be of durable stuff. Among historic sites, urban sites can be expected to yield the most artefacts. Population density will have been higher in cities than in other areas, and activities like trade and manufacturing that produce many artefacts are common in cities.

Case study – Parliament buildings, Upper Canada

In Canada's city of Toronto, a heavily developed urban property, long known to be the location of the first and second Parliament buildings of Upper Canada, built in 1797 and 1820, respectively was on the verge of beginning another stage in its industrial use (see Dieterman and Williamson 2001). Prevailing thought assumed it was unlikely that any archaeological heritage resource remained intact due to the urban setting and the extent of institutional and industrial development that had taken place on the site. However, a local heritage advocacy group persisted and the City of Toronto was persuaded to retain an archaeological heritage consultant to assess the property and to search for any surviving remains of the parliamentary complex prior to its redevelopment as a car dealership.

Background research and archaeological test excavations identified the remains of the first and second Parliament buildings of Upper Canada. Techniques that were used included historic documentation and archival research, artefact identification and distributional analyses, stratigraphic and subsurface archaeological feature identification, identification of historic construction techniques, as well as lithographic, botanical, and faunal analyses (Dieterman and Williamson 2001).

This case study demonstrates that urban properties with extensive development histories can still retain areas that contain archaeological heritage resources dating from their earliest uses and that a detailed understanding of the development history and use of a subject property is required prior to concluding it has no archaeological heritage potential.

Case Study – Philadelphia Independence Hall, USA

Over the past several years, the Independence National Historical Park in downtown Philadelphia, Pennsylvania, which contains the World Heritage Site of Independence Hall, has been the site of intense activities associated with the construction of the National Constitution Centre. The non-profit organisation that is raising $185 million to build and operate the Centre was required by federal law to sponsor inventory and evaluation of archaeological resources, and to mitigate any destruction of resources that might be caused by the construction. Indeed, in such a highly visible location, some degree of archaeology was inevitable. Soon, artefacts poured out of the first test pits, which were widened to reveal large areas where the colonial landscape remained much as it appeared when covered two centuries ago. As archaeologist Douglas Mooney said, "... we found evidence of the entire colonial-era city block preserved almost intact below ground surface".

Artefacts associated with Colonial life were recovered in plenty: clothing, shoes, newspapers, muskets, cups, tableware, coins, jewellery, gaming pieces, trade beads, buttons, needles, food remains and toys. Historians found evidence of social diversity that surprised many. The wealthy white elite lived there alongside former slaves, as well as immigrant labourers, shopkeepers, and scientists. The Philadelphia Inquirer did a series of stories on the excavation. All archaeologists involved in the research spoke in superlatives about the finds. One called it "the greatest urban archaeological find of our lifetime". More than one million artefacts have so far been taken from the ground.

After sponsoring five million dollars of archaeological research – an almost unprecedented figure in American archaeology – the president of the National Constitution Centre said, as reported on 30 April 2002 by the *Philadelphia Inquirer*, „I don't think we could justify taking more funds away from the building project. This is not a museum about the 18th-century life on the ... block". In the fall [northern autumn] of 2003, the National Park Service acknowledged that they were responsible for the completion of archaeological work, a proclamation that was worrisome to many most concerned with the research. On 14 November 2003, the *Philadelphia Inquirer* quoted Anthony Ranere, professor of archaeology and anthropology at Temple University, as saying: "It's hard to evaluate what they'll be able to do. It's unbelievable, and it's worrisome". The National Park Service remains vague about how they will complete cataloguing and preservation of artefacts, along with analysis of the myriad finds, and finally sponsoring an academic analysis of what they mean to American histo-

Detail of 1872 panorama of Philadelphia, Independence Hall left (NPS website)

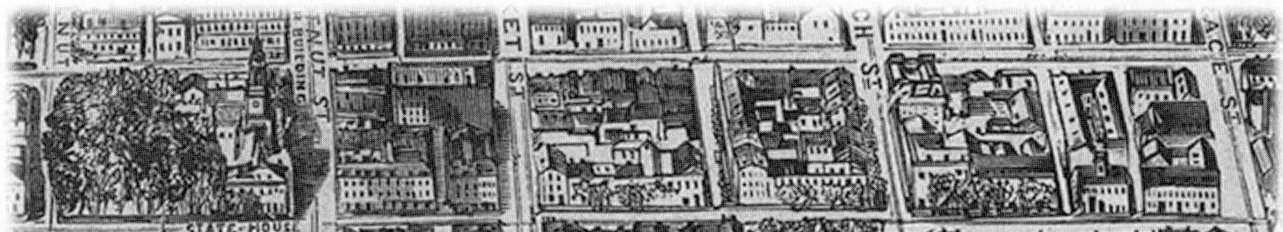

ry. Regarded as the 'lead preservation agency' for all others in federal, state, and local governments, the Park Service has suggested that it will utilise its own archaeologists, now in short supply after years of reducing the number of federal employees; or that it will contract for these specialised services with funding that has yet to be identified.

According to United States federal preservation law, failure to complete cataloguing, analysis, and reporting of findings recovered in archaeological investigations constitutes an adverse impact on irreplaceable cultural resources – in much the same way as does looting or destruction of such resources during unmonitored construction. The situation described in Philadelphia is extreme, in regards to the great importance of the archaeological remains uncovered there, far from unique.

ICOMOS ICAHM - International Committee on Archaeological Heritage Management

Authors: Eastern Europe - Zbigniew Kobylinski (Vice-President), Poland; Alexander Smirnov, Russia; Martin Tomasek, Czech Republic; Juris Urtans, Latvia; East Asia – Akira Ono (Vice-President), Japan; Masatoshi Kishimoto (Associate member), Japan; North America - Douglas Comer, (Vice-President), USA; Christophe Rivet, (Secretary) Canada; Marilyn Truscott (Associate Member), Australia.

References

Frank A. Dieterman and Ronald F. Williamson 2001, *Government on Fire: The History and Archaeology of Upper Canada's First Parliament Buildings.* Eastend Book, Toronto.

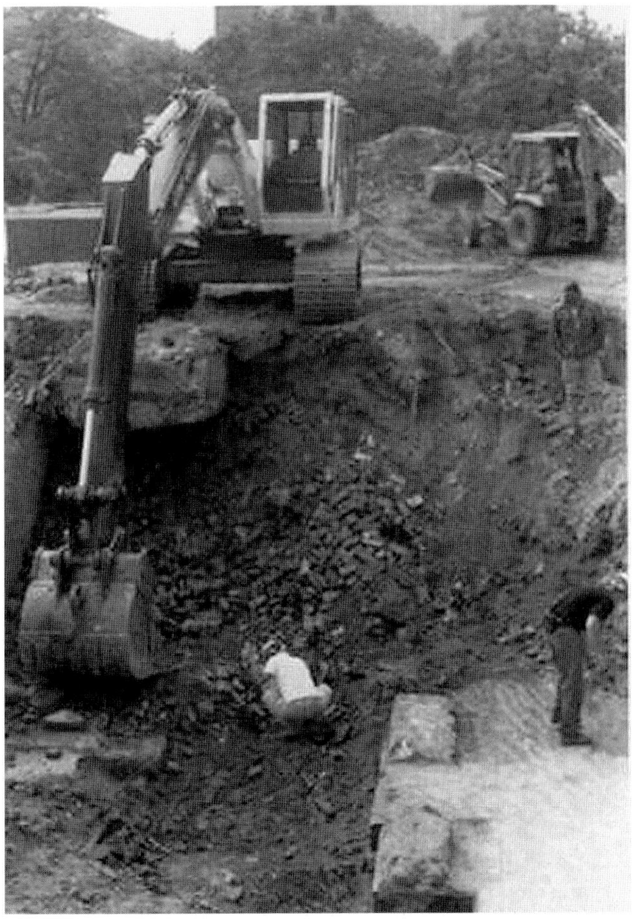

Excavation at Independence Park Visitors Centre, Philadelphia (photo: NPS, Jed Levin)

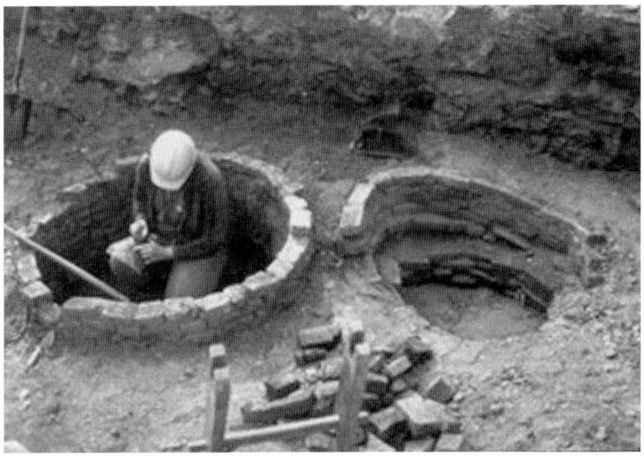

Shallow features can be destroyed by modern construction, Independence Park Visitors Centre, Philadelphia (photo: NPS, Paul Inashima)

ROCK ART

Rock art, the most widespread cultural heritage of humanity, is constantly attracting a growing interest from research and management institutions, education and tourism bodies and also from an aware public. Research is steadily expanding within universities and other research institutions. This is above all noticeable from the increasing number of students' papers and doctoral theses dealing with rock art in recent years. This is a greatly encouraging fact for any specialist involved in this complex and delicate subject. However, some fundamental changes that affect the chosen subject of study also seem to have occurred lately. This concerns the funding situation, especially in Europe where the traditional funds from universities and research councils have become considerably smaller affecting the possibilities and choices of the preferred research aim. Most of the main funding is now accumulated within the research and education programs of the European Commission and Union. This change of research funding provider has affected quite considerably not only the possibilities of following a traditional academic career but also the choice of research topics and contexts in rock art.

The latter phenomenon is evident from a growing number of applications and approvals for European Union financed projects in previous years in the Mediterranean and Nordic countries. Sometimes these projects are based on co-operation between these two regions. Hopefully, this widening of the sphere of participators has had a positive influence also on the target topics and scope of studies. It has been further promoted by the fact that prehistoric rock art in Europe and especially that from the Neolithic and the Bronze Age share many features of chronology, context and imagery, such as between Bohuslän and Lombardy and different parts of Spain and Norway.

The most significant outcome of this intensified European cooperation seems to be a shift of focus from traditional university research topics, such as dating and the meaning of rock art to those dealing with the conservation and management of the sites. It is perhaps better described as an enhancement of an already existing research trend where aspects of documentation and management have become increasingly important. In many countries including Norway, Spain, Great Britain and in the USA research on the management of rock art as part of a wider archaeological arena has become established more or less as a discipline of its own.

It has sometimes been argued that this may not be to the advantage of 'pure' rock art research that should be directed towards the meaning and interpretation of rock art itself. This topic will most probably also be a matter of debate in the future. But it seems obvious that management and research are two sides of one and the same coin. Without public investment in the development of management, including the protection and conservation of rock art sites, there would soon be very few sites left on which to do research. And without research there would soon be very little of interest to tell the educated public about the meaning and further archaeological implications of rock art. It seems that one key factor in further integrating these two fields is documentation itself.

Documentation, whether performed using traditional methods such as rubbing or tracing or with modern high-tech laser-scanning, provides researchers with the possibility to get to know rock art *in situ* with all its detail and additional artistic values. Details are often revealed which are crucial to understanding the meaning and therefore the interpretation of the message conveyed in the rock art. Applied in a conscious and careful way high-tech methods can be a considerable aid to recording and storing this information, as well as in bringing it from its natural location in the landscape into the laboratory where it can be subject of further analysis and study.

It is important to stress that this development of cross-border research is not unique to Europe, however strong it may be there at the moment. In Southern Africa a partially similar situation is taking place with the Southern African Rock Art Project (SARAP) that was initiated in 1995 at a joint ICOMOS/WHC meeting in Harare in Zimbabwe, focusing on the need for a common regional management strategy for rock art. The main aim of SARAP has become that of identifying a rock art site in each Southern African country eligible for a serial nomination to the World Heritage List. After having received funding for this purpose from the Norwegian development aid agency NORAD in 2000/2001, a group of sites for nomination were selected consisting of Kondoa in Tanzania nominated in 2000, Brandenburg and Twyfelfontain in Namibia (being nominated), Drakensberg of South Africa nominated in

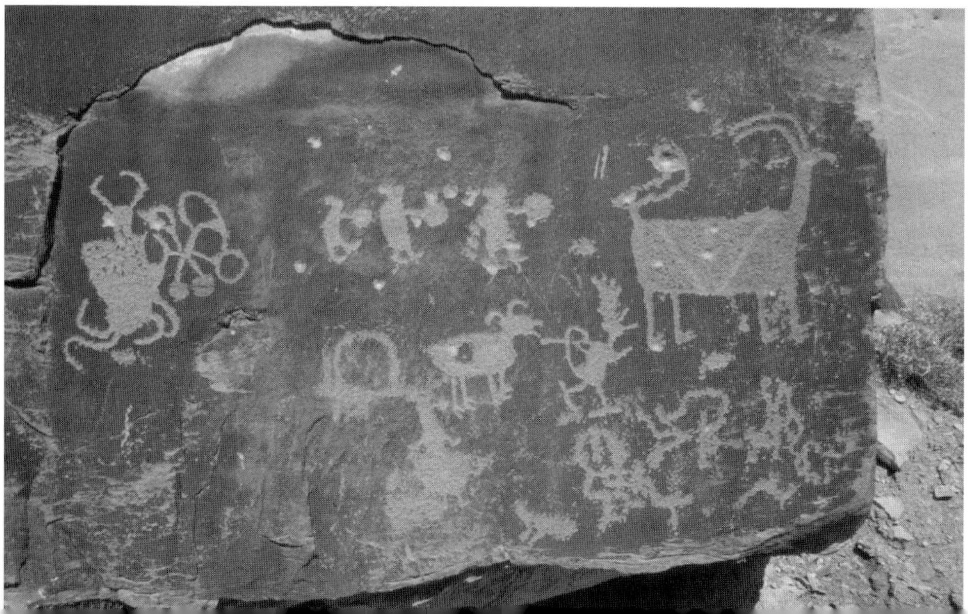

Nine Mile Canyon, USA (photo: Jean Clottes)

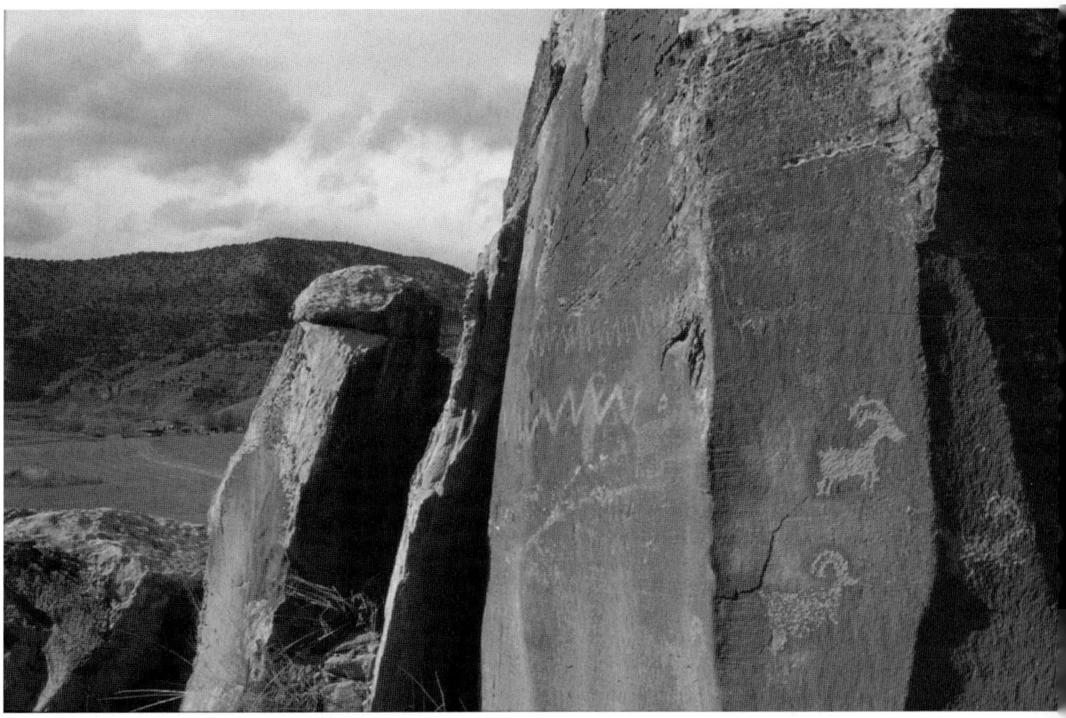

Nine Mile Canyon, USA (photo: Jean Clottes)

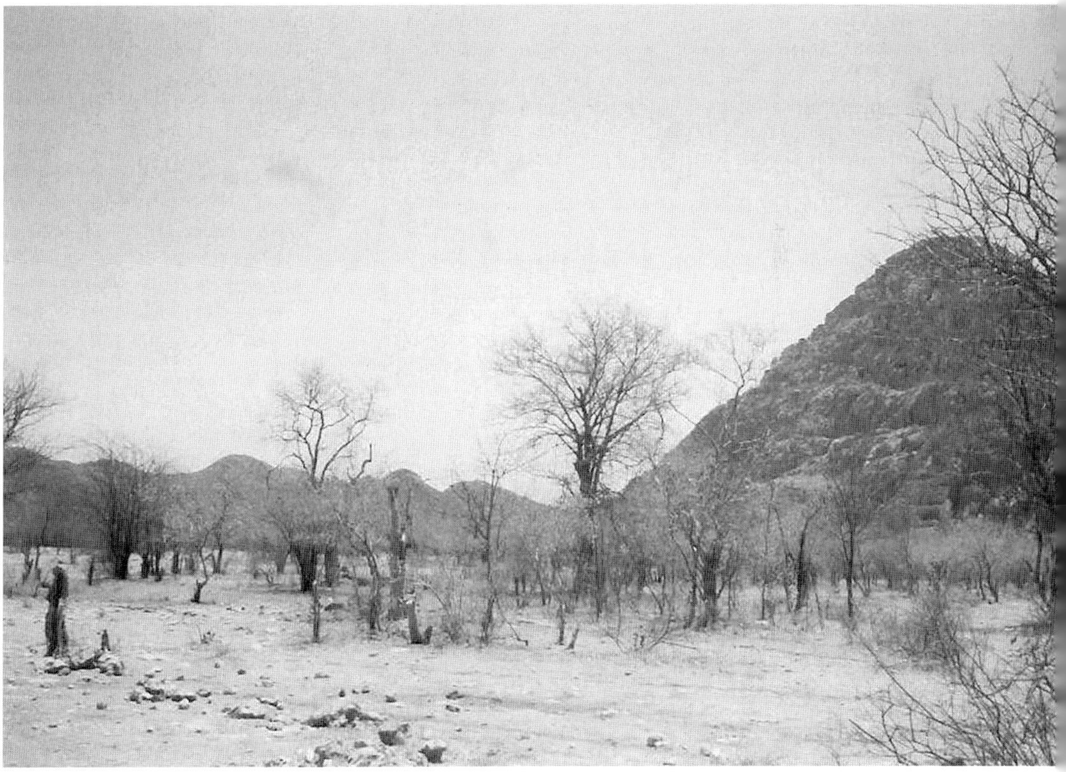

Tsodilo Hills World Heritage site, Botswana (photo: M C Truscott)

1999, Tsodoli of Botswana nominated in 2000, Dedza-Chongoi of Malawi nominated in 2001. Nominations are in progress for the rock paintings of Matopos in Zimbabwe, Kasama in Zambia and Manica province in Mozambique (see Deacon 2004).

This important and progressive initiative of the Southern African countries is also an attempt to fill the well-known gap of rock art sites from developing countries on the World Heritage List. There is now a consensus that such a gap exists not only in Africa but also in certain parts of Asia and the Americas, although the situation is slowly but steadily improving. Other than the above African sites, there are also sites such as Zalavruga of the coastal region in Karelian Russia, Gobustan in Azerbaijan and Seimuly Tash in Kyrgyzstan, the latter probably being the most outstanding site of all. In China there are several rock art sites concerned, one being Helan Shan. In the Americas are also several of which one of the most important is Nine Mile Canyon in the USA.

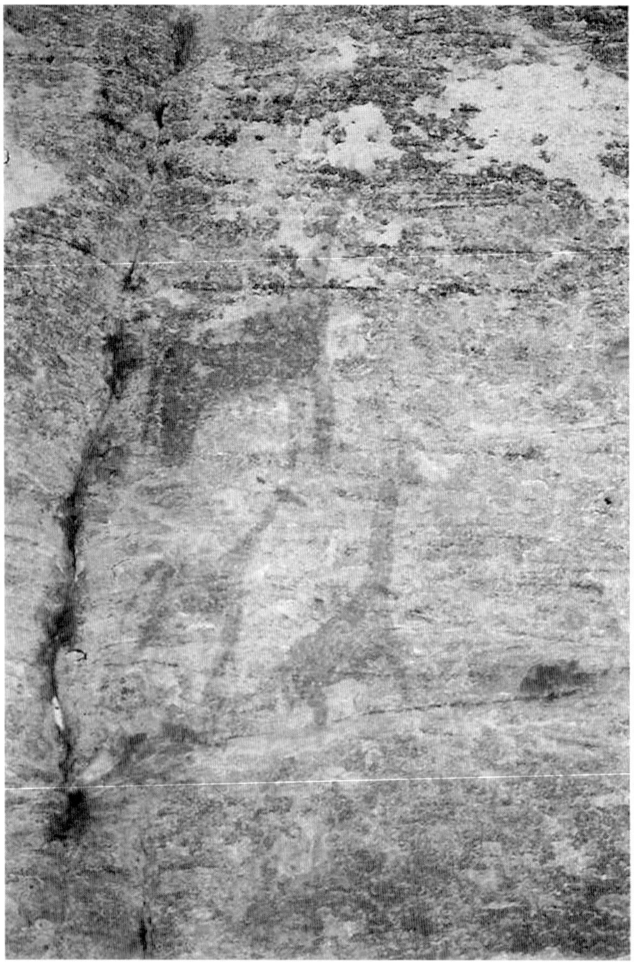

Tsodilo Hills World Heritage site, Botswana (photo: M C Truscott)

This complex of sites is now being severely threatened by a governmental initiative to exploit the water resources. A similar threat has developed at the impressive site of the Burrup Peninusula, at Dampier in Australia now immediately threatened by mining infrastructure. Further examples from various parts of the world could also be mentioned.

A difficulty often occurring in nominating sites to the World Heritage List and especially in developing countries is the problem of survey and documentation of the rock art panels. This basic information and data needed for the identification, evaluation and verification of the sites and their condition is often completely missing or incomplete. If it exists it has often been collected and recorded a long time ago in the days of colonialism and in a form and in media that are not conducive for a nomination to the World Heritage List today. In this sense, it is correct to say that the concept of 'rock art at risk' does not signify only the immediate threats to sites posed by increased deterioration caused by worsening climatic conditions or human intervention with intensified infrastructural development and planning. At nominated sites, it should also include the situation regarding their survey and documentation, as inadequacies and shortcomings in that respect may cause problems in the evaluation process and make the establishment of a site's 'outstanding universal value' difficult or impossible. Such a lack of documentation may very well pose as big a threat to the future of a rock art site as the above human factors. Once nominated and inscribed on the World Heritage List a site would have a much brighter future regarding funding for management and research. If the nomination process fails there is a big risk that such a site will lose much of its positive appeal.

Therefore, in order to counteract these problems and to improve the current situation there is an immediate need for some guidelines in this area. A first step could be to define and establish a common documentation standard – a minimum standard – that could be easily applied almost anywhere without high costs and technical problems. Such methods have already been developed in some of the European Union projects based on traditional paper rubbing and plastic tracing records that are scanned and computerised to enable subsequent treatment and use. Similar efficient methods have also been developed in Southern Africa to record rock paintings. This need for simple and reliable recording methods is also matched by an equal need for a general and easily accessible database recording system. Such a system is under development by CAR – ICOMOS in co-operation with the Centro Camuno di Studi Preistorici on whose earlier WARA system it is partly based. In contrast to that system, it will however focus more on basic information about the rock art and its documentation than the symbols, and its meaning and interpretation.

The World Heritage site of Valcamonica has been the focus of earlier Rock Art at Risk reports. Also this year it has been the focus of a Reactive Monitoring Mission jointly undertaken by ICOMOS and the World Heritage Centre as a result of several suggestions of site mismanagement. Although the mission report is still in preparation some important observations can already be made. Many panels have been recorded at the site throughout the years, yet there is an obvious lack of a basic reliable and readily accessible documentation system. Such a system should be based on the refined recording methods using plastic tracings that were developed by the CCSP's research institutes in the valley. The system currently in use by the responsible state authority, the Sopraintendente in Milan, is based on digital photos and is not well-suited to record images and scenes, although it might be appropriate for recording erosion and other damage. Another observation is that state authorities, such as that in Milan, should put more effort into initiating and co-ordinating research already being undertaken by various players, rather than put too much emphasis on doing such activities themselves. Otherwise they may end up in a situation where they do not contribute to an expansion of areas of research but instead limit them. This would in turn pose new threats to the Valcamonica rock art, which would be unacceptable since this is one of the original centres of such activities.

Ulf Bertilsson
President of CAR-ICOMOS

References

Bertilsson, U 2004, Recent trends in rock art management and research of the Nordic countries – a personal overview. In Bertilsson, U, and L McDermott (eds) The Valcamonica symposiums 2001 and 2002. *Rapport från Riksantikvarieämbetet 2004:6*, pp. 100-113.

Deacon, J 2004, Southern African Rock Art in the New Millennium. Bertilsson, U, and L McDermott (eds) The Future of Rock Art – a World Review. *Rapport från Riksantikvarieämbetet 2004:7* pp. 120-131.

EARTHEN ARCHITECTURE
Yemeni Mudbrick at Risk

Wadi Hadhramaut in the former People's Democratic Republic of Yemen (South Yemen) is recognized internationally for its spectacular mudbrick tower houses. The walled city of Shibam, with its densely packed ten-story un-reinforced mudbrick high-rises, was designated a World Heritage site in 1982. Seyoun (the regional capital) is dominated by the Kathiri sultan's palace, now the Museum of the Hadhramaut, whereas Tarim is characterized by its eclectic complex of mudbrick mansions. The mansions, the product of a wealthy merchant class, date from the 1870s to the 1930s and interpret imported colonial styles (Neo-Classical, Baroque, Rococo, Mughal, Art Nouveau and Art Deco) in the local construction technology of load-bearing mudbrick and lime plaster. The significance of the Tarimi mansions lies in their collective representation of a period of time when there was extensive interaction with the Indian Ocean trade routes and Southeast Asia.

In the early 1970s, the then Marxist government expropriated twelve of the Tarimi mansions. These were mostly reused as housing for the poor. Two decades later, when the civil war united North and South Yemen, the mansions were returned to their rightful owners. By this time, however, the mansions had suffered from lack of maintenance and the families were not compensated for the damage. As a consequence, the owners did not feel responsible for the needed repairs. In addition, each mansion is owned by literally dozens of inheritors, many of who no longer live in Tarim. The result has been abandonment and 'demolition by neglect'.

Since 2000, the Tarimi mansions preservation project has been working to reverse the tide for this collection of buildings. Initially, a feasibility study was performed by the co-directors, Pamela Jerome[1] and Dr Selma al-Radi.[2] The feasibility study identified significant structures and their ownership context, as well as evaluating their condition and adaptive reuse potential. It also recommended that a documentation training program be instituted to record the structures. The initial feasibility study was funded by the New York City-based Samuel H Kress Foundation. This study was updated at the request of UNESCO in March 2004, identifying a total of fifty mansions.

The next step was to get the buildings listed on the World Monuments Fund (WMF) 100 Most Endangered Sites list (the Watch List) where they stayed for two consecutive two-year cycles from 2000–2004. Simultaneously, additional international exposure was accomplished by presenting the project at several conferences, as well as developing a website (www.learn.columbia.edu/tarim). Through interaction with stakeholders, local interest has also been stimulated.

Since 2002, the Tarimi mansions preservation project has begun documenting the most significant of the buildings using both conventional and digital media. This work is being funded by the American Institute for Yemeni Studies (AIYS) through grants provided by the US State Department's Bureau of Educational and Cultural Affairs, and the Samuel H Kress Foundation. The project trains Columbia University graduate students and personnel from Yemen's General Organization of Antiquities and Museums (GOAM), who work side by side with American conservators. Measured CADD drawings are produced along with digital photographs, 35 mm slides and condition assessments.

The assessments have led to emergency stabilization efforts funded by the US State Department's Ambassador's Fund for Cultural Preservation and the Yemeni organization, the Social Fund for Development (SFD). The 'Ishshah palace, documented during the December 2002-January 2003 season, has had several col-

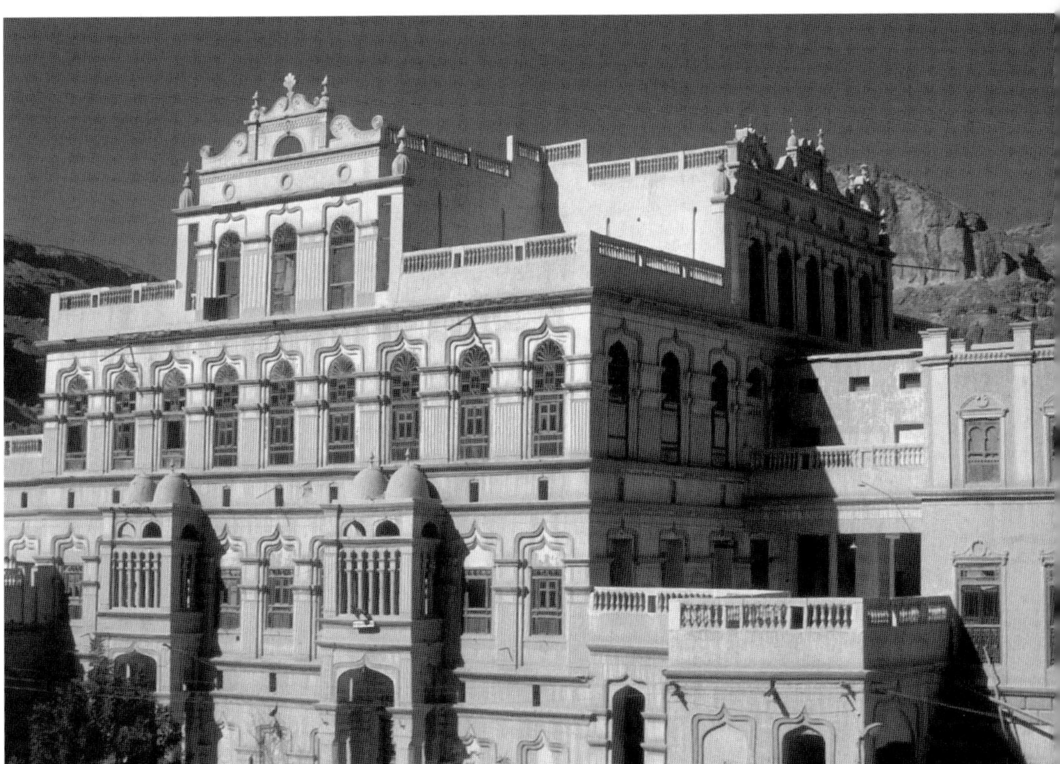

The main building of the 'Ishshah palace, Yemen, designed by Sayid Alawi Abu Bakr al-Kaf

lapsed areas reconstructed under the administration of the Tarimi mansions preservation project. This included the reconstruction of a large area of the west elevation, the northwest kitchen wing and the northeast wing of Dar Dawil, the oldest building of the 'Ishshah complex. The 'Ishshah is probably the most significant of the Tarimi mansions; it was the seat of family patriarch 'Umar bin Shaikh al-Kaf who amassed his fortune in Singapore and built several of the mansions. The 'Ishshah is currently on long-term lease to the Tarim branch of the Yemeni Society for History and Heritage Protection which presents it to the public as a house museum, the only one in the valley.

Dar al-Salam, an Art Deco masterpiece designed by 'Umar's cousin and gentleman architect, Sayid Alawi Abu Bakr al-Kaf, has been proposed for reuse as the headquarters of the future Association of Mud Masons. In January 2004, a ribbon cutting ceremony was held at Dar al-Salam as part of the Günter Grass ceremony. Nobel Prize winner Günter Grass donated a portion of his prize towards the establishment of the Association of Mud Masons. Training programs are planned in cost estimating, reading of architectural plans and apprenticeship to permit the masons to compete against concrete contractors for government bids, as well as produce the next generation of craftsmen. While Dar al-Salam was documented during the December 2003-January 2004 season, a hole in one of the roofs was repaired and electricity and plumbing introduced with funds from the SFD.

In addition, the undermined entrance portico of the adjacent Hamtut mansion was stabilized and the front yard cleaned and leveled in preparation for the Günter Grass event, which was held in the Hamtut's courtyard. The Hamtut will be the subject of the upcoming season's documentation and is proposed for reuse as the Center for Visiting Scholars.

The Tarimi mansions preservation project was removed from the WMF's Watch List and awarded a Certificate of Outstanding Achievement. The award ceremony was held in January 2004 in the rebuilt western section of the 'Ishshah mansion. Both events were attended by government officials, representatives of the municipality, and stakeholders and received extensive press coverage.

As a result of the attention shed on the mansions by our project, the Yemeni government is considering purchasing some of the most significant abandoned mansions. We are also encouraging the government to draft legislation that would protect the historic city of Tarim while controlling the aesthetics of new concrete construction. Although a good start has been made, much remains to be done in order to ensure the future of the Tarimi mansions.

Pamela Jerome
US/ICOMOS Specialized Committee on Earthen Architecture

[1] Adjunct associate professor, Columbia University's Graduate School of Architecture, Planning and Preservation and director of preservation, Wank Adams Slavin Associates LLP.

[2] Research fellow, New York University's Institute of Fine Arts and co-director of al-'Amiriya Madrasa Restoration Project.

POLAR HERITAGE

Two major causes of deterioration of heritage sites in the polar areas – human impacts and natural forces – are not new threats. However, the situation today is that both of these threats are increasing at a pace not seen before. The new wave of tourism to the remotest areas of the world also includes the previously shielded regions of the Arctic and Antarctic. This has brought benefits to cultural heritage protection by the spread of information and interest which, in turn, leads to support back home for heritage conservators and managers working with polar heritage places. On the other side of the picture is the often unavoidable wear and tear on these fragile sites, as well as increased access by unplanned visits, which unfortunately in extreme cases can inflict unthinking or intentional damage.

Greater access to heritage places is also a result of the warmer summers over the last decade or so, producing less sea ice and longer shipping seasons. Previously the ice acted as a barrier, preventing ships from approaching more remote shores and regions. The clear indications of climate change around the world are expected to have a particular effect on polar areas. Increasing temperatures, increased precipitation as rain during the summer months, more storms and less sea ice to moderate the impacts of wave action, are already inflicting damage and destruction to Arctic heritage places. It is unfortunate in this regard that most heritage places were established by the sea at the time, which usually was the easiest, and in many cases the only access to the region, if only during a very short period in summer. Coastal erosion has always taken place, and sites have been lost into the sea, but the rate of loss today is increasing alarmingly and protective measures for sites are often not viable.

The two case studies presented here address these problems and challenges, the one from the Norwegian Arctic archipelago of Svalbard and the other from the north-west Canadian coast. They stand as examples of many other similar cases around the Arctic.

'Haudegen' – A German Marine Weather Station in Svalbard – slowly decaying!

During World War II, because meteorological data for the North Atlantic were not available from foreign weather services, Germany maintained several weather stations in the Arctic. Between September 1941 and September 1945 the German Navy and the German Air Force had their own stations installed on Spitsbergen and Hopen (Svalbard), East Greenland and Franz Josef Land.

Station 'Haudegen' at Wordiebukta (Wordie Bay) in Rijpfjord on Nordaustlandet, Svalbard operated from 1944 to 1945 and is the only German station that was not destroyed after its detection. The base hut was erected 150 m from the shore on the western foothill of Lookout Rock, using six prefabricated walls and trusses in a pattern of cubes 3 m x 3 m x 2.2 m. The hut was also given a double thickness of walls, floor and roof covered with a tarpaulin.

The completed hut measured 6 m x 9 m, and consisted of the team leader's room, a dormitory with seven beds, a mess-hall, kitchen, battery-charging room, wireless room with three beds, workshop, porch and toilet, store for coal and wood, and outer porch. Solid boxes were used to make a table and benches in the mess hall, and they also served as shelves for a library of about 200 books and for various supplies. The hut was surrounded by a walkway, which was built of stacked provision cases covered by canvas. With this insulation the hut was strengthened against being blown away during heavy westerly winter storms. Camouflage netting was draped over the entire building and the nearby weather screen. During winter the snow cover totally concealed the station within the landscape.

A small wooden hut was built close to the station to house the hydrogen generating plant. It had two rooms, one for the plant and another for a sauna that was also used as a laundry. The hydrogen was needed for the daily meteorological radiosonde balloon ascents to investigate the meteorological conditions in the upper air. A depot and an emergency radio station were located in another small hut made from empty wooden boxes covered by sheet metal and rocks. This was situated on Lookout Rock, 80 m east of the station and 100 m above it.

Unfortunately, the roof of the base hut was not waterproof. The painted tarpaulin cover became porous with rain and frost and the material of the walls also proved to be unsatisfactory during the first cold period. Moisture formed on the inside as impermeable hardboard material was used instead of the wood used in earlier versions of these prefabricated cubes.

When the sun returned and the snow disappeared, the camouflage was set up again and a military lookout was established on Lookout Rock. Electrically detonated mines were also installed around the station.

On 7 May 1945 the men of 'Haudegen' were informed of Germany's surrender. Weather observations however were continued, transmitting without code to become part of the world meteorological service. When the men finally surrendered to the captain of a Norwegian sealer, they were ordered to leave behind provisions and clothing for four men for three months, so that the 'Haudegen' base could be used as a future refuge hut. So its location in one of the outermost areas of Svalbard saved the station from being destroyed. The windows and the door of the hut were carefully barricaded against polar bears, and the military installations, especially the mines, were disabled.

In 1985 an expedition from the Norwegian Defence Museum (Oslo) salvaged artefacts from the weather station 'Haudegen'. The station buildings were still there, but showed signs of damage by bears, visitors and weather. Provisions and equipment had been ransacked and scattered around the entire area. The kitchen stove and the radio equipment had been stolen, while the books of the extensive library were thrown around the mess-hall. Only some less significant artefacts were left in the vandalised emergency radio hut. The lifeboat remained undisturbed on the beach south of the station, and a metal box with the station logbook and other documents were unearthed nearby and taken to Oslo.

Today 'Haudegen' is in a bad state and will continue to decay slowly. Its earlier isolation is now shattered and it has become one of the scheduled tourist sites for cruises to Svalbard, being visited almost every two years depending on ice conditions. Although the Cultural Heritage Act for Svalbard protects all places and material dating from before 1946, and the Tourist Regulations emphasise heritage protection, this is not observed by every private expedition. Polar bears and the natural elements continue to attack the buildings. Today, 'Haudegen' is the only existing German overwintering station in the Arctic and it represents a modern type of prefabricated hut, which other countries used later in modified forms during the International Geophysical Year (1957-1958).

Something must be done soon to protect the station and to preserve it as polar cultural heritage.

A project financed by the Fritz-Thyssen-Foundation has now been established to document 'Haudegen'. Unpublished diaries, pictures and even film in the private possession of the expedition leader's family are being analysed to describe the station at the time of its operation. The site's current condition is to be recorded with the help of geodetic methods and photography, during a proposed field expedition. This information will be used for future decisions and actions regarding the site's conservation in co-operation with the Norwegian authorities.

Climate change in the western Canadian Arctic threatens cultural resources

In 2001 the Intergovernmental Panel on Climate Change (www.ipcc.ch) stated that:

Climate change in the Polar Regions is expected to be among the largest and most rapid of any region on Earth, and will cause major physical, ecological, sociological, and economic impacts, especially in the Arctic.

The recent trend towards warmer weather in the Arctic is magnified in the Beaufort Sea area in the western Canadian Arctic. The Beaufort Sea extends eastward from the north coast of Alaska, USA, north of Canada's Yukon Territory to the Mackenzie River Delta, north of Canada's Northwest Territories.

The western Canadian Arctic has warmed by 1.5° C over the past 100 years. Global circulation models predict further warming of the global atmosphere throughout the 21st century. In the Canadian Arctic, winter temperatures are expected to rise by 5° C–10° C, summer temperatures will increase 2° C–5° C, and precipitation will increase by 15%–25%.

The observations of Arctic residents, being based on traditional knowledge, reinforce this scientific analysis. The Inuvialuit, Inuit of the western Canadian Arctic, have said that they can no longer predict the weather. These indigenous people are highly dependent on living off the land, harvesting game, fish and plant materials in a traditional manner. Over recent decades they have observed increasingly intense late summer and autumn storms that have brought sea level surges and a battering of shorelines by the steadily thinning sea ice.

The shores of the Beaufort Sea are largely made up of sedimentary deposits bound together by permafrost. As warmer temperatures erode this permafrost, the rate of slope failure and shoreline erosion increases. In recent years, erosion has consumed more than 10 metres of shore in some areas of the Beaufort Sea region. Rising sea levels will have a long-term impact as well. The hamlet of Tuktoyaktuk, the main transportation hub for the western Canadian Arctic, has suffered severe erosion and flooding despite three attempts at shore stabilisation and protection since 1976. The recent exposure of Inuvialuit graves along the receding shoreline has upset the community.

A consequence of climate warming in the region is a decrease in the extent and mass of Arctic sea ice and an increase in the length of the melt season. This has had a damaging effect on seal populations and inevitably will impact on polar bears that feed on them along the margins of the permanent ice pack. Changes have been noticed in the migration patterns and breeding cycles of other mammals, birds and sea life. Further ecological, economic and sociological impacts are expected as the Northwest Passage becomes more easily navigable across the north of America and commercial shipping and other water traffic becomes more viable.

In response to these changes many agencies and institutions are stepping up their Arctic study programs and initiating new ones. McGill University in Canada has started a program to study and monitor the deterioration of ground ice in the Beaufort Sea region. Using photogrammetric methods and global positioning surveys (GPS) in the field, they have computed increased horizontal coastal retreat rates of 0.67 m to 1.03 m a year from 1954 to 2000. One focus for study is Herschel Island, one kilometre off the Yukon coast.

Herschel Island was named in 1826 by the noted Arctic explorer, Sir John Franklin, after the British scientist, Sir John Herschel. There is evidence of human occupation at least 1000 years before Franklin arrived. The Inuvialuit name for the island is Qikiqtaruk.

Late in the 19th century, in relentless pursuit of the depleting stocks of whales in the North Pacific, whalers discovered one of the last refuges in the Beaufort Sea of the prized Bowhead whale. Bowheads were coveted for their baleen, or whalebone, the 'plastic' of the time. American commercial whalers found a good harbour at Pauline Cove on Herschel Island and established a settlement there in 1890 amongst the Inuit, who provided necessary survival skills and local foods such as fish and Caribou.

In 1893–94, at the height of Beaufort Sea whaling, it is estimated that there were 1500 people over-wintering on the island. Today there are 13 standing structures that date to 1893, as well as over one hundred Inuit and whalers' graves and the archaeological remains of prehistoric dwellings. One of the most ancient and rich archaeological sites has been named the 'Washout Site' because of its destruction in the 1980s by encroaching waves.

The south-facing slopes above Pauline Cove have suffered severe slumping due to melting ground ice. A large Inuit graveyard at the base of one slope has taken the brunt of this activity, known as 'solifluction'. An active layer of melted silts is sliding down over sub-surface ice, tumbling and exposing coffins. Extreme surface water run-off is adding to this damage.

Violent late summer and autumn storms have endangered a number of structures from the historic settlement, along the spit of Pauline Cove. Sea ice has been driven up against the Northern Whaling and Trading Company Store, leading to the dismantling of a sheet-metal clad shed along the west side of the building in 2000. The floor frame of the shed was left in place, along with industrial, neoprene sand bags, in an attempt to stabilise the low-lying shore of the spit, which is being reshaped and eroded. This effort proved in vain and in 2003 the building and adjacent Canada Customs Warehouse were braced, lifted and moved back from the shore. These buildings will need to be moved further back in 2004 as well as a hunters' and travellers' survival cabin.

If weather patterns continue in the current direction a decision will eventually have to be made about the value and viability of conserving the heritage resources on Herschel Island and in other areas of the Arctic. It is hoped that environmental studies will call attention to and help predict the impacts of this climate change and allow for better planning for the protection and long term care of polar heritage.

Susan Barr, President IPHC
Cornelia Lüdecke, University of Hamburg
Doug Olynyk, Historic Sites Coordinator,
Tourism Yukon, Canada
ICOMOS Polar Heritage Committee

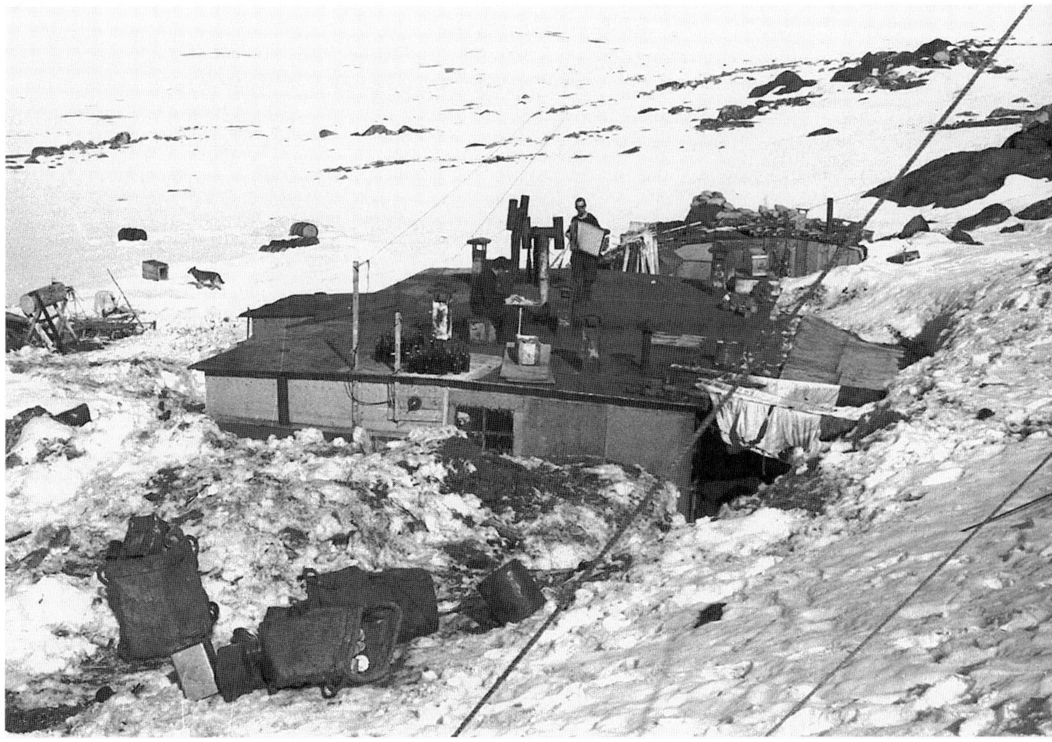

'Haudegen' Station in Nordaustlandet (Svalbard), spring 1945 (photo in possession of E. Dege, Kiel)

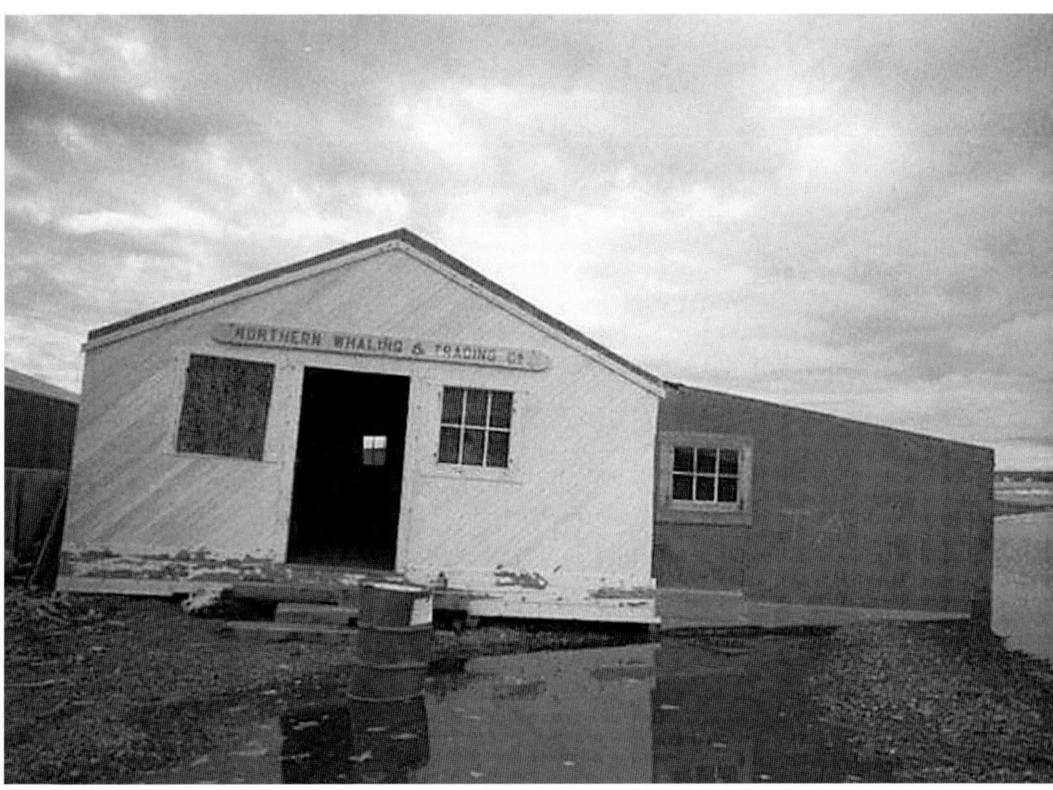

Northern Whaling and Trading Company Store, Pauline Cove, Western Canada Arctic, prior to dismantling of shed addition in 2000

CONTACT INFORMATION

ICOMOS
International Council on Monuments and Sites
Conseil international des monuments et des sites
49–51, rue de la Fédération
75015 Paris – France
Tel: 33 (0)1 45 67 67 70
Fax: 33 (0)1 45 66 06 22
e-mail: secretariat@icomos.org
http://www.international.icomos.org

UNESCO
United Nations Educational, Scientific and Cultural Organization
Organisation des Nations Unies pour l'éducation, la science et la culture
Division of Cultural Heritage
1, rue Miollis
75732 Paris cedex 15 – France
Tel: 33 (0)1 45683793
Fax: 33 (0)1 45685596
http://www.unesco.org

ICOM
International Council of Museums
Maison de l'UNESCO
1, rue Miollis
75732 Paris cedex 15 – France
Tel: 33 (0)1 47 34 05 00
Fax: 33 (0)1 43 06 78 62
e-mail: secretariat@icom.org
http://www.icom.org

ICCROM
The International Centre for the Study of the Preservation and Restoration of Cultural Property
Via di San Michele 13
00153 Rome – Italy
Tel: 39 06 585531
Fax: 39 06 58553349
e-mail: iccrom@iccrom.org
http://www.iccrom.org

DOCOMOMO
International Working Party for Documentation and Conservation of Buildings, Sites and Neighbourhoods of the Modern Movement
International Secretariat
President: Maristella Casciato
Institut français d'architecture
Palais de la Porte Dorée
293 av. Danmesnil
75012 Paris – France
http://www.docomomo.com

ICBS
International Committee of the Blue Shield
Secrétaire ICBS Secretary
Christiane Logie
boulevard de l'Empereur 4
1000 Brussels – Belgium
Tel/Fax: 32 (0) 2 519 54 40
e-mail: christiane.logie@kbr.be.

TICCIH
The International Committee for the Conservation of the Industrial Heritage
Secretary: Stuart B. Smith
'Chygarth', 5 Beacon Terrace
CAMBORNE, Cornwall TR14 7BU, UK
Tel/Fax: 44 1 209 612 142
e-mail: TICCIH@correa.gencat.es
http://www.mnactec.com/TICCIH/

Published so far: *Heritage at Risk, ICOMOS World Report 2000 on Monuments and Sites in Danger,* Munich 2000, K.G. Saur Verlag, ISBN 3-598-24240-9
Heritage at Risk, ICOMOS World Report 2001/2002 on Monuments and Sites in Danger, Munich 2001, K.G. Saur Verlag, ISBN 3-598-24241-7
Heritage at Risk, ICOMOS World Report 2002/2003 on Monuments and Sites in Danger, Munich 2003, K.G. Saur Verlag, ISBN 3-598-24242-5

Heritage at Risk Reports on the internet: www.international.icomos.org/risk/risk2000.htm
www.international.icomos.org/risk/2001/index.html
www.international.icomos.org/risk/2002/index.html

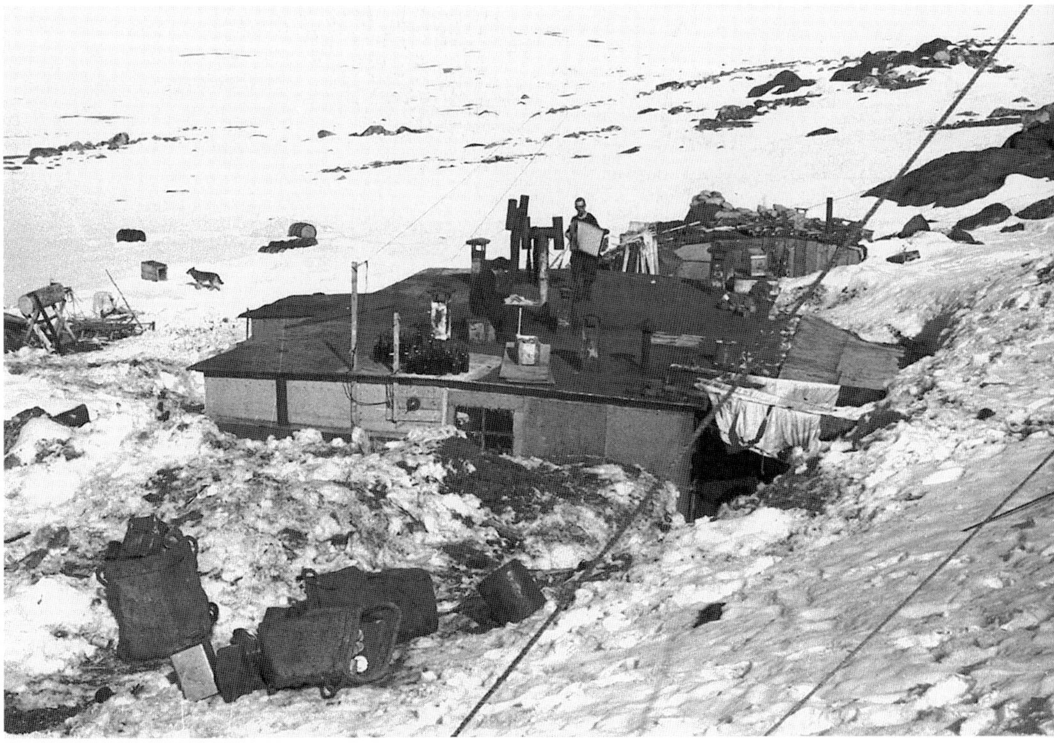

'Haudegen' Station in Nordaustlandet (Svalbard), spring 1945 (photo in possession of E. Dege, Kiel)

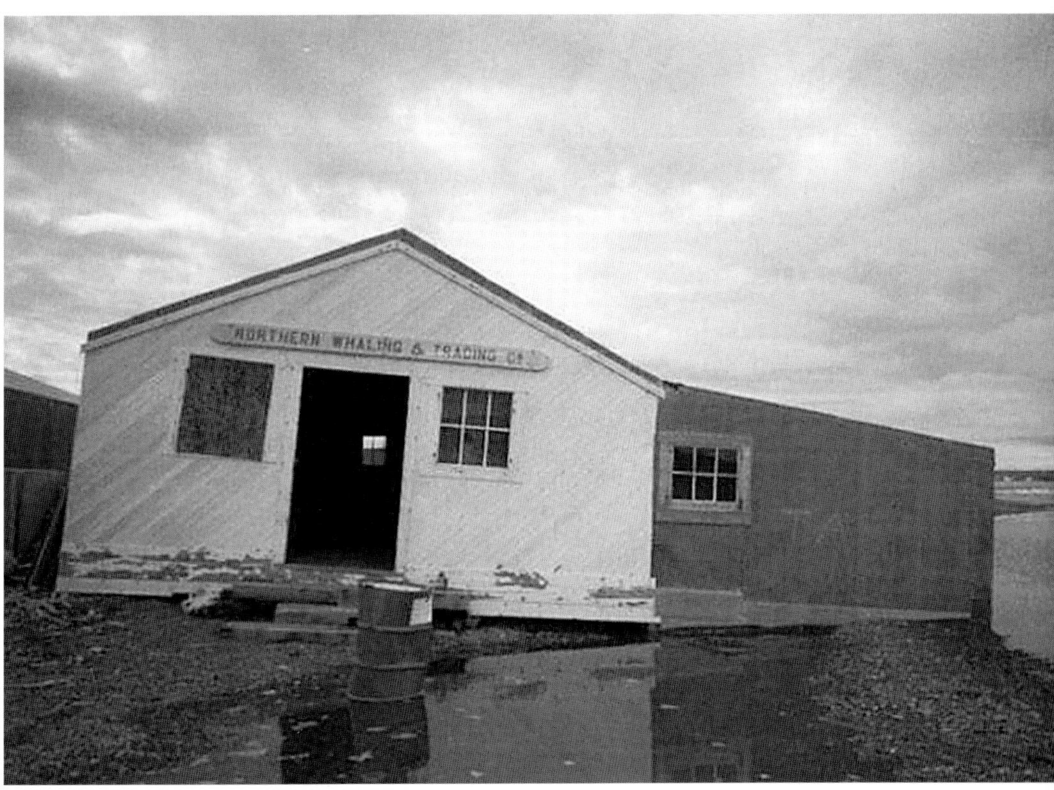

Northern Whaling and Trading Company Store, Pauline Cove, Western Canada Arctic, prior to dismantling of shed addition in 2000

CONTACT INFORMATION

ICOMOS
International Council on Monuments and Sites
Conseil international des monuments et des sites
49–51, rue de la Fédération
75015 Paris – France
Tel: 33 (0)1 45 67 67 70
Fax: 33 (0)1 45 66 06 22
e-mail: secretariat@icomos.org
http://www.international.icomos.org

ICOM
International Council of Museums
Maison de l'UNESCO
1, rue Miollis
75732 Paris cedex 15 – France
Tel: 33 (0)1 47 34 05 00
Fax: 33 (0)1 43 06 78 62
e-mail: secretariat@icom.org
http://www.icom.org

DOCOMOMO
International Working Party for Documentation and Conservation of Buildings, Sites and Neighbourhoods of the Modern Movement
International Secretariat
President: Maristella Casciato
Institut français d'architecture
Palais de la Porte Dorée
293 av. Danmesnil
75012 Paris – France
http://www.docomomo.com

TICCIH
The International Committee for the Conservation of the Industrial Heritage
Secretary: Stuart B. Smith
'Chygarth', 5 Beacon Terrace
CAMBORNE, Cornwall TR14 7BU, UK
Tel/Fax: 44 1 209 612 142
e-mail: TICCIH@correa.gencat.es
http://www.mnactec.com/TICCIH/

UNESCO
United Nations Educational, Scientific and Cultural Organization
Organisation des Nations Unies pour l'éducation, la science et la culture
Division of Cultural Heritage
1, rue Miollis
75732 Paris cedex 15 – France
Tel: 33 (0)1 45683793
Fax: 33 (0)1 45685596
http://www.unesco.org

ICCROM
The International Centre for the Study of the Preservation and Restoration of Cultural Property
Via di San Michele 13
00153 Rome – Italy
Tel: 39 06 585531
Fax: 39 06 58553349
e-mail: iccrom@iccrom.org
http://www.iccrom.org

ICBS
International Committee of the Blue Shield
Secrétaire ICBS Secretary
Christiane Logie
boulevard de l'Empereur 4
1000 Brussels – Belgium
Tel/Fax: 32 (0) 2 519 54 40
e-mail: christiane.logie@kbr.be.

Published so far: *Heritage at Risk, ICOMOS World Report 2000 on Monuments and Sites in Danger,* Munich 2000, K.G. Saur Verlag, ISBN 3-598-24240-9
Heritage at Risk, ICOMOS World Report 2001/2002 on Monuments and Sites in Danger, Munich 2001, K.G. Saur Verlag, ISBN 3-598-24241-7
Heritage at Risk, ICOMOS World Report 2002/2003 on Monuments and Sites in Danger, Munich 2003, K.G. Saur Verlag, ISBN 3-598-24242-5

Heritage at Risk Reports on the internet: www.international.icomos.org/risk/risk2000.htm
www.international.icomos.org/risk/2001/index.html
www.international.icomos.org/risk/2002/index.html